D0080435

Introduction to World Religions

Introduction to World Religions

THIRD EDITION

Updated and revised by Tim Dowley

General Editor: Christopher Partridge

Fortress Press

Minneapolis

INTRODUCTION TO WORLD RELIGIONS
Third Edition

Copyright © 2018 Fortress Press. All rights reserved. Except for brief quotations
in critical articles or reviews, no part of this book may be reproduced in any manner
without prior written permission from the publisher. Email copyright@1517.media or
write to Permissions, Fortress Press, PO Box 1209, Minneapolis, MN 55440-1209.

Scripture quotations marked NIV are from the Holy Bible, New International Version,
copyright © 1973, 1978, 1984 International Bible Society. Used by permission of
Zondervan and Hodder & Stoughton Limited. All rights reserved. The 'NIV' and
'New International Version' trademarks are registered in the United States Patent and
Trademark Office by International Bible Society. Use of either trademark requires the
permission of International Bible Society. UK trademark number 1448790.

Scripture quotations marked Good News Bible are from the Good News Bible (GNB)
© American Bible Society 1966, 1971, 1976.

Scripture quotations marked Revised Standard Version is taken from the Revised
Standard Version of the Bible, copyright 1952 2nd edition, 1971 by the Division of
Christian Education of the National Council of Churches of Christ in the United
States of America. Used by permission. All rights reserved. Scripture quotations
marked KJV are from the King James Version.

Cover image: Buddhist prayer beads/Antoine Taveneaux/Wikimedia
Cover design: Laurie Ingram

Print ISBN: 978-1-5064-4594-6
eBook ISBN: 978-1-5064-4601-1

The paper used in this publication meets the minimum requirements of American
National Standard for Information Sciences — Permanence of Paper for Printed
Library Materials, ANSI Z329.48-1984.

Manufactured in Canada

CONSULTING EDITORS

Dr Veikko Anttonen
Professor of Comparative Religion,
School of Cultural Research,
University of Turku, Finland

Dr Eric S. Christianson
Formerly Senior Lecturer in Biblical Studies,
University College Chester, UK

Dr Diana L. Eck
Professor of Comparative Religion and
Indian Studies, Harvard Divinity School,
Cambridge, MA, USA

Dr Gavin Flood
Professor of Hindu Studies and
Comparative Religion,
University of Oxford, UK

Dr Andreas Grünschloß
Professor of Religious Studies,
Göttingen University, Germany

Dr Robert J. Kisala,
Associate Professor, Nanzan University,
Nagoya, Japan

Dr Anthony N. S. Lane
Professor of Historical Theology and
Director of Research,
London School of Theology, UK

Dr Nicholas de Lange
Professor of Hebrew and Jewish Studies,
University of Cambridge, UK

Dr Mikael Rothstein
Associate Professor of Religious History,
University of Copenhagen, Denmark

Professor Lamin Sanneh
D. Willis James Professor of Missions and
World Christianity and Professor of History,
Yale Divinity School, New Haven, CT, USA

Baron Singh of Wimbledon CBE

Dr Garry W. Trompf
Emeritus Professor in the History of Ideas,
University of Sydney, Australia

Dr Linda Woodhead
Professor of Sociology of Religion,
Lancaster University, UK

Contents

PART 1
UNDERSTANDING RELIGION

PART 2
RELIGIONS OF ANTIQUITY

PART 3
INDIGENOUS RELIGIONS

PART 4
HINDUISM

PART 5
BUDDHISM

PART 6
JAINISM

PART 7
CHINESE RELIGIONS

PART 8
KOREAN AND JAPANESE RELIGIONS

PART 9
JUDAISM

PART 10
CHRISTIANITY

PART 11
ISLAM

PART 12
SIKHISM

PART 13
RELIGIONS IN TODAY'S WORLD

Contributors

The late Sir Norman Anderson, formerly Director of the Institute of Advanced Legal Studies, University of London, UK: *The Law of Islam*

Dr Veikko Anttonen, Professor of Comparative Religion, School of Cultural Research, University of Turku, Finland: *Norse Shamanism*

David Arnold: *I am a Jew*

Dr George Bankes, formerly Keeper of Ethnology, The Manchester Museum, University of Manchester, UK: *Land of the Aztecs and Incas*

Dr Robert Banks, formerly Home L. Goddard Professor of the Ministry of the Laity, Fuller Theological Seminary, Pasadena, California, USA: *The Covenant*

Dr Axel-Ivar Berglund, Professor in Missiology and Cultural Anthropology, Uppsala University, Sweden: *The Bangwa*

Dr John H. Berthrong, Associate Professor of Comparative Theology, Boston University School of Theology, MA, USA: *Chinese Religions*

Resham Singh Bhogal: *I am a Sikh*

Dr Barbara M. Boal, formerly Lecturer in Primal Religions, Selly Oak Colleges, Birmingham, UK: *Indigenous Religions in Asia, The Cao Dai and the Hoa Hoa*

Dr Fiona Bowie, Honorary Research Fellow, Department of Archaeology and Anthropology, University of Bristol, UK: *The Anthropology of Religion, Ritual and Performance*

Rt Revd Colin Buchanan, previously Bishop of Woolwich, London, UK: *Christianity: Worship and Festivals*

John Mohammed Butt, Islamic scholar and broadcaster, Muslim chaplain at Cambridge University: *Consultant on Islam*

Dr Jeremy Carrette, Professor of Religion and Culture, University of Kent, England: *Critical Theory and Religion*

Dr Eric S. Christianson, formerly Senior Lecturer in Biblical Studies, University College Chester, UK: *Judaism: Sacred Writings*

Dr George Chryssides, Research Fellow, University of Birmingham, UK: *New Religious Movements*

Chua Wee Hian, formerly Senior Pastor, Emmanuel Evangelical Church, London, UK: *The Worship of Ancestors*

Dr Dan Cohn-Sherbok, Professor Emeritus of Judaism, University of Wales, UK: *Judaism: Beliefs, The Holocaust*

The late Harvie M. Conn, Professor of Missions, Westminster Theological Seminary, Philadelphia PA, USA: *Sinkyo*

Dr Geoffrey Cowling, formerly Senior Lecturer in History, Macquarie University, New South Wales, Australia: *Judaism: A Historical Overview*

Dr James L. Cox, Professor of Religious Studies, University of Edinburgh, Scotland: *Inuit, African Indigenous Religions*

Dr Clyde Curry Smith, Professor Emeritus of Ancient History and Religion, University of Wisconsin, USA: *The Ancient Religions of Greece and Rome*

Dr Douglas Davies, Professor in the Study of Religion, Department of Theology and Religion, University of Durham, UK: *Myths and Symbols, The Golden Temple*

Dr Andrew Dawson, Senior Lecturer in Religion, Lancaster University, UK: *South American Indigenous Religions*

The late Dr Richard T. France, formerly Principal, Wycliffe Hall, Oxford, UK: *Jesus, Christianity: Sacred Writings*

Dr Theodore Gabriel, Honorary Research Fellow, Department of Religious Studies, University of Gloucestershire, UK: *Hinduism: Sacred Writings, Hinduism in the Modern World, Islam: Science, Art, and Culture*

Daniel Guy, MA, University of Cambridge, UK: *Summaries*

Dr Malcolm Hamilton, Senior Lecturer, Department of Sociology, University of Reading, UK: *The Sociology of Religion*

Dr David Harley, former Principal, All Nations Christian College, Ware, Herts, UK: *Judaism: Family and Society*

Dr Elizabeth J. Harris, Senior Lecturer, Comparative Study of Religions, Liverpool Hope University, UK: *Buddhism: Beliefs, Family and Society, Buddhism in the Modern World*

Dr Graham Harvey, Reader in Religious Studies, The Open University, UK: *Understanding Indigenous Religions*

Dr Paul Hedges, Senior Lecturer in Theology and Religious Studies: *Theological Approaches to the Study of Religion*

John R. Hinnells, Emeritus Professor of Theology, Liverpool Hope University, UK: *Zoroastrianism, Zoroastrian Beliefs*

Jason Hood: *I am a Christian*

The late Åke Hultkrantz, Professor of Comparative Religion, University of Stockholm, Sweden: *Religion before History, Nomads of the Steppes*

Dr Lynne Hume, Associate Professor in the School of History, Philosophy, Religion and Classics, University of Queensland, Australia: *Australian Aboriginal Religions*

Ronald Hutton, Professor of History, University of Bristol, UK: *The Religion of the Celts*

Dr Edward A. Irons, Director of the Hong Kong Institute for Culture, Commerce and Religion, Hong Kong: *Christianity in Contemporary China*

Dr Sewa Singh Kalsi, Lecturer in Sikh Studies, University of Leeds, UK: *Sikhism: Sacred Writings, Beliefs, Worship and Festivals, Family and Society*

Mohammed A. Khan: *I am a Muslim*

The late Dr David Kerr, formerly Professor in Missiology and Ecumenics at the Centre for Theology and Religious Studies at Lund University, Sweden: *The Unity and Variety of Islam, Islam: Worship and Festivals*

Dr Anna S. King, Reader in Theology and Religious Studies, University of Winchester, UK: *Hinduism: Beliefs*

Magdalen Lambkin, PhD student at the University of Glasgow, Scotland: Consultant, *Understanding Religion*

Carl Loeliger, Senior Lecturer in Religious Studies, History Department, University of Papua New Guinea: *Melanesia*

Dr David Lyon, Professor of Sociology, Queen's University, Kingston, Canada: *Religion and Globalization*

Dr Russell T. McCutcheon, Professor of Sociology of Religion, University of Alabama, USA: *What is Religion?*

Dr Alister McGrath, Professor of Theology, Ministry, and Education at Kings College London, UK: *Christianity: A Historical Overview*

Dr I. Howard Marshall, Professor Emeritus of New Testament Exegesis, University of Aberdeen, UK: *Christianity: Beliefs*

A. R. Millard, Rankin Professor Emeritus and Honorary Senior Fellow, School of Archaeology, Classics and Egyptology, University of Liverpool, UK: *The Ancient Near East*

Dr Moojan Momen, independent scholar and author, UK: *The Baha'i Faith*

The late Dr J. W. E. Newbery, formerly Professor Emeritus (Native Studies), University of Sudbury, Canada: *South American Indigenous Religions*

Dr Christopher Partridge, Professor of Religious Studies, University of Lancaster, UK: *Phenomenology and the Study of Religion, Rapid Fact-finder*

Naren Patel: *I am a Hindu*

Dr Robert Pope, Reader in Theology, University of Wales, Trinity St David, UK: *Religion and Politics*

Samani Charitra Prajna: *I am a Jain*

Dr Michael Pye, formerly Professor of the Study of Religions, University of Marburg (Philipps-Universität), Germany: *Japanese Religions*

Dr Elizabeth Ramsey, Lecturer, Liverpool Hope University College, UK: *Judaism: Worship and Festivals, Judaism in the Modern World*

Dr Peter G. Riddell, Professorial Dean of the BCV Centre for the Study of Islam and Other Faiths, Melbourne, Australia: *Islam: Sacred Writings, Beliefs*

John Ruffle, Keeper, Oriental Museum, University of Durham, UK: *Ancient Egypt, Egyptian Temples: Houses of Power*

Joan E. Rule, formerly Senior Lecturer in English, Dauli Teachers' College, Papua New Guinea: *The Foe of Papua New Guinea*

Dr Tinu Ruparell, Associate Professor, Department of Religious Studies, University of Calgary, Canada: *Hinduism: Philosophy*

Very Revd Michael Sadgrove, Dean of Durham Cathedral, UK: *Branches of the Church*

Dr Emma Salter, Course leader, Religion and Education, University of Huddersfield, UK: *Jainism: A Historical Overview, Sacred Writings, Beliefs, Family and Society, Worship and Festivals, Jainism in the Modern World*

Paul Seto: *I am a Buddhist*

Helen Serdiville: *I am a spiritual seeker*

Dr Christopher Shackle, Emeritus Professor of Modern Languages of South Asia, University of London, UK: *Sikhism: A Historical Overview, Sikhism Today*

Revd Dr David Smith, Senior Research Fellow, International Christian College, Glasgow, UK: *Contemporary Christianity*

Canon Dr Anthony C. Thiselton, Emeritus Professor of Christian Theology, University of Nottingham, UK: *From Existentialism to Postmodernism*

Revd Angela Tilby, Diocesan Canon, Christ Church, Oxford, UK: *Rapid Fact-finder*

The late Revd Dr Harold W. Turner, formerly Director of the Centre for New Religious Movements in Selly Oak Colleges, Birmingham, UK: *Holy Places, Sacred Calendars*

Dr Alana Vincent, Lecturer in Jewish Studies, University of Chester, UK: Consultant, *Judaism*

Dr David Waines, Professor of Islamic Studies, University of Lancaster, UK: *Islam in the Modern World*

Dr Morten Warmind, Lecturer, Department of Cross-cultural and Regional Studies, University of Copenhagen, Denmark: *The Religions of Scandinavia*

Dr Maya Warrier, Lecturer on Hinduism, University of Wales, Trinity St David, UK: *Hinduism: A Historical Overview, Worship and Festivals, Family and Society*

The late Revd Dr William Montgomery Watt, former Professor of Arabic and Islamic Studies, University of Edinburgh, UK: *Islam: A Historical Overview*

Dr Fraser N. Watts, Starbridge Lecturer in Theology and Natural Science, University of Cambridge, UK: *The Psychology of Religion*

Dr Paul Williams, Emeritus Professor of Indian and Tibetan Philosophy, University of Bristol, UK: *Buddhism: A Historical Overview, Sacred Writings*

Revd Dr Marvin R. Wilson, Harold J. Ockenga Professor of Biblical and Theological Studies, Gordon College, Wenham, MA, USA: *Branches of Judaism*

Dr Linda Woodhead, Professor of Sociology of Religion, Lancaster University, UK: Christianity: *Family and Society, Secularization and Sacralization*

Revd Dr John-David Yule, Incumbent of the United Benefice of Fen Drayton with Conington, Lolworth, and Swavesey, Cambridge, UK: *Rapid Fact-finder*

Benjamin Zephaniah, poet, Lincolnshire, UK: *I am a Rastafarian*

List of Maps

List of Time Charts

List of Festival Charts

List of Illustrations

Preface to the First Edition

In the small, complicated world of the twenty-first century there is a widespread and growing awareness of the significance of religions and beliefs. This has been accompanied by an increasing desire for, and arguably a need for, reliable and accessible knowledge. Not only have religions contributed to the foundation of civilizations throughout history, but also they have directly influenced contemporary international relations and significant world events. Whether one thinks of the globalization of 'fundamentalisms', religiously motivated politics, the emergence of numerous new religions, or our increasingly plural societies, the informed twenty-first-century citizen cannot afford to neglect acquiring some understanding of religious belief and practice.

This book is a collection of insightful, stimulating and accessible introductions to the histories, beliefs and practices of religions from pre-historic times to twenty-first-century developments. As well as being accessible, the articles are accurate and authoritative, having been written by an international team of acknowledged experts. Moreover, making the religions visible, the book is richly illustrated with numerous photographs, maps and diagrams. Consequently, there are few, if any, volumes to rival it as an attractive, readable and reliable resource for those wanting basic introductions to the world's religious traditions. It is particularly suitable for teachers, students, interested laypeople, and professionals who need clear, accurate, comprehensive overviews of the world's principal religious beliefs and practices.

Those familiar with earlier editions of this book will immediately see that this edition has been completely revised. Not only has much of it been rewritten in order to bring it up to date with current scholarship, but the layout has also significantly changed, with each of the principal religions given its own discrete section. A further particularly stimulating feature of this new edition is the inclusion of short articles written by 'ordinary' believers about what their faith means to them and how their lives are shaped by their beliefs. In other words, the short 'insider' articles in the book seek to take readers 'under the skin' of faith traditions, by allowing individual believers from around the world to speak for themselves. Although, of course, they only allow a single believer's perspective (with which other believers may disagree), they do enable some understanding of what it means to be a believer within a particular faith.

While the sections dealing with particular religions are not absolutely identical, being shaped to a large degree by the emphases within the faith, there has been an effort to ensure that all such sections address the following principal areas: (1) historical overview; (2) sacred writings; (3) key beliefs; (4) worship and festivals; (5) family and society; and (6) developments in the modern world. Therefore, if you read through any section in its entirety you will come away with a good introductory knowledge of these six principal areas of the respective faith.

As well as sections on particular religions, the book begins with an important section on the study of religion, in which readers are introduced to some of the key thinkers in the history of the modern study of religions and to some of the key issues and approaches taken to the study of religion. Again, the Rapid Fact-Finder at the end of the book, which many readers have found particularly useful, has been thoroughly updated. Finally, the last main section includes discussions of some particular developments in the modern world, such as the emergence of new religions and alternative spiritualities, the impact of postmodernism on religious thought, and issues surrounding the decline of once dominant forms of religion (such as Christianity in the Western world). Again, these articles draw on the latest research and thinking in their respective areas and thus provide important introductions to religion in the modern world.

CHRISTOPHER PARTRIDGE, 2005

Preface to the Second Edition

This new, revised edition adheres to the aims of the original book. However, before undertaking the launch of this updated version, the publisher solicited in-depth opinions from a panel of leading academics, teachers, and instructors who have previously used the text, in an effort to maximize its usefulness and accuracy. As a result, we have redesigned and re-arranged the book radically, to make things clearer and easier to follow, and created much new cartographic and other visual material.

In summary, for this edition we have:

- Completely re-designed the entire book, with a larger format, more readable typeface, and clearer layout
- Radically re-organized the book into broadly chronological order. Korea and Japan now have a separate chapter. Bahá'í is now covered in the final section, and Zoroastrianism with Ancient Religions (though there are of course modern adherents)
- The section on Judaism has been carefully re-written and re-arranged, to make it clearer, more readable and up-to-date
- The text has been comprehensively revised, re-styled, checked, and re-edited throughout
- Each section of the text has been reviewed, in consultation with current expert authorities
- Important new text has been added — for example on theological approaches to the study of religion
- The glossary has been expanded and painstakingly re-checked
- 20 completely new full-colour maps have been created and introduced
- 10 invaluable timelines have been added
- The book has been completely re-illustrated, with new full-colour photographs throughout
- Summaries, study questions, and suggested further reading for students have been added to each section
- Quotations have been increased in both number and variety

It is the hope of the editor that this book in its new form will open up the study of World Religions to a new generation of readers and students.

TIM DOWLEY
DULWICH, LONDON 2013

Preface to the Third Edition

The third edition of *Introduction to World Religions*, edited and revised by Tim Dowley, and originally edited by Christopher Partridge, builds on the structure and organization of the second Fortress Press edition (2013). The third edition features a redesigned format and color spectrum. It includes a new chapter on "Women and Religion" and a newly revised section on "Religions in Today's World," which brings the textbook up-to-date with contemporary issues and questions.

PART I
UNDERSTANDING RELIGION

SUMMARY

Belief in something that exists beyond or outside our understanding – whether spirits, gods, or simply a particular order to the world – has been present at every stage in the development of human society, and has been a major factor in shaping much of that development. Unsurprisingly, many have devoted themselves to the study of religion, whether to understand a particular set of beliefs, or to explain why humans seem instinctively drawn to religion. While biologists, for example, may seek to understand what purpose religion served in our evolutionary descent, we are concerned here with the beliefs, rituals, and speculation about existence that we – with some reservation – call religion.

The question of what 'religion' actually is is more fraught than might be expected. Problems can arise when we try to define the boundaries between religion and philosophy when speculation about existence is involved, or between religion and politics when moral teaching or social structure are at issue. In particular, once we depart from looking at the traditions of the West, many contend that such apparently obvious distinctions should not be applied automatically.

While there have always been people interested in the religious traditions of others, such 'comparative' approaches are surprisingly new. Theology faculties are among the oldest in European universities, but, while the systematic internal exploration of a religion provides considerable insights, many scholars insisted that the examination of religions more generally should be conducted instead by objective observers. This phenomenological approach was central to the establishment of the study of religion as a discipline in its own right. Others, concerned with the nature of society, or the workings of the human mind, for example, were inevitably drawn to the study of religion to expand their respective areas. More recently, many have attempted to utilise the work of these disparate approaches. In particular, many now suggest that – because no student can ever be entirely objective – theological studies are valuable because of their ability to define a religion in its own terms: by engaging with this alongside other, more detached, approaches, a student may gain a more accurate view of a particular religion.

CHAPTER 1

What Is Religion?

Although no one is certain of the word's origins, we know that 'religion' derives from Latin, and that languages influenced by Latin have equivalents to the English word 'religion'. In Germany, the systematic study of religion is known as *Religionswissenschaft*, and in France as *les sciences religieuses*. Although the ancient words to which we trace 'religion' have nothing to do with today's meanings — it may have come from the Latin word that meant to tie something tightly (*religare*) — it is today commonly used to refer to those beliefs, behaviours, and social institutions which have something to do with speculations on any, and all, of the following: the origin, end, and significance of the universe; what happens after death; the existence and wishes of powerful, non-human beings such as spirits, ancestors, angels, demons, and gods; and the manner in which all of this shapes human behaviour.

Because each of these makes reference to an invisible (that is, non-empirical) world that somehow lies outside of, or beyond, human history, the things we name as 'religious' are commonly thought to be opposed to those institutions which we label as 'political'. In the West today we generally operate under the assumption that, whereas religion is a matter of personal belief that can never be settled by rational debate, such things as politics are observable, public, and thus open to rational debate.

THE ESSENCE OF 'RELIGION'

Although this commonsense distinction between private and public, sentiment and action, is itself a historical development — it is around the seventeenth century that we first see evidence that words that once referred to one's behaviour, public standing, and social rank (such as piety and reverence) became sentimentalized as matters of private feeling — today the assumption that religion involves an inner core of belief that is somehow expressed publicly in ritual is so widespread that to question it appears counterintuitive. It is just this assumption that inspires a number of people who, collectively, we could term 'essentialists'. They are 'essentialists' because they maintain that 'religion' names the outward behaviours that are inspired by the inner thing they call 'faith'. Hence, one can imagine someone saying, 'I'm not religious, but I'm spiritual.' Implicit here is the assumption that the institutions associated with religions — hierarchies, regulations, rituals, and so on — are merely secondary and inessential; the important thing is the inner faith, the inner 'essence' of religion. Although the essence of religion – the thing without which someone is thought to be non-religious – is known by various names (faith, belief, the Sacred, the Holy, and so on), essentialists are in general agreement that the essence of religion is real and non-empirical (that is, it cannot itself be seen, heard, touched, and so on); it defies study and must be experienced first-hand.

THE FUNCTION OF 'RELIGION'

Apart from an approach that assumes an inner experience, which underlies religious behaviour, scholars have used the term 'religion' for what they consider to be curious areas of observable human behaviour which require an explanation. Such people form theories to account for why it is people think, for example, that an invisible part of their body, usually called 'the soul', outlives that body; that powerful beings control the universe; and that there is more to existence than what is observable. These theories are largely functionalist; that is, they seek to determine the social, psychological, or political role played by the things we refer to as 'religious'. Such functionalists include historically:

- Karl Marx (1818–83), whose work in political economy understood religion to be a pacifier that deadened oppressed people's sense of pain and alienation, while simultaneously preventing them from doing something about their lot in life, since ultimate responsibility was thought to reside in a being who existed outside history.
- Émile Durkheim (1858–1917), whose sociology defined religious as sets of beliefs and practices to enable individuals who engaged in them to form a shared, social identity.
- Sigmund Freud (1856–1939), whose psychological studies prompted him to liken religious behaviour to the role that dreams play in helping people to vent antisocial anxieties in a manner that does not threaten their place within the group.

Although these classic approaches are all rather different, each can be understood as *functionalist* insomuch as religion names an institution that has a role to play in helping individuals and communities to reproduce themselves.

Karl Marx (1818–83).

THE FAMILY RESEMBLANCE APPROACH

Apart from the *essentialist* way of defining religion (i.e. there is some non-empirical, core feature without which something is not religious) and the *functionalist* (i.e. that religions help to satisfy human needs), there is a third approach: the *family resemblance* definition. Associated with the philosophy of Ludwig Wittgenstein (1889–1951), a family resemblance approach assumes that nothing is defined by merely one essence or function. Rather, just as members of a family more or less share a series of traits, and just as all things we call 'games' more or less share a series of traits — none of which is distributed evenly across all members of those groups we call 'family' or 'games' — so all things — including religion — are defined insomuch as they more or less share a series of delimited traits. Ninian Smart (1927–2001), who identified seven dimensions of religion that are present in religious traditions with varying degrees of emphasis, is perhaps the best known proponent of this view.

'RELIGION' AS CLASSIFIER

Our conclusion is that the word 'religion' likely tells us more about the user of the word (i.e. the classifier) than it does about the thing being classified. For instance, a Freudian psychologist will not conclude that religion functions to oppress the masses, since the Freudian theory precludes coming up with this Marxist conclusion. On the other hand, a scholar who adopts Wittgenstein's approach will sooner or later come up with a case in which something seems to share some traits, but perhaps not enough to count as 'a religion'. If, say, soccer matches satisfy many of the criteria of a religion, what might not also be called religion if soccer is? And what does such a broad usage do to the specificity, and thus utility, of the word 'religion'? As for those who adopt an essentialist approach, it is likely no coincidence that only those institutions with which one agrees are thought to be expressions of some authentic inner experience, sentiment, or emotion, whilst the traditions of others are criticized as being shallow and derivative.

So what is religion? As with any other item in our lexicon, 'religion' is a historical artefact that different social actors use for different purposes: to classify certain parts of their social world in order to celebrate, degrade, or theorize about them. Whatever else it may or may not be, religion is at least an item of rhetoric that group members use to sort out their group identities.

RUSSELL T. MCCUTCHEON

CHAPTER 2

Phenomenology and the Study of Religion

There is a long history of curiosity and scholarship regarding the religions of other people. However, the study of religions is a relative newcomer to academia. Greatly indebted to the impressive work and influence of the German scholar Friedrich Max Müller (1823–1900), the first university professorships were established in the final quarter of the nineteenth century. By the second half of the twentieth century, the study of religion had emerged as an important field of academic enquiry. In a period of history during which the rationalism of the earlier part of the century saw a decline, and in which there was increased interest in particularly non-Christian spirituality, since 1945 there has been a growth in courses in the study of religion offered in academic institutions. Moreover, work done in other disciplines has increasingly converged with the work done by students of religion (see the discussion in this book of 'The Anthropology of Religion', 'The Psychology of Religion', 'The Sociology of Religion', and 'Critical Theory and Religion').

These factors, amongst others, have made it possible for the study of religion in most Western universities to pull away from its traditional place alongside the study of Christian theology and establish itself as an independent field of enquiry. Whereas earlier in the century the study of non-Christian faiths was usually undertaken in faculties of Christian theology, and studied as part of a theology degree, there was a move – particularly in the late 1960s and 1970s, when the term 'religious studies' became common currency – to establish separate departments of religious studies. Whilst in the United States and most of Western Europe religious studies tends to be considered a subject completely distinct from theology, in the United Kingdom it is quite common for universities to offer degree programmes in 'theology and religious studies', and the lines between the two disciplines are not so heavily drawn.

RELIGIONSPHÄNOMENOLOGIE

Phenomenology is distinct from other approaches to the study of religion in that it does not necessarily seek to understand the social nature of religion, it is not concerned to explore the psychological factors involved in religious belief, nor is it

especially interested in the historical development of religions. Rather its main concern has been descriptive, the classification of religious phenomena: objects, rituals, teachings, behaviours, and so on.

During the Kumbh Mela festival in the holy city of Haridwar the Guru in his decorated chariot is escorted by holy men and pilgrims visiting the River Ganges, India.

The term *Religionsphänomenologie* was first used by the Dutch scholar Pierre Daniel Chantepie de la Saussaye (1848–1920) in his work *Lehrbuch der Religions-geschichte* (1887), which simply documented religious phenomena. This might be described as 'descriptive' phenomenology, the aim being to gather information about the various religions and, as botanists might classify plants, identify varieties of particular religious phenomena. This classification of types of religious phenomena, the hallmark of the phenomenological method, can be seen in the works of scholars such as Ninian Smart (1927–2001) and Mircea Eliade (1907–86). Descriptive phenomenology of the late nineteenth and early twentieth centuries tended to lead to accounts of religious phenomena which, to continue with the analogy, read much the same as a botanical handbook. Various species were identified (higher religion, lower religion, prophetic religion, mystical religion, and so on) and particular religious beliefs and practices were then categorized, discussed, and compared.

As the study of religion progressed, phenomenology came to refer to a method which was more complex, and claimed rather more for itself, than Chantepie's mere cataloguing of facts. This later development in the discipline – which was due in part to the inspiration of the philosophy of Edmund Husserl (1859–1938) – recognized how easy it is for prior beliefs and interpretations unconsciously to influence one's thinking. Hence, scholars such as Gerardus van der Leeuw (1890–1950) stressed the need for phenomenological *epoché*: the 'bracketing' or shelving of the question about the ontological or objective status of the religious appearances to consciousness. Thus questions about the objective or independent truth of Kali, Allah, or the Holy Spirit are initially laid aside. The scholar seeks to suspend judgment about the beliefs of those he studies in order to gain greater objectivity and accuracy in understanding. Also central to phenomenology is the need for empathy (*Einfühlung*), which helps towards an understanding of the religion from within. Students of a religion seek to feel their way into the beliefs of others by empathizing with them. Along with this suspension of judgment and empathy, phenomenologists spoke of 'eidetic vision', the capacity of the observer to see beyond the particularities of a religion and to grasp its core essence and meaning. Whilst we often see only what we want, or expect, to see, eidetic vision is the ability to see a phenomenon without such distortions and limitations. Hence, later phenomenologists did not merely catalogue the facts of religious history, but by means of *epoché*, empathy, and eidetic vision sought to understand their meaning for the believer. Although phenomenologists are well aware that there will always be some distance between the believer's understandings of religious facts and those of the scholar, the aim of phenomenology is, as far as possible, to testify only to what has been observed. It aims to strip away all that would stand in the way of a neutral, judgment-free presentation of the facts.

THE IDEA OF THE HOLY

Some scholars have gone beyond this simple presentation of the facts and claimed more. A classic example is Rudolf Otto's (1869–1937) book *Das Heilige* (*The Idea of the Holy*, 1917). On the basis of his study of religions, Otto claimed that central to all religious expression is an a priori sense of 'the numinous' or 'the holy'. This, of course, necessarily goes beyond a simple presentation of the facts of religious history to the development of a particular philosophical interpretation of those facts. The central truth of all religion, claimed Otto, is a genuine feeling of awe or reverence in the believer, a sense of the 'uncanny' inspired by an encounter with the divine. Otto did more than simply relate facts about religion; he assumed the existence of the holy – accepting the truth of encounters with the supernatural.

> *'Numinous dread' or awe characterizes the so-called 'religion of primitive man', where it appears as 'daemonic dread.'*
>
> Rudolf Otto, *The Idea of the Holy*

For some scholars, for example Ninian Smart, such an assumption is unacceptable in the study of religion. To compromise objectivity in this way, Smart argued, skews the scholar's research and findings. What the scholar ends up with is not an unbiased account of the facts of religion, but a personal *theology* of religion.

NEUTRALITY

Whilst Otto's type of phenomenology clearly displays a basic lack of objectivity, it is now generally recognized that this is a problem intrinsic to the study of religions. Although many contemporary religious studies scholars would want to defend the notion of *epoché* as an ideal to which one should aspire, there is a question as to whether this ideal involves a certain naivety. For example, the very process of selection and production of typologies assumes a level of interpretation. To select certain facts rather than others, and to present them with other facts as a particular type of religion, presupposes some interpretation. What facts we consider important and unimportant, interesting or uninteresting, will be shaped by certain ideas that we hold, whether religious or non-religious. To be an atheist does not in itself make the scholar more objective and neutral. Hence, the belief in detached objectivity, and the claim to be purely 'descriptive', are now considered to be naive. The important thing is that, as we engage in study, we recognize and critically evaluate our beliefs, our presuppositions, our biases, and how they might shape the way we understand a religion (see 'Critical Theory and Religion').

INSIDERS AND OUTSIDERS

Another important issue in contemporary religious studies is the 'insider/outsider' problem. To what extent can a non-believer ('an outsider') understand a faith in the way the believer (an 'insider') does? It is argued that outsiders, simply because they are outsiders, will never fully grasp the insider's experience; even people who experience the same event at the same time will, because of their contexts and personal histories, interpret that experience in different ways. However, some scholars have insisted there is a definite advantage to studying religion from the outside — sometimes referred to as the 'etic' perspective. Members of a religion may be conditioned by, or pressurized into accepting, a particular — and often narrow — understanding of their faith, whereas the outsider is in the scholarly position of not being influenced by such pressures and conditioning. Impartiality and disinterest allow greater objectivity.

There is undoubtedly value in scholarly detachment. However — while the scholar may have a greater knowledge of the history, texts, philosophy, structure, and social implications of a particular faith than the average believer — not to have experienced that faith from the inside is surely to have a rather large hole in the centre of one's understanding. Indeed, many insiders will insist that scholarly 'head-knowledge' is peripheral to the 'meaning' of their faith. Hence, others have noted the value of studying a religion as an 'insider', or at least relying heavily on the views of insiders — sometimes referred to as the 'emic' perspective.

RESPONSE THRESHOLD

In order to take account of the emic perspective, along with the emphasis on participant observation (see 'The Anthropology of Religion'), some have spoken of the 'response threshold' in religious studies. The crossing of the response threshold happens when insiders question the scholar's interpretations: etic interpretations are challenged by emic perspectives. An insider's perspective – which may conflict with scholarly interpretations – is felt to carry equal, if not more, weight. Wilfred Cantwell Smith (1916–2000) has even argued that no understanding of a faith is valid until it has been acknowledged by an insider. Religious studies are thus carried out in the context of a dialogue which takes seriously the views of the insider, in order to gain a deeper understanding of the insider's world view.

BEYOND PHENOMENOLOGY

In his book entitled *Beyond Phenomenology* (1999), Gavin Flood has argued that what is important in studying religions is 'not so much the distinction between the insider and the outsider, but between the critical and the non-critical'. Flood makes use of theories developed within the social sciences and humanities. With reference to the shift in contemporary theoretical discourse, which recognizes that all knowledge is tradition-specific and embodied within particular cultures (see 'Critical Theory and Religion'), Flood argues, firstly, that religions should not be abstracted and studied apart from the historical, political, cultural, linguistic, and social contexts. Secondly, he argues that scholars, who are likewise shaped by their own contexts, always bring conceptual baggage to the study of religion. Hence, whether because of the effect research has on the community being studied, or because the scholar's own prejudices, preconceptions, instincts, emotions, and personal characteristics significantly influence that research, the academic study of religion can never be neutral and purely objective. Flood thus argues for 'a rigorous metatheoretical discourse' in religious studies. Metatheory is the critical analysis of theory and practice, the aim of which is to 'unravel the underlying assumptions inherent in any research programme and to critically comment on them'.

Metatheory is thus important because it 'questions the contexts of inquiry, the nature of inquiry, and the kinds of interests represented in inquiry'. In so doing, it questions the idea of detached objectivity in the study of religion, and the notion that one can be a disinterested observer who is able to produce neutral descriptions of religious phenomena, free of evaluative judgments. Hence, scholars need always to engage critically with, and take account of, their own assumptions, prejudices, and presuppositions.

This means that holding a particular faith need not be a hindrance to the study of religion. One can, for example, be a Christian theologian and a good student of religion. But for scholars such as Flood, the important thing is not the faith or lack of it, but the awareness of, and the critical engagement with, one's assumptions: 'It is critique rather than faith that is all important.'

It is worth noting that recent work, mainly in France, sees new possibilities for the philosophy of religion through a turn to phenomenology. Much of this work has been done in response to the important French Jewish philosopher Emmanuel Levinas (1905–95). The names particularly associated with this turn are Jean-Luc Marion, Dominique Janicaud, Jean-Luc Chretien, Michel Henry, and Alain Badiou. Marion, for example, has written on the phenomenology of the gift in theology, Badiou has responded to Levinas arguing against his emphasis on the importance of 'the other', and Chretien has written on the phenomenology of prayer.

CHRISTOPHER PARTRIDGE

CHAPTER 3

The Anthropology of Religion

Anthropology approaches religion as an aspect of culture. Religious beliefs and practices are important because they are central to the ways in which we organize our social lives. They shape our understanding of our place in the world, and determine how we relate to one another and to the rest of the natural, and supernatural, order. The truth or falsity of religious beliefs, or the authenticity or moral worth of religious practices, are seldom an issue for anthropologists, whose main concern is to document what people think and do, rather than determine what they ought to believe, or how they should behave.

RELIGION AND SOCIAL STRUCTURE

The belief in a supreme God or a single God is no mere philosophical speculation; it is a great practical idea.

Maurice Hocart

An early observation in the anthropology of religion was the extent to which religion and social structure mirror one another. Both the French historian Fustel de Coulanges (1830–89), drawing on Classical sources, and the Scottish biblical scholar William Robertson Smith (1846–94), who studied Semitic religions, demonstrated this coincidence in form. For example, nomadic peoples such as the Bedouin conceive of God in terms of a father, and use familial and pastoral imagery to describe their relationship with God. A settled, hierarchical society, by contrast, will depict God as a monarch to whom tribute is due, with imagery of servants and subjects honouring a supreme ruler. These early studies influenced the French sociologist Émile Durkheim (1858–1917), whose book *The Elementary Forms of the Religious Life* (1912) was foundational for later anthropological studies of religion. Rather than seeing religion as determining social structure, Durkheim argued that religion is a projection of society's highest values and goals. The realm of the sacred is separated from the profane world and made to seem both natural and obligatory. Through collective rituals people both reaffirm their belief in supernatural beings and reinforce their bonds with one another.

The totemism of Australian Aboriginals, which links human groups with particular forms of animal or other natural phenomena in relations of prohibition and prescription, was regarded by many nineteenth-century scholars as the earliest form of religion, and as such was of interest to both Durkheim and the anthropologist Edward Burnett Tylor

(1832–1917), who postulated an evolutionary movement from animism to polytheism and then monotheism. However, as evolutionary arguments are essentially unprovable, later work built not on these foundations, but on the more sociological insights of Durkheim and anthropologists such as Alfred Radcliffe-Brown (1881–1955) and Sir Edward Evan Evans-Pritchard (1902–73).

Evans-Pritchard sought to retain the historical perspective of his predecessors, while replacing speculation concerning origins with data based on first-hand observations and participation in the life of a people. His classic 1937 ethnography of witchcraft, oracles, and magic among the Azande in Central Africa demonstrated that beliefs which, from a Western perspective, appear irrational and unscientific – such as the existence of witches and magic – are perfectly logical, once one understands the ideational system on which a society is based.

SYMBOLISM

While Durkheim was avowedly atheist, some of the most influential anthropologists of the later twentieth century, including Evans-Pritchard, were or became practising Roman Catholics. This is true of Mary Douglas (1921–2007) and Victor Turner (1920–83), both of whom were particularly interested in the symbolic aspects of religion. They were influenced not only by Durkheim and Evans-Pritchard, but more particularly by Durkheim's gifted pupils Marcel Mauss (1872–1950) and Henri Hubert (1864–1925), who wrote on ceremonial exchange, sacrifice, and magic.

> *Man is an animal suspended in webs of significance he himself has spun. I take culture to be those webs.*
>
> Clifford Geertz, *The Interpretation of Cultures: Selected Essays* (New York, 1973)

In her influential collection of essays *Purity and Danger* (1966), Douglas looked at the ways in which the human body is used as a symbol system in which meanings are encoded. The body is seen as a microcosm of the powers and dangers attributed to society at large. Thus, a group that is concerned to maintain its social boundaries, such as members of the Brahman caste in India, pays great attention to notions of purity and pollution as they affect the individual body. In examining purity rules, Douglas was primarily concerned with systems of classification. In her study of the Hebrew purity rules in the book of Leviticus, for example, Douglas argued that dietary proscriptions were not the result of medical or hygiene concerns, but followed the logic of a system of classification that divided animals into clean and unclean species according to whether they conformed to certain rules – such as being cloven-hooved and chewing cud – or were anomalous, and therefore unclean and prohibited. Like Robertson Smith, Douglas observed that rituals can retain their form over many generations, notwithstanding changes in their interpretation, and that meaning is preserved in the form itself, as well as in explanations for a particular ritual action.

In the work of Mary Douglas we see a fruitful combination of the sociological and symbolist tradition of the Durkheimians and the structuralism of Claude Lévi-Strauss (1908–2009). Lévi-Strauss carried out some fieldwork in the Amazonian region of Brazil, but it is as a theoretician that he has been most influential, looking not at the meaning or semantics of social structure, but at its syntax or formal aspects. In his four-volume study of mythology (1970–81), he sought to demonstrate the universality of certain cultural themes, often expressed as binary oppositions, such as the transformation of food from raw to cooked, or the opposition between culture and nature. The structuralism of Lévi-Strauss both looks back to Russian formalism and the linguistics of the Swiss Ferdinand de Saussure (1857–1913), and forwards to more recent psychoanalytic studies of religion, both of which see themselves as belonging more to a scientific than to a humanist tradition.

RITUAL AND SYMBOL

On the symbolist and interpretive side, Victor Turner (1920–83) produced a series of sensitive, detailed studies of ritual and symbols, focusing on the processual nature of ritual and its theatrical, dramatic aspects, based on extensive fieldwork among the Ndembu of Zambia carried out in the 1950s. Clifford Geertz (1926–2006) was equally concerned with meaning and interpretation, and following a German-American tradition he looked more at culture than at social structure. Geertz saw religion as essentially that which gives meaning to human society, and religious symbols as codifying an ethos or world view. Their power lies in their ability both to reflect and to shape society.

Recently, important changes have stemmed from postmodernism and postcolonial thinking, globalization and multiculturalism. Anthropologists now often incorporate a critique of their own position and interests into their studies, and are no longer preoccupied exclusively with 'exotic' small-scale societies; for instance, there is a lot of research into global Pentecostalism and its local forms. The impact of new forms of media in the religious sphere has also become a significant area of study.

FIONA BOWIE

MYTHS AND SYMBOLS

One dimension of religions which has received particular attention by scholars has been that of myths and symbols. If we had just heard a moving piece of music, we would find it strange if someone asked us whether the music were true or false. Music, we might reply, is neither true nor false; to ask such a question is inappropriate. Most people know that music can, as it were, speak to them, even though no words are used.

As with music so with people. The question of what someone 'means' to you cannot fully be answered by saying that he is your husband or she is your wife, because there are always unspoken levels of intuition, feeling, and emotion built into relationships. The question of 'meaning' must always be seen to concern these dimensions, as well as the more obviously factual ones.

Myths

Myths take many forms, depending on the culture in which they are found. But their function is always that of pinpointing vital issues and values in the life of the society concerned. They often dramatize those profound issues of life and death, of how humanity came into being, and of what life means, of how we should conduct ourselves as a citizen or spouse, as a creature of God or as a farmer, and so on.

Myths are not scientific or sociological theories about these issues; they are the outcome of the way a nation or group has pondered the great questions. Their function is not merely to provide a theory of life that can be taken or left at will; they serve to compel a response from humanity. We might speak of myths as bridges between the intellect and emotion, between the mind and heart – and in this, myths are like music. They express an idea and trigger our response to it.

Sometimes myths form an extensive series, interlinking with each other and encompassing many aspects of life, as has been shown for the Dogon people of the River Niger in West Africa. On the other hand, they may serve merely as partial accounts of problems, such as the hatred between people and snakes, or the reason for the particular shape of a mountain.

One problem in our understanding of myths lies in the fact that the so-called Western religions – Judaism, Christianity, and Islam – are strongly concerned with history. They have founders, and see their history as God's own doing. This strong emphasis upon actual events differs from the Eastern approaches to religion, which emphasize the consciousness of the individual. Believing in the cyclical nature of time, Hinduism and Buddhism possess a different approach to history, and hence also to science.

In the West, the search for facts in science is like the search for facts in history, but both these endeavours differ from the search for religious experience in the present. In the West, history and science have come to function as a framework within which religious experiences are found and interpreted, one consequence of which is that myths are often no longer appreciated for their power to evoke human responses to religious ideas.

The eminent historian of religion Mircea Eliade (1907–86) sought to restore this missing sense of the sacred by helping people to understand the true nature of myths. The secularized Westerner has lost the sense of the sacred, and is trying to compensate, as Eliade saw it, by means of science fiction, supernatural literature, and films. One may, of course, keep a firm sense of history and science without seeking to destroy the mythical appreciation of ideas and beliefs.

Symbols

Religious symbols help believers to understand their faith in quite profound ways. Like myths, they serve to unite the intellect and the emotions. Symbols also integrate the social and personal dimensions of religion, enabling individuals to share certain commonly held beliefs expressed by symbols, while also giving freedom to read private meaning into them.

We live the whole of our life in a world of symbols. The daily smiles and grimaces, handshakes and greetings, as well as the more readily acknowledged status symbols of large cars or houses – all these communicate messages about ourselves to others.

To clarify the meaning of symbols, it will help if we distinguish between the terms 'symbol' and 'sign'. There is a certain arbitrariness about signs, so that the word 'table', which signifies an object of furniture with a flat top supported on legs, could be swapped for another sound without any difficulty. Thus the Germans call it *tisch* and the Welsh *bwrdd*.

A symbol, by contrast, is more intimately involved in that to which it refers. It participates in what it symbolizes, and cannot easily be swapped for another symbol. Nor can it be explained in words and still carry the same power. For example, a kiss is a symbol of affection and love; it not only signifies these feelings in some abstract way; it actually demonstrates them. In this sense a symbol can be a thought in action.

Religious symbols share these general characteristics, but are often even more intensely powerful, because they enshrine and express the highest values and relationships of life. The cross of Christ, the sacred books of Muslims and Sikhs, the sacred cow of Hindus, or the silent, seated Buddha – all these command the allegiance of millions of religious men and women. If such symbols are attacked or desecrated, an intense reaction is felt by the faithful, which shows us how deeply symbols are embedded in the emotional life of believers.

The power of symbols lies in this ability to unite fellow-believers into a community. It provides a focal point of faith and action, while also making possible a degree of personal understanding which those outside may not share.

In many societies the shared aspect of symbols is important as a unifying principle of life. Blood, for example, may be symbolic of life, strength, parenthood, or of the family and kinship group itself. In Christianity it expresses life poured out in death, the self-sacrificial love of Christ who died for human sin. It may even be true that the colour red can so easily serve as a symbol of

The cross is the central symbol of Christianity.

danger because of its deeper biological association with life and death.

Symbols serve as triggers of commitment in religions. They enshrine the teachings and express them in a tangible way. So the sacraments of baptism and the Lord's Supper in Christianity bring the believer into a practical relationship with otherwise abstract ideas, such as repentance and forgiveness. People can hardly live without symbols because they always need something to motivate life; it is as though abstract ideas need to be set within a symbol before individuals can be impelled to act upon them. When any attempt is made to turn symbols into bare statements of truth, this vital trigger of the emotions can easily be lost.

Douglas Davies

CHAPTER 4

The Sociology of Religion

The sociological study of religion has its roots in the seventeenth- and eighteenth-century Enlightenment, when a number of influential thinkers sought not only to question religious belief, but also to understand it as a natural phenomenon, a human product rather than the result of divine revelation or revealed truth. While contemporary sociology of religion has largely abandoned the overtly critical stance of early theoretical approaches to the truth claims of religion, the discipline retains the essential principle that an understanding of religion must acknowledge that it is, to some degree at least, socially constructed, and that social processes are fundamentally involved in the emergence, development, and dissemination of religious beliefs and practices.

METHODOLOGICAL AGNOSTICISM

While some sociologists consider that some religious beliefs are false, and that recognition of this is crucial to a sociological understanding of them, the dominant position in the sociology of religion today is that of 'methodological agnosticism'. This method states that it is neither possible, nor necessary, to decide whether beliefs are true or false in order to study them sociologically. Theology and philosophy of religion, not sociology, discuss questions of religious truth. The conditions which promote the acceptance or rejection of religious beliefs and practices, which govern their dissemination and the impact they have on behaviour and on society, can all be investigated without prior determination of their truth or falsity.

ROOTS IN INDIVIDUAL NEEDS

Theoretical approaches in the sociology of religion can usefully – if a little crudely – be divided into those which perceive the roots of religion to lie in individual needs and propensities, and those which perceive its roots to lie in social processes and to stem from the characteristics of society and social groups. The former may be further divided into those which emphasize cognitive processes – intellectualism – and those which emphasize various feelings and emotions – emotionalism.

In the nineteenth century, intellectualist theorists such as Auguste Comte (1798–1857), Edward Burnett Tylor (1832–1917), James G. Frazer (1854–1941), and Herbert Spencer (1820–1903) analyzed religious belief as essentially a pre-scientific attempt to understand the world and human experience, which would increasingly be supplanted by sound scientific knowledge. The future would thus be entirely secular, with no place for religion.

Emotionalist theorists, such as Robert Ranulph Marett (1866–1943), Bronislaw Malinowski (1884–1942), and Sigmund Freud (1856–1939), saw religions as stemming from human emotions such as fear, uncertainty, ambivalence, and awe. They were not attempts to explain and understand, but to cope with intense emotional experience.

ROOTS IN SOCIAL PROCESSES

The most influential sociological approaches that consider the roots of religion lie in society and social processes, not in the individual, are those of Karl Marx (1818–83) and Émile Durkheim (1858–1917).

For Marx, religion was both a form of ideology supported by ruling classes in order to control the masses, and at the same time an expression of protest against such oppression – 'the sigh of the oppressed creature'. As a protest, however, it changed nothing, promoting only resignation, and promising resolution of problems in the afterlife. Religion is 'the opium of the people', in the sense that it dulls the pain of the oppressed and thereby stops them from revolting. Hence, the oppressed turn to religion to help them get through life; the ruling classes promote it to keep them in check. It will simply disappear when the social conditions that cause it are removed.

> Religion is the sigh of the oppressed creature and the opium of the people.
>
> Karl Marx, *A Contribution to the Critique of Hegel's Philosophy of Right* (Deutsch-Französische Jahrbücher, 1844).

Durkheim saw religion as an essential, integrating social force, which fulfilled basic functions in society. It was the expression of human subordination, not to a ruling class, as Marx had argued, but rather to the requirements of society itself, and to social pressures which overrule individual preferences. In his famous work *The Elementary Forms of the Religious Life* (1912), Durkheim argued that 'Religion is society worshipping itself.' God may not exist, but society does; rather than God exerting pressure on the individual to conform, society itself exerts the pressure. Individuals, who do not understand the nature of society and social groups, use the language of religion to explain the social forces they experience. Although people misinterpret social forces as religious forces, what they experience is real. Moreover, for Durkheim, religion fulfils a positive role, in that it binds society together as a moral community.

MAX WEBER AND MEANING THEORY

Later theoretical approaches in the sociology of religion have all drawn extensively on this earlier work, attempting to synthesize its insights into more nuanced approaches, in which the various strands of intellectual, emotional, and social factors are woven together. A notable example is the work of Max Weber (1864–1920), probably the most significant contributor to the sociology of religion to this day. His work included one of the best-known treatises in the sub-discipline, *The Protestant Ethic and the Spirit of Capitalism* (1904–05), and three major studies of world religions.

Weber's approach to religion was the forerunner of what has become known as 'meaning theory', which emphasizes the way in which religion gives meaning to human life and society, in the face of apparently arbitrary suffering and injustice. Religion offers explanation and justification of good and of bad fortune, by locating them within a broader picture of a reality which may go beyond the world of immediate everyday perception, thereby helping to make sense of what always threatens to appear senseless. So those who suffer undeservedly in this life may have offended in a previous one; or they will receive their just deserts in the next life, or in heaven. Those who prosper through wickedness will ultimately be judged and duly punished.

RATIONAL CHOICE THEORY

The most recent, general theoretical approach in the sociology of religion, which synthesizes many previous insights, is that of 'rational choice theory'. Drawing upon economic theory, this treats religions as rival products offered in a market by religious organizations – which are compared to commercial firms – and leaders, to consumers, who choose by assessing which best meets their needs, which is most reliable, and so on. This approach promises to provide many insights. However, it has been subjected to trenchant criticism by those who question whether religion can be treated as something chosen in the way that products such as cars or soap-powders are chosen, rather than something into which people are socialized, and which forms an important part of their identity that cannot easily be set aside or changed. Furthermore, if religious beliefs are a matter of preference and convenience, why do their followers accept the uncongenial demands and constraints they usually impose, and the threat of punishments for failure to comply?

SECULARIZATION AND NEW MOVEMENTS

The sociology of religion was for many decades regarded as an insignificant branch of sociology. This situation has changed in recent years, especially in the USA. Substantive empirical inquiry has been dominated by two areas: secularization and religious sects, cults, and movements. It had been widely assumed that religion was declining in modern industrial societies and losing its social significance – the secularization thesis. This has

Hare Krishna Festival of Chariots in Trafalgar Square, London. Hare Krishna is one of many New Religious Movements.

been questioned and found by many — especially rational choice theorists — to be wanting. The result has been intense debate. The dominant position now, though not unchallenged, is that the secularization thesis was a myth.

Central to this debate is the claim that — while religion in its traditional forms may be declining in some modern, Western industrial societies — it is not declining in all of them, the USA being a notable exception; and that novel forms of religion are continuously emerging to meet inherent spiritual needs. Some new forms are clearly religious in character. Others, it is claimed, are quite unlike religion as commonly understood, and include alternative and complementary forms of healing, psychotherapies, techniques for the development of human potential, deep ecology, holistic spirituality, New Age, the cult of celebrity, nationalist movements, and even sport. Whether such things can be considered forms of religion depends upon how religion is defined, a matter much disputed.

A second crucial element in the secularization debate is the rise of a diversity of sects and cults – the New Religious Movements – which have proliferated since the 1960s and 1970s. For the anti-secularization – or 'sacralization' – theorists, this flourishing of novel religiosity gives the lie to the thesis; while for pro-secularization theorists, such movements fall far short of making up for the decline of mainstream churches and denominations. Whatever their significance for the secularization thesis, the New Religious Movements – and sects and cults in general – have fascinated sociologists, whose extensive studies of them form a major part of the subject.

Heavy concentration on New Religious Movements has been balanced more recently by studies of more mainstream religious churches and communities, and by studies of the religious life of ethnic minorities and immigrant communities, among whom religion is often particularly significant and an important element of identity. Added to the interest in new forms of religion and quasi-religion, such studies make the contemporary sociology of religion more diverse and varied than ever.

MALCOLM HAMILTON

CHAPTER 5

The Psychology of Religion

Three key figures dominate the psychology of religion that we have inherited from the pre-World War II period: William James, Sigmund Freud, and C. G. Jung.

WILLIAM JAMES (1842–1910)

The undoubted masterpiece of the early days of the psychology of religion is the classic *Varieties of Religious Experience*, written by William James at the end of the nineteenth century. James assembled an interesting compendium of personal reports of religious experience, and embedded them in a rich and subtle framework of analysis. He thought religious experience was essentially an individual matter, the foundation on which religious doctrine and church life were built. However, from the outset his critics argued that religious experience is in fact interpreted within the framework of inherited religious teaching and shaped by the life of the institution. James hoped to put religion on a scientific basis, through the scientific study of religious experience, although he was unable to make a really convincing case for accepting religious experience at face value. Despite these issues, even his critics have never doubted the quality of his work, which is as hotly debated now as when it was first written.

SIGMUND FREUD (1856–1939)

Another important figure in the development of the psychology of religion was Sigmund Freud, although his approach was very different from that of James. Freud built his general theories upon what patients told him during their psychoanalysis, although he reported only one case study in which religion played a central part. This was the so-called 'wolf man', in whom religion and obsessionality were intertwined, which led Freud to suggest that religion was a universal form of obsessional neurosis. In fact, Freud's psychology of religion was hardly based on data at all; it was a blend of general psychoanalytic theory and his own personal hostility to religion. He wrote several books about religion, each taking a different approach. The clearest is *The Future of an Illusion*, which claims that religion is merely 'illusion', which for him is a technical term meaning wish-fulfilment.

Freud's successors have argued that what he called illusion, including religion, is in fact much more valuable than he realized to people in helping them to adjust to life.

C. G. JUNG (1875–1961)

Freud's approach to religion was continued in modified form by Carl Gustav Jung. Whereas Freud had been a harsh critic of religion, Jung was favourably disposed to it. However, his approach to religion was so idiosyncratic that many have found him an uncomfortable friend. Jung made a distinction between the ego – the centre of conscious life – and the self – the whole personality that people can potentially become. For Jung, the self is the image of God in the psyche, and the process of 'individuation' – that is, development from

Sigmund Freud (1856–1939).

ego-centred life to self-centred life – is in some ways analogous to religious salvation. Jung was evasive about the question of whether there was a god beyond the psyche, and usually said it was not a question for him as a psychologist. Jung took more interest in the significance of Christian doctrine than most psychologists and, for example, wrote long essays on the Mass and on the Trinity.

Religious ideas … are illusions, fulfilments of the oldest, strongest, and most urgent wishes of mankind.

Sigmund Freud, *The Future of an Illusion* (London: Hogarth, 1962).

THE PSYCHOLOGY OF RELIGION TODAY

The psychology of religion went relatively quiet around the middle of the twentieth century, but has been reviving in recent decades. It has become more explicitly scientific, and most psychological research on religion now uses quantitative methods. There are currently no big psychological theories of religion, but important insights have been obtained about various specific aspects of religion. The following examples give a flavour of current work.

- *Individual differences.* One useful distinction has been between 'intrinsic' religious people – those for whom religion is the dominant motivation in their lives – and 'extrinsic' religious people – those for whom religion meets other needs. Intrinsics and extrinsics differ from one another in many ways. For example, it has been suggested that intrinsically religious people show less social prejudice than non-religious people, whereas extrinsically religious people show more.

- *Religious development.* Children's understanding of religion follows a predictable path, moving from the concrete to the abstract. However, acquiring a better intellectual understanding of religion is not necessarily accompanied by a more spiritual experience. In fact, spiritual experience may actually decline as children grow up. There have been attempts to extend a development approach to religion into adulthood. For example, James Fowler developed a general theory of 'faith development'. Although this has identified different approaches to faith in adults, it is not clear that higher levels of faith necessarily follow the earlier ones, nor that they are superior.
- *Mental health.* Despite Freud's view that religion is a form of neurosis, scientific research has shown that there is often a positive correlation between religion and health, especially mental health. It is most likely that religion actually helps to improve people's mental health, although this is hard to prove conclusively. Religion probably helps by providing a framework of meaning and a supportive community, both of which enable people to cope better with stressful experiences.
- *Conservative and charismatic Christianity.* There has been much interest in both fundamentalism and charismatic religion. One key feature of fundamentalism is the 'black and white' mindset that maintains a sharp dichotomy between truth and falsehood, and between insiders and outsiders. The charismatic phenomenon that has attracted most research interest is speaking in tongues. It seems very unlikely that this is an actual language; it is probably more a form of ecstatic utterance. One line of research has explored the social context in which people learn to speak in tongues, and another the unusual state of consciousness in which people surrender voluntary control of their speech.

Although psychology has generally taken a detached, scientific view of religion, there are other points of contact. One is the incorporation of psychological methods into the Christian church's pastoral care, begun by Freud's Lutheran pastor friend, Oskar Pfister (1873–1956). Another is the dialogue between religious and psychological world-views, an aspect of the more general dialogue between science and religion. Some psychologists consider that humans are 'nothing but' the product of their evolution or their nervous systems, whereas religious faith emphasizes their importance in the purposes of God.

FRASER WATTS

CHAPTER 6

Theological Approaches to the Study of Religion

During the development of the study of religion as a new discipline in the twentieth century, the pioneers of the field were often at pains to stress that what they did was different from theology. As such, it might be asked whether a theological approach even belongs within the study of religion. Many scholars today, who emphasize it as a scientific or historical discipline, distance themselves from any notion that theology, in any form, has a place within the study of religion. For others, the relationship is more ambiguous, while some scholars even argue that theological approaches are essential to understanding, and so truly studying, religion.

WHAT DO WE MEAN BY 'THEOLOGY'?

It is best to start by defining what we mean by 'theology' in relation to the study of religion. We will begin with some negatives. First, it does not mean a confessional approach, where the teachings of one school, tradition, or sect within a religion are taught as the true, or correct, understanding of that religion. Second, theology does not imply that there is any need for a belief, or faith content, within the person studying in that idiom. It is not, therefore, under the classic definition of the medieval Christian Anselm of Canterbury (1033–1109), an act of 'faith seeking understanding'.

We come now to the positives. First, it is about understanding the internal terms within which a religion will seek to explain itself, its teachings, and its formulations. We must be clear here that 'theology' is used loosely, because while it makes sense as a Christian term – literally it is the study of God – and can be fairly clearly applied to other theistic traditions, it is also used elsewhere to talk about broadly philosophical traditions related to transcendence. Accordingly, people use the term 'Buddhist theology' – although others question whether this usage is appropriate, but space does not permit us to engage in such disputes here. Second, it means engaging with empathy with questions of meaning as they would make sense within the religious worldview, and so goes beyond reasoning and relates to a way of life. Here, we see clear resonances with phenomenological approaches, where we seek to understand a religion on its own terms.

Anselm of Canterbury (1033–1109).

Indeed, without a theological viewpoint, it can be argued that the study of religions fails, because on the one hand it is either simply reductionist, that is to say it explains via some chosen system why the religion exists, what it does, and what it means — as tends to be the case with some parts of the sociology or psychology of religion. Or, on the other hand, it becomes merely descriptive, telling us what rituals are performed, what the ethics are, what the teachings are, how it is lived out, and so on — a simply phenomenological approach. A theological approach looks into the religion, and seeks to understand what it means to believers within its own terms, and how that system works as a rational worldview to those within it.

INSIDER AND OUTSIDER

Two important pairs of distinctions are useful to consider how theological approaches are applied. The first, developed by the anthropologist Kenneth Pike (1912–2000), and often applied to religion, concerns what are called 'emic' and 'etic' approaches. An emic approach attempts to explain things within the cultural world of the believer. An etic approach is the way an external observer would try and make sense of the behaviours and beliefs of a society or group in some form of scientific sense. Within anthropology, these basic distinctions are seen as part of the tools of the trade. Unless she enters into the thought-world of a group, culture, and society, the anthropologist will remain forever exterior, and will not understand what things mean to those in that group. Moreover, emic understandings can help inspire etic description, and assess its appropriateness. Clearly, in the study of religion, this originally anthropological distinction suggests that an emic, or theological, approach is justified.

Our second pair of distinctions is the notion of 'Insider' and 'Outsider' perspectives. These are, respectively, concepts from somebody who is a believer (an Insider), and a non-believer, that is, the scholar (an Outsider). This differs from the emic/etic distinction, because they are always perspectives of the Outsider: the scholar. As such, an emic theological approach is different from the confessional theology of an Insider. However, this distinction is often blurred. Field anthropologists speak of spending so much time within the group or society they study that they often almost become part of that group, and part of good fieldwork is about entering the life world of those studied. This applies equally to scholars of religion, especially those engaged in fieldwork.

Another issue is that scholars may be believers within a religion, and so may inhabit both Insider and Outsider worlds. This raises many interesting questions, but here we will note simply that the notion of the detached, impartial, and objective scholar is increasingly questioned. Issues raised by critical theory have suggested that every standpoint will always have a bias, and some have argued further – notably the Hindu scholar, Gavin Flood – that a religious point of view, if openly acknowledged, can form part of the broader study of religions. Moreover, religious groups are often affected by what scholars of religion say about them. Therefore, Insider worldviews and Outsider descriptions – etic or emic – become intertwined in a dance that affects each other. As such, the question of how a theological approach fits into, or works within, religious studies is far from simple.

ALWAYS 'TAINTED'?

Scholars such as Timothy Fitzgerald, Tomoko Masuzawa, and Tala Asad have argued that the supposedly secular study of religion has always been 'tainted', because it developed in a world where Christianity dominated – often with a particular kind of liberal theology – so that no study of religion is entirely free from theology. Certainly, some foundational figures, such as Mircea Eliade, had a religious worldview, and a lot of mid-twentieth century work developing the phenomenology of religion, or comparative religion, made assumptions about a religious realm that underlay all traditions. However, it is arguable whether all scholars of religion then and since are affected in this way, while a case can be made that it was not solely Christian assumptions that affected the study of religion, but that such assumptions were shaped by the encounter with various religious traditions. As such, while we must be suspicious of some categories within the study of religion, we do not need to assume that everything has a Christian basis. Indeed, Frank Whaling argues we must also not forget that many religions have a lot to say about other religions, and this leads into theorizing on comparative religion, comparative theology, and the theology of religions within a confessional standpoint which is not entirely separate from understanding a religion and its worldview.

The relationship of the study of religions and theology varies in different countries. For instance, in Germany the two tend to be starkly polarized, with theology departments being — at least traditionally — strictly confessional, normally Roman Catholic or Protestant, and the study of religions — understood as a primarily reductionist secular discipline — is always separate from theology. In the UK, the ancient universities started to admit non-Anglican Christian denominations from the nineteenth century, and so lost their confessional stance, with seminaries for training priests becoming separate or linked institutions. For this reason, it was easier to start teaching theology from a generic standpoint, which could integrate other religions as part of the curriculum, and so there are many combined departments for theology and the study of religion. The USA tends to have a more separate system, although there are places where an active study of religion discipline exists within a theology department. Obviously, such regional differences affect the way a theological approach to the study of religion is accepted or understood.

PAUL HEDGES

CHAPTER 7

Critical Theory and Religion

Our knowledge of 'religion' is always politically shaped, and never an innocent or a neutral activity. Knowledge about religion can always be questioned, and scholars of religion are finding that 'religion', and talk about 'religion', is involved with questions of power. Critical theory questions knowledge about 'religion', and reveals the social and political nature of such ideas.

DEFINING CRITICAL THEORY

Critical theory arises from a long tradition in Western thought which has questioned the truth and certainty of knowledge. It carries forward the work of the 'three great masters of suspicion', Karl Marx (1818–83), Friedrich Nietzsche (1844–1900), and Sigmund Freud (1856–1939). Following Marx, critical theory is aware that all knowledge is linked to economic and political ideology; following Nietzsche, it understands that all knowledge is linked to the 'will to power'; and following Freud, it understands that all knowledge is linked to things outside our awareness (the unconscious). The ideas of these three great thinkers influence, and are carried forward in, the work of critical theory. All three started to question the view that knowledge was neutral and rational.

There are two basic understandings of 'critical theory', a strict definition and a loose definition. The former relates to the Frankfurt School of Critical Theory, an important group of German intellectuals who tried to think about society according to the ideas of Marx and Freud.

Friedrich Nietzsche (1844–1900).

They included Theodor Adorno (1903–69) and Max Horkheimer (1895–1973), who jointly published *Dialectic of Enlightenment*, a seminal work in which they questioned Western rational thought since the Enlightenment. What did it say about the potential of human knowledge if it could lead to the ideology of Nazi Germany and the horrors of the Holocaust? Culture was understood to be formed by propagandist manipulation.

The loose definition incorporates a wider range of critical theories, which emerged – largely in France – after the student riots of 1968 in Paris. This date is a watershed in modern Western intellectual history because it reflects, among many things, a shift in the thinking about state power and the control of ideas. It was an event that brought the questions of 'power' and 'politics' to the question of knowledge and truth.

POST-STRUCTURALISM

The critical thinking that emerged in 1968 in France is known as 'post-structuralism' because it comes after an intellectual movement known as 'structuralism'. Structuralism held that one could identify a given number of structures in myth, language, and the world. Post-structuralists argued that these structures were not 'given' in the fabric of the world, but created by different societies at different points of history and in different cultures. Michel Foucault (1926–84) examined the historical nature of ideas, showing that the ways we think about the world are related to political institutions and regimes of power. Jacques Derrida (1930–2004) showed that our ways of representing the world in texts holds hidden contradictions and tensions, because language is unstable and built upon assertions of power, not truth. The instability of language refers to the discovery that the meaning of words in a dictionary simply means other words, rather than something indisputable and fixed in the world, and that meanings are simply asserted or agreed, rather than having a strong foundation given for all time. These two prominent thinkers brought knowledge under question, and enabled scholars of religion to uncover how what is and what is not classified as 'religion' can benefit certain groups of people within society.

Critical theory is thus not an abstract and disengaged way of thinking, but an active ethical responsibility for the world and the way we think about the world. It shows the link between ideas and political practices.

> *Religion is a political force.*
> Michel Foucault

THE END OF PHENOMENOLOGY

Before critical theory, the study of religion often consisted of representing different religious traditions, and understanding them according to their rituals, beliefs, and practices. This is known as 'the phenomenology of religion', and is arguably still dominant in school and university programmes of study. Such an approach assumed that knowledge is neutral, and that different issues can be presented without too much difficulty. It was also assumed by many scholars that one does not need a 'theory' or 'theoretical position' –

a way of understanding knowledge and the world – to represent a religious tradition or a set of ideas. There was an assumption that language neutrally represented the external world according to a direct correspondence between the subject in representation (words) and the object in the external world (things) – in this case 'religious' things. However, knowledge and the categories used to represent the world and religion are now seen to be carrying hidden assumptions, with implications for gender, society, politics, colonial history, race, and ethnicity. All knowledge is now seen as reflecting a particular viewpoint or bias about the world; the production and acquisition of knowledge is never neutral. Hence, after critical theory, there is no neutral presentation of ideas about religion.

Critical theory is a way of thinking about how our dominant conceptions of religion come to be dominant or hegemonic. It seeks to identify the hidden positions within our knowledge, and to recognize that all ideas about religion hold a theoretical position about knowledge, even if that position is denied or not apparent. Critical theory offers a way of exploring 'religion' through a set of critical questions about the world and the ideas under discussion. It is not limited to the study of religion, but applies to all ways of thinking about the world, and even questions the boundary between different disciplines of knowledge. Critical theory is not a sub-discipline of religious studies – like the sociology, anthropology, or psychology of religion – but cuts across all these areas and questions all types of knowledge.

Critical theory questions the very idea of 'religion' as a Western – even Christian – category that assumes that belief is more important than how people live, which in turn is used to make assumptions about what people outside Christianity believe. This is seen as a distortion of other cultures. To correct such a view, critical theory considers traditions and cultures outside the bias of such an idea, which assumes there is something special and distinctive we can call 'religion' or 'religious'. For example, scholars question the Christian missionary interpretation of other cultures, and ask whether Hinduism is a 'religion' or the culture of South Asia. In turn, we may question whether Western capitalism is a culture or a religion. Critical theory draws attention to how knowledge is related to political ideas, and questions the domination of Western ideas (particularly European-American ideas) over other ways of seeing the world in different cultures and periods of history. It explores the way ideas powerfully rule the world and the 'truth' people have about the world.

RELIGION, POWER, AND CULTURE

Critical theory shows that the ways we think about religion are bound up in questions of power. Religious studies is now involved in exploring how the history and abuses of colonialism influenced the emergence of religion as an idea; how state power, political regimes, and the globalized world of capitalism affect this process; and how the mass media alter what we mean by religion, and uncover those activities and groups within society not recognized as religious. Critical theory exposes the abuses of power in history, and examines who benefits from thinking about the world in certain ways. It identifies those who are marginalized and unable to speak for themselves.

By examining race, gender, sexuality, and economic wealth one can see how ideas about religion often support those in power, usually the ruling educated elite of white, Western men. Thinking and writing about ideas from the position of the exploited radically changes the subject and the writing of history. Such a process questions, for example, the narrative of Christian history from its Roman-European bias, and examines Christianity through its African – particularly Ethiopian – traditions, highlighting the importance of Augustine as an African. It explores the involvement of Buddhist monks in political activism, and uncovers how the Western media distort the understanding of Islam. Critical theory also identifies ways of life outside the mainstream traditions, and explores the indigenous or local traditions around the world, which are suppressed by multinational business interests for land and oil.

Critical theory questions the boundary between religion and culture, and argues that what people do – rather than what they believe – is more important in understanding. The distinction between the religious and the secular is seen as an ideological or political tool. According to this view, the category of 'religion' can be applied to all cultural activities, such as football, shopping, fashion, club-culture, and film. The historical roots of social institutions – such as government, schools, hospitals, and law – are shown to carry ideas that can be classified as religious, even if they are not transparent. Critical theory radically alters the understanding of religion and shows the importance of the idea to world history. After critical theory, the study of religion becomes a political activity, an account of how powerful organizations in different parts of the world shape the way we understand and classify the world.

JEREMY CARRETTE

Orthodox priests at a Christian festival at Timket, Ethiopia.

CHAPTER 8

Ritual and Performance

Like myths and symbols, ritual and performance is an area that has particularly interested religious studies scholars. Ritual is patterned, formal, symbolic action. Religious ritual is usually seen as having reference to divine or transcendent beings, or perhaps ancestors, whom the participants invoke, propitiate, feed – through offering or sacrifice – worship, or otherwise communicate with. Rituals attempt to enact and deal with the central dilemmas of human existence: continuity and stability, growth and fertility, morality and immortality or transcendence. They have the potential to transform people and situations, creating a fierce warrior or docile wife, a loving servant or imperious tyrant. The ambiguity of ritual symbols, and the invocation of supernatural power, magnifies and disguises human needs and emotions. Because rituals are sometimes performed in terrifying circumstances – as in certain initiation rituals – the messages they carry act at a psycho-biological level that includes, but also exceeds, the rational mind. Symbols and sacred objects are manipulated within ritual to enhance performance and communicate ideological messages concerning the nature of the individual, society, and cosmos. Rituals are fundamental to human culture, and can be used to control, subvert, stabilize, enhance, or terrorize individuals and groups. Studying them gives us a key to an understanding and interpretation of culture.

Anthropologists and religious studies scholars sometimes look at rituals in terms of what they do. For instance, Catherine Bell (b. 1953) distinguishes between:
• rites of passage or 'life crisis' rituals
• calendrical rituals and commemorative rites
• rites of exchange or communication
• rites of affliction
• rites of feasting, fasting, festivals
• political rituals

Another approach is to focus on their explanatory value. Mircea Eliade (1907–86) was interested in ritual as a re-enactment of a primal, cosmogonic myth, bringing the past continually into the present. Robin Horton emphasizes the reality of the religious beliefs behind ritual actions. Using the Kalabari of Nigeria as an example, he insists that religious rituals have the power to move and transform participants because they express beliefs that have meaning and coherence for their adherents. Taking a lead from Durkheim (1858–1917), other scholars claim that rituals are effective because they make statements about social phenomena. Maurice Bloch, writing about circumcision rituals in Madagascar, makes the interesting observation that because a ritual is not fully a statement and not fully an action it allows its message to be simultaneously communicated and disguised. In some cases ritual symbols may be full of resonance, as Victor Turner demonstrated for Ndembu heali ng, chiefly installation, and initiation rituals in Central Africa. In other cases the performance of the ritual itself may be what matters, the content or symbolism having become redundant or forgotten over time, as Fritz Staal has argued for Vedic rituals in India.

> *No experience is too lowly to be taken up in ritual and given a lofty meaning.*
>
> Mary Douglas

PATTERNS IN RITUAL

A key figure in the study of ritual is Arnold van Gennep (1873–1957), who discerned an underlying patterning beneath a wide range of rituals. Whether we look at seasonal festivals such as Christmas, midsummer, or harvest, or 'life crisis' rituals that mark a change in status from one stage of life to another, such as birth, puberty, marriage, or mortuary rituals, we see beneath them all the threefold pattern of separation, transition, and reintegration. Van Gennep also noted that there is generally a physical passage in ritual as well as a social movement, and that the first time a ritual is celebrated it is usually more elaborate than on subsequent occasions, as it bears the weight of change of status.

Victor Turner took up van Gennep's schema, emphasizing the movement from social structure to an anti-structural position in the middle, liminal, stage of a rite of passage. In the middle stage, initiands often share certain characteristics. There is a levelling process — they may be stripped, or dressed in such a way as to erase individuality, hair may be shaved or allowed to grow long. Neophytes are often isolated from the everyday world, and may undergo certain ordeals that bind them to one another and to those initiating them. Turner coined the term 'communitas' to describe a spontaneous, immediate, and concrete relatedness that is typical of people in the liminal stage of a rite of passage. Liminality can also be institutionalized and extended almost indefinitely, as for instance in the military, monastic communities, hospitals, or asylums.

MALE AND FEMALE INITIATION

Bruce Lincoln has criticized both van Gennep and Turner's models as more relevant to male than female initiations, pointing out that women have little status in the social hierarchy, and therefore the middle stage of a woman's initiation is less likely to stress anti-structural elements. Rather than being brought low as a prelude to being elevated, her lowlier place within society is reinforced. A woman is more likely than her male counterparts to be initiated singly, and to be enclosed within a domestic space. Women are generally adorned rather than stripped, and the nature of the knowledge

Malagasy children, Madagascar.

passed on during initiation is likely to be mundane rather than esoteric. Rather than separation, liminality, and reintegration, Lincoln proposes that for women initiation is more likely to involve enclosure, metamorphosis or magnification, and emergence.

A ritual is a type of performance, but not all performances are rituals. Richard Schechner (b. 1934) has pointed out that whether a performance is to be classified as ritual or theatre depends on the context. If the purpose of a performance is to be efficacious, it is a ritual. If its purpose is to entertain, it is theatre. These are not absolute distinctions, and most performances contain elements of both efficacious intention and entertainment. At the ritual end of the continuum we are likely to have an active 'audience', who share the aims and intentions of the main actors. Time and space are sacred, and symbolically marked, and it is the end result of the action that matters — to heal, initiate, aid the deceased, or whatever it may be. In a theatrical performance, the audience is more likely to observe than participate, and the event is an end in itself. It is performed for those watching, and not for, or in the presence of, a higher power or absent other.

FIONA BOWIE

QUESTIONS

1. What is a religion, and why can the term be problematic?

2. Why did many phenomenologists reject theological approaches to religion?

3. An atheist will always be a more objective student of religion than a believer. How far do you agree or disagree with this statement?

4. What problems might you encounter in studying a religion as an outsider?

5. What did Marx mean when he referred to religion as 'the sigh of the oppressed creature'?

6. How do Marx and Weber differ in their perceptions of religion?

7. Explain Durkheim's view of the role of religion in society.

8. Why has there been renewed interest in the sociology of religion in recent years?

9. What can psychology tell us about why people may hold religious beliefs?

10. How has Critical Theory influenced our understanding of religion since the 1960s?

FURTHER READING

Connolly, Peter (ed.), *Approaches to the Study of Religion*. London: Continuum, 2001.

Eliade, Mircea, *The Sacred and the Profane: The Nature of Religion*. New York: Harcourt, Brace, 1959.

Fitzgerald, Timothy, *The Ideology of Religious Studies*. Oxford: Oxford University Press, 2000.

Flood, Gavin, *Beyond Phenomenology: Rethinking the Study of Religion*. London: Cassell, 1999.

Geertz, Clifford, 'Religion as a Cultural System', in Michael Banton, ed., *Anthropological Approaches to the Study of Religion*, pp. 1–46. London: Tavistock, 1966.

Kunin, Seth D., *Religion: The Modern Theories*. Baltimore: Johns Hopkins University Press, 2003.

Levi-Strauss, Claude, *Myth and Meaning*. Toronto: University of Toronto Press, 1978.

McCutcheon, Russell T. ed., *The Insider/Outsider Problem in the Study of Religion*. London: Cassell, 1999.

Otto, Rudolf, *The Idea of the Holy*. London: Oxford University Press, 1923.

Pals, Daniel L., *Eight Theories of Religion*. New York: Oxford University Press, 2006.

Van der Leeuw, Gerardus, *Religion in Essence and Manifestation*. London: Allen & Unwin, 1938.

TIMELINE OF WORLD RELIGIONS

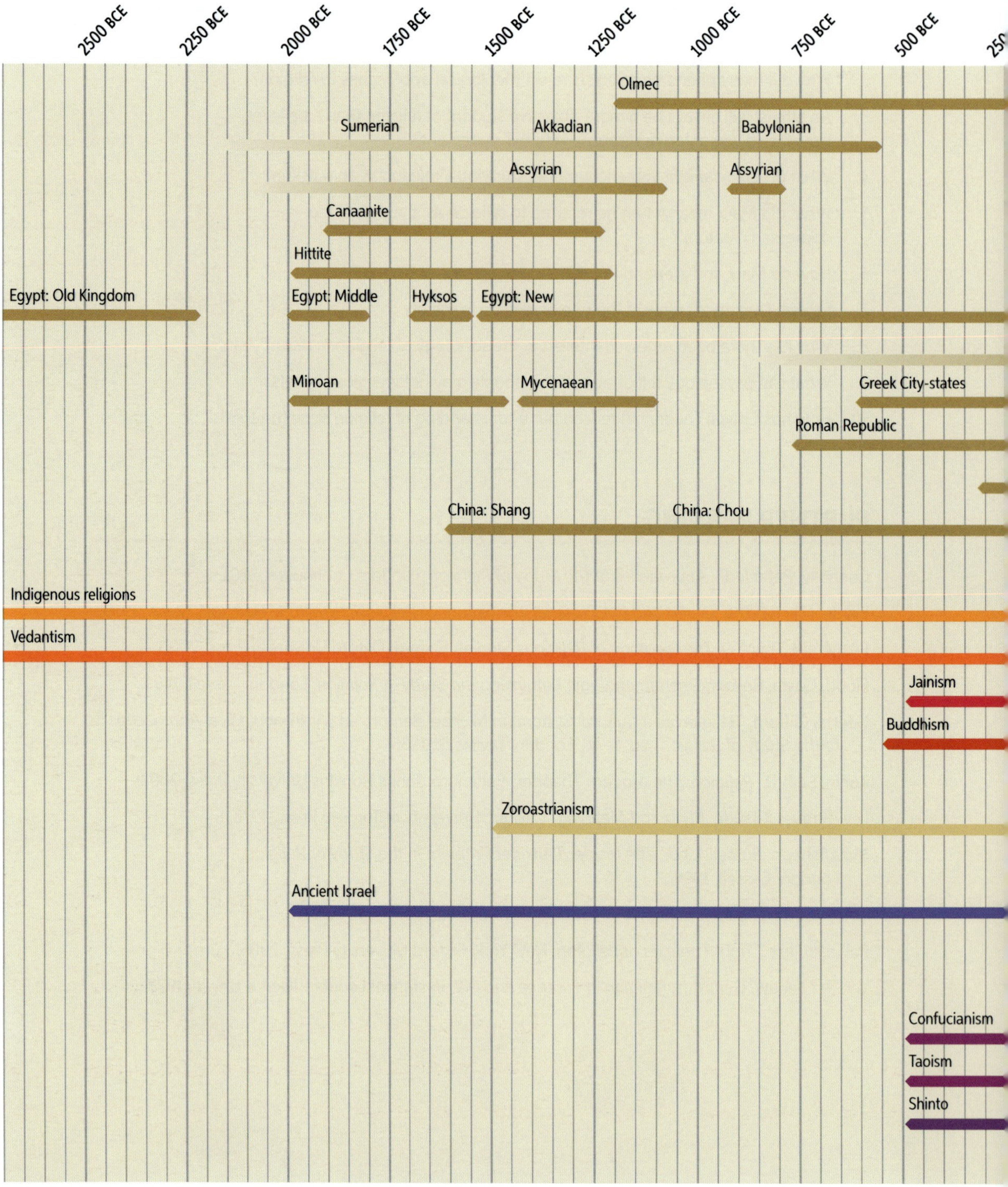

| | 2500 BCE | 2250 BCE | 2000 BCE | 1750 BCE | 1500 BCE | 1250 BCE | 1000 BCE | 750 BCE | 500 BCE | 250 |

Olmec

Sumerian   Akkadian   Babylonian

Assyrian   Assyrian

Canaanite

Hittite

Egypt: Old Kingdom   Egypt: Middle   Hyksos   Egypt: New

Minoan   Mycenaean   Greek City-states

Roman Republic

China: Shang   China: Chou

Indigenous religions

Vedantism

Jainism

Buddhism

Zoroastrianism

Ancient Israel

Confucianism

Taoism

Shinto

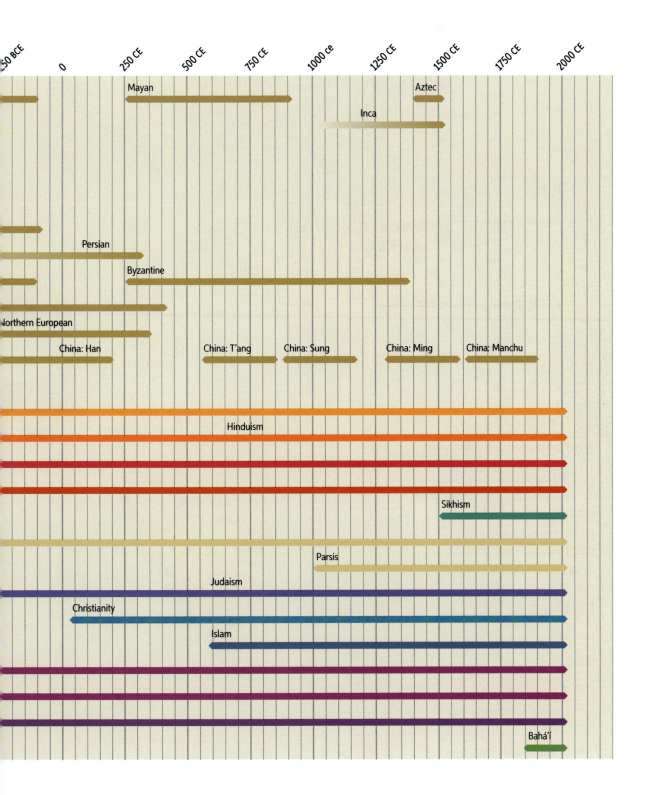

Timeline showing world religions and civilizations across time from 250 BCE to 2000 CE:

- **Mayan** (circa 250 CE – 800 CE)
- **Aztec** (circa 1450 CE – 1500 CE)
- **Inca** (circa 1000 CE – 1500 CE)
- **Persian**
- **Byzantine**
- **Northern European**
- **China: Han**
- **China: T'ang**
- **China: Sung**
- **China: Ming**
- **China: Manchu**
- **Hinduism**
- **Sikhism**
- **Parsis**
- **Judaism**
- **Christianity**
- **Islam**
- **Bahá'í**

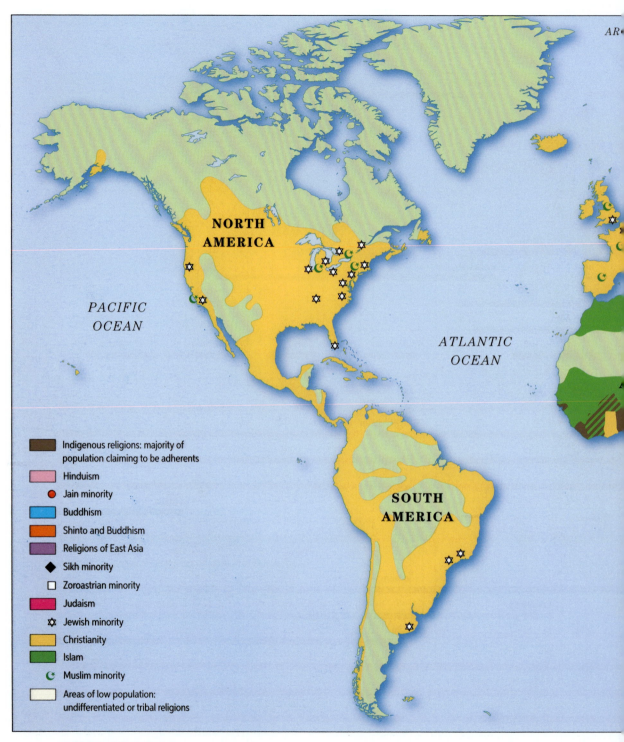

The World's Religions

INTRODUCTION TO WORLD RELIGIONS

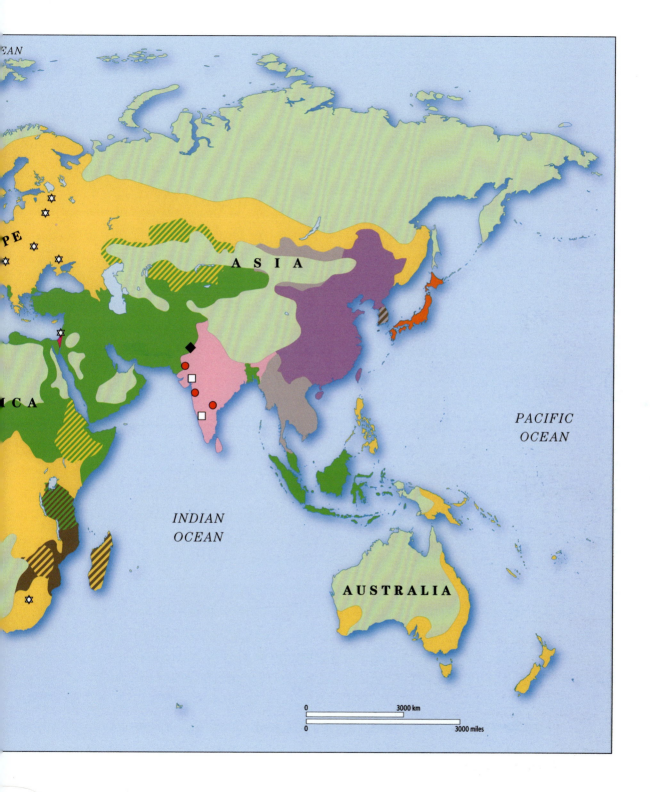

PART 2
RELIGIONS OF ANTIQUITY

SUMMARY

Evidence suggests that, for as long as humanity has walked the earth, we have been drawn towards religious belief of some kind. Whilst some have even suggested that traits which might be called religious are observable in parts of the animal kingdom, archaeologists today believe that our ancestors, perhaps as far back as *Homo erectus* – between 500,000 and a million years ago – engaged in some ritualistic behaviour. Evidence from early *Homo sapiens*, such as the widely distributed 'Venus' figures, suggests that the basic needs of nomadic hunter-gatherer societies, such as fertility and successful hunting, were the chief preoccupation of their religions. From around 12,000 years ago, humans began to settle down and farm the land, and evidence such as early temples and complex burial rituals demonstrates that our religious instincts were subjected more and more to organisation.

Around 3000 BCE, the development of writing in many places was accompanied by the ascent of the great civilizations. Generally, this resulted in more systematic traditions, with whole families of gods and goddesses, often hierarchical, with specific roles, and served by professional priests in dedicated – and increasingly elaborate – temples. The use of text also made possible the transmission and preservation of detailed mythologies. The ancient Egyptians, for example, thought of the world's origin in terms of land emerging from a universe of water. It was common for the religions of antiquity to be tied closely to the state; indeed, many civilizations deified not only illustrious predecessors, but also reigning rulers, such as the Roman emperors. However, in many cultures state religions coexisted with popular folk beliefs, meaning that a person's religion was often a marker of their status. It is, of course, impossible to generalize about the huge diversity in early religion, but one thing almost all share. With the exception of a few late survivors, such as the old faiths of the Baltic people, which lasted to the eighteenth century, or Zoroastrianism, which still claims many adherents, they were displaced by the new religions that came to dominate, and still do so today.

CHAPTER 9

Religion Before History

Most religions are known to us through written sources. 'Prehistoric' means that we are dealing with the time before recorded history; that is, before there were written records about myths, rituals, and beliefs.

Writing was developed in the ancient civilizations of the Near East, China, and Central America. The literate era started about 3000 BCE in the Old World, and shortly after the birth of Christ in the New World. For the sake of convenience, we may designate all religions before 3000 BCE as prehistoric.

'RELIGIOUS' BEHAVIOUR

The question of the origins of religion will not concern us here. Earlier evolutionists thought there had been an original, non-religious phase in human history. Their information has, however, proved to be false. All we can say is that some groups, for example the Maasai in Kenya, appear to lack a belief in life after death.

Some students of religion consider that religious consciousness was born during the time when humankind first appeared. Others find traces of 'religious' behaviour even in the animal kingdom. Despite some startling progress in animal-behaviour studies (ethology) and the study of early humankind (palaeoanthropology), nothing certain can be said about these. All that we know is that some early human cultures seem to have contained traces of religious orientation.

PREHISTORIC SOURCES

The main difficulty in any approach to prehistoric religion lies, of course, in the absence of written sources from this extensive period in the history of humankind. The prehistorian is referred to silent survivals of the past: bone materials, stone arrangements, rough stone figures, rock drawings, and similar materials. Such objects are difficult to decipher.

For example, it is difficult to tell whether a Danish bog find from the Iron Age – be it a well-preserved human body or a golden dish – was or was not used as a gift or offering, since there are no documents from that time to illuminate what really happened.

Some modern archaeologists even question whether Denmark, or even Scandinavia, had a religion during the Bronze Age. We shall never know for certain what the people of those days thought.

However, there are means to come closer to an understanding of at least some general ideas of those distant times. Let us first see how the prehistoric source materials can be classified. The difficulty of such a classification is obvious: we cannot know if a particular type of artifact — an axe, say, or a wagon — ever had a ritual purpose. Nevertheless, a survey of materials that seem to qualify as connected with religion calls for a division along the following lines:

- burial places and burial finds
- deposition of offerings
- representations of deities, spirits, and cultic figures (carved idols, reliefs, rock paintings, rock drawings, etc.)
- remains of constructions with religious associations, such as altars, temples, or foundations of world pillars

Archaeologists usually point out that this material can be interpreted only by analogy. The prehistoric material must be placed in a context which may suggest its original meaning. Of course, all such conclusions are hypothetical; the history of prehistoric research has seen a succession of interpretations. The methods of archaeological reconstruction have become more refined, comparisons with the world of the science of the peoples of humankind (ethnology) more restricted in scope, and ecological perspectives more decisive. Nevertheless, much of our reconstruction of prehistoric religion remains guesswork. Almost every interpretation of beliefs can be, and has been, contested.

PRELITERATE RELIGIONS

The prehistoric era of religion stretches from the beginning of humankind — probably about two or three million years ago — until approximately 3000 BCE. During all this time religious knowledge was transmitted through the spoken word — beliefs and myths — and through imitative behaviour — rituals. This somewhat restricted how much knowledge could be accumulated, although it is amazing how much tribal keepers of oral traditions are able to memorize.

> There is nothing more ancient in the world than language. The history of man begins, not with rude flints, rock temples or pyramids, but with language. The second stage is represented by myths as the first attempt at translating the phenomena of nature into thought. The third stage is that of religion or the recognition of moral powers, and in the end of One Moral Power behind and above all nature.
>
> F. Max Müller, *Contributions to the Science of Mythology* (London, 1897).

In many prehistoric societies the fight for subsistence may likewise have precluded the growth of sophisticated religious thought, although there are examples of primal societies with a good deal of leisure time at their disposal. We therefore find some basic differences between representatives of preliterate and literate religions; for instance, the former value repetition in myth and ritual, the latter develop dogma and may go in for intricate speculations.

The main differences between prehistoric and historic religions are, however, that the former are organized around the perspectives of the hunter, food-gatherer, fisherman, or early farmer, whereas historic religions represent the world-view of the developed civilizations, beginning with Egypt, Mesopotamia, and China. In other words, prehistoric religions were at home in small-scale tribal societies, where family or kin-groups meant more than other forms of social organization, and where the influence of natural forces had a tremendous impact on daily life and religion. Such primitive societies still linger on today, and it is possible to link the types of these societies with prehistoric periods.

HUNTERS AND FARMERS

The first period is the Palaeolithic, or Old Stone Age, during which people were hunters, food-gatherers, and fishermen. Latter-day hunting societies have been organized along similar lines, and the patterns of their religions are probably reminiscent of those of Palaeolithic times.

The Palaeolithic was followed by the Neolithic, or New Stone Age, about 10,000 BCE. This was the time when many hunters turned into primitive farmers. In the following millennia, pastoral nomadism developed out of this agriculture, in places where the cultivated lands met the grasslands and deserts. The world of the farmers and herdsmen is still with us, and there is every reason to expect that their religious practices resemble those of their prehistoric predecessors. These analogies between past and present are very rough and ready. Ecological, technological, social, and historical differences may cast doubts upon their validity. But they do give us certain clues on which to base our interpretation.

BEFORE 30,000 BCE

It is extremely difficult to tell from the finds at our disposal what religion was like during the long period called the Early, or Lower, Palaeolithic, before 30,000 BCE. This was the time of the pre-human members of the family of humankind, the early hominids such as *Australopithecus africanus*, *Homo habilis* (2,500,000 BCE), *Homo erectus* (1,600,000 BCE), and *Homo neanderthalensis* (100,000–30,000 BCE). Perhaps originating in Africa – only Africa has the earliest skeletons and a continuous succession of species – the hominids spread to Europe, where they appeared before 1,000,000 BCE, and to Asia; Peking man and Sangiran man in Indonesia were both representatives of *Homo erectus*.

We have some information about the modest cultural achievements of early humankind. For instance, we know that two-and-a-half million years ago groups of hominids in East Africa used choppers, scrapers, and other stone utensils that they had shaped themselves. They practised division of labour between the sexes and food-sharing. However, their religious ideas – if any – are unknown to us. This is what we might expect, for people's cultural capacity at this early time was crude, and they did not express clear religious ideas that can be recognized as such by today's archaeologists. We have neither burials, drawings, nor stone monuments to guide our search; however, the toolmaking of these early individuals suggests they possessed creative intelligence, and therefore – very possibly – a form of religion.

PEKING MAN

Many prehistorians have assumed that the Peking representative of *Homo erectus*, who lived about half a million years ago, had some concept of religion or magic. The cave discovered near Chou Kou Tien contained human skulls broken at the *foramen magnum*, which gives easy access to the brain, which it would seem was extracted and eaten. If this was the case – of course, we cannot be sure – the motive was religious or magical rather than for food, for there were many animals to hunt. Such cannibalism, when practised in present-day primal societies, usually implies the incorporation of the dead person's vigour and power.

This is a very hypothetical interpretation, and, unfortunately, practically all finds from the Lower Palaeolithic that lend themselves to a religious interpretation are subject to the same difficulty. Take, for instance, the discoveries of circles of mammoth skulls in Russia and Ukraine. We are familiar with similar skull arrangements from North America in historical times, the circles of buffalo skulls on the plains that were important in worship. However, the Palaeolithic mammoth skulls may simply have served as weights on the tent-cloths, instead of stones. In several instances there are bone circles surrounding fireplaces, and in these cases a religious purpose is probably out of the question.

NEANDERTHAL MAN

Almost all the early remains that may have religious significance are associated with 'Neanderthal man' and the last 50,000 years of the Lower Palaeolithic – the so-called Mousterian period. Neanderthal people buried their dead with proper ceremonies, and seem to have believed in some kind of life after death. In the cave of Shanidar, northern Iraq, a dead person was buried under a heap of stones, resting on a bed of many flowers. At Techik Tach, Turkestan, a child was buried surrounded by five pairs of horns of the mountain goat, apparently placed in a circle. A cave at Monte Circeo, Italy, contains a human skull within a small circle of stones, one of the so-called 'skull burials' that continue throughout the Palaeolithic period.

Grave gifts are common in many instances – for example, at La Chapelle-aux-Saints, France. Towards the end of the Mousterian period, the dead were buried in a contracted position – 'flexed burials' – and painted with red ochre. Both these features may reflect belief in a future life: a return to the womb of Mother Earth, a continued existence in

> *Religion in one or other of its many aspects is a universal phenomenon and it appears to be virtually as old as the human race itself.*
>
> E. O. James, *The Beginnings of Religion* (1958).

another world through the red 'blood'. Studies of certain modern peoples support these interpretations, but others are of course possible.

From this time also we have evidence of sacred objects: round fossils and pieces of iron pyrites. One round fossil from Tata, Hungary, is engraved with two lines, forming a cross; this could be the first clear evidence of the idea of a quartered universe, a concept widely represented in both Old and New World cosmology.

Even in recent times some Arctic peoples have worshipped bears, and it is possible similar religious beliefs were represented in Central Europe – in France, Switzerland and Italy – in Mousterian times. In the Drachenloch Cave, Switzerland, bear skulls have been found enclosed in a stone coffin covered by stone slabs, which looks like a bear burial. Some reputable scholars, including Koby, Leroi-Gourhan, and Kurtén, insist, however, that the cave-bears in question died a natural death in their winter lairs, and that the apparent 'burial chests' are due to natural rockfall from the ceiling of the cave. This is a plausible explanation, but the 'cultic' interpretation seems no less plausible. Other finds in Dordogne, France, and Weimar, Germany, suggest deliberate burial of bears – brown bears in these cases. The main idea behind bear ceremonialism is that the dead animal will return to life, or persuade its relatives to make themselves available to the hunter, provided it has received a correct burial. The pattern of burial has been taken from human burials.

HOMO SAPIENS

Neanderthal people belonged to Europe, the Middle East, North Africa, and northern Asia. They were slowly replaced by another species, *Homo sapiens* – our own direct ancestors – who had already spread over the continents before the end of the Lower Palaeolithic: Siberian peoples entered the New World as early as 60,000 years ago, or perhaps even earlier, and Australia received its population from Indonesia more than 30,000 years ago. This is of importance for our reconstruction of religious history, as it means the main structures of American and Australian hunting religions go back to the Lower Palaeolithic. It may even imply that totemism and high-god beliefs, which both appear in these religions, are equally old.

At the beginning of the Upper Palaeolithic period – about 30,000 years ago – Neanderthal people had left the scene in Europe and modern humankind, *Homo sapiens*, took over. The main periods were the Aurignacian (from 30,000 BCE), Solutrean (from 20,000 BCE) and Magdalenian (15,000–10,000 BCE). Now the religious patterns which we glimpse in earlier periods take a more discernible form. The world-view is still that of hunting peoples, but it varies in different parts of Eurasia. The religious developments in Africa, southern Asia, Australia, and America are as yet hidden from us.

The burial customs give clear evidence of a belief in life after death. For example, in caves near Menton, south-east France, some 'flexed' skeletons were found, stained with iron oxide, adorned with rows of pierced shells and bracelets, and equipped with quartzite tools and flint knives. Skeletons from Italy to Russia testify that the dead were buried with their most precious property; no doubt, they were thought to take it with them to another world.

THE MOTHER GODDESS

It is from this time – the Gravettian period, 25,000 BCE – that the famous sculpted 'Venus' figurines in ivory, bone, and stone appear. They are distributed from France to eastern Siberia, and best known of them is the Venus from Willendorf, Austria. They all have characteristic, distorted features: the parts of the body which serve sexual and child-bearing functions – the breasts, hips, buttocks, and private parts – are excessively enlarged, whereas little attention is paid to the face, arms, and legs.

It has been suggested that these fat-rumped – 'steatopygous' – figures are simply representatives of mortal women, portrayed in the fashion of the time. This is scarcely probable: the emphasis on the sexual parts shows clearly that these Venuses were supposed to represent deities of fertility, growth, and fruitfulness. Here we have for the first time representations of a deity – the mother goddess – conceived as one or many.

There is a seemingly puzzling question here. How could the mother goddess – forerunner of Ishtar, Cybele, and Artemis – be such a prominent divinity in a hunting culture? The answer is simple. In recently studied northern Eurasian cultures, the women had similar birth goddesses protecting them during pregnancy and childbirth. Many Siberian tribes believed in a mother of the wild animals, a mistress who protects the wild creatures to whom she has given life. We also know women played a very important role during the Stone Age as mothers, housekeepers, and gatherers of roots and berries.

Do these figurines prove that the concept of a male god was introduced later than the concept of a goddess? Such a conclusion seems unwarranted. Before the emergence of the Middle Eastern city-states, the Supreme Being was never represented in art, as far as we can tell. A diffuse sky-god was not easy to picture. We know that bull-roarers have been used to imitate the voice of the Supreme Being, or the voices of dead ancestors, in some modern primal hunting religions in Australia, South Africa, Brazil, and California. Some perforated, ornate stone slabs found in Upper Palaeolithic caves may have been similar bull-roarers, symbolizing the presence of the Supreme God or other supernatural beings. However, this is far from certain.

CAVE PAINTINGS

The most telling artistic creations from the Upper Palaeolithic are the engravings and paintings on cave walls. These first appear in the Aurignacian period, but receive their full development in the Magdalenian, and their focus is in southern France and northernmost Spain. The most famous and numerous rock paintings date from 15,000 to 11,000 BCE, the time of the caves of Lascaux in the Dordogne, Niaux, Les Trois-Frères, and Montespan in Ariège, France, and Altamira, northern Spain.

Eighty per cent of the figures depicted are animals, of which most are horses and bison, the hooved fauna of the frosty plains. Reindeer occur only at a late stage, as the glaciers made their last push forward. The composition of these beautiful and realistic animal scenes has been interpreted in various ways. Despite alternative speculations, it seems reasonable to believe the animals refer to hunting ritual and hunting magic. Hunting was the major occupation of Palaeolithic man, and ceremonies to secure a successful hunt were certainly part of the hunting craft, just as they have been among traditional hunters up to the present day. Only four per cent of the pictured animals show arrows, or wounds resulting from arrows. This does not necessarily mean they cannot be associated with hunting magic. Among primal peoples, hunting ceremonies are often complicated, and real magic – indicating the anticipation of success in the hunt – is only part of a wider pattern. It was believed mere representation of an animal form might lead to the kill.

Why did this animal ceremonialism take place in caves, often in the depths of scarcely accessible inner chambers? We do not know, but it may have to do with the fact that – in widespread tales – the animals

Stone Age cave paintings at Bhimbetka, Bhopal, Madhya Pradesh, India, are approximately 30,000 years old.

INTRODUCTION TO WORLD RELIGIONS

are supposed originally to have come from underground, or to have once been secluded in caves. Some wall-scenes depict human beings in animal disguise, possibly representing ritual performers – perhaps magicians, ritual dancers, or mythical beings. Well-known is the 'sorcerer' of the cave of Les Trois-Frères: an image of a human being with reindeer antlers, long beard, bear's paws, and a horse's tail. This figure has been interpreted as a shaman, or god of the cave, but his position in the picture, over a great number of animals, makes it more likely he was a lord of the animals, master of the game.

> *The prehistoric paintings discovered in southern France and in Spain reveal that our ancient ancestors were trying to decipher the meaning of life and the world from their primitive dwelling places.*
>
> Joseph Kitagawa, *The Quest for Human Unity* (1990).

All these interpretations are, of course, tentative. There is a host of pictures that do not easily lend themselves to interpretation, such as pictographs of headless animals – even a sculpture of a headless bear – of women dancing around a phallic man, and so on. However, such representations strengthen the impression that Upper Palaeolithic European religion was concerned with animals and sexual fertility – natural subjects in a religion chiefly concerned with hunting. We can say the same of animal ceremonialism in Siberia in the same era: reindeer skeletons were carefully buried in anatomical order. Such hunting rites have survived in this area into the twentieth century. As in the bear rites, the aim has been to restore the animal to a new life in this world or hereafter.

From the end of the Palaeolithic, or the Mesolithic, we have evidence in northern Germany of what appear to have been sacrifices to the supernatural rulers of the reindeer. Reindeer were submerged in a lake close to present-day Hamburg, weighted down with stones. It is unlikely these reindeer were caches for the hunters, as has also been suggested.

THE NEOLITHIC PERIOD

The Neolithic period (10,000–3,000 BCE) is, strictly speaking, the time when objects of stone were no longer chipped, but ground and polished. More important, from about 10,000 BCE people changed to producing, rather than hunting or gathering, their own food. The population of the world was probably around 10 million. The climate had changed – the melting of the ice was in full flux – and the warmer weather made possible new inventions in subsistence.

Agriculture was born, possibly as a consequence of the gathering of seeds by the women. This new way of life made it possible for a rapidly-growing population to settle in one place, to live in villages, and practise pottery-making and weaving. Village life had a tremendous impact on religion, as did the new food sources, the products of agriculture – or horticulture, as primitive agriculture is sometimes called.

The Neolithic period provides us with archaeological materials from the whole world. Farming began in at least three independent centres, one of which is the Middle East, on the mountain slopes of the Fertile Crescent. Wheat and corn were cultivated here, and dogs and goats domesticated. The taming of animals slowly developed into pastoral nomadism on the outskirts of the area. In the north, where the grasslands were wide and open, horse riding was introduced in about 900 BCE. Another centre of agriculture was South-East Asia, homeland of the cultivation of root crops such as yams. Close by, in Assam, rice was introduced as a staple food which quickly spread to China and the surrounding areas. A third centre was Central America, where the cultivation of maize began around 5000 BCE.

The religions of the Neolithic peoples were closely adapted to these three agricultural civilizations and spread with them. When pastoral nomadism appeared on the scene, a new profile of religion was formed that changed the course of world religions.

> *… in the deep reaches of the prehistory of Homo erectus, there are telltale signs of beliefs about the afterlife.*
>
> Ninian Smart,
> *The World's Religions* (1989).

DEATH AND BURIAL

If we concentrate on the West Asian-Mediterranean Neolithic religions, we see how the archaeological finds fit this picture. People lived in villages and similar settlements; outside these, true cemeteries have been found, although in some cases the bodies were buried under the floors of the houses. Graves were provided with gifts and offerings, such as beads, shells, utensils such as ivory combs, and female figurines – perhaps symbolizing servants for the next life, or protective goddesses.

The closer we come to the time of developed civilizations, the more differentiated are the burials according to rank or class. Social distinctions – 'stratification' – developed as political organization based on kinship was succeeded by one based on territory, and a surplus of products made it possible for some to become relatively rich and important. This development was reflected in the burial customs.

'Inhumation' was now common, where the body was interred in the ground like grain, to arise again in another world. Coffins became more frequently used as time went by. Towards the end of the Neolithic, cremation was practised here and there, perhaps associated with a more spiritual view of the afterlife.

In some early Neolithic burials, the heads of the dead were removed and placed in a circle, facing the centre. This seems to be the last survival of an old Palaeolithic tradition. The beliefs behind this arrangement are hidden from us; perhaps it is linked to the circle as a symbol of the universe.

MALE AND FEMALE

Many female sculptures – fat-rumped and violin-shaped figures in bone, clay, and terracotta – testify to the prominence of fertility cults. Figurines from Romania (5000 BCE) show a mother with her child, later a favourite motif in the Egyptian and Christian religions. In some places there are also phallic statuettes, representing the male companion of the fertility goddess. The female statuettes are, however, in the majority, reflecting the elevated position of the woman, and so also of the goddess, in a matrilineal, agrarian society. The functions of the mother goddess were now adapted to farming needs: she appeared as goddess of earth and vegetation.

Other fertility divinities were also portrayed, sometimes through animal masks, sometimes in sculpture. Serpentines around the goddess hint that she was a snake-goddess; in later Cretan culture the goddess raises her hands holding snakes. The snake was a fertility symbol in historical times in Europe, the Middle East, India, and China – where the dragon was too.

Another divinity is probably represented in the bull effigies with human masks found in the Balkans. The cult of the bull – symbol of fertility – seems to have been distributed across the Mediterranean and Middle Eastern world. In historical times, it became associated with gods such as Baal and Dionysus, and with the supernatural master of the bull figures in Zoroastrian religion, where Mithra is represented as killing the bull to rejuvenate the world. The bullfights of south-western Europe are probably echoes of ancient rituals in the worship of the bull-cult.

PRIESTS AND TEMPLES

This was the time when a form of priesthood evolved, and when temples of wood, stone, and clay became common. The casual sacrificing places of the earlier nomadic hunting culture

Prehistoric dolmen – single-chamber megalithic tomb – in field in Ireland. It would originally have been covered with an earth mound.

were superseded by large buildings for divine service. Here were kept altars, vessels, inscribed objects, vases with paintings of ritual scenes, sculptures in clay, and – later on – copper and gold. All these were used in the rituals.

In Ukraine and surrounding areas, archaeologists have found both the remains of temples and clay models of temples. For instance, at Sabatinovka, in the Southern Bug Valley, Ukraine, Russian prehistorians discovered a temple dating from about 5000 BCE. Built of wattle and daub, it occupied about seventy square metres. A large, rectangular room, with a floor plastered with clay, contained at the back a clay altar, upon which sixteen big-buttocked female figurines were found, seated on horn-backed stools. Beside the altar was a clay chair, perhaps intended for the high priest.

European and West-Asian Neolithic developments are paralleled in East Asia, and are connected with the Chinese Neolithic period. But the developments in South-East Asia are more difficult to follow. In America, the fertility religion of the horticulturists was simply a transfer of the conceptual world of the hunter to that of the planter; agrarian rituals did not vary much from hunting rituals in post-Columbian eastern North America. However, some mythological motifs connected with the 'maize mother' point to links with Indonesia. In large areas of agricultural America, the Neolithic period continued until the arrival of Columbus, and even beyond that date.

Neolithic aligned stones, or menhirs, at Carnac, Brittany, France, dating from c. 4500 BCE.

INTRODUCTION TO WORLD RELIGIONS

HOLY PLACES, SACRED CALENDARS

The places where the gods are revealed or act, and the times when they do so, are central to religious experience.

The place of a vision, healing, miracle, or sign tends to be set aside as a special holy space where the gods may be expected to act again. This may begin as a mere cleared circle in the grass, where people come with prayers and offerings. Symbolic objects representing the divinity, altars for offerings and sacrifices, and buildings to protect both images and altars and to serve as a 'house for the god' may then be added. As the shrine is elaborated, it may become a vast temple space with massive structures.

Such sacred places have a symbolic significance. They may be regarded as the 'centre of the world', or 'navel of the earth', as the meeting-place between the gods and humankind, and the earthly replica of the heavenly realms. The inner cell where the image rests is the 'most holy place', often followed by a series of courts, with degrees of lesser holiness, to the entrances.

Ascent from the earthly to the heavenly realm is symbolized by vertical features – massive stairways, sacred pillars or trees, and sanctuaries on holy mountains. Similar ideas may attach to sacred caves, groves, healing wells, mysterious rock formations, and the tombs of saints or martyrs. Since divine power is more accessible at sanctuaries, these become places of pilgrimage.

The synagogues, churches, and mosques of Judaism, Christianity, and Islam, however, should be seen as meeting-places for the worshippers, not as sacred dwelling-places for God. They may have a historical or devotional value, but they do not possess a special 'holiness' because God is more active there than anywhere else.

Distance in time separates people from the divine creative acts of the past. In many religions this is overcome by regular recital of sacred myths, retelling what the gods did in creating the world, giving the land, and showing how to make fire, to hunt, farm, build, and live together. The recital brings these foundation events to life again. Similarly, periodic rituals re-enact – and so renew – the actions of the gods.

Together, myths and rites make up great religious ceremonies, which are timed by the rhythms of the seasons or of the heavenly bodies. The most basic is the new year renewal rite, when both human and earthly vitalities, which have been used up, corrupted, or attacked by evil forces, are purified and given fresh life from the spirit world.

Calendars first developed as schedules telling when to be ready for the next renewal of divine blessing or power. Calendars, however, could not tell the right time to secure divine blessing on activities such as building a new village, making war, trading, travel, marrying, or anything else of special importance. For these, diviners sought to read the signs of divine approval in the position of the stars (astrology), the flight of birds, by casting lots, consulting oracles, and in many other ways. Divination is therefore important where people feel totally dependent on gods who do not otherwise disclose their will.

Religions with scriptures, such as Judaism, Christianity, and Islam, have other means of revelation, and have often opposed divination. On the other hand, they have their calendars of times for renewal, whether in daily devotions, weekly worship, or annual renewals of experience of the divine blessing.

Harold Turner

MEGALITHS

Towards the end of the Neolithic era, structures composed of large stones – or 'megaliths' – were erected in Europe. Most of these were probably burial structures: the striking tombs – 'dolmens' – consisting of a large, flat stone supported on uprights, and the passage graves, are found on islands and shores of the Mediterranean and western Europe. However, in addition to the megalithic tombs there are also huge stones in alignment – or 'menhirs' – as at Carnac, in Brittany, France. Their purpose is unknown; possibly they marked ritual procession routes. Some large constructions, such as the Hal Tarxien stone buildings in Malta, were evidently temples. Chalk sculptures found in them show realistic human features with some kind of gowns, and may represent gods and goddesses and their priests.

Other megalithic structures give the impression of having had astronomical functions. Possibly they helped to determine the calendar and the agricultural seasons, always important to the farmer. For instance, Stonehenge, on Salisbury Plain, England, has a circle of sarsen stones, some of which line up with the sunrise at midsummer. Whatever calendar purpose Stonehenge had, it was also a place of worship; archaeologists have suggested fertility-gods and goddesses were probably worshipped there.

A section of the circle of sarsen stones at Stonehenge, Wiltshire, England.

INTRODUCTION TO WORLD RELIGIONS

Megalithic monuments have been found from Britain in the west to Assam in the east, and reached South-East Asia, Polynesia, and — according to some scholars — even the New World. Certainly, the Egyptian pyramids and the Mayan pyramids in Yucatan, Mexico, resemble each other, and both served as burial chambers. All over Eurasia and America, astronomers and prehistorians have identified stone constructions as observatories and megalithic calendars. If this is true, it is almost certain that astronomy was pursued within the frame of religious and ceremonial interests.

THE GREAT CIVILIZATIONS

These megalithic monuments are — like the Bronze-Age finds that date from approximately the same time — stepping stones to the era of the great civilizations, or 'high cultures'. The latter started on the river plains of Egypt, Mesopotamia, and other Near Eastern areas around 3000 BCE, and introduce the age of history, that is, of writing. With people living in towns, central political power, large economic surpluses, and strict class differentiation characterize these new kingdoms. In the religious sphere they are distinguished by sacred kings, a priestly hierarchy, developed ritual, hecatombs of blood-sacrifices, and imposing temple buildings. Their religious world is populated by great gods and goddesses — usually arranged in hierarchical order under a supreme god — and their realm of the dead is stratified.

We have come a long way from the simple stone arrangements of the Palaeolithic peoples. Despite the 'Neolithic revolution', it is a continuous road that leads from the simple beliefs of Palaeolithic hunting groups to the polytheism of the great ancient kingdoms.

ÅKE HULTKRANTZ

CHAPTER 10

Land of the Aztecs and Incas

'Pre-Columbian' is a term generally applied to Central and South America before its conquest by Spain in the sixteenth century CE. In much of Central America – now mainly the modern states of Mexico and Guatemala – and the central Andes – largely modern Peru and highland Bolivia – high cultures with polytheistic religions developed. In both areas, however, there were two levels of religion: the common people had their local shrines at which offerings were made, but there were also the organized state religions, with temples and systematic theologies. What we know about these religions comes from archaeology, contemporary native documents – such as the Aztec and Maya codices – and Spanish accounts. The origins of formalized religions in both Mexico and Peru can be traced back as early as 1200 BCE to temple structures with associated cults.

CENTRAL AMERICA

The Olmecs

Between about 1200 and 500 BCE a people called by archaeologists the Olmecs lived on the Gulf Coast of Mexico. They built ceremonial centres, for example La Venta, which were carefully planned temple communities. At La Venta, a group of buildings was arranged symmetrically along one axis, with a clay pyramid, shaped like a fluted cone, at the south end.

Olmec religion seems to have centred on the jaguar in various guises. At La Venta, three identical mosaic pavements made from blocks of green serpentine were discovered, each laid out in the form of a stylized jaguar face. As soon as each had been finished, it was covered up. These could have been some kind of offering to the beast.

On the lid of a stone coffin, or sarcophagus, at La Venta, a jaguar mask is depicted, with feathers for eyebrows and a forked tongue of the type found only in snakes. This seems to show the jaguar as part bird and part snake, suggesting that he may be the ancestor of the Mexican god Quetzalcoatl, usually shown as a plumed serpent. It also suggests that, in Olmec times, different animals were combined to form one god, an idea basic to Central American deities.

The Olmec jaguar could also assume human characteristics. A carving from the site of Potrero Nuevo, Mexico, shows his union with a woman, an act that was believed to have produced a race of half-human and half-jaguar creatures. The human element is generally childish, with a paunch and stubby limbs, onto which are grafted the jaguar characteristics: fangs, sometimes claws, and a snarling mouth, turned down at the corners. The heads are often cleft at the top. These hybrid creatures were probably deities, possibly of fertility.

The Maya

Successors to the Olmecs were the Maya, a Central American people who lived in the semi-tropical rain forest of the Guatemalan department of El Petén and adjacent parts of Mexico and Belize. The Maya developed an elaborate state religion based on ceremonial centres and cities containing temples, whilst alongside this there existed a native folk religion. The earliest temples were built about 200 BCE at Tikal and Uaxactun; however Maya culture and religion fully developed during the Classic Period, between 300 and 900 CE, after which the state religion largely collapsed, though the folk one has partially survived.

Mayan religion was – and still is – a contract between human beings and their gods. The gods helped humans in their work and provided them with food, but in return expected payment, usually in advance. Prayer was directed towards material ends, such as obtaining rain to make the crops grow.

There seems to have been little difference – except in scale – between preparations for an important ceremony in a village and at a ceremonial centre or city. Before all ceremonies there had to be sexual continence,

The Mayan temple at Tikal, Guatemala, rises 154 feet (47 metres) high and was completed around 740–750 CE.

fasting, and usually confession. Continence involved husbands and wives sleeping apart for a specified period; if this was not observed, both the ceremony and the guilty person might be jeopardized. In antiquity, the body was painted black – the colour of unmarried men – during fasting.

Many forms of sacrifice played a part in Mayan religion, involving offerings of one's own blood, that of human or animal victims, or produce such as maize. Human sacrifice involved extracting the heart while the living victim was held down by the arms and legs. The rain-gods preferred small offerings, such as miniature corn grindstones, and in the case of human sacrifice, children.

Mayan deities usually only wanted recognition in the form of frequent offerings. Few of them were human in form, and most showed a mixture of human and animal features. For example, the all-important *Chacs,* or rain gods, are shown in the Mayan codices as long-nosed gods with snake features. Gods such as the *Chacs* were conceived of in fours, each associated with a compass direction and a colour. For example, there was one *Chac* for the east, with the colour red.

These gods of the Maya possessed a dual character – benevolent and malevolent – and also sexual duality. The *Chacs* are generally masculine, but one is sometimes shown as female. The Maya marshalled their gods indiscriminately in large categories, and a god could belong to two diametrically opposed groups. The sun-god was mainly a sky-god, as might be expected. However, at night this god passed through the underworld on the way east from the point of sunset to that of sunrise, and during this passage became one of the nine lords of the night and the underworld.

Teotihuacan

Teotihuacan was a large city that flourished in the Valley of Mexico at much the same time as the Mayan zenith, between 300 and 700 CE. To judge from the number and size of the temples there, it appears to have been a theocracy, and seems to have fallen to outside invaders about 700 CE.

Religious symbolism features strongly on the temple walls of Teotihuacan. The rain-god, Tlaloc, or 'the one who makes things grow', is frequently depicted, suggesting this god was held in great esteem. One fresco shows him with a spectacle-like mask over his face and fangs protruding from his mouth. The other deity who features prominently at Teotihuacan is Quetzalcoatl, who can be seen on a temple façade bearing his name, and is surrounded by sea-shells and snail-shells. He may have represented the waters of the earth.

The Toltecs

The Toltecs were a coalition of nations in north-central Mexico who established their capital at Tula, about 50 miles/80 kilometres north of Mexico City, about 980 CE. The fifth ruler of the Toltecs, the semi-legendary Ce Acatl, was a priest-king who took the name of the god Quetzalcoatl. Soon after his accession, he was expelled by devotees of the god Tezcatlipoca and migrated with his followers to Yucatan, where he founded Chichen Itza. The two principal Toltec pyramids – the Castillo at Chichen Itza, and the Temple of the Morning Star at Tula – illustrate how religious life changed after the collapse of the theocracy at

Teotihuacan. At the foot of the stairway of each pyramid was a large colonnaded hall, where warriors could gather together at religious festivals to use their own altar platforms and sacrificial stones. Theocracy had been largely superseded by militarism.

Among the Toltecs, Quetzalcoatl became a sky symbol instead of one of water. Another Toltec deity was a combination of the eagle and jaguar, representing the earthly warrior caste. The latter had the duty of feeding the sun and morning star with the hearts and blood of sacrificial victims.

Aztec religion traced several important elements back to Toltec times. Both Toltec and Aztec religion displayed a close connection between kingship and warriorhood on the one hand, and fire, the sun, and the morning star on the other. The Aztecs also continued the Toltec method of human sacrifice, by which the victim was held down on a low stone block, the chest opened with a knife, and the heart torn out.

The Aztecs

The Aztecs migrated into the Valley of Mexico in the late twelfth century, and founded their capital city of Tenochtitlan about 1370 CE. However, they did not start their political expansion until after 1430 CE. The Aztecs believed that two primordial beings originated everything, including the gods: Ometecuhtli, 'Lord of the Duality', and Omeciuatl, 'Lady of the Duality', who both lived at the summit of the world, in the thirteenth heaven. These two produced all the gods and all humankind. However, by the time of the Spanish Conquest, the two primordial beings had largely been pushed into the background by a crowd of younger and more active gods.

Some of the pyramids of Teotihuacan, the huge archaeological site 30 miles north-west of Mexico City, Mexico.

… the central rites of the empire, presided over by the emperor himself, were human sacrifices in which the victim's chest would be opened and the still quivering heart torn out and presented to the gods.

Ninian Smart,
The World's Religions (1989).

The Aztecs believed that the gods in turn created the earth, during which the most important act was the birth of the sun at Teotihuacan, through the self-sacrifice of a little leprous god. The remaining gods followed his example of sacrifice, to provide the blood needed to set the sun moving across the sky. To keep the sun moving on its course, it had to be fed daily with human blood. The Aztecs regarded sacrifice as a sacred duty towards the sun, without which the life of the world would stop. Therefore constant human sacrifices — mainly of war captives — had to be provided. It is thought that more than 20,000 were slain each year.

There was a strong solar element in Aztec religion. Huitzilopochtli, the tribal god of the Aztecs, and god of the warriors, personified the sun at its height. In contrast was the rain-god Tlaloc, the supreme god of the peasants. Tlaloc was rated equal with Huitzilopochtli, and their high priests were equal in status. Thus Aztec religion combined both ancient and modern elements, in the form of the old rain-god and the later tribal one.

Aztec warriors who were sacrificed or who died in battle were believed to join the sun in the sky for four years, after which they were reincarnated as hummingbirds. When peasants died, they went to Tlalocan — a lush tropical paradise. Those who did not get to either of these places went to Mictlan, a cold, twilit underworld.

CENTRAL ANDES

Chavin

Between 600 and 300 BCE a cult involving the worship of a supernatural feline being spread through northern, central, and part of southern Peru. It appears to have emanated from a stone-built temple at Chavin de Huantar, in the north Peruvian highlands.

The temple at Chavin is riddled with interior galleries, some of which contained offerings of fine pottery, guinea pigs, and llamas, as well as sea shells. In the oldest part of the temple is a gallery containing a tall, sculptured standing stone, carved on which is a stylized feline – probably a jaguar – in human form, with snakes representing the eyebrows and hair. The upturned lips of this creature have earned it the name 'The Smiling God'.

Another version of the Chavin feline is the 'Staff God': a standing feline figure with a large rectangular head and outstretched arms, holding a type of staff in each hand. The fingers and toes have claws, while snakes represent the hair. This could have been a nature-god who was thought to live up in the sky with the eagles and hawks, also carved on pillars at Chavin.

The Moche

The Moche people revived the Chavin feline cult on the coast of north Peru during the first millennium CE. They made many pots showing fanged humans, often with snake belts. Frequently they are depicted fighting a monster, part human and part animal, which they generally defeat. Human prisoners were sacrificed to these fanged beings. There seem to have been a number of other animal deities, such as one which was part owl and part human. The moon also was probably an important deity.

Tiahuanaco

The ruins of the city of Tiahuanaco are on the eastern side of Lake Titicaca, just in present-day Bolivia. Most of the buildings there are ceremonial and were erected during the period 200–500 CE, when the city's influence was widespread.

The principal deity of Tiahuanaco appears to have been a standing figure that is carved on a monolithic gateway. In each hand he holds a vertical staff with eagle-headed appendages. His radiating head-dress includes six puma heads, and from his belt hang a row of trophy heads suggesting human sacrifice. This figure could represent Viracocha, the creator-god of Inca mythology.

The Chimu

The Chimu established a kingdom on the coast of north Peru between 1200 CE and their conquest by the Incas in the 1460s. Their greatest divinity was the moon, believed to be more powerful than the sun, since she appeared both day and night. The sun was believed to be an inferior supernatural being. Several constellations were highly regarded: Fur, or the Pleiades, was the patron of agriculture, while the sea, Ni, was also very important. White maize flour and red ochre were offered to Ni, with prayers for fish and for protection against drowning. The feline cult of earlier times appears to have largely died out by this period.

The Incas

The Incas first established themselves in the Cuzco area about 1200 CE. However, their conquest of highland and coastal Peru was not completed until about 1470 CE, by which time their empire covered some 400,000 square miles/one million square kilometres.

In the Inca Empire there were numerous local shrines, which were allowed to exist alongside the state religion. Some of these were of great antiquity, and a few – such as the oracle at Pachacamac – were noted for their pronouncements. There were numerous Inca shrines around Cuzco, ranging from natural features such as hills to temple buildings.

The Inca state religion was largely concerned with ritual and organization – particularly that of the food supply – rather than with mysticism and spirituality. Divination was essential before taking any action, and almost every religious rite was accompanied by sacrifices – usually of maize beer, food, or llamas, but occasionally of virgins or children.

The Inca emperor Pachacuti instituted the worship of a creator-god called Viracocha, or Huiracocha. Viracocha created the sun, moon, other supernatural beings, and all humankind. He was the theoretical source of all divine power, and had supernatural beings such as the sun to help administer his creation.

The cult of the sun was very important to the Incas. He was thought of as a male god, Inti, who protected and matured the crops. Sun temples were established along with fields to support the religious officials. These temples also housed the images of all the other sky-gods, such as the thunder-god who was the servant and messenger of the sun.

In contrast to many Central American peoples, the Incas and their predecessors had a widespread ancestor cult. Elaborate offerings, including food and drink, were placed with the dead. The mummies of Inca emperors were preserved in their palaces and brought out at festivals. The Incas believed that, after death, virtuous people went to live in the 'upper world', Janaq Pacha, which was rather like earth, while sinners went to the 'lower world', Uku Pacha, where they were cold and had only stones to eat.

THE SPANISH CONQUEST

At the height of its political power and cultural achievements, the Inca Empire was destroyed by the Spanish invasion of 1532. The Inca ruler was deposed and killed, and within fifty years the last vestige of Inca resistance had ceased. Roman Catholic Christianity, imposed by force, officially displaced the old religion. However, it lingered on among the people, and some of its features are still recognizable in present-day indigenous beliefs.

GEORGE BANKES

CHAPTER 11

The Ancient Near East

CRADLE OF CIVILIZATION

Mesopotamia is the Greek name for the land of the Tigris and Euphrates rivers, the area now ruled by Iraq and Syria. To the north are the mountains of Turkey, and to the east the Zagros range looms over the plains. On the west the steppe country reaches out to the Arabian Desert, while the two great rivers drain through marshes and lagoons to the Persian Gulf in the south.

Mesopotamia was a region, therefore, that had no easily defensible frontiers. Throughout historical times fierce hill-folk raided from the east, and hungry herdsmen from the steppe overran the fertile lands from the west and south. This pattern began as soon as people realized the possibilities of cultivating the rich soil and harvesting the fish of the rivers here. The northern part of Mesopotamia receives enough rain each year for farmers to grow grain and find pasture for their flocks, and people have lived in the hills and near the rivers since the Neolithic age, about 12,000 years ago.

The south – ancient Babylonia – depends upon artificial irrigation, by drawing the water from the rivers and carefully controlling it, in order to grow any crops. It appears this skill was put into practice there about 5000 BCE, from which time we can trace a steady development of settled life, until we find great cities flourishing by the rivers and canals during the fourth millennium BCE. From these cities traders and colonists spread up the Euphrates into Syria, eastwards into Persia, and south down the Gulf, carrying with them the inventions and ideas of their culture.

Amongst these was writing – one of the greatest inventions of all time. It was apparently the need to organize and administer the large settlements and their vital irrigation systems that stimulated the development of writing in Babylonia, and, at the same time – possibly by imitation – in Egypt. Without written documents, relatively little can be learned about the life and religion of a long-dead society; the objects surviving from an ancient religion can easily be misunderstood without the precise information that written texts can give.

THE SUMERIANS

The Babylonian cuneiform writing on clay tablets was produced for the dominant people of the south, the Sumerians. Theirs are the earliest religious beliefs we can learn about in Mesopotamia, but it is impossible to be sure that any feature is purely Sumerian, because the land was always inhabited by a mixture of races. Indeed, apart from their language, there is very little that can be called distinctively Sumerian.

In Uruk, the city of about 3000 BCE best known from excavations by archaeologists and from the earliest texts, there were two main temples. One was for Anu, the supreme god, the king of heaven; the other was for Inanna, the great mother, goddess of fertility, love, and war. Inanna was undoubtedly the principle of life, worshipped from time immemorial, the goddess found depicted on paintings, carved in stone, and modelled in clay in almost every prehistoric dwelling-place.

The temples employed large numbers of people, and owned large estates. Beside the farmers and herdsmen, there were craftsmen making fine objects for use in the temple

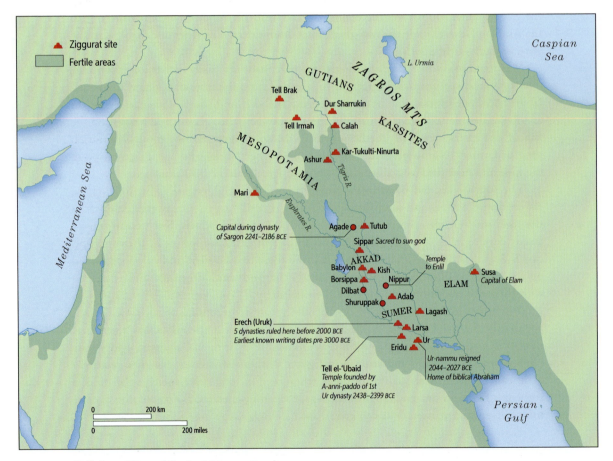

Religious Sites of Ancient Mesopotamia

services, weavers making clothes for the sacred statues and for the priests, and scribes keeping check on all the temple affairs. The priests had an important place in city life, the high priest sometimes being the king of the city. This seems to have been the normal structure of temple life in the Babylonian cities for many centuries.

Each major city in the south was the centre for worship of a particular deity. During the third millennium BCE, beside Anu and Inanna at Uruk, there were Enlil, lord of the atmosphere, who was worshipped at Nippur, and was, next to Anu, the chief of the gods; Enki, ruler of the fresh waters that come from beneath the earth, who had his shrine at Eridu; the sun-god, Utu, whose home was at Larsa; and the moon-god, Nanna, who lived at Ur. In some places the chief deity was simply called 'Lord of the City X'.

Ancient theologians organized the relationships between the gods and goddesses. Each principal god had a family and servants, who were honoured with temples and chapels too. For example, Enlil's son, Ninurta, was lord of Lagash. The less important deities had shrines inside the larger temples, but were also revered in small shrines set amongst the houses of the citizens.

The temples dominated the cities. When a temple grew old, or was thought to be too small, a new one was built, often on the ruins of the previous one. Over the years, the temples came to be set up above the surrounding houses, on platforms that covered the earlier buildings. The most important part was the holy room, where the statue of the god stood.

SUMERIAN MYTHS

Between 3000 and 2000 BCE, Sumerian poets told stories about the gods, probably setting them to music. Some of these myths survive, a few in copies made about 2500 BCE, many in copies of around 1700 BCE.

The gods of the Sumerians were the powers of nature as revealed in the world. So the sun-god was the sun and the power within it. Just as human activities are limited, so the gods were each restricted to their own sphere. The myths show the gods fighting to hold their places against evil powers that want to break down their ordered way of life, quarrelling over their areas of influence, engaging in trickery, and showing every kind of human emotion and vice.

Like most people, the Sumerians asked why the world existed, and why humankind was made. Several myths gave answers. In one, Enlil separated the heaven from the earth. On the earth he made a hoe to break the soil, and out of the hole made by his hoe sprang people, like plants. Another myth tells how Enki and the mother goddess created humans. The gods were tired of the work they had to do, tilling the ground and digging canals to grow the crops for food. Enki had the idea of making a clay figure which the mother goddess would bring to birth. This was done, resulting in humankind. Ever since, people have had to work the ground in order to grow food for the gods and for themselves.

This myth goes on to tell how the god and goddess drank too much beer in their celebration. They quarrelled, and the goddess boasted she could spoil their creation. Enki challenged her, boasting that he could find a place for any creature she made. The goddess produced all sorts of cripples and freaks, but Enki found each a place in society. So the story not only explained why human beings were made, but also offered a reason for the existence of the deformed.

Another topic the poets took up was the story of Dumuzi, later known as Tammuz, a shepherd who wooed and married the goddess Inanna. Afterwards, Dumuzi was carried off to the world of the dead. There is more than one version of this story. In the clearest, Dumuzi was the substitute provided by his wife who had dared to enter the realm of the dead in order to obtain her release. In other versions, Dumuzi was captured by police from the underworld.

There follow in all the stories great lamenting for the dead god, and attempts to restore him to life. The idea that he did rise from the dead is hard to find in the Sumerian texts. It is likely that the story arose from the cycle of nature, when the fresh growth of spring dies in the summer heat. Certainly the story was significant for the Sumerians. In many cities it was retold each year, as the king performed a symbolic marriage with a priestess, in a rite aimed at securing prosperity for the year.

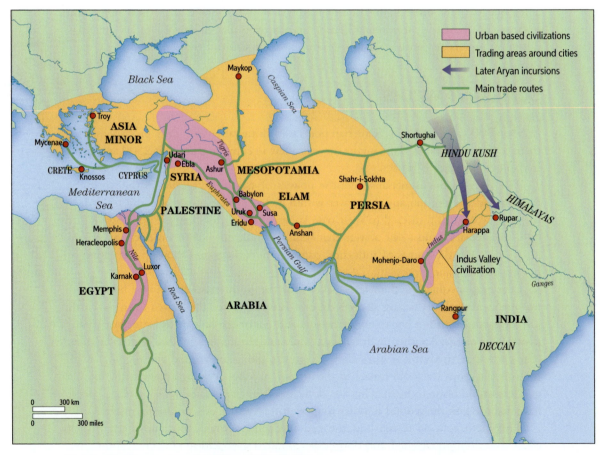

The Fertile Crescent and the Rise of City Religions

THE AKKADIAN EMPIRE

During the third millennium BCE Semitic peoples settled in Babylonia in increasing numbers. They mixed with the Sumerians, adopting their culture and their writing. From 2300 BCE they came to dominate Mesopotamia, when Sargon of Akkad set up the first Semitic empire. This was a time of high artistic achievement, and probably the time when the Sumerian stories began to be put into the Semitic language we call Akkadian. Semitic compositions, too, were recorded in writing. These Semites identified some of their gods with the Sumerian ones. Thus Anu was equated with El, the chief god; Inanna with Ishtar; Enki was known as Ea, a name that seems to mean 'living'; and the sun and moon became Shamash and Sin.

Sargon's dynasty fell to mountain raiders, and a new line of kings arose, at Ur, in modern Iraq, where they built for the moon-god a magnificent temple-tower, or ziggurat, which still rises over the ruins. Further invaders ended Ur's rule, and made the Semitic Akkadian, or Babylonian, language the normal one, ending the use of Sumerian outside of the schools. In the schools, many of the Sumerian myths were copied out as writing exercises, alongside a growing number of tales in Akkadian — some new compositions and some new forms of the ancient Sumerian stories.

THE GILGAMESH EPIC

Most famous are those stories that tell of the great King Gilgamesh, who had ruled Uruk — there is now evidence to suggest — about 2700 BCE. Somehow he captured the storytellers' imaginations and became a legendary figure. In Sumerian there are several separate stories about him; in Akkadian one long epic, whose basic theme is the problem of mortality. Gilgamesh did great deeds, but — forced to recognize he would die one day — he set out on a quest for immortality. After many adventures, he came to the place where lived an old man, the Babylonian equivalent of the biblical Noah. This man, Ut-napishtim, was the only mortal who had gained immortality. But Gilgamesh was disappointed, for the man was incredibly old, and lay on his back doing nothing. Perhaps immortality was not so good after all!

Ut-napishtim explained to Gilgamesh how he had reached this state. The gods had created humankind, but people then disturbed them with their noise. Unable to quell the din, the gods decided

Gilgamesh said: 'O barmaid, let me not see the death I constantly fear.'

The barmaid said to him, to Gilgamesh:

'Gilgamesh, where are you wandering to?

You will not find the life you seek.

When the gods made mankind,

They set death aside for men,

But they kept life in their own hands.

So, Gilgamesh, do you fill your belly,

Be happy day and night,

Take pleasure every day,

Day and night dance and play.

Wear clean clothes,

Wash your head, bathe in water,

Attend to the child who holds your hand,

Let your wife be happy with you.

This is what man's lot is.

The Epic of Gilgamesh

to destroy humankind by a great flood. Enki, who had made humankind in the first place, warned his particular devotee, Ut-napishtim, telling him to build a large boat in which he might escape. When the flood came, Ut-napishtim, his family, and a variety of animals were safe. After the flood, the ship grounded on a mountain in the north-east of Mesopotamia, and the gods rewarded Ut-napishtim with immortality. But Gilgamesh could not have that experience.

Ut-napishtim told Gilgamesh how to get a plant that might make him young again. Gilgamesh found it, and was taking it home to Uruk to test on an old man, when he put it on the ground while he had a swim. A snake ate it, and went away, sloughing its skin. The power of the plant was proved, but there was no other, and Gilgamesh could only go home with the thought that his noble deeds would live long after his death.

This story summarizes the outlook of the Babylonians: for them, life on earth was the main concern, life after death a vague and shadowy concept. They thought of the world of the dead as a place of dust and gloom. Yet it was necessary for the dead to be properly buried; otherwise, they would return to haunt their relatives. Offerings were made for the dead, too, partly to keep their memories alive.

BABYLONIAN RELIGION

This present life was entirely under the control of the gods: to have success or happiness, it was essential to keep the gods in good humour. There were special days of festival when worshippers would attend ceremonies at the temple, or carry the statues through the streets. Sacrifices could be made to show devotion, or ask for help. Ordinary people could not simply walk into the presence of a great god, but had to be introduced by an intermediary. Such a scene is engraved on cylinder seals current during the Third dynasty of Ur and following centuries. The owner of the seal would identify with the figure on it, and pray for the god's blessing. But the gods were unpredictable: Babylonians could hope, but have no assurance of divine favour. This led to the development of another aspect of Babylonian religion that is not yet extinct: the taking of omens.

The Babylonians, like the Sumerians before them, believed they could find

Reconstruction of the celebrated Ishtar Gate to the ancient city of Babylon.

out about the future from all sorts of strange happenings. In the birth of monstrosities, the movements of animals, the shapes of cracks in the wall, and of oil poured into a cup of water, they saw the fingers of the gods pointing to the future. If a man wanted to marry, or a king to go to war, the omens would be consulted. One common way was to examine the liver of a sacrificed animal. If the form was exactly as it had been once before, then the events that followed on that occasion, if good, suggested it was a good omen; if bad, that the proposed action should not be taken.

A special class of priests was trained to take, and interpret, the omens, and they built up an enormous encyclopedia about them. In watching the skies, they learned a lot about the stars, and became able to predict eclipses and correct the calendar. They also originated fortune-telling by astrology.

THE ASSYRIAN EMPIRE

In northern Mesopotamia, the state of Assyria grew strong about 1400 BCE, and, after an interval, became the dominant power in the Near East, from 900 to 612 BCE. The Assyrian kings tried to copy the Babylonians, whose culture was much older. They worshipped the same gods, but the chief god – identified with Enlil – was Ashur, the god of the original capital.

When the Assyrians conquered other lands, they did not interfere in the local religion, and, if the people were submissive, they allowed them to continue their own customs. If they revolted, their gods might be taken away captive, to be set in the Assyrian temples. Usually they were respected, and they were sometimes returned when a once-rebellious land was made to submit.

MARDUK OF BABYLON

Assyria fell to the Babylonians, or Chaldeans, of whom Nebuchadnezzar is the most famous ruler. He rebuilt Babylon and the great temple of Marduk, the patron god of the city. Marduk had risen to prominence under Hammurabi of Babylon in about 1750 BCE, and was popular when Babylon's power was greatest. In his honour, the Babylonian creation story was written.

This story describes the beginning of the world, when all was sea. The gods borne by the sea disturbed her, and she planned to destroy them. They chose a champion to fight her lieutenant, but he failed. Another was chosen and failed. Then Marduk – a god of no importance – offered a plan, and succeeded. His prize was the kingship of the gods. His gift to the gods was the creation of humankind – aided by his father Enki-Ea – to do the work they so disliked. The poem ends with a long list of Marduk's powers.

The Persians who subsequently conquered Babylon kept the local religion alive, and in a few centres it flickered on until the first century CE. Some of the gods and goddesses continued to be worshipped by local people until the coming of Islam to Iraq.

Warrior Marduk, whose anger is like a flood,

Whose forgiveness is like a loving father's,

I am sleepless through speaking but

not being heard,

I am depressed from calling but

receiving no answer.

This has made my heart grow weak,

And made me bent like an old man.

Great lord, Marduk, forgiving god,

Who among all kinds of men,

Can understand his nature?

Who has not been at fault,

who is there who has not sinned?

Who can know the way of a god?

O that I were careful not to sin,

O that I would seek the places of life always!

Mankind is set by the gods on a hapless course,

To endure what the gods inflict upon him.

If I, your servant, have sinned,

If I have passed the divine bounds,

What I did in my youth, forget it,

whatever it was,

And absolve my fault, remove my wrong,

Lighten my troubles, relieve my distress …

Warrior Marduk, let me live to sing your praise!

Part of a prayer to Marduk

CANAANITE RELIGION

Canaan was the name for the Holy Land from about 1800 to 1200 BCE. The people living there were a mixture of races: basically Semitic, with close relatives in Syria to the north. After Israel took control of the land, by about 1100 BCE, some of the Canaanites maintained separate states in the north, in the area the Greeks called Phoenicia, modern Lebanon. Their culture and religion continued to flourish there, and influenced the neighbouring lands.

Temples, religious objects, and inscriptions unearthed there tell us something about the religion of the Canaanites and Phoenicians, while other information is given by Hebrew, Greek, and Latin books. Ancient Israel was warned to avoid all contact with Canaanite religion, in fact, to wipe all traces of it from the land in which they were to settle (Exodus 23:23–33).

Excavations have uncovered remains of many small temples in the towns of Canaan. They were single rooms, with a niche opposite the doorway where a statue of the deity might stand. Other rooms in front of, or beside, the shrine could be for the priests, or for storage. In a few cases, the thickness of the walls suggests there was an upper storey, and models in pottery show that some temples had towers, presumably for special rites — perhaps the worship of the sun or the stars.

Where the temple had a courtyard, it is likely the worshippers stood there while the priests alone entered the sanctuary. A large altar may have stood in the courtyard, with a smaller one inside the building. Animal bones suggest the animals commonly sacrificed were lambs and kids, while at one place piglets had been slaughtered. Liquid offerings of wine and oil were also made, and incense was burned.

In some temples, stone pillars stood as memorials to the dead, while other pillars were symbols of the gods. They were objects of worship, covered with fine cloth, and carried in procession for the faithful to see. Their ancient name, *bethel*, 'house of god', suggests that the god was supposed to live in them.

Statues of gods and goddesses were carved in stone or wood, or moulded in metal. They were overlaid with gold, dressed in expensive clothes, and decorated with valuable jewellery given by the devotees. They have not survived, but many small bronze figures are still to be seen – probably copies of the larger images that stood in the temples. These small ones were made for the worshipper to offer at the temple, or to use in private devotions at home. When new, most of them were probably plated with gold or silver. The most common figures are cheap pottery representations of a naked female, thought to be the mother goddess, giver of fertility, which were used as charms.

UGARIT EVIDENCE

To the north of ancient Canaan, but sharing much of the same culture, lay the merchant city of Ugarit. Excavations there since 1929 have yielded much information about the local religion. In particular, clay tablets, written about 1200 BCE, have added an important dimension to our understanding of Canaanite thought that could not be obtained from the material remains alone.

These texts from Ugarit contain stories about the gods, and instructions about their worship. We learn that the Canaanite gods were, like many others of the Ancient Near East, powers of the natural world. At their head was El, whose name means simply 'god'. He was the father of gods and humans, and his wife, Asherah, the mother goddess. El appears in some of the myths as an old man, too old to act effectively, bullied by his wife and his children. In one story he is shown in a drunken stupor; in another he marries two girls who bear him two sons, Dawn and Dusk.

El had a daughter, Anat, who personified war. One poem tells how she slaughtered the people of a city, tied their heads to her waist, and waded up to her thighs in their blood, laughing with joy. Anat was also the goddess of love, and is described in some stories as the lover of her brother, Baal, the best known of the Canaanite gods. His name means 'master' or 'lord', and he was actually the god of the weather, Hadad, 'the thunderer'.

POPULAR RELIGION

It is difficult to discover what ordinary people believed, or how they worshipped. In offering sacrifices, the person could share in the meat at a cultic banquet with the priest and the god, the sacrifice being a sign of devotion, the payment of a vow, or an offering for pardon. Beside the chief gods, there were many spirits and demons, who had to be placated or warded off. Dead relatives, too, required regular commemoration, to prevent their ghosts from haunting the living.

Many priests served at small shrines on hilltops – the 'high places' mentioned in the Bible – and in every town and village. These men, and others, cast spells and forecast the future, telling the anxious inquirer if it was a lucky day for a business venture, a war, or a wedding. Divination was a skill Canaanites learned with the help of Babylonian manuals, and applied in every possible way.

According to Hebrew and Greek writings, popular worship included ritual prostitution and other excesses. Child sacrifice was believed by the Romans to be a custom of the Phoenicians, and the people of Israel were instructed not to 'pass their chil dren through fire to Molech', another form, apparently, of infant sacrifice (see, for example, Leviticus 18:21). Remains of such offerings have come to light in the ruins of Carthage, North Africa.

A happier side of Canaanite religion can be seen in the titles 'merciful' and 'gracious' applied to El. The main impression, however, is of gods and goddesses who were wilful and capricious, like their human followers. Whatever the Canaanites might do, they could not be sure of divine approval or blessing, for they could not know their gods.

MOAB, EDOM, AND AMMON

When the Israelites took control of Canaan, other peoples were settling in adjacent lands. Along the coast, in the south-west of Palestine, were the Philistines; eastwards, across the Jordan, were Edomites, Moabites, and Ammonites; while the Aramaeans occupied Syria to the north.

The religions of all but the Aramaeans are little known, for these people have left very few inscriptions, and their cities have not been extensively explored. The Bible speaks of Chemosh as the national god of Moab, and a little more can be discovered about him from the famous Moabite Stone. This inscription, engraved about 830 BCE, describes Chemosh in much the same way as the God of Israel is depicted; he is angry with his land, so hands it over to an enemy, then he gives relief, and the enemy is defeated. Booty and captives were dedicated to him by the victorious king of Moab, Mesha (see 2 Kings), who set up the stone in a temple of Chemosh at Dibon. When under attack, another king of Moab sacrificed his son, in a bid to arouse Chemosh's aid (2 Kings 3:27). It was to Moab that the seer Balaam was brought to curse Israel (Numbers 22).

Clay figures of humans and animals, and especially of the 'mother goddess' type, are found in Moab, Edom, and Ammon, just as in Canaan and Israel. From the little known of Moabite religion, similarities with Canaanite beliefs are evident, although the position of Chemosh as a national god is more like the position of Israel's deity. It is reasonable to assume that Edomite and Ammonite religions, of which even less is known, were very like the Moabite one. Edom's national god was Qaus, and his name formed part of personal names borne by Edomites, such as Qaus-gabbar: 'Qaus is mighty'.

In Ammon – the name is preserved in modern Amman – the people worshipped Milcom, who may be identified with the Molech to whom Canaanites offered children. As for the Philistines, the Old Testament suggests that they adopted Canaanite gods, such as Dagon (Judges 16:23–24) and Baal-zebub (2 Kings 1:2). A small temple uncovered at Tel Aviv is similar in design and furnishings to Canaanite shrines, except it contained Philistine pottery.

ARAMAEAN RELIGION

The Aramaeans of Syria also absorbed the religion of the people of the land. Hadad was revered as the chief god of Damascus, with the added title Ramman, or Rimmon, 'Thunderer'. He was also called Baal-shamen, 'Lord of heaven'. Beside him was his consort, Athtar. El continued to have worshippers, who gave him the title 'Creator of heaven and earth'. The 'Queen of heaven' was a name for the mother goddess. In course of time, these Semitic deities were identified with Greek, and then with Roman, gods, and some took over the attributes of others. Under the Roman Empire, magnificent temples were built for the gods at the main centres, and some still stand, most notably at Baalbek, Lebanon, where Baal-shamen was equated with Zeus and Jupiter, as the sun-god, while the goddess Atargatis, a fusion of Athtar and Anat, became Venus.

The Meshe Stele, or Moabite Stone, set up around 840 BCE by King Mesha of Moab, in modern Jordan.

At Palmyra, the caravan city between Damascus and the Euphrates, a powerful state existed during the first century BCE and the first three centuries CE. Baal-shamen was important there, in addition to a triad of local deities, Bol – or Bel – Yarihbol, and Aglibol, the last two being the sun and the moon. Appropriately for a trading city, Gad, 'good luck', was prominent, too. The great temple of Bel still stands, its size and extensive outbuildings showing the wealth of the city and the large number of staff employed in the cult.

The priests were organized in groups, the highest being the priests of Bel, and presided at sacred meals that followed sacrifices. This was an ancient practice, followed by the Canaanites, when the priests, the offerers, and the gods were all thought to eat and drink together. Wealthy citizens gave funds for the banquets to be held regularly, expecting thereby to gain merit. Admission was by small clay tokens bearing suitable pictures and inscriptions. As elsewhere in the Ancient Near East, the people of Palmyra buried their dead with care, recording their names so that their memory might not be lost.

THE HITTITES

From about 2000 BCE until 1200 BCE, most of the area of modern Turkey was controlled by an Indo-European people called the Hittites, although that name really belonged to another, non-Indo-European, group. A third people, the Hurrians, possibly related to the modern Armenians, mixed with the Hittites, and influenced their religion and culture from 1450 BCE. After the end of Hittite power, the language and religious beliefs continued for a long time in parts of Turkey, being known to writers of the Roman period.

The country is mountainous, each town being distinct. As a result, each town had its own god or goddess, usually the deified elements – the sun, storm, and so forth – whom the citizens worshipped in the main temple of the place. A Hittite myth makes clear how the gods depended upon their human servants: when a disaster befell the land, the gods starved because sacrifices were interrupted! All sorts of other powers claimed attention: the spirits of earth, of grain, of fire, of seeing, of hearing, and magic spells were recited to win their aid, or ward off their evil.

At the capital city, Hattusha, modern Bogazköy, the king led the cult of the storm-god and the sun-goddess, the national deities. The king was both high priest and deputy of the storm-god, and high priest of all the other gods. He was expected to attend the major annual festival of each deity in that god's city. Elaborate rituals were performed, to ensure he was cultically pure for such occasions. If the king did not attend, or committed some other error, a catastrophe could overtake the land. The causes of divine anger might be petty, as when the god's robe was worn out, or significant, such as the breaking of an oath, and could be discovered only by asking the god to give a sign through an omen of some sort. Only in such ways could people learn the mind of the gods, and hope to gain their goodwill.

ALAN MILLARD

CHAPTER 12

Ancient Egypt

LAND OF THE PRIEST-KING

Ancient Egypt is the name given to the civilization in the lower reaches of the Nile Valley, from about 3100 BCE to 30 BCE, when the Romans occupied Egypt. It covers periods of strength, such as the Old Kingdom (c. 2700–2200 BCE), when a line of powerful rulers left their pyramids as monuments; the Middle Kingdom (c. 2000–1800 BCE), another time of strong central government, with influence amongst Egypt's neighbours; and the New Kingdom (c. 1550–1225 BCE), when Egypt was one of the dominant countries of the Near East. It also covers periods of weakness, when Egypt was torn by internal strife and occupied by foreign powers. Obviously such changes in political strength and economic fortunes over 3000 years meant that philosophical and religious attitudes also changed, but there are enough consistent features for us to be able to talk about Egyptian religion as a whole.

THE EARLIEST PERIOD

Writing was not practised in Egypt until about 3100 BCE, when a single central government was established. What we know about Egyptian religion before then, therefore, has to be deduced from objects found by archaeologists. These take us back another 2000 to 3000 years, and mainly consist of amulets, usually connected with hunting or fertility. Animal tusks, worn as pendants, were probably intended to protect the hunter and make him successful; earthenware figures of naked women were meant to ensure plenty of healthy children.

Some pictures painted on pots, or scratched onto rocks, seem to suggest religious rituals, but without a written explanation it is impossible to understand them fully. Sometimes they seem to refer to ceremonies or figures that we recognize from later periods, and it is fairly safe to assume that the basic beliefs and practices did not greatly change in the historical period.

EGYPTIAN GODS

The gods of ancient Egypt — as they are represented in the temples and tombs — present a bewildering complexity of strange forms, half animal, half human. In fact we know very little about Egyptian religious beliefs, since there are no studies of Egyptian theology made by the ancient Egyptians themselves.

Many of the Egyptian gods represented strong forces in the natural world. Egypt's prosperity depended on the daily reappearance of the sun and the annual flooding of the river, and these natural forces, with others, were thought of as gods needing to be cajoled and encouraged by sacrifice and worship. The Egyptians often portrayed them as animals: for example, they chose the hawk, which flies high in the sky, as a representation of the sun; and the cobra, which was often found basking on the hot threshing floors, as a symbol of the harvest goddess.

At an early stage, other characteristics were associated with some of the gods. The ibis-headed god, Thoth, was thought of as the god of scribes and writing; Khnum, the ram-headed deity, was considered the creator of humankind on his potter's wheel, and so on. How these special attributes came to be given to particular deities is not clear, but they seem to be established in these roles at an early date.

The gods were often associated with particular cities, which probably dates back into the prehistoric period, when Egypt was a series of individual communities. As these communities came together into larger political units, so their local deities gradually became important in the nation as a whole. For example, the god Amun, from the city of Thebes, was a kind of national god, protecting and leading the whole nation for a time during the New Kingdom, while Thebes was the home city of the ruling family.

This was not exclusive, however. The town-folk of other communities would continue to worship their own local god, and also feel free to pray to any other god who might offer special favours. So a scribe who hailed from Denderah might accompany the king to the temple of Amun at Thebes after some notable victory, but would pay his respects to Hathor whilst at Denderah. He would also pray to Thoth, the god with a special interest in writing, for help in his career.

There are also references to 'God' or 'The God', who seems to have been an unnamed universal divine power, who controlled the universe and upheld good against evil.

THE 'REFORM' OF AKHENATEN

For a short while, from about 1375 to 1350 BCE, there was an attempt to impose a form of monotheism. The pharaoh Amenophis IV, who is variously described as a visionary or a lunatic, gradually built up the worship of the Aten, or the sun's disk, until he was the only god whose worship was tolerated. The other gods were proscribed, their temples closed, their priesthoods disbanded, and their names erased from all monuments where they could be found. The worship of Amun, in particular, was strongly attacked, while the Aten was regarded as the source of all life. This gift of life was passed to the king,

who changed his name to Akhenaten – which means 'the one who is beneficial to the Aten' – and to his family, and thence to the people.

Pyramids at Giza, Cairo, Egypt.

This 'reform' probably had some political cause, such as an attempt to stabilize and unite the nation, but was also influenced by Akhenaten's bizarre personality. It was apparently not popular; the priests would certainly have been against it, since it deprived them of their living, and it survived only briefly after Akhenaten's death. The power of the priests of Amun could not so easily be destroyed. This period was exceptional, since normally the gods seemed happy to exist side-by-side, even when ideas claimed on their behalf appear contradictory.

OTHER GODS

As well as the 'mainstream' gods, other deities were adopted by the Egyptians. Some private individuals who had distinguished themselves in some way were deified. The king or pharaoh was also thought of as a god; he was referred to as 'The Good God', but this was a restricted idea of divinity because he was, plainly, mortal. Very few rulers actually had a statue placed in the temple shrine as an object of worship. The fact that the king could be both god and priest indicates some of the contradictions of Egyptian religion.

Animals too form an interesting aspect of Egyptian religion, with actual practice varying according to place and time. In some cases, all the animals of one species were regarded as sacred, and were mummified and buried in huge numbers: baboons, crocodiles, ibises, even cats and dogs received this treatment on occasion. In other cases, one individual animal was singled out as the incarnation of a god. There were several places where a particular bull was selected, perhaps because it had some distinctive markings, and then taken into the temple, pampered throughout its life, and mummified and ceremonially interred at death.

FESTIVALS AND SERVICES

The festivals and daily services in the temples show that the Egyptians thought of their gods as having the same needs and instincts as themselves. The day began with a ritual in which the god was wakened by a choir. The night attire was then removed from the image of the god, which was washed, dressed, and offered food and drink. After this, the god might be called upon to receive visitors, deliver oracles, or undertake some other duties. We may assume that his behaviour and decisions reflected the views and wishes of the priests, who could claim to interpret them on his behalf. He would receive other offerings of food during the day, and eventually be put to bed for the night in his shrine.

The daily routine was broken by festivals. Some were short, involving only a special offering, or a procession inside the temple. Others involved long journeys by river to the temple of another god. Amun, for example,

Avenue of goat-headed sphinxes leading from the Karnak temple complex to the Temple of Luxor, Egypt.

went by boat from his great national temple at Karnak to the smaller shrine at Luxor, which was regarded as his private home, where he stayed for several days with his consort, Mut, and then returned along the processional way. Hathor travelled nearly 100 miles by boat from Denderah on her annual visit to the temple of Horus, at Edfu.

The festivals which involved processions along the river or in the town were treated as holidays by the people, who lined the route to cheer and wave at the god's shrine. Some travelled on long pilgrimages to attend. One writer records 700,000 pilgrims gathering for a festival. Some festivals we know only by name; it is intriguing to try to imagine what happened on 'The Day of Smelling Onions'!

The actual images of the gods that were the centre of this worship have not survived. They may have been of stone or fine metal, probably richly ornamented. At festivals they were carried, hidden from public gaze, in ornate wooden shrines in a large model boat, which was borne on the shoulders of several bearers. For the river journeys, they travelled in special boats built of wood, but shaped to resemble the early reed boats, a reminder that these festivals had their origin in very early times.

The priest who performed all the religious ceremonies was in theory the king. All the temple reliefs show him making the offerings, but in fact, of course, they would be made by his deputies. The priesthood was at first a duty taken on by the local dignitaries, working according to a roster; but gradually a professional priesthood was set up. At certain periods, when the king was weak, the high priest of Amun or another major god was the real ruler of Egypt.

In addition to the high priest, there was a whole range of other clergy, with carefully graded ranks and titles. Women served as priestesses, and of course there were numerous other people in the temple service, ranging from choristers and librarians to cooks and gardeners.

EGYPTIAN MYTHS

There is no ancient Egyptian sacred book, equivalent to the Bible or *Qur'an*, that was accepted as a revelation of divine truth. The Egyptians had their myths, like those of the ancient Greeks, telling the story of the relationships between the gods — but very few have survived intact. All we have are short, scattered references, which can sometimes be pieced together to tell the whole story, though we cannot be sure that we have it correct.

Various creation myths abounded, for example. The Egyptians generally imagined the universe as originally filled with water, from which a hill arose on which life began. This was no doubt derived from what they observed each year, as the Nile flood subsided. Thereafter the stories become extremely complex. Different gods were thought to have somehow emerged from the hill or the water, and in various ways to have created other gods. Many of the great temples were claimed to be built on this primeval hill.

An interesting claim was advanced by the priests of Memphis on behalf of their god Ptah. They declared he was the great god, who somehow was also the great watery

EGYPTIAN TEMPLES: HOUSES OF POWER

The outward appearance of an Egyptian temple was not particularly elegant. To those of us whose ideas are coloured by Gothic cathedrals or Greek temples, they appear more like power stations than temples. This in fact reflects their purpose. They were less concerned with telling people outside about the majesty and power of the god to whom they were dedicated, and more concerned with the ritual that went on inside. This ritual was intended to ensure that the gods would continue their favour towards Egypt, which was therefore the prime consideration in the design of the building.

The plan of the temple

The two main types of temple were the cult temple, dedicated to a particular god, usually the principal god of the city or area, and the funerary temple, dedicated to the memory of a dead king who was treated as a god. To all intents and purposes, the plans of these two types were the same.

The temple was thought of as the house of the god, and its plan was similar to the houses of nobles and officials. These usually consisted of a number of reception rooms, leading to the private family rooms, and ultimately to the owner's bedroom. In the temples the same types of room were used, with large courts and halls corresponding to the reception room, and the shrine corresponding to the main bedroom. The chief difference was that the rooms of the temple were laid out in a straight line, so that processions could pass from the main gate to the sanctuary without awkward bends.

Some temples were in use for several hundreds of years, and were extended and altered, demolished and rebuilt during that time; but the same general arrangement was followed throughout. Even those cut in the rock cliffs of Nubia, such as the temples of Ramesses II at Abu Simbel, kept to the same basic plan. A few exceptions occurred, as when, for example, two deities of equal rank occupied the same temple at Kom Ombo; a double aisle and twin shrines were provided.

The temples represented Egypt in miniature. The great monumental entrance was similar in shape to the hieroglyph which stood for the horizon, or limits of the country. On the outside walls of this gate we see the king destroying his foreign enemies. Inside, the halls were decorated as huge thickets, the floors painted to represent water, and the ceilings painted with stars. Egyptian architects did not use vaulting, so the flat stone blocks that formed the ceilings had to be supported by closely arranged pillars, which were based on plant shapes, usually with papyrus or lotus capitals.

Ritual purity

As far as possible, the temple was cut off from the outside world, to protect its ritual purity. At the foundation ceremony, a pit was filled with clean sand containing magic amulets, which warded off any evil influence that might attack from below. The corners of the building were further protected by foundation deposits, consisting of animal sacrifices, groups of model tools, and other items. A high wall protected the temple estate, and the building itself was erected within another wall and an ambulatory, or corridor, which formed a further protective layer around it.

Elaborate precautions were even taken to remove rainwater from the roof, with a complex series of channels and huge gargoyles. The shrine itself was often constructed as a separate building within the main temple, complete with its own roof, so it was again separated from contact with the world outside.

Within the main building various rooms were set aside for special purposes. There would be a library for the papyrus rolls with the ritual texts, a vestry for the special clothing, and store-rooms for the chalices, censers, and other vessels used in the rituals. Often, in addition to the main god who occupied the central shrine, there were other gods, perhaps members of the family, who shared the temple. Their images were kept in smaller shrines, built around the central shrine in the sanctuary area.

Deepening mystery

The walls of the temple were decorated with relief carvings of scenes from the temple rituals, and the words that were recited at the rituals were also inscribed on the walls. From the position of these carvings within the temple, it is sometimes possible to tell the uses of the different rooms. These carvings were not just a large-scale service book; the ceremony that was performed when the completed building was formally presented to the god included an 'Opening of the Mouth' ritual, by which all these carvings were given life and everlasting effectiveness. So the mere portrayal of the ritual supposedly guaranteed it would continue for ever, even if the priests ceased to perform it.

As the worshippers moved from the temple entrance to the sanctuary, the air of mystery gradually deepened. The size of the rooms was reduced in stages, the roof level became lower, and the floor was stepped up. Daylight was also gradually excluded. From the open court one passed to courts lit by a clerestory, or openings in the first wall, which was sometimes only constructed half-way to the roof. The innermost rooms were completely cut off from daylight. It is easy to imagine how the flickering, leaping light of torches playing on the richly painted figures and hieroglyphs on the walls must have combined with the singing and incense to create a feeling of awe and wonder in the worshippers. The roof of the temple was also important. Some ceremonies – involving, for instance, the union of the divine image with the sun – were performed there. Special stairs, with shallow steps, were used, so that the image of the god could be carried up to the roof in a small, portable shrine. Small roof-top chapels were built for these ceremonies.

Shrines

Outside the main building of the temple, but within the enclosure wall, were many other buildings. These may still be seen in some temples, such as Karnak and Denderah. These include small shrines and chapels, often one where a divine marriage and birth ritual was enacted. There was also housing for the priests, slaughter-yards, and bakehouses where offerings were prepared, a well that provided holy water, and a sacred lake on which other rituals would be performed, rather like medieval mystery plays.

John Ruffle

universe from which the other gods were born, their acts of creation being simply the carrying out of his will.

Ancient Egyptian bas relief showing Pharaoh Seti ("he of Seth") I offering incense to Osiris, whose wife Isis is standing behind him.

As well as the myths, there are prayers and hymns to the gods, which read very much like the Old Testament psalms. Books of wisdom are also known, which – rather like the biblical book of Proverbs – range from practical and moral advice to general theological reflections on the nature of life.

There are also many magical spells, which may be counted as religious, since they invoke the gods and try to persuade them to give help and protection from all sorts of evils.

THE AFTERLIFE

Several of the wisdom books encourage their readers to live according to a moral and ethical code of personal piety, partly because this is the way to earn respect from one's fellows, partly because it is pleasing to 'the god'. Living a good life was also thought to be a way of ensuring a safe passage to the afterworld. There are many representations of a judgment scene, in which the dead person's heart is weighed in a balance against a feather, which represents truth. The result was recorded by Thoth, the scribe of the gods, in the presence of Osiris, and those who failed were destroyed for ever. This judgment was not, however, a great incentive to piety, since the result could be influenced by correctly reciting an incantation, in which the person denied ever committing a whole range of sins.

The Egyptians seem always to have had a belief in an afterlife. The very earliest tombs contain items of food and equipment, and, later on, the decoration of the tombs tells us how the Egyptians thought such a life would be. Generally, it was thought to be similar to this world, but better – with successful hunting and harvests, rich banquets and pretty girls.

The idea went through various stages of development. At first it was thought the king would spend his afterlife alongside the sun-god Re, also known as Ra, on his daily journey across the heavens. Soon, however, his future became linked with the god Osiris, and each king in turn, as he died, became identified with him. Gradually this privilege was extended, first to the nobles, and later to all classes, so that each person, on their death, somehow became identified with Osiris.

The story of Osiris himself was not recorded in full until the Greek writer Plutarch (c. 100 CE) recounted how the good King Osiris was murdered by his jealous brother, Seth. With the help of his wife, Isis, and other gods, Osiris eventually became the ruler of the afterworld, and a symbol of continued life after death. There are several references to the story in Egyptian literature that make it clear there were differing versions of this account.

The journey to the afterworld was fraught with difficulty: all sorts of obstacles lay in the way, and demons were ready at every turn to seize the traveller. A successful journey was assured by possession of a papyrus roll containing a series of incantations that could be recited to allow the dead person to pass when an obstacle or demon was encountered. These books are usually called *The Book of the Dead*, although there are several different titles and versions. Copies were placed with the dead in the tomb, ready for use, or at different periods they were inscribed inside the coffin or on the tomb walls.

It was, of course, plain to the Egyptians that the physical body remained in this world, and that it was the person's spirit that passed on. They thought this spirit needed the body as a kind of base, and for this reason made elaborate attempts to preserve the body by mummification. It was particularly serious if a body was lost at sea, or destroyed by fire, although in extreme cases a statue or portrait of the departed might serve as a substitute.

The funeral ritual included a ceremony called 'The Opening of the Mouth', in which the mouth and other openings of the body were magically treated, to ensure that the dead might continue to use their bodies to feed, see, hear, and so on. The same ceremony performed over statues and paintings endowed them with a form of life in the afterworld.

JOHN RUFFLE

CHAPTER 13

Zoroastrianism

A HISTORICAL OVERVIEW

The story of Zoroastrianism begins in the third millennium BCE with the Indo-Europeans. Somewhere to the east of Europe about 3000 BCE a group of tribes began to split up: some travelled south and settled in Greece and Rome, others went north and settled in Scandinavia, and others went east to Persia — now Iran — and India. Because of this common descent, the ancient languages of these countries have a similar pattern. The important group for Zoroastrian studies is the third one, which settled in India and Persia, a people called the 'Indo-Iranians' by scholars, though they referred to themselves as the *Aryas* — Aryans — 'the noble ones'. They travelled eastwards in two main waves. The first, in approximately 2000 BCE, passed through northern Persia, leaving only a few settlers there, with the main body carrying on into north-west India, where they gradually overthrew the Indus Valley civilization. The second wave of Indo-Iranians settled in Persia about 1500 BCE.

The religion of the Indo-Iranians provides the background to Zoroastrianism, just as ancient Israelite religion does to Christianity. The Indo-Iranians were nomads, journeying on foot from pasture to pasture with their herds, not staying long enough to build temples, travelling light, so they did not have statues of the gods. Theirs was a religion of the mountain-top, with the dome of the sky for their temple, using the ordinary household fire as the focus for their ritual offerings. Their imagery was drawn from wind and storm, from sun and rain. Their gods were not thought of in human form, but as the forces which surround humankind.

ZARATHUSHTRA

Zoroaster is the name by which the West knows the prophet of ancient Persia, more correctly called Zarathushtra. It was usual to date him about 600 BCE, but the evidence of language is persuading more scholars nowadays to date him about 1200 BCE, which means he lived when Persia was emerging from the Stone Age, and would make him the first of the great prophets of the world's religions.

Zarathushtra was a descendant of the first wave of Indo-Iranians. His people had become settled agriculturalists and were threatened by the second wave of Indo-Iranian settlers. We know little of the prophet's life. He was a priest — interestingly, the only one of the great prophets who was — he was married and had several children. At the age of thirty he had the first of a series of visions, which inspired him to preach a new message. His teaching was at first rejected, he suffered persecution, and was forced to leave his home. It took ten years before he made his first convert, his cousin. Then his message found favour with a local king, Vishtasp, and Zarathushtra's religion became the official teaching of a small kingdom somewhere in north-east Persia, in what was formerly part of southern Russia — the precise location is not known. Zarathushtra's religion in time spread throughout Persia and became the official religion of what was, for 1000 years, one of the major world empires.

ZARATHUSHTRA'S TEACHING

Zoroastrians believe their prophet is the one chosen by God to receive his unique revelation, which is contained in seventeen hymns, the *Gathas*. Obviously the prophet gave more teaching than this, but all that has survived is a fragment cast into verse form to help memorize the words, in an age and region where writing was unknown. These hymns are now the central part of a major act of worship, *yasna*.

Perhaps the distinctive feature of Zarathushtra's teaching is his emphasis on personal religion, inspired presumably by his conviction that God had called him and appeared to him personally. All men and women — both sexes have the same duties in Zoroastrianism — have a personal responsibility to choose between good and evil. On the basis of the exercise of their free-will, they will be judged in the hereafter. Those whose good thoughts, words, and deeds outweigh the evil will go to heaven, regardless of their social status; those whose evil thoughts, words, and deeds outweigh the good will go to hell, again regardless of their social status.

A similar prophetic emphasis can be seen in the badge Zarathushtra took for the religion. For the Indo-Iranians, a sacred cord was the symbol of priesthood, as it still is with the Brahmans in India. Zarathushtra made this and a sacred shirt, made of white cotton and rather like a vest, the symbolic armour which all believers should wear at all times after initiation, to remind them of the battle they must fight against evil.

GOOD AND EVIL

God, Zarathushtra taught, was the wholly Good Creator of all things: of sun, moon, and stars, of the spiritual and material worlds, of humans, and of animals. Ahura Mazda, the Wise Lord, is the bountiful sovereign, the friend not only of Zarathushtra, but of everyone. He is in no way responsible for evil in the world; this comes from Angra Mainyu, the Destructive Spirit, whose nature is violent and destructive, who created the demons,

*This I ask Thee. Tell
me truly, Lord. Which
man in the beginning
was the father of truth
during the creation?
Which man did fix the
course of the sun and of
the stars? ... Through
whom does dawn exist,
along with midday and
evening, [all of] which
remind the worshipper of
his purpose? ... Which
man, O Wise Lord,
is the creator of the
good mind...? By these
[questions], O Wise
Lord, I am helping to
discern Thee to be the
Creator of everything.*

Yasna 44:3–5, 7

rules in hell, and who has opposed God from the beginning. In Zoroastrianism the 'Devil' is not a fallen angel, for that would make the Good Creator ultimately responsible for evil – an inconceivable idea for Zoroastrians. The world is the battleground in which the forces of good and evil do battle. The world and humankind were created by God to aid him in this battle.

God also created a number of heavenly beings, foremost among them Amesha Spentas, the Bounteous Immortals, or the sons and daughters of God, as they became known. In some ways they resemble the Christian idea of archangels, which belief some scholars think was influenced by Zoroastrianism. But like the gods of the Indo-Iranians, there is an important abstract dimension to their nature, as their names show. They are: Vohu Manah, Good Mind; Asha, Righteousness; Armaiti, Devotion; Kshathra, Dominion; Haurvatat, Wholeness; and Ameretat, Immortality. These are not only heavenly beings, but also ideals to which the righteous should aspire. So by sharing in the good mind, by a life of devotion and righteousness, people share in God's dominion and attain wholeness and immortality.

Each of the Bounteous Immortals is thought to protect, and to be represented by, one of the seven creations which together constitute the Good Creation of God: the sky, waters, earth, plants, animals, humanity, and fire. At important acts of worship, a representative of each creation, and therefore of the Bounteous Immortal, is present, so that the earthly and heavenly worlds are both symbolically present.

Zarathushtra taught that the world was essentially good, but spoilt at present by the attacks of evil. He looked forward to the day when the battle with evil would reach its climax, when good would triumph, and the world would be restored to the perfect state its Creator gave it. At the last, the dead will be raised and judged, the wicked will go to hell, and the righteous dwell with God in perfection for eternity.

PERSIA AND THE SPREAD OF ZOROASTRIANISM

The first 700 years after the death of the prophet are shrouded in mystery; there simply are not the sources to reconstruct Zoroastrianism's early history. It appears to have spread across the Persian plateau, largely through the movements of tribes, and through tribal battles. The Medes came to power in western Persia in the seventh century BCE, and the Persians in the sixth century, by which time Zoroastrianism was evidently a power in the land.

Persia emerges into the light of history in 559 BCE, when Cyrus ascended the throne of a small Persian kingdom called Anshan, in the south-west of the country. In 550 he seized the throne of the Medes, and then captured the fabulously wealthy king of Lydia, in distant Anatolia, modern Turkey. Finally in 539 the mighty Babylonian Empire capitulated to him, and Cyrus rose to become ruler of what was then the world's largest empire, establishing for himself a widespread reputation for tolerance and justice. The Achaemenid dynasty which ruled Persia after him continued to uphold these ideals – and also spread Zoroastrianism throughout the realm.

The people largely responsible for its propagation were the Magi, the priestly tribe of the Medes, who continued in office throughout all periods of the Zoroastrian history of Persia. The Magi acted as royal chaplains, and travelled with all important delegations. They also lived in the many Persian settlements in various parts of the empire. So when Matthew's Gospel refers to wise men – Magi – visiting the infant Jesus, his readers would understand well the significance of that. The later Christian legend that they were kings is wrong.

The Achaemenid Empire was brought to an end by Alexander the Great in 331 BCE, who in Persian history is known as 'Alexander the accursed', because he killed priests and burned down the royal palace of Persepolis. He said he wanted to unite the cultures of Persia and Greece, but he and his successors, the Seleucids, are remembered as the foreign interlopers who intruded into Persian life.

THE PARTHIAN EMPIRE

A native Persian dynasty – known as the Parthians because of the region in Iran they came from – gradually expelled Seleucid power from the land in the middle of the second century BCE. The Parthians have not received the attention they deserve, mainly because the archaeological and written sources are so few. Yet they ruled Persia for about 400 years, with an empire as large as that of their more famous Achaemenid forebears – stretching at times from North India to what is now Turkey – and were the largest power to confront the might of Rome. They had good relations with Israel; invading the land in 40 BCE, they deposed the hated Herod and put a Jew in his place. The Romans returned two years later and restored Herod. At the time of Jesus, the Parthians had made Zoroastrianism the most powerful religion of the then known world. It was during the Parthian period that the first moves were made to collect together the ancient traditions and sacred literature that made up the Zoroastrian holy book, the *Avesta*.

In 224 CE the ruler of a province in south-west Persia rebelled against the Parthians. The resulting new Sasanian Empire – also known as the Sassanid Empire – was named after a legendary ancestor, Sasan, and ruled Persia until the Muslim invasion in the seventh century. The Sasanians left behind a wealth of material splendour and a number of writings, creating the impression that this was the most glorious epoch in the history of Zoroastrian Persia. The high priest was a major power behind the throne, determining much of imperial policy. After Constantine and his successors made Christianity the official religion of the Roman Empire in the fourth century CE, providing a religious basis for its unity, a comparable unity was deemed necessary in the major Eastern empire. Zoroastrianism had always stressed the unity of church and state, and this was developed to the full in Sasanian times.

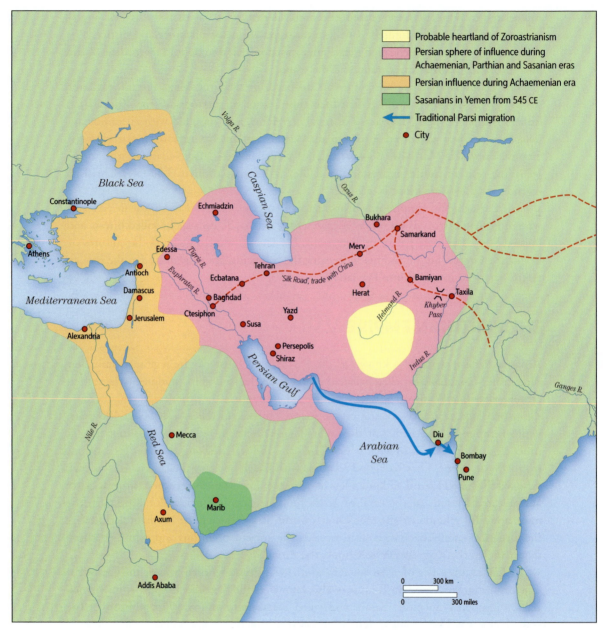

Legend:
- Probable heartland of Zoroastrianism
- Persian sphere of influence during Achaemenian, Parthian and Sasanian eras
- Persian influence during Achaemenian era
- Sasanians in Yemen from 545 CE
- Traditional Parsi migration
- City

Black Sea

Caspian Sea

Volga R.

Oxus R.

Constantinople

Echmiadzin

Bukhara

Samarkand

Athens

Edessa

Tigris R.

Merv

Antioch

Euphrates R.

Tehran

'Silk Road', trade with China

Bamiyan

Taxila

Damascus

Ecbatana

Baghdad

Herat

Khyber Pass

Mediterranean Sea

Ctesiphon

Yazd

Helmand R.

Jerusalem

Susa

Indus R.

Alexandria

Persepolis

Shiraz

Ganges R.

Nile R.

Persian Gulf

Diu

Red Sea

Mecca

Arabian Sea

Bombay

Pune

Marib

Axum

Addis Ababa

0   300 km

0   300 miles

Zoroastrianism

THE ISLAMIC CONQUEST

The Arab armies of the new Muslim religion entered Persia in 633 CE, only one year after the death of Muhammad. At first they came for booty, but later battles were aimed at permanent conquest. The intention was primarily to enforce submission to the rule of Islam. In theory, religions which the Muslim authorities recognized as 'people of a book', that is, those who had received a revelation from God – mainly Jews and Christians – were allowed to continue their religion, subject only to the imposition of an extra tax. But the position of Zoroastrianism as a religion of a book was less clear, and as the new Islamic world empire took hold, the position of Zoroastrians in their own land became increasingly threatened. Education, promotion, and equality before the law were all denied to the followers of Zarathushtra, who were forced gradually to retreat into the obscurity of desert villages. So the religion of the land became associated with poverty and backwardness.

Zoroastrians, as the oppressed poor, were often the subjects of vicious attacks from Muslims. Even in the twentieth century, under the protective Pahlavi dynasty, 'infidel-baiting' was common in remote villages far from official gaze. Any Zoroastrian venturing alone into a Muslim quarter could expect verbal – and often physical – abuse. Persecution, oppression, poverty, injustice, and isolation are the conditions Zoroastrians have faced in their own land for nearly 1400 years of Muslim rule. It is a tribute to their courage, determination, and faith that any followers of Zarathushtra remain in present-day Iran. They are mainly in Tehran and in the villages of the Yazdi plain, and total about 25,000 – although government figures are much higher.

PARSIS AND IRANIANS

The worldwide population of Parsi and Iranian Zoroastrians today is reckoned to be no more than 115,000. The main base of the religion today, in numerical terms, is India, among the Parsis and Iranis, with around 65,000 people. In the tenth century CE a small band of the faithful set out to seek a new land of religious freedom, preferring to leave Persia rather than give up the religion of their forefathers. The term 'Irani' is used for those Zoroastrians who fled Iran because of increasing religious persecution between the eighteenth and twentieth centuries and settled in India. There they have lived in peace and security, in time even achieving a position of wealth and power, which they used to campaign for and support their co-religionists back in the homeland.

JOHN HINNELLS

CHAPTER 14

Zoroastrian Beliefs

The tenth century was a time of literary activity among the Zoroastrians of Persia. A number of texts were produced to encourage, inspire, and instruct the faithful, in the contemporary language known as Pahlavi, or Middle Persian. The holy book, the *Avesta*, was in a language which only a few learned priests understood. Translations, summaries, and explanations were produced, as well as defences of the faith against Muslim, Christian, and Hindu teachings. Although they were written in the ninth and tenth centuries, they can be taken as the definitive statements of traditional Zoroastrian thought. These Middle Persian texts codify, elaborate, and systematize the teaching of Zarathushtra himself, from which they stem.

CREATION

The Middle Persian forms of the names of God and the 'Devil' – ancient Ahura Mazda and Angra Mainyu – are Ohrmazd and Ahriman. Ohrmazd, it is taught, dwells on high, in perfect goodness and light; whereas Ahriman dwells for eternity in darkness, below in the abyss. Battle between these two primal spirits was inevitable, so Ohrmazd created the heavenly and material worlds to aid him in the battle. First he created the heavenly beings, then the world in purely spiritual form, that is, invisible and intangible. In Zoroastrian belief, the material world is not evil or corrupt; rather it is the visible, tangible manifestation of the spiritual creation. It is the creation of God, therefore it is good.

The essential characteristics of evil are violence, chaos, and the will to destroy. When Ahriman saw the good creation of God, he tried to destroy it, afflicting it with misery, suffering, disease, and death. None of these evils, therefore, came from God, nor were they part of his plan for creation. They are unnatural afflictions, wrought by a wholly independent 'Devil', who seeks to ruin the perfection of the divine creation.

In the myth of creation it is said that Ahriman defiled all parts of creation: the ordered creation was afflicted with chaos; the round, flat earth was shaken so that valleys were opened up,

Then I recognised you, O Mazda, in [my] thought as being the beginning and the end …

Yasna 31:8

and mountains raised; the sun was dislodged from its ideal noonday position; fire was afflicted with smoke; the archetypal man and bull were afflicted with suffering and death. Ahriman was apparently triumphant. Then a miracle occurred: the dying bull and man emitted sperm; from the bull's seed grew cattle, from man's came a plant whose leaves grew, separated, and formed the first human couple. In Zoroastrian thought human beings are literally at one with their environment.

THE COSMIC BATTLE

Then Ahriman sought to escape from the world, but found he was trapped within it. Thus the cosmic battle between good and evil is now fought out in the arena of world history. For the first 3000 years after Ahriman's attack, the two forces were quite evenly balanced, in what is known as 'the period of mixture' – that is, of good and evil. Then the prophet Zarathushtra was born. With the revelation of the Good Religion, the defeat of Ahriman was assured; from this time on, the defeat of evil began. But in Zoroastrian thought this does not come suddenly and unexpectedly; it is a further 3000-year conflict, as Ahriman makes a desperate bid to destroy all that is good.

This final fling is in vain. At thousand-year intervals three saviours appear: each born of a virgin who had been impregnated with the prophet's seed, preserved in a lake where the maidens bathed. They are, therefore, of the line of the prophet, though born of a virgin. A part of the evil creation is destroyed by each of them, until the third saviour raises the dead and introduces the last judgment. From this, humanity will return to heaven and hell for a limited period, before re-emerging to pass through a stream of molten metal – the final ordeal before all dwell in total perfection with Ohrmazd.

During these cataclysmic events the heavenly forces will have been engaged in the final battle with the demonic powers, finally overcoming them. The molten metal, which had already restored the earth to its original state, by reducing mountains and filling up the valleys, and which finally tested humankind, now fills up hell. So Ahriman is rendered powerless for eternity. For the first time Ohrmazd becomes all-powerful. Evil is wiped out. So, in the myth, the earth ascends to the moon, the heaven descends to the moon; neither is done away with. Zoroastrians do not speak of 'the end of the world', for that would be the end of what God made. Instead they look forward to the 'renovation of creation', the time when heaven and earth join together to make what is literally the best of both worlds.

THE DESTINY OF HUMANKIND

In Zoroastrian thought the individual faces two judgments. One comes after death, when his or her thoughts, words, and deeds are weighed in the balances. If good outweighs evil, then the person's own conscience guides him or her across the Bridge of the Separator, or Chinvat Bridge, to heaven. If evil predominates, then his or her conscience leads him trembling to the bridge, from which he or she falls into the abyss of hell. The second judgment is after the resurrection.

There are two sides to human nature, the physical and the spiritual, both the creations of God. The individual must be judged, rewarded, or punished in both aspects of his or her being. The first judgment after death is evidently one in the spirit, because the body can be seen to remain on earth. But hell is not eternal in Zoroastrian belief. The purpose of punishment, Zoroastrians believe, must be corrective. In hell, Zoroastrians believe, the punishment is made to fit the crime; so a cruel ruler who tortures or starves his people is himself tortured and starved in hell. But at the resurrection, all return from heaven or hell to face their second judgment, this time in the body; and again they return to heaven or hell as appropriate, so they may be physically rewarded or corrected.

The purpose is that the whole person – body and soul – should be so corrected that he or she may dwell, in the perfection of a united being, with God. Man and woman are a divine creation, intended to be fellow-workers with God; their final destiny must be with God. During their earthly life they have complete free-will to act as they choose, to support the forces of good or evil. They can live contrary to their nature; but they cannot, in eternal terms, change that nature. Through judgment, heaven, and hell, they are corrected and rewarded, for their part in the great battle between good and evil.

BODY AND SOUL

A person's foremost duty is to make his or her body the dwelling-place of the Bounteous Immortals, seeking to reflect the generous, creative spirit of God, and to reject the negative path. To do this, they must keep the spiritual and material sides of their nature in balance. So people have a religious duty to expand God's material creation as well as to support his spiritual creation. A man should marry and have children; he should seek to expand his herds and the natural environment through agriculture. To remain celibate is sinfully to refrain from this duty. On the other hand, he should not abuse the divine gift of marriage through lechery. In Zoroastrian belief, a monk is as great a sinner as a lecher – both deny what God wills. A man should not fast so that the spirit is exalted over the body, nor should he be gluttonous and exalt the body over the soul. The health of body and soul are interdependent, and should be cared for equally.

The world is God's good creation, and it is people's religious duty to care for and enjoy that creation; for Zoroastrians believe that 'misery drives away the divine'. The spirit of happiness permeates not only

> *Yes, there are two fundamental spirits, twins which are renowned to be in conflict. In thought and in word, in action, they are two: the better and the bad … When these two spirits first came together they created life and death, and how, at the end, the worst existence shall be for the deceitful, but the best thinking for the truthful person … Of these two spirits, the deceitful one chose to bring to realization the worst things. [But] the very bounteous spirit, who is clothed in the hardest stones, chose the truth …*
>
> Yasna 30:3–5

Zoroastrian ethics, but also their rituals. If evil is associated with death and decay in the material

Zoroastrian Tower of Silence, near Yazd, Iran.

world, then people have a duty to avoid contact with any matter that aids these evils. Dirt, rotting, and dead matter are places where death — and therefore evil — is present. The housewife cleaning the home, rites associated with birth, marriage, and death, standards of personal hygiene — all are concerned with the great cosmic battle between good and evil. In this way each individual, a fellow-worker with Ohrmazd, seeks to wipe out evil and restore the world to its God-created perfection.

Since death is seen as the temporary triumph of evil, Parsi Zoroastrians in India normally do not bury, burn, or drown their dead, as all these are seen as agents of pollution and therefore evil. Instead bodies are exposed, naked, in a *dakhma*, a circular, stone tower, open to the sky, known in English as a 'Tower of Silence', where they are devoured by birds of prey, and the skeletal remains dry in the heat of the sun. Later, the remains are moved to a circular pit lined with lime and black salt, where over time they turn to dust.

Zoroastrianism is a religion concerned with the good God, the good creation, and the goodness of humankind; its followers often call it 'The Good Religion'. Everyone is responsible for his or her own part in the cosmic battle, and for his or her own destiny. It is a religion of stalwart determination — which is perhaps what has enabled it to survive for so long, despite a millennium of oppression.

JOHN HINNELLS

FIRE TEMPLES

Fire has been the focus of Zoroastrian rites and devotions from earliest times. The nomads used the household fire as the centre of their rites, having the sky as their dome, not a man-made temple. Temples were first introduced into Zoroastrianism by the Achaemenid monarch Artaxerxes II (404–359 BCE), probably in imitation of Babylonian practice. He also introduced the cult of statues, but this was too radical a break with tradition for it to succeed. Instead of man-made statues, Zoroastrians placed the divinely created 'icon' of fire at the centre of their holy buildings. Temple worship was, then, a late entry into the religion.

There is no set time of day for temple worship, nor any fixed ritual to perform. For the laity it involves essentially a personal pilgrimage. Before entering the temple, worshippers wash and offer prayers, so they are clean physically and spiritually. The prayer room itself is very simple. Against one wall there is the sanctuary, marked off by ceiling-high walls, with a door for the priest to enter and windows for the faithful to see through. The sacred fire is kept burning in a large vessel, sometimes as much as 6 feet/2 metres high. Ordinary worshippers approach the door of the sanctuary, touch the ground with the forehead, leave an offering of wood for the fire, and take a pinch of ash from a ladle left by the priest. They then stand to offer their prayers in private. There is no congregational worship; prayer is offered by each person directly to God. While the priests are expected to undertake 'higher' ceremonies on behalf of laypeople, the ordinary Zoroastrian's duty is the life of good thoughts, words, and deeds; the daily prayers, the practice of rituals, and the inspiration of a personal pilgrimage to the temple.

CHAPTER 15

The Ancient Religions of Greece and Rome

The ancient history of Greece covers some 6000 years or more of development, from the first permanent settlement based upon grain agriculture, until Greece was absorbed by Rome. Within this immense period, only the last 2000 years at most are definitely Greek by language. The ancient history of Rome, by contrast, begins in the eighth century BCE and extends into the fifth century CE, and the Latin language is present over that whole span.

MINOAN-MYCENAEAN CIVILIZATIONS

When barley and wheat entered the larger European and Mediterranean worlds, they were accompanied by those who understood their cultivation. These people's way of thinking included observing the seasonal cycle, and its ritual correlation with preparing, planting, weeding, and harvesting; or breeding, pasturing, tending, and milking. In this we see the base for all later development of religious ideas.

EARLY BRONZE AGE

For the earliest phase of the Bronze Age on the Greek mainland, objects of religious significance are minimal, but there is much better evidence from the group of islands called the Cyclades. Best known of all Cycladic objects are the marble figurines, the two most common being the elongated female and the abbreviated 'fiddle-shaped' version, which emphasizes only the necklace and the sexually-explicit features. Although the figurines are usually less than twelve inches (thirty centimetres) tall, several life-sized examples also exist, broken at the neck and knee to fit into the grave.

MINOAN CRETE

There is evidence of royal palace complexes. The palace rulers are said to be 'theocratic', because excavations have revealed no separate structures that can be called 'religious' within these palaces. But in 1979, during the excavation of a small site at Anemospilia, not far from Knossos, Crete, there was found the first example of a tiny Minoan temple, originally destroyed in an earthquake.

The Minoans seem to have worshipped bulls and sacrificed them. 'Bull-leapers' performed dangerous acrobatics over a bull for religious purposes, as is often portrayed in wall-paintings, seals, bronze, and terracotta. These ceremonial games took place in the large central courts of the palaces.

The palaces also contained 'pillar crypts', decorated with the double-headed axe – the chief Minoan religious symbol – possibly from its use in animal sacrifices. The double axe was a woodman's tool rather than a weapon, and examples have been found with other carpentry tools. Storage magazines were sometimes connected with the pillar crypts. In the floor of one crypt at Knossos were 'temple repositories', containing faience figurines handling snakes. Snakes were used as house-guardians, and so became the sacred animal of the household-goddess.

CITADELS OF THE MYCENAEANS

The Minoan epoch came to an end disastrously, probably when the volcanic island of Thera erupted with extreme violence in about 1450 BCE. The Late Bronze Age, or Late Helladic Era, belongs to the Mycenaeans, both on the mainland and the islands, including Crete. The Middle Bronze mainland had been dominated by Minoan cultural influence, but as the Late Bronze Age began we find the *tholos* tomb-builders. There are no surviving indications of the dwellings of these aristocratic warrior-rulers, though they may well have been built on the sites on which the Mycenaean palaces were to appear. Their *tholos* tombs were underground beehive-shaped vaults, entered by way of a long, gently-sloping tunnel, and topped by an earth mound.

The Mycenaean palace complexes are neither towns nor houses, but fortified centres for developing valley communities. What most distinguishes these complexes from their Minoan predecessors is their location on high citadels, and their massive fortification walls. Five major sites on the mainland are known: Thebes, under the modern city; Athens, levelled for the fifth-century acropolis; Tiryns and Pylos, both well-preserved; and Mycenae, the best example, though part of the palace itself has collapsed down the slope.

The new ingredient in the Late Bronze Age is the earliest written texts, in a script called 'Linear B', which was deciphered in 1952, and shown to be an archaic form of Greek. The Linear B texts give an entirely new dimension to investigation. To date, tablets have been found only at Knossos, Pylos, Mycenae, and Thebes. They include inventory lists of people and their occupations, livestock, and agricultural produce, land

The Palace of Knossos, Crete.

ownership — with some usage — textiles, vessels, furniture, metals and military equipment, and a grouping defined as 'proportional tribute and ritual offerings'. It seems commodities could serve as either tribute or offering, and that these were assessed seasonally, according to fixed schedules, that receipts varied from assessments and, most important of all, that there were functionaries of all sorts, as well as deities known by name or title. Poseidon is of considerable importance, as is 'the Lady' of different places. Zeus, Hera, Ares, Hermes, Athena, Artemis, Dionysus, and a few other classical deities are named. Among the great variety of functionaries who made up this administrative complex, a 'priestess' or 'priest' is very occasionally mentioned.

THE EPICS OF HOMER

There is a gap at the end of the Bronze Age, with the destruction of the Mycenaean world. The palace bureaucracies disappeared. Pottery remains from this period are very few. We have nothing that documents the religious response to reality, except the 'epic interlude': the unsurpassed poetry of Homer, regarded by many later Greeks almost as sacred scripture. The epic language is peculiar, in that it was apparently not a spoken dialect, nor equivalent to any of the historic dialects found in inscriptions or subsequent literature. It was, however, designed to be recited. The nearly 28,000 lines of Homer which form the *Odyssey* and the slightly longer *Iliad* constitute the surviving bulk of this epic form, with its strict metre.

> *We must dedicate to Poseidon ... that he might take pity on us, and not pile up a huge mountain over our city.*
>
> Homer, *Odyssey* 13.180–83

THE HOMERIC GODS

The gods are portrayed in essentially human terms, but they do not grow old and are immortal. The gods have power – *daimon* – to change their appearance, size, and attributes beyond the bounds of the human form they may take. Their awesome status prompted dread, fear, shame, or reverence. In response, humans were impelled to pray, entreat, praise, take an oath, make sacrifice of a victim, or pour out a libation of grain or wine. Many of these activities can be tied quite naturally to daily domestic routine. The communication between gods and humans may be direct, or via an intermediary – including the god in disguise as a human friend – or by a dream. The gods may be consulted through an agent accomplished in the art of divining, most commonly through birds or the interpretation of dreams. Lightning, thunder, or falling stars may also serve as omens. And places where there was an oracle, such as Dodona, with its great oak tree at which people listened for the voice of Zeus, played a lesser role.

> There is a land called Crete in the midst of the wine-dark sea, a fair country and fertile, seagirt, and there are many peoples, innumerable; there are ninety cities … and there is Knossos, the great city, the place where Minos was king for nine-year periods, and conversed with great Zeus.
>
> Homer, *Odyssey* 19.172–74, 178–79

Life in Homer takes on some specific burden which humans must bear, sometimes even the delusion with which the gods affect them. The human characters tend to explain the course of events as the destiny imposed by the gods – even if, as Helen says to Hector, 'hereafter we shall be made into things of song for the men of the future'. With gifts and prayers, these gods may be implored to change the situation. The god might sometimes do so, or might merely turn his head away in rejection; for these gods – even Zeus himself – are equally bound by fate. Whatever else may be granted, humans are not permitted to escape death, which is their final destiny. Within that framework, all phenomena – religious and otherwise – are set. Although the gods manipulate human actions, they neither make nor change human nature.

HOMERIC HEROES

Heroes seek honour, glory, and renown, believing that to obtain these is of much greater worth than life itself. The burial of the dead is of great importance. They require that last honour, even though their souls go immediately to the underworld – Hades – lest they become the gods' curse upon the living. In Homer, the funeral would seem to include cremation – if that of a warrior, dressed in his full armour – and some kind of interment of the burned remains, accompanied by lamentations. A mound was heaped over the grave, with a stone indicating the dead person's profession. The funeral rites were commonly accompanied by athletic contests, such as chariot-racing, boxing, wrestling, close-combat with sword and shield, weight-throwing, and spear-throwing – and betting on all of these!

The obverse side of heroic life is an overbearing, presumptuous pride, violence, and transgression. Although it cannot be shown that in any final sense – other than death – recompense is required for sin, there are nevertheless hints at some larger levels of justice and decency, which the gods love in preference to cruelty, or to excessive glorification over slain men. Since fate determines all, the anger of the gods, like the anger of humans towards one another, must work out its destined course. Yet their full destructive anger may be averted by means of prayer, libation – a poured-out drink offering – and sacrifice. The gods may be offended by perverse judgments, refusal or neglect of funeral rites, brutal conduct in a host's home, and murder of a guest. Ultimately, the values of society are vindicated by the gods.

> Since there are three brothers born by Rheia to Kronos, Zeus and me, and the third is Hades, lord of the dead, all was divided among us three ways, each given his domain: I, when the lots were shaken, drew the grey sea to live in forever; Hades drew the lot of the mists and the darkness, and Zeus was allotted the wide sky, in the cloud and the bright air. But Earth and high Olympos are common to all three.
>
> Homer, *Iliad* 15.187–93

THE CITY-STATE

The Mycenaean age ended in destructive violence brought about by human efforts around 1100 BCE and, with it, not only palace and palace art, but also the Linear B script, pass into obscurity. The archaic phase of classical Greece opens on a new world, with the coming of alphabetic writing. The fundamental factor is a devastating decline in total population. Whereas some 320 inhabited sites are known from the thirteenth century BCE, many of them large centres, only forty are known from the eleventh century, and all of these are small.

What remained intact through that major change was a legacy of technology, in the mundane matters of mixed farming, building, carpentry, boat-building, spinning, weaving, pottery, and metallurgy. The shift from bronze to iron carried with it the 'hateful strife of evil war', rather than healthy competition among hard-working neighbours.

Greece was divided among the Hellenes into at least twelve separate regions, and the Greek language into five major linguistic blocks. It is not surprising that Greece consisted ultimately of no fewer than 158 independent city-states. Most were quite small, and incapable of sustaining a total population above 10,000. By colonial expansion, even more city-states were founded throughout the greater Mediterranean basin.

URBAN RELIGION

By the sixth century BCE, 'a new god had captured the Acropolis, and had, by an imperceptible passage, merged with the original deity' (Lewis Mumford). What he had in mind was the city (*polis*) itself. Just as ordinary men insinuated themselves by warfare into political life, so the city assembly (*ekklesia*) insinuated itself into what religious structure was still considered relevant. Yet several major groups remained outside the pale of citizenship-participation: the women, the children, the large cluster of slaves

descended from suppressed indigenous inhabitants or taken captive in war, and the resident aliens.

View from the Acropolis, Mycenae, Greece.

Official city religion is clearly manifest in the very layout and architecture of the city. The lofty citadel, *acropolis*, which had been the Mycenaean fortress and palatial residence, was now abandoned – left for the gods alone. The new city lies within the plains whose agriculture supports its economy. The centre of life is the marketplace, *agora*, whose purpose reveals that economics is central to this renewed urban life, and whose architecture reflects the necessity for public access. Although public inscriptions bear witness of dedication and piety to the official religion, no gods dwell there. At some distance from the city centre, or perhaps on the old acropolis, decorative and elaborate temples were created and maintained, with more than a hint that a major function was as treasury for the wealth of the city.

The growth of temples typifies this new era of the growth of the city-state, and of law and order. The decorative arts were used to portray mythical events that expressed this sense of order. Victory over the great uncivilized forces was personified in the victory of lapiths against centaurs, or of their legendary ancestors against Amazons. The final form of Greek mythology is the end product of the creative formation of the Greek city-states. Their nature is also reflected in the temple architecture, with its basic patterns or 'orders'.

At the individual level of society, from the Geometric period onwards, come marker-stones, *stela*, especially those set up at graves. Thus names and titles, genealogies and deeds enter into history. Objects of all kinds were dedicated to the gods, but the funeral stele is fully human.

TEMPLE STYLES

The history of temple styles is summarized in three successive 'orders': Doric, Ionic, and Corinthian. The columns of these orders are increasingly elaborate and highly embellished. As Gisela Richter has stated: 'A central hall was provided with a columned porch, practically always in front and often also at the back; pilasters terminated the side walls of the central hall. Rows of columns were placed in front, at the back, and sometimes all around to form a colonnade; occasionally columns were added also in the interior to support the roof.' The pitched roof created triangular space at each end of the pediment, which came to be decorated, often with a central mythological theme for the particular temple.

Even the largest temples are quite small: few exceed one hundred feet (thirty metres) in overall width, or much more than twice that in length. The inner hall, being open only in one direction, could not have allowed easy access to many people at once. Clearly the major purpose was to provide a space for the great statue of the god who was worshipped.

> I am Demeter the honoured, the greatest benefit and joy to undying gods and to mortals. But come now, let all the people build me a great temple and beneath it an altar under the steep walls of the city, above Kallikhoron, on the rising hill. I myself shall introduce rites so that later You may propitiate my mind by their right performance.
>
> Homeric *Hymn to Demeter* 268–74

PAINTING AND SCULPTURE

Vase-painting styles developed from the earlier black-figure to red-figure techniques. Athenian examples dominate both varieties. Some shapes in the black-figure style were exclusively intended for ritual use: as grave-offerings, or for other uses at funerals, or for use in marriage ceremonies.

Although illustration focused on a god or myth, that is no guarantee of explicit religiou sness. The world of vase-painting is basically secular, reflecting the structure of the city-state. Yet, as well as maenads – the ecstatic female followers of Dionysus – and their attendant satyrs, with the onset of the red-figure phase, women of all sorts, increasingly in domestic scenes, are more often portrayed.

Temples are rare in these paintings; but altars with sacrifice are often shown. The deities invoked are rarely to be seen, and the attendants cannot be distinguished from those in domestic life. Since there was no explicit ceremony, marriage processionals indicate that event. Funerals show chiefly the laying out of the body, the women mourning – only the men approaching in ritual gesture. The strange phenomenon of the *herm* – that unhewn pillar, seldom with any other features than a human head and an erect penis, which stood everywhere throughout the city, outside the doors of ordinary houses – is illustrated in scenes beginning with its carving to the perfunctory act of worship made by passers-by. Similarly, the phallus-bearing celebrants in some revelry, often dedicated to Dionysus, are commonplace. Erotic scenes, both hetero- and homosexual, were considered appropriate subjects even on votive and funeral plaques.

THE GREEK WORLD-VIEW

Although the fifth century BCE has often been interpreted as a crucial age for human civilization, its achievements were built on the whole period from the time of Homer. The boundary is not only the turn of a century, but the life and death of one man, Socrates (469–399 BCE). Before Socrates, it was thought that all things were made out of one or more of the four basic ingredients: air, earth, fire, and water. The one fully preserved example of pre-Socratic cultural inquiry is Herodotus (c. 490–430), who divided the known world into five intellectual components. The Greek was set over and against the Egyptian, Libyan, Scythian, and Persian – collectively considered as 'barbarian', that is, incapable of Greek language and hence of civilized Greek thought.

Pre-Socratic understanding turned on the assumed relationship between nature and custom, but this broke down in the crisis which accompanied the destructive half-century of war among the Greek city-states.

The literary response to the Peloponnesian War is provided by two groups of Athenian writings. The first consists of plays, cast in metrical poetry, portraying the actions of the gods in relation to humans, especially in the growing horror of a world at war. Beginning with the self-esteem which all Greeks shared from their common resistance to the Persian invasions, all the cherished assumptions of Greek society were questioned by Aeschylus (525–456), Sophocles (497–405), and Euripides (485–406), as Athens, whose democracy had become imperialistic in regard to its allies, struggled with Sparta, whose militaristic regime championed the freedom of the other city states. The second, prose, grouping came to be called 'Sophist', and taught rhetoric, 'the art of persuasion'. The major surviving fifth-century author in whose work these ingredients are found is Thucydides (c. 455–400 BCE).

Both analyses – poetic and prose – arrive at the role of the irrational in human affairs, and particularly in power politics, for in both Thucydides and Euripides we are introduced to the pathology of human nature under stress. Human affairs cannot

> There was a time when undisciplined was human life, kindred to beasts, servant to brute strength; there was no reward for good, nor punishment for evil ... Then it was, someone wise in intellect discovered for humans fear of gods, that awe might restrain evil ones, even those doing things in secret ... So now, if you want to do some evil, even in secret, you will not escape these gods.
>
> Critias, *Sisyphus* fragment

The Parthenon, Athens, dedicated to the maiden goddess Athena, patron of the city.

ultimately be blamed on the gods, though perhaps some fortune or necessity controls the mysterious past that has produced the present disastrous situations at both the urban and the individual levels. When human nature is aroused to do something – anything – it is not possible to turn it aside, either by law or fear of punishment. Consequences cannot be anticipated. This somewhat sceptical approach was accompanied by a sense that the Olympian gods were remote – and scarcely model examples of ethical behaviour.

TALKING ABOUT RELIGION

The ridicule of the gods in the plays of Aristophanes (c. 450–385) attracted no apparent criticism at the time, although dedications to the gods continued to be made in the state's official inscriptions. But after the defeat of Athens in the war, the trumped-up charges against Socrates were said to be not acknowledging the gods worshipped by the state, and introducing new divinities or an educational atheism which served to corrupt the young men from their attitudes as good citizens.

It is less than clear what, in their own times, either Plato (c. 429–347) or Aristotle (384–322) contributed to religious thought. Aristotle's treatise format has a greater precision than Plato's dialogues, and his discussion of fundamental substance as the basic constituent of reality served the growing sense of the nature of God, so that *Metaphysics* contains reference to the 'unmoved-mover' – God – as First Cause.

By the fifth century, there was an unprecedented enlargement of religious vocabulary. From Herodotus comes a word for 'religious observance', almost 'religion' itself, and a verb 'to observe religiously', or to worship, to do religion. In contrast, by the time of Theophrastos (371–287), a word was in common use whose meaning, 'fear of', or 'reverence for', divinity, already had such negative overtones that it could designate the 'superstitious' person. Interestingly, the era produced no words for 'believing in' gods.

RULERS BECOME GODS

Hellenization was taking place even before the advent of Alexander the Great (356–323), though it was his conquest of the vast Persian Empire in the East which brought the process to fruition. Alexander founded some seventy cities on the Greek pattern, mostly named after himself, 'Alexandria'. With easy transport and communication within the empire, Greek being the common language, Hellenization opened up the Mediterranean world to Eastern influences, including religious beliefs. This era was one of conspicuous luxury among the rich and powerful, while inflated prices and lower wages were the lot of the poor. At the very top of the society were the Hellenized rulers, who declared themselves to be divine. Alexander, whose heroic deeds could not be doubted, was believed to have been received among the gods upon his death, like Heracles before him. This soon degenerated into automatic deification for the king.

MYSTERIES AND HEALING CULTS

The specific technical term 'the mysteries' first occurs in Herodotus and the tragedians, though their usage had clearly grown out of urban ceremonial and temple festivals. By Hellenistic times, however, the process of initiation was open to all Greek-speaking people who were not ritually impure and could afford the initiation fee. Ultimately, the mysteries – meaning those primarily of Eleusis near Athens, commonly called 'Greater' – must be said to lie in the initiate, to whom something real is revealed, rather than in the ritual act or paraphernalia. The total complex included 'things said', 'things shown', and 'things performed'.

Initiation promised happiness, perhaps simply in a glorious vision of the god. Although at first no particular good life was implied beyond death, the mystery religions were highly syncretistic, and tended to absorb Eastern myths which hinted that this happiness continued into an afterlife, perhaps by a unification with the gods, or by a deification of the human. But no kind of group association followed, and no moral demands were required for this bliss – except purity at the cult, and silence ever after on 'the mysteries'.

The mythological and ritual complex at Eleusis, involving the goddess Demeter and her daughter, was tied to cereal grain. The processional and festival celebration,

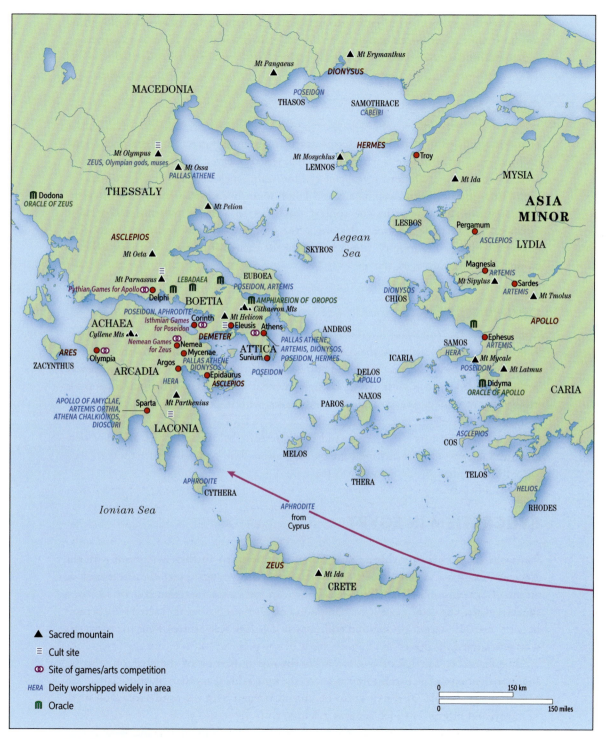

Map labels:

Mt Erymanthus

Mt Pangaeus

DIONYSUS

MACEDONIA

POSEIDON
THASOS

SAMOTHRACE
CABEIRI

HERMES

Mt Olympus
ZEUS, Olympian gods, muses

Mt Ossa
PALLAS ATHENE

Mt Mosychlus
LEMNOS

Troy

MYSIA

Mt Ida

ASIA
MINOR

THESSALY

Dodona
ORACLE OF ZEUS

Mt Pelion

Aegean
Sea

LESBOS

Pergamum
ASCLEPIOS

LYDIA

ASCLEPIOS

Mt Oeta

SKYROS

Magnesia
ARTEMIS

Mt Parnassus
Pythian Games for Apollo
Delphi

LEBADAEA

EUBOEA
POSEIDON, ARTEMIS

DIONYSOS
CHIOS

Mt Sipylus
Sardes
ARTEMIS

Mt Tmolus

BOETIA

AMPHIAREION OF OROPOS

Cithaeron Mts

APOLLO

ACHAEA

Cyllene Mts

POSEIDON, APHRODITE
Isthmian Games
for Poseidon
Corinth

Mt Helicon
Eleusis
Athens

ANDROS

SAMOS
HERA

Ephesus
ARTEMIS

ARES

Nemean Games
for Zeus
Nemea
Mycenae

DEMETER

ATTICA
Sunium

PALLAS ATHENE,
ARTEMIS, DIONYSOS,
POSEIDON, HERMES

ICARIA

POSEIDON

Mt Mycale
Mt Latmus

ZACYNTHUS

Olympia

Argos

ARCADIA
HERA

PALLAS ATHENE
DIONYSOS
Epidaurus
ASCLEPIOS

POSEIDON

DELOS
APOLLO

Didyma
ORACLE OF APOLLO

CARIA

APOLLO OF AMYCLAE,
ARTEMIS ORTHIA,
ATHENA CHALKIOIKOS,
DIOSCURI

Sparta

Mt Parthenius

PAROS

NAXOS

LACONIA

ASCLEPIOS
COS

APHRODITE
CYTHERA

MELOS

THERA

TELOS

HELIOS

Ionian Sea

APHRODITE
from
Cyprus

RHODES

ZEUS

Mt Ida
CRETE

Legend:

▲ Sacred mountain

☰ Cult site

⊕ Site of games/arts competition

HERA Deity worshipped widely in area

🏛 Oracle

0   150 km

0   150 miles

Cult Centres of Ancient Greece

which was the context for initiation, took place in September-October – the ploughing season. Unlike other Greek temples, the one at Eleusis was meant for a large gathering, and could hold up to 10,000 people.

ORACLES

Herodotus tells us that the most ancient oracular site in all Greece, and the only one in his time, was that at Dodona, with its great oak tree. Preserved inscriptions of questions asked of the oracle at Dodona reveal concern for health, including successful pregnancies. There were also oracles at Amphiaraus and Trophonius. In each case, some kind of earth-fault or warm spring provides the context for belief in a divine presence and a cultic sacrifice. After this, the inquirer – sleeping at the spot – received by dream an appropriate response to his or her inquiry. Individuals brought their own private concerns; officials consulted about matters of state.

DIVINE HEALING

The temple-cult of Asclepios, the god of healing, was set up principally in times of great need, especially by city-states threatened by disease. It thrived because rich people who were healed rewarded the cult with wealth, though payment was not required from the poor. It became the most widespread of all the newer cults, with important centres at Pergamum and Corinth, as well as Epidauros and Kos. Apart from the environment of cleanliness and pure air, a combination of exercise, cold baths, rest, herbal prescriptions, and diet were employed, along with dreams induced by suggestion. The god was understood to have visited the suppliant while he or she slept.

SYNCRETISM IN EGYPT

Two cults from Egypt provide an interesting illustration of further syncretism with the Ancient Near East. The cult of Serapis was created in Egypt under the Ptolemies, as an intentional fusion of the Greek mysteries with the native Egyptian cult of Osiris, a funerary deity. The name itself was a compound of Osiris and Apis, the sacred bull. Serapis became a manifestation of the one god; attached to his cult-centres were functionaries who proclaimed the power and mighty deeds of the god.

The second cult is that of Isis, originally the personification of the pharaoh's throne. In the ancient myth, she became important as the king's divine mother, in whose lap he sat, a 'madonna-and-child' image. She also became associated with the royal succession myth of Osiris and Horus, in which she was a deliverer.

Under the impact of Hellenistic syncretism, these two cults of Isis and Serapis may be brought together. These deities had the power of deliverance from war, prison, pain, wandering, shipwreck, even death, and were believed to guide humankind, for they saw the manifold deeds of both the wicked and the just. They were expected to grant to the righteous, where such righteousness is individual virtue, appropriate sacrifice, and a share of blessings received.

ROME EXPANDS

Historically, the event that marked the beginning of Roman achievement was the sacking of the city of Rome in 387 BCE by the same marauding Gauls who helped eliminate the Etruscans. Until then, the central Mediterranean had suffered rivalry among the Greeks of Magna Graecia in southern Italy, the Phoenicians centred on Carthage, and the Etruscans, with the conflict focused on Sicily. It was the disruption of this balance of power that permitted Rome to move swiftly, deploying the sword, founding colonies, and building roads, to bring all Italy south of the River Po under their rule withi n a century.

> *Go proclaim to the Romans it is heaven's will that my Rome shall be capital of the world; accordingly they must cherish soldierliness, and they must be assured, and transmit to posterity the assurance, that no human power can withstand Roman arms.*
>
> Romulus in *Livy* 1.16

The historical character of Rome, which took shape in the centuries between the two sackings of the city – by Gauls in 387 BCE and by Goths in 410 CE – is best described on two levels: the social institutions on which the structure of urban life rests, and the buildings in which the structure was contained. At the first level, the focus of attention is on the army, the law, the populace, and the religion. The architectural needs of each caused the city's buildings to be erected.

RELIGION OF HEARTH, FIELD, AND CITY

Just as the myth of Rome as the city of cities was to dominate the political aspect of Roman self-understanding, so the myth of their own religiousness was to dominate their personal and cultic insights. Cicero (106–43) put it clearly: 'If we compare ourselves with other peoples, in various things we appear equal or even inferior, except that of religion, meaning the worship of the gods, in which we are by far superior.' 'Religion' (*religio*) is a Latin concept; there was no exact equivalent in Greek.

Latin authors could speak of a person as having a 'religious nature free of superstition'; or affirm 'it is proper to be religious but not to be superstitious', contrasting the positive and negative elements of belief. On the other hand, the late Republic came to be sceptical of older religious forms that were still practised. Authors, with the bondage of religious duties in mind, could affirm that religion is that from which the soul (Lucretius), or oneself and one's household (Livy), ought to be freed.

The documented evidence provides little knowledge of early Roman domestic religion. The structure of the laws – especially those relating to women and marriage, children and inheritance – bears out the links of household and hearth, with paternal

... there are many things in philosophy which have not yet been satisfactorily explained, particularly that most obscure and most difficult question concerning the nature of the gods, which is so extremely important both for a knowledge of the human soul and also for the regulation of religion.

Cicero, *The Nature of the Gods* 1.1

domination expressed in religious custom and ritual. The 'Twelve Tables', the oldest law code, are strictly civil.

To the Romans, gods were functions. Irrespective of what myths might have been attached to a particular deity, the Roman concern was to assign the precise office, so that the office – rather than the older personification – received appropriate worship.

The communal religion was related to the basic agricultural economy, and so was dependent upon the Etruscans and others, for Rome developed too late to foster more than the mythology of her own creation. This religion was primarily that of the state, with the city personified as the chief deity. The Romans were aware of the need to accept some foreign gods, especially Greek, into their state-cult, and they modified these deities to fit their functional need. Livy (59 BCE–17CE) claims the first celebration in Rome of a public offering of a sacred meal to images of Greek deities placed on couches (*lectisternium*) took place in 399 BCE. In contrast to Greek pairing of such deities as divine couples, symbolizing sacred marriage, the Romans indiscriminately paired Apollo with his mother Larona, or Mercury with Neptune. It was not until 217 BCE that the traditional Twelve Olympians were appropriately paired, but with Latin names and given an *interpretatio Romana*, on pretence of confusing foreign deities with their own.

Three of the oldest deities – Jupiter, Juno, and Minerva – were worshipped in an impressively large

Temples on the Capitoline Hill, Rome.

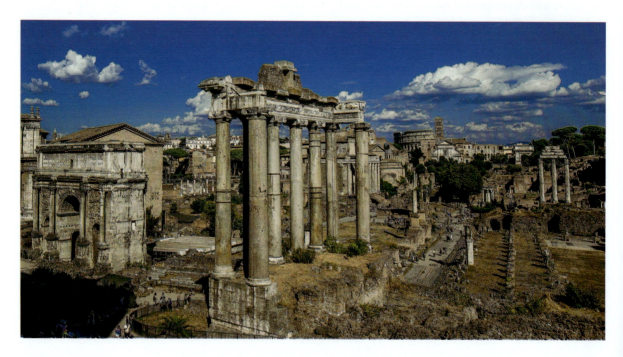

INTRODUCTION TO WORLD RELIGIONS

temple on the Capitoline Hill, and are thus known as the 'Capitoline Triad'. The temple was dedicated to Jupiter the Best and Greatest (*Jupiter Optimus Maximus*): his was the central hall of worship, flanked by those of Juno and Minerva to the right and left.

Other deities followed in the remaining centuries BCE, in response to various communal needs or crises, such as the cult of Aesculapius (Greek, Asclepios) to overcome pestilence in 293–291, or that of the Cybele, to counteract Hannibal's military threat in 204. At the turn of the era, Augustus (63 BCE–14 CE) could still be described as one who 'treated with great respect such foreign rites as were ancient and well-established, but held the rest in contempt'. This distinction of old versus new in matters of religion was characteristic. Conservatism was maintained by the high priest (*pontifex maximus*); open-mindedness was fostered by the *viri sacrisfaciundis*, religious officials responsible for the introduction of a new idea when it was most appropriate.

Foreign elements could be brought into Rome; equally, those already present might be suppressed, or driven out. The official Senate decree of 7 October 186 BCE severely limited the celebrations of the Bacchanalia, and the number of its followers. This applied not only to Rome, but also to its allies, and arose from the supposed threat of societies that met in secret or conducted secret rites. Among legitimate groupings within Rome were various associations of pontiffs, augurs, and auspices; flamens, or special priests for individual gods; and the vestal virgins.

BELIEF AND PHILOSOPHY

Cicero wrote *On the Nature of the Gods* in 45 BCE, in the form of a dialogue among several of the intellectual positions of his day: Sceptic, Epicurean, and Stoic. Two important traditions are absent: the Peripatetic – if the Stoics were really different from Aristotle as he was by then understood – and the Cynic position, which was merely described.

The importance of the various positions lies simply in the fact that religion until then had no explicit intellectual content; it hinged exclusively on ritual – right doing, not right thinking, and certainly not yet right believing. For until the first century BCE, the vocabulary of belief was hardly coined. The value of this practical religion can be quite bluntly stated: 'Men describe Jupiter as best and greatest not because he makes us just or temperate or wise, but because he makes us healthy, rich, and prosperous.'

For the relatively few who were caught up in the discussion, or could read, or for the larger audience to whom philosophical views were preached by itinerants, there began that transformation by which religion came to mean an intellectual consideration

> It is hard to say whether the birthday of the most divine Caesar is more joyful or more advantageous; we may rightly regard it as like the beginning of all things, if not in the world of nature, yet in advantage. There is nothing that was decaying and declining to unfortunate state that he did not restore, and he gave a fresh appearance to the whole universe, which would have been content to accept its own ruin if there had not been born the universal blessing of all – Caesar Augustus. The birthday of the god was the beginning of the good news (euangelion) to the world on account of him.
>
> Roman Proconsul to Provincial Assembly of Asia, 9 BCE

of god, gods, and the world. The several philosophies ask essentially three questions: 'What is the nature of the world?', 'How do I know the world?', and 'How am I to live in the world?' Although theologically they produced different systems in response, they began with similar assumptions in answer to these questions:

> *Matter is the sole reality.*
>
> *Senses are the sole source of knowledge.*
>
> *Being untroubled and undisturbed is the nature of happiness or pleasure.*

The Epicurean position was that gods exist – but they have no concern for the world. The Stoic position was that the world is ruled by a divine rationality (*logos*), manifest as fate and providence, and closely related to human reason. Scepticism was a by-product of the Platonic Academy, sharing in the common assumptions. Its appeal was to the one who 'suspends judgment about things that are either good or bad by nature, or that are to be practised or not practised, and in so doing he resists the dogmatic tendency, and follows without strong convictions either way the observances of everyday life', achieving thereby the desired untroubled state. Cynics are 'dog-like' (*kunikos*) because they substitute for a system a way of life blatantly rejecting all imposed values: they identified the ideal life with that of nature. Taking nothing but the beggar's knapsack and staff, delighting in flouting all standards of decency, they wandered about with a minimum of food or shelter, often functioning as missionaries by preaching on street corners.

IMPERIAL CULT

When Virgil (70–19 BCE) wrote the *Aeneid* to honour the Emperor Augustus, by linking him with Rome's past, Augustus not only restored the Hut of Romulus, but absorbed into himself the whole religious tradition of the city, by assuming the ancient office of *pontifex maximus*. A temple of Roma and Augustus at Ostia expresses the result. Throughout the time of the empire, even the older gods of the state cult, with the exception of the major deities – Jupiter, Juno, and Minerva – gave way to the increasingly dominant cult of the imperial house.

Republican Rome, even with its dictators, had avoided the absolute rule of Hellenistic kings. A precedent was set by the Roman Senate on the assassination of Julius Caesar in 44 BCE, when he was enrolled among the gods. The deification of his successor, Augustus, had been demanded in parts of the empire – especially the east – while Augustus was still alive, and divine honours were accorded him in some places. Though the Senate's action in proclaiming Augustus divine followed the precedent, Tiberius (42 BCE–37 CE), who succeeded him, stoutly resisted deification, and so much angered the Senate that he was not even acclaimed as a god upon his death. Thereafter, apart from Nero and the three unsuccessful military contenders for his position, all the early emperors received a place among the gods: even Caligula (12–41 CE), who had assumed

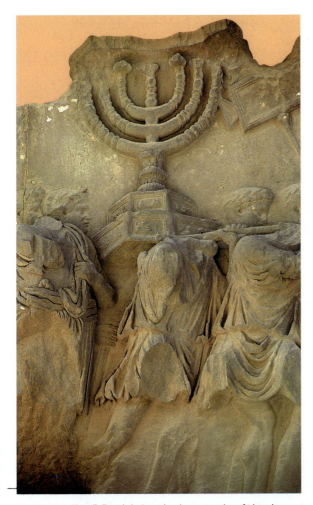

Herod's Temple in Jerusalem in a procession of triumph through their city; relief from the Arch of Titus, Rome.

it for himself while living, and Domitian (51–96 CE), who did likewise, though without reaffirmation by the Senate.

From the days of Augustus, oaths of allegiance to the emperor were required from Roman businessmen making money in the provinces. These show him as already 'son of a god', and express loyalty not only to him but 'to his children and descendants'. From the coronation of Caligula, the oath includes Augustus between 'Zeus the Saviour' and 'the holy Virgin of our city' – *Athena Polias*. Such oaths were engraved in bronze – at the oath-takers' expense – and mounted for all to see.

EVIDENCE FROM POMPEII

The disastrous eruption of Vesuvius began on the morning of 24 August, 79 CE, and by evening had buried the two flourishing cities of Pompeii and Herculaneum, and the coastal resort of Stabiae. The Latin poet Martial asserted that 'even for gods this was going too far'. Many other cities of the ancient Mediterranean world have been destroyed and buried, but none so completely preserved in the process. The religious evidence from Pompeii is of two principal forms: buildings – both official buildings, innumerable domestic shrines, and wayside altars – and works of art – frescoes, inscriptions of all sorts, including graffiti, and, from Herculaneum, a prodigious papyri library, chiefly devoted to the religious philosophy of the obscure Epicurean Philodemus (c. 110–40 BCE).

Family cults flourished. Nearly every house and workshop had its private shrine, *lararium*, normally housing busts of ancestors and other traditional household gods, the *Lares* and *Penates*. The simple rites at these shrines were part of daily life, under the care of the paternal head of the household, and would have included rituals for important family events, such as the coming of age of the heir. Many plaques and statues have been found, representing various minor deities – Faunus, Silvanus, Flora, Priapus, and so on – largely concerned with fruitfulness and reproduction, plenty and gain. Wreaths of fruit, or horns of plenty – *cornucopiae* – were commonplace. So too was the phallus,

Hence it is that throughout wide empires, provinces, and towns, we see each people having its own individual rites and worshipping the local gods ... but the Romans one and all.

Minucius Felix, *Octavius* 6.23

either alone, or gigantically displayed on a little deity, often with scales to weigh its fullness.

Official cults were more elaborate, but their remains fewer. Pompeii had ten temples, but three had been wrecked in the earlier earthquake of 62 CE, and were still unrepaired at the time of their burial. One had been converted to the use of a private association; two were dedicated to the imperial cult, one to the most recently enrolled member, Vespasian (9–79 CE), who died just a month before the eruption, and the other to Fortuna Augusta. Graffiti reflect people's nonchalant attitude towards this cult: 'Augustus Caesar's mother was only a woman!' Of the remaining four temples, only that dedicated to the cult of triune Isis, her consort, Serapis, and their divine child, Harpocrates, showed the signs of prosperity coming from popular support. Wall-size frescoes indicate the religious life within this sanctuary, conducted by its white-robed, shaven-headed priests.

Apart from the buildings designed for religious use, we have the houses of rich and poor, in which were displayed not only wealth, and varying taste and styles, but also frescoes or mosaics of religious themes. The most important of these is the sixty-roomed 'Villa of the Mysteries': one room presents on three walls twenty-nine near life-size figures, subdivided into ten group scenes, acting out a complex Bacchic ritual. This was entirely a woman's rite. It is impossible to say what place this great house, or its spectacular scene, played within the religious life of the city – perhaps somewhere in between the few great temples and the numerous little shrines.

Remains of the ancient Roman basilica, Pompeii, Italy.

The preserved ruins of Ostia, the port of Rome, show a different array within this religious mix, including, by the third century CE, not less than fifteen Mithraea – shrines devoted to Mithras.

PHILOSOPHICAL RELIGION

Roman religion was thus a complex mixture from varied sources. Later in the third century CE, the mix was to receive a more systematic treatment, blending the religious and philosophical elements into a form of Neo-Platonism, of which Plotinus (205–69) was founder, and Porphyry (232–305) his expositor. This revived Platonism was a blend of elements from the traditions of Plato himself, Pythagoras, Aristotle, and the Stoics. World-mind, World-soul, and Nature are the descending levels of reality between the Ultimate One, which is the ground of existence and the source of values, and Bare Matter. All these ingredients lie within human nature, whose purpose is to achieve unification, in a kind of ecstatic union with the One. This rare union was believed to occur as a result of prolonged effort of the will and understanding. Plotinus makes little explicit reference to religious ritual, or particular gods, though the writings of his followers do contain hymns to certain gods. The result is the philosophical equivalent of the 'mysteries'.

> *Those who would learn about the gods need to have been well educated from childhood and must not be bred up among foolish ideas; they must also be good and intelligent by nature, in order that they may have something in common with the subject.*
>
> Sallust, *Concerning the Gods and the Universe* 1

THE UNCONQUERED SUN

Of the thirty-five Roman emperors between 192 and 284 CE, only three reigned for more than ten years, and only one died a natural death. All the others died of unnatural causes, at the hands of troops or counter-claimants, after a reign of less than a year in at least twelve cases. Consequently, few of these imperial figures lived long enough, or died in such a way, as to receive deification. Most of the emperors, even the stronger ones, preferred to rule under the aegis of some greater deity, since they had perceived that to be declared divine themselves hardly secured them a long life. The most important such god is Aurelian's choice: *Sol Invictus*, the 'Unconquered Sun'.

It was a mere matter of time before the one resilient religion would be imposed upon the state. This took place in the Edict of Milan, issued in 313 jointly by Licinius and Constantine. Christian worship, like any other, was now allowed to take place freely; and the Christian church, alone among the competitive cults, was singled out for 'compensation from our benevolence'. It was its organization that gave it an edge over all alternatives from the authorities' viewpoint, for Christianity – as Arnold Toynbee has said – 'was singular in building up for itself a world-wide administrative organization, instead of letting each local group of converts go its own way'.

THE END OF ANTIQUITY

The remoulding of the Roman Empire as Christian in all senses took more than a century, though Theodosius I had proscribed other religions by 381 CE. The old forms, however, lingered on in several ways. Initially 'pagan', *paganus*, had meant a rural-, in contrast to an urban-, dweller, and Christianity had made little headway in the former environment before it became the state religion. By this later date, the term came to designate civilians in general, over against soldiers, and thus took on its 'religious' connotation. Several remnants of the older religion survived for a while. The short-reigned Julian (361–63) was the last non-Christian emperor.

The older traditions at more subtle levels died out in the educational replacement of one *mythos* by another, but survived in terms of human nature and its response to the realities of the agricultural economy. At the level of fundamental assumptions, little really seemed to matter, for as the Roman historian Sallust (86–c. 36 BCE) said, there are 'universal opinions, by which I mean those in which all men, if rightly questioned, would concur; such opinions are that every god is good and impassive and unchangeable'.

Rome itself, however, had become less advantageous as the capital. Once it proved vulnerable to Visigothic assault, in 410, it was but a matter of time before the imperial government was withdrawn to a safer location. The sacking of the city after 800 years precipitated a crisis of ideas for a state newly allied to the Christian religion. Augustine of Hippo (354–430) in his *City of God*, carefully sifted all the religiousness of the ancient city and its empire; what was worthwhile was baptized into Christ, the rest was to be put aside for ever. The city, now greatly reduced in dignity and size, became the Christian Rome. Its bishop became the sole remaining officer of rank, when the imperial government of the West was transferred north to Ravenna, and then in 476, when the Western Empire itself ceased to exist. Rome's change of hands is well illustrated when its bishop, Leo the Great (r. 440–61), assumed the defunct urban title of *pontifex maximus*, 'Supreme Pontiff'. The Christian church was the final successor to the ancient religion which was the city, and in such terms the primacy of the church at Rome came to be declared.

CLYDE CURRY SMITH

CHAPTER 16

The Religion of the Celts

Until about fifty years ago, scholars were reasonably confident about who the ancient Celts were, and what could be agreed about their religion. They were a family of peoples speaking similar languages who occupied Europe north of the Alps and south of the River Elbe, with extensions into Mediterranean lands. They were warlike, with a ruling military aristocracy, creative, producing a marvellous art characterized by fluid lines and abstract figures, impetuous, and emotional. They were also intensely spiritual, believing in a mixture of gods and goddesses, of whom the greatest was Lugh, identified with the sun, intelligence, skills, and arts. Traces of his worship have been found from Ireland to what is now eastern Germany.

This religion was dominated by a highly trained and learned priesthood, the Druids, who presided over ceremonies and had an important role as scholars, lawgivers, and arbitrators. They taught that, when humans die, their souls pass into new bodies and are reborn into this world. At the same time, they conducted large-scale human sacrifice by a range of cruel means, including the burning alive of victims in huge wicker images. Their most important festivals were on the days that opened the seasons, at the beginning of November, February, May, and August, with the year starting on the first of these, the modern Halloween. They preferred not to build temples, but worshipped in natural groves of trees. All this information comes from a mixture of archaeological finds, the writings of the ancient Greeks and Romans, and the medieval literature of the Celtic peoples who became the Irish and Welsh: a varied group of sources, but one that can present a coherent picture.

WHO WERE THE CELTS?

The view of the subject that was dominant in the 1960s has virtually collapsed. Experts now recognize that the term 'Celts' was originally used by the Greeks as a vague label for barbarians living north of the Alps and Danube, and was not applied to types of language until the end of the seventeenth century, and no ancient writer ever described Celts as living in the British Isles. It is now accepted that the distribution of Celtic languages does not seem to match the distribution of what has been called Celtic art, and neither matches that of material culture. None of these ranges seems to have any relevance to racial types.

It seems as though ancient peoples living along the Rhine and Elbe who have traditionally been called Celtic had more in common with their neighbours across the rivers, whom scholars, following the Romans, have called 'Germanic', than with their remote linguistic relatives in places such as Ireland or Spain. The term 'Celtic' is still valuable as a label for types of language, and therefore of literature, and for modern cultural politics; but as a label for ancient societies and cultures, it is more or less dead, most experts now preferring the cumbersome but precise formula 'late pre-Roman Iron Age' to describe the groups to whom it was formerly applied.

WHO WERE THE DRUIDS?

So what was the religion of ancient north-western Europe in the 'late pre-Roman Iron Age'? Again, the old certainties have crumbled. It has been repeatedly noted that all the sources of information we possess are suspect. Some of the Greek and Roman writers who described that religion lived at the time when it was still active, but all may be accused of distortion for propaganda purposes. Those who hailed the Druids as philosophers and scientists tended to live at the opposite end of the Mediterranean world, and may have been making a romantic idealization of them with which to entertain or criticize their own society. The alleged Druidic belief in a form of reincarnation could be a projection of Greek ideas onto much simpler native traditions. On the other hand, those who wrote of the Druids' addiction to human sacrifice may have been seeking to destroy their reputation in order to justify the Roman conquest of their lands. Their identification with groves appears after that conquest, and may simply reflect the fact that they had been reduced to a secret religion lingering in the woods. The medieval Irish and Welsh texts were all composed centuries after the conversion of those peoples to Christianity and may be fantasies about an almost-forgotten past, rather than echoes of it reliably preserved in oral tradition.

The worship of Lugh seems to have been confined to Ireland and Spain, and apparent traces of his name further east could just be linguistic errors. There is no good evidence for generally worshipped, 'pan-Celtic', deities. As for the four festivals, they represent an Irish system that may not have been observed elsewhere, and there is no real proof that the New Year was celebrated at Halloween even in Ireland. There is plenty of evidence in the structure of monuments and in literature that at least as much importance was attached to the summer and winter solstices, all over northern and western Europe, as to the four quarter days.

LOCAL DEITIES

So what can be said with certainty? The best evidence consists of the inscriptions left by the native populations of the north-western provinces of the Roman Empire, which express religious belief in a distinctively local way that does seem genuinely to reflect an older native tradition. These can be compared with the Greek, Roman, Irish, and Welsh sources and with other material remains. They show an intense localism in which every tribe, stream, hill, and wood had its own deity or deities. Of 375 native gods identified by the 1980s in the Roman period of what is now France, 305 are recorded just once. Some were honoured across large regions – a cross-legged, antlered god in central and eastern France, a young horseman god in the east midlands of England – but none seems to have had a wider range than that. Certain stereotypes were very widespread, however, such as a god of smiths, a patron god who protected the people and land of a particular district, and a god of trading and communication. Goddesses were more closely identified with the natural world, being spirits of hills, rivers, and woods, but there were still plenty of nature-gods and goddesses of human activities. Both sexes of deity were associated with war, although it is possible that gods were more identified with leadership in it, and goddesses with its raw emotions.

WORSHIP AND SACRIFICE

It is certain that the Druids had a leading role in religion and society, although we cannot be exactly sure what it was, or what they taught. It is very likely that worship was carried on in groves of trees; and springs, rivers, and lakes were certainly considered sacred, because offerings of precious metalwork were thrown into them. The earth itself was venerated, gifts of food and drink being deposited in the pits used for storing grain each time one was taken out of use, as if to thank the soil for its bounty. On the other hand, shrines and temples were certainly erected, ranging from huge circles of wooden posts in Ireland, and small rectangular huts – perhaps just houses for deities – in British settlements, to huge sanctuaries enclosed by ditches and ramparts in northern France, and stone-built temples with carvings and statues in Provence.

Animal sacrifice was certainly practised – as it was all over the ancient world – and it is significant that the most popular victims were horses and dogs, which form the closest emotional bonds with humans: they would have been sacrifices in the modern sense of the word. The killing of humans is also likely, because it was found in many parts of the ancient world, and the Romans themselves had only banned it in 97 BCE. The number of human bodies, skulls, or long bones found buried at settlements and fortresses, or displayed at the French sanctuaries, are probably the remains of the victims, although it is just possible that they had belonged to honoured warriors. The careful deposition of personal possessions in graves strongly suggests a widespread belief in a continuation of life after death.

That is all that can be said at present, although continuing archaeology may well resolve some of the mysteries and enable the development of more secure knowledge. What matters most is that, however accurate or distorted they may have been, the references to this religion in Greek, Roman, Welsh, and Irish writings have shaped the self-image of Europeans, and inspired the art and literature of later times. They have become part of the world's cultural heritage. The ancient reality has left little solid evidence of itself, but the dream of what it might have been has been one of the great inspirations of Western humanity.

RONALD HUTTON

CHAPTER 17

The Religions of Scandinavia

THE NORSE GODS

The period of the Norse gods is best narrowed down to the Viking Age, from roughly 800 CE until the arrival of Christianity in Scandinavia around 1000 – a little sooner in Denmark and somewhat later in Sweden. There are signs of continuity from the Iron Age, at least from Roman times, but there is a clear change in the language used from around 800. It is therefore reasonable to consider the pre-Christian Viking Age on its own terms.

SOURCES

The few sources from the period are especially informative and extremely important, in that they confirm the existence of belief in indigenous gods before Christianity. Most of these sources are simply place names, which include references to the gods and inscriptions of personal names containing the names of deities or invoking a particular deity. There are also a few helpful non-Scandinavian descriptions: for example, an Arabic traveller describes a funeral in 923, in which deities and religious rites are mentioned, and a German monk writes of a temple. A large proportion of the most revealing sources for understanding pre-Christian religion in Scandinavia have come to us from Iceland, having been preserved by the Icelandic scholar Snorri Sturluson (1179–1241).

The most informative sources are two series of poems in very different styles, which together provide the fullest account available of the beliefs of any pre-literate peoples. Unfortunately, the precise date of their composition is unknown – sometime between 800 and 1200. Although the poems often do provide an author and a precise date, scholars now believe these may have been forged at a later date.

- One group is a collection of about thirty-seven poems about gods and heroes, traditionally called the *Elder* or the *Poetic Edda*.
- The other is a collection of writings known as Scaldic poetry, consisting mostly of praise poems to kings or short verses about everyday life.

Because these poems constantly allude to the gods, goddesses, and rituals of Norse mythology, they provide a relatively good understanding of ancient Scandinavian religion.

A gifted writer with a keen sense of humour, Snorri wrote a handbook on Scaldic poetry, which he called the *Edda*, and which is now referred to as the *Younger Edda* or *Prose Edda*. It contains a complete Norse cosmology — an understanding of the cosmos from the perspective of Norse religion — and many stories about the Nordic gods. Although it is the most popular source for understanding Norse religion, must not be forgotten that Snorri was a Christian thinker, writing in a medieval scholarly context, rather than a Viking writer in a pre-Christian context.

Another important source is provided by the Danish scholar Saxo Grammaticus (c. 1150–1220), whose Latin work, *Gesta Danorum* — 'History of the Danes' — contains much mythological material about deities and heroes, which, he claimed, he had learned from Icelanders. Although this is actually an older source than Snorri's *Edda*, and Saxo uses some of the same stories as Snorri, it is not used nearly as much by scholars. Other sources used to investigate pre-Christian customs and religious life can be found in the Icelandic saga-literature. However, this material was principally written in the 1200s and 1300s, and it is evident that the anonymous writers had very limited knowledge of actual religion in pre-Christian Scandinavia.

Early sources confirm the existence of deities that were widely worshipped and those that were more localized. The distribution of belief in a particular god or goddess can often be gauged from their appearance in place names. For example, Ull — described by Snorri as a minor ski god — is found in place names in Norway and Sweden, but not in Denmark, which is flat and thus not known for skiing. The god Thor, on the other hand, was worshipped all over Scandinavia. Several inscriptions in memory of dead men invoke Thor, with a prayer that he bless the memorial. Indeed, Thor is the only figure mentioned as a god in indigenous pre-Christian, Scandinavian sources.

The German monk Adam of Bremen, who wrote around 1070, was told of a magnificent temple in the town of Uppsala, Sweden, where 'pagan' rites were still performed at this time. He describes three gods — Thor, Odin, and Freyr — each with an emblem and a function. Thor has a sceptre and decides the weather; Odin has a spear and is a war deity; and Freyr, a fertility deity, has an enormous phallus. From later sources we know that Adam must have mistaken Thor's hammer for a sceptre, but this lends credibility to his description, which is evidently not based on mythological tales. Adam further relates that great festivals, at which participation was mandatory, and which included human and animal sacrifice, took place at Uppsala every ninth year at the vernal equinox.

NORSE COSMOLOGY

Much of what we know about ancient Norse cosmology comes from medieval sources. In Snorri and the Eddic poems, particularly a unique poem called the *Völuspá* ('The Prophecy of the Sibyl'), a strange creation story is told. First, there was only heat and cold; where these met, an immense giant, Ymir, came into being. The different parts of Ymir's body could

Copy of a ninth-century statue of Thor with his hammer *Mjollnir*, found in Iceland.

have children with each other, and as a result, a race of giants was born. Ymir was fed by a cow, who licked the salty earth. Where the cow licked the earth, a man came into being, named Bor. Bor begat a son, called Bur, who was the father of Odin, Vili, and Ve. These three killed Ymir and made the cosmos from his body: his flesh is the soil; his blood the sea; his skull the heavens, and so on. In the middle, the gods fashioned Middle Earth for humans, while the gods live in Asgard, and the giants in Udgard. Eventually the gods, who became known as Æsir, battled another race of deities called the Vanir. They ended up exchanging hostages, and three of the Vanir joined the Æsir – Njord, along with his daughter Freyja, and his son Freyr.

The world in which we live is one of nine worlds, all of which are linked to an immense, self-renewing ash-tree called Yggdrasil. Adam tells of a great tree in Uppsala which probably represented Yggdrasil. It is said Yggdrasil has a root in each of the different worlds. Our world, Midgard (or, as popularized in J. R. R. Tolkien's *Lord of the Rings*, 'Middle Earth'), is predominantly populated by humans, while other worlds are populated by giants, elves, gods, dwarves, and so on. Often there is conflict between these worlds. Because Yggdrasil provides sustenance to the different worlds – even the great god Odin had to hang in its branches to gain wisdom from it and learn how to read the hidden runes – it seems to be greater than all the deities.

ÆSIR – THE GODS

Odin is king of the gods, sitting in his great hall, Valhalla – The Hall of the Slain – where he brings all great human warriors. Although he is the god who gives victory to warriors and leaders, he is capricious, and just as likely to snatch it away again. Odin is preparing for the battle at the end of the world, and is portrayed as a lord, feasting on an endless supply of pork and drinking mead. He is glib and treacherous, always searching for wisdom. Indeed, he only has one eye, having surrendered the other for a single drink from the spring of wisdom and understanding owned by the giant Mimir. He is also a performer of *seid*, a ritual described as shamanistic. Many stories are associated with Odin, including notions of shape-shifting, heroic warfare, strangulation, and death, as well as poetry and wisdom. Devotion to him perhaps explains grim stories of ritual killings by noose and spear.

In Norse religion, giants such as Mimir and Suttung, whose mead Odin stole, represent forces of chaos. Because they are so old, they are also very wise. Interestingly, wisdom itself is perceived as a chaotic force.

- Thor, the slayer of giants, appears to have attracted the most widespread devotion. If the leaders and warriors looked to Odin as their patron, common people looked to Thor as their protector. He is the thunder-god, full of chaotic and destructive energy. In later Northern religion, the 'black Thor' — possibly so called because of the colour of his images — was understood to be the principal enemy of the 'white Christ'. His symbol, the hammer *Mjollnir*, 'The Crusher', was used at weddings, and as a protective amulet. Stories speak of Thor going on adventures with his *Mjollnir* to protect humans. The most entertaining of Snorri's stories describes his battles with giants, often aided by the shadowy and enigmatic Loki.
- Loki is probably best understood as a trickster: he often sets a story in motion. It was Loki who, by a trick, secured the death of Balder, Odin's son, and fairest of the gods.

Other gods of the Æsir are less prominent:
- Tyr seems to have been an important war god.
- Balder seems to do little, apart from famously dying, through the agency of Loki.
- Bragi is associated with poetry.

The goddesses are less exciting, and seem less important:
- Sif, Thor's wife, has hair of gold.
- Idun, Bragi's wife, keeps the apples of youth.
- Frigg, Odin's wife, is exceedingly wise.

Several groups of less personal 'forces' are referred to as female. Most famously the Valkyries, 'Choosers of the Slain', are said to help Odin collect the finest warriors from among the dead and serve them mead in Valhalla.

Among the Vanir, the goddess Freyja, 'The Lady', stands out as a particularly dynamic deity. She is a trophy, often desired by the giants, but shows independence in her sexuality, which is proverbial; like Odin, in the Eddic poems she is significantly connected with death and shamanism.

The fertility god Freyr, 'The Lord', is known chiefly because of a story where he falls in love with a giantess; so in love is he that he is in danger of dying; his servant Skirnir, 'The Shining', therefore coerces the maiden into sleeping with him.

Finally, Njord is connected with the bounty of the sea.

RELIGIOUS RITUALS AND FESTIVALS

Religious life seems to have been made up of great feasts at significant times of the year, determined by the sun. All the people from a district met at a central place to sacrifice, eat, and drink together. Formal oaths were sworn, and contracts made on holy ground. The leader of the feast seems also to have been the political leader. Both human and animal sacrifice were probably part of the ritual. Adam of Bremen records that victims were hung in trees.

An Arabic account of a funeral, by Ahmad ibn Fadlan in 923, describes such a sacrifice. The victim, who is – significantly – a slave-girl, immediately becomes an important figure in the community, and is treated with great respect. At the time of the funeral, she is brought to a state of ecstasy, and lifted up to look into the realm of the dead. After this, she is taken to the funeral ship with the dead man and plied with alcohol. Six men then have intercourse with her then strangle her, while she is also stabbed in the ribs by the priestess. A myth describes Odin as hanging in a tree, pierced with a spear, during his quest for wisdom. Because this myth incorporates stabbing, strangling, and hanging in trees, it supports the theory that this was the preferred form of sacrifice.

MORTEN WARMIND

CHAPTER 18

Nomads of the Steppes

Some 3000 years ago the wide steppes of southern Russia were sparsely populated by Indo-European peoples: the Cimmerians west of the Caspian Sea, the Persians east of it. Around this time, or soon after, the northern Persians, or Scythians, developed into horse-riding nomads.

This had tremendous historical consequences. Not only did they, in the seventh century BCE, overrun the Cimmerian lands, so their territory now stretched from present-day Romania to Turkestan, but they also opened communications between East and West, so that religious ideas and art forms — 'animal style' — streamed across the open steppes. Long after the disappearance of the Scythians, this road to China constituted a major link between Western Christian and Eastern religious ideas; from the first century CE, the famous 'silk route' partly followed the same way.

In the fifth century BCE, the Greek historian Herodotus gives interesting information on Scythian religion. The foremost divinities were the Sky Father, Papa, married to Mother Earth, Api. Among other deities — all apparently heavenly beings — were the fire- and war-gods. There were no images of the gods, altars, or temples. The gods received animal sacrifices — usually horses — which were strangled, and their meat cooked over a fire made on their bones. A piece of the meat was thrown into the fire.

The Scythians had a war-god, represented by an iron sword raised on a heap of brushwood. To him were sacrificed cattle and horses in large numbers, as well as prisoners of war; their blood was poured over the god's sword. Herodotus also mentions diviners, who, however, were killed when they were unsuccessful.

When a king died, his corpse was carried on a wagon around the tribes of his domain, followed by his wives and servants in a long procession. He was finally buried in a wooden chamber, together with several court servants — who were strangled — his horses, and some golden bowls. An enormous earth mound was heaped over the burial place. The bereaved cleansed themselves by entering a tent filled with steam from hemp seeds that had been thrown on red-hot stones.

This is the earliest description we have of a religion of horse nomads; its essentials fit well with what we know of later religions among equestrian pastoralists. Horse nomadism spread to the Mongol and Turko-Tataric tribes east of the Scythian area and on the plateaux of central Asia. Here, the war-like religion of the plains joined the traditional hunting religions, with master-of-the-animals concepts and shamanism, and formed a new type of religion.

THE MONGOLS

A good illustration of this kind of religion is offered by the Mongols of central Asia. From tribal beginnings in north-east Asia, they ousted the Turkish peoples of Mongolia and built up an empire that in the thirteenth and fourteenth centuries CE stretched from the Amur River to the Volga and beyond – the greatest empire the world had seen. Their primitive beginnings, nomadic way of life, and stratified patriarchal society were all reflected in their religion.

Their supreme god was Tengri, a name by which both the god and the blue sky were designated. Prayers were directed to him by lone supplicants bowing down on mountain-tops, and juniper incense was burned in his honour. Like other nomadic high gods, Tengri was not represented by pictures. Nor did he create the world. In all central Asia the beginning of the world was referred to two creators, one a good spirit (not Tengri), the other a devil. This story of creation was diffused from Europe to North America, and was sometimes combined with the flood myth, sometimes with the myth of a primeval sea.

'Tengri' is, however, also a word for everything 'heavenly', wonderful, or marvellous, and for ninety-nine tengri gods that in particular protect the herds. For instance, Ataga tengri gives luck in horse-breeding, another tengri protects the cows, still another the yaks. Manaqan tengri is the guardian of the wild game.

Landmarks such as mountains, lakes, and rivers were worshipped – the mountains particularly inspired great awe. Passes and mountain-tops were residences of spirits, and whoever passed by had to propitiate these spirits by throwing a stone on a pile of rocks, a so-called 'obo'. The ground was sacred, and libations were poured out for Mother Earth.

LEADERS

Dead princes and tribal ancestors had their own shrines. Chingis Khan – better known as Genghis Khan (d. 1227 CE) – the mighty ruler of the Mongols, was considered of heavenly descent. A statue representing him was raised on a wagon in the military camp, and horses were dedicated to him. Sometimes he was mentioned as Tengri himself, sometimes as a culture-hero who had initiated all cultural and religious institutions. Offerings were also made to other deceased great princes by their descendants: most often horses were impaled above their graves. The Mongols of the Golden Horde in southern Russia suspended horse-skins upon poles over the graves of their great leaders.

At the entrance of their tents the Mongols placed house idols made of felt, '*ongons*', to whom they offered milk. There also was a 'fire mother' to whom butter was offered regularly. At the end of the year, she also received a bone from a sheep, and ritual hymns were addressed to her. Fire was supposed to have cleansing power.

The tribal leaders were also shamans, that is, experts who cured diseases and who divined hidden knowledge while in a trance. Shamanism, a heritage from very ancient times, was strongly integrated with ancestor-worship – the shaman's guardian spirits were his ancestors – and concentrated on the exorcism of evil spirits. Shamans performed many of the customary sacrifices.

Of the Mongol and Turkish tribes that invaded Europe during the first Christian millennium, the Huns were known for their belief in Tengri, and the Magyars – Hungarians – for their high-god beliefs and shamanism.

SLAVIC RELIGIONS

From their ancient homes in Poland and White Russia, the Slavs spread over Eastern Europe during the first millennium of the Christian era. They were organized in numerous tribes, which, as time passed, formed themselves into larger groups. Of these only the western Slavs – formerly living east of the Elbe – and the Russians have left traces in the history of religions. What they believed is not clear, however, and interpretations differ widely among scholars.

We can only guess what the religion of the Russians was like before the emergence of the Russian grand duchy in the ninth century. The most well-known god seems to have been Perun, a god of thunder and lightning, and apparently a Supreme Being. His position was probably reinforced when, in about 980, Vladimir the Great, who was of Viking descent, created two cultic centres for him, one in Kiev, the other in Novgorod. In Kiev, together with a few other gods, Perun was represented in wood on a hill outside the princely palace, his image adorned with a head of silver and a beard of bronze. Cattle and even human beings were sacrificed to this god. When Vladimir was baptized in 988, this image was dragged into the River Dnieper and the sacrificial grove destroyed. The cult of the thunder-god had obviously been influenced by the cult of Thor in Scandinavia; Kiev was effectively a Viking colony.

Other Russian gods were Svarog and Dashbog, father and son, both representing the sun and the fire. The common element in their names, *bog* – compare the Indian *bhaga* – stands for 'richness' and 'god'. Volos is mentioned as the god by whose name one swears solemn oaths.

Folk beliefs in Russia, Poland, and the Balkans have probably also preserved elements of ancient Slavic religion. Best known are vampires, dead people who suck the blood of the living, and werewolves, human beings transformed into wolves. *Rusalki* are maidens who have suffered premature death; bogs are the abodes of *bagnik* and *bolotnik*, old and dirty men. Also commonly referred to are river-maidens, *vila* – seen as beautiful and cunning.

WESTERN SLAVIC TEMPLES

In the western Slavic area the old religion continued until 1168, when the temple in Arkona, on the River Rügen, was destroyed by King Valdemar I of Denmark. Unlike the Russians, the west Slavs built temples to their gods, probably very late, and possibly influenced by Germanic peoples. The temple clergy seem to have enjoyed high prestige. In Arkona, for instance, only the priest was allowed into the temple, where he made libations and, at the harvest, sacrifices of meat. He also performed divination; for instance, he took omens from the movements of the white horse dedicated to the chief god, Svantevit, 'the sacred lord'.

The west-Slavic gods were very warlike and all-knowing, the latter quality expressed by their statues having several heads or faces. Thus, Svantevit's huge image had four heads, two looking ahead, two looking backwards. Triglav, in Stettin, modern Szczecin, had three heads; Rugievit, at Garz, on the Rügen, one head with seven faces — and seven swords hanging from his belt; Porsevit, at the same place, had five heads, and so on. The idea of multi-headed gods is truly Slavic: even in late Serbian folklore there is a three-headed mysterious nightly rider, Trojan, probably named after the Roman Emperor Trajan.

The temples sometimes contained precious things. Triglav's statue was made of gold, although Svantevit's image at Arkona was wooden, and chopped up and burnt by the Christian king, Valdemar. In the temple belonging to the war-god Jarovit of Wolgast, a shield was preserved that was brought out every time they prayed for victory in battle. Sacred groves grew next to the temples. In Stettin, Triglav had a sacred oak with a spring beneath. The god Proven, who was venerated at the site of Oldenburg, north of Eutin, owned a grove of sacred oaks surrounded by a wooden fence; here the prince executed justice in the middle of his subjects, just as the Germanic kings did under an oak.

BALTIC RELIGIONS

The old religions of the Baltic peoples — the Latvians, Lithuanians, and now-extinct ancient Prussians — lived on until very recent times. Lithuania did not turn Christian until the fifteenth century, while in Latvia the sacred groves and the cult of Perkons — god of thunder and fertility, closely related to the Slavic Perun, Perkunas in Lithuania — survived until the eighteenth century. It was still possible to observe these indigenous religions in Baltic lands until the end of the nineteenth century. Baltic religions are interesting because they are believed to have been very close to the original Indo-European religion of Persia and India. The heavenly god, Dievs, has his counterpart in the Indian Dyaus, and Perkunas is identical with the Indian Parjanya.

A feature of Baltic religions is that there are many female divinities, whereas Slavic religions are noted for their lack of goddesses. Among a host of 'mothers' are Mother Earth, Zemes māte, and the Fire Mother, Uguns māte. The Sun, Saule in Latvia, is represented as a beautiful maiden with golden hair who rides in a wagon drawn by horses. Laima and Mara, St Mary, are important goddesses of fate and guardians of human beings. Laima receives sacrifices of dogs, sheep, and pigs, and blesses the fields and cattle.

Besides Dievs — who is thought of as a farmer with a family — there are other sky-gods, such as Usinsh, a god associated with the spring, and a patron of horses.

Among terrestrial gods should be mentioned the earth-god, Zemes Dievs, who has developed into a lord of the farmstead, and the fertility-god, Jumis, represented by a double-ear of corn. Jumis is connected with the harvest feast in the autumn, when he is identified with the last sheaf of the cornfields.

ÅKE HULTKRANTZ

QUESTIONS

1. Why does studying prehistoric religion present us with so many problems?

2. How far does the evidence of religion in the Neolithic period (c.10,000–3000 BCE) reflect the needs of the societies of that era?

3. Why was sacrifice such an important part of the religion of the Maya and the Aztecs?

4. Why was the development of writing so important to religion?

5. Describe the different ways divination and astrology were used in ancient religions.

6. What does the long-term failure of the religious reforms of Amenophis IV of Egypt tell us about the status of religion in Egyptian society?

7. What factors were responsible for the decline of Zoroastrianism from its peak?

8. Explain how Zoroastrianism's understanding of divine judgment differs from the role of the gods in Greek and Roman religion.

9. Why did the religious traditions of ancient Rome die out?

10. Why are older interpretations of the religions of the Celts so unreliable?

FURTHER READING

Beard, Mary, J. North, and S. Price, *Religions of Rome*, 2 vols. Cambridge: Cambridge University Press, 1998.

Easterling, P. E. and J. V. Muir, eds, *Greek Religion and Society*. Cambridge: Cambridge University Press, 1985.

Hart, George, *Egyptian Myths*. Austin: University of Texas Press, 1997.

Hassig, Ross, *Time, History, and Belief in Aztec and Colonial Mexico*. Austin: University of Texas Press, 2001.

Hutton, Ronald, *The Pagan Religions of the Ancient British Isles: Their Nature and Legacy*. Oxford: Blackwell, 1991.

Lane Fox, Robin, *Pagans and Christians: In the Mediterranean World from the Second Century AD to the Conversion of Constantine*, 2nd ed. London: Penguin, 2006.

Lindow, John, *Norse Mythology: A Guide to the Gods, Heroes, Rituals, and Beliefs*. Oxford: Oxford University Press, 2001.

Miller, Mary, and Karl Taube, *The Gods and Symbols of Ancient Mexico and the Maya: An Illustrated Dictionary of Mesoamerican Religion*. London: Thames & Hudson, 1993.

Pinch, Geraldine, *Egyptian Mythology: A Guide to the Gods, Goddesses, and Traditions of Ancient Egypt*. Oxford: Oxford University Press, 2004.

Rose, Jenny, *Zoroastrianism: An Introduction*. London: I. B. Tauris, 2011.

PART 3
INDIGENOUS RELIGIONS

SUMMARY

The prominence today of a handful of religions with a huge number of followers throughout the world can easily blind us to the existence of the huge number of religions which exist only in small communities, whether in a particular region or even a single village. Unsurprisingly, diversity abounds among indigenous religions, meaning it is inappropriate to generalize when considering their features, or to imagine it is possible to use them to outline a supposed evolution of religious types, as many scholars in the past did. Many have raised concerns about considering indigenous religions as 'religions' at all, especially because local languages often have no concept of 'religion' as it is understood in the West.

Nevertheless, commonalities are to be found. One concept that permeates many indigenous societies is that of respect for others, for one's elders, or ancestors. Many native North American communities, for example, place great value on their ancient wisdom, and consider living elders as a link to this. Many indigenous communities have highly-developed conceptions of sacred and profane space. Australian aborigines, for instance, consider the landscape to have been shaped by their ancestors. Commonly, the life and wellbeing of the community is the primary concern of religious life, and the purpose of ritual reflects this. Equally, shamans are often valued for their role in preventing the subversion of the common good by means such as witchcraft.

Today, of course, many small indigenous religions have been wiped out, as a result of the growth of religions such as Christianity; but in many places they have adapted to this challenge, or even adopted some aspects of the incomers. This reflects the strength of some local religions: far from being stuck in time, many have – throughout their history – adapted to new challenges facing the communities they serve.

CHAPTER 19

Understanding Indigenous Religions

Indigenous religions make up the majority of the world's religions. They are as diverse as the languages spoken, the music made, and the means of subsistence employed by the many and various people who find them meaningful and satisfying. The number of people who might be counted as members of indigenous religions may not form the majority of the world's religious people – some of these religions exist only in one small village – but they are far from insignificant when considered altogether.

This overview is intended to improve approaches to, and understanding of, indigenous religions such as those discussed in the 'case studies' in this section. It is important to note that not all indigenous religions are the same. Just as there are hundreds of indigenous languages in North America or in Papua New Guinea, so there are many different ways of being religious.

Few indigenous languages have a word like 'religion', and some people have drawn the conclusion that it is inappropriate to speak of 'religion' with reference to indigenous cultures. But if we think of religions as particular ways of living in, and particular ways of seeing, the world, then we can find religion in the ordinary, everyday lives of many people who do not use the word. In fact, it is unusual for adherents of any religion to separate their religious beliefs and practices from their everyday lives – so indigenous people are not so very different. It is also noteworthy that religions are not all about seemingly strange ideas and peculiar practices, although these are often the things that stand out when we encounter something new to us. There is nothing wrong with noticing 'strange things', as long as we also pay attention to the more everyday ways in which people speak of what makes their lives meaningful and interesting.

TRADITION AND CHANGE

As a result of the spread of transcultural or global religions – for example Buddhism, Christianity, and Islam – some indigenous religions have been destroyed, rejected, or abandoned. Some indigenous people have accepted the arriving religion on their own terms, and slotted it into an indigenous understanding. Many indigenous religions have been adapted to the presence of more powerful, or dominating, religions and continued with considerable vitality and creativity. While many people are returning to their 'traditional ways', others are engaging in both an indigenous and another, newer, religion.

Such processes, which keep religions continuously relevant, are not only interesting in themselves, but provide the most recent example of the quite ordinary fact that all religions continuously change. 'Tradition' does not mean nothing ever changes; rather, it means one generation sets standards by which the next might judge the value of an idea or practice before changing. Indigenous religions are not the fossilized remains of the earliest, or first, religions. They are rarely simple or simplistic, and should not be mistaken for the basic building blocks from which 'more advanced' religions were built or evolved. Hence, earlier terms – such as 'primitive religion' or 'primal religion' – detract from a proper, and respectful, understanding of the vibrant ways in which people understand, and engage with, the world. Similarly, it is unhelpful to speak of groups that might include millions of people as 'tribes', and of their religions as 'tribal religions'. Indigenous religions are not stuck in the past, nor do they make sense only when practised in their original homelands. Although indigenous religions are severely affected by colonialism, they continue to provide resources for people surviving and thriving in the new, globalized world.

RESPECT

The notion of respect is important in discussing indigenous religions. Elders continuously encourage younger people to show respect in particular ways to those who deserve it. Asking who is respected, and how respect is shown, can be quite revealing about what is of central importance. In many parts of Africa, for example, beer is offered to those one respects. Native Americans did not traditionally use alcohol, and continue to give gifts of tobacco or sage to respected people. In some cultures it is appropriate to be reserved when first meeting another person; in others it is permissible to act quite intimately. Knowing whether to touch someone else at all, and in what way, is important. Do you shake hands or press noses? Do you hand people gifts – or place them on the ground in front of them?

WHO IS A PERSON?

Important as these questions are, the more radical question is 'Who is a person?' Most cultures understand humans are not the only kind of person. Christians, Jews, and Muslims, for example, consider God and angels to be persons of considerable importance. Of course, this nicely illustrates the point that not all persons are the same, and that there are different ways to approach particular persons. There are indigenous religions in which teachings about a God who created the world are significant. There are many more in which everything we see is the result of the creative activities of many other persons. Perhaps a single creator, or a creative process, started it all, but then life developed as each living being, or person, played their part. Trees separated sky and land, mountains arose to shape the land, coyote or jaguar or a robin tamed fire, corn taught planting cycles and ceremonies, humans built towns, and so the world became the way it is. And similar processes continue to change the world, making it important that people learn to act responsibly and respectfully. All this is commonplace in a great variety of indigenous religions.

What needs more careful thought is the implication that there is a great variety of creative persons. Some of these might be recognized as being like the God monotheists acknowledge, others are more polytheistic deities, often encountered in the kind of intimate, everyday matters for which some academics use the word 'immanence' — the divine within the world and everyday experience. Many significant persons are humans: elders, priests, shamans, grandparents, rulers, and so on. Although ancestors are important, it is important to note that among indigenous people this word typically refers to those from whom a particular person or family is descended, and rarely means 'all those who have died'. This can cause difficulties, because some museum scientists consider that all human remains belong to 'humanity' universally. The difference between these 'scientific' and indigenous ways of speaking — and the resulting confusion — is illustrated in references to 'our ancestors' by those museum officials who reject requests for the return of particular remains to their places of origin. Such misunderstandings also illustrate tensions familiar from wider concerns about globalization.

If ancestors are pre-eminent among the community of human persons in many indigenous cultures, and deserve appropriate displays of respect, they are far from alone in being categorized as 'persons'. In many, but not all, indigenous cultures, words equivalent to 'person' can refer to animals, plants, rocks, clouds, and more. Having learned from Ojibwe people in southern-central Canada, Irving Hallowell (1892–1974) coined the influential term 'other-than-human persons'. That is, in Ojibwe understanding, the world is inhabited by a vast community of persons, only some of whom are human. There are human-persons, tree-persons, rock-persons, cloud-persons, and so on. From a rock-person's perspective there might be 'other-than-rock persons', such as some humans, with whom it is possible — and even desirable — to communicate. Many indigenous peoples have similar understandings of the nature of life and personhood.

EXCHANGING GIFTS

Children brought up in particular indigenous religions may have to be taught to distinguish between persons and objects, but religious education is rarely presented as lectures and lists. More commonly, children are taught how to act towards other persons. Just as they receive gifts from, and give gifts to, older relatives, they learn that the process of giving and receiving is a vitally important element of the relationships that mark people as different from mere 'things'. Gifts are given as signs of respect and love to those more powerful, or more esteemed, than us. Gifts are received as signs of support, help, and compassion from those more powerful, or esteemed, than us. Gifts initiate, maintain, and further relationships between people. Gifts carry obligations and create ongoing relationships. Just as Ojibwe children might offer respected elders gifts of tobacco, elders might offer tobacco to respected rocks or eagles, or to sage plants from which they wish to cut leaves. Gift processes thus demonstrate who are considered to be persons, who is expected to act personally towards other persons.

POWER DYNAMICS

Gift is also central to the dynamics of power. Understandings of power are also a common theme in discussions of indigenous religions. Although the history of Western scholarship contains misunderstandings of indigenous ideas about power, the theme is an important one. Some scholars have claimed that many indigenous people have 'primitive' and mistaken notions about mystical powers being something like electricity. Often these scholars have not listened attentively to their hosts, who have been explaining the social dynamics by which people interact. For example, social – not mystical – powers are usually at stake in Polynesian references to *mana* and Ojibwe references to *manitou*. Again, this usage is not alien to Westerners, who are familiar with the language of 'empowerment'. There are more and less powerful persons. More power manifests itself as more ability to perform certain roles – for example, making pots or speeches – and brings with it the responsibility to act respectfully and to the benefit of others.

> Mau e ki mai, he aha te mea nui?
>
> Maku e ki atu,
>
> he tangata, he tangata, he tangata.
>
> *If you ask what is the greatest thing*
>
> *I will tell you*
>
> *it is people, people, people.*
>
> Taitokerau Whakatauki – Maori

SHAMANS AND WITCHES

Person, gift, and power are also central to common problems to which indigenous religions proffer solutions. For example, some indigenous people understand it is possible to cause harm by performing particular rituals, such as witchcraft and sorcery. Solutions might be found among some people by recourse to diviners, while others employ shamans. For the indigenous people, these specialists are adept at finding knowledge unavailable to others, and require careful – and sometimes frightening – training for their role. In response to questions about whether such practices are superstitious, indigenous people might point to the fact that rather different questions are important in indigenous communities. The interesting question for them is not why a grain store collapsed: everybody knows that grain stores collapse because termites eat their supports away. The important

> 'A ńlọ wá ìmò, òtító, àti òdodo.
>
> *We are going in search of knowledge, truth, and justice.*
>
> A line of Ifa divination text – Yoruba

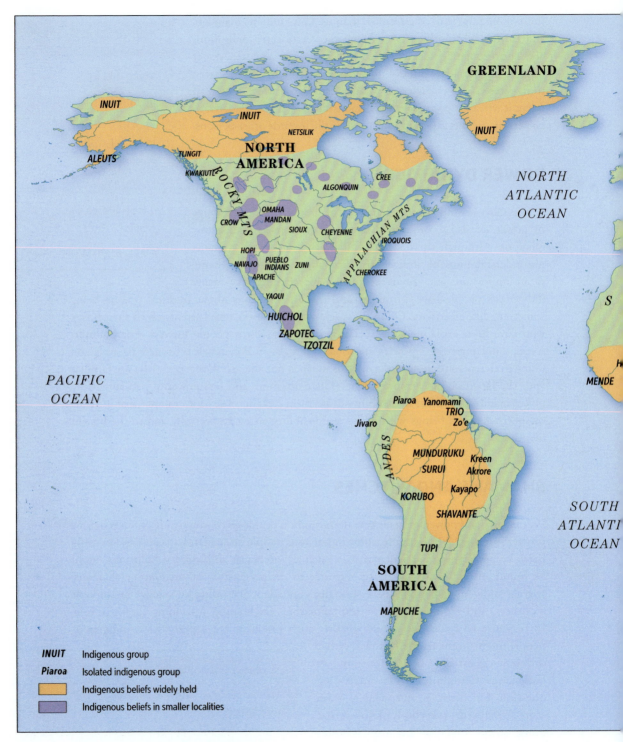

Indigenous Religions Worldwide

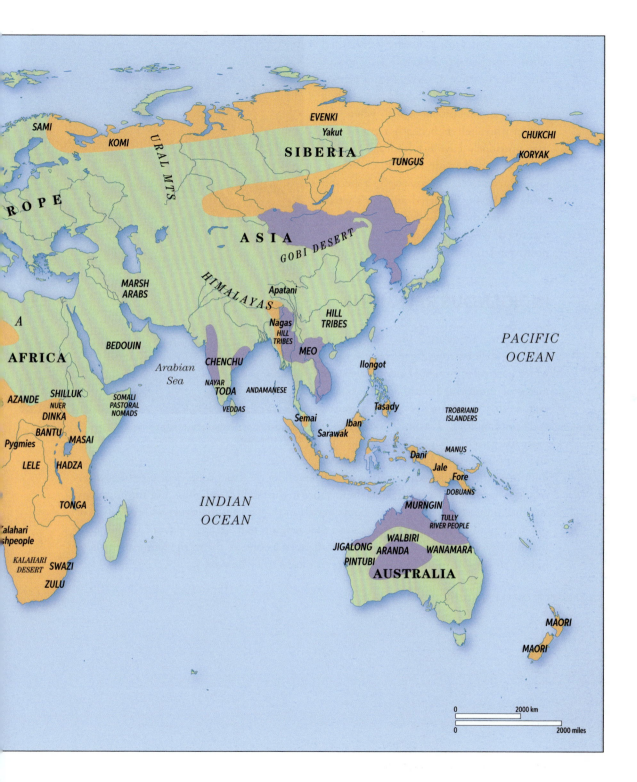

SAMI

KOMI

EVENKI

Yakut

CHUKCHI

KORYAK

URAL MTS.

SIBERIA

TUNGUS

ROPE

ASIA

GOBI DESERT

PACIFIC
OCEAN

HIMALAYAS

Apatani

MARSH
ARABS

A

AFRICA

BEDOUIN

Nagas

HILL
TRIBES

HILL
TRIBES

MEO

Ilongot

Arabian
Sea

CHENCHU

NAYAR
TODA

ANDAMANESE

Tasady

TROBRIAND
ISLANDERS

AZANDE

SHILLUK

NUER

DINKA

SOMALI
PASTORAL
NOMADS

VEDDAS

Semai

Iban

Sarawak

MANUS

BANTU

MASAI

Dani

Jale

Pygmies

Fore

LELE

HADZA

DOBUANS

INDIAN
OCEAN

MURNGIN

TONGA

TULLY
RIVER PEOPLE

Kalahari
shpeople

WALBIRI

JIGALONG

ARANDA

WANAMARA

KALAHARI
DESERT

SWAZI

PINTUBI

ZULU

AUSTRALIA

MAORI

MAORI

0   2000 km

0   2000 miles

question, as they see it, is why it collapsed when this person sheltered beneath it, rather than earlier or later. In indigenous religions, talk of witchcraft arises in a personal and relational world, where the person who shelters beneath a grain store may previously have insulted an ancestor or a witch, and made himself or herself liable to disaster. Alternatively, a person aware of having incurred another's wrath might offer the kind of gifts commonly identified as 'sacrifices' to restore a more positive relationship.

INDIGENOUS RELIGIONS

Indigenous religions, like all other religions, may be considered to be ways in which particular groups of people seek the means of improving health, happiness, and even wealth for themselves, their families, and communities. Finding out what a particular group means by health, wealth, and happiness, and how they go about

1831 painting by George Catlin of native American Ojibwe Chief of the Plains.

improving these, will greatly enhance understanding of that group's culture. Indigenous religions have been of considerable importance in the study of religions and anthropology, and their adherents are now participants in rich and significant dialogues with members of other religions or none. The recognition that religion may be largely about the etiquette by which people relate to one another can be seen as one of the most significant gifts of indigenous people to understanding what it means to be human.

GRAHAM HARVEY

CHAPTER 20

Indigenous Religions in Asia

CASE-STUDY I

Asian tribal peoples do not separate the sacred and secular. Their religious concepts are expressed in ritualized activities involving the community. These concepts and actions do not result from verbal 'beliefs'. In this they differ from 'religion' as we know it in the world's major faiths.

The key to understanding Asian tribal worldviews is 'relationship': with gods and spirits; with fellow human beings; with nature. These cannot be separated: they form one whole. Each group has religious practices appropriate to themselves and their environment, most often seeking to restore the good order that was created 'in the beginning'. So the practices of tribal groups stretching across Asia and the neighbouring islands vary widely.

SHAMANS

Shamans dominate religion in Siberia, where people believe in a high god, beyond all good and evil. Chosen by the spirits from certain families, male and female shamans enter rigorous training. Their souls leave the body by ecstatic trances to communicate with the spirits. They bring back instructions to correct the erring and restore harmony between people, the spirit world, and everything created. This harmony is fundamental to their beliefs. Similar beliefs are held by the Ainus of northern Japan, the mountain peoples of Taiwan and, to some extent, the Hakka of China.

NOMADIC GROUPS

Many people think the nomadic groups are descendants of Asia's ancient peoples who have preserved traditional ways down the ages. Today they live in small bands in remote, forested hill-country, where they were probably pushed long ago by more highly organized immigrants. They include very small tribes in west-central and south India and in Chota Nagpur, and they are also found on the Andaman Islands, and scattered in remote forest and swamp areas of coastal Cambodia. Better known, perhaps, are the small groups of Semang-Negritoes and their neighbours, the Senoi, inhabiting the jungle hills of northern and central peninsular Malaysia; also the Aëtas-Negritoes of Luzon, Mindanao, and Mindoro in the Philippines. Other hunter-gatherer groups can be found wandering in central Kalimantang, the Celebes, and eastern Sumatra.

Such groups may be made up of one elder and his family, or several families. Scarcity of food dictates size. However much they roam, they usually keep within their own boundaries. Food is always shared equally – roots, tubers, leaves, and fruits from the forest, possibly fish speared or trapped. Small game is hunted by bow-and-arrow, except on the Malaysian peninsula, where Senoi blowgun and poisoned dart have also been adopted by the Semang.

The Mah Meri people belong to the Senoi sub-group of Malaysia, and most live along the coast of South Selangor.

INTRODUCTION TO WORLD RELIGIONS

LAND AND RITUAL

Their home area of land and its produce has great religious significance. However far they wander, they return repeatedly to the place they regard as their own. Many, such as the Malaysian Senoi hill-people — widely known as *Sakai*, 'slave' — have changed to slash-and-burn cultivation for part of each year. They still live in very temporary shelters during food-collecting expeditions, but cultivation demands settled base-camps at some seasons, which changes their religious attitude to the land and to the spirits.

The Senoi, like other hill-cultivators, are surrounded by taboos and work restrictions as soon as they choose which trees to fell and fire to prepare a hill-plot. Through a series of rituals, they seek the spirits' help in securing a good crop, until the final harvest celebration. These rituals are performed by the whole community; for instance, all are in 'quarantine' on the first day of planting. Similarly, one person's sickness involves everybody; for the person's soul has wandered out of the group and must be brought back. The shaman employs the power of certain herbs and plants disliked by the spirit world to drive away the evil and call back the wandering soul.

TABOO

In cases of serious illness the whole group is involved in taboos and ritual observances, perhaps in days and nights of music and spirit-possessed dance. Finally, when blood sacrifice has been offered, the spirit is driven out. If the patient dies, another set of pollution observances begins. Deaths, like births, are full of danger, and the group must isolate itself, both for its own safety and that of its neighbours. If any member breaks the taboo, terrifying tropical storms will follow. These come from a supreme god, but the Senoi have little idea of a hierarchy of spirit beings. To them, the presence of ancestor-spirits is vague and unwelcome. Safety and well-being depend on the unity and harmony of the living community.

Tribes with more complex social structures, and more settled and advanced economic patterns, develop a stronger pattern of rituals, which demands ritual specialists for proper celebration. Though certain rites may be performed for the individual, they still involve the wider community. The Kondhs provide an example.

> *The elements of the taboo … are always the same: certain things, or persons, or places belong in some way to a different order of being, and therefore contact with them will produce an upheaval at the ontological level which might well prove fatal.*
>
> Mircea Eliade, *Patterns in Comparative Religion* (1958).

THE KONDHS

The Kondhs — or Kui, as they call themselves — live in the jungle-covered Eastern Ghats of Orissa, India, and number more than a million. Traditionally, they supported themselves by slash-and-burn hill-plots, and by hunting and gathering during the dry

Taboo is a sort of warning: 'Danger! High voltage!' Power has been stored up, and we must be on our guard. The taboo is the expressly authenticated condition of being replete with power, and man's reaction to it should rest on a clear recognition of this potent fullness, should maintain the proper distance and secure protection.

Gerardus van der Leeuw,
Religion in Essence and Manifestation (1938).

'hungry season'. Paddy-cultivation has now steadily increased.

In 1835 the British East India Company first encountered the Kondhs' constant human sacrifices to satisfy the earth's demands. Kondh myths taught that only in return for this costliest form of sacrifice would the earth deity grant them fertility of crops, animals, and healthy children.

The creator-god, Bura, formed the earth-goddess, Tari, as his companion, but found her sadly lacking in wifely attentions. She tried in vain to prevent his creating the world and humankind. All was paradise in the created world, except for her growing jealousy, which led to a fierce conflict between the two. All the Kondhs, except a small minority, believed the earth-goddess had won, although she let the creator keep second place. She taught the arts of hunting, war, and cultivation only in return for human blood, her 'proper food'.

Buffalo now replace human victims, and – though declining – this ritual continues. Strips of flesh are hacked from the victim and buried in the village and in neighbouring villages, to release her gift of fertility. Many villages were formerly at war. Brief, strict peace-pacts are therefore made for each annual stage of this three- or four-year ritual, ensuring cooperation for the set few days. In some areas, this ritual is still annually celebrated in each district, also at certain farming seasons, or when the health of the people or its livestock is affected. This binds the people together as Kondhs, when otherwise the strongest unit is the lineage group.

A number of myths and dialogues show how the Kondhs tried to avoid the earth-goddess's demands: 'We will die rather than give you human beings!' But breaking the relationship with her also involved breaking the relationship with the land – bringing drought and famine – and with humankind, bringing pestilence and death. Hence she always made them submit, as the means of recreating harmony and well-being.

Being chosen by the spirits, taught by them to enter a trance and fly with one's soul to other worlds in the sky or clamber through dangerous crevasses into subterranean worlds; being stripped of one's flesh, reduced to a skeleton and then reassembled and reborn; gaining the power to combat spiritual enemies and heal their victims; to kill enemies and save one's own people from disease and starvation – these are the features of shamanic religions in many parts of the world.

Piers Vitebsky (2000)

KONDH RITUALS

The Kondhs try to use mystical powers in many other rituals, to increase or restore relationship – thus strength and well-being – in the district, village, kin-group, or household:

- Rituals between the high god, humankind, and the land. These follow the farming calendar, from ground preparation and sowing, to reaping and threshing; also taboo-lifting rituals on hunting and gathering wild produce.
- Rituals to seek the blessing and help of the ancestors. These may involve other clans: such as marriage or the taking of a second wife, or the removal of an entire village with its ancestors, if problems and pestilences show the need.
- Rituals to guard against loss of well-being through pollution. Ritual impurity runs the full gamut from small household avoidances to incest, which pollutes the earth and everybody in the area. All births and deaths pollute, but most serious for the Kondhs are deaths before due time, by tiger-mauling, in childbirth, or by hanging, falling from a tree, or drowning. These place the entire village in 'quarantine', traditionally for a month, but nowadays for a shorter period, while priest and people undergo daily purification rites.
- Rituals to safeguard life. The danger may come from high-ranking spirits: gods of the hill, of smallpox, of boundaries, of iron (war), or hunting. These are stronger than spirits of springs, trees, and lesser hills. Offence against them rapidly brings disaster. Also life-destroying is an overpowering belief in evil eye, sorcery, and witchcraft. These powers — neutral in themselves — become evil and deeply feared when someone uses them against their fellow, for this reverses Kondh beliefs about community well-being. Counter-rituals by 'witch-detectives' may return the evil to its originator, but the victim may nevertheless fall sick or die.

Seers communicate with the spirits through trances or divination, to find out who caused the problem and why. Priests perform the rituals, sacrificing cocks, goats, pigs, or buffalo. A spirit-chosen keeper of the village's shrine-stones performs many annual purification rituals. Many villages also have groves sacred to the hill-god or guardian spirit. The household head is priest for ancestor rites, and some look after bronze emblems of animals, reptiles, or other household spirits.

ONE COMMUNITY

The ancestors, the unborn, and the living all form one community; the same daily activities continue in the shade-world. Death in old age with a full funeral gives the best hope of passing peacefully to the ancestors. The dead are also rehabilitated into the bereaved home in the form of a spider, found near the funeral pyre. Sudden death in the feared forms mentioned earlier rules out being accepted by the ancestors. This results in unbearable loneliness for the now dangerous spirit. For the Kondhs, it is as necessary to live in community after death as before it. The manner of death — not good or evil behaviour in this life — decides the future life.

BARBARA BOAL

CHAPTER 21

The Foe of Papua New Guinea

CASE-STUDY 2

In the tribal religion of the Foe, in the Southern Highlands of Papua New Guinea, there is an awesome, seldom-named being, Siruwage, and a chief spirit, Ama-a Hai Ta-o, 'Old Man in East', but neither is earth's creator and there is no creator worship.

There are, in addition, three groups of spirits who live in fixed places:

- the evil things, *maame gai*
- the *hisare*
- the *hibu yii*

Certain men in each village make a special relationship with one of these groups of spirits, and others pay them to make an offering on their behalf.

THE EVIL THINGS

The 'evil things' inhabit a clump of trees, a big rock, or some unusual natural feature. For example, in around 1967, on a point of land on the south-east side of Lake Kutubu, in a swampy area of wild bamboo, a man named Igare, from Gese village, found a small area with red cordyline shrubs growing neatly. This, all agreed, must be a spirit house, so it was regarded as a place of the 'evil things'. Those who made a relationship with the evil things, and who had the right spells for them, were in their favour and would not be harmed. But those who roused their anger would get swollen legs or a swollen stomach. Children whose parents had garden-houses in the area were warned not to go near, or to make a noise, for fear of making them angry.

Further up the lake, some *hisare* spirits live. In the waters of the lake live a number of fearsome water spirits, the *guruka*. Men who make a relationship with the *hisare* spirits also make contact with these *guruka*. After the *hisare* people have danced with the *hisare* spirits, the *guruka* will come up from the water and dance. They will bring cassowary feathers, or perhaps human bones, and present them to the *hisare* people, acting for the spirits. According to the gift, the following month a cassowary will be caught, someone will die, or some similarly appropriate event will occur.

Hibu yii men built a house in their village, and at secret ceremonies the *hibu yii* spirits appeared to them. In many villages this is no longer practised.

WANDERING SPIRITS

Other spirit beings wander from place to place. The *soro* are spirits of the air who wander here and there at will, always on the lookout for some harm to do to humans. Children are afraid of the spirits of the air, being sure they could carry them off, or do dreadful things; but adults make it plain that they must work in company with the spirits who live within the living (*baisese*). A pair or group of *baisese* must work with at least one spirit of the air. If someone has an enemy, their spirit will go out, find another person's spirit, find a spirit of the air, and then go to do damage. For example, in about 1960 a stone was thrown into a man's sleeping area. He realized his spirit was leaving him, pressed into service by a fellow villager's spirit, and said 'There'll be a man harmed at Hegeso village,' naming the man. Two days later the man was dead.

SPIRITS OF THE DEAD

Most feared of all are the spirits of the dead, which include the spirits of men slain, mostly in inter-village fighting, and the spirits of those who have died from other causes. Both can cause harm and serious illness, entering into a person's body in the form of stones and wood that will cause death.

The spirits of the slain, *bauwabe*, are the most potent. These spirits live 'up above' and are always painted all over with red. People who make offerings to a spirit of the slain find that their spirit appears to them in a dream or vision, guaranteeing success and help. But if a man and his kinsmen are enemies of a man who is slain, his spirit appearing to them means trouble. If a person has a bad ulcer or abdominal pain, this is clearly the work of the spirit of the slain.

The spirit of someone who has died in any other way — *amena denane* — goes 'east', but wanders back and hovers around, at least for a time. It can cause sickness, but not death. An exasperated mother may say to a child, 'If you don't stop, the spirit will come with a bamboo, collect your tears, and drink them — and if they're sweet cause you lots of harm.'

Medicine men once claimed to be able to 'suck out' the stones and sticks implanted by the spirits. They were paid in strings of cowries, or with a pig. This cult died a natural death: the prices charged were high, and the number of cures not impressive. At local health centres, on the other hand, drugs such as penicillin and chloroquine produced dramatic cures free of charge. Certain medicine men would also, for a fee, chant away a spirit said to be causing sickness. This practice also appears to have been largely discontinued.

SORCERY

The sorcerer is greatly feared. In a group of two or three hundred people, complete and electric silence resulted when a well-known sorcerer produced a small bamboo of sorcery material bought from sorcerers in the west to cause the death of named men. Foe sorcerers have three main methods.

The first method, 'hitting the skin with a stick', is the most potent; the man will die in one or two days. Sorcery material from the bamboo, generally a fine, white, powdery substance, touches the skin of the doomed man, either by means of a stick, or by being shaken on him while he is asleep. If it can be put into his bamboo of water or his food, it works just as well.

In the second method, pieces of the man's belongings – a fragment of his cane leg-band, or of the leaves or cloth covering his buttocks – are put in the bamboo of sorcery material, which is placed in the fork of a tree, where it wears slowly away. Or it may be placed in a large ant-mound on a tree trunk, or in a small running stream. As the friction or the eating takes place, the man will sicken and die over a period of four or five months.

The third method – white sorcery – is done with a set of small white stones. The sorcerer obtains a tree gum, and says his spell as he rubs it into the stones. This also causes death.

JOAN RULE

CHAPTER 22

Australian Aboriginal Religions

CASE-STUDY 3

Australia is a vast continent that was peopled sparsely by its indigenous inhabitants before the advent of Europeans. When Europeans did arrive, they found a very different land from the one they had left, and an indigenous population that held religious views and lifestyles they found almost impossible to comprehend. The archaeological record of human life on the continent reaches back at least 40,000 years, white colonization little more than 200 years.

LAND AND CREATION

Central to Aboriginal beliefs are stories that tell of their relationship to the land, of totemic ancestors that once lay beneath the land and who, in the creative period, or founding drama, gave form to the formless and instituted unchangeable laws that humans were to follow for all time. The ancestors gave shape to an existing, yet formless world; they were self-created and creative, possessing special powers that could be used for good or harm. When they rose up from beneath the land, they journeyed across, under, or over it, leaving tangible expressions of their essence, or power, in the land itself. Where they stopped to urinate, for example, one might find a waterhole; where they sat, one might find a shallow depression; where they slept might be a rock; where they bled, ochre deposits were left; where they dug in the ground, water flowed and springs formed; where they cut down trees, valleys were formed. These primordial beings, the ancestors of living Aborigines, instituted tribal laws for their progeny to follow, and, when they completed their travels, they returned into the land whence they had come. Because all things share a common ancestral life force that is sacred, everything is interconnected, the living to the non-living, the sentient to the non-sentient, within a sacred geography that provides visual evidence of ancestral presence.

Aboriginal beliefs about the origins of the universe, and the place of humans in that universe, are conveyed in stories to do with the ancestors, and relayed through ceremonial performance, art, dance, and song. Songlines consist of a number of songs that follow

Aboriginal rock painting in Kakadu National Park, Northern Territory, Australia.

INTRODUCTION TO WORLD RELIGIONS

tracts of land pertaining to particular ancestors and their associated journeying, and those areas of land are associated with particular species of animals, birds, and other phenomena, and their connections to humans. Everything is linked, in an all-encompassing system of interrelatedness, and a network of tracks that cover the continent.

THE DREAMING

When Frank Gillen and Baldwin Spencer encountered the Arrernte Aborigines in central Australia in the late nineteenth century, they tried to understand what they referred to as their *Altyerrenge/Alcheringa* – the fundamental religious concepts that permeated every aspect of Aboriginal life and death. The closest translation these two white men could arrive at was 'Dream times', because it seemed to them that the Arrernte were talking about a past period of a vague and 'dreamy' nature, yet one that was still present. They realized that the *Altyerrenge* was of great importance to Aboriginal culture, but also that 'Dream times' – which later became 'the Dreaming' or 'Dreamtime' – did not adequately convey the meaning of the Aboriginal term. W. E. H. Stanner described the Dreaming as 'everywhen', to convey the sense of a non-linear, ever-present aspect to the Dreaming. Other Aboriginal language groups throughout Australia use similar concepts, and so the term 'Dreaming' came to have a universal application. Aborigines are more likely to give specific language names to the concept, or to call it their 'Law'. T. G. H. Strehlow aptly described it as 'eternal, uncreated, sprung out of itself'.

Since different parts of the landscape were created by particular ancestral beings, there is a plurality of Dreamings. Access to the Dreaming can come about through various means: participation in ceremonial performance, song, dance, or ritual, and via dreams and other methods. The significance of Dreaming stories is conveyed through these means, and according to an individual's position in the scheme of sacred knowledge. For example, a song might have several layers of meaning: at the basic level, men, women, and children have access to the public nature of a story conveyed in the song; at another level, a sacred meaning would be conveyed; and at a secret-sacred level, only those who have undertaken a specific initiation in either 'men's business' – knowledge about the Dreaming pertaining to men – or 'women's business' – knowledge about the Dreaming pertaining to women – would be privy to the deepest levels of meaning. Similarly, paintings also have layers of meaning, from public to esoteric knowledge, held by only a few senior people. The most secret, restricted knowledge is owned, or known, by senior men who are experts in 'men's business' and by senior women who are experts in 'women's business'.

> *I am not painting just for my pleasure; there is the meaning, knowledge, and power. This is the earthly painting for the creation and for the land story. The land is not empty, the land is full of knowledge, full of story, full of goodness, full of energy.*
>
> Marika, quoted in Wally Caruana and Nigel Lendon, *The Painters of the Wagilag Sisters' Story* 1937–97 (National Gallery of Australia, Canberra, 1997).

OWNERSHIP

The concept of 'ownership' has relevance only to knowledge, not to ownership of land. Ownership of knowledge extends to everything that is non-material: the right of someone to paint certain designs, to sing a song, or to tell a story. The expression 'keeping up country' means that the people who come from a specific area, or 'country', and are associated with it through the Dreaming, must look after it in the form of stewardship or custodianship – by continuing the rituals, following the songlines, and maintaining a proper relationship with the ancestors of that 'place'.

Legal recognition of traditional ownership is an ongoing concern for Aboriginal people, many of whom were displaced from their original lands after colonization. This is a major issue for Aboriginal people, still under debate in courts of law throughout Australia.

ABORIGINES AND CHRISTIANITY

After 200 years of colonization and Christianization through missionary influences, a great many Aboriginal people are now Christian, or combine tenets of Christianity with indigenous beliefs and practices. Their stories of the Dreaming, their displacement, and their sometimes traumatic experiences as a result of European presence, are all depicted in their distinctive art – which now consists of traditional methods such as dot paintings and abstract designs – Christian influences, and political statements about their lived experiences.

LYNNE HUME

CHAPTER 23

Melanesia

CASE-STUDY 4

Melanesia is the area of the Pacific Ocean from the western end of New Guinea – Irian Jaya – to Fiji in the east, from the northernmost islands of Papua New Guinea to New Caledonia in the south, and includes Irian Jaya, Papua New Guinea, the Torres Strait Islands, the Solomon Islands, the New Hebrides, and New Caledonia. There are no fewer than 1200 vernacular languages among its roughly 5 million inhabitants.

More than a century of close contact with foreign cultures and Christianity has changed Melanesian indigenous religion, but has not everywhere reduced its vitality and pervasiveness.

WORLD VIEW

Melanesians make no distinction between the 'religious' and the 'secular', between the 'natural' and the 'supernatural'. Their religion can be seen as a particular view of the universe, and a set of relationships with it, including people, gods, spirits, ghosts, magical powers, totems, the land, and features of the landscape, living creatures, trees, plants, and all physical objects, all of which are in some sense potential sources of power.

Relationships with people and ancestral spirits are universally the most important, for at the centre of life is the community of people and spirits. This community, along with clan and extended family, and links with a particular piece of land, give a person identity and security, a reason for living, a sense of history, and an approach to the future. All rituals of birth, initiation into adult life, marriage, and death are directed towards maintaining these relationships.

Melanesian primal religion aims at life, fertility, prosperity, harmony, control, and balance in all relationships between people and spirits, and in this world rather than

> *If a stone is found to have supernatural power, it is because a spirit has associated itself with it; a dead man's bone has with it mana, because the ghost is with the bone; a man may have so close a connection with a spirit or ghost that he has mana in himself also, and can so direct it as to effect what he desires.*
>
> R. H. Codrington,
> *The Melanesians* (1891).

the next. However, as with many other religions, not all its activities match these ideals. Narrow concern with family and clan, suspicions and hostility between and within groups, and in some areas between the sexes, have helped foster seemingly harsh and inhuman practices.

MYTHS AND STORIES

Melanesian primal religion features a range of migration and other stories, legends and myths, songs, prayers and incantations, all transmitted orally. Parts of this repertoire are known only by initiated males, or adult women, or by specialists such as priests. Especially sacred knowledge is restricted to elderly initiated people. There is a variety of creation stories, but little speculation about the origins and nature of the universe. Many people believe that important parts of culture – social, economic, and political life – were created for, or given to, the people by gods.

Not all Melanesian peoples have believed in a god of the whole universe, or in a powerful god or gods, or that god or the gods are interested in human activities. While some believe gods to be creators who continue to care for the world, many believe in a variety of spirit beings, including evil 'ghosts', demons, and witches – not widespread – many of which can harm or kill people. Ancestral spirits are important everywhere; some societies look forward to the return of the dead, others fear it. Some societies regard the spirits of the recent dead as dangerous; others think they are friendly towards the living. They believe elaborate rituals in honour of the dead – mourning, food offerings, dances, exchanges of pigs, food, and valuables – will ensure that the dead will protect the living. Where beliefs in totems occur, the totems – animals, birds, fish, trees, plants – are sometimes seen as ancestors, sometimes simply as emblems.

RITUAL AND MAGIC

Rituals vary from simple acts linked with everyday activities, such as hunting, gardening, and fishing, to complex rituals, festivals, and festival cycles, lasting days, weeks, even months and years. In the major activities, initiated men take the central role; women and juniors have only minor roles. The pig figures in many of these rituals and festivals. Food, drink, and sexual taboos accompany most important rituals. Some peoples believe rituals force the spirits or gods to act; others believe the gods are free to act as they will.

Magic has a place in most societies. The sorcerer is an important person in many Melanesian societies; deaths are often credited to his activity, since a death is usually regarded as being caused by

> *A man is a good fighter, not because of his own strength or resources but because of the strength he gets from the mana of some dead fighter; this mana may lie in the little stone amulet hanging around his neck, in some leaves fastened to his belt, or in some spoken formula. The fact that a man's pigs multiply or his garden thrives is due to his possessing certain stones containing the particular mana of pigs and of trees.*
>
> Mircea Eliade, *Patterns in Comparative Religion* (1958).

someone. Every Melanesian society includes people with special ritual responsibilities, temporary, permanent, or hereditary.

For Melanesians, sacred places can include features of the landscape, such as caves, pools, streams, and rocks, but also artificial constructions varying from simple structures to large elaborate buildings, such as the Sepik ancestral spirit houses.

In some societies, ethics and religion seem to have no connection; in others, the spirits and gods are clearly concerned with behaviour. Ethical conduct is the particular interest of the god Datagaliwabe among the Huli people of the Southern Highlands of Papua New Guinea.

CARL LOELIGER

CHAPTER 24

South American Indigenous Religions

CASE-STUDY 5

This overview concerns the religious world views of the indigenous peoples of Central and South America, focusing upon those disparate and diverse communities whose tribal practices and geographical remoteness have until relatively recently helped to preserve much of a cultural heritage that very substantially predates European 'conquest' (1492–). Because of the linguistic and cultural diversity of these communities, examples have been introduced from as many different contexts as possible, with indigenous sources cited regarding their most popular name. The majority of examples relate to peoples inhabiting the forested highlands and lowlands of northern/central South America, with broader representation gained by referring to assorted groups in Tierra del Fuego and Patagonia in the south and the Central American isthmus to the north. A proper appreciation of the practices and belief systems of these indigenous groups requires an awareness of an overarching worldview, consisting of an enormously complex interaction of situated socio-cultural processes and localized economico-political dynamics.

TIME AND SPACE

Conceiving time as linear rather than cyclical, these indigenous peoples make sense of the present with reference to the foundational events of a primordial past. Here, a mythical period of momentous upheavals engenders an increasingly variegated world, in which flood, fire, and violence mould and reshape the cosmos. Indigenous mythologies represent the world as the intended product of pre-existent deities, such as Temáukel of the Ona, or as an unintended result caused by their godly and semi-divine offspring, as with Kumai of the Baniwa. The transition from mythical pre-history to human time is often effected through the foundational practices of mythical cultural heroes, such as Elal of the Tehuelche. Within this period of momentous change and unfolding differentiation, tribal traditions are established, and classificatory systems formulated — the ambiguities, contradictions, and maladies of which continue to find their basis in the primeval period. The recalcitrant disorder of the present is framed by the ambivalent discontinuities of a mythic past.

The indigenous cosmos is spatially divided into a series of overlapping tiers, some of which are further subdivided. The number of strata differs from culture to culture, with the Kógi having as many as nine divisions, the Siona and Waiwai five, the Tapirapé and Baniwa four, and the Toba, Matsigenka, and Pemón three. At its simplest, the universe has the earth sandwiched between the heavenly terrain of the gods above, and the subterranean world below. With the Baniwa, the heavenly realm comprises a lower 'Other World', adjacent to the earth, and a more distant 'Other Sky'. The underworld can also be layered, as with the Campa's partition of it into two. Although any particular stratum may be divided laterally, the earthly tier is most commonly subjected to such treatment, with prominent environmental features, such as mountains, lakes, and dense parts of the forest, and mythical places, such as the Avá-Chiripá's 'land without evil', accorded extra-special status.

THE PHYSICAL MIRRORS THE SUPERNATURAL

The physical space and moral environment of indigenous peoples is ordered to reflect mythico-cosmic space-time. The Kayopó village, for example, both in its design and external orientation to the surrounding forest, exemplifies physical space as a microcosm upon which temporal heritage and spatial hierarchy write themselves, through individual lives and social processes. As with the village, so too the human individual is held to mirror the cosmic order of things. The indigenous self is seen in a wide variety of ways. The Waiwai, certain Guaraní groups, and the Toba talk of the self as having two principal elements, rendered 'souls' by most scholars. The Avá-Chiripá, Matsigenka, and other Guaraní groups understand the self as comprised of three primary components. Whatever the structure, indigenous conceptions of the self and its constituent parts serve at least two basic functions:

- As within many other mythico-religious systems, they allow for continuity in the face of spatio-temporal change. Whether awake or asleep, as with the nocturnal roamings of the Matsigenka 'free soul' and the Toba 'image soul'; alive or dead, as with the post-mortem ascension of the Waiwai 'eye-soul' to Kapu; in this world or another, as with the 'soul flight' of shamanic ecstasy, partitioned conceptions of the self help to preserve a continuity of personal identity.

- They help to situate the individual amidst a multiple configuration of mythical, temporal, and spatial reality. Whether unified, dualistic, or tripartite, these views of the self serve generally to articulate an understanding of the individual as constituted through the continuous interplay of its divine origins, base corporeality, and personal-social processes. They thereby allow for relations with other spheres of existence both in this life and the next, ground the individual in the corruptible materiality of this world, and preserve a personal identity which is derived from more than its heavenly-physical origins. The indigenous self exists as a nodal point at which mythical, spatial, and temporal dynamics intersect.

Indigenous Groups of South America

SUPERNATURAL BEINGS

Alongside humankind and the flora and fauna surrounding it, the indigenous universe is populated by a broad array of supernatural beings. Whilst taxonomy differs from people to people, the following categories are generally representative:

- Inhabiting the higher strata of the cosmologies, often remote from everyday human activity, are — for some tribes — uncreated/pre-existent deities such as Kóoch of the Tehuelche, Ñanderuvusú of the Guaraní, and Nanderú Guazù of the Avá-Chiripá.

- These divine beings are accompanied by a pantheon of lesser deities, whose origins and characteristics are usually connected with celestial, climatic, totemic, and otherwise routine phenomena — as with Gidosíde, the Ayoreo moon goddess; Karuten, the Tehuelche god of thunder; the black monkey of the Arawak or the tiger of the Goajiros; and Pel'ek of the Toba, the owner of the night.

- Although indigenous deities involve themselves in the general ordering of human affairs, and are at times difficult to differentiate from the more numerous category of 'spirits', it is the latter who most directly influence day-to-day affairs. Usually occupying the lower strata of the cosmos, the spirits of animals, plants, and elementals — for example, of water — along with those of deceased human beings, are regarded as primary causal forces, potentially influencing every facet of personal well-being, interpersonal relations, and social reproduction.

- Experienced through dreams or visions, encountered at night in the village or by day in the forest, the spirits of the indigenous world view are central to the dynamics of a human world which is, after all, nothing but a pale imitation of the 'real world' they inhabit. Whilst benevolent and malevolent forms exist, within the indigenous mindset spirits are, by and large, morally ambivalent in their dealings with humans. However, with adequate inducements and the appropriate opportunities they are quick to make their ubiquitous presence felt. The prevalence of widespread supernatural causality demands constant and careful handling, and most indigenous peoples turn to ritualized activity, managed by the local shaman, to limit or coordinate the impact of the spiritual upon the material.

THE SHAMAN

Although intended — as opposed to accidental and undesired — engagement with indigenous spirits is not restricted to formal shamanic activity, the shaman is the primary agent in human-supernatural interaction. Selected by way of heredity, as with the Putumayo, or shamanic preference, as with the Avá-Chiripá, shamans undergo rigorous and prolonged training. Lasting anywhere from less than five years — as with the Matsigenka, Siona, and Chiquitano — to more than ten — as with the Kógi, Arecuna, and Taulipáng — shamanic apprenticeship comprises an extended period of isolation and instruction, coupled with numerous ordeals and disciplinary regimes. In effect, literal marginalization, sexual abstinence, emetically induced purgation, and narcotically managed disruption to sleep and hygiene patterns reconstitute the shamanic novice as one who is to live and function at the personal and spiritual margins of everyday life. Yet the shaman is an 'outsider within', for the overwhelming role accorded supernatural causality entails that the shaman's place is thoroughly intertwined within the warp and woof of daily routine.

The Tapirapé, for example, hold shamanic activity to be central to biological reproduction, believing the shaman to be responsible for the safe transit from other realms of the souls of those newly conceived. Like many other indigenous communities, the Baniwa regard serious illness as a direct result of spirit assault. Whether induced at the behest of other – usually shamanic – human beings, or resulting from the breaking of any number of food, hygiene, and social taboos, an attack by spirits can only be properly dealt with through recourse to one trained in the arts of the supernatural spheres. In addition to the almost daily routine of preventing, diagnosing, or curing serious illness, the shaman is a focal point of communal festivals, such as harvest; rites of passage, such as female menarche and male coming of age; socio-economic reproduction, such as successful hunting; and political processes, such as assuaging internal discord or inter-tribal dispute.

Differentiation of shamanic specialisms is a varying phenomenon among indigenous peoples. The Jívaro and Wakuénai distinguish two classes of shaman, whereas the Ishír, Winikina-Warao, and Desana have three types. The grounds for such differentiation differ from tribe to tribe, with the most popular distinctions related to abilities to heal or injure, the frequenting of different supernatural realms, or the relationship with particular spirits, often relative to the use of specific hallucinogenic agents.

Whatever his – and the indigenous shaman is overwhelmingly male – title, role, or place in society, the shaman executes his responsibilities by drawing upon a vast range of knowledge acquired through initiation, apprenticeship, and practice. In addition to memorizing the structures of the numerous cosmic realms, the shaman must master the techniques of ecstasy, dream, and vision through which other worlds are visited, and the services of their supernatural inhabitants engaged. The shaman thereby provides a heavily ritualized service, the execution of which demands combining a vast cosmological knowledge with gruelling physical regimes, diagnostic lore with curative techniques, and socio-economic practices with religious performance.

Central to successful shamanic practice are the alliances forged by the indigenous shaman with spiritual forces from other worlds. Generally occupying the higher strata of the cosmos, 'guardian spirits' serve as powerful allies to the shaman, offering protection from supernatural assault, and information as to the probable causes of individual malady and social disturbance. Visiting their domains in person, a shaman communicates with his guardian spirits by transporting his soul through the media of naturally occurring, ritually induced, and narcotically stimulated dreams, trances, and visions. Complementing the overarching support of a particular shaman's set of guardian spirits may be any number of auxiliary spirits, principally of animals and plants. Resident within the shaman himself, auxiliary spirits play a diagnostic role, but come into their own as active agents in the curative techniques called upon in shamanic practice. The principal relationship between a shaman and his auxiliary spirits is one of mutually beneficial exchange. Here, the resident spirits get to enjoy whatever hallucinogenic agents are used in ritualized shamanic activity, in return for their aid in resolving problems. In this instance narcotics, such as tobacco and ayahuasca – *Banisteriopsis caapi* – are not simple hallucinogens, but commodities of a highly ritualized exchange forming the central component by and around which other forms of shamanic performance, such as chant and dance, are ordered.

The shaman's ability to persuade, co-opt, suborn, and manipulate agents of the spirit world, subsequently exploiting these alliances and relationships for the betterment of his community, furnishes a practical corollary to indigenous belief in widespread supernatural causality. Triadic in nature, shamanic activity is:

- mimetic, in that its recapitulation of received tradition reappropriates for the present the powerful forces of primordial times;
- restorative, in that these forces align current practices with primeval order;
- creative, in that the correlation of past and present staves off disorder and assures futurity.

Integral to the indigenous worldview, shamanic practice exemplifies indigenous existence as a nodal point through which a multiple configuration of mythico-religious forces write themselves upon human space-time.

ANDREW DAWSON

CHAPTER 25

Native North Americans

CASE-STUDY 6

Contrary to popular belief, indigenous religions are today reviving in many parts of the world. The superior attitude which spread European civilization over the globe, spurred on by Western Christianity and materialism, was discredited in the twentieth century. Native faith-ways – scorned, forbidden, almost destroyed – reached their lowest point at the end of the nineteenth century.

Today disregard for the earth, for community, and for spirituality have brought the whole human enterprise into jeopardy. Arising like the phoenix from the ashes, tribal peoples are gathering again in their ceremonial circles, remembering discarded teachings, renewing the traditional ways. As they do so, perhaps they are laying the foundations for what they themselves are calling 'the fourth world', and a hope for a new beginning on the earth.

Wisdom, for such people, is found in the past, in the long experience of the race, in tradition. A very frequent expression in their ceremonies is, 'it is said …', by which is meant the teaching of the ancients. The teachers are the Elders, who are closest to those things of the past that are important. For tribal people, life is one. The sacred is very real – and specially real in some times and places. But the sacred is not divided off from times and places called secular; all life is sacred. All things are 'indwelt' to some degree. The whole range of life is open to spirit.

ONE GREAT SPIRIT

The tribal peoples of North America proclaim the One Great Spirit. Their thought and action is governed by the circle, which they see as basic in nature: the shape of moon and sun, the wheeling stars above them, the rotating seasons, the actions of birds and animals. 'Everything tries to be round.' This form is evident in everything they do – in myth, ceremony, art, and community organization. Essential to the circle is its centre, from which it is created. This is the symbol of the Great Spirit, reflected in all the dances around the fire, drum, or pole, and in ceremonies such as the sacred pipe.

TWO-NESS

Tribal people also reflect upon the two-ness of life and nature. Native North Americans symbolize this by a divided circle, as in the Plains shields, and in many forms of art and craft. Nature presents itself in pairs: dark and light, cold and hot, male and female, good and bad, and so on. These are not contradictory, but complementary. This twoness is expressed in the myths, such as that of the two sons of Mother Earth; in the totems of the west coast, such as Sisutl of the Kwakiutl, the two-headed serpent which punishes and protects; in the Thunderbird, threatening and caring; and in ceremonies, such as the forked pole of the Sundance.

But the two are always seen as aspects of the one, the circle. They are different, but they appear in balance, in harmony — the overriding virtue. Contentment is found not by conflict, but by coming to terms. An example of this is the native Arctic-dwellers, the Inuit. Intruding whites complain about a harsh, cruel environment, and when they go north take with them all manner of technologies to beat the climate. The Inuit, on the other hand, live face to face with nature, and, when untouched by the intruder, are happy. They have found harmony with their surroundings, and treat the ice and snow as friends, not enemies.

TRIANGLE ON CIRCLE

Give and take is the basis of all healthy relationships, and can be symbolized as a triangle on a circle. Tribal people search for support that will make their ventures succeed. This help is obtained in ceremonies whose action is three-sided. For example, a Mohawk community is threatened by drought, and corn withers in the fields. Help lies with the Thunderbeings; the rain must be sought with their aid by means of the rain dance. The community gathers in the fields, the drum and shaker sound, the dance begins, prayer is sung, water is sprinkled, and the rains come. The same give and take, between human need, heavenly power, and particular action, is found in all ceremonies for healing, guidance, and power.

When we killed a buffalo, we knew what we were doing. We apologized to his spirit, tried to make him understand why we did it, honouring with a prayer the bones of those who gave their flesh to keep us alive, praying for their return, praying for the life of our brothers, the buffalo nation, as well as for our own people.

John Lame Deer, twentieth-century Sioux shaman

THE FOUR POWERS

Native peoples in North America, as elsewhere, tended to see the structure of the world, and of the powers that control it, as four-sided. The symbol they used for this is a circle, with four points on the circumference.

Lame Deer, a present-day Sioux, explains:

Four is the number that is most sacred [wakan]. Four stands for the four quarters of the earth ... the four winds ... seasons ... colours ... four things of which the universe is made – earth, air, water, fire. There are four virtues which a man should possess … We Sioux do everything by fours …

Into this structure of fours is gathered and classified all life's variety. It is made one – the circle – through the 'great law of sacrifice', in which each part depends upon, and contributes to, all the others. 'One dies that another may live.' The 'wheel' is the pattern of all ceremonies, because it symbolizes the variety of life in the wholeness of life. This concept of unity in variety, and variety within unity, is basic to the goal of harmony and balance in life, seen by tribal people as the foundation of all health, peace, and well-being in the world.

> *Every object in the world has a spirit and that spirit is wakan. Thus the spirits of the tree or things of that kind, while not like the spirit of man, are also wakan. Wakan comes from the wakan beings. These wakan beings are greater than mankind in the same way that mankind is greater than animals. They are never born and never die … Mankind can pray to the wakan beings for help … The word Wakan Tanka means all of the wakan beings, because they are all as if one. Wakan Tanka Kin signifies the chief or leading wakan being, which is the Sun. However, the most powerful of the wakan beings is Nagh Tanka, the great Spirit who is also Taku Skanskan.*
>
> Sword, *Wakan*, trans. Burt Means

MYSTERY OF SEVENS

A 'mystery of sevens' lies at the root of ancient wisdom, and is found among indigenous cultures in all parts of the world, including the tribal people of North America. We hear of the seven sacred rites of the Sioux, the seven prophecies, or fires, of the Ojibwa Midewiwin, and the seven stopping-places in their ages-long migration westward. We hear of cycles of seven years and seven-times-seven years, and we hear of the seven Grandfathers.

The seven Grandfathers, found in Ojibwa mythology, are symbolized in the teaching staff, hung in the centre of the ceremonial circle, and made up of three straight sticks bound together at their centres. These sticks have six points, standing for the four directions plus the 'above' power – sky – and the 'below' power – earth, with a seventh at the crossing-point. It is the 'here' place of power, the self, the power within. This is not to say that the individual is the centre of all, but that all the powers are available to, and are flowing through, individuals. The powers come to them in visions and dreams, and are working through them in teachings and ceremonies.

Finally, there is the simple quartered circle, the symbol of wholeness. When taking part in the ceremonies, as the sweet grass is burned, the water drunk, the pipe smoked, one hears from each worshipper the words 'All my relations'. All are related to each, and each to all. Participants are conscious that the whole universe is around them, sharing in their need and their prayer.

J. W. E. NEWBERY

CHAPTER 26

Inuit

CASE-STUDY 7

Inuit cultures extend from the Pacific coast of Alaska to the Siberian and Alaskan sides of the Bering Sea, and from there thousands of kilometres north and east along Canada's Arctic coast into Labrador and Greenland. The population of the Inuit people within this vast region is put at around 125,000. Many scholars persist in lumping Inuit peoples under the generic term 'Eskimo', originally a term of ridicule meaning 'eaters of raw flesh'. The word 'inuit', which is used now as a term of self-designation, means 'real people'. The Inuit claim a common ancestry in eastern Siberia and Asia, probably appearing in Alaska little more than 2,400 years ago, and spreading eastward rapidly. The Inuit economy was characterized by the manufacture of harpoons, skin clothing, oil lamps, and skin-covered boats — kayaks or umiaks — the Inuit hunting sea mammals along the coasts and seas, or in inland regions hunting caribou or fishing.

Despite the natural resources available to the Inuit, because of the extreme climate, and in many places the barrenness of the land, a fragile relationship with nature existed. The people depended on their skill and ingenuity in hunting and fishing to ensure adequate supplies of food and materials. This tenuous relationship with the land explains why, in the traditional worldview, life, spirit, or soul — *inua*, or personhood — was attributed to the animals and fish which provided the primary sources for sustenance. Spirits were thought also to inhabit the instruments used in hunting and fishing, and to be connected to the weather, particularly the winds blowing from the cardinal directions, which brought quite distinct climatic conditions.

The shaman, who acted as a mediator between the spirit world and the human community, was the central religious practitioner. Some traditional stories relate that the world was originally thin and permeable, hardening since its creation by the mythic Raven, thus making communication between the human and spirit worlds more difficult. As the earth thickened, the need for shamans to cross the boundaries between the spirit and human worlds became imperative. The role of the shaman was to gather under his control various spirits, which could be utilized to ensure that

Subsistence is our spiritual way of life, our culture.

Old Inuit woman testifying to Canadian Judge Thomas Berger

the needs of the community were met. The shaman would go into a trance in rituals, often leave his body, travel to other worlds in the sky, such as the moon, or beneath the earth, or under the sea, and return having persuaded the spirits of the animals or fish to cooperate during the annual hunting and fishing seasons.

Inuit with sledge dogs in Greenland.

Inuit indigenous religions were suppressed in many parts of the circumpolar region, under the anti-superstition programme of the former Soviet Union, under the direction of government-appointed missionary teachers in Alaska, and since the eighteenth century by Danish missionaries in Greenland. In some places, Inuit culture was virtually eradicated, including language, and of course the practice of shamanism. Today, a revival of Inuit culture is occurring in some areas, with younger people learning the indigenous languages, participating in traditional dances, and affirming cultural values such as honouring elders, fostering a reciprocal relationship with animals, and re-establishing subsistence patterns of life.

JAMES COX

CHAPTER 27

Norse Shamanism

CASE-STUDY 8

Shamanism is a socio-religious system in which a religious functionary called 'shaman' plays a central role. Shamans have ritual mastery over spirits, which are believed to inhabit human beings and nature, and are skilled practitioners of a technique that induces a state of trance in order to create a connection between the human and the non-human worlds. In short, 'shaman' is the name given to the specialist in spirits whose domain of expertise comprises both the visible and the invisible world.

Shamanism is practised in small-scale societies in which hunting and agriculture are dominant forms of subsistence. As a cultural phenomenon, shamanism is most commonly associated with the traditions of the Arctic and Subarctic zones, and of Central and East Asia. In the geographical area of so-called classical shamanism in the Eurasian north, from Greenland to the Bering Straits, in the Arctic and Subarctic zones, the shaman is a person who possesses the necessary technical competence, traditional knowledge, and psychic tendency to go into an ecstatic trance and establish contact with the spirit world, as defined by the particular religion. By falling into a trance, and separating the spirit from the corporeal body, the shaman is believed to cure the sick, escort the souls of the dead to the underworld, foretell the future, and transcend time and space, as well as the boundaries between the living and the non-living, in order to find something lost or to assist hunters in tracking down prey.

In Old Norse, the term *seidr* was used to denote witchcraft. In Norse shamanism, *seidr* can denote both natural rock or stone formations, and man-made wooden columns around which ritual actions are organized. Most *seidr* objects are stone formations, erratic boulders, weathered rocks, or conspicuous, anthropomorphic stones on the banks of a river or a lake. Salient natural features and locations have

> Culture is man's major mode of adaptation at the same time that culture alters, and to a degree provides, the ecological situation to which we adapt; and religion, as a part of culture, is one kind of cultural adaptation, and a rather special one. All the religions, perhaps, began as crisis cults, the response of society to problems the contemporary culture failed to resolve.
>
> Weston LaBarre, *The Ghost Dance: Origins of Religion* (New York: Doubleday, 1970).

been perceived as boundaries, edges, crossroads, openings, and fissures: places where a channel from

The rocky Hvalnes coast, southern Iceland.

this world to the other can be opened up. Places which shamans employ to exit and re-enter the world of ordinary reality are holes and openings in the ground, caves, and fissures between rocks.

Seidr stones contain cracks, hollows, excrescences, and flat 'shelves' caused by weathering. These have functioned as altars, on which reindeer, deer, and fish were sacrificed. Similarly, the indigenous Saami gods were believed to have their abode on the *seidr*. The *seidr* sacrificial sites were closely connected with economies based on reindeer pastoralism, hunting, and fishing. Depending on the specific location in the territory of the individual Saami groups, observances at the *seidr* sites were performed either by several reindeer-herding communities (*sii'dâ*), by members of a family, or by individuals. The motif of the world tree, Yggdrasil, is a salient feature, which is represented in shamanistic practices, not only among the peoples of the North, but also among the ancient Germanic tribes. A mythical world tree was believed by some to support the heavens.

VEIKKO ANTTONEN

INTRODUCTION TO WORLD RELIGIONS

CHAPTER 28

African Indigenous Religions

CASE-STUDY 9

The continent of Africa covers more than 11.5 million square miles/30 million square kilometres and has a population of more than 1000 million. The diversity of religions in such a vast region is immense and extremely complex. Islam has been present in most of North Africa since the seventh and eighth centuries CE and, following the spread of European colonialism in the eighteenth and nineteenth centuries, Christianity has been growing rapidly throughout the sub-Saharan regions. As a result, it is accurate to say that no 'indigenous' religion exists in Africa today, if we mean by the term 'indigenous' that which is original, archaic, or unchanging.

In fact, the religious expressions of African peoples have always been dynamic, changing just as societies have changed, and taking different forms as contact is made with other African peoples, and as economic modes and power structures have evolved. Indigenous, therefore, is not a term referring to some original African religiosity: it designates what we are able to know historically about the religious life and practices of particular African societies prior and subsequent to extensive encounters with Islam and the colonial West, and through a study of those practices which persist among contemporary African peoples. The indigenous religions of Africa thus are known through a wide combination of methodologies, including the study of historic documents, analysis of oral traditions, archaeological evidence, phenomenological classifications, and anthropological fieldwork.

> *The African is notoriously religious.*
>
> J. S. Mbiti, Kenyan theologian

CHARACTERISTICS

Although wide variations exist, most scholars of African indigenous religions identify eight characteristics that practitioners hold in common, particularly those living in the sub-Saharan regions.

- Because African indigenous religions are coextensive with their societies, and based largely on kinship relationships, religion cannot be separated from other cultural practices. Society, in its widest sense, is thought to include not only the living, but what the community understands to be a variety of spiritual forces, foremost among which are the ancestors.

- The impossibility of segregating the religious from the social means that – to outsiders – the visibility of African indigenous religions is low. What people in the West typically regard as secular, such as planting and harvesting crops, is connected closely to religious understandings in Africa.
- The multi-stranded nature of thought that is used to explain the misfortunes, illnesses, and catastrophes which commonly afflict communities can appear unsystematic and unanalytical to an outsider. For example, if the remedy prescribed by a traditional healer or diviner fails, other diviners are consulted, who may offer quite different solutions. Sometimes explanations relate to violations of social norms that occurred long before the present generation was alive, and thus cannot be remembered by the living. These ways of resolving human crises are not thought by the participants to be irrational, since the multi-stranded nature of thought means many apparently contradictory explanations are believed and acted on at the same time.
- Rituals are performed primarily to guarantee tangible benefits in this life only. African indigenous religions are pragmatic, concerning themselves with securing and maintaining largely material advantages, which promote the well-being of the community as a whole. Communication with a variety of spirits in rituals is intended to achieve this end.
- Reciprocity between the community and the spirits defines the primary way that such tangible benefits are acquired and maintained. Generally this means the community must provide gifts to the spirits, usually in the form of sacrificed animals, as a sign of respect and remembrance; in return the spirits provide protection and material gains for the community.
- Beliefs are not articulated, but remain implicit. Hence, there are no doctrines, theologies, claims to truth, or factional disputes between sects. African indigenous religions are non-missionary in their intent.
- African indigenous religions readily adopt ideas, beliefs, and practices from other religions. They have an open mind, importing their deities and rituals readily, and integrating them into their own complex systems.
- African indigenous religions are adaptive: they are able to accommodate to new factors, including modernization. In the modern religious scene in Africa, most believers have expanded their original religious perspectives to include that of an imported religion, usually Christianity or Islam. The widespread popularity of African-founded churches, often referred to as African Independent or African-initiated Churches, confirms the process of adaptation of traditional beliefs and practices to missionary religions.

CONTENT

Although it is possible to outline the substantive features or general content of the religiosity of African peoples, summarized in the following six points, it must be kept in mind that these do not constitute a coherent doctrinal system, or a kind of 'African systematic theology'.

- Reality is regarded as dynamic: centres of power are located in natural phenomena, animals, and humans. Some societies may acknowledge one source of power behind these, but the overriding concern is to ensure that such power enhances the quality of human life, rather than diminishing it. An example of the positive use of power is when ancestors provide ample rain to ensure the abundance of crops and the health of the cattle. Witchcraft is always identified with a power that diminishes the quality of a community's life.
- African indigenous religions can be called a form of humanism, because religious activity focuses on how positive benefits for society can be enhanced. Forces seen as spiritual – whether deities, ancestor spirits, or nature spirits – are understood primarily in connection with their ability to guarantee human well-being.
- This humanism is communal and not individualistic. Fulfilment comes for individuals as they participate in family and community relationships.
- Because religion focuses on communal well-being, Africans are concerned with the present moment and not with a future existence after death. There is no sense of the past moving through the present to some future event; the past and the future find their meaning in the present. Hence, distance from the present is more important than the direction time takes.
- Maintaining good health defines a dominant concern for African societies. When good health fails, methods for healing must be identified and employed. Healing has to do with the preservation and/or restoration of human vitality in the context of the community as a whole. Ultimately, health depends on right human relationships and harmony with the spirit world, particularly the ancestors.
- The fundamental concerns of African societies with health and well-being are expressed primarily through ritual activity. Festivals, feasts, dances, and artistic expressions celebrate communal existence, both of the living and the dead.

Taken together, the characteristics of African indigenous religions and the basic content within the African way of life lead to the following core definition: African indigenous religions are localized, kinship-based, non-missionary religions with inarticulate, multi-stranded, and pragmatic beliefs aimed at securing optimal material health for the community, primarily through ritual activity.

INTERVIEW WITH A DIVINER

This definition is exemplified vividly by an interview the present author conducted in Zimbabwe in 1992 with a traditional healer and diviner, or *n'anga*, a woman of about fifty, who was the chosen medium of the spirit of her deceased father. When the interview began, the *n'anga* was seated outside her hut with her daughter and granddaughter, wearing a simple dress and a sweater. She explained that the people in the region come to her with many different problems, such as sickness, poor crops, death, infertility, and problems at school. She indicated that her deceased father speaks to these people through her, and tells them why they are having problems, and what to do about it. She started doing this about three years earlier, following a long illness no one had been able to cure. During a special ritual prescribed by a *n'anga*, she became possessed by her father, and then recovered completely. Since then, she has helped other people.

The present author's questions seemed to confuse her. When asked how her father takes control of her, she replied simply: 'He does.' Asked if her father – as an ancestor spirit – has special knowledge that he did not have when he was alive, and whether he was in communication with other ancestors, she began to appear uncomfortable, turning away and shaking a little. Further questions followed: 'Does your father carry messages to higher ancestor spirits, even to God? Do any people come to you who are victims of witchcraft?' The woman muttered something to her daughter, let out a very loud belch, and began to shake. Her daughter announced she was now possessed and needed to put on her clothes. They then entered the nearby hut, from which a deep voice could be heard asking, 'Who are these people? Why are they asking my daughter such hard questions?'

The *n'anga* returned from the hut, no longer dressed in simple village attire, but wearing a skirt of animal skins, a hat of eagle feathers, a black cloth over her shoulders and around her waist, and with rattles tied on the side of her legs. She was holding a dark walking stick, about three feet [one metre] in length, with designs on the top. She walked with heavy steps, like a man, and spoke in a deep voice. She was then asked the same questions that had been posed earlier. The reply was, 'These are questions that cannot be answered.' Then a practical problem was raised, and the atmosphere suddenly became quite relaxed. The present writer indicated he had lost his wallet somewhere in his travels around the region. He asked if the woman, now possessed and acting as the medium for her father's spirit, could help retrieve it.

What followed was a dramatic presentation and explanation. The medium said that, on the way to the Chief's home, at a local shop, someone in the crowd spotted the wallet and said to himself, 'Ah, *murungu* (white person)! I will be rich.' He slipped the wallet out of the back pocket and left the shop. When he looked in the wallet, however, he was disappointed, because there was very little money in it. He threw it in some red soil beside the road. Another person came along and spotted it. He also thought, 'Ah, I will be rich!' When he found no money in it, he threw it back into the red soil. That is what happened, said the spirit medium, and the wallet will never be found. During the whole time she was telling this story, she was acting it out. She showed how the man had slipped the wallet out of the back pocket, how he hurriedly left the shop, how he opened it, and expressed disappointment before throwing it by the road. When the medium finished, she sat down again, with her legs crossed like a man. She then stood up and announced: 'I am returning to a mountain near Great Zimbabwe.' At that, the woman re-entered the hut, appearing shortly after in her simple dress and sweater. When asked if she remembered being possessed by her father, she said she did not remember anything.

For the spirit medium, the possession had nothing to do with revealing knowledge of the other world, nor with constructing a systematic diagram of the relationships between ancestor spirits. Its purpose was entirely practical, to alter the enquirer's experience, if possible, in favour of health and well-being. This does not mean her reactions to the analytical questions posed were simplistic; indeed, she illustrated the type of rationality characteristic of the indigenous religions of Zimbabwe. Her responses were pragmatic, concerned with the present – never speculative in a cosmological sense – and employed the spirit world only to influence experience in the here-and-now material existence.

CONCLUSION

If the definition of African indigenous religions presented and exemplified in this article accurately captures their essence, we would expect to detect these emphases, to a lesser or greater extent, in all forms of African religions, including Christianity and Islam. By identifying these central characteristics and core elements, therefore, the student of religions in Africa is provided with key concepts for analysing the multiple, complex, and often bewildering expressions of religion found throughout this immense and culturally diverse continent.

JAMES COX

CHAPTER 29

The Bangwa

CASE-STUDY 10

The Bangwa of Lebialem Division, South-West Province, Cameroon, occupy a mountainous region that stretches from the grassfield plateau of Eastern and North-West Provinces to the Cross-River Basin in the south-west. An entrepreneurial people, with origins in both the lowland forest zone and the grassfields, they have linguistic, cultural, and historical links with surrounding groups. The Bangwa are traders as well as farmers and hunters. European contact was first made at the beginning of the twentieth century, and there has been a permanent mission presence in Lebang (Fontem), the largest of the Bangwa villages, since the mid-1960s.

Traditional religious practices focus on *belem* (singular, *ndem*), translated as both 'gods' and 'ancestors'. There is a hierarchy of sacred places, '*fuandem*', such as waterfalls or other natural features, where a chief or sub-chief makes offerings for the fertility and well-being of the land. Most people live in scattered compounds – extended family homes – the larger of which will have a 'house', or *ndia ndem*, for the household or threshold god or gods, *ndem bo*, at which a compound head can make offerings of food and drink on behalf of his family. Ancestral skulls are exhumed and kept by a man's successor and, less formally, women's skulls might pass to women. They are kept in a special house in the compound, and are 'fed' and consulted about important decisions, using various forms of divination.

The Nweh language makes no distinction between witches, sorcerers, animals, and spirits (*lekang*). Everyone has a witch animal or spirit in the stomach that remains dormant unless sent out either consciously or unconsciously. Chiefs and other powerful individuals can use their ability to transform themselves into wild animals through witchcraft to confront their enemies or fight other witches.

Around 10 per cent of the population of Lebialem are baptized Christians, mostly Roman Catholics. Many Bangwa now live outside their home area, in the larger towns of Cameroon, in Europe, and in the USA, most regarding themselves as Christian. The first-generation emigrants retain strong emotional and kinship links with their home villages, and value their language and culture. Both Christians and non-Christians take the performance of traditional ceremonies, such as the wake, or 'cry die', very seriously,

and will try to travel back to their natal or parental villages for a funeral celebration. Polygyny remains common and, in terms of church membership, problematic. Because of their marital status, many fervent Christians cannot be baptized, or are excommunicants, while the widespread baptism of children in mission schools produces what are disparagingly referred to as 'baptized pagans'. What we see with the Bangwa is a people bringing their traditional worldview into their Christian practice, and vice versa, in a dynamic and creative process of transformation.

FIONA BOWIE

Ancient Bangwa shamanistic sculpture from Cameroon.

CHAPTER 30

The Zulu

CASE-STUDY 11

Recent studies on African traditional beliefs have shown convincingly that African ideas and religious convictions are not primitive in an evolutionistic sense. Nor are they 'backward' and without sense. Thoughts and beliefs, expressed in rituals and in life-attitudes, make sense and are fully logical, if they are seen from the angle of those who live these thought-patterns.

Zulu, who live on the east coast of South Africa, and belong to the Nguni family of Bantu-speaking people, are a good illustration of how an African traditional religion can adapt and accommodate itself to new ideas and symbols.

> A man may suffer from his mother's discipline, but a Zulu son would never accuse his mother of bewitching him. And although some modern Zulu men have accused their fathers of witchcraft, this is regarded as a sign of the degeneration of modern times.
>
> Geoffrey Parrinder

THE LORD-OF-THE-SKY

Early literature on Zulu religious ideas, dating back some 100 years, seems to indicate that Zulu of that time hardly entertained thoughts of a god in the sky; the preoccupation was with the shades. Due chiefly to the presence of, and challenge by, Christian missions, there has developed among traditional Zulu an idea of the Lord-of-the-Sky, *iNkosi yezulu*.

This Lord is believed to be the eternal from whom flows power and might. The Lord-of-the-Sky is the source of both good and evil, is both kind and generous, but also erratic and unpredictable. In times of crisis, such as drought or childlessness, Zulus turn to him; but he also sends lightning that will strike 'the one he wants to be his slave up there in heaven'. He will cause barrenness 'because the woman has irritated him, sometimes by talking too much, sometimes because the Lord-of-the-Sky is fretful'.

The chameleon is linked with the Lord-of-the-Sky; it too is unpredictable. It continually changes colour. It has five legs — the tail is said to be a leg because it coils around branches — and has eyes that look in different directions at the same time! 'How

could such a thing as a chameleon be created? There can be no sympathy with the one that made such a creature as this.'

A traditional healer, or Sangoma priest, in Mantegna, Swaziland, Africa, who uses animal bones and skins and summons spirits.

Although the Lord-of-the-Sky can be approached, he must be avoided, lest you become insane. Only on special occasions should he be approached, and then only after long preparation. Certain well-known hills in Zululand are recognized as his. On these no cattle graze, and people rarely ascend them.

> *Only when we plead for rain will we go up this mountain. First there must be fasting and much prayer. When everybody is ready and the set day arrives, we gather at the foot of the hill. Everybody is quiet. We climb with awe, looking down and walking humbly. Then prayer is offered by the rain-doctor. We kneel or lie down when he speaks to the Lord-of-the-Sky. When he has finished we return, without speaking. We do not talk, for the one in whose presence we are is fearful.*

THE BROODING SHADES

In the lives of the Zulu people, the shades play an all-important role. But in times of crisis, the shades brood over their descendants 'as a hen broods over her chickens'. The chief occasions are childbirth, puberty, marriage, death, and burial. Diviners are constantly brooded over by the shades, but because they 'eat the right medicines, they do not become mad. All other people would have gone mad long ago, if they had been in the same situation.'

When a hen broods over her eggs, the chickens eventually hatch. Likewise the brooding of the shades heralds the emergence of a different person.

> *It is like this. There is the bride. She is one kind of person. At marriage, when*
> *the shades brood, she becomes another person. She is now the wife. When they*
> *brood again, she changes from the childless to the mother of a child.*

Zulu diviners claim they see things upside down. Shades are believed to be pale-coloured; in the world of the shades, dark stands for light and light for dark. Shades are said to like gall 'because gall to them is sweet as honey'. People work during daytime, the shades are active at night. The right hand is left, and the left is right, in the world of the shades. So diviners, servants of the shades, often use the left hand when divining. Up stands for down and down for up.

These reversals and opposites make sense in the context of a flat earth viewpoint — the global concept is, after all, relatively recent, even in Europe. If Zululanders believe we live on top of a pancake-like world, it follows that those who live on the other side are opposite. On top, people walk with their heads upward and feet downward; in the underworld they move upside down. When it is night on top, it is daytime underneath. Hence people were buried at night, not to avoid the grave-site being known to thieves and evil-minded people, but so that the deceased can reach the land of the dead 'at a time when he can see in this new country'.

AXEL-IVAR BERGLUND

QUESTIONS

1. Why is interpreting indigenous religions as 'primitive religions' from which 'more advanced' examples later emerge so problematic?

2. Why is the concept of respect so pervasive in indigenous religions?

3. Why do so many indigenous religions regard witchcraft and sorcery as problematic?

4. Why might it be more appropriate to refer to 'beliefs' rather than 'religion' when considering indigenous traditions?

5. Explain why land is so important to Australian aborigines.

6. Explain and compare the role of shamanism in two different indigenous traditions.

7. Why do African religions often lack a distinction between the sacred and the secular?

8. Explain the relationship of the religion of the Bangwa with Christianity.

9. Compare and contrast the beliefs of three indigenous religions.

10. Why is the pairing of opposites in nature so important to native North Americans?

FURTHER READING

Burridge, Kenelm, *New Heaven, New Earth: A Study of Millenarian Activities*. Oxford: Basil Blackwell, 1986.

Durkheim, E., *The Elementary Forms of the Religious Life*. New York: Free Press, 1965 (1915).

Evans-Pritchard, E. E., *Nuer Religion*. London: Oxford University Press, 1956.

Harvey, Graham, *Shamanism: A Reader*. New York: Routledge, 2002.

Herdt, Gilbert H., ed., *Rituals of Manhood: Male Initiation in Papua New Guinea*. Berkeley: University of California Press, 1982.

Martin, Joel W., *The Land Looks After Us: A History of Native American Religion*. New York: Oxford University Press, 2001.

Ray, Benjamin, *African Religions*, 2nd ed. Englewood Cliffs, NJ: Prentice-Hall, 1999.

Turner, Victor, *The Ritual Process*. Ithaca: Cornell University Press, 1969.

PART 4
HINDUISM

SUMMARY

The religion today known as Hinduism may be almost as old as Indian civilization itself: archaeological evidence suggests continuities between the religion of the Indus Valley society of 2500–1500 BCE and the Hinduism of today. The Vedic texts, from the period that followed, provide the basis for some of the central themes of Hindu belief, including *samsara*, the doctrine that all creatures are reborn repeatedly unless the cycle can be broken through liberation (*moksha*), and *karma*, the notion that actions in one life are rewarded or punished in the next. The Vedic religion was hierarchical, and centred around sacrificial offerings. In time, sacrifice was largely replaced by *puja*, the personal devotion of an individual to a particular deity.

Hinduism has a vast body of sacred texts, from the early Vedas onward, and generally is divided into the more authoritative *Sruti* – revealed scripture – and the less authoritative *Smriti* – which includes Epics such as the *Mahabharata* (including the *Bhagavad Gita*) and the *Ramayana*. A hierarchy of sorts also exists amongst the many gods of India, with Vishnu and Shiva enjoying a privileged position – although there is no consensus as to whether there are in fact many gods, or whether the many are merely different representations of the one God, *Brahman*.

Today, like so many religions, Hinduism has a following throughout the world, largely because of the many Indian diaspora communities. Despite this, the subcontinent remains hugely important for Hindus, in part because of the value placed on the many sacred sites in the country, such as the River Ganges, and in part because of the strong ties that bind the wider community. Within India itself – now a secular democracy – there exists something of a division between those at ease with recent developments, such as secularization and the changing role of women, and the emergent Hindu nationalists – often deeply hostile to other religions in the region, particularly Islam – who seek a stronger role for religion in public life.

CHAPTER 31

A Historical Overview

The term 'Hinduism' as we understand it today refers to the majority religion of the Indian subcontinent. The present understanding of Hinduism as a 'world religion' has come about only since the nineteenth century, when Hindu reformers and Western orientalists came to refer to the diverse beliefs and practices characterizing religious life in South Asia as 'Hinduism'. Yet this classification is problematic, as Hinduism possesses many features characteristic of 'indigenous religions': it has no single historical founder, no central revelation, no creed or unified system of belief, no single doctrine of salvation, and no centralized authority. In this sense, it is different from other 'world religions'. Huge diversity and variety of religious movements, systems, beliefs, and practices are all characteristic features of 'Hinduism'. Also, there is no clear division between the 'sacred' and 'profane' – or natural and supernatural: religion and social life are inseparable and intertwined. Nevertheless, most scholars would agree there are unifying strands that run through the diverse traditions that constitute it. Although the term Hinduism is recent, the diverse traditions that it encompasses have very ancient origins that extend back beyond the second millennium BCE.

> *Hinduism is a living organism liable to growth and decay and subject to the laws of nature. One and indivisible at the root, it has grown into a vast tree with innumerable branches.*
>
> Mahatma Gandhi, *Hindu Dharma* (New Delhi: Orient Paperbacks, 1987).

THE INDUS VALLEY CIVILIZATION

The earliest traces of Hinduism can be found in the Indus Valley civilization which flourished from 2500 to about 1500 BCE along the banks of the River Indus, which flows through present-day Pakistan. Archaeological excavations in this area have revealed evidence of what appears to be a highly developed urban culture with sophisticated water distribution, drainage and garbage disposal technologies and well-developed systems of farming, grain-storage and pottery. Little is known about the religion of this civilization. The large number of terracotta figurines unearthed through excavations suggest a continuity between the iconographic features of these images and those of such later Hindu deities as Shiva and the mother goddess. Given the lack of systematic evidence for such continuity, however,

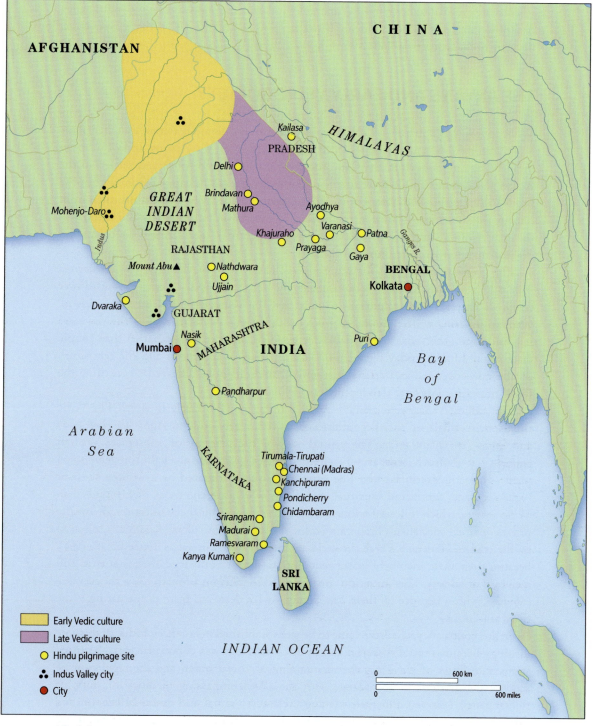

Hinduism

CHINA

AFGHANISTAN

HIMALAYAS

Kailasa

PRADESH

Delhi

GREAT
INDIAN
DESERT

Brindavan
Mathura

Ayodhya

Varanasi
Patna

Khajuraho

Prayaga

Gaya

Mohenjo-Daro

Indus

RAJASTHAN

Mount Abu ▲

Nathdwara

Ujjain

BENGAL

Kolkata

Dvaraka

GUJARAT

Nasik

MAHARASHTRA

INDIA

Puri

Mumbai

Ganges R.

Pandharpur

*Bay
of
Bengal*

*Arabian
Sea*

KARNATAKA

Tirumala-Tirupati
Chennai (Madras)
Kanchipuram
Pondicherry
Chidambaram

Srirangam
Madurai
Ramesvaram
Kanya Kumari

**SRI
LANKA**

INDIAN OCEAN

Early Vedic culture
Late Vedic culture
Hindu pilgrimage site
Indus Valley city
City

0   600 km

0   600 miles

scholars are inclined to be cautious. Archaeological evidence suggests that the Indus Valley civilization declined rather suddenly between 1800 and 1700 BCE, perhaps because of flooding or inadequate rainfall.

THE ARYANS AND EARLY VEDIC SOCIETY

What followed is a matter of considerable controversy. Some maintain that the Indus Valley civilization came to be replaced by the culture of the Aryans, Indo-European invaders, or migrants from the Caucasus region, who moved south and settled in the Indian subcontinent. Others believe the Aryan civilization developed from within the Indus Valley culture and was not introduced from outside. Whether Aryans came from outside the subcontinent or not, the history of Hinduism as we understand it today is the history of the next 2000 years of Aryan culture, often interacting with, but always dominating, non-Aryan cultures in the area.

The language of the Aryans was Sanskrit. Knowledge of the early Aryans derives primarily from early Sanskrit compositions, the Vedas, a corpus of texts compiled over hundreds of years. It is important to note that the Vedas were oral for thousands of years before being written down. In South India, the oral performances of the Vedas are still important; the Vedas are articulated, embodied, and performed, rather than simply read. Many Hindus today regard the Vedas as timeless revelation and the repository of all knowledge, and as a crucial marker of Hindu identity. The Vedas constitute the foundation for most later developments in Hinduism.

The earliest Vedas were mainly liturgical texts, used primarily in ritual. The Vedic rituals were rituals of sacrifice, addressed to such early gods as Agni (the fire god) and Soma (the plant god). The central act was the offering of substances – often animals, but also such items as milk, clarified butter, grain, and the hallucinogenic soma plant – into the sacrificial fire. The ritual was usually initiated by a wealthy sponsor (*yajamana*), and conducted by ritual specialists, who were the most highly ranked in Vedic society, which followed a fourfold system of hierarchical classification. Below the priests or ritual specialists (Brahmans) came the warriors or rulers (*Kshatriyas*), followed by the traders (*Vaishyas*). These three classes (*varna*) were known as 'twice-born' (*dvija*), because their male members underwent initiation that confirmed their status as full members of society. This initiation rite separated them from a fourth class, the servants (*Shudras*), who – because of their 'low' status – were debarred from perpetuating Vedic ritual traditions.

In due course, Aryan culture came to be well established in northern India. Brahmanic ideology became central to social and political life, and was concerned with the ritual status and duties of the king, the maintaining of social order, and the regulation of individual behaviour in accordance with the all-encompassing ideology of duty, or righteousness (*dharma*). Dharmic ideology related to ritual and moral behaviour, and defined good conduct according to such factors as one's class (*varna*) and one's stage of life (*ashrama*). It operated simultaneously at several levels: the transcendental, and therefore eternal (*sanatana dharma*), the everyday (*sadharana dharma*), and the individual and personal (*svadharma*). Neglecting *dharma* was believed to lead to undesirable social, as well as personal, consequences.

THE LATER VEDIC PERIOD

Alongside the performance of Vedic ritual, speculation arose about its meaning and purpose. These speculations were developed in the later Vedic texts – the *Aranyakas* and *Upanishads* – which tended to see the observance of ritual action as secondary to the gaining of spiritual knowledge. Central to this approach was the *karma-samsara-moksha* doctrine:
• all beings are reincarnated into the world (*samsara*) over and over again;
• the results of action (*karma*) are reaped in future lives;
• this process of endless rebirth is characterized by suffering (*dukkha*);
• liberation (*moksha*) from this suffering can be obtained by gaining spiritual knowledge.

Gaining spiritual knowledge thus came to assume central importance, and the self-disciplining and methods of asceticism necessary for gaining it were developed in Hinduism's traditions of yoga and world renunciation. Ascetic groups known as strivers (*sramanas*) were formed during this period, seeking liberation through austerity. Buddhism and Jainism, both of which rejected the authority of the Vedas, originated in these groups. Whereas monastic institutions developed in Buddhism from its inception, similar institutions appeared within the Hindu pale only later, possibly in the eighth and ninth centuries CE, when – according to Hindu belief – the theologian Shankara (c. 788–820 CE) founded monastic centres in the four corners of India, and instituted the first renunciatory order of the Dasanamis.

Alongside early Hinduism's elaboration of systems of ritual, and its teachings about liberation/salvation involving yoga and meditation, there developed highly sophisticated philosophical systems, the *darshanas*, comprising mainly Samkhya and Yoga, Mimamsa and Vedanta, and Nyaya and Vaisheshika. These in turn generated a multitude of metaphysical positions, and traditions of rigorous philosophical debate, within the parameters of Vedic revelation and the doctrine of liberation. One of the most important of these Indian philosophical traditions today is the philosophy of non-dualism (*advaita vedanta*), propounded by Shankara, the most famous of Indian philosopher-theologians.

SECTARIAN WORSHIP

Through much of the first millennium CE, sectarian worship of particular deities grew and flourished in India. Vedic sacrifice came to be increasingly marginalized, giving way – though never disappearing completely – to devotional worship or *puja*. *Puja* is a ritual expression of love or devotion (*bhakti*) to a deity, often a personal god or goddess, with whom the devotee establishes an intense and intimate relationship. Corresponding to the growth of Hindu theism and devotionalism, Sanskrit narrative traditions grew and flourished, the most important of which were the Hindu epics or *itihasas* – the *Ramayana* and the *Mahabharata* – the Puranas – devotional texts containing, among other things, mythological stories about the gods and goddesses, and treatises on ritual worship – and devotional poetry in several Indian regional languages, most notably Tamil. One of the most important developments at this time was the composition of the *Bhagavad Gita*, the 'Song of the Lord', contained in the *Mahabharata*. This work, perhaps the most famous of the Hindu scriptures, expresses in narrative form the concerns of Hinduism: the importance of *dharma*, responsible action, and the maintenance of social order and stability, combined with the importance of devotion to the transcendent as a personal god.

Temple cities grew and flourished in this period, serving not only as commercial and administrative hubs of kingdoms, but as ritual centres, with the temple located at the heart of the town and, therefore, of the kingdom. Kings sought to derive legitimacy for their rule through their royal patronage of these ritual sites, dedicated to one or the other of the major Puranic deities. Large temple complexes stood testimony to a king's dharmic rule over his kingdom, which was often modelled on the ideal of divine kingship symbolized by the great god Vishnu. Sectarian devotional groups emerged, dedicated to the worship of Vishnu (*Vaishnavas*), Shiva (*Shaivas*), and the goddess Devi (*Shaktas*).

HINDUISM DURING BRITISH COLONIAL RULE

These theistic traditions continued to flourish, to lesser or greater degrees, through much of the following period, when large sections of the Indian subcontinent were conquered and ruled by Muslim rulers. The rule of the last Muslim emperor in India came to an end in the eighteenth century, and British forces, initially in the form of the East India Company, and later the British crown, stepped in to assume power. By the middle of the eighteenth century, British power was at its peak. Hindu traditions, which had tended to be relatively insular in the intervening period, now responded actively to the British and, more importantly, Christian presence in their midst. Hindu reform movements arose, led by such figures as Ram Mohan Roy (1772–1883), Dayananda Sarasvati (1824–83), and Vivekananda (1863–1902), all seeking to restore the perceived glory of Hinduism's ancient past. It was at this time that Hinduism came to be defined in the terms by which we understand it today – a world religion, with a distinct identity. These reform movements, often collectively referred to as the Hindu renaissance, absorbed Christianity's rationalist elements, and paid particular attention to social and ethical concerns. Most of these movements were closely linked with the increasingly vocal Indian nationalist movement, which brought about the end of British colonial rule, and established India as an independent nation state in 1947.

RELIGIOUS NATIONALISM IN CONTEMPORARY INDIA

Though India defined itself as a secular state on gaining independence, it has experienced a resurgence of religious nationalism, particularly since the 1980s, expressed in *Hindutva* ('Hinduness'), the ideology of Hindu nationalists who call for a state in which civic rights, nationhood, and national culture would be defined by Hinduism. Their politicized, activist religious nationalism has precedents in various movements of organized Hinduism that arose in British India. Today the Sangh Parivar, a 'family' of social and political organizations, works to propagate *Hindutva*, with its political wing, the Bharatiya Janata Party (BJP, 'Indian People's Party'), winning enough support to head a coalition government between 1998 and 2004.

A significant act of religious violence in recent times was the destruction of the Mughal Babri mosque in Ayodhya in 1992, by supporters of *Hindutva* demanding the setting up of a temple dedicated to the Hindu deity Rama at the site, which they believe to be Rama's birthplace. Several violent incidents between Hindus and Muslims have been precipitated by this temple/mosque controversy.

BEYOND INDIA'S FRONTIERS

Yet many Hindus are not greatly concerned, as 'Hindu-ness' is not something they explicitly think about. Running counter to these chauvinist and violently exclusivist forms of Hinduism, other forms of Hindu belief and practice adopt a more inclusive, universal orientation, emphasizing values such as social justice, peace, and the spiritual transformation of humanity – though Hinduism has in fact always been inclusive, encompassing many traditions and practices. Some recent manifestations of Hinduism, especially in the form of Indian gurus addressing Western and/or multicultural audiences, have transcended nationalistic boundaries in their teaching and philosophy.

Hinduism has also transcended national boundaries in another sense. While Hinduism has long flourished beyond the Indian subcontinent, in places such as Java and Bali, in the twentieth century the Hindu diaspora spread markedly, establishing communities in host cultures across the globe. This geographical transcendence of boundaries does not always parallel ideological dispositions and orientations, however. Religious nationalism often strikes deep roots in diaspora communities, such that India as a geographical entity comes to be perceived, in the imagination of Hindus abroad, as their sacred, or holy, land, which they identify with conceptions of a Hindu religious polity, and therefore a Hindu nation state.

MAYA WARRIER

HINDUISM TIMELINE

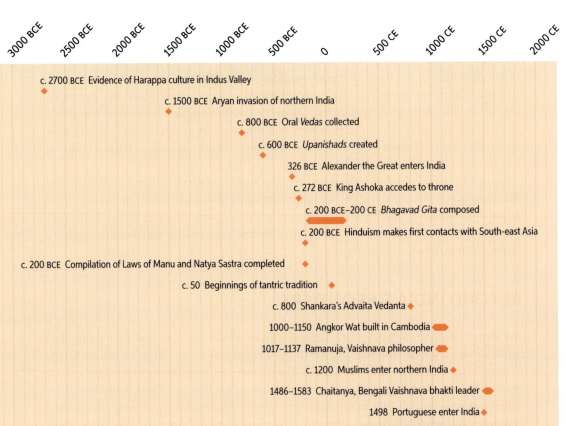

3000 BCE — 2500 BCE — 2000 BCE — 1500 BCE — 1000 BCE — 500 BCE — 0 — 500 CE — 1000 CE — 1500 CE — 2000 CE

c. 2700 BCE Evidence of Harappa culture in Indus Valley

c. 1500 BCE Aryan invasion of northern India

c. 800 BCE Oral *Vedas* collected

c. 600 BCE *Upanishads* created

326 BCE Alexander the Great enters India

c. 272 BCE King Ashoka accedes to throne

c. 200 BCE–200 CE *Bhagavad Gita* composed

c. 200 BCE Hinduism makes first contacts with South-east Asia

c. 200 BCE Compilation of Laws of Manu and Natya Sastra completed

c. 50 Beginnings of tantric tradition

c. 800 Shankara's Advaita Vedanta

1000–1150 Angkor Wat built in Cambodia

1017–1137 Ramanuja, Vaishnava philosopher

c. 1200 Muslims enter northern India

1486–1583 Chaitanya, Bengali Vaishnava bhakti leader

1498 Portuguese enter India

1757 British rule established in Calcutta

1828 Ram Mohan Roy founds Brahmo Samaj

1836–86 Ramakrishna Paramahamsa

1875 Dayanand Sarasvati founds Arya Samaj

1893 Vivekananda at World's Parliament of Religions, Chicago

1926–2011 Satya Sai Baba

1948 Mahatma Gandhi assassinated

1998 Hindu nationalist party BJP wins Indian national election

CHAPTER 32

Philosophy

Hindu philosophy, the oldest continuing tradition of Indian thought, stretches back to sacred texts written between 900 and 400 BCE known as the *Upanishads* — literally 'to sit beneath', as at the feet of a teacher. These texts are reflections on the deeper meaning of the rites, hymns, and ritual prescriptions found in earlier Vedic writings. However, they were soon regarded as a genre of Vedic literature in their own right, and it is here that we first encounter a developed theory of *karma* (action, making; law of cause and effect) and *moksha* (liberation from the cycle of rebirth).

THE *ASTIKA* SCHOOLS

Hindu philosophy developed through debate between schools of Hindu thought and, importantly, with Jain, Carvaka (materialist), and Buddhist thinkers. During the classical period of Hindu philosophy (100 BCE to 1000 CE) the six *astika* schools ('orthodox', in accepting Vedic authority) condensed and cemented their distinctive views. These are usually paired:

- *Purva-mimamsa* — Vedanta
- *Samkhya* — Yoga
- *Nyaya* — *Vaisheshika*

It should be noted that these pairings bring together a larger number of schools, and are less to do with Indian philosophical schools themselves, and more the result of the way Indian thought has been studied in the West since the nineteenth century.

> *The wise call him a man of learning whose every activity is free from desire and specific intention; his actions are consumed in the fire of knowledge.*
>
> Bhagavad Gita 4:19

While it greatly oversimplifies historical Indian thought to impute consensus, it is useful to isolate a few central notions that serve as building blocks for the six 'orthodox' philosophical perspectives (*darshanas*) above. A key philosophical question in Indian thought, addressing, among other issues, being (ontology), knowledge (epistemology), morality (ethics), God (theology), and even beauty (aesthetics), is 'Who are we?' To understand the various responses, we need to consider three central presuppositions of Hindu thought:

- the cyclical nature of time
- an essential connection between microcosmic and macrocosmic levels of reality
- a principle of causality

In Hindu philosophy the universe has neither beginning nor end. It issued forth from *Brahman* (the ultimate, divine 'ground of Being'), and will eventually return to *Brahman*, only to repeat the cycle again. If time itself revolves in an endless cycle, then all of creation also exists in a cyclical way. So life is followed by death, giving rise to a new life, and so on. This cycle of birth and rebirth (*samsara*) is deducible from any observation of the natural world, and is an example of how events at the microcosmic level of individual lives, seasons, and generations are seen to be intimately connected to the macrocosmic level of the great ages of history (*yugas*), the cosmic creations and dissolutions, and indeed time itself. Furthermore, the causal principle of *karma* connects each event in *samsara*, so that events in this cycle affect events in subsequent cycles, just as they themselves are already affected by events in previous cycles. Time, causality, and the micro- macrocosm are linked: what one does, and how one chooses, has a necessary — if miniscule — effect on the entire universe.

DHARMA AND MOKSHA

The three presuppositions inform two other primary concepts: *dharma* and *moksha*.
- *Dharma* ('to uphold') is understood to be the moral and metaphysical foundation of the universe. Acting in accordance with one's *dharma*, which is not always easy to determine, connects one's activities and life to one's social structure and environment. Fulfilling one's dharmic duties is necessary, but not sufficient, for *moksha*.
- To attain *moksha* — ultimate liberation, the goal of human existence — is to attain complete freedom from the samsaric cycle of birth and rebirth, and all the dissatisfaction, suffering, and death — as well as the joys and pleasures — which go with it.

The *Samkhya*–Yoga school sees *moksha* as one's return, through yogic discipline, to an original, blissful state of pure spirit (*purusha*), separated from matter (*prakriti*). For the *Nyaya*–Vaisheshika school, more interested in logical reasoning and the right understanding of reality, *moksha* is gained through right understanding of the universe, and of one's real nature as a simple collection of material and non-material qualities: it means returning to an undifferentiated state of being, free from change and suffering — a vision harshly criticized by the *Mimamsa*–Vedanta school, which compared it to the existence of a stone. This last school saw *moksha* as the fulfilment of one's dharmic duty, resulting in the cessation of rebirth, and the realization of one's true relationship with *Brahman*.

VEDANTA

Only Vedanta now commands a large following. Of the dozen or so Vedantic schools, three are of particular interest:
- *Advaita* (non-dualism)
- *Vishishtadvaita* (non-dualism of particulars)
- *Dvaita* (dualism)

The great Hindu philosopher-saint Shankara (c. 788–820 CE) expounded an austerely non-dualistic (*advaita*) system. In his short life, he established monasteries in the four corners of India, and a monastic order of ten divisions, and was held by some of his followers to be an incarnation of the Hindu deity Shiva. He has had inordinate influence on modern Hinduism, through such Neo-Vedantic exponents as Dayananda Sarasvati (1824–83), Swami Vivekananda (1863–1902), and even Gandhi (1869–1948). *Advaita* holds that one's true self (*atman*) is literally identical to *Brahman*. Whereas Judaism, Christianity, and Islam are dualistic, maintaining a strong distinction between God and the human soul, between God and the world, and between the individual and the world, for Shankara's *advaita Vedanta*, all is one, and any perceived dualism is the result of ignorance. We are working within an illusory interpretation (*maya*) of the world, but through the hearing and study of the Vedas — particularly the *Upanishads*, the *Bhagavad Gita*, and the *Brahmasutras* — we can come to a correct and liberating knowledge of the world and of our own true nature as identical with *Brahman*.

Ramanuja (1077–1157) is often compared with Thomas Aquinas (1225–74), such was the depth and subtlety of their respective systems. Ramanuja revered the South Indian poet/saint traditions of the Alvars, and proposed that, although

Mahatma Gandhi, Indian nationalist leader and proponent of non-violent civil disobedience, outside 10 Downing Street, London.

identical to *Brahman*, the individual *atman* retains its particular qualities, just as a unified body retains its particular parts (*Vishishtadvaita*). He recognized that simultaneous unity and difference (*bheda-abheda*) is essential in a monotheistic tradition which claims ultimate unity between God and the devotee, but also values devotional love towards God.

Madhva (c. 1197–1276) wrote commentaries on a number of sacred texts, and established a new, dualistic interpretation of Vedanta. The *dvaita vedanta* school maintains that the perfect *Brahman* could not be identical to the imperfect, created *atman*: there must be a fundamental distinction between the individual self and God. One can only talk of such identity in the way one talks of the relationship between a devoted lover and his or her beloved. A Vaishnavite, Madhva took both the evidence of our senses and the reality of difference seriously. Any view which claimed real unity with the divine threatened the transcendence of God, and undervalued our own experience.

There was – and remains – lively debate. The question of who we ultimately are provided for Hindu philosophers a gateway into profound discussions of the nature of reality, knowledge, truth, and goodness which continue to guide and instruct today.

TINU RUPARELL

CHAPTER 33

Sacred Writings

Hindu scriptures comprise a vast corpus of literature, dating from 1300 BCE to modern times. Most of the scriptures are in Sanskrit – a word meaning 'refined' – a classical Indian language now used only by scholars and for ritual purposes. There is also a considerable amount of religious literature in regional Indian languages, and variants of the original texts, which emphasize a particular aspect of Hindu belief. For example, the *Adhyatma Ramayana* is a version of the popular epic *Ramayana* that stresses devotion (*bhakti*). What follows does not exhaust the many diverse categories of Hindu sacred writings, but outlines the major elements of a vast array of texts, dealing with various aspects of belief, ritual, and tradition in Hindu society.

Hindus generally divide their scriptures into two categories: heard or revealed (*Sruti*) and remembered (*Smriti*). *Sruti* scriptures are believed to be communicated directly by God to ancient Indian sages; *Smriti* scriptures are less authoritative, and consist of texts such as the Hindu epics –the *Ramayana*, and the *Mahabharata*; the *Dharma Sutras* – books of law, concerned with customs and correct conduct – and *Puranas* – mythology.

THE VEDAS

The Hindu canon is usually termed Veda, from the root *vid*, meaning 'knowledge'. The Vedas comprise four main types: The Vedic *Samhitas*, *Brahmanas*, *Aranyakas*, and *Upanishads*.

1. The Vedic *Samhitas*, classified as the *Rig, Sama, Yajur* and *Atharva* Vedas, are the earliest known Hindu religious literature (1300–200 BCE), consisting mainly of praises to various deities of ancient Hinduism, led by Indra, king of the gods.

2. The *Brahmanas* stipulate the details of, and explain the significance of, rituals (*yaga* or *yajna*), especially the fire ritual, in which oblations were poured out, or cast into fire, to be conveyed to the gods. The prominence of Agni, the god of fire, and of the Brahman priest in these texts indicates the growing importance and complexity of the fire ritual in early Indian religion.

3. The *Aranyakas* ('forest books') provide analysis and interpretation of the fire ritual, whereby a correspondence is drawn between the ritual and the cosmos. The ritual, moreover, is understood to have an intrinsic power, by which the gods are to some extent bypassed. Indeed, the *Aranyakas* also represent a transition from the

ritualistic *Brahmanas* to the far more contemplative and philosophical themes of the *Upanishads*, tending to move away from the polytheism of the *Samhitas* towards a more philosophical, monistic, or pantheistic understanding of reality, in which despite appearances all is one. Hence, the *Aranyakas* and the *Upanishads* mark a growing resistance to the ritualism of the fire sacrifice, and a preference for more contemplative and spiritual forms of worship.

4. The *Upanishads* (*upa* = alongside, *nishad* = set) are commentaries and elaborations of the ideas encountered in the Vedic *Samhitas* and *Brahmanas*. Four major themes can be identified: internal sacrifice, the idea of the *atman* (similar to 'soul' or 'self'), *Brahman* (non-personal divine being), and monistic theology, which equates the *atman*, and indeed the whole cosmos, with *Brahman* – everything is *Brahman*. The previous emphasis on the importance and intricacy of the fire ritual is overshadowed by an emphasis on personal spiritual development. In religious terminology, *tapas* or *pranagnihotra* – sometimes described as the oblation of one's body in the fire of one's breath – is shown as much more efficacious and powerful than the external *yajna*. The *atman-Brahman* identification has tremendous implications for the Hindu's understanding of the nature of God, the cosmos, and the liberation – or 'salvation' – of the individual.

> *Then was not non-existence nor existence: there was no realm of air, no sky beyond it. What stirred, and where? What gave shelter? Was water there, unfathomed depth of water?*
>
> *Death was not then, nor was there anything immortal: no sign was there of the day's and night's divider. That One, breathless, breathed by its own nature: apart from it was nothing whatsoever.*
>
> *Darkness there was: at first concealed in darkness this. All was indiscriminate chaos. All that existed then was void and formless: by the great power of heat was born that One.*
>
> *Thereafter rose Desire in the beginning, Desire, the primal seed and germ of Spirit. Sages who searched with their heart's thought discovered the bond of existence in the non-existent . . .*
>
> *Who truly knows and who can here declare it, whence it was born and whence comes this creation? The gods came later than this world's creation. Who knows then whence it first came into being?*
>
> *He, the first origin of this creation, whether he formed it all or did not form it, Whose eye controls this world in highest heaven, he verily knows it, or perhaps he knows not.*
>
> The Creation Hymn, *Rig Veda* 10.129,
> transl. Ralph T. H. Griffith, 1896, adapted

DHARMA SUTRAS

Of the *Dharma Sutras* (literally, aphorisms relating to duties), the most important is the compendium of law known as *Manava Dharma Shastra* (The laws of Manu), which stipulate the duties, laws, and regulations binding on all categories of Hindus, whatever their caste (*varna*), stage of life (*ashrama*), or gender. Because ideas of salvation in Hinduism involve adherence to these laws, regulations, and duties, it is vital for Hindus to know and understand them. In other words, devout Hindus seeking release from *samsara* — the cycle of lives, deaths, and reincarnations — need to obey the *Dharma Sutras*.

THE EPICS

Perusal of the two epics of Hinduism, the *Ramayana* and the *Mahabharata*, is deemed a sacred duty, and helpful in progressing towards liberation/salvation (*moksha*) from the cycle of worldly life. These epics, allegedly written by the ancient sages Valmiki and Vyasa, are deemed by scholars to be compilations of folk-tales, songs sung by minstrels, and heroic stories composed in honour of kings. However, the editing of these scriptures was highly skilful and, despite their complexity and bewildering multiplicity of themes, they seem to point to a central theme of salvation of the world, and the continual war between good and evil in the universe. The stories are threaded into a central theme of a world slowly, but inexorably, declining to an age of destruction. The Battle of Kurukshetra is a climactic event in the *Mahabharata*, for instance, marking the beginning of the age of evil (*Kaliyuga*), and witnessing the gradual decline of honour, compassion, and chivalry during its denouement. In the *Ramayana*, the war between Rama and Ravana symbolizes the confrontation between the forces of good and evil in the world. In both, the principal characters are either gods or demi-gods and demons. Although the gods ultimately win, they have to compromise, and often resort to devious stratagems to achieve their victory. The end result is a tainted world, in which even the gods are not entirely free from unethical actions.

Both epics have common features: a righteous prince excluded from kingship and exiled; a climactic battle between forces of good and evil; the intervention of God on behalf of the good; in spite of many reverses, the ultimate triumph of good over evil. The epics present many ideals and heroic role models to Hindus, and are generally Vaishnavite, extolling the god Vishnu.

THE *BHAGAVAD GITA*

The *Bhagavad Gita* ('song of the Lord') is a small part of the epic *Mahabharata*. Nevertheless, it is a highly influential scripture within Hinduism, and has acquired almost an independent standing of its own. It is a discourse between Krishna, the incarnation (*avatar*) of the god Vishnu, and his devotee Prince Arjuna, the greatest warrior in the *Mahabharata*. The discussion is obviously an insertion into the epic, and many scholars consider it to be an *Upanishad*.

Above all, the *Bhagavad Gita* is an irenic scripture, which seeks to unite the major theological strands of Hinduism. It says that all ways to salvation are equally valid: the way of enlightenment (*jnana marga*), the way of altruistic righteous action and progression through the caste hierarchy (*nishkama karma marga*), the way of meditation (*yoga marga*), and the way of devotion (*bhakti marga*). However, it argues that the way of devotion (*bhakti*) is the highest of all paths and – for the first time in Hinduism – it reveals that the devotee is greatly loved by a gracious God. Consequently, it also proposes a radical rethinking of traditional Hindu concepts of salvation (*moksha*), in that it argues that it is open to all castes, and to men and women.

THE *PURANAS*

The *Puranas* – 'ancient stories' – are, again, a vast body of literature. Traditionally, there are eighteen *Puranas* which have been classified as associated with the gods Vishnu, Brahma, and Shiva, as well as many associated with minor deities and with holy places, such as particular temples or sacred sites. The contents are wide-ranging, including, for example, genealogies, law codes, descriptions of rituals, and pilgrimages to holy places. They are not merely a collection of old tales, as the name *Purana* seems to suggest, but narratives that highlight a theistic stance and vision.

THEODORE GABRIEL

CHAPTER 34

Beliefs

What we now know as Hinduism has developed into a rich, pluralist religious culture, with a great variety of customs, forms of worship, gods and goddesses, theologies, philosophies, stories, art, and music. Many Hindus believe its essential teachings remain the same down the centuries; however, diversity within Hinduism has led some scholars to talk of Hindu religions rather than a single Hindu religion, 'Hinduisms' rather than 'Hinduism', and even to abandon the term 'Hinduism' altogether. Moreover, many different Hindu voices and traditions compete globally to define the essential beliefs of Hinduism.

Hindus generally accept that they share common beliefs, principles, and structures. For many, however, Hinduism is not so much a system of beliefs as a way of life, a religious culture, a spiritual and intellectual quest, and an intense identification with the myriad ways in which the sacred is present in India. If asked about their beliefs, they often begin by talking about ethical teachings: kindness and truth; hospitality to the guest; respect for the family — and particularly for elders and parents. They may go on to consider beliefs in particular gods or goddesses, the authority of important sacred texts, the merit of pilgrimage, or the doctrine of *karma*. Some — not all — may accept the social hierarchy of the four *varnas* (caste system) and certain principles of purity and pollution. Any study of popular Hindu beliefs begins with the gods and goddesses of Hinduism.

GOD, GODS, AND GODDESSES

Hindus may be polytheistic, monotheistic, or monistic — believing that all reality is actually one. There are even orthodox Hindus who are atheistic. Many Hindus believe there is one God (*Brahman*) who can be worshipped in many forms. God can, for example, appear as a baby, a friend, a king, a mother, or a lover. God can manifest as male or female, or in non-human form; be worshipped as without form (*nirguna Brahman*) or with form (*saguna Brahman*); appear through icons and images (*murti*), or in human shape as a living saint or *guru*. Some Hindu gurus, such as Vivekananda (1863–1902), have even taught that God is embodied in the form of the universe, and in all sentient beings: hence, in serving others we are – quite literally – serving God.

Statue of Ganesha, the elephant-headed god.

God is sometimes understood in a threefold way, as *Trimurti*. The *Trimurti* consists of Brahma (the creator), Vishnu (the sustainer), and Shiva (the destroyer). However, not only is Brahma seldom worshipped, but nowadays the *Trimurti* is often replaced by a group of five gods: Vishnu, Shiva, Devi, Surya, and Ganesha.

The two pre-eminent gods, worshipped by Hindus everywhere, are Shiva and Vishnu. Vishnu is principally associated with the preservation of the cosmos and its proper order. He is, therefore, linked to kingship, and to the maintenance of *dharma* – law, order, righteousness. He is probably most frequently worshipped in his incarnations (*avatar*) as Rama and Krishna.

Shiva, 'the auspicious', is both the lord of *yogis* (ascetics) – depicted with matted hair, a body smeared with ashes, and meditating in a cremation ground – and also the divine lover. He is worshipped most commonly in the form of the phallus (*linga*). He has two sons: Ganesha, the elephant-headed god, and Skanda, or Murugan. Shiva reveals the ultimate nature of reality, the polarities of life and death, creation and destruction, the ascetic and the erotic, on whose interrelationship the whole of life depends.

Vaishnavism (devotion to Vishnu), Shaivism (devotion to Shiva), and Shaktism (devotion to the Goddess, or Devi) are the best-known traditions within Hinduism. However, Hindus often have a chosen deity (*ishtadev*) who, for the devotee, can take on the aspects of the ultimate god. Such gods and goddesses are worshipped both as distinct beings with their own stories and iconography, and as forms of the one ultimate reality (*Brahman*). Hindus may worship many gods, but they also believe all gods are one.

GODDESS WORSHIP

Goddess worship is one of the most distinctive traditions of Hinduism, going back to prehistoric times. *Shakti* (power, strength, force) is a term used to refer to the power of any deity, and is also the activating energy incarnated in goddesses. All goddesses can be seen as distinct deities, or as diverse forms of (Maha)devi, the (Great) Goddess. The Goddess (*Adyashakti*) is worshipped as the Supreme Being, but also as the consort of a male god.

Detail of a statue of Shiva, displaying the dynamic feminine aspect of the supreme Divine, Shakti.

The consorts of the three great gods are Lakshmi, Sarasvati, and Parvati.

Sometimes scholars draw a distinction between independent goddesses, who are dangerous and 'hot', and wifely goddesses, who are restrained and 'cool'. For many Hindu women Sita, the wife of Rama, is the model Hindu wife, whose resolute integrity and courage are today emphasized by the Indian women's movement.

The land of India itself is worshipped as 'Divine Mother' (*Bharat Mata*), and is further sanctified by *Shaktipithas* (centres of Goddess worship), and by great rivers like the Ganges, which are worshipped as bestowers of prosperity and liberation.

AVATARS

Avatars are manifestations (literally 'descents') of God. They periodically intervene to fight evil, and ensure that the universe functions in accordance with *dharma*. The best loved are Krishna and Rama (*avatars* of Vishnu).

Krishna is worshipped as a child, as the god of erotic mystical love, and as the hero of the epic *Mahabharata*. While the youthful Krishna with his flute entrances the world with his play (*Krishna-lila*), in the *Bhagavad Gita* Krishna reveals himself as the great teacher and supreme god (Vishnu).

Rama is worshipped as the ideal ruler and the restorer of *dharma*. Always popular in northern India, Rama, has latterly become the principal god of Hindu nationalism. His reign (*Ram Rajya*) is invoked as a golden period of justice, harmony, and prosperity.

IMAGE WORSHIP

While many Hindus acknowledge that *Brahman* is the ultimate reality, the vast majority also worship divine beings and images. Many believe that the power (*shakti*) of a deity is actually present in that deity's image (*murti*). Therefore, in worshipping before an image, worship is offered to the deity whose power is in the image, and also to the deity as an image. When an image is consecrated, the ceremony transforms images of stone, metal, and wood into embodiments of God. Hindus go to the temple for *darshana*, the 'sight' or 'vision' of the deities. It is believed that *darshana* brings good fortune, grace, and spiritual merit. It also makes possible an intimate, loving relationship between deities and their devotees. During ritual worship (*puja*), the gods are served and cared for as honoured guests by the offerings made to their images.

DHARMA

Hindus today often refer to Hindu beliefs and practices as *sanatana dharma* (eternal religion), or Vedic *dharma* (Vedic religion). *Dharma* may mean the social order, or the cosmic order, but equally it can refer to personal behaviour and attitudes. At the simplest level, it means the individual's religious and social duties, according to status and stage of life. The *Bhagavad Gita*, for example, teaches that it is better to do one's own duty imperfectly than that of another well.

SAMSARA

Many Hindus, particularly those in the higher castes, believe in the endless cycle of rebirth (*samsara*). Efforts to bring the cycle to an end are at the core of many Hindu religious practices. The picture of a world as a place where the eternal soul is perpetually reincarnated has dominated the Indian imagination for over three millennia.

KARMA

Central to the teaching about reincarnation, *karma* is the taken-for-granted belief that one's actions determine one's condition in this life and rebirth in the next. Every action has its inevitable fruit or consequence. *Karma* is thus inseparable from *dharma* and *samsara*. To summarize the belief: good deeds result in good *karma*, which produces good fortune in this life and a good birth in the next life; bad deeds result in bad *karma*, which may lead to much less desirable rebirths in the next life, as a human lower down the social hierarchy, as an animal, or even as an unfortunate soul suffering the torments of one of the many hells.

> To see the universal and all-pervading Spirit of Truth face to face one must be able to love the meanest of creation as oneself.
>
> Mahatma Gandhi, *An Autobiography* (Harmondsworth: Penguin, 1982).

There are ways in which *karma* may be overridden. Devotion to a deity is perhaps the most potent, whilst religious rituals and meritorious action may also cancel past sins. Some Hindus withdraw from the world and practise non-engagement. However, the *Bhagavad Gita* teaches that adherence to one's duty, combined with internal renunciation of attachment to, or desire for, the results of one's actions, can lead to liberation (*moksha*) from the cycle of *samsara*.

Karma can lead to either fatalism or ethical activism. It can be seen as an uncontrollable, impersonal determinant of the human condition; or can encourage people to feel responsible for their own fate, and promote a dynamic view of action in the world.

THE THREE PATHS

The three paths – *margas* or *yogas* – to spiritual fulfilment are: *jnana* (knowledge, insight, wisdom), *karma* (action) and *bhakti* (ecstatic devotion). Some Hindus consider each of the three paths requires exclusive concentration, and is sufficient for liberation. However, many modern teachers and gurus teach a *yoga* of synthesis, arguing that the three paths are linked, and liberating knowledge may be obtained through all.

Jnanayoga — the path of wisdom/knowledge — liberates from *karma* and rebirth, and indeed from sickness, old age, and death. It leads to the overcoming of ignorance and the realization of *Brahman*. The pursuit of wisdom implies religious practice, meditation, self-purification, and above all study of the scriptures. The Vedas, and particularly the *Upanishads*, provide knowledge of *Brahman*, and of our true condition. Indeed, the famous teaching of the *Upanishads* is that in soul (*atman*) humans are identical with *Brahman*. According to some Hindu schools, if humans realize this truth, they can be liberated-in-life (*jivan-mukta*).

Karmayoga — the path of work — enables ordinary people everywhere to give spiritual meaning to their everyday lives. It is associated for many with the *Bhagavad Gita's* teaching that action can be a positive means of personal transformation, if people perform their duty selflessly, and act without the desire for status or reward. Gandhi reinterpreted *karmayoga*, by equating

A Hindu pilgrim sits beside the River Ganges, Varanasi, India.

it with social commitment and struggle, and found in the *Gita* authority for his philosophy of non-violence and peaceful resistance to British rule.

Bhaktiyoga — the path of loving devotion — is characterized by an intense personal relationship between the deity and devotee. Selfless love of God consumes past *karma*, and results in a state of intimate, blissful, and loving communion with the deity. Vaishnavas often speak of *prapatti* — complete self-surrender in love — to Vishnu. God-intoxicated saints are depicted as immersed in blissful devotion. Today many busy Hindus follow the path of *bhakti*: their spiritual discipline (*sadhana*) may vary, but is broadly characterized by selfless service and loving devotion to God.

THE FOUR GOALS

Hinduism offers four legitimate goals (*purusartha*) for human beings which, taken together, are believed to ensure spiritual and social harmony:

I. *Artha* — worldly wealth and success — is a proper goal, if pursued without desire, anger, and greed. Kautilya's *Artha Shastra*, written in the third to fourth century BCE, argues that prosperity is the basis of a well-ordered state, and people need *artha* if they are to practise religion. Thus pursuing an occupation, accumulating wealth, governing and so on are justified if they do not violate *dharma*.

2. *Kama* – pleasure, desire – is also a legitimate goal, if it accords with *dharma*. This is the pursuit of pleasurable activities, including sexuality, play, recreation, the arts, and literature. The *Kama Sutra*, written in the third or fourth centuries CE, deals at length with erotic techniques, the arts of pleasure, and seduction.

3. *Dharma* – virtue, morality – has two levels: it is both one's own particular set of duties (*svadharma*) and the absolute morality, valid universally. When profit and pleasure are pursued for themselves, outside of *dharma*, they lead to social chaos.

4. *Moksha* – spiritual liberation – is the ultimate Hindu quest: release from the bondage of suffering and rebirth (*samsara*).

Some Hindus believe these goals are interconnected and that no goal is primary. Others believe they form an ascending hierarchy, with *moksha* transcending – even opposing – the other three. Whatever one's understanding, this system of the four goals implicitly recognizes the complexity of human drives and aspirations.

> *Just as a person casts off worn-out garments and puts on others that are new, even so the embodied soul casts off worn-out bodies and takes on others that are new. Weapons do not cleave the Self, fire does not burn the Self. Waters do not drench the Self, winds do not parch the Self. The Self is the same forever: unmanifest, unthinkable, still.*
>
> Bhagavad Gita II, 22–25

DEATH AND THE AFTERLIFE

Hindu beliefs about the afterlife are complex. Most Hindus believe they will be reborn into another body, according to their *karma*. However, *moksha* – salvation or ultimate spiritual fulfilment – may be understood in different ways: as final union with *Brahman*; as a perfectly blissful state; as communion with God; or as liberation in some heavenly realm or paradise. Many Hindus may find the concept of salvation, or liberation after death, a very distant ideal.

Moreover, ancient understandings of the afterlife persist, and Vedic views are implied in the death ritual. Funerary rites of passage, and memorial rituals for the dead, indicate a belief in the continued existence of ancestors (*pitr*), who are benefited and pleased by offerings made by their descendants. There are also popular beliefs about the journey of the soul after death; the multiplicity of heavens and hells, and the role of the god of death (Yamraj or Dharmaraj) as judge; and restless or malicious ghosts (*pret, bhuta*) who may possess or disturb the living.

TIME

Hindu, Buddhist, and Jain beliefs about the vastness of time, and the age of the universe, in some senses coincide with modern scientific understanding. The classical Hindu view is of gradually deteriorating conditions, until finally the world is destroyed by fire and

To conquer the subtle passions seems to me harder far than the physical conquest of the world by force of arms.

Mahatma Gandhi, *An Autobiography*

returns to chaos. The world itself perpetually undergoes cycles of evolution, from a state of non-differentiation, through a series of ages, to its dissolution (*pralaya*) back into the unevolved state, from which the cycle starts again. This process of evolution and dissolution is a 'day of Brahma': each day of Brahma divides into the fourteen 'periods of the Manu'; each of the fourteen periods of Manu divides into four great ages; each of the four great ages divides into four *yugas*. The passing of the *yugas* is marked by progressive moral and physical deterioration. We are now in the middle of the last, and worst, age: the *Kaliyuga*. Hence, that there is apparent moral decline, suffering, famine, and war is no surprise to Hindus; indeed, the orthodox view is that life will get worse as we progress through the *yuga*.

GURUS

The *guru* – spiritual teacher – is a figure of the greatest importance in Hinduism, the object of *darshan* and worship, and comes in all shapes and sizes, traditions and orders. Some may assert their status by virtue of their charisma, others are initiated into a long-established lineage (*sampradaya*). Many have carried their spiritual message to the West, helping to extend the bounds of Hinduism. One of the best known gurus was Sathya Sai Baba, worshipped as an *avatara* of Sirdi Sai Baba, and of Shiva and Shakti. There have also been women gurus, such as Sarada Devi (1853–1920), widow of Ramakrishna, Mira Alfassa (1878–1973), Mother of the Aurobindo organization, Ananda Mayi Ma (1896–1982), and Mata Amritanandamayi (b. 1953).

ANNA S. KING

CHAPTER 35

Worship and Festivals

YAJNA

In early Vedic times, worship usually took the form of a sacrificial ritual (*yajna*), addressed to nature gods such as the sun god, Surya; the rain god, Indra; the god of fire, Agni; or the Soma god, believed to reside in a probably hallucinogenic plant of the same name. These rituals involved the sacrifice of animals such as goats and cows, or the pouring of oblations of such items as clarified butter, honey, and milk into a sacrificial fire, accompanied by the chanting of Vedic hymns and prayers. The early Vedas are liturgical texts, which set out in great detail the method of ritual observance. These rituals were intended to please the gods through worship, and to ensure the well-being of the sponsor or patron of the sacrifice — the *yajamana* — and his family.

PUJA

Yajnas are something of a rarity in the contemporary Hindu world; far more commonly observed is *puja*, a ritual of devotional worship regularly conducted at temples, usually by Brahman priests, and often observed privately at household shrines. *Puja* may be addressed to any of the manifold gods and goddesses in the Hindu pantheon, important among whom are the great gods Vishnu and Shiva, and the goddess Shakti, all of whom appear in myriad forms and aspects in Hindu mythology, and across the contemporary Hindu sacred landscape.

> *Whatever you do, or eat, or give, or offer in adoration, let it be an offering to me; and whatever you suffer, suffer it for me.*
>
> Bhagavad Gita 9.26

Temples dedicated to the different Hindu gods and goddesses usually contain a sanctified image of the deity, and to this image the ritual of *puja* is addressed. During *puja*, the priest ritually purifies himself and the shrine, invokes the presence of the deity in the image, and then worships the image by ritually bathing and adorning it, feeding it symbolically, and waving a flaming lamp in a circle around it in a ritual of light. This is usually accompanied by the chanting of Sanskrit mantras, the blowing of conches, and the ringing of bells. In Hindu households, the family usually observes an abbreviated form of this ritual.

The relationship between the image and the divine presence is, in the Hindu world, often a complex one. For most Hindus, the image is symbolic of the divine presence; but for many, it is also the divine presence, manifesting itself in tangible form. Moreover, Hindus seldom agree on the importance of *puja*. While some see it as an act of great religious significance, others see it as a largely unnecessary, outward expression of religious piety, and prefer instead a more inward-oriented mode of spiritual development. Besides *puja*, other modes of worship commonly practised in Hindu society include *bhajana* – the singing of hymns – and the recitation of the *sahasranama*, the thousand names of the gods and goddesses.

Part of the huge Hindu temple complex at Angkor Wat, Cambodia – the world's largest religious monument – built by the Tamil king Suryavarnman II in the twelfth century CE.

I am the same to all beings, and my love is ever the same; but those who worship me with devotion, they are in me and I am in them.

Bhagavad Gita 9.29

INTRODUCTION TO WORLD RELIGIONS

Festivals of Hinduism

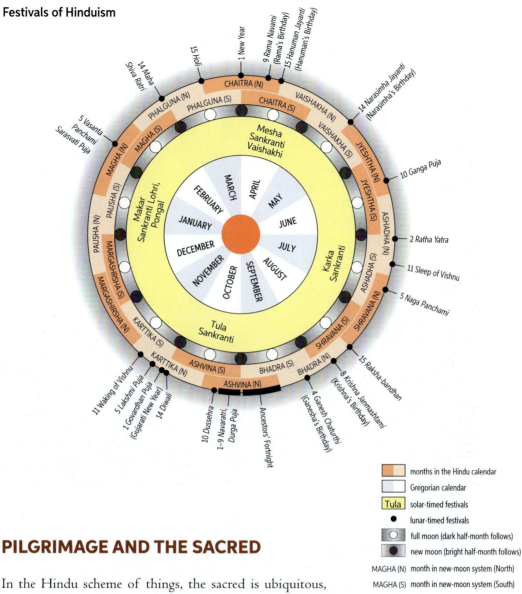

Legend:
- months in the Hindu calendar
- Gregorian calendar
- Tula — solar-timed festivals
- ● lunar-timed festivals
- ○ full moon (dark half-month follows)
- ◑ new moon (bright half-month follows)
- MAGHA (N) — month in new-moon system (North)
- MAGHA (S) — month in new-moon system (South)

Festival labels (from the outer ring):
- 14 Maha Shiva Ratri
- 15 Holi
- 1 New Year
- 9 Rama Navami (Rama's Birthday)
- 15 Hanuman Jayanti (Hanuman's Birthday)
- 14 Narasimha Jayanti (Narasimha's Birthday)
- 5 Vasanta Panchami / Sarasvati Puja
- 10 Ganga Puja
- 2 Ratha Yatra
- 11 Sleep of Vishnu
- 5 Naga Panchami
- 15 Raksha-bandhan
- 8 Krishna Janmashtami (Krishna's Birthday)
- 4 Ganesh Chaturthi (Ganesha's Birthday)
- Ancestors' Fortnight
- 1–9 Navaratri, Durga Puja
- 10 Dussehra
- 14 Diwali
- 1 Govardhan Puja (Gujarati New Year)
- 5 Lakshmi Puja
- 11 Waking of Vishnu

Hindu month names (outer ring):
CHAITRA (N), CHAITRA (S), VAISHAKHA (N), VAISHAKHA (S), JYESHTHA (N), JYESHTHA (S), ASHADHA (N), ASHADHA (S), SHRAVANA (N), SHRAVANA (S), BHADRA (N), BHADRA (S), ASHVINA (N), ASHVINA (S), KARTTIKA (N), KARTTIKA (S), MARGASHIRSHA (N), MARGASHIRSHA (S), PAUSHA (N), PAUSHA (S), MAGHA (N), MAGHA (S), PHALGUNA (N), PHALGUNA (S)

Inner ring (solar festivals):
Mesha Sankranti / Vaishakhi, Karka Sankranti, Tula Sankranti, Makar Sankranti / Lohri, Pongal

Gregorian months: JANUARY, FEBRUARY, MARCH, APRIL, MAY, JUNE, JULY, AUGUST, SEPTEMBER, OCTOBER, NOVEMBER, DECEMBER

PILGRIMAGE AND THE SACRED

In the Hindu scheme of things, the sacred is ubiquitous, contained not only in temples and sacred images, but also in nature — in stones, trees, mountains, and rivers. Every once in a while the sacred 'manifests' itself in the form of a mysterious rock, stream, or spring, and the site of such manifestation becomes a place of worship. Pilgrims flock to such places during auspicious months of the Hindu calendar, and mythological stories grow about the miraculous nature of the pilgrimage site. Particularly important in the Hindu cosmology are sacred rivers, and holy towns and cities situated along their banks, which are seen as places of crossing (*tirtha*) between the mundane and the sacred, and between the worlds of the living and the dead. The water of the Ganges in North

Hindu pilgrims gather on the banks of the holy River Ganges at Varanasi, India, to perform their morning religious rituals.

INTRODUCTION TO WORLD RELIGIONS

India is believed to be especially potent in this respect, and a single dip in the river is believed to earn for the worshipper untold spiritual merit.

The sacred often manifests itself in living things too. The cow, the monkey, and – in some parts of India – even the snake and the rat are believed to be sacred and therefore worshipped. Yet more common is the worship of men and women believed to be holy, and therefore capable of performing miracles that can transform the lives of devotees, and ensure their well-being. Many such holy figures attract an extensive following, and head vast spiritual empires extending across regional and national boundaries.

FESTIVALS

The Hindu (lunar) calendar year is punctuated by a series of religious festivals. Temple festivals are usually marked by processions, when worshippers carry the deity's image through the temple town or village, offering devotees a chance to glimpse it in all its glory. Other festivals – which celebrate landmark events in Hindu mythology – include:

Image of Durga, a popular fierce form of the Hindu goddess, depicted with up to eighteen arms.

- *Janmashtami* (July–August): the celebration of the birthday of the popular Hindu god, Krishna.
- *Ganesh Chaturthi* (August–September): a festival dedicated to the elephant-headed god, Ganesh, the remover of obstacles.
- *Dussehra* (September–October, towards the end of the monsoon): marking the victory of Rama and his monkey army over the demon-king Ravana. It encompasses *Navaratri* – also known as 'the festival of nine nights' – which in Bengal culminates in a grand celebration dedicated to the worship of the goddess Durga.
- *Diwali* (October–November): the festival of lights, following shortly after *Dussehra*. Hindus throughout the world illuminate their homes with lamps and exchange gifts.

- *Shivaratri* (January–February): a festival during which Shiva is worshipped.
- *Holi* (February–March): a spring festival, during which people drench one another in water and coloured powder.

Besides these, there are several localized festivals observed in different parts of the Hindu world. The *Kumbh Mela*, perhaps the most popular of these, attracts pilgrims in vast numbers to its four sites in North India – Hardwar, Nasik, Ujjain, and Allahabad – where it is celebrated on a rotational basis once every three years. The *Purna Kumbha Mela* takes place once every twelve years in the holy town of Allahabad. Billed as the 'biggest gathering on earth', in 2001 more than 40 million people gathered on its busiest days.

MAYA WARRIER

CHAPTER 36

Family and Society

Caste and joint family are often seen as the central features of traditional Hindu social organization. The caste system orders Hindu society hierarchically, such that different social groups are ranked in a relationship of superiority or inferiority to each other in terms of their levels of purity. Every Hindu is born into the caste of his or her parents. Traditionally, caste groups were – by and large – occupational groups, and the nature of one's occupation determined one's level of purity. Ritual, worship, and scholarship in sacred texts, seen as the purest pursuits, were the preserve of the 'purest' and 'highest' of castes, the Brahmans. At the opposite end of the hierarchy were the so-called 'untouchables', who, by virtue of the 'impurity' attaching to their occupations – scavenging, tanning leather and the like – were considered too polluting to be incorporated into mainstream society, and were therefore excluded from everyday social life. Between these two extremes ranged a vast and varied spectrum of caste rankings. In traditional Indian village society, caste determined most aspects of one's life – where one lived, with whom one could legitimately interact, with whom one could share food, and whom one could marry. As a result, social mobility, especially for those on the lowest rungs of society, was highly restricted.

THE JOINT FAMILY

Just as caste determined one's place in society, so status within the joint family determined one's place within the household. In the joint family system, two, often three, or even four generations of a family lived together, as part of the same household, sharing common living space and kitchen facilities, drawing from a common pool of financial resources, and sharing responsibilities for the upkeep of the family home. The head of the household was usually the oldest male member of the family. In the traditional Hindu family system, family property passed down the male line; the women of the family seldom owned or controlled family property. Indian epic narratives, such as the *Mahabharata* and *Ramayana*, dwell at great length on familial roles and duties as

> For the sake of the family, one may abandon an individual. For the sake of a village one may abandon a family. For the country's sake, one may abandon a village. For the sake of the soul, one may abandon the world!
>
> *Mahabharata* 2.55.10

husband, wife, father, mother, son, daughter, brother and so on, thus providing traditional models for good conduct in familial contexts.

MARRIAGE

Traditionally, a woman derived her identity from the male authority figures in her life: usually her father before her marriage, her husband after marriage, and her sons in her old age. Marriage was – and remains to this day – a central institution, ordering and regulating the Hindu social system. Conventionally, marriage is seen, not as the formalizing of a romantic relationship between the individuals concerned, but as an arrangement between families of the same, or similarly ranked, caste groups within the caste hierarchy. The bride, seen in most Hindu communities as a 'gift' from her parents to the family of the

I AM A HINDU

I was born a few years after India gained independence, in a village in Gujarat, India, just outside the town of Dandi – famous for Gandhi's Salt March protest against the British colonial government. I came to England when I was eleven, because my father was employed in a car factory in Coventry. Although I attended school in India from the age of five, I found schooling in England difficult, mainly because I knew little English. However, I quickly learned the new language and settled in.

At sixteen, I joined a local engineering company, and began an apprenticeship. After five years, I successfully concluded it, and was encouraged to apply to Sussex University. After being awarded a degree in Mechanical Engineering, I returned to the company, and worked my way up to become one of their chief engineers, which has led to my travelling to various parts of the world.

As a Hindu, I believe in one God who has many incarnations (*avatars*). I believe in all these gods, but – like many Hindus – focus on a particular god who has become special to me: Krishna, a very popular god within Hinduism. I am particularly moved and helped by the many stories about Krishna. My belief in God has encouraged me to be a helpful, contributing member of society. For instance, I assisted in starting a cricket club for young people, and I have been its secretary for thirty years. I did this because, as a Hindu, I wanted to put something back into the community from which I have benefited so much. I believe that, if I lead a good life, helping others, and worshipping God, as a result of reincarnation I will be reborn into a better life.

I do not believe it is necessary to visit the temple every day to keep in touch with God. God is with me every hour of the day. I pray to God in my thoughts wherever I am, and reflect on my beliefs, and whether what I'm doing is good for me or for other people. I do this, not only because they are good things to do, but also because they will contribute to a good reincarnation. That said, I like to be in the temple whenever I can, serving my community. I find that regular attendance helps my religious life, by expanding my thoughts, and helping to make me less selfish and to see the best in others. This is what faith means to me. It is a faith I learned particularly from my mother, a traditional Hindu; she has been the greatest influence on my religious upbringing.

When we moved to Cheltenham, we were the first Hindu family, and there was no temple. We had a shrine in our house, but had to return to Coventry for important festivals, celebrating there as we had done in India, if on a smaller scale. Finally, in 1975, the growing groom, often brings wealth – in the form of dowry – to the groom's family. Her parents, in popular belief, derive spiritual merit by gifting their daughter to the groom's family. Although in some instances it is permissible for the woman to 'marry up' into a family of higher social standing than her own, the reverse, where the woman marries someone from a lower caste, is considered taboo.

FAMILY AND SOCIETY TODAY

While the institutions of caste and joint family still prevail in contemporary Hindu society, they have undergone vast changes, mainly due to changes in economic organization. The status of women in society too has undergone some measure of change, although several traditional ideas regarding the woman's role in the family still prevail. In modern

Hindu community in Cheltenham established their own temple, an occasion of much rejoicing and celebration.

In 1976 I returned to India, where I met my wife, a traditional Hindu from Gujarat. Already a devout Hindu, after our marriage I became more involved in the activities of the temple, as its secretary and now its treasurer. Because of my work, I do not participate in worship in the temple every day, but attend at least three times a week. When I retire, I will attend worship in the temple far more regularly.

In our home, we have a temple-like shrine, at which my mother and my wife perform *puja* every day. After bathing in the morning, I also pray there for a short time. I observe fasting on special occasions, but am not too particular about my diet. My wife and my mother are far more traditionally Hindu in this respect. My faith is more interior than exterior: I am less concerned about outward symbols, such as dress, than I am about what I think and do. That said, I do often wear traditional Indian dress for *puja* and other religious functions.

I do not have time to attend scripture study regularly. Once or twice a year I attend scripture reading and exposition in Coventry. I would like to go regularly to a local reading of Hindu sacred texts, but none is available, although scholars from the Hare Krishna

temple in Watford are sometimes invited to explain Hindu texts locally.

I visit India most years, and whenever I go I make a point of visiting places of pilgrimage or particular temples. My aspiration is to visit most of the temples and sacred places in South India, which I believe are the original Hindu temples. My goal, when I retire, is to devote my life to seeking inner peace through prayer and meditation.

My wife is more devout than I am, and observes all the Hindu calendar events, and my family life is firmly based on Hindu religion and culture. My faith has helped strengthen my relationship with my wife, mother, and sisters. Together we observe all the Hindu festivals and celebrations, such as *Navaratri* and *Janmashtami*, and key ceremonies (*samskars*) such as cyclical funerary rites (*sraddha*). I took my father's ashes to India to scatter in rivers and on the land, especially in our hometown.

As a Hindu community we are very close-knit. We all get to know about the sickness, death, and other problems faced by other Hindu families. The close friendships we have mean we are always ready to support each other in times of need.

Naren Patel

Hindu society, one's caste need no longer determine one's occupation, income, or social status. Particularly in urban contexts, where modern occupations and workplaces afford employees some degree of autonomy from caste restrictions, caste often ceases to be the all-important marker of one's identity. The joint family system likewise worked best when occupations were hereditary, and different generations of a family derived their income from the same source of livelihood. With urbanization and industrialization generating new, and more numerous, job opportunities, and modern educational institutions imparting new skills to recruits from diverse backgrounds, it has been possible for younger generations not only to break away from their hereditary familial occupations and move into new kinds of employment, but also to set up independent nuclear families of their own. With more and more women entering educational institutions and the employment sector, they too need less support from the male members of their families. They are thus, to some degree, able to assert their independence and autonomy from the traditional family structure.

While in several instances the nuclear family has come to replace the joint family, the idea of the joint family retains a powerful hold over the Hindu imagination. Families tend to be closely networked across generations, and older members of the family, although they may not live in close proximity to younger members, continue to exercise considerable authority over the latter. Parents still have a major say in determining same-caste life partners for their sons and daughters, even though the concept of the 'love marriage' as opposed to the 'arranged marriage' is gaining increasing popularity in the contemporary Hindu world. Families come together on occasions such as birth, wedding, and death ceremonies, reinforcing a sense of solidarity as a group. Hindu epic stories, such as the *Mahabharata* and *Ramayana*, are often retold today in the form of television serials and dance dramas, bolstering the ideal of the joint family in popular thinking.

MAYA WARRIER

CHAPTER 37

Hinduism in the Modern World

Hinduism, the most ancient world religion, has been subject to many changes in the course of its long history. The rise and fall in prominence of some ancient gods, such as Indra, King of gods, and Varuna, god of the sea; the decline in importance of the fire sacrifice; the rise in popularity of the *bhakti* (devotional) tradition in the sixth century CE are all instances of this. In the nineteenth and early twentieth centuries Hindu reformers such as Vivekananda (1863–1902), Ram Mohan Roy (1772–1833), Mohandas (Mahatma) Gandhi (1869–1948), and Sarvepalli Radhakrishnan (1888–1975) advocated an ethical form of Hinduism, which campaigned against social practices such as *sati* – the self-immolation of widows on their husbands' funeral pyres – and child marriage, and displayed the influence of Western values. In modern times, Hinduism has moved away from this puritanical type of religion, which decried many ancient beliefs as superstitious, and has returned with full vigour to traditional Hinduism.

ASTROLOGERS AND GURUS

A large number of Hindus now defend traditional Hindu mores and practices. Contemporary Hindus are not worried about being labelled 'superstitious', and openly consult astrologers and gurus. The increased veneration of gurus has given rise to the cult phenomenon in modern Hinduism. Some prominent gurus, such as Swami Prabhupada, Bhagavan Rajneesh, and Satya Sai Baba, established popular new religious movements that have spread beyond India, attracting a considerable following from Westerners, although, technically, conversion into Hinduism is impossible, because Hindus are – as a result of their *karma* – those born into Hindu families and into a particular caste. Non-Hindus do not have a caste identity; hence, traditionally Hindu missionary activity was aimed at recovering Hindus who had lapsed into Christianity or Islam, and required a purification ritual, or *shuddi*. However, in the modern world, new cults and movements have emulated Christians, by engaging in mission to non-Hindus. Many of these new Hindu movements have been successful in recruiting Westerners.

POLITICIZATION

One of the most striking modern developments has been the politicization of Hinduism, and the rising militancy among some factions, perhaps a natural consequence of the emergence of Hindu nationalism in a country so long under the yoke of Muslim and Christian powers. Independence for India in August 1947 ended around 400 years of such rule and, although the Indian leaders opted for a secular, or religiously neutral, nation, the vast majority of the population is Hindu. With the passing of time, the secular ideals of Jawaharlal Nehru (1889–1964) – first Prime Minister of India – and Gandhi have become less valued, and today many view India as a Hindu, rather than a secular, multi-religious, nation.

This shift toward Hindu nationalism should be seen in the context of the rise of Muslim nationalism in the subcontinent, and the perennial dispute over Kashmir, the Muslim-majority state located between India and Pakistan. Hindu nationalistic parties such as the RSS (Rashtriya Swayam Sevak Sangh/National Self-Service Association), the VHP (Vishwa Hindu Parishad/World Hindu Organization) and BJP (Bharatiya Janatha Party/Indian People's Party) promote India as a Hindu

The Birla Mandir, or Laxmi Narayan, Hindu Temple, Delhi, India, built between 1933 and 1939.

INTRODUCTION TO WORLD RELIGIONS

state, and believe Hindu religion, ideology, and values should predominate. This has increased pressure on the religious minorities and created division. The actions and claims of more militant sections of Hindu nationalist organizations, such as the Bajrang Dal, have been denounced by Hindu intellectuals as uncharacteristic of Hindu religion and culture, with its image of tolerance, and willingness to absorb beliefs and practices from other religions and philosophies. The militants have an ideology based on *Hindutva* ('Hindu-ness'), which raises problems for the religious minorities, and raises the possibility of a Hindu theocratic state, alienating the millions of non-Hindus in the nation.

The appeal of the Hindu nationalistic ideology is more evident among the less literate and rural sections of the Hindu community, who constitute the majority of the Indian populace. This combination of political power and militant religious nationalism has led to tension in some areas of India where several faith communities live alongside each other. The massacre of Muslims in Gujarat in 2002 was allegedly condoned, and even abetted, by the Hindu nationalist state government. Hindu nationalists seek the Hinduization of Indian polity, culture, and education. This trend, often termed 'saffronization' — saffron being a colour associated with Hinduism — is growing stronger, although opposed by the Indian intelligentsia, who argue against the politicization of religion, its identification with the nation and growing hostility to other faiths.

THE HINDU DIASPORA

A significant development in Hinduism has resulted from the migration of many Hindus to the West. Because these diaspora communities are minorities, a defensive, more fervent type of Hinduism has emerged. For example, in southern states of the USA, where there is a strong conservative Christian culture, Hindus have challenged what they see as the misrepresentation of Hindu concepts and practices in school textbooks.

Westernized Hindu ideas, when imported back to India, have been responsible for an increased awareness of mystical traditions, sacred sites, and some esoteric forms of Hindu spirituality. There has been a burgeoning interest in pilgrimage to sacred shrines, such as the Sabarimala Temple in Kerala, and great festivals, such as the *Kumbh Mela*. There has also been an increase in pilgrims visiting gurus in search of miracles.

THE CASTE SYSTEM

Modern Hinduism has also seen a strengthening of the caste system. At the turn of the twentieth century, a campaign by Hindu reformers such as Dayananda Sarasvati (1824–83), Vivekananda, and Gandhi sought to reform what they saw as the chauvinism and discrimination of the caste system. Caste did not disappear, but it was felt to be out of date and incompatible with modern egalitarian ideals. For some, the conversion of 'untouchables' to Christianity, Islam, or Buddhism seemed to threaten the predominance of Hinduism in the subcontinent. Under Gandhi's influence, the Indian constitution and laws guaranteed privileges to the untouchables in education and employment. In recent years this has faced opposition by 'forward communities', who claim positive discrimination policies have undermined the economic status of their own communities. In some areas there have been caste wars between the *savarnas* – those belonging to the *varna* or caste system – and the *avarnas* – the untouchables. Both the untouchables and the *savarnas* have now organized into vote banks to achieve political influence.

Revisionist thinking now emphasizes the positive side of the caste system. Even practices such as *sati* have been praised by fundamentalists, despite a growing feminist movement within Hinduism. On the other hand, there is a phenomenon termed 'sanskritization', which has seen untouchables and tribal peoples of India attempting to Hinduize their religious practices. Some untouchable and tribal groups are beginning to abandon their traditional deities and practices to build temples and worship Hindu deities, such as Vishnu and Shiva, possibly in an attempt to enter the Hindu fold, or gain higher status for their community. The Indian constitution has made the restriction of entry of untouchables to Hindu temples illegal, and some untouchables have undertaken Hindu theological training and demanded entry to the priesthood, even at *savarna* temples.

Meanwhile, other untouchable and tribal groups have retained their traditional pantheon and ritual praxis, but attempted to identify their deities and practices with Hindu gods and worship, by reinterpreting their mythology and ritual proceedings. The leaders of the Muthappan cult of northern Kerala, for example, have reinterpreted the Muthappan deities as Vishnu and Shiva, although originally tribal gods of the forest dwellers of the region.

WOMEN IN MODERN HINDUISM

Nineteenth-century and twentieth-century social reformers spearheaded efforts to achieve the liberation of women, at considerable risk. Ram Mohan Roy's campaign resulted in the banning of *sati*. Ishwar Chandra Vidyasagar married a widow, to set an example of improving the lot of people treated as virtually dead – widows lived in seclusion, were not allowed to remarry, had to forgo all adornments, and were looked on as inauspicious. Gandhi, for the first time in modern India, brought Indian women into the public arena, in his campaign for independence. Women took part in public demonstrations and in the civil disobedience movement. The momentum gained has not been lost: the traditional image of the Hindu woman – domesticated and subservient to father and husband – is changing rapidly. Women are well represented in the employment sector and in government, and there has been a move to set quotas for women members of the *Lok Sabha* (parliament). A Vanitha Commission (Woman's Commission) in Kerala State is looking into women's grievances, including molestation or 'eve teasing' in public places, discrimination in employment, and their position in the family.

Traditionally, the role of the woman was in the home, serving her husband and nurturing her children. Hindu mythology often emphasized this image. Female figures such as Sita, the virtuous and long suffering wife of Rama, and Savithri, who pleaded successfully to

Yama, the god of death, for the life of her husband, were held up as paradigms of womanly behaviour. Modern Hindu women do not adhere to these norms; they are out in public, competing against men in all fields, even in occupations traditionally viewed as exclusively male, such as law, engineering, and the police and armed forces. Feminist groups such as the Working Woman's Forum are active in trying to achieve equality. Film directors such as Mira Nair and Deepa Mehta have made films highlighting the aspirations of Indian women and the problems they face, such as *Fire* (1996) and *Monsoon Wedding* (2001), provoking controversy among right-wing Hindu groups.

THEODORE GABRIEL

QUESTIONS

1.   What continuities are there between early Vedic religion and modern Hinduism?

2.   Explain the different views of the role of *Brahman* in Hinduism.

3.   Explain the different views of the nature of human existence held by the three main Vedantic schools (*Advaita*, *Vishishtadvaita*, and *Dvaita*).

4.   What role do the *Ramayana* and *Mahabarata* play in helping to attain liberation?

5.   Explain why some believe the term 'Hinduisms' to be more appropriate than 'Hinduism'.

6.   Why are Shiva and Vishnu considered to be so important?

7.   Why do Hindus understand *moksha* (liberation) in a variety of different ways?

8.   Explain some of the different roles of the guru in Hinduism.

9.   Why are some geographical sites seen as sacred in Hinduism?

10. Why has the caste system been so important in Hinduism and Indian society?

FURTHER READING

Biardeau, Madeleine, *Hinduism: The Anthropology of a Civilization*. Delhi: Oxford University Press, 1989.

Blurton, T. Richard, *Hindu Art*. Cambridge: Harvard University Press, 1992.

Hiriyanna, Mysore, *The Essentials of Indian Philosophy*. London: Allen and Unwin, 1985.

Kinsley, David R., *Hindu Goddesses: Visions of the Divine Feminine in the Hindu Religious Tradition*. Berkeley: University of California Press, 1988.

Lopez, Donald S. Jr., ed., *Religions of India in Practice*. Princeton: Princeton University Press, 1995.

Mittal, S., and G. Thursby, eds., *The Hindu World*. New York: Routledge, 2004.

Narayan, R. K., *Ramayana: A Shortened Modern Prose Version of the Indian Epic*. New York: Viking, 1972.

Swami Prabhavananda and Frederick Manchester, trans., *The Upanishads*. New York: Signet, 2002.

Swami Prabhavananda and Christopher Isherwood, trans., *Bhagavad-Gita: The Song of God*. New York: Signet, 2002.

von Stietencron, Heinrich, 'Hinduism: On the Proper Use of a Deceptive Term', in Gunther D. Sontheimer and Hermann Kulke, eds., *Hinduism Reconsidered*, pp. 11–27. New Delhi: Manohar, 1989.

Williams, Raymond Brady, ed., *A Sacred Thread: Modern Transmission of Hindu Traditions in India and Abroad*. Chambersburg, PA: Anima, 1992.

PART 5
BUDDHISM

SUMMARY

Buddhism, it is now generally believed, emerged into the world sometime around the fifth century BCE, in northern India, and is derived from the teachings of one man – Siddhartha Gautama – known to his followers by the title Buddha. Central to the Buddha's teachings was the idea that one had to experience dissatisfaction or suffering in order to understand that these have a cause: the egocentric desire for satisfaction, pleasure, or even life itself. Once this understanding is reached, followers of the *Dharma*, 'the teaching', can begin their quest for enlightenment, *nirvana*, by following the Buddhist moral code, and by meditating in order to purify the mind. As a non-theistic religion, Buddhism does not concern itself with the existence of a creator, in the Western sense at least, teaching that attainment of *nirvana* is a person's route out of the endless cycle of death and rebirth.

A variety of different schools and monastic traditions emerged within Buddhism, from *Theravada*, the earliest surviving monastic school, to *Tantra*, which advocates the use of ritual magic to control hidden forces or aid the path to *nirvana*. One of the most important traditions is *Mahayana*, through which some seek not only to achieve *nirvana* but actually to become a Buddha. Regional variations also emerged, as Buddhism spread outward from India across much of eastern Asia. In many cases, these variations are closely related to local religious traditions, or are even the product of wider syncretism, such as the Cao Dai in Vietnam, which has roots not only in Buddhism but also Catholic Christianity, Confucianism, and Taoism. In recent decades, Buddhism has faced suppression in many Asian countries, perhaps most notably in Tibet, where rule by Maoist China led to severe repression of the local traditions. Alongside this, though, Buddhism has experienced growth elsewhere, buoyed both by migration and Western interest in the religion.

CHAPTER 38

A Historical Overview

Buddhism is the '-ism' that is named after the Buddha. 'Buddha' is not a personal name, but a title meaning 'the one who has awakened'. The Buddha was a historical individual who lived and died some centuries BCE, although it is difficult to be precise about his exact dates. The common traditional date for the Buddha's birth is 563 BCE, and the sources agree he lived in North India for eighty years. However, modern scholarship questions the reliability of this date, and most historians place his birth eighty to a hundred years later, and his death around 400 BCE. The Buddha's clan-name was Gautama, but later tradition called him Siddhartha in Sanskrit, or Siddhattha in the Pali language, in which many early Buddhist works were written.

'Buddhism' is an English name for a religion that its followers often simply refer to as the *Dharma* (Pali, *Dhamma*), which can be taken here as meaning both 'the teaching' and 'the way things are'. It was discovering this, and teaching it, that made Siddhartha Gautama 'the Buddha'. Whereas Western discussions tend to stress the importance of its founder (Buddha + ism, no doubt on the model of Christ + ianity), Buddhists prefer to emphasize not him, but rather what he taught; for them the obvious place to start is the teaching. This teaching, they say, leads people to understand how things truly are, and thence to a radical reassessment of their lives. The Buddha simply awakened to this truth and taught it. In this he was not unique, for — it is said — others had awakened before him, and there will be many, many after him too.

> *Hatred is never quenched by hatred; by non-hatred alone is hatred quenched. This is an Eternal Law.*
>
> *Dhammapada*, v. 5

WHO WAS THE BUDDHA?

To start with the life story of the Buddha is the Western tradition. Even if we start with it here too, this life story should not be read as historical fact, though we can reasonably take it that Siddhartha Gautama lived and died. He was considered by his followers to have achieved the fullest possible understanding of reality, an understanding that is true freedom. The historicity of the rest is difficult to assess. Some of it we know is very unlikely to have happened, but Buddhism has always been more interested in the ways in which the life story illustrates Buddhist teachings than in its literal historical truth.

The legendary account of the Buddha's life developed gradually in the centuries after his demise. In that account, he is a prince who is protected from all knowledge of the nasty things of life. However, in the Pali sources he is simply a highborn Shakyan who had little awareness of suffering as he grew up, but the shock of discovering old age, sickness, and death led him to renounce worldly pursuits. He had married and had a son, but left his family and took to the life – not uncommon in India then as now – of a wandering seeker. He sought the final truth that would lead to complete freedom from suffering – a harsh life of meditation, study, and asceticism. Food – and very little of it – came from asking for alms. But eventually Siddhartha, looking within, in deep meditation, reached the truth he sought. He came to 'see it the way it really is', and this truth set him free. He was now the awakened one, the Buddha. The Buddha gathered around him a group of disciples and wandered northern India, teaching all who would listen. Eventually, in old age, the Buddha died. But for him death was nothing; for he was now free from death, as he was free from all other forms of unpleasantness, imperfection, and frustration. After death, there is nothing more to say.

Chinese Buddha figurine.

WHAT DID HE TEACH?

The life story of the Buddha is all about things appearing one way and really being another. The Buddha taught that 'seeing things the way they really are' is the way to overcome every sort of unpleasantness, imperfection, and frustration. These are all classed under the expression *dukkha* (Pali), a term which in the everyday context of the time meant literally 'pain' or 'suffering'. He taught that, when we look deeply, we can see that all our lives are, one way or another, at root simply *dukkha*. The Buddha was uninterested in the question of God; and Buddhist tradition has been unanimous that a creator-God, in the sense in which he is thought to exist by Christians, for example, simply does not exist. Suffering, for Buddhists, is the result of our ignorance, not understanding the way things really are, and we all live our lives in the light of that failure in understanding. The central dimension of such misunderstanding lies in our not appreciating that everything in our experience is by its very nature impermanent. Alongside impermanence – in fact, logically and doctrinally prior to it – is conditionality: the teaching that things arise and pass away in dependence upon conditions. Suffering results from holding on, trying in our experiences and in our lives to 'fix things' so they do not break up and cease to be. Clearly we are doomed to failure. We need to learn to let go let go of attachment and a fixed sense of selfhood; but this letting go has to occur at a very deep level indeed, since we have been confused and suffering in this manner for infinite lifetimes.

For Buddhists, human experience consists of a flow of consciousness, with associated mental contents such as feelings and intentions, and a body that is ever changing too. Any further unchanging element, called a 'self' (Pali, *atta*; Sanskrit, *atman*), would appear to be unnecessary. Indeed, it could lead to a dangerous form of self-grasping, the very opposite of letting go. Rather, Buddhist tradition teaches 'not-self' (Pali, *anatta*; Sanskrit, *anatman*). At death the body ceases, but the ever-flowing continuum of consciousness and its mental accompaniments continues and 'spins', as it were, another body in accordance with one's good or bad deeds (*karma*). Such 'rebirth' means that one is yet again subject to suffering – old age, sickness, death and so on. This process ceases only with letting go at the deepest possible level, attained through meditation. It is a letting go that springs from seeing things as they truly are, and completely reversing one's almost instinctive and frantic patterns of grasping after things. This cessation Buddhists call 'enlightenment' (Pali, *nibbana*; Sanskrit, *nirvana*).

MONASTIC TRADITIONS AND DOCTRINAL SCHOOLS

Central to the Buddha's vision of the way forward was an order of monks and nuns – known as the *Sangha* – living on alms, and expressing in their state of renunciation their commitment to the radical transformation we all need. In time, monasteries were established, together with a monastic rule, to regulate the conduct of the *Sangha*, and promote the peace and harmony necessary in order to follow the Buddha's path. The Buddha did not appoint a successor, reportedly declaring that the teaching – the *Dharma* – should be his successor. But after his death, with time, disagreements occurred, initially over the monastic rules. Where disputes over the rule could not be reconciled, monks in the minority were required to depart, forming their own groups based on variants of the monastic rule. Eventually, a number of different monastic traditions were formed. The best known of these – and the only one of the early Indian Buddhist monastic traditions to survive to the present day – is the 'Way of the Elders' (*Theravada*), found nowadays in, for example, Sri Lanka, Thailand, Cambodia, and Myanmar (Burma).

In Buddhism, 'schism' (*sanghabheda*) technically concerns monastic rule, not doctrinal disagreement, which is relatively less serious. Nevertheless, as time passed, different doctrinal positions also evolved, sometimes followed by identifiable schools – for example the school known as *Pudgalavada* ('Teaching the *pudgala*'). The point of contention here was that of the 'person' (*pudgala*). Advocates urged that, although the Buddha taught 'not-self', there still exists something – albeit difficult to specify what – called the *pudgala*, as something in some sense really there 'in' us. Others viewed this *pudgala* as just a self in disguise, and an abandonment of a central part of the Buddha's teaching. Further issues of debate involved who or what the Buddha himself was. Some urged that a Buddha is really much more extraordinary than people realize. For example, although he seems to teach, really he is permanently in meditation. He has no need to sleep, to defecate, or even to eat, but only does these things in order to act in accordance with the expectations of the world. Many such topics were debated in early – and even later – Buddhism, as the Buddha's followers sought to put his teaching into practice, and to explain it clearly to others. Indeed, also discussed was the relative importance of practising the *Dharma* for one's own freedom from all suffering, as opposed to compassionately teaching it to others.

> Let none deceive another, not despise any person whatsoever in any place. Let one not wish any harm to another out of anger or ill-will …
>
> Let thoughts of boundless love pervade the whole world: above, below and across, without any obstruction, without any hatred, any enmity.
>
> From the *Metta Sutta*, The Discourse on Loving Kindness, *Sutta Nipata*, verses 6 and 8

WHAT IS MAHAYANA BUDDHISM?

To understand early Buddhist history it is thus necessary to distinguish doctrinal dispute and debate – that is, doctrinal schools – from behavioural disharmony and schism – monastic traditions. Different again, and appearing in the literature from about the first century CE, is the greatest internal development within Buddhism, the growth of the *Mahayana*: the 'Great Vehicle' or perhaps 'the Vehicle that leads to the Great'. Mahayana Buddhism is not a doctrinal school; within the Mahayana there are many doctrinal schools. Moreover the Mahayana is to be distinguished from a monastic tradition. There is no such thing as a distinct set of Mahayana monastic rules (*vinaya*). For example, monks in India holding to the Mahayana perspective would be ordained and live in accordance with any one of the sets of monastic rules that had already developed, and were sometimes to be found in monasteries with others who did not hold to the Mahayana perspective.

Hence it makes no sense to speak of two 'schools' of Buddhism, Theravada and Mahayana. Theravada is a monastic tradition; Mahayana is not. They are not comparable phenomena: there could in theory be a Theravada follower of Mahayana. However, in their practice Mahayana and Theravada are very different phenomena, with different scriptures and practices. Mahayana can best be thought of as a vision of what Buddhism is really, finally, all about. Mahayana appears first in texts – writings known as *Mahayana sutras* – claiming, controversially, to be the word of the Buddha himself. Crucially, what gradually emerges in these writings is a distinction between simply being free from all suffering – in other words, enlightened – and actually being a Buddha. A Buddha is spiritually more than just free from his own suffering; a Buddha is also perfectly compassionate. Thus to be a Buddha is better than simply being enlightened. This is not only because of a Buddha's great compassion,

Stone Buddha in Buddhist temple, Bangkok, Thailand.

but also because of the many marvellous – indeed miraculous – abilities a Buddha possesses in order to help others. But it takes many, many lifetimes of spiritual striving to become a Buddha. Thus, those who aim for the highest goal should seek not just their own freedom from suffering and rebirth, but should also vow to follow the long path to Buddhahood. This path is to be followed over very many rebirths, willingly taking on their attendant sufferings, in order eventually as a Buddha better to be able to help others.

The Mahayana, in a nutshell, is the way of those who aspire to become perfect Buddhas, which is said to be for the benefit of all sentient beings – all those with consciousness. Those who vow to do this are known as *bodhisattvas*, perhaps originally meaning 'one who is capable of awakening'. Mahayana sources go into great detail about the stages of the path that a *bodhisattva* must follow in order to become a Buddha.

With time, the Mahayana also elaborated on the ways in which a Buddha is superior to someone who has simply put an end to his or her own suffering, developing further the idea that a Buddha is really much more than he appears to be. Even his death was just a show, put on in order to give a 'skilful teaching' of impermanence. For the Mahayana, the Buddha – indeed infinite Buddhas – are still around, living on higher planes – 'Pure Lands' – from which, through their great compassion and with miraculous powers, they are available and willing to help those who have need of them. With them are advanced *bodhisattvas*, who are also full of compassion and able to help others. Some of these Buddhas and 'celestial' *bodhisattvas* are named, such as Avalokiteshvara, a *bodhisattva* who is said to be the very incarnation of compassion, or Mañjushri, likewise the very incarnation of wisdom and insight.

BUDDHISM BEYOND INDIA

Significant to the history of Buddhism in India was the conversion of the great Emperor Ashoka (third century BCE), which gave the religion important imperial patronage – although scholars now discount the view that he attempted to make Buddhism the state religion. From the time of Ashoka, Buddhism began to migrate further afield, according to tradition reaching Sri Lanka at this time. It subsequently spread into South-East Asia, reaching China along the Central Asian trade routes during the early centuries CE, spreading to Korea and other countries of East Asia, and reaching Japan in the sixth century CE. Buddhism came to Tibet from various directions – including India and China – probably from about the seventh century. In India, however, for various reasons not yet fully understood, but possibly partly related to the rise of devotional theistic forms of Hinduism, as well as the impact of Islam on India, Buddhism declined, almost ceasing to exist from about the fourteenth century. It has revived in recent centuries, and Buddhism has also now taken on a global dimension. Perhaps the most well known modern Buddhist is the Dalai Lama of Tibet (1935–), a former winner of the Nobel Peace Prize.

It is common, although misleading, to speak of the Buddhism of, for example, China, Japan, and Tibet as Mahayana, as opposed to the Theravada Buddhism of, for example, South-East Asia. As we have

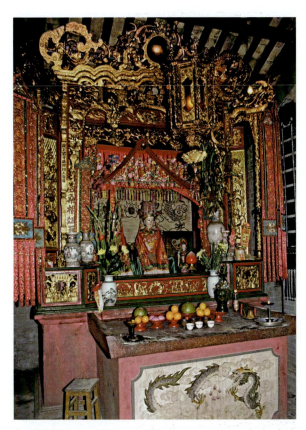

Buddhist shrine, Macao, Asia.

seen, these are not comparable phenomena. Nevertheless, many Mahayana scriptures were transmitted to, and usually given unquestioning authority in, China, Japan, and Tibet. Unlike in South-East Asia, Buddhists in those countries could be expected to express adherence, in one way or another, to the Mahayana vision as embracing their highest and final aspirations.

ZEN

Particularly characteristic of East Asian Buddhism is the tradition known in Japan as *Zen*. Zen – the word itself is related to 'meditation' – is known for stressing direct, non-verbal, intuitive insight, expressed through arts such as painting, but sometimes also employing humour and shock tactics to bring about awakening. This awakened 'Buddha-nature', it is urged, is already present within all of us, if we did but realize it. Also important in, for example, Japanese Buddhism is the tradition of Shinran (thirteenth century CE). For Shinran, the awakening of a Buddha is quite beyond unenlightened capabilities; only by completely letting go of reliance on ourselves, and trusting in the Buddha's salvific ability, can the already-enlightened nature of the Buddha (a Buddha known here as *Amida*) shine

BUDDHISM TIMELINE

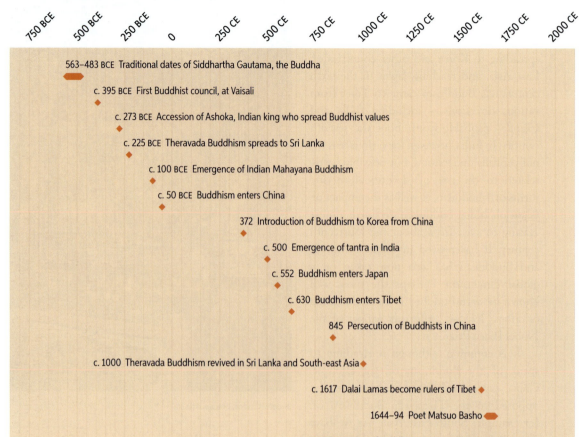

750 BCE   500 BCE   250 BCE   0   250 CE   500 CE   750 CE   1000 CE   1250 CE   1500 CE   1750 CE   2000 CE

563–483 BCE Traditional dates of Siddhartha Gautama, the Buddha

c. 395 BCE First Buddhist council, at Vaisali

c. 273 BCE Accession of Ashoka, Indian king who spread Buddhist values

c. 225 BCE Theravada Buddhism spreads to Sri Lanka

c. 100 BCE Emergence of Indian Mahayana Buddhism

c. 50 BCE Buddhism enters China

372 Introduction of Buddhism to Korea from China

c. 500 Emergence of tantra in India

c. 552 Buddhism enters Japan

c. 630 Buddhism enters Tibet

845 Persecution of Buddhists in China

c. 1000 Theravada Buddhism revived in Sri Lanka and South-east Asia

c. 1617 Dalai Lamas become rulers of Tibet

1644–94 Poet Matsuo Basho

c. 1900 Beginning of Buddhist missionary activity in the West

1952 World Fellowship of Buddhism founded

1959 Chinese take over Tibet, destroying temples and monasteries; Dalai Lama and others flee to India

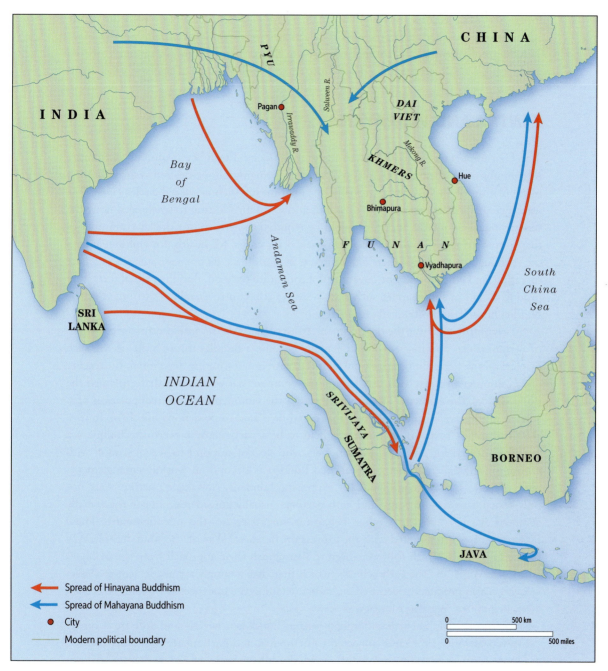

Legend:
- Spread of Hinayana Buddhism
- Spread of Mahayana Buddhism
- ● City
- Modern political boundary

Spread of Buddhism to South-east Asia

forth. According to this teaching, humans have to let go completely of even the subtle egoism that encourages them to think they can achieve anything spiritually worthwhile – including enlightenment – through their own efforts. Being a monk or nun, or even meditating, is finally irrelevant, a distraction, and a possible source of egoistic attachment.

TANTRA AND VAJRAYANA

The final important development to mention is *Tantra*. From the beginning Buddhists, in common with their peers, accepted magic – bringing about desired results through manipulation of hidden forces, usually by ritual means such as sacred circles (*mandalas*), utterances of power (*mantras*), visualizations and so on. In addition to teaching, among the services Buddhist monks and nuns might be required to perform for the lay communities that supported them would be magical rituals – for crops, for health, for children and so on. Although this was not their main interest as Buddhists, its appropriateness, as an act of caring, and efficacy was not questioned. From quite early on, Buddhist ritual texts were produced, and in some circles such texts were – again controversially – attributed to the Buddha himself, and often called *tantras*.

Also controversial was the development, from perhaps the seventh century CE or earlier, of certain *tantras* claiming one could actually become a Buddha through the use of such magical means. Secret initiations were required, with unquestioning devotion to the teacher (*guru*), in order to learn their use. Even more controversial were *tantras* that explained the possibility of this supreme attainment through the employment and manipulation of a sort of subtle, psycho-physical body that everyone is said to possess within them. In this, the ritual use of sexual intercourse was held to be a particularly powerful technique – a practice reserved for advanced practitioners who do not respond to sexual stimuli with craving or attachment. Since an awakened Buddha is beyond all worldly entanglements and confusions, also recommended – expressing humanity's awakened nature – are not only sexual activity – in ways, and with partners, usually considered outside the socially accepted norm – but also other behaviour surprising to the unenlightened. These developments – often linked with the expression *Vajrayana* (Way of the Thunderbolt, Way of the Diamond), which followers used to distinguish their approach from the *Mahayana* (the Great Way), and the early schools, which they disparagingly termed 'Hinayana' (lesser vehicle) – also produced a genre of literature detailing the unexpected exploits of certain awakened tantric 'persons of magical power' (*siddhas*).

Not surprisingly, such developments within Buddhism were – and still are – highly controversial. With time, and subjected to orthodox, and particularly monastic, control, the more controversial dimensions of Tantric Buddhism were 'tamed' and absorbed into the wider Mahayana spiritual context of great compassion and wisdom. It is in this form that one finds today the widest and most well known presence of *tantra*, in the Buddhism of Tibet.

PAUL WILLIAMS

INTRODUCTION TO WORLD RELIGIONS

CHAPTER 39

Sacred Writings

The Buddha himself wrote nothing; he simply taught. He sometimes taught his vision of the world, humanity's place within it, and the spiritual and moral way to freedom — eventually complete freedom — from incompleteness, frustration, and suffering. At other times he settled disputes among his followers, or legislated for the best sort of life to live to attain this complete freedom. According to Buddhist tradition, soon after the Buddha's death those monks who had achieved the goal — enlightenment (Pali, *nibbana*; Sanskrit, *nirvana*) — met to recite what they remembered of the Buddha's discourses at the First Buddhist Council. (It is often stated there were three such councils in classical times, although only two are accepted by all Buddhist traditions.)

ORAL TRANSMISSION

The emphasis from the beginning was on memory and recitation. For the first few centuries, the Buddhist scriptures were handed down orally — which partly explains the importance in Buddhism of the oral transmission from teacher to pupil — rather than in written form. Different groups of monks specialized in preserving different texts, or collections of scriptures; and transmission through oral recitation in groups proved to be a very effective way of preserving the Buddha's words — at least as accurate as writing, since interpolation of additional — and perhaps controversial — material or omission is much more difficult, as it would immediately be noticed. According to one Buddhist tradition, the scriptures were not written down until the first century BCE. The decision to resort to writing was perhaps partly due to fear in time of social and political stress that the teachings might become lost through the death of significant numbers of important reciters by disease, war, or famine — something that seems to have happened, for example, with some of the scriptures of Jainism.

THE BUDDHIST CANON

The texts recited at the First Council form the basis of the Buddhist scriptural canon. They are divided into:

sutras (Pali, *sutta*) – the general discourses of the Buddha and, sometimes, the teachings of his authorized followers

vinaya – texts relating to the structure and discipline of the monastic order.

With time, a further section of the canon was added, the *abhidharma* (Pali, *abhidhamma*): perhaps 'higher [or 'more precise'] teaching'. This section consists mainly of works that develop an elaborate description of how the psycho-physical world looks when seen 'as things really are' by an enlightened person, rather than through everyday unenlightened vision. The canonical *abhidharma* texts probably date from after the death of the Buddha, but all claim direct origin from him.

These three sections together form the 'Three Baskets' (Pali, *Tipitaka*; Sanskrit, *Tripitaka*), which are themselves subdivided. For example, in the Pali Canon, the *sutra* 'basket' is divided into four sections – plus one supplementary section – known as *Nikayas*. Perhaps the best known of these is the 'Collection of Long Discourses' (*Digha Nikaya*).

It was some centuries before the canon became more or less closed, such that – at least in theory – no more works could be added to it and given the prestige of 'coming directly from the Buddha himself'. Some scholars think the *Sutta Pitaka* was closed 150 years after the Buddha, while the other sections were closed later. There are also some Buddhist texts which have all the authority of canonical scriptures, but are not technically part of the canon at all – for example the monastic rule, still recited regularly by monks and nuns.

DIFFERENT VERSIONS

There is a tradition that the Buddha recommended preserving and transmitting his teachings in local languages rather than Sanskrit, the pan-Indian language of education. Hence, from quite early times, Buddhist scriptures were in a number of languages and also underwent translation. Moreover, as the various Buddhist monastic traditions and doctrinal schools were formed, different versions of the canon began to appear, often in different Indian languages. Nowadays, the comparative study of different canonical versions of recognizably the same text forms a fruitful area of scholarly research.

Scriptures require some sort of authoritative body to preserve and transmit them down the ages. In Buddhism, particularly in the Indian world, this has always been the monastic order, the *Sangha*. The only Buddhist monastic tradition to have survived from the early centuries to the present day is the 'Way of the Elders' (*Theravada*); the canon preserved by the *Theravada* – the sole version to have survived in its entirety and in its ancient Indian language – is the 'Pali Canon', written in the *Pali* language. Although old – and of inestimable importance for the study of Buddhism – the Pali Canon is only one of a number of Buddhist canons that existed in ancient times. Other individual canonical works, or collections, have survived, either in other Indian languages, or in ancient translations, for example into Chinese or Tibetan, made as part of Buddhist missionary activity.

With time, and with greater reliance on writing than on oral transmission, certain Buddhist traditions and schools in India started to preserve their scriptures in Sanskrit, which is why Buddhist terms are often given in both their Sanskrit and Pali forms — usually very similar: for example, *nibbana* (Pali), *nirvana* (Sanskrit). As Buddhism spread across India, using just one language made sense, rather than relying on different translations in different areas. Educated people would be familiar with Sanskrit, and a monk with a Sanskrit text could take it anywhere, without needing to have it translated, explaining in the vernacular what the text meant to less educated people as part of his teaching mission. This change to the use of Sanskrit can be seen occurring in the greatest post-canonical scriptural development in Indian Buddhism, the appearance of the Mahayana *sutras*. A number of the early Mahayana *sutras* show signs of having been translated into Sanskrit out of other Indian languages, in which, presumably, they were originally composed.

Stupa (dome) of the ninth-century CE Mahayana Buddhist temple of Borobudur, or Barabudur, Magelang, Central Java, Indonesia.

APOCRYPHAL SCRIPTURES

The earliest form in which we know Mahayana Buddhism is in its scriptures. Indeed, for followers of Mahayana, scriptural support appears to be older by some centuries than archaeological evidence. Mahayana *sutras* are apocryphal, and their ideas often seemingly new and radical. As apocryphal *sutras*, although they claim to be the words of the Buddha himself, this claim is hotly disputed within Buddhism, and the extant versions of these *sutras* cannot possibly be that old. Elements of at least some early Mahayana *sutras* may have originated in inspiring, meditative visions and revelations, held to be from a Buddha, who was thus thought to be still accessible to us on some 'higher plane'.

Although there may have been attempts to add such *sutras*, they are not included in any official canon preserved by any known Indian monastic tradition.

Apocryphal *sutras* were not created in India alone. For example, many Mahayana apocryphal *sutras* were composed in China, and unknown in India in classical times. Even today, outside areas usually associated with Mahayana — for example, the monastically Theravada world of Sri Lanka — apocryphal Buddhist *sutras* are still produced, claiming to spring from some sort of special revelation, but not accepted as canonical by the mainstream, local Buddhist monastic order.

It has been suggested that the origin and survival of Mahayana as a movement required the existence of writing. Religions often produce controversial texts claiming to be the words of, or in some sense inspired by, their founder; but such works disappear unless taken up and preserved by enthusiasts down the ages. In traditional Buddhism, canonical works have been preserved and transmitted to future generations by the monastic *Sangha*. But the *Sangha* was unlikely to preserve apocryphal texts, and certainly not texts such as the early Mahayana *sutras*, which inclined sometimes to be critical of the existing monastic hierarchy. Hence, so long as the canon was transmitted orally, the preservation of significant new perspectives — such as that of Mahayana, claiming the authority of the Buddha — was all but impossible. However, the writing down of the scriptures made possible the preservation and transmission of apocryphal works and perspectives. A written text could survive, providing someone was willing to preserve it.

TANTRAS

The other major corpus of apocryphal, scriptural literature in Buddhism claiming the authority of the Buddha himself consists of the *Tantras*, texts associated with the use of ritual magic. Their origins in Buddhism — they are also found in Hinduism and Jainism — are obscure, and the earliest *Tantras* are certainly some centuries later than the earliest Mahayana *sutras*. This literature is very large. To practise the ritual prescriptions of these texts, which in time came to include techniques for attaining enlightenment as well as more mundane magical activities, requires initiation, close instruction from a teacher (*guru*), and vows of secrecy. Tantric texts involve the use of such methods as magical diagrams, utterances (*mantras*), and visualizations. *Tantras* have become linked with, and in places such as Tibet assimilated into, Mahayana; but recent research has also found tantric literature in Myanmar (Burma) and Cambodia, countries not normally associated with Mahayana perspectives.

Asked by some citizens of Kalama for guidance, the Buddha said: 'Be not led by reports or tradition or hearsay. Be not led by the authority of religious texts, nor by mere logic or inference, nor by considering appearances … But, O Kalamas, when you know for yourselves that certain things are unwholesome (akusala) and wrong and bad, then give them up … And when you know for yourselves that certain things are wholesome (kusala) and good, then accept them and follow them.'

Anguttara Nikaya 3.65 (i 188).

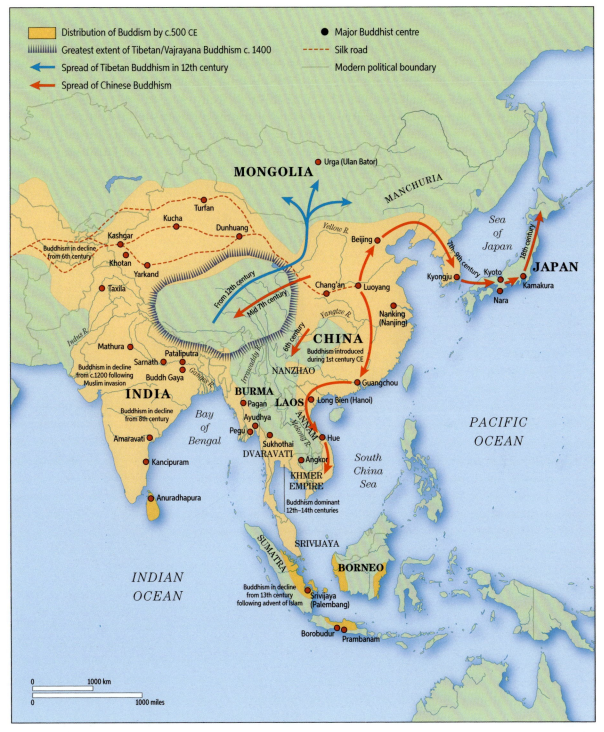

Legend:

- Distribution of Buddhism by c.500 CE
- Greatest extent of Tibetan/Vajrayana Buddhism c. 1400
- → Spread of Tibetan Buddhism in 12th century
- → Spread of Chinese Buddhism
- ● Major Buddhist centre
- --- Silk road
- — Modern political boundary

MONGOLIA

Urga (Ulan Bator)

MANCHURIA

Turfan

Kucha

Dunhuang

Yellow R.

Kashgar

Beijing

Sea of Japan

Khotan

Yarkand

Buddhism in decline from 6th century

From 12th century

Mid 7th century

Chang'an

Luoyang

6th century

7th-9th century

Kyongju

Kyoto

Nara

Kamakura

18th century

JAPAN

Taxila

Indus R.

Mathura

Nanking (Nanjing)

Sarnath

Pataliputra

Buddhism in decline from c.1200 following Muslim invasion

Buddh Gaya

Ganges R.

CHINA
Buddhism introduced during 1st century CE

NANZHAO

INDIA

Buddhism in decline from 8th century

Bay of Bengal

BURMA

Pagan

LAOS

Long Bien (Hanoi)

Guangchou

Irrawaddy R.

Amaravati

Ayudhya

Pegu

Sukhothai

Mekong R.

ANNAM

Hue

PACIFIC OCEAN

Kancipuram

DVARAVATI

Angkor

South China Sea

KHMER EMPIRE
Buddhism dominant 12th–14th centuries

Anuradhapura

INDIAN OCEAN

SUMATRA

SRIVIJAYA

BORNEO

Buddhism in decline from 13th century following advent of Islam

Srivijaya (Palembang)

Borobudur

Prambanam

0 _____ 1000 km

0 _____ 1000 miles

The Spread of Chinese and Tibetan Buddhism

SHASTRAS

In addition to scriptures – those accepted by all as canonical, and those of disputed authority, held by some as apocryphal – Buddhist literature also includes a vast number of exegetical treatises, often known as *shastras*. These have been produced by great scholars of various Buddhist traditions and schools, to clarify difficult points of interpretation, to defend their understanding against rivals and alternatives, or, like the 'Treasury of Abhidharma' (*Abhidharmakosha*), to serve as critical compendia of the Buddhist doctrine and path. Such exegetical treatises have been produced in each country in which Buddhism has been established, and are very important for the study of Buddhist doctrinal history.

PAUL WILLIAMS

CHAPTER 40

Beliefs

A disciple of the Buddha, Malunkyaputta, complained that the Buddha had not answered some of the most important questions of life – Is the world eternal? Is the soul the same as the body? and so on. The Buddha replied with a story.

> *A man is wounded by an arrow thickly smeared with poison. His friends and relatives brought a surgeon to him. The man said, 'I will not let the surgeon pull out this arrow until I know whether the man who wounded me was a noble, a brahman, a merchant or a worker. I will not let the surgeon pull out the arrow until I know the name and clan of the man who wounded me … until I know whether the he was tall or short or of middle height … until I know whether the bow that wounded me was a longbow or a crossbow … until I know whether the bowstring that wounded me was fibre or reed or sinew or bark …*
>
> *All this would not be known to the man and he would die.*

Abridged from the *Culamalunkya Sutta, Majjhima Nikaya* 63 (I, 246).

So, the Buddha added, will those die who insist they must know the answers to speculative questions about the nature of reality before starting to live the holy life. For such questions are not beneficial to the real task, the cessation of suffering.

This story points to the heart of what Buddhism is about. Buddhism is less a set of beliefs than a path, leading from suffering to the cessation of suffering, from ignorance to compassion and wisdom. The Buddha's first invitation to those who wished to follow him as monks or nuns in the fifth century BCE was: 'Come, live the holy life, in order that you make an end of suffering.' The only credal statement in Buddhism, therefore, is:

> *I go to the Buddha for refuge;*
> *I go to the Dhamma for refuge;*
> *I go to the* Sangha *[the Buddhist community] for refuge.*

These are the 'Three Jewels' or 'Three Gems': anyone who places them at the centre of life, by 'going for refuge' to them, is a Buddhist. The *Dhamma* (Pali; Sanskrit, *Dharma*) – literally, 'that which constitutes', or 'the way things are' – is what the Buddha 'awoke to' at his enlightenment, and what he taught for forty years after. For Buddhists, it is the truth about the nature of existence; the truth that upholds the cosmos; the truth that all Buddhas have taught. Across the different schools of Buddhism, the *Dhamma* is expressed in a variety of ways; however, there are elements that all schools hold in common.

LIVING THE HOLY LIFE

Living the holy life involves a way of seeing reality and a way of acting. The way of seeing begins with experience rather than metaphysics: the experience that something in life is dislocated, flawed, unsatisfactory, and full of suffering, and the realization that one reason for this is that everything is impermanent. We are separated from loved ones. We lose our strength. We grow old, sicken, and die. Everything we cherish – youth, strength, possessions, relationships – passes away. Buddhism speaks of three defining characteristics of existence: impermanence (Pali, *anicca*; Sanskrit, *anitya*), unsatisfactoriness (Pali, *dukkha*; Sanskrit, *duhkha*), and not-self (Pali, *anatta*; Sanskrit, *anatman*). The characteristic of not-self arises when the concept of impermanence is applied to the self. As with all external phenomena, everything in our bodies and minds is changing, everything is conditioned. There is no unchanging 'self', 'soul', or ego. Mahayana Buddhists use the word 'emptiness'. All things – the self included – are 'empty' of their own nature.

> Whatever harm an enemy may do to an enemy, or a hater to a hater, an ill-directed mind inflicts on oneself a greater harm.
>
> Dhammapada, v. 42

This is the start of the Buddhist view of existence, but not the end. The message of the Buddha was that the suffering or unsatisfactoriness of life is not haphazard, random, or immovable. It has a cause, as all other phenomena have a cause, and if this cause is eradicated, suffering will not arise. The cause abides within the mind, and the Buddha identified it as 'craving': self-centred desire for sensual pleasures and life itself. Remove this craving, and suffering will cease, giving way to the liberation of *nibbana* (Sanskrit, *nirvana*). It is this 'view' that forms the first three of the Four Noble Truths:

- The Noble Truth of *Dukkha*: that there is an incompleteness and unsatisfactoriness at the heart of existence;
- The Noble Truth of the Origin of *Dukkha*: that the cause is craving or thirst (Pali, *tanha*; Sanskrit, *trsna*), the thirst for sensual pleasures, the thirst for continued existence, and the thirst for annihilation;
- The Noble Truth of the Cessation of *Dukkha*: that there is an end, based on the law of cause and effect – that is, if craving is destroyed, *dukkha* cannot arise;
- The Noble Truth of the Path to the Cessation of *Dukkha*: the Eightfold Path (see below).

The Buddhist view of the world is, therefore, of a world dis-eased (that is, ill at ease), a world entrapped in craving, where *dukkha* reigns supreme because people have not seen the *dhamma*, the truth about existence. It is a world where people are trapped in mental prisons of their own making. But it is a world where liberation awaits all who can change the way they look at the world and work towards freedom from the craving that is rooted in ignorance and expressed through greed and hatred.

THE WAY TO LIBERATION

The Noble Truths are the 'house' into which everything else fits in Buddhism.

The Fourth Noble Truth is the Noble Eightfold Path, the way to the ending of suffering:
- right view
- right resolve
- right speech
- right action
- right livelihood
- right effort
- right mindfulness
- right concentration or meditation

This is often reduced to just three categories: morality (Pali/Sanskrit, *sila*); concentration or meditation (Pali/Sanskrit, *samadhi*); and wisdom (Pali, *panna*; Sanskrit, *prajna*). Sometimes the following verse from the *Dhammapada*, a text known and loved throughout the Buddhist world, is quoted:

> The avoidance of evil, the undertaking of good, the cleansing of one's mind;
> this is the teaching of the awakened ones.

Dhammapada, v. 183

MORALITY

Morality is the bedrock of the Buddhist path. It involves 'the avoidance of evil, the undertaking of good'. Without moral discipline, the holy life cannot be lived. Most lay Buddhists place the following five precepts at the centre of their life:
- to abstain from harming any living being
- to abstain from taking what is not given
- to abstain from sexual misconduct
- to abstain from false speech
- to abstain from anything that clouds or intoxicates the mind, such as drugs and alcohol.

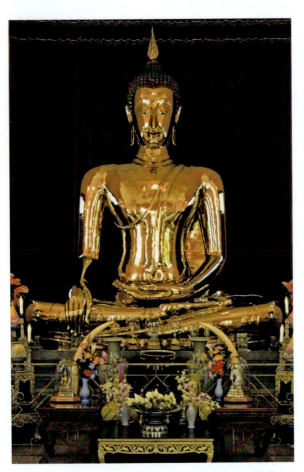

The Golden Buddha, Phra Phuttha Maha Suwan Patimakon, is the world's largest solid gold statue, and sited at the Temple of Wat Traimit, Bangkok, Thailand. It was created roughly 700 years ago.

Many would insist that these precepts involve not only abstention, but cultivation. A commitment not to harm involves the development of loving-kindness and compassion. The commitment to abstaining from taking what is not given involves recognizing the dignity and worth of other people, as does abstaining from sexual misconduct. Abstaining from false speech involves cultivating honesty and integrity.

An ancient text in the Theravada tradition, the *Karaniyametta Sutta*, describes loving-kindness in the following way: 'Just as a mother would protect her only child at the risk of her own life, even so cultivate a boundless heart towards all beings.' One way to do this is to meditate on loving-kindness (*metta*). The first step is to imagine oneself surrounded by loving-kindness. Then this loving-kindness — sometimes imagined as a white, warm light — is thrown further and further outwards into the world. First of all those dear to the meditator are brought to mind. Then the radius widens, eventually reaching those who are disliked, or even hated. It is a transformative practice that spills into everyday conduct.

Morality, for many Buddhists, is also linked with the law of action, the law of *karma* (Sanskrit; Pali, *kamma*), that moral action will produce good fruit, and unwholesome action bad fruit. This does not mean Buddhist morality is essentially selfish. Rather, self and other are seen to be interconnected. What is good for others is good for self; what would not be done to oneself would not be done to another.

MEDITATION

The task of meditation is to cleanse the mind. It ties in with the heart of the Buddha's message: that the cause of our dis-ease lies in our craving, in the three unwholesome roots of greed, hatred, and delusion. Since it is our minds and hearts that generate this craving, according to Buddhism, the only way to uproot craving is to work on the mind and heart. Buddhism offers numerous meditation methods, but these can be reduced to two main practices: tranquillity meditation (Pali/Sanskrit, *samatha*) and insight meditation (Pali, *vipassana*; Sanskrit, *vipasyana*).

Tranquillity meditation is not unique to Buddhism. It is a method through which an object of meditation is used to concentrate the mind and gain one-pointedness. The most popular object is the breath: some Buddhists pay attention to the breath as it enters and leaves the nostrils; others watch the rise and fall of the abdomen. The meditator sits with the back upright; in some traditions the eyes are closed, in others they remain partly open. When the mind wanders away from the object, it is brought back, gently and non-judgmentally, to the breath. Traditionally, forty other meditation objects can be chosen, under the direction of a teacher. This kind of meditation may lead to what Buddhists call 'meditative absorptions' or *jhanas* (Pali; Sanskrit, *dhyanas*), states of intense absorption and mental refinement.

Vipassana means 'seeing clearly' – seeing the body and the mind clearly – and is unique to Buddhism, and distinct from altered states of consciousness. Its aim is direct verification of the *Dhamma* through observation of the body and the mind. Many exercises have been developed within the Buddhist tradition to aid this. One method used widely is 'bare attention', or 'choiceless awareness', a form of mindfulness that emphasizes the present moment. Whatever arises in the mind and the body becomes the object of meditation, of awareness. It may be a reaction of attraction or aversion to an external noise, a feeling of pain in the legs, or thoughts of hatred, jealousy, or love. Nothing is judged good or bad, nothing clung to. Everything is watched, noted, and allowed to pass; its impermanence and not-self seen. The

The Pure Mind

All that we are is the result of what we have thought: it is founded on our thoughts, it is made up of our thoughts. If a man speaks or acts with an evil thought, pain follows him, as the wheel follows the foot of the ox that draws the carriage.

All that we are is the result of what we have thought: it is founded on our thoughts, it is made up of our thoughts. If a man speaks or acts with a pure thought, happiness follows him, like a shadow that never leaves him.

'He abused me, he beat me, he defeated me, he robbed me' – in those who harbour such thoughts hatred will never cease.

'He abused me, he beat me, he defeated me, he robbed me,' – in those who do not harbour such thoughts hatred will cease.

For hatred does not cease by hatred at any time: hatred ceases by love, this is an old rule.

The world does not know that we must all come to an end here: but those who know it, their quarrels cease at once.

He who lives looking for pleasures only, his senses uncontrolled, immoderate in his food, idle, and weak, Mara (death) will certainly overthrow him, as the wind throws down a weak tree.

He who lives without looking for pleasures, his senses well controlled, moderate in his food, faithful and strong, him Mara will certainly not overthrow, any more than the wind throws down a rocky mountain.

The Dhammapada 1.1–8, transl. by Max Müller and Max Fausböll, 1881, adapted.

greed, hatred, and delusion in everything is seen, as well as what
triggers them. Each period of meditation becomes a voyage of
Thai Buddhist temple.
discovery into the way the mind and body function. Other methods include noticing the
impermanent or insubstantial nature of experience, and dismantling the experience of
selfhood by examining it in the light of Buddhist teachings.

Buddhists believe meditation is the principal means through which greed, hatred,
and delusion or ignorance can be uprooted and transcended. Central to 'delusion'
(Pali, *moha*) is the belief that we have an unchanging 'I' or ego that has to be placed at
the centre of all things, to be protected, promoted, and pampered. Meditation shows
that the things we believe to be 'self' – our feelings, our thoughts, our pain – are
impermanent and empty.

REBIRTH

Buddhists stress that there is continuity after death, but that the ultimate goal of religious
practice is not an after-death state. The term most often used is 'rebirth', which most
Buddhists prefer to 'reincarnation', since they do not believe there is an unchanging soul

to reincarnate, but rather an ever-changing process of cause and effect. Death is believed to lead continually to rebirth after rebirth, until greed, hatred, and delusion are eradicated. For the Theravada Buddhist, one can be reborn into any of five realms:

1. the hells;
2. the animal world;
3. the realm of the hungry ghosts;
4. the realm of humans; and
5. the realm of the gods.

Mahayana Buddhists have added another heavenly realm:

6. that of the demi-gods.

> Monks, there are to be seen beings who can admit freedom from suffering from bodily disease for one year, for two years, for three, four, five, ten, twenty, thirty, forty, fifty years; who can admit freedom from bodily disease for even a hundred years. But, monks, those beings are hard to find in the world who can admit freedom from mental disease even for one moment, save only those in whom the asavas ('corruptions' such as ignorance) are destroyed.
>
> *Anguttara Nikaya* Text ii, 143.

Each realm is linked to a particular emotion or characteristic, and they are states of mind as well as states of being. So one who is in the grip of hatred and anger is, in one sense, already in the hell realm.

The goal of the Buddhist path is to go beyond all of these realms by attaining *nirvana*, through eradicating greed, hatred, and delusion. Some Buddhists see this as a well-nigh impossible immediate goal. For them, rebirth in a heavenly realm, through following the five precepts and developing loving kindness, is goal enough. Others insist that *nirvana* is possible in this very life. Whether it is seen as possible now, or in the distant future, all Buddhists speak of it with joy and wonder. *Nirvana* is the end of suffering and rebirth, attained when the fire of craving is put out. It is the highest ethical state, but also beyond all human ethical constructs. It is defined by wisdom and compassion, yet beyond anything that the unenlightened person can conceive. It is absolute security and bliss. It is liberation. Some Mahayana Buddhists link it with realizing one's Buddha nature. Theravada Buddhists speak of reaching the state of the *arahat*. What happens after death to those who have realized their Buddha nature, or reached the state of the *arahat*, is left open. The message of the texts is that it is beyond all human concepts.

Some Buddhists in the Mahayana tradition have an additional goal: the liberation of all beings. They take what is known as the *bodhisattva* vow, an aspiration to achieve enlightenment not for oneself alone, but for the sake of all beings. This is sometimes envisaged as a commitment to stay within the realm of birth and rebirth until all beings have been liberated.

ELIZABETH J. HARRIS

CHAPTER 41

Family and Society

The original call of the Buddha was: 'Come, live the holy life in order that you make an end of suffering.' Some who heard this renounced home and family to become celibate monks and nuns (Pali, *bhikkhus*, *bhikkhunis*; Sanskrit, *bhiksu*, *bhiksuni*). Others remained within their family as lay followers. A clear division emerged between the two, summed up in the verse from the Pali Canon about the peacock and the swan:

The blue-necked peacock which flies through the air never approaches the speed of the swan. Similarly, the householder can never resemble the monk who is endowed with the qualities of a sage who meditates, aloof, in the jungle.

Sutta Nipata, v. 221

THE FOURFOLD SOCIETY

Those with no responsibilities to their families were believed to be on the fast track to *nirvana*, because they could more easily free themselves from attachments, and from the attraction and aversion that attachments generate. Householders, generally speaking, were on the slower track, forced into wealth creation and worries about survival. However, that did not mean they were unimportant, or that they could not reach high levels of religious purity. The canonical texts contain many examples of strong, spiritual laypeople. Early Buddhism spoke about the 'Fourfold Society – monks, nuns, laymen, and laywomen – with a relationship of interdependence between them:

- Monks and nuns were dependent for food and other requisites on laypeople.
- Householders were taught the *dhamma* (Pali; Sanskrit, *dharma*) by the ordained, and gained a 'field' for the making of merit (Pali: *punna*; Sanskrit, *punya*). The concept of merit derives from the law of action (Pali, *kamma*; Sanskrit, *karma*), according to which good action produces good

Just as a mother would protect her only child at the risk of her own life, even so cultivate a boundless heart towards all beings.

From *The Discourse on Loving Kindness*, Sutta Nipata, v. 149

consequences. Monks and nuns were a 'field' for merit-gaining, because good consequences were ensured for any who were generous to them.

This fourfold system still exists in many Asian countries with a Buddhist majority. The order of nuns was lost in countries such as Sri Lanka and Myanmar (Burma), but action by Buddhist women in recent decades is bringing it back. In the twentieth century, Buddhist movements without orders of traditional monks or nuns developed, such as Rissho Kosei-kai and Soka Gakkai in Japan, and the Friends of the Western Triratna Buddhist Order in Britain and elsewhere. However, the last distinguishes between 'members' — *Dharmacari* and *Dharmacarini* — male and female 'followers of the *Dharma*' — who follow a limited rule of discipline — and 'friends'. However, the majority of Buddhists still operate within a system in which there is a clear distinction between those who renounce family ties and the laity.

Yet, when Buddhist societies are compared to each other, there is tremendous variety. As Buddhism spread from India, it became rooted in diverse cultures. Buddhism in Japan and China, for example, feels very different, culturally,

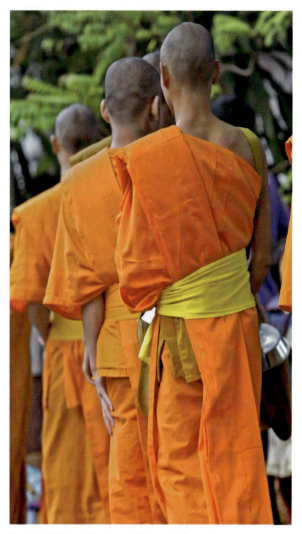

Young Buddhist mendicant monks in Luang Prabang, Laos.

from Buddhism in Sri Lanka. Globalizing forces, and the entry of Buddhism into the West, are causing more changes, as Buddhists adapt, innovate, and sometimes retrench. To generalize about family and society within Buddhism is therefore difficult.

FAMILY

In all Buddhist communities, the family is most important. However, in most traditional Buddhist societies, marriage is a secular matter. It is linked with the worldly, and takes place without the presence of a religious officiant. There is no concept of sacred vows made before God, since Buddhism is not a theistic religion in the strict sense of the word. For the same reason, divorce in some Buddhist communities — at least before the period of European colonialism — was a straightforward, mundane matter, that gave rights to the wife unknown to Western women at the time. Under the influence of colonialism, Christianity, and globalization, changes have occurred. Some Buddhist brides in Sri Lanka, for instance, now wear white, a colour traditionally linked with funerals and sterility. Religious verses are sung during the ceremony, and occasionally monks are involved. Also, divorce has become much more difficult.

Children are greeted with joy. Although there is a recognition that the love and attachment connected with parenting has a cost, and is a cause of pain (*dukkha*), positive images of parenthood permeate all schools of Buddhism. Because of the Buddhist belief in rebirth, children are seen as coming into the world with a history. They are not the parents' 'possession', for they have had previous lives. There is also a belief that human life is precious, a not-to-be-missed opportunity to progress spiritually. In the Tibetan tradition especially, focusing on the preciousness of human life is part of meditation practice.

Family relationships, according to one ancient Theravada text, the *Sigalovada Sutta*, are to be regulated according to reciprocal sets of duties that almost touch on the modern concept of human rights. Wives are to offer hospitality to the extended family, show faithfulness, look after the goods brought by their husbands, and carry out their duties with skill. Husbands should in turn show respect, courtesy, and faithfulness, give authority to their wives, and provide 'adornments' such as clothing and jewellery. Servants are to do their work well and rise before their employers, but employers in turn are to assign their employees work according to their strength, look after them in sickness, supply them with food and wages, and give them leave. Times have changed since this discourse was written, but its underlying ideals remain influential in Buddhist families and in the wider society, particularly in Theravada countries.

> To those in the kingdom who are engaged in cultivating crops and raising cattle, let your majesty distribute grain and fodder; to those in trade, give capital; to those in government service assign proper living wages.
>
> Advice given to a king troubled by lawlessness, from the *Kutadanta Sutta, Digha Nikaya*, 5: I 135.

SOCIETY

The traditional Buddhist image of the state is of a monarch, influenced by the *Dhamma* and advised by the monastic *Sangha* (community), creating wellbeing in society through a wise legal system and economic justice — ensuring the poor have a means of livelihood, for instance. The spread of democratic models has changed this, although in some countries the monastic *Sangha* still sees itself as an adviser to the state. It could be argued, however, that Buddhism has always had a democratic model to offer — the monastic *Sangha*, inspiration for which could have come from some of the more republican models of governance in the Buddha's own society. Today Buddhism is practised within a number of different political models.

One stereotype of Buddhism is that it encourages withdrawal from society, because of its emphasis on non-attachment. This is misleading: for the Buddhist, non-attachment is non-attachment to all that plays havoc in society: selfishness, greed, hatred, anger, violence, and jealousy. It has nothing to do with lack of compassion or apathy. In fact, one of the contributions Buddhism offer to the world is its emphasis on the compassion and lovingkindness that can flow when greed and hatred, jealousy and competitiveness, are controlled and transcended. One of the first steps is the ability to empathize with others:

> All tremble at violence; to all life is dear. Comparing [others] with oneself, one should not kill nor cause others to kill.
>
> *Dhammapada*, v. 130

ELIZABETH J. HARRIS

THE CAO DAI AND THE HOA HAO

In the late nineteenth and early twentieth centuries, Vietnamese nationalism was firmly, sometimes harshly, repressed by colonial French occupiers. The intellectuals who traditionally led nationalist movements began in the 1920s to profit financially from the situation and to enjoy privileged status like the French. Organizations then arose under new forms of nationalist leadership, seeking to end French domination and to establish a republic. Some of them followed Communist principles, but three were under the religious leadership of monks and priests: the Cao Dai, the Hoa Hao and, less important, the Binh Xuyen. All three feared and hated things foreign. They were products of local education, and aimed not only at expelling foreigners but also establishing local rule by religious leaders – something quite new to the Vietnamese pattern of rule by the privileged.

During the 1930s, the Communist Party of Indo-China (CPI) began to gain sympathy abroad. At this point the three religious movements began armed opposition to the French colonial forces. The Cao Dai held the Mekong Delta, the Hoa Hao the border of Cambodia, and the Binh Xuyen the Saigon area.

From 1941 until the end of World War II, Japanese military commanders directed the French colonial forces for the Vichy government in France. For a brief period in 1941, the combined French and Japanese all but defeated the local troops; but during the remainder of the war the latter gained strength. After the final defeat of the Japanese, the USA – in the grip of anti-colonial convictions – aided the Communist-controlled Viet Minh, led by Ho Chi Minh (1890–1969), and Vietnamese independence was declared on 2 September 1945.

Because American and French interests in Vietnam were at variance, a decade of confused political, cultural, and religious action and reaction resulted, leading finally to the Geneva Accord of 1954 and the partition of North and South Vietnam. The Communist Viet Minh held the North, while the South was under the nationalist government of Ngo Dinh Diem (1901–63). Close on a million refugees

from North to South added to the confusion. The French, as part of their opposition to Diem, had supplied arms to the Cao Dai, Hoa Hao, and Binh Xuyen; but by 1956, with American aid, Diem had smashed the military strength of the three sects. Their followers, numbering about a quarter of the total population, were resentful, but remained active in a less military context.

Out of the maze of political aims, cultural diffusion, and varied religious beliefs that form the background to twentieth-century Vietnam, four principal religious groups emerged to play a significant part in more recent years: the Buddhists, the Roman Catholic Church, the Cao Dai, and the Hoa Hao.

The Cao Dai

The Cao Dai sect arose from a séance communication received by Ngo Van Chieu (1878–1926), an administrator for the French in Cochin China, in 1919. In 1926 the sect was formally organized by a wealthy compatriot and Mandarin, Le Van Trung (d. 1935). Cao Dai means 'Supreme Palace' or 'High Altar', and denotes the name of the supreme God.

Strikingly syncretistic, Cao Dai is also known as 'The Third Amnesty' of God. It was preceded by a first (Eastern) amnesty with Buddha and Lao-tzu, and a second (Western) amnesty with Moses and Jesus Christ. Cao Dai is the third and unsurpassable manifestation of God in the historical process of revelation; it requires no human representatives – God communicates directly through trance to certain devotees. In its characteristic hierarchical structure, it follows the pattern of the Roman Catholic Church, with its own pope dwelling in a village outside Tan Ninh city, near Saigon, where an ornate cathedral was built in 1937, at the foot of a high mountain. Its dignitaries include a full ranking-list of priests, bishops, and cardinals.

In addition to Catholicism and Buddhism, Cao Dai combines Confucianism, Taoism, and traditional cults of spirits and ancestors. Spiritualistic elements have a striking importance, especially contacts with the dead. Amongst a host of additional figures revered in its pantheon are Victor Hugo, Sun Yat Sen, Joan of Arc, Louis Pasteur, and Jean Decoux, the French Admiral of World War II who administered Vietnam for the Japanese. Its breadth thus appeals to the integrated view of peasant peoples; entire village communities have become its followers. The wealthy Le Van Trung had, like Buddha, renounced the luxurious life; but for villagers to whom poverty is nothing new, it is the magical elements that prove attractive.

The ethic of Cao Dai is based on the underlying concept of the transmigration of souls. Cao Dai revived traditional Buddhist rules regarding vegetarianism, attitudes towards animals, and rules for social behaviour. Fraternity and charity, however, are much stronger than in Buddhist ethics and practice. There is also a strongly marked temple cult, with numerous rites. Prayers, incense offerings, meditation, and exorcisms are of great importance. Female celebrants are permitted, and matrilineal descent is important.

The religious symbol of the community is Cao Dai's eye over the globe. Its initially rapid expansion led to struggles for leadership. Despite splitting into several sects, Cao Dai has continued to grow, and its numbers are claimed to be more than 5 million.

The Hoa Hao

This neo-Buddhist sect was started by Huynh Phu So, in the village of Hoa Hao, Vietnam, near the Cambodian border. Born in 1919, he was the son of a leading Roman Catholic peasant in the local community, and received religious training as a young man, in the hope of improving his poor health. In 1939 he experienced a violent nervous spasm, from which he emerged, not only cured, but with great power to preach and teach a new religion. Claiming to be the incarnation of several past heroes, he set this religion on a supposedly ancient foundation, which also indicated a political role for himself and his followers. He combined a revised form of Buddhist rituals with a teaching that no intermediary or holy place is necessary for direct prayer to the Almighty.

There are four main precepts in his sect's teaching:
- honour for one's parents
- love of one's country
- respect for his interpretation of Buddhism
- love towards one's fellows

Not in temples, but in teaching-centres spread over former South Vietnam, his teachings were communicated in forms attractive to the peasant population. They sometimes had nationalistic overtones, and strangely predicted the coming of Americans two decades ahead of their arrival. Viewed in the 1940s as a 'living Buddha', his reputation rapidly drew followers to the sect. The French, however, saw him as a focus of political unrest, detained him in a psychiatric hospital, and later under house arrest. This enhanced his reputation, and from his home he taught many groups of pilgrims. A few days before a French plan to exile him to Laos could be put into action, his followers, aided by Japanese secret police, moved him to Saigon, where he was kept out of French hands.

Later it became obvious that the various nationalist movements, including Cao Dai and Hoa Hao, would each seek supremacy in the power struggle. By the late 1960s, increasingly disillusioned nationalist urban intellectuals joined the Hoa peasants' religious movement, though it remained fundamentally of rural appeal. By the time Huynh Phu So was murdered by Communists in April 1947, sub-sects had arisen which were far more active and united within themselves than were the sub-sects in the Cao Dai. The new sub-sects rejected the bribery and betrayal that discredited some Cao Dai leaders – who also suffered disunity and decline after the death of their pope in 1959. The vigorous teaching activities of Hoa Hao continued to appeal to the large rural population in the Mekong Delta, and the sect has remained a powerful force in southern Vietnam.

Barbara Boal

I AM A BUDDHIST

I was born in Brisbane, Australia, into a Roman Catholic family, and have Japanese, Irish, and English ancestry. For seventeen years I strove to be a good Catholic boy, until the time of the Vietnam War. All the Christian religious teaching I had received included as a central premise the commandment, 'Thou shall not kill.' I was therefore confused when I learned that Australia had introduced conscription for seventeen-year-old boys. This seemed to me to be hypocrisy and made me question the religion I had taken for granted. Eventually, I decided to explore my Japanese heritage.

I had already become interested in the martial arts of judo and karate. However, as I pursued my interest, I learnt that *karate* means 'empty hand' and *judo* means 'the gentle way'; that it is not violence and coercion that lead to success, but rather becoming so developed and aware that one cannot be hurt. However, much training is required to remain focused and alert. There is a saying concerning being attacked by a sword, 'The beginner can only see where the sword is, and cannot move. The master sees everywhere that the sword is not, and quietly moves there.'

Later I discovered the calm, smiling, accepting faces of the Buddha statues, which attracted me strongly. Here, in front of them, was a place where I could sit, and no one was going to criticize me; where I could let my guard down and just be a boy – relaxed and happy. Over the years, the Buddha faces became more real, as I began to meet Buddhist monks and nuns, people who could explain in great detail why and how they looked so peaceful. In essence, it was because they had given up worrying. 'If something can be done, then do it. Do not worry. If something cannot be done, then it cannot be done. Do not worry.'

This is one of the most valuable things I have discovered as a Buddhist. It is always possible to do something useful in every situation. No matter how difficult or impossible something might seem, there is always an explanation, and always something to do next. For example, if I fail at a task and feel awful, Buddhist teaching instructs me to examine who I think I am. Am I just a collection of other people's judgments, good or bad? Or do I truly have a reality and an essence that is already complete and whole, yet is at the same time developing with everything – good or bad – that I do? This deep understanding helps me to move forward in life. If suddenly there is a mountain in front of me – whether literally or figuratively – I can either sit down defeated or start climbing upwards step by step. It is only by climbing a mountain that one becomes a good mountain climber. The same is true of every human situation. I can only become a more compassionate person by acting compassionately, a good leader by leading well, a good follower by learning to give loyalty to those who have been appointed to lead.

My Buddhist teacher tells me I must learn to love problems like chocolate! He means that problems provide opportunities to develop the wisdom to see the best way forward in every situation. Although the experience of happiness should be fully enjoyed, it is impermanent and constantly changing – just like problems. Nothing lasts forever.

After many years, I have learnt that, if my heart and my mind are truly in a compassionately wise state, the results will usually be effective and useful to myself and other people. To this end, I start each day with prayers and readings from the Buddhist lineage that I follow – the Tibetan Gelugpa lineage of His Holiness the Dalai Lama. I try, as my teacher advises, to sit in formal meditation for at least forty-five minutes each day. In this way, I can set my motivation and focus for the coming day, which on a 'normal' day is full of competing demands on my time, energy, and attention. Although I have a formal time of meditation, I seek to stay in a 'meditative state of mind' all day, which is the goal of all spiritual practice: to live the faith in the 'real world' and thereby show that it is alive and well.

In the evening, I briefly review what has happened during the day, and determine to try to be even more mindful the following day. Also, I pray that the Buddhas and gurus will watch over me throughout the night, and teach me in my dreams. This is a way of reaching through the limited conceptual mind into the core being of who I really am, and why I am really here – not the collection of public facades that I have to wear for my various roles and positions.

There are four special days of the Buddhist year on which I fast:

1. *Wesak*,
2. The Descent to teach in this world,
3. The day of the Buddha's first teaching – the Four Noble Truths,
4. Tibetan New Year.

I also try to fast on all full moon days – many Buddhists still use a lunar calendar. During the two weeks when the moon is waning, I practise reducing my negative activities; and in the two weeks of the waxing moon, I practise developing my positive qualities.

Over Christmas, I often go on a retreat and fast for forty-eight hours, drinking just a little fruit juice or black tea. I find it relatively easy, especially if I do it in a Buddhist centre, with no television, radio, or music to distract me. I am not a strict vegetarian, although some Buddhists are. As one who follows a Tibetan tradition, I am not required to be. The Tibetans, because of their environment, are not vegetarian: not many crops grow above the snow line, and yak meat is very warming in a stew. That said, the overall emphasis in Buddhism is always to try to reduce harm with every thought, word and deed.

Every week I go to my local temple to hear my teacher discuss his views on the scriptures and how to apply them in modern life. This keeps me in touch with 'real reality', rather than the reality of the newspapers and television.

Paul Seto

CHAPTER 42

Buddhism in the Modern World

What can Buddhism offer to the contemporary world? In what ways is it challenging society? In what ways is it reinforcing the traditional? To answer these questions it is first necessary to look at some of the forces that have influenced the development of Buddhism in the last two hundred years.

EUROPEAN COLONIALISM

Sri Lanka (Ceylon) was the first predominantly Buddhist country to be affected by European colonialism. When the British occupied Colombo in 1796, Sri Lanka had already known two colonial powers: the Portuguese and the Dutch, though both ruled only part of the island. The British brought the whole under foreign rule, by bringing down the previously independent Kandyan Kingdom in 1815. Myanmar (Burma) was the second Buddhist country to be affected by European colonialism. In 1795, the Burmese authorities allowed a British Resident in Yangon (Rangoon). Three Anglo-Burmese wars followed, until in 1885 all of Myanmar came under British rule. Independence for both Sri Lanka and Myanmar came in 1948. Cambodia, Laos and Vietnam were the third Buddhist areas, coming under French rule. For Cambodia, the process began in 1864, and by the 1890s the French had almost complete control over the internal running of the country. Significant also was Western penetration into China: between 1839 and 1865 the West, through military action and forced treaties, gained rights of residence and, in some parts of the country, jurisdiction.

This imperialistic movement affected Buddhism in two main ways. Firstly, Western visitors to these countries started to study Buddhism and interpret it to the West, working in tandem with European-based orientalists. In the early years of the nineteenth century, some drew on oral sources in Asia, but, as the century progressed, the texts took precedence, leading to an increasingly textualized interpretation of Buddhism in the West. Secondly, Asian Buddhism itself underwent revival, as it attempted to resist the Christian missionary activity that accompanied colonialism. In Sri Lanka, for instance, archival records suggest that Buddhists at first sought coexistence with Christians; they were willing to procure Buddhist texts for them and teach them the language of the texts, Pali. When they discovered, however, that the missionaries would use their knowledge to undermine Buddhism, hospitality turned to confrontation, and to the development of 'Protestant Buddhism' – a form of Buddhism that both 'protested' against Christianity and borrowed elements from it, from the Young Man's Buddhist Association and hymns to Protestant Christianity's emphasis on texts and devaluing of ritual. Myanmar witnessed a similar revivalist development, influenced by Sri Lanka, and in both countries revival movements and independence movements gave strength to each other. At the beginning of the twentieth century, Chinese Buddhism also underwent revival, again in response to the impact of the West, although its impact was lessened by the growth of secular ideologies.

SECULAR IDEOLOGIES AND AUTHORITARIANISM

In the middle years of the twentieth century, Buddhism in Cambodia, China, Korea, Laos, Tibet, and Vietnam was adversely affected by secular ideologies, Communism in particular. Communist leaders in China, after the establishment of the Chinese People's Republic in 1949,

Buddhist prayer flags on the mountainside, Nepal.

simply expected Buddhism to die away. When it did not, particularly from 1966–76, the years of the Cultural Revolution, there were violent attacks on Buddhist leaders and religious buildings.

It was the British withdrawal from India that gave Communist China the opportunity to invade Tibet. The process began in 1950 and culminated in 1959, when China imposed direct rule on the country and the Dalai Lama fled. Systematic suppression of Tibet's Buddhist heritage followed: the looting of monasteries; the destruction of libraries and religious images; the execution of some monks; and the torture and imprisonment of others. In the late 1970s, there was some relaxation of this policy, leading to a limited renewal of Buddhism in the country.

Cambodia gained its independence from the French in 1953. In 1975, Phnom Penh fell to the Khmer Rouge under Saloth Sar (Pol Pot, 1925–98). Although before victory the Khmer Rouge had seemed to praise Buddhism, after 1975 Buddhism was systematically dismantled, together with everything else that evoked Cambodia's former culture. Almost all Buddhist temples were razed, Buddhist monks were killed or given degrading labour, and Buddhist libraries gutted. In the Buddhist Institute in Phnom Penh, 40,000 documents were destroyed. When the Vietnamese defeated Pol Pot in 1979, the country was in ruins, and there was only a handful of Buddhist monks left.

Since 1979, Cambodia has painstakingly – and in the context of ongoing violence and war – attempted to rebuild its Buddhist heritage, gaining help from countries such as Sri Lanka, Japan, and Germany. The first priority was to rebuild the temples, after which came teachers and books. In 1992, the Buddhist Institute was re-opened. A deeper challenge than any of these has been to spark an interest in spiritual values in those Cambodians who had only known violence.

BUDDHISM ENTERS THE WEST

One consequence of China's invasion of Tibet was that thousands of Tibetans fled the country. Most went to India, Nepal, and Bhutan, but some travelled to Europe and America, internationalizing the Tibetan story, and spreading Tibetan forms of Buddhism. For instance in 1967 two Tibetans – Chogyam Trungpa Tulku Rinpoche (1939–87) and Dr Akong Tulku Rinpoche (b. 1939) – founded Kagyu Samye Ling monastery, near Eskdalemuir, southern Scotland, which has now become the largest Tibetan Buddhist centre in Europe, attracting numerous Westerners, a good number of whom have become monks and nuns.

Tibetan Buddhism, however, was not the first form of Buddhism to enter the West. In the nineteenth century, Buddhists came to British universities from countries such as Sri Lanka and Myanmar. Then, in 1893, the Anagarika Dharmapala (1864–1933), a key figure in the Buddhist Revival in Sri Lanka, visited Britain – although his principal goal was to attend the World's Parliament of Religions in Chicago – returning in 1896 and 1907. The first formal Buddhist mission to Britain, however, came from Myanmar in 1908, led by the second British person to become a Buddhist monk, Venerable Ananda Metteyya (Allan Bennett, 1872–1923), who was then living in Myanmar. The Buddhist Society of Great Britain and Northern Ireland was formed to welcome him. Allan Bennett had come to Buddhism through theosophy, and through Edwin Arnold's poem on the Buddha, *The Light of Asia*, published in 1879. This poem's presentation of the Buddha as compassionate hero drew on both Theravada and Mahayana textual sources and attracted countless readers.

The history of Buddhism in Britain and the West between 1908 and 1959 is a complex one. In 1924, the work of the Buddhist Society of Great Britain and Northern Ireland was taken over by a lawyer, Christmas Humphreys (1901–83), who combined it with a Buddhist centre he had started within the Theosophical Society, to form the Buddhist Lodge. In 1943 this was renamed The Buddhist Society, London, which continues today as the Buddhist Society. One of the inspirations for Christmas Humphreys was Daisetz Teitaro Suzuki (1870–1966), the Japanese Zen master who did more than any other person to bring Zen Buddhism to laypeople in the West. As a young man, he lived in La Salle, Illinois, but in 1921 became Professor of Buddhist Philosophy at Otani University, Tokyo. Following World War II, he resumed contact with the West, influencing a generation of Westerners, and producing more than thirty volumes on Buddhism and Zen in English.

Almost all schools of Buddhism are now present in the West, and new Buddhist organizations are emerging to meet the needs of Westerners. In Britain, for instance, Theravada Buddhism has a strong presence, with monasteries and educational centres catering for Buddhists from Sri Lanka, Thailand, Myanmar, and for Western converts. The Japanese Mahayana schools are represented – Zen, Pure Land, Tendai – and also newer lay movements such as Soka Gakkai, with its many Western followers, and Rissho Kosei-kai. The different Tibetan schools have also taken root, and there are movements such

Young Buddhist monks in Cambodia.

as the one founded in 1967 by the British Buddhist, Sangharakshita (Dennis Lingwood, b. 1925), the Triratna Buddhist Order, which aims to offer a Buddhism to Westerners that combines the best of all schools. Never in the history of Buddhism has one area of the world received so many forms of Buddhism within the same short time span.

Asian countries such as Thailand and Japan have been particularly affected by the internationalization of capital, and the individualism and consumerism that has followed in its wake. Since the mid-twentieth century, both countries have experienced phenomenal economic growth, which has led to an undermining of Buddhism's emphases on non-greed and community. On the other hand, new counter-cultural Buddhist voices have emerged, challenging forms of Buddhism that place individual well-being above the health of the whole community.

BUDDHISM, WAR, AND PEACE

Conditioned by forces such as those mentioned above, Buddhists are entering many contemporary debates. Their contribution falls into two broad categories: the dynamics of social engagement, and the benefits – and indeed necessity – of meditation as a way of preventing hatred, anger, and violence.

In Cambodia, after the fall of Pol Pot, in a situation of ongoing violence, a remarkable Buddhist movement, The Coalition for Peace and Reconciliation, grew up under the leadership of Maha Ghosananda (1929–2007), a monk who escaped the Pol Pot regime because he was in Thailand in 1975. During the 1990s, annual peace walks, or Pilgrimages for Truth (*Dhammayietras*), were held, passing through areas still torn by conflict. Monks and nuns, laywomen and men, took part, sometimes risking their lives as they walked through crossfire. Such costly witnesses for peace have characterized Buddhism in the modern world. However, Buddhists have not stood for non-violence in all situations.

The monk's vow

I shall eat whatever is given to me with appreciation.

From *The Monastic Code of Discipline, Vinaya IV 189*

Buddhism's nonviolent stance sets it against war in general. However, like followers of other faiths, Buddhists have struggled when this principle comes up against pressing and complex issues, and some strands of Buddhism developed a philosophy of the 'just war'. At times, this justification of war has seemed to predominate over nonviolence. For example, Japanese Buddhists aligned with – or at least did not resist – the militarization of Japan in the middle years of the twentieth century, an attitude criticized by Buddhists born later in the century, after the horror of Nagasaki and Hiroshima. In Sri Lanka, some Buddhist monks and laypeople have supported a military solution to the ethnic war that ravaged the country after 1983, arguing that defence of Buddhism is justified if it is seen to be threatened, though other Sri Lankan Buddhists have rejected this stance.

BUDDHISM AND WOMEN

In the Buddha's time, women received higher ordination and became nuns (Pali, *bhikkhunis*; Sanskrit, *bhiksunis*). This higher ordination was lost in Sri Lanka and Myanmar, and never transmitted to countries such as Tibet and Thailand. Even without higher ordination, however, women have left their families to become nuns, but have not officially been able to follow the complete *bhikkhuni* rule of discipline. This began to change after the founding in 1987 of Sakyadhita ('Daughters of the Buddha'), an international organization of Buddhist women. At Sakyadhita conferences, fully-ordained nuns from Mahayana countries such as Taiwan and Korea met 'contemporary nuns' from countries such as Sri Lanka. This eventually led to ordination ceremonies, at which nuns from countries such as Taiwan, together with sympathetic Theravada monks, ordained nuns from countries that had no higher ordination. This is a story still in process.

Restoring to all Buddhist women the opportunity to gain higher ordination is not simply about regaining lost 'rights'; it is about affirming what women can contribute to Buddhism. Whether all Buddhist women gain the option to renounce as fully-ordained nuns or not, Buddhist women are now coming together with urgency to meditate, to co-operate in joint projects, and to share their vision of a world transformed by the Buddha's teaching.

ENGAGED BUDDHISM

In 1989, the International Network of Engaged Buddhists was formed. Its founders included Sulak Sivaraksa (b. 1933), a lay Buddhist from Siam – he will not call himself Thai – and Thich Nhat Hanh (b. 1929), an exiled monk from Vietnam, who founded the Order of Interbeing in 1965. The Network asserted that Buddhism was not only about individual peace and liberation, but also about creating a better world now. Drawing on Buddhist concern for the elimination of suffering and the concept of interconnectedness, it sought to draw attention to the fact that the causes of much oppression, poverty, and suffering lay in unjust structures and the corporate greed of the rich. Engaged Buddhist movements are now found throughout the world. The members of the Amida Trust in Britain, for instance, draw inspiration from the Pure Land Tradition of Japan – which emphasizes that rebirth in the 'Pure Land', from where it will be easy to attain *nirvana*, is possible through relying on the compassion of the Buddha Amitabha – but direct this towards working for a 'Pure Land' here and now, a task they link with the original message of the Buddha.

Engaged Buddhists insist that meditation and social engagement go hand in hand, in line with the Buddha's message that we need to know how our minds and hearts work, if we are to act with wisdom rather than with greed and hatred. A growth of meditation centres catering for laypeople in Asia and the West is putting this message across strongly. In traditional Asian Buddhism, meditation practices – except for the most elementary – were linked with monastic life. Now, whether in Sri Lanka, Thailand, the USA, or Europe, meditation is becoming an important part of life for laypeople as well.

INTERFAITH RELATIONS

Although mistrust of Christianity is found in countries such as Sri Lanka, where Buddhists have experienced aggressive Christian missionary activity, many Buddhists across the world are involved in building bridges of understanding between faiths. Rissho Kosei-kai, for instance, a Japanese Buddhist lay movement started in 1938, was one of the founders of the World Conference on Religion and Peace in 1970, a pioneering international interfaith organization. In 1987 the US-based Society for Buddhist-Christian Studies was formed, and in October 1997 the European Network of Buddhist-Christian Studies.

Buddhism is changing, partly due to the interpenetration of Western and Eastern forms of Buddhism. The result is that Buddhism has become a positive, dynamic force in the world; one of the insights it can offer the world is that social engagement and compassionate action must go hand in hand with work on self, the work of meditation, the work of wisdom.

ELIZABETH J. HARRIS

QUESTIONS

1. Why is human experience so important for a follower of Buddhism?

2. Explain how the Four Noble Truths help Buddhists attain *nirvana*.

3. What is Mahayana Buddhism?

4. What is the difference between Theravada and Mahayana Buddhism, and why are they not directly comparable?

5. Why did Sanskrit become so important in Buddhism?

6. What is Tantric Buddhism and why is it regarded as controversial?

7. Why is abstention so important in Buddhist morality?

8. What is Cao Dai, and how does it differ from other Buddhist traditions?

9. Explain the role of meditation in Buddhism.

10. Explain some of the different ways that Buddhism has been affected by encounters with the West.

FURTHER READING

Blomfield, Vishvapani, *Gautama Buddha: The Life and Times of the Awakened One*. London: Quercus, 2011.

Bui, Hum Dac, and Beck, Ngasha, *Cao Dai: Faith of Unity*. Fayetteville, AR: Emerald Wave, 2000.

Dalai Lama, *How to Practice: The Way to a Meaningful Life*. Trans. and ed. Jeffrey Hopkins. New York: Pocket Books, 2002.

Fisher, Robert E., *Buddhist Art and Architecture*. London: Thames & Hudson, 2002.

Gunaratana, Bhante H., *Mindfulness in Plain English*. Boston: Wisdom Publications, 2002.

Harvey, P., An Introduction to Buddhism: Teachings, History and Practices. Cambridge: Cambridge University Press, 1990.

Lopez, Donald S. Jr., *The Story of Buddhism: A Concise Guide to its History and Teachings*. New York: HarperCollins, 2002.

Queen, Christopher S., and King, Sallie B, eds., *Engaged Buddhism: Liberation Movements in Asia*. Albany: State University of New York Press, 1996.

Thich Nhat Hanh, *The Heart of the Buddha's Teaching*. New York: Broadway, 1999.

Williams, Paul, *Buddhist Thought: A Complete Introduction to the Indian Tradition*. New York, Routledge, 2000.

PART 6
JAINISM

SUMMARY

Jainism, like Hinduism and Buddhism, emerged from the Vedic culture of northern India, about the fifth century BCE, and is based around the teachings of Mahavira, whom Jains venerate as the twenty-fourth *jina* ('conquerer') of the last cosmic cycle. Jains hold that all living beings have a soul, and that these souls, undergoing a continuous cycle of death and rebirth, can only be liberated if the individual adopts the lifestyle of an extreme ascetic, in order to become omniscient, following the example of Mahavira himself. In the years after Mahavira's death, Jains broke into two main sects, Digambara and Shvetambara, which are divided by their views on scripture – Shvetambara Jains believe their canon descends directly from *The Twelve-limbed Basket*, the collection of Mahavira's teachings, while Digambara Jains believe this has been lost – and by the question whether there have been female *jinas*. Monasticism has an important role in Jainism, because of the value placed on asceticism, and the co-dependence of ascetics and the laity is central to the structure of traditional Jain society. Because of their belief that all living beings have souls, Jains are bound by a strict code of ethics, centred on the principle of non-violence, which forbids causing harm to any creature.

In the centuries after Mahavira's death, Jainism spread out through India, which remains its primary home to this day. Diaspora communities do exist, though these are small, and somewhat restricted by the absence of ascetics, who may travel only on foot. Alongside this, Jains – whether living in India or elsewhere – often have to compromise on some of the stricter ethical rules in order to live everyday lives in the modern world.

CHAPTER 43

A Historical Overview

Jainism originated in India, its name deriving from the term *jina* (conqueror). *Jinas* are also called *tirthankaras* – the terms are synonymous – meaning 'ford-makers'. The *jinas*, or *tirthankaras*, are religious teachers who, Jains believe, have attained enlightenment and omniscience by conquering *samsara*. Their state of omniscience means their teachings have indisputable authority, and can provide Jains with a crossing or ford – hence 'ford-maker' – from *samsara* to liberation.

Early in its history, Jainism split into two main sects: Digambara Jainism predominates in South India, Shvetambara in North-West India. Some scholars suggest the difference in beliefs and practices emerged gradually, the sects bifurcating after the Council of Valabhi, at Saurashtra, in the fifth century CE, during which the Shvetambara canon was fixed, in the absence of any Digambara representation. Today, Jainism has many different branches, most of them associated with either Digambara or Shvetambara Jainism.

THE *JINAS*

Twenty-four *jinas* are born and preach during the third and fourth phases of each half of the cosmic cycle. Jains of the Digambara sect believe all twenty-four *jinas* of the last cosmic cycle were men; Shvetambara Jains believe the nineteenth *jina*, Mallinath, was a woman. The twenty-fourth, and most recent, *jina* was called Mahavira. Jain tradition states that, just a few years after Mahavira's death, the cosmos entered the fifth phase of its regressive half-cycle, which will last for approximately 21,000 years. The first *jina* of the next group of twenty-four will not be born until the third phase of the next progressive cycle. Historians of religion sometimes associate Jainism's point of origin with the birth of Mahavira. Jains themselves subscribe to a timeless history, in which Mahavira is one of a perpetual cycle of spiritual masters. Textual evidence verifies Mahavira as a historical figure who was contemporary with the Buddha. Evidence also supports the historicity of the twenty-third *jina*, called Parshva, who lived in Varanasi about 250 years before Mahavira.

MAHAVIRA

Jain temple on Mount Shatrunjaya, near
Palitana, 'City of Temples', Gujarat, India.

Mahavira lived towards the end of the Vedic period, when religious culture centred on rituals to preserve the health and prosperity of individuals, as well as cosmic equilibrium and political stability. Rituals, which sometimes involved animal sacrifice, were commissioned by high-caste householders, but performed by members of the priestly caste (Brahmans), who monopolized religious authority and had an important status in Indian society. From about the seventh century BCE, a number of 'renouncer' traditions (*shramana*) emerged. Breaking with Vedic culture, they shifted the emphasis of their religious practice from external ritual to renunciation and asceticism. Jainism and Buddhism are two examples.

Mahavira lived and preached near Patna, in the state of Bihar, and died aged seventy-two. Historians date his death at around 425 BCE; Digambara Jains believe he died in 510 BCE, Shvetambara Jains in 527 BCE. Jains celebrate five auspicious moments in Mahavira's life: his conception, birth, renunciation, enlightenment, and final spiritual liberation (*moksha*). These five auspicious events, which occur in the lives of each of the *jinas*, are thought to authenticate the *jina's* identity as a *jina*.

Mahavira's life story and teachings are recorded in Jain scriptures. The *Kalpasutra* describes how, after Mahavira's previous incarnation as a celestial being, Indra, the king of the gods, arranged for Mahavira to be transported to his mother's womb. Shvetambara Jainism tells how Mahavira was mistakenly delivered to a Brahman woman before reaching his

On reaching the most excellent asoka tree, he [Mahavira] ordered his palanquin to be placed beneath it. Then he came out of the palanquin. Thereafter, with his own hand, he took off his wreaths, fineries, and ornaments. Having taken them off, he himself tonsured his head in five handfuls.

Kalpa Sutra, trans. K. C. Lalwani
(Motilal Banarsidass, 1999) verse 116

intended mother, Trisala, who was the wife of King Siddhartha. *Jinas* are always born into the caste of warriors and noblemen, in contrast to Vedic culture, in which holy men were always Brahmans. The impact of Mahavira's renunciation is enhanced by the luxurious lifestyle that he left. Trisala had a series of auspicious dreams during her pregnancy, which were interpreted as predictions that Mahavira would be a great political or spiritual leader.

Humans and gods rejoiced when Mahavira was born. Indra took the infant to Mount Meru, at the centre of the universe, where he was anointed and consecrated. Mahavira was originally named Vardhamana ('increasing'), because his family had prospered during his mother's pregnancy. Much later he was given the name Mahavira ('great hero') in recognition of the strict asceticism he practised as an adult. Shvetambara tradition recalls that, when Mahavira was a young man, he married Princess Yasoda, who bore him a daughter. Digambara tradition denies this: when Mahavira was thirty, the gods beseeched him to pursue his destiny as a *jina*. Heeding them, Mahavira was initiated as an ascetic, the gods officiating at the ceremony. As part of his initiation, Mahavira renounced all his possessions, and even pulled the hair from his head. Novice Jain ascetics still pull the hair from their heads during their initiation ceremonies.

For the rest of his life, Mahavira wandered homeless and without possessions. Digambara tradition states he was naked from the outset. Shvetambara tradition tells how his white robe caught on a bush, and Mahavira was too deep in contemplation to notice its disappearance. He depended on alms from villagers for sustenance, although the people he encountered often abused him. He practised non-violence, undertook extreme fasting, and meditated continually on the nature of the soul. After twelve and a half years, Mahavira attained enlightenment and omniscience.

Mahavira's enlightenment is a vital moment in Jain history, because it was from this point that his career as the twenty-fourth *jina* began. The assemblies (*samavasarana*) at which he preached are depicted frequently in Jain art. Mahavira took the central position, surrounded in concentric rings by his congregation, who consisted of gods, humans, and animals. Mahavira faced east, but so that the whole congregation could hear and see him, the gods replicated his image to face each cardinal point. According to Digambara Jainism, Mahavira's body emitted a divine sound (*divyadhvani*) during his sermons, which his disciples translated for the congregation.

During his life, Mahavira is believed to have established a Jain community of 36,000 nuns, 14,000 monks, 318,000 laywomen, and 159,000 laymen. His first disciples were three Brahman priests: Indrabhuti Gautama and his two brothers, Agnibhuti and Vayubhuti, who converted after Mahavira defeated them in debate. They were soon joined by a further eight Brahman converts, bringing the total of Mahavira's closest disciples to eleven. These eleven disciples had hundreds of disciples of their own, who also converted to Jainism. Mahavira's eleven closest disciples all attained enlightenment under his guidance.

ASCETIC AND LAY COMMUNITIES

Soon after Mahavira's death, the community of Jain ascetics began to branch into groups. Having taken a vow of non-possession, they depended for survival upon alms from a laity who shared their values of non-violence and vegetarianism, and lay communities probably developed in tandem quite early. Inscriptions describing donations by tradesmen and artisans date from the beginning of the Common Era. By the fifth century CE, alms-giving had escalated from food offerings into the construction of ascetics' dwelling-halls. By the eleventh century CE, numerous ascetic communities existed, each led by a religious teacher (*acharya*), and supported by a lay following. In Shvetambara Jainism, an *acharya's* religious authority was — and continues to be — authenticated by a lineage traced back to Mahavira's disciple, Sudharman.

> *Still in meditation, [Mahavira] attained the supreme knowledge and faith, kevala by name, unsurpassed unobstructed, unlimited, complete, and full.*
>
> *Then Sramana Bhagavan Mahavira became the venerable, victor, omniscient, all-knowing, all observing.*
>
> Kalpa Sutra verses 120 and 121.

THE SPREAD OF JAINISM IN INDIA

Jains soon began to migrate from the north-east to other regions in India, ascetics to uphold their vows as wandering mendicants, the laity to pursue mercantile opportunities. Some followed a western caravan route towards Delhi, Mathura, and finally Gujarat; others followed the southern caravan route towards Orissa, Chennai, and Mysore. Mathura was an important Jain centre for trade and culture from about 100 BCE to 100 CE, perhaps even earlier; an inscription dated 157 CE at a Jain shrine here implies the shrine was already of considerable antiquity by that date. By about the fourth century CE, pressure from the ruling Gupta Empire and international trading opportunities led some Jains to travel further west to Valabhi, which became an important centre of Shvetambara Jainism.

Jain presence in South India is confirmed from about the second century BCE by inscriptional evidence at Kalinga. Digambara Jainism continued to be a major religious and cultural influence in South India for almost a millennium. By the sixth century CE, Jains were largely divided by geography and sect: Shvetambara Jains in the west, Gujarat, Rajasthan, and Punjab; Digambara Jains in the south, Maharashtra, and Karnataka. Very few Jains remained near Mahavira's homeland in the north-east.

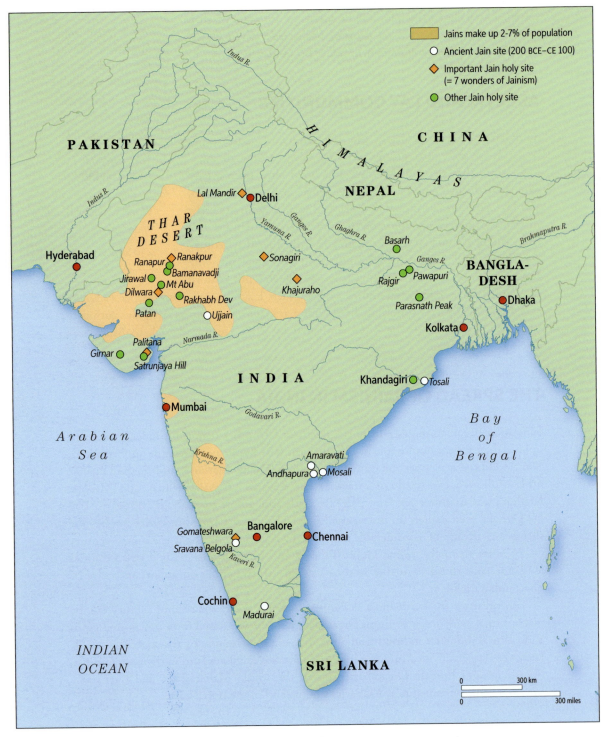

Jainism in India

Jains make up 2-7% of population
○ Ancient Jain site (200 BCE–CE 100)
◆ Important Jain holy site (= 7 wonders of Jainism)
● Other Jain holy site

PAKISTAN

CHINA

HIMALAYAS

NEPAL

BANGLA-DESH

Indus R.

Lal Mandir ● Delhi

THAR DESERT

Hyderabad

Ranapur ◆ Ranakpur
◆ Bamanavadji
Jirawal ● Mt Abu
Dilwara ◆
Rakhabh Dev
Patan ○ Ujjain

Yamuna R.

Ganges R.

Ghaghra R.

◆ Sonagiri

◆ Khajuraho

Basarh

Ganges R.

Brahmaputra R.

Rajgir ● Pawapuri

Parasnath Peak

● Dhaka

Kolkata

Palitana
Girnar ●
◆
Satrunjaya Hill

Narmada R.

INDIA

Khandagiri ● ○ Tosali

Mumbai

Godavari R.

Arabian Sea

Krishna R.

Bay of Bengal

Amaravati ○
Andhapura ○ ○ Mosali

Gomateshwara ○
Sravana Belgola

Bangalore ● ● Chennai

Kaveri R.

Cochin ●
○ Madurai

INDIAN OCEAN

SRI LANKA

0   300 km
0   300 miles

ROYAL PATRONAGE

The development of Jainism benefited from periods of royal support. King Srenika, who ruled in Bihar during the period that Mahavira preached, was sympathetic to Mahavira's message. The pro-Jain Nanda dynasty, followed by the Chandragupta Maurya dynasty, ruled in Bihar until the third century BCE. In Gujarat, King Vanaraja, who had been raised by a Shvetambara ascetic, established Jainism as the state religion from 746 CE to 806. Jain ascetics sometimes forged links with royal patrons, such allegiances affording protection to Jain communities, and helping to promote Jainism. Acharya Hemachandra (1087–1172) was court scholar to Jayasimha Siddharaja, King of Gujarat (1092–1141), and to Siddharaja's heir, Kumarpala, who ruled until 1165. With Hemachandra at his side, Kumarpala employed Jain values in the running of his kingdom. He took Jain lay vows, practised vegetarianism, outlawed animal slaughter, and erected Jain temples – for example, at Taranga Hill, in Gujarat.

Digambara Jains in South India enjoyed almost seven centuries of political stability, under the rule of the Ganga dynasty in Karnataka, which came to power in 265 CE, with the assistance of a powerful ascetic called Simhanandi. Two other southern dynasties that supported Jainism were the Rashtrakutas in the Deccan, between the eighth and twelfth centuries CE, and the Hoysalas in Karnataka, between the twelfth and fourteenth centuries. During periods of royal patronage, Jainism in North and South India grew in wealth and political influence. However, by the thirteenth century, this influence began to wane, under increasing Muslim rule and the Hindu *bhakti* movement.

HERESY AND REFORM

By about the fourth century CE, the spiritual ideal of wandering Jain ascetics was jeopardized by ascetics who lived permanently in monasteries. In Shvetambara Jainism these sedentary mendicants were called *caityavasi* (temple-dwellers). Temple-dwelling ascetics questioned the religious validity of perpetual wandering, and argued that their presence preserved Jainism, by keeping Jain temples active. However, their behaviour was challenged by reformed Jains, who upheld the value of non-possession, and who regarded sedentary mendicants as lax and irreligious. In 1024 a reformed ascetic called Jinesvara Suri defeated in debate a temple-dwelling ascetic at the royal court in Patan, Gujarat. During the mid-fifteenth century, a famous layman from Gujarat called Lonka Shah established the Lonka Gaccha. These Jains sought to return to Mahavira's teachings, which, according to Lonka Shah's interpretation, meant no *caityavasi*, and no use of temples and images during worship.

During the twelfth century, an institution of clerics developed within Digambara Jainism. *Bhattarakas* ('venerable ones') underwent minimal ascetic initiation. They managed temple ritual and temple-dwelling ascetics, supervised vow-taking by the laity, maintained libraries, and oversaw lay religious education. *Bhattarakas* also acted as emissaries between Jain communities and other religious and political authorities, and, in this role, often wielded significant political influence. *Bhattarakas* are credited with negotiating political protection for Jains, and for promoting Jainism through the spread of education and publications. However, as an institution, *bhattarakas* are regarded retrospectively as an emblem of spiritual decline in Jainism, because their claim to religious authority was not verified by the moral authority of ascetic renunciation. By the early twentieth century, most of the thirty-six *bhattaraka* seats in India had become obsolete.

EMMA SALTER

LEADERS AND ENLIGHTENMENT

Indrabhuti Gautama and Sudharman were the only two of Mahavira's eleven closest disciples to survive him. Tradition tells how Indrabhuti Gautama's enlightenment was obstructed by his supreme attachment to Mahavira. He was initially distraught by Mahavira's death, but his passion ceased within a few hours, when he realized the truth of Mahavira's *moksha*, and he became enlightened too. Jains celebrate the combined events of Mahavira's *moksha* and Indrabhuti Gautama's enlightenment during a festival in November called Dipavali.

Sudharman led the ascetic community, until he too achieved enlightenment and was succeeded by his disciple Jambu, who also attained enlightenment. Early in the Common Era, Jains started to believe that, since Jambu, enlightenment was no longer possible during the current cosmic era. This protects Jainism's claim that its spiritual leaders were omniscient, because no living person's omniscience can be tested.

JAINISM TIMELINE

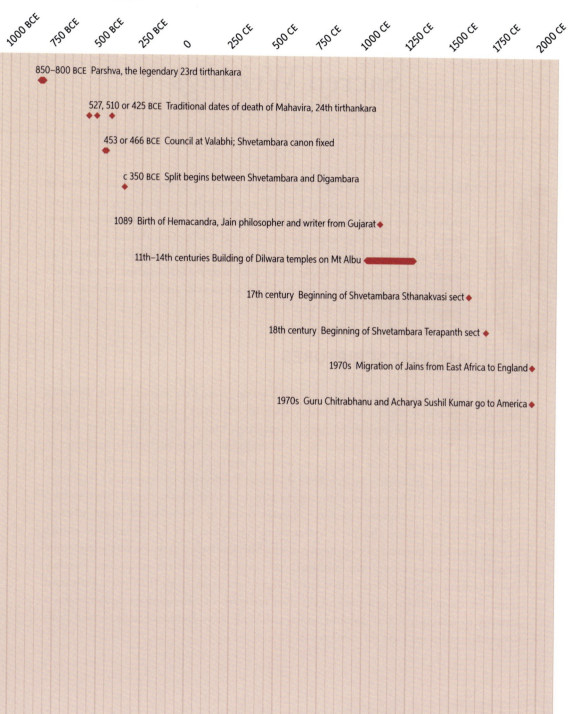

1000 BCE 750 BCE 500 BCE 250 BCE 0 250 CE 500 CE 750 CE 1000 CE 1250 CE 1500 CE 1750 CE 2000 CE

850–800 BCE Parshva, the legendary 23rd tirthankara

527, 510 or 425 BCE Traditional dates of death of Mahavira, 24th tirthankara

453 or 466 BCE Council at Valabhi; Shvetambara canon fixed

c 350 BCE Split begins between Shvetambara and Digambara

1089 Birth of Hemacandra, Jain philosopher and writer from Gujarat

11th–14th centuries Building of Dilwara temples on Mt Albu

17th century Beginning of Shvetambara Sthanakvasi sect

18th century Beginning of Shvetambara Terapanth sect

1970s Migration of Jains from East Africa to England

1970s Guru Chitrabhanu and Acharya Sushil Kumar go to America

CHAPTER 44

Sacred Writings

Jain sacred writings are not a tidy affair. Jainism has no single textual equivalent to, for example, the Christian Bible. Throughout Jainism's history, a variety of religious texts has become regarded as sacred: some are ancient texts, but many reflect the teachings of relatively recent saints. In Jainism, the sacredness of a text is not judged necessarily by its antiquity, but by the religious value of its content, and by its use during worship. Jains may regard as sacred writings both an ancient scripture written by an illustrious ascetic, and a nineteenth-century hymn written by a pious layman.

ANCIENT SCRIPTURES

It is not known when ancient Jain scriptures (*agamas*) were first written down. Jainism's ancient scriptural tradition began orally. Each of Mahavira's disciples is said to have compiled an oral recension of Mahavira's teachings, known collectively as the *Twelve-limbed Basket*. Early texts were written in Ardhamagadhi, a form of Prakrit, and later in Sanskrit. The current extant Jain canon was not written by a single person at a single point in history, although it is accepted by Jains as a reflection of Mahavira's teachings.

Digambara and Shvetambara Jainism do not refer to the same canon. Shvetambara Jains believe their scriptures descend directly from the *Twelve-limbed Basket*, whereas Digambara Jains believe this early literature to have been lost by the second century CE, and therefore question the authority of the Shvetambara canon. Nevertheless, some Digambara ascetics accept the authority of some Shvetambara scriptures. Possibly the migration to South India dislocated Digambara Jains from their early scriptural tradition, though some scholars suspect their rejection of Shvetambara scripture was a strategy to establish a clear division between the two sects. Evidence suggests that both scriptural traditions have the same roots.

THE DIGAMBARA CANON

The oldest text accepted by Digambara Jainism is the *Scripture of Six Parts*, which originated with the recollections of the ascetic Dharasena, who lived during the second century CE. Soon after, another ascetic, Gunabhadra, composed the *Treatise on the Passions*. These are the only two texts Digambara Jains accept as belonging to the ancient scriptural tradition; both discuss the nature of the soul and its liberation from *samsara*.

Over the centuries texts written by revered Digambara ascetics have been collated into a corpus of literature that has acquired canonical status. This is organized into four groups, known as the *Expositions*:

1. One of the most famous texts in the first group is the *Universal History*, which describes among other things the origins of Jainism and society, and the lives of Mahavira and the other *jinas*. The *Universal History* was written during the eighth century by an ascetic called Jinasena and his pupil Gunabhadra. Shvetambara Jainism has its own version of the *Universal History*.
2. The second exposition includes texts about cosmology.
3. The third exposition includes texts about codes of behaviour for ascetic and lay Jains. Some of the most important texts in this group were composed by a famous Digambara *acharya* called Kundakunda, whom some historians place in the eighth century CE, although Digambara tradition places him several centuries earlier.
4. The fourth exposition includes a broad range of metaphysical works and devotional hymns.

THE SHVETAMBARA CANON

The Shvetambara canon was formed during three councils at which senior Shvetambara ascetics — but no Digambara ascetics — recited what they could remember of the oral tradition, and their recollections were recorded and collated into textual scripture. The first council was held in Patna, 160 years after Mahavira's death; the second, 827 years after his death, was held simultaneously at Mathura, in the north, and at Valabhi, in the west. This led to some discrepancies, but Shvetambara Jains generally accepted the Mathura version as the first official canon. The third council, at which the Shvetambara canon was finally closed, was held at Valabhi, during the first half of the fifth century. The problem for scholars attempting to reconstruct the early Shvetambara canon is that no lists of the texts accepted at any of these councils remain.

The Shvetambara canon is organized into three groups:

1. The *Purva*, the tradition of lost scripture that Digambara and Shvetambara Jains accept as authoritative.
2. The *Twelve Limbs*, of which the twelfth text is lost.
3. A group divided into five categories of subsidiary texts that originate not with Mahavira's disciples, but with later ascetic teachers.

This is a broad and inclusive outline of the Shvetambara canon; not all Shvetambara Jains accept all these texts as authoritative. For example, two branches of Shvetambara Jainism, Sthanakvasi Jains and Terapanthi Jains, reject texts that advocate image worship.

Mahavira Temple, Osian, near Jodhpur, India.

TATTVARTHASUTRA

One important text accepted by both Digambara and Shvetambara Jainism is the *Tattvarthasutra*, written during the fourth or fifth century CE by the ascetic Umasvati, about whom little is known, although Digambara and Shvetambara Jains both claim he belonged to their sect. The *Tattvarthasutra* was the first significant Jain text to be written in Sanskrit, and the first to organize the main aspects of Jain doctrine into a single volume. The opening verse of the *Tattvarthasutra* identifies the essence of Jain

> *The enlightened world-view, enlightened knowledge, and enlightened conduct are the path to liberation.*
>
> Umasvati, *That Which Is (Tattvartha)*, trans. Nathmal Tatia (HarperCollins, 1994) verse 1.1.

doctrine as correct faith, correct knowledge, and correct conduct – a triad that became known as 'the three jewels of Jainism'.

ATTITUDES TO SCRIPTURE

Historically, only ascetics were allowed to study scripture. Laypeople were precluded, because they couldn't read the non-vernacular language of the texts, and because scriptural study without the qualification of ascetic rigour was considered dangerous. The laity encountered sacred literature at religious lectures delivered by ascetics, and through their devotional practices. Partly as a result of this, Jainism lays claim to a substantial quantity of devotional texts written by laypeople in their vernacular languages. More recently, attitudes have changed, and edited editions of some sacred Jain texts have been published, which has widened access for lay Jains and non-Jains. However, a vast corpus of sacred literature remains the exclusive domain of ascetic communities.

EMMA SALTER

CHAPTER 45

Beliefs

Much of Jain doctrine is concerned with the nature of the soul, and its liberation from bondage. Every living being has a soul that is trapped in *samsara*, the continuous cycle of birth, death, and rebirth that binds a soul to its worldly existence. A soul bound in *samsara* is believed to be suffering, even if the body in which it is incarnated enjoys a happy life, because bound souls are unaware of their true nature, which is omniscience and absolute bliss. Omniscience is pure and simultaneous knowledge of all things. Once a soul becomes fully aware of its true nature, it is released from *samsara* and becomes a liberated soul — *arhat* or *kevalin* — that endures no more incarnations, and suffers no further worldly entrapment. The *jinas* were *arhats* who were distinguished by their vital roles as religious teachers.

When the physical body in which a liberated soul is incarnated dies, the liberated soul attains *moksha*, a state of absolute purity and perfection, and is called *siddha*. *Siddhas* do not have physical bodies; they reside at the topmost part of the universe, where they exist in a constant state of omniscience and bliss, and have no further dealings with mundane, worldly affairs. The soteriological goal of Jainism is to attain *moksha* and become *siddha*.

BONDAGE

Souls are trapped in *samsara* because of the effects of *karma*. In Jainism, *karma* is believed to be physical matter that permeates the entire universe, but which is so fine that it is imperceptible. Under certain conditions, *karma* 'sticks' to the soul, and obscures the

> The five causes of bondage are: deluded world-view, non-abstinence, laxity, passions, and the actions of the body, speech, and mind. Because of its passions, the soul attracts and assimilates the material particles of karmic bondage. The result is bondage.
>
> *Tattvarthasutra verses 8.1 to 8.3*

soul's knowledge of its true, pure nature, as dust on a mirror prevents the mirror from giving a clear reflection. A soul generates energy by motivating the body to perform mental, verbal, or physical actions, and this energy attracts free-floating *karma* towards the soul.

Karma is unable to stick to the soul of its own accord. For this to happen, *kashaya* — which translates loosely as 'passion', and includes feelings of anger, pride, deception, and greed – needs to be present. The soul produces *kashaya* in response to attachment, of which there are two types: attraction to an event or thing, and aversion to an event or thing. Eventually *karma* 'stuck' to the soul matures and produces an effect – a mental, verbal, or physical action, usually reflecting the activity by which it was attracted – before falling naturally away. This is why Jains sometimes refer to the circumstances of peoples' lives as resulting from their *karma*.

Karma sometimes produces unpleasant results, sometimes pleasing results, but – as all *karma* traps the soul in *samsara* – it is anomalous to describe any *karma* as 'good'. The action *karma* induces the soul to take generates energy that attracts more *karma* towards the soul. The soul's response of attraction, or aversion, to the action causes more *karma* to stick to the soul, and so the cycle continues. Thus, *karma* traps the soul in *samsara* because it deludes it of its own pure nature, and entangles it in a perpetual cycle of action and reaction. A soul has to be reincarnated over and over again, to expel the *karma* it has accrued, whilst at the same time continuing to accrue more *karma*. The type of *karma* accrued determines the soul's next incarnation.

LIBERATION

Jains state that the binding effect of *karma* is not the same as predestination – in which a person has no free will to affect the events of her or his life – because the soul is an intellectual force that exerts free will by the way it chooses to respond to life's events. Jains aim to control the type and quantity of *karma* attracted to their soul through their religious practices. Strategies for overcoming the mechanism of bondage therefore provide a moral framework for Jains to live by.

Jains do not depend upon an external figure of salvation, but have to take personal responsibility for their own liberation. Mahavira's teachings describe *how* Jains can cleanse their souls of *karma*, but Mahavira cannot undertake the process *for* them. The path of religious practice leading to liberation, *moksha marg*, is charted by the *gunasthanas*, fourteen stages of purity through which a soul has to pass on its way to *moksha*:

- The fourth stage is a vital turning point in a Jain's spiritual journey, because at this stage a Jain experiences *samyak darshana*, true insight. Jains interpret the experience of *samyak darshana* differently: for some, it is a deep personal commitment to their religion, for others, religious commitment coupled with a spiritual experience of communion with their soul.
- The *anuvratas* (lay vows) are taken at the fifth *gunasthana*, and the *mahavratas* (ascetic vows) at the sixth *gunasthana*. Jains believe only ascetics can attain liberation. Shvetambara Jains believe women ascetics can attain liberation, whereas Digambara Jains believe liberation can be achieved only by men.
- At the thirteenth *gunasthana*, all deluding *karma* is finally dispelled, and the soul attains omniscience.
- At the moment of death, all *karma* associated with embodiment is exhausted, and the liberated soul attains *moksha*. This is the fourteenth *gunasthana*.

Jains believe that, in this part of the universe, and during the current cosmic era, it is not possible to progress beyond the seventh *gunasthana*.

GOD AND DIVINITY

Jains do not believe in a creator-God, so Jainism is sometimes described as atheistic. This is a misrepresentation. In Jainism, liberated souls are venerated as divine being, and it is these — and most specifically the *jinas* — whom Jains worship. The hierarchy of beings worthy of veneration is expressed in the *Panch Namaskara Mantra*:

> *I bow before the* arhats
> *I bow before the* siddhas
> *I bow before* acharyas
> *I bow before ascetic teachers*
> *I bow before all ascetics*
> *This fivefold salutation*
> *Which destroys all sin*
> *Is pre-eminent as the most auspicious of all auspicious things.*

adapted from P. S. Jaini, *The Jaina Path of Purification*

The recital of this, the most popular and widely used mantra in Jainism, is incorporated into most patterns of worship, and is accepted, with small variations, by all Jain sects. The *arhats* — embodied, liberated beings — are the first to receive veneration, because they perpetuate Jain teachings. *Siddhas* have attained *moksha*, and so no longer engage in worldly affairs.

THE SOUL

Physical bodies consist of matter: they cannot act, think, or respond to the world, unless 'inhabited' by a soul, which is their sentient force. The soul is the only type of substance in the universe that has the capacity for consciousness — which is its fundamental quality. Two other qualities of the soul are energy and bliss. Only liberated souls can fully experience bliss.

Jains believe all living beings have a soul. They also believe the entire universe is permeated by infinite, minute, life monads that exist alongside more substantial life forms, such as plants, animals, humans, celestial beings, and hell beings. When a living being dies, its soul is immediately reincarnated into another body, although not necessarily of the same type. For example, a human being may not necessarily be reincarnated as another

> *Morality is perfect forgiveness, humility, straightforwardness, purity (freedom from greed), truthfulness, self-restraint, austerity, renunciation, detachment, and continence.*
>
> *Tattvarthasutra* verse 9.6

human being. Although souls are not material, they expand or shrink, to fit precisely the size and shape of their current corporeal form. Just as the light from a lamp will fill different size rooms, so a soul will fill different size bodies.

Souls are eternal, which means they can be neither created nor destroyed, and every soul is likely to have experienced every conceivable embodiment, millions of times over. Jains therefore generally adopt an attitude of respect to all living beings, in the belief that one may have been similarly incarnated in a previous life, and that most beings have the potential of becoming *siddha* in a future incarnation. Jains believe all living beings – no matter how small – have the capacity for suffering, because all living beings have a soul, and are therefore conscious. Causing harm to another soul is believed to generate an influx of *karma* to one's own soul. For this reason, Jains take great lengths to avoid harmful behaviour. Non-violence is Jainism's principal ethical value, and the emphasis Jains give to it has earned them a reputation for compassion and tolerance. Their commitment to non-violence, combined with their belief in the ubiquity of life, has resulted in many of Jainism's characteristic religious practices, such as vegetarianism. Jainism's doctrine of non-violence is said to have inspired Mahatma Gandhi in his peaceful protest for India's freedom from British rule.

COSMOLOGY

Jains believe the cosmos is uncreated and eternal. It is dualistic, consisting of consciousness, determined by the presence of souls, and that which is not conscious, which includes both matter and aspects that are neither material nor conscious, for example, space, time, motion, and non-motion.

Matter has shape, colour, taste, smell, and density. From a philosophical perspective, Jainism regards matter as both permanent and temporary. It is permanent, because the physical atoms that make up material substances are constant so can be neither created nor destroyed; at the same time it is temporary, because substances with particular qualities and modes are formed when atoms combine, but when the combined atoms dissipate, the substance they have formed is destroyed. Atoms then rejoin in different combinations, to form new substances, with different qualities and modes.

The Jain cosmos is finite in size, but vast beyond human imaginings. Its shape is sometimes described as two drums balanced on top of each other, or as a human figure, standing legs apart and hands on hips. At the base of the cosmos are seven realms of hell, inhabited by hell beings who suffer hideous tortures, as a result of the bad *karma* they have accrued during previous incarnations. Above the seven realms of hell is a middle realm, *madhya loka*, the smallest cosmic realm, and the domain of human habitation. Above *madhya loka* are seven celestial realms, inhabited by celestial beings who live in great luxury and splendour, as a result of the meritorious *karma* they have accrued during previous incarnations. At the very top of the cosmos is *siddha loka*, also known as *isatprabhara* – 'the slightly curving place' – where liberated souls, free from *karma*, reside in a state of *moksha*.

From a soteriological perspective, *madhya loka* is the most significant cosmic realm, because it is where humans live. Liberation is only possible from a human incarnation, and then only as an ascetic. *Madhya loka* undergoes perpetual cyclical phases, like a wheel constantly rotating. There are six phases of ascent, during which *madhya loka* becomes increasingly more spiritual and human suffering decreases, followed by six phases of descent, during which spiritual purity declines and suffering increases. Twenty-four *jinas* are born and preach in *madhya loka* during the third and fourth phases of each half cycle. It is only possible to attain *moksha* during these phases, because during the other phases society is either in such a state of suffering that it cannot accept the possibility of liberation, or in such a state of contentment that it cannot accept the necessity for liberation. Jains believe our world entered the fifth phase of the descending cycle soon after Mahavira's death. Only one region in *madhya loka* — called *mahavideha*— is immune to the cycle of ascent and descent. Here a *jina* — currently Simadhar Svami — is always preaching, so *moksha* can be attained at any time. The structure and mechanism of the cosmos explains why liberation is not currently possible in our world, but encourages religious effort, by the opportunity of rebirth in *mahavideha*.

EMMA SALTER

CHAPTER 46

Family and Society

There are more than three million Jains in the world, the majority of whom live in India. Digambara Jains live predominantly in the Deccan, Delhi, East Rajasthan, and neighbouring Madhya Pradesh; Shvetambara Jains live predominantly in Mumbai, Delhi, Rajasthan, Gujarat, and Madhya Pradesh. There are also Jain communities in East Africa, Europe, and North America.

Jain religious society is organized into a fourfold structure of female ascetics, male ascetics, laywomen, and laymen, a pattern said to have been established by the first *jina*, Rishabha, also called Adinatha, and re-established by the subsequent twenty-three *jinas*. The inclusion of ascetic and lay communities in Jain religious society indicates that both communities share the same goal of spiritual liberation.

There are numerous Jain sects, most of which are associated with Digambara or Shvetambara Jainism, and have their own ascetic and lay communities. The origin of different sects often lay with reformers, who established a new ascetic lineage after a reinterpretation of doctrine or practice. For example, the seventeenth-century reformer Lavaji founded the Sthanakvasi branch of Shvetambara Jainism, when he broke from the Lonka Gaccha, because they had returned to the practice of image worship.

ASCETIC COMMUNITIES

Ascetic communities are hierarchical. The spiritual head and leader of an ascetic order is called an *acharya*. *Acharyas* and other senior ascetics may have many lay disciples, as well as their ascetic followers. Novice ascetics are at the bottom of the hierarchy. Throughout Jain history, far more women than men have taken ascetic initiation. Despite this, they are usually regarded as subordinate to their male counterparts, even if they are older, or have been an ascetic longer. Much earlier in Jain history, children sometimes took ascetic initiation. In modern times, only adults are allowed to become ascetics, and only after they have been granted permission by their next of kin.

Before initiation is permitted, a Jain layperson has to progress through eleven stages of renunciation (*pratimas*), under the supervision of an *acharya*. This includes taking five lay vows, the *anuvratas*, which are a less rigorous version of the ascetics' vows. The

Pilgrim entering an ancient marble Jain temple, Ranakpur, Rajasthan, India.

INTRODUCTION TO WORLD RELIGIONS

ceremony at which a novice ascetic is fully initiated is called *diksha*. Lay and ascetic communities come together to celebrate and perform ascetic initiation, during which the novice wears luxurious clothes, similar to wedding finery, and is treated like royalty. This final extravagance emphasizes the material sacrifice the novice makes as she or he renounces all possessions and association with worldly life, including familial contact. The novice takes five ascetic vows (the *mahavratas*):

1. Non-violence
2. Truthfulness
3. Not taking anything that has not been given freely
4. Celibacy – fidelity for the lay Jain
5. Non-attachment to worldly possessions – restriction of wealth and possessions for the lay Jain

Finally the novice ascetic plucks the hair from her or his own head, as a symbol of commitment to the ascetic way of life. Then the new initiate undertakes a period of fasting, which is broken the first time she or he seeks alms.

To uphold their vows of renunciation, ascetics have no permanent home, and are permitted to spend only a few days in any one place. In small groups, they walk between towns and villages, where they receive donations of food from Jain laypeople. They take shelter in lodging halls (*upashraya*) built exclusively for them by the lay community. Their vow of non-violence means they are allowed to travel only on foot, because motorized transport may harm insects and other small creatures, and they cease their wanderings temporarily for the monsoon season (approximately July to October) when travelling would risk breaking their vow of non-violence, because of the proliferation of insect life. It is during this period that they have a sustained period of contact with the lay community. For this reason, many Jain festivals, in which ascetics and laypeople take part, occur during the monsoon season.

Jain ascetics renounce all worldly attachments, but do not live in solitude. Instead, ascetics are public figures, under more or less constant scrutiny by their lay followers. They have no money, and are not allowed to prepare food themselves, so they have to maintain contact with lay communities, on whom they depend for their material needs, whilst lay Jains depend on ascetics for their spiritual needs. Ascetics deliver sermons to the laity – usually from the local *upashraya* – counsel laypeople in religious matters, and administer vows of fasting and other austerities. Lay people also accrue spiritual merit by providing ascetics with food and shelter. Lay Jains regard ascetics as worthy of veneration, because they embody Jainism's doctrinal message as living paradigms of the religious ideal.

> *The universe is peopled by manifold creatures who are, in this round of rebirth, born in different families and castes, for having done various actions ... Sometimes they become nobles or outcasts and untouchables, or worms and moths, or ... ants.*
>
> Uttaradhyayana Sutra, *That Which Is (Tattvartha)*, trans. Nathmal Tatia (London: HarperCollins, 1994).

LAY COMMUNITIES

Jain lay society is divided by sect and caste. Interaction and intermarriage between Jains of different sects is rare in India, although it is more frequent amongst diaspora communities, because of a greater need for solidarity. In India, intermarriage between Jains and Hindus of the same caste is not uncommon. The Jain marriage ceremony and funeral rites are similar to their Hindu equivalent. Jains believe religious qualities are judged by a person's conduct, not by their birth status, so caste division is restricted to a secular, societal role. However, in practice many Jain sects prohibit low-caste Jains from taking ascetic initiation. Sthanakvasi Jainism is an exception.

Commitment to non-violence means that Jains are prohibited from entering professions associated with causing harm to other living beings. For example, a Jain would never operate a slaughterhouse, or trade in leather goods. Apart from this restriction Jains enter all types of professions. In India many are traders or financiers.

In modern times, it is rare for lay Jains to take lay vows, unless they intend to initiate as mendicants in the future. Nevertheless, the practice of non-violence is a strong influence in their daily lives. Jains are vegetarian, and many also avoid eating potatoes, which they believe to contain millions of tiny life-forms, and root vegetables, because harvesting them may cause harm to earth-dwelling creatures. Jain households tie small muslin bags over their taps to filter their water, to avoid ingesting and harming water bodies. Jains living in countries where tap-water is not fit for drinking boil and re-filter their water for health purposes. Non-violence also extends to proactive endeavours, such as charitable donations.

EMMA SALTER

CHAPTER 47

Worship and Festivals

In Jainism, worship is directed towards ascetics, because their commitment to renunciation and non-violence is thought to represent the religious ideal taught by Mahavira and the other *jinas*. Lay Jains venerate ascetics, and ascetics venerate their superiors. The *Panch Namaskara Mantra*, which is recited by ascetic and lay Jains, venerates all ascetics, from the novice to the liberated soul. Ascetics are believed to have progressed further along the path of liberation — *moksha marg* — than lay Jains, and therefore to have attained a higher level of spiritual purity.

Whenever a lay Jain meets an ascetic, whether at a public sermon or private interview, she or he performs a rite of veneration, *guru-vandan*, bowing twice to the ground before the ascetic, and reciting a short prayer of veneration. Often the ascetic will then offer a blessing. Devout Jains visit ascetics' lodgings daily to perform *guru-vandan*. Theoretically, lay Jains do not personalize their veneration towards one particular ascetic, because all Jain ascetics are equal representatives of Jainism's religious ideal; in practice, they sometimes revere a particular ascetic as their special guru.

VENERATION OF THE *JINAS*

The twenty-four *jinas* were perfect, liberated ascetics, who taught the path of liberation, and attained *moksha*, and are thus the principal focus of worship. Jains worship the *jinas* during rituals called *puja*, and also express their veneration of them in a rich tradition of devotional songs.

Shvetambara Jains of the Terapanthi and Sthanakvasi sects, and Digambara Jains of the Taranapanthi sect, do not use images of the *jinas* during worship, as they do not believe the practice to have been sanctioned by the *jinas*. Ascetic and lay Jains who belong to these sects perform their worship in plain halls, usually attached to the ascetics' lodgings, venerating the *jinas* through *mantra* chanting, meditation, and scriptural study. If available, a senior ascetic teacher may provide a focal point; otherwise a scriptural text may be used as a substitute. In either case, it is the *jinas'* teachings that are the focus of veneration.

Other Shvetambara and Digambara sects use images of the *jinas* during their worship. Usually crafted in marble or metal, they depict the twenty-four *jinas* as identical to each

other; with robust male physiques, broad shoulders, and narrow waists — always meditating, either sitting or standing. A symbol carved at the base

Stone statue of an elephant outside the ancient Jain temple of Indra Sabha, carved out of solid rock, at Ellora Caves, near Auranabad, India, between the fifth and tenth century CE.

of each image identifies which *jina* it represents: for example, images of Mahavira are identified by a lion, whilst images of Parshvana — the twenty-third *jina* — have a canopy of cobra hoods. Digambara images are plain and naked, depicting the *jinas* in their ascetic role; Shvetambara images depict the *jinas* as nobility, before they became ascetics, and so are bejewelled, dressed in royal regalia, and adorned with gold or silver crowns. A Digambara or Shvetambara temple is often very ornate and beautiful, and usually dedicated to a single *jina*, an image of whom is the focal point. Large temples may also house images of other *jinas* and associated deities.

Most ritual worship in the temple is non-congregational. One simple ritual — *darshan* — involves gazing upon the image of a *jina* with a feeling of devotion and humility. Another ritual — *aarti* — is usually performed in the evening, and involves placing five small candles — representing five different types of knowledge — on a special tray. Worshippers then wave the tray in clockwise, circular motions before the image, while singing devotional hymns. Another ritual many Jains perform daily is the '*puja* of eight substances'.

As liberated beings, who have transcended worldly affairs, the *jinas* take no reciprocal role during worship. Worship does not appease them, nor do they respond to it by granting favours. Despite this, Jains feel immense love and devotion towards the *jinas*. The most important aspect of Jain worship is the devotional sentiment of the worshipper, regardless of ritual patterns, and whether or not an image is present. For this reason, Jains have to perform their own worship; no one else can do it on their behalf. Substances used during rituals are not offerings from the worshipper to the *jinas*, who have no use for them, but gestures of renunciation on the part of the worshipper. This is one reason why ascetics cannot perform temple rituals; they own nothing, and therefore have nothing to renounce.

FESTIVALS

Festivals are a time when lay Jains worship collectively, and often lay and ascetic communities come together. Most Jain festivals celebrate an aspect of the lives of the *jinas*: for example, *Mahavira Jayanti* in March/April celebrates Mahavira's birthday. Jains share some festivals with Hindus, and in mid-October celebrate *Diwali*. For Jains, however, *Diwali* signals the start of a new ritual and commercial year ,and celebrates Mahavira's transcendence to *moksha* and the enlightenment of his disciple Gautama.

PARYUSHAN

Paryushan ('abiding') is an important Shvetambara festival, closing the old year. It occurs in August/September, and lasts for eight days. Jains may attend the temple more often than usual, and some observe fasts, ending in a celebratory feast on the last

THE PUJA OF EIGHT SUBSTANCES

This ritual varies slightly between Jain communities, and is usually performed in the morning after bathing.

- Upon entering the temple, the worshipper bows before the *jina* image, while saying *nisihi* ('abandonment'), signifying that she or he has left the mundane world and entered the sanctity of the temple.
- The worshipper then circumambulates the image three times clockwise.
- Shvetambara Jains anoint the image with milk mixed with water, and, while reciting special prayers, use the third finger of their right hand to apply camphor and sandalwood paste to nine parts of the image in the following order: left and right big toes, right and left knees, right and left wrists, right and left shoulders, crown, forehead, throat, chest, and navel. Digambara Jains do not touch their *jina* images, so for this part of the ritual they sit before the image, pouring water – or a mixture of milk and water – from one vessel into another, and reciting prayers.
- Shvetambaras and Digambaras place a fresh flower by the image, and, in a circular motion, waft incense, followed by a camphor lamp.
- The worshipper then performs a joyous dance before the image, while waving a yak-tail fan.
- Next, the reflection of the *jina's* image is observed in a hand-held mirror.
- The worshipper then places a handful of dry rice on a special plate, forming it into the shape of a swastika, representing four possible incarnations: human, animal, celestial being, or hell being. Some food – usually sweets, fruit, or nuts – and sometimes a small amount of money, is placed on top of the rice swastika.
- At the end of the ritual, the worshipper says *nisihi* again, perhaps spends some time in spiritual contemplation, and usually sounds a bell upon departure.

> *The observer of vows should cultivate friendliness towards all living beings, delight in the distinction and honour of others, compassion for miserable, lowly creatures and equanimity towards the vainglorious.*
>
> *Tattvarthasutra* by Umasvati chapter 7 verse 6.

day of the festival. Fasting is an important and frequently performed religious practice amongst Jain laity. It is usually women who fast, men often claim to be restricted by their professional obligations. In addition to spiritual benefits, the completion of an arduous fast may improve the social prestige of the family of the person fasting. Pious lay Jains may stay at the mendicants' lodgings, having taken temporary vows of asceticism, and others make a pilgrimage to a holy site, such as Mount Shatrunjaya, in Gujarat, or Shravana Belagola, in Karnataka.

Ascetics deliver sermons daily for the first three days of *Paryushan,* and twice daily for the remaining five days. On the fourth to seventh days, this involves a public reading of the *Kalpasutra,* the Shvetambara scripture containing histories of the twenty-four *jinas.* The description of Mahavira's birth, on the second day of the reading, is accompanied by an elaborate ritual and great celebration.

On the final day, Jains perform *pratikraman,* a congregational ritual that is a communal statement of atonement and repentance for any harmful actions that may have been committed during the year. For more pious Jains, *pratikraman* is also a daily practice. At the end of *Paryushan,* many Jains send cards or emails to relatives and friends, seeking forgiveness for any wrong-doing. A devout Jain carries no grudge or quarrel over into the new year.

The equivalent Digambara festival is called *Dashalakshanaparvan* ('Festival of Ten Religious Qualities') and lasts ten days. The ten chapters of the *Tattvarthasutra* are recited publicly, with laypeople taking an active role, as there are relatively few Digambara ascetics. Towards the end of the festival, a special *puja* with flowers is performed to Ananta, the fourteenth *jina.* On the last day, rites of atonement are performed, similar to those of *Paryushan.*

ASCETIC PRACTICES

By taking ascetic initiation, a Jain dedicates her or his life to spiritual progression. The vows of renunciation ascetics take mean they no longer have a secular role in society; their worldly possessions are replaced with those things necessary for their ascetic lifestyle. For Digambara ascetics, this is a broom made from naturally shed peacock feathers and a water pot. They do not wear robes; *Digambara* literally meaning 'sky-clad', that is, naked. It is socially unacceptable for women to be 'sky-clad', which is one reason Digambaras – unlike Shvetambaras – do not accept that women can attain liberation. Shvetambara ascetics receive a set of simple white robes, a bowl for collecting alms, and a broom made from naturally shed cow-tail hair. As well as relinquishing worldly possessions, renunciation also means giving up anything that may be pleasing to the senses, such as tasty food, or comfortable living quarters.

Ceiling of the marble Jain temple at Ranakpur, Rajasthan, India, dedicated to Adinatha.

I AM A JAIN

I am a Jain nun, and have been practising Jainism for nineteen years. I joined my monastery when I was eighteen. Jain ascetic life is very simple: I have two sets of clothes; I eat pure vegetarian food in handmade wooden bowls; I have no monetary assets – no property, no bank balance; I have given up family attachments; and I am happy, having no desires for material possessions.

I did not become a nun because I was unhappy. I had incredibly happy moments with my parents, my two sisters and brother. I was born in Chennai, in southern India. My father is a physician and radiologist, my mother a housewife. We always said prayers and meditated for an hour on Sunday. The inspiration of my family, and the religious environment in which I was brought up, made a deep impression on me and developed within me. My parents are not only followers of the Jain religion, but have applied Jain principles throughout their lives. Their deep spirituality and religious commitment influenced me a lot.

Eventually I started to learn more about Jainism, by discussing and spending time with many Jain monks and nuns who visited Chennai. Their simple way of life appealed to me. After finishing my education at high school, I sought the permission of my parents to join the training institution for nuns. I had to wait a couple of years, to convince my parents of my commitment to the religious life: they needed to be sure this was what I really wanted. I wanted a life that was peaceful, purposeful, productive, and progressive. I wanted

something special, that gave me a feeling of contentment and fulfilment. Finally, I chose this path. In the Jain training centre, I read not only the holy scriptures, but also comparative studies of different religions, philosophies, and ideas. I studied for a Master's degree in comparative religion and philosophy at the Jain Vishwa Bharati Institute at Ladnun, in Rajasthan. This period of study helped me to understand my beliefs and values with more clarity.

After six years of training, my spiritual gurus, Acharya Tulsi and Acharya Mahaprajna, initiated me, at a gathering of thousands of people. It was a deeply spiritual celebration. I took vows of non-violence, truth, non-stealing, celibacy, and non-possession. It is a lifelong commitment, with self-discipline and self-control. That day I was so happy – my dream was coming true. I was at the feet of my guru, receiving blessings for this new journey of spiritual enlightenment. I was dressed in a white robe and my head was shaved. I was named 'Samani Charitra Prajna'.

Acharya Tulsi and Acharya Mahaprajna established the Saman Order in 1980. Their vision was to propagate and reinforce the message of non-violence, peace, and harmony throughout the world. In Jainism, we believe that water, air, fire, earth, and plants are living beings. Although it is not possible to be completely non-violent, we try to prevent unnecessary violence by our actions, words, and thoughts. Acharya Tulsi established a new form of monastic life. The lifestyle of a *saman* or *samni* is very similar to that of a monk or nun in other Jain monastic communities, but there are differences. For example, we use transport to educate and enhance human life and values at the global level.

As a *samni*, my lifestyle is totally different from that of a secular person. I spend four to five hours a day in meditation, prayer, chanting, and reading the holy scriptures. Twice a day, before sunrise and after sunset, I recite a special prayer known as *pratikraman*, in which I ask for forgiveness from, and give forgiveness to, all living beings; if I have committed sins, or violated any kind of vows, I repent and resolve not to repeat them. I freely admit my flaws and mistakes, and seek to improve myself.

I observe *preksha* meditation every day. A scientific technique, it is aimed at transforming my inner personality; it is known to have an impact on the endocrine system, by changing the biochemicals and balancing the hormones. It helps me a lot, enabling me to eliminate negative emotions and regenerate positive qualities, and benefits me by relaxing me and giving me peace of mind. As a *samni,* I do not eat and drink before sunrise or after sunset. This has a basis in science, as it has been shown sunlight is needed for good digestion.

Along with the daily practice of meditation and prayer, once a year I celebrate eight special days of spiritual enhancement and uplifting of my soul. This is called *paryushan* – 'being closer to your soul' – and is practised not only by monks and nuns, but by the whole Jain community. We listen to sermons, fast day and night, and practise living simply, with detachment from the material world and self-control. The last day of *paryushan* is very important, because this is the day when we recall all our past mistakes and sins, ask forgiveness from those against whom we have sinned, and give forgiveness to those who have sinned against us.

Jainism emphasizes a process of self-purification. All my efforts are focused on freeing the soul from the bondage of *karma*.

As a *samni*, ten months a year I travel extensively in India and overseas, lecturing at universities, colleges, national and international conferences, and to various associations. I have often participated in interfaith dialogues and discussions, and have conducted many camps, workshops, and seminars on stress management, anger management, the science of living, and ailments such as diabetes, high blood pressure, anxiety, obesity, allergies, and heart attacks. The rest of my time I spend in the presence of my guru, whose holy presence clarifies many doubts and queries.

I am very happy I have dedicated my whole life to a good cause, and to be following the message of non-violence, and a soul-oriented religion that emphasizes human values.

Samani Charitra Prajna

Of the five ascetic vows, the most famous is commitment to non-violence: not harming any creature — however small or seemingly insignificant — by action, speech, or thought, and not condoning such actions by others. Ascetics use their broom to sweep gently the ground before them free from insects, so they do not tread on them. During the rainy season, they do not travel, because the risk of harming creatures is too great. Terapanthi and Sthanakvasi Shvetambaras wear cloth mouthshields, to protect tiny airborne creatures from being harmed by their breath. During alms collection, donations are accepted only if they meet the ascetics' strict ethical requirements, food being inspected for insects and other impurities prior to consumption. Collecting or eating alms after dark is prohibited, because cooking-fires may lure insects to their deaths. Jain commitment to non-violence also includes honesty, respect, and compassion towards others.

Ascetic practices, which can be internal or external, are believed to 'burn off' *karma* already attached to the soul. Internal practices develop spirituality, and are met by the six obligatory actions. External practices involve enduring physical hardships. The most frequently performed is fasting, which includes total abstinence from food for a designated period, reduction — for example, eating every other day — or denial of certain types of food. The most dramatic form is *sallekhana* (elective fasting until death). The ascetic meditates throughout, to maintain a state of equanimity, which is believed to result in a meritorious rebirth. Ascetics are permitted to perform *sallekhana* only if they are already facing death by terminal illness or old age, and the process must be overseen by a senior ascetic. Few perform *sallekhana*, but those who do are highly celebrated.

EMMA SALTER

CHAPTER 48

Jainism in the Modern World

Jainism is a dynamic religion, remaining relevant in the modern world, by responding to social change, and to scientific and technological innovations. Some Jains embrace modernization, while others prefer to uphold established traditions; the different points of view have sometimes led to tension within the Jain community. The estimated 100,000 Jains living outside India face additional challenges, in that Jain ascetics play a vital role in the religious practices of Jain laypeople, yet are allowed to travel only on foot, and not permitted to travel outside India.

SOCIAL CHANGE AND MODERNIZATION

Changing social values have influenced traditional Jain practices. For example, most Jain sects no longer allow children to take ascetic initiation. Jains sometimes attempt to demonstrate the validity of Jain doctrine by reference to current social issues, such as associating vegetarianism with healthy living, or associating non-violence with cultural tolerance.

Jainism has also responded to scientific discoveries. Some Jains have suggested science proves the truth of Jain doctrine and, therefore, the authority of the *jinas*, because Jain teachings about the formation of matter from particles correspond with scientific discoveries about atoms. Where science and doctrine are not reconciled, as with the structure of the cosmos, Jains have to decide whether to accept scientific discovery and reclassify their doctrinal beliefs as mythical, or reject scientific discovery and hold fast to their doctrinal beliefs.

Technological advances have presented Jains with new ethical dilemmas. Some progressive mendicants use microphones during their sermons, to ensure the entire congregation can hear them; while other mendicants refuse to use electrical equipment, out of concern that electricity may harm tiny airborne creatures. Advances in printing, publishing and information technology have made Jain literature increasingly accessible to a broad readership that includes lay Jains and non-Jains. Some Jains hope this will further the understanding of Jainism, while others are concerned that sacred texts may be misinterpreted, or treated irreverently. Modernization also obliges Jains to rethink the motivation behind certain religious practices. For example, today most lay Jains live in houses or apartments where it is no longer appropriate to suggest eating after dark increases the risk of harming insects. If they do not eat after sunset, they have to justify this as exercising discipline and respect for tradition, rather than as an act of non-violence.

Today many Jains are well educated; religious rituals that appear to hold little meaning beyond tradition may not satisfy them. However, numerous independent educational programmes are being established in India and abroad, to teach lay Jains about Jainism, and revitalize their commitment, by explaining the doctrinal reasons for their religious practices. The first Jain university was established in 1970 at Ladnun, Rajasthan, under the direction of Acharya Tulsi (1914–97).

THE JAIN DIASPORA

Towards the end of the nineteenth century, many Indian people emigrated to East Africa, where they established homes and businesses. By 1926, a Jain temple had been built in Nairobi, Kenya, and another was constructed in Mombasa in 1963, indicating the religious community's growth. However, during the late 1960s and 1970s, Indian people were persecuted by East African political regimes, and many fled to Britain and North America, where they took up citizenship, while endeavouring to establish a communal identity.

To Jains who do not live in India, the absence of ascetics presents a difficulty, since ascetics have religious authority, and play a vital role in the religious practices of Jain laypeople, offering instruction, administering vows, performing initiation and consecration ceremonies, and giving laypeople the opportunity to gain spiritual merit through alms-giving. Some diaspora Jains travel to India, either regularly or occasionally, to be in the presence of

MODERN JAIN LEADERS

Shrimad Rajachandra (1867–1901) was a Jain layman and guru from Gujarat who taught the importance of devotion to an authoritative guru for achieving liberation. His followers turn to spiritual laypeople instead of to ascetics. As lay gurus have no travel restrictions placed upon them, the Shrimad Rajachandra movement has transferred well to diaspora communities.

Kanji Swami (1889–1980), also from Gujarat, was initiated as a Sthanakvasi ascetic in 1913. He later relinquished his ascetic status to become a Digambara layman, although he never married. Kanji Swami attracted a huge following, which is one of the most successful movements in modern Jainism. Like the Shrimad Rajachandra movement, the Kanji Swami Panth is a lay organization that places little emphasis on the role of ascetics, and therefore has an important place among diaspora Jains.

Acharya Mahaprajna (1920–2010), who succeeded Acharya Tulsi as spiritual leader of Terapanthi Jainism, instigated numerous reforms, and established a class of 'semi-ascetics': partially-initiated men and women who may travel abroad to teach and administer to lay Jains.

Chitrabhanu (b. 1922) was a Shvetambara ascetic in India who relinquished his status and settled in North America in the 1970s, establishing an extensive community of lay followers, who regard him as an authoritative guru.

> It doesn't matter if you become a Jain, aspire to become a good man, a moral person.
>
> Acharya Tulsi

ascetics, though family, work, and financial restraints make such trips difficult for many. This difficulty is compounded by ascetics being peripatetic for eight months of the year. Some modern movements have — consciously or not — addressed the problem of ascetic absence. Terapanthi Jainism, the followers of Chitrabhanu, Shrimad Rajachandra, and Kanji Swami all have different organizational structures, but each is an example of progressive and modernized Jainism.

EMMA SALTER

QUESTIONS

1. What is the role of a *jina*?

2. Explain the main points of disagreement between Digambara and Shvetambara Jains.

3. Why is asceticism so important in Jainism?

4. Explain why Jains do not believe enlightenment is possible during the current cosmic era.

5. Why is the Digambara scriptural canon so much smaller than the Shvetamara canon?

6. Explain the Jain conception of *karma* and its role in trapping a soul in *samsara*.

7. Why do Digambara and Shvetambara Jains have different views about the role of women?

8. Why do Jains have such a strong position on non-violence?

9. What attracts Jains to an ascetic lifestyle?

10. Why does modern life pose so many problems for strict Jains?

FURTHER READING

Carrithers, Michael, and C. Humphrey, *The Assembly of Listeners: Jains in Society*. Cambridge: Cambridge University Press, 1991.

Cort, John E., *Jains in the World: Religious Values and Ideology in India*. New York: Oxford University Press, 2004.

Dundas, Paul, *The Jains*. New York: Routledge, 2002.

Jaini, Padmanabh, *The Jaina Path of Purification*, 2nd ed. Columbia, MI: South Asia Books, 2001.

Laidlaw, James, *Riches and Renunciation: Religion, Economy, and Society among the Jains*. New York: Oxford University Press, 1996.

Vallely, Anne, *Guardians of the Transcendent: An Ethnography of a Jain Ascetic Community*. Toronto: University of Toronto Press, 2002.

PART 7
CHINESE RELIGIONS

SUMMARY

For as long as humans have lived in China, the country has had its own, highly distinctive, religious traditions. This distinctiveness is in part due to the fact that the belief systems of China grew up in almost complete isolation from those elsewhere, resulting in none of the idea-sharing common in Western religions. Yet, if the religions of China have little in common with those of the rest of the world, they have much in common with each other, with the result that a very particular Chinese outlook is identifiable. From the very earliest traditions – about which little is known – comes the conception of the balance of nature, well known today as yin and yang; while all Chinese traditions emphasize a supernatural concern with the wellbeing of humankind. As a result, Chinese traditions have tended to focus more on their conception of ethics than on speculation about the existence of a benign, or vengeful, deity, leading many in the West (wrongly) to consider the Chinese traditions not to be religion at all, but schools of philosophy.

While the ethical teachings of Confucius himself were augmented to some extent by later prophets, especially Mencius and Hsün-tzu, the Taoist religion emerged almost as a foil to Confucianism's emphasis on service to society, concerned with seeking a mystical unity with the Tao – a metaphysical absolute – by the contemplation of nature. Both traditions – Taoism especially – also changed through the influence of Buddhism. The extent of crossover between these three traditions in China is such that today many see no problem in being a member of all three. In the twentieth century, all three traditions struggled to survive the emergence of Maoist Communism, and the onslaught of the Cultural Revolution, while in more recent years the re-emergence, and rise, of Christianity has been one of the major results of the relaxation of state proscription.

CHAPTER 49

Chinese Religions

SAGES AND IMMORTALS

Chinese religion is unique. This is partly due to the fact that – alone among the great religions of humankind – Chinese religion first developed in isolation, without the influence of the other great world religions. Confucianism and Taoism (or Daoism), two of the three faiths of China, developed their distinctive forms before there was any significant contact with the rest of the world. For this reason, Chinese religion has taken a form which often seems quite unlike any other. For example, neither Confucianism nor Taoism is like Judaism, Christianity, or Islam – monotheistic religions with God at the centre. Confucianism, especially, became a religion without any great speculation on the nature and function of God. For this reason, it was often not even considered to be a religion. However, it is clear Confucianism is a religion, and that it was the dominant tradition of pre-modern China.

THE SHANG

The earliest forms of Chinese religion are not clear. We know hardly anything definite about the religion of the great Shang dynasty (1766–1122 BCE), the first historical dynasty. But although we know little of the detail, we are certain religion played a very important part in the life of the Shang. In fact, the Shang lived in a world of spirits and powers, who directly influenced the lives of the living – their success or failure – and who required sacrifice and appeasement.

The Shang sought to fathom the wishes of these spirits through a complicated system of divination. We still have the records of these divinations, the famous 'oracle bones'. The diviner, at the request of the king, would put a question to the spirit, and record the question and its answer on the carapace of a turtle or the shoulder-blade of an ox. The Shang were concerned to know the will of the spirits for just about everything they did.

Although the nature of Shang religion is clouded in mystery, a certain continuity remains between the Shang and later Chinese religion. There is a persistent belief in the balance of nature, an idea that was later explicitly defined as the famous concepts of *Yin* and *Yang*: the forces of dark and light, of soft and hard, of female and male. Another important idea which continues throughout the history of Chinese religion is a constant concern for the well-being of the people, an idea that later became the concept of *t'ien-ming* or the Will of Heaven.

Prior to the rise of Confucianism, certain elements of the Shang and Chou dynasties took more definite shape. If there is one idea that informs the entire history of the development of Chinese religion, it is a 'consciousness of concern'. Even in the western Chou and eastern Chou, one finds the persistent claim that high Heaven itself has concern for the well-being of the people. In fact, Heaven is said to hear and see, as the people hear and see, and hence to have a most active concern for them.

This sense that concern is the basis of the cosmos makes Chinese religion different from such religions as Judaism, Christianity, or Islam, where a sense of awe, or dread, of a supreme power informs religious consciousness. Chinese religion has always had a close connection with the ethical thought of the people; a sense of concern and participation pervades the Chinese understanding of humanity's relationship to the transcendent and with other people.

PHILOSOPHY OR RELIGION?

In Chinese terms, what then are Confucianism and Taoism? Are they philosophies or religions? Do they have any kind of mystical traditions that seek to aid the faithful to achieve the perfected aims of a religious life?

There is a common Chinese distinction that is helpful in answering this question: the distinction between the terms *chia* (schools of thought, philosophy) and *chiao* (teaching, religion). The former refers more to the great thinkers and their teachings, and the 'great traditions'; the latter to the religious and, by extension, to the unique ways in which the great traditions have been appropriated by the people at grass-roots level. A distinction between the great intellectual traditions and the cultic and devotional side of religious life has been made in all the Chinese traditions: Confucianism, Taoism and also Buddhism, after its introduction into China in the second century CE.

The Chinese traditions have never felt the need to contrast *chia* and *chiao* in a hostile fashion; in a very characteristic way, they are said to represent two different parts of one continuum. They are different yet related. In traditional China, each of the great religions operated on both levels: there were great Confucian, Taoist, and Buddhist philosophers, as well as masters of the various religious arts of meditation, liturgy, and ritual.

CONFUCIANISM

The Latinized name, Confucianism, is a Western invention which has come down from seventeenth-century Jesuit missionaries. Interestingly, these early Western missionaries clearly saw the religious nature of Confucianism, even if they did not agree with its traditions and rituals.

The Chinese term for Confucianism, *Ju* (scholars, literati, with the special meaning of Confucian from the T'ang dynasty), points to its broader character as intellectual culture. It is usually regarded as philosophy (*chia*), although such terms as *Ju-chiao*, *K'ung-chiao* (*K'ung* being Confucius's family name), or *Li-chiao* (*Li* referring to Confucian rituals) are also used. All these terms refer to those elements of worship, ritual, and sacrifice that are religious teachings, which is, of course, what *chiao* itself refers to.

> *The master said, 'I have transmitted what was taught to me, without making up anything of my own. I have been faithful to and loved the Ancients.'*
>
> Confucius, *Analects*

CONFUCIUS

Confucianism is best known for its moral philosophy, represented by Confucius (551–479 BCE), Mencius (371–c. 289 BCE), and Hsün-tzu (fl. 298–238 BCE), and is clearly grounded in religion – the inherited religion of the Lord-on-high, or Heaven. Even the great rationalist Hsün-tzu sees society founded on the penetrating insight of the sagely mind. Although Confucianism is less known for its mysticism, the *Book of Mencius*, as well as other works, cannot be fully understood except in the light of mysticism. The *Chung-yung*, one of the 'Four Books' which became the basis for Confucian self-cultivation in the southern Sung (1126–1279 CE), explicitly states that the sage, having realized true integrity (*ch'eng*), becomes one with Heaven and Earth. Confucian moral metaphysics reaches over into the religious quest for unity with the ground of being.

Nonetheless, Confucianism gives primary emphasis to the ethical meaning of human relationships, finding and grounding the moral in the divine transcendence. The perfect example of this is Confucius himself, who is best remembered as a great teacher, and the basis of whose teaching was the concept of humanity (*jen*). Just as compassion is the greatest Buddhist virtue, and love the Christian, *jen* is the ultimate goal of conduct and self-transformation for the Confucian. Whereas most of Confucius's teachings stress the ethical dimension of humanity, he made it clear that it was Heaven itself which protected him and gave him his message: 'Heaven is the author of the virtue that is in me.'

> *His life was glorious, his death bewailed. How can such a one ever be equalled?*
>
> Confucius, *Analects*

MENCIUS

Confucius stands as a prophet, giving an ethical teaching grounded in religious consciousness, whereas Mencius projects the image of a teacher of mysticism. He proclaims an inner doctrine, alluding to the presence within the heart of something greater than itself: 'All things are present in me. When I reflect upon myself in all sincerity, my joy is boundless.' What was an implicitly religious message in Confucius becomes explicit in Mencius. For example, Confucius is said not to have discussed the relationship between human nature and the Way of Heaven, whereas Mencius made his whole system of thought revolve around these two concepts, attempting to show how the very essence of the Way of Heaven, the divine power of the cosmos, became human nature. He felt that if this human nature could be correctly cultivated and nurtured, even the common person could become a sage.

The Confucian classics (there are thirteen) prefer to discuss the work of spiritual cultivation in terms of emotional harmony and psychic equilibrium – a harmony of due proportions, rather than the absence of passions. The 'Doctrine of the Mean' (*Chung-yung*), one of the 'Four Books', distinguishes between two states of fundamental mind, the 'pre-stirred' state (before the rise of emotions), and the 'post-stirred' state (after contact with the things and events of the world). The meaning best expressed by the concept of true integrity (*ch'eng*) lies in the harmony of emotions that have arisen, but resembles the equilibrium of the 'pre-stirred' state. The *Chung-yung*, as we have seen before, claims this harmony puts a person in touch with the cosmic processes

Stone statue of Confucius from temple in Shanghai, China.

of life and creativity: 'If they can assist in the transformation and nourishing process of Heaven and Earth, they can thus form a trinity with Heaven and Earth.'

HSÜN-TZU

The third founding father of Confucianism, Hsün-tzu, is best remembered for his doctrine of ritual action (*li*). If Confucius begins Confucianism with the dramatic – almost prophetic – demand that we live a life of *jen*, or perfect humanity, and Mencius expands upon the concept of *jen*, to show this is a life of heightened inter-subjectivity and intuition into the boundless joy of the enlightened sage, Hsün-tzu provides the practical side of Confucian religion. It is his genius to demonstrate the power of correct ritual action needed to transform the human heart, which is prone to err, into the mind of a sage. In doing so, Hsün-tzu provides a model for daily life that supports the religious

> Everything has its own destiny, and it is for us to accept our destiny in its true form.
>
> Mencius

Which is the greatest service? The service of parents is the greatest. Which is the greatest of charges? The charge of oneself is the greatest. I have heard of keeping oneself, and thus being able to serve one's parents. But I have not heard of failing to keep oneself, and yet being able to serve one's parents.

Mencius

and ethical intuitions of Confucius and Mencius. Without a life of ritual – a liturgy of daily life ennobled by humility and graced by beautiful conduct – the supreme insights of religious geniuses such as Confucius and Mencius would be impossible to maintain.

In the course of time, the meaning of the word 'Heaven' becomes ambiguous, shifting from the early reference to a supreme deity (the *Analects* of Confucius), to a vacillation between that and moral force (Mencius), to the universe itself (Hsün-tzu).

NEO-CONFUCIANISM

Confucian mysticism, especially in its second great phase, Neo-Confucianism, leans more and more in the direction of pantheism, as is borne out by the later philosopher, Chang Tsai (1020–77). Here Confucian religion and mysticism show the imprint of Taoist – and Buddhist – influences; yet Chang Tsai still shows a profoundly Confucian bent to his mystical vision of the unity of the world, by expressing this as one of a perfected family. In this vision, all the world becomes related to him as his own family. The note of inter-subjective concern sounded by Confucius and Mencius is reaffirmed.

The first great flowering of Confucianism produced such diverse thinkers as Mencius and Hsün-tzu, while Neo-Confucianism gave us Chu Hsi (1130–1200) and Wang Yang-ming (1472–1529). Both the latter started from a desire to reform the Confucianism of their day, and then sought to give practical guidance for the perfection of the mind. Their schools, respectively, were called 'the teaching of principle' (*li-hsüeh*) and 'the teaching of mind' (*hsin-hsüeh*). In fact, both were primarily concerned with the task of achieving sagehood: the great debate between them centred on how to achieve this.

Chu Hsi believed we must go through a long and arduous process of self-cultivation and ethical activity in order to reach *jen*. He stressed the method of 'the examination of things' (*ko-wu*) as the best means to achieve this end. But this was more than a scientific interest in the material matters of the cosmos; it was to be an examination of all the various ethical and spiritual states of the mind, an attempt to know the self, in order to perfect the original nature, which he held to be good.

Chu Hsi expressed his spiritual goal in this way:

> *The mind of Heaven and Earth, which gives birth to all things, is humanity (jen). Man, in being endowed with matter-energy, receives this mind of Heaven and Earth, and thereby his life. Hence tender-heartedness and humanity are part of the very essence of his life.*

CHINA TIMELINE

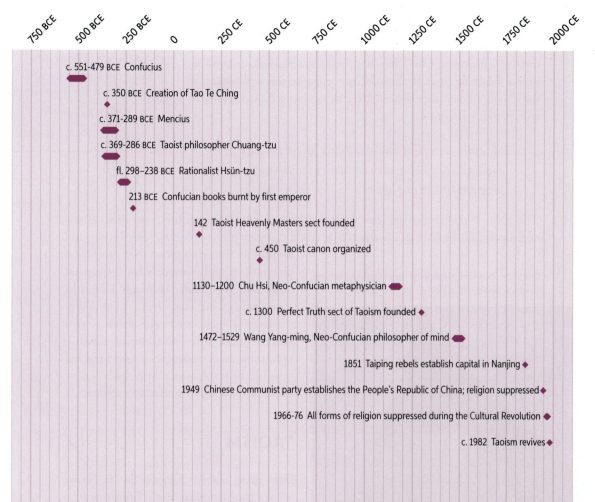

750 BCE · 500 BCE · 250 BCE · 0 · 250 CE · 500 CE · 750 CE · 1000 CE · 1250 CE · 1500 CE · 1750 CE · 2000 CE

c. 551-479 BCE Confucius

c. 350 BCE Creation of Tao Te Ching

c. 371-289 BCE Mencius

c. 369-286 BCE Taoist philosopher Chuang-tzu

fl. 298–238 BCE Rationalist Hsün-tzu

213 BCE Confucian books burnt by first emperor

142 Taoist Heavenly Masters sect founded

c. 450 Taoist canon organized

1130–1200 Chu Hsi, Neo-Confucian metaphysician

c. 1300 Perfect Truth sect of Taoism founded

1472–1529 Wang Yang-ming, Neo-Confucian philosopher of mind

1851 Taiping rebels establish capital in Nanjing

1949 Chinese Communist party establishes the People's Republic of China; religion suppressed

1966-76 All forms of religion suppressed during the Cultural Revolution

c. 1982 Taoism revives

Wang Yang-ming agreed on the goal of sagehood, but rejected Chu Hsi's gradualist method. For Wang, only the 'enlightenment experience' of the absolute unity of our minds with the mind of the Tao (or Dao) would suffice to achieve sagehood. All other methods, including Chu Hsi's attempt at gradual self-cultivation, were a waste of time, if they did not provoke this realization of the enlightenment experience. After Wang himself had had such an experience he wrote:

> My own nature is, of course sufficient for me to attain sagehood. And I have been mistaken in searching for principle in external things and affairs.

The great Neo-Confucians gave Confucianism a new lease of life, providing a new explanation of the Confucian vision that could compete philosophically with Taoism and Buddhism. But, even more, they provided a practical set of life-models for the earnest seeker of sagehood. Although Chu Hsi consulted gradualism, and Wang Yang-ming immediate experience, both sought that moment when the human mind — precarious in its tendencies to good and evil — would be transformed into the Mind of Heaven, the state of perfected excellence.

Human nature is disposed to goodness, just as water flows downwards. There is no water but flows down, and no men but show this tendency to good.

Mencius

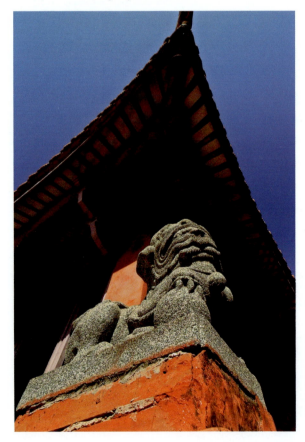

One of the stone lions guarding the Tainan Confucius Temple, Taiwan, originally built in 1665.

TAOISM

The great Taoist religion is, in many ways, the opposite of Confucianism. Confucianism seeks to perfect men and women within the world, a goal of the secular as sacred; whereas Taoism prefers to turn away from society to the contemplation of nature, seeking fulfilment in the spontaneous and 'trans-ethical'. The Tao, a metaphysical absolute, appears to have been a philosophical transformation of an earlier personal God. The way it teaches leads to a union with itself — a way of passive acceptance and mystical contemplation. Such is the teaching of the great Taoist thinkers, Lao-tzu and Chuang-

RUSSIA

MONGOLIA

CHINA

Yellow R.

⊛ Beijing ⊛

NORTH
KOREA

Birthplace of
Confucius,
551 BCE

⊛ Seoul

Qufu ⊛

SOUTH
KOREA

JAPAN

● Kaifeng

Birthplace of
Mencius,
c.371 BCE

TIBET

HIMALAYAS

NEPAL   BHUTAN

Ganges R.

Yangtze R.

● Nanjing

⊛ Quzhou ●

Wuyuan ●

Birthplace of Zhu Xi,
1130–1200 CE

⊛ Taipei
⊛ ⊛

INDIA

MYANMAR

⊛
Hong Kong

PACIFIC
OCEAN

Irrawaddy R.

*Bay
of
Bengal*

LAOS

THAILAND

CAMBODIA VIETNAM

*South
China
Sea*

PHILIPPINES

*INDIAN
OCEAN*

BRUNEI ⊛
⊛

MALAYSIA ⊛

Kuala Lumpur

⊛
⊛ ⊛

BORNEO

SUMATRA

CELEBES

NEW
GUINEA

INDONESIA

Jakarta   JAVA

⊛

TIMOR

Area of Mencius' travels

Area of Zhu Xi's travels

Confucian/Neo-Confucian influence

Cao Dai

⊛ Major Confucian temple

⊛ Major Confucian academy

● City

Modern political boundary

0   500 km

0   500 miles

Confucianism in East Asia

tzu, about whose lives little is know n, if indeed they ever existed. This is perhaps fitting for men who allegedly chose a life of obscurity, and taught a way of silence.

Taoism is not just passive contemplation. The texts of Lao-tzu and Chuang-tzu (also the name of the book, *Chuang-tzu*) served a later generation of religious-minded thinkers, anxious to transcend the limited conditions of human existence, whose ambition was to 'steal the secret of Heaven and Earth', to wrench from it the mystery of life itself, in order to fulfil their desire for immortality.

The goal of the Confucian was to become a sage, a servant of society, while the goal of the Taoist was to become an immortal (*hsien*). They revived belief in personal deities, practising a ritual of prayer and appeasement, and fostered the art of alchemy – an external alchemy, which 'internalized' the golden pill of immortality – and sought it through yoga and meditation. They also saw sexual hygiene as another means of prolonging human life.

This new Taoism has been called 'Taoist religion', to distinguish it from the classical philosophy of Lao-tzu and Chuang-tzu and its acceptance of both life and death. This Taoist religion developed its own mystical tradition, embellished with stories of marvellous drugs and wonder-working immortals, of levitations and bodily ascensions to heaven. Basing itself on the early texts – the *Lao-tzu*, *Chuang-tzu*, *Huai-nan-tzu*, and *Lieh-tzu* – the Taoist religionists created long-lasting religious institutions.

Some of these groups still exist today, and trace their roots back to the Taoist movements at the end of the second century CE. With their esoteric and exoteric teachings, their lines of orthodox teachers, their social organizations, they more closely resemble the other great religious traditions of humankind. But their persistent Chinese style comes through: they seek unity with the Tao which cannot be named.

THE TAO

How can Taoism be distinguished from its great sister religion, Confucianism? One major goal of all the various schools and sects of Taoism was the quest for freedom. For some, it was freedom from the political and social constraints of the emerging Confucian state; for others, the more profound search for immortality; and for others, the search for oneness with the Tao itself. This Tao was the sum total of all things which are and which change, for change itself was a very important part of the Taoist view of reality. As the *Chuang-tzu* tells us, the Tao is 'complete, all-embracing, the whole: these are different names for the same reality denoting the One'. This One, this totality of the Tao, worked as a liberating concept for the Taoists; within the ceaseless flux of the Tao, they found the power to live life in a spontaneous fashion. Probably the most famous statement of the freedom of the Taoist immortal is that of Lao-tzu, where he says, 'The ways of men are conditioned by those of Heaven, the ways of Heaven by those of the Tao, and the Tao came into being by itself.' The Tao

> The highest good is like that of water. The goodness of water is that it benefits the ten thousand creatures; yet itself does not scramble, but is content with the places that all men disdain. It is this that makes water so near to the Way.
>
> Tao Te Ching

is therefore the principle of the universe, and also a pattern for human behaviour, often called 'uncontrived action' (*wu-wei*).

> All things alter and change,
> Never a moment ceasing,
> Revolving, whirling, and rolling away,
> Driven far off and returning onward,
> Like the mutations of cicada,
> Profound, subtle, and illimitable
> Who can finish describing it?

'The Owl', Chia Yi (200–168 BCE)

> *Tai gave them birth; the power of the Tao reared them, shaped them according to their kinds, perfected them, giving to each its strength. Therefore, of the ten thousand things, there is not one that does not worship Tao and do homage to its power.*
>
> *Tao Te Ching*

The Taoist imagination was totally unfettered by the confines of Confucian etiquette or sensibility, and provided the magic garden of the Chinese people. Some took this magic very seriously, while some found that this, too, was just another illusion of the changing Tao. For example, at the end of a report of a magical spirit journey attributed to King My of the Chou dynasty, the magician who has been his guide for the trip explains:

> *Your majesty feels at home with the permanent, is suspicious of the sudden and temporary. But can one always measure how far and how fast a scene may later turn into something else?*

Or, as the next story in the *Lieh-tzu* puts it:

> *The breath of all that lives, the appearance of all that has shape, is illusion.*

But unlike many of the great religions of India and the East, the Taoists never felt that the Tao could be called a conscious god.

> *How can the Creator have a conscious mind? It spontaneously takes place, but seems mysterious. The breath and matter collect together, coagulate, and become shape: constant with transformation it continues on without ever ceasing.*

TAOISM TODAY

Throughout its history, the diverse masters of Taoism have sought, in various ways, to become part of this 'self-so-ness' of reality. Life rolls on by itself in an unbroken wave of creative spontaneity; neither the Confucian Heaven, nor the rule of earthly kings and emperors, nor the folly of demons or goblins can defy it.

Being of themselves as they are
Silently brings them about,
Gives them serenity, gives them peace,
Escorts them as they go and
welcomes them as they come.

The true immortal lives to learn a life in tune with the Tao.

In all Taoist religion there is a poetic touch, a realization that life is a beautiful – and frightening – panorama of transformations. No religion has been more successful at invoking the sense of wonder that these transformations cause to human beings. Set within their mountain retreats and their lake pavilions, the Taoists have truly been the poets of nature. The great T'ao Ch'ien (365–427 CE) expresses this sense of wonder, tinged with serene resignation and hope.

Just surrender to the cycle of things,
Give yourself to the waves of the Great Change,
Neither happy nor yet afraid,
And when it is time to go, then simply go,
Without any unnecessary fuss.

Today this sense of poetic beauty, and desire to achieve oneness with the Tao, still informs the

An old cleaner at a Taoist temple at Chengdu City, Sichuan Province, China.

INTRODUCTION TO WORLD RELIGIONS

Taoist religion. Because of the great revolutionary changes in China, and the determined animosity of Maoism towards traditional 'superstition', it was difficult to tell if and how Taoism could survive on the Chinese mainland. In recent years, however, a distinct *détente* concerning religious affairs has been noticeable.

CROSS-FERTILIZATION

The great Chinese religions have always influenced each other's development. In early China, great debates and arguments went on between the Taoists and Confucians, helping both sides develop their own distinctive attitudes. The picture becomes more complicated with the introduction of Buddhism into China. Both Taoism and Confucianism borrowed a great deal from the new Indian religion, with the Taoists reforming their religious structures, founding monasteries, and writing a huge canon of sacred texts in imitation of Buddhist models.

The great Neo-Confucian revival in the twelfth and eleventh centuries CE would also be unthinkable without the stimulus and challenge of Buddhist philosophy. Although the Confucians did not borrow nearly as much as the Taoists from the Buddhists, they were certainly stimulated to work out their own mature philosophic response to Buddhist thought – and on the practical level learned a great deal about meditation, which they called 'quiet-sitting', from the Buddhists.

The heyday of cross-fertilization of religions in China came in the Ming dynasty (1369–1644), when many religious thinkers, such as Lin Chao-en (1517–98), sought to effect a harmonization of the three great religions of China, declaring that the three religions are one. Lin sought to combine the best features of Taoist and Buddhist meditation with a Confucian sense of shared concern for fellow creatures, in a uniquely Chinese type of religious synthesis that is still present in China today. It would not be far wrong to say that most religious Chinese are, in fact, a mixture of all three great religions; the syncretists had such an effect that no one thinks it odd to be Buddhist, Taoist, and Confucian at the same time.

Finally, there is an element of Western culture in modern China's intellectual development (see 'Christianity in Contemporary China'). Religious and secular Western influence will, no doubt, have just as great an impact on China – witness the tremendous transformative power of Maoist thought, based in part on Marxist concepts – as did Buddhism. It is impossible to say what will survive; but we can be certain that what will emerge will be distinctively Chinese.

JOHN BERTHRONG

CHAPTER 50

Christianity in Contemporary China

A century ago, the Chinese still regarded Christianity as an imported, 'foreign' religion. Today, throughout large swathes of the countryside, China resembles a Christian culture: the country is dominated by a single political party, with near-absolute powers, yet in many ways the multitude of local communities can largely control their own fates. Towns allow traditional beliefs and practices of all religions to flourish, even if such expressions are not allowed in the cities.

Out of a total population of 1,330 billion in 2010, it has been estimated that approximately 85 million are Protestants, and another 21 million Catholics.[1] If these estimates are accurate, China – with more than 105 million Christian believers – would contain the third largest Christian population in the world, after the USA and Brazil.

SINICIZATION

Chinese Christianity, like Chinese Buddhism, has undergone a process of 'sinicization', or indigenization, becoming an embedded part of the Chinese cultural landscape. While worship, ritual, preaching, and other elements of religious culture retain their recognizable Christian character, they are now also stubbornly Chinese. Many of the categories familiar in other parts of the world do not apply here.

The first thirty years of Communist rule, from 1949 to the end of the Cultural Revolution in 1978, showed how firmly Christianity had become rooted, especially in the Chinese countryside. Local preachers and networks of worshippers sprang up, many completely cut off from outside contact. They often had limited knowledge of the Bible, or traditional doctrine, but taught the message. With some liberalization in the post-Mao era, the Chineseness of China's Christianity only strengthened, though it is not immune to the forces of globalization.

> *I believed in Christ in 1997 when my son was ill and I was seeking his healing. Later, this eight-month-old did not get well and was taken by the Lord ... He caused me to understand that following Christ is not just so we can get bodily healing, but something far more important – healing of our spiritual sicknesses.*
>
> Zhou, farmer

---

1 Jason Mandryk, *Operation World*, Colorado Springs: Biblica Publishing, 2010, p. 215.

International Christian organizations maintain relations with Chinese groups; some have entered and spread their teachings without official approval; and many English teachers in China are sent to spread the Christian message.

Yet Chinese Christianity is unique. About 80 per cent of believers live in rural areas, often poor, with no resources to build churches or purchase Bibles or hymnals. The educational level is low, and many clergy prefer to work in urban environments, leaving congregations dependent on oral teaching, and with a weak grasp of doctrine or the church's broader role in society. Sermons often focus on filial piety, a recurring topic throughout Chinese history. Other topics include forbearance, forgiveness, and obedience – mixing easily with local folk traditions.

As with many Chinese religions, Christianity is primarily a female activity. Approximately 70 per cent of believers are female, although women do not make up the same proportion of church leaders. A 'cultural Christian' is an indigenous term from the 1980s for certain academics who, unlike practising church Christians, were relatively free to write and publish on Christian topics. It came to mean an academic who might secretly be a Christian, but for workplace reasons did not want to publicize this. Ironically, cultural Christians, though rarely church members, are seen by many Chinese as legitimate spokespeople for Christianity.

Religion was equated by the post-1949 Chinese state with superstition, feudalism, and imperialism – and simply not allowed. Yet people clung to their beliefs, and this approach softened. Since 1978, state control has been increasingly liberalized. The official church structure, the Three Self Church, has reopened churches throughout the countryside and in cities, and worship is allowed. Significant numbers of believers are not under the Three Self umbrella: they may belong to banned groups and their offshoots, or their leaders may choose not to cooperate with the official church structure. However, the term 'underground church' – used widely in the 1980s – is not an accurate description today; often rural believers meet in the open, or in homes, simply because no buildings are available.

CHRISTIAN MISSIONS TO CHINA

Christianity has been present in China from as early as 635, when a Nestorian Christian community was established in the capital Chang An (now Xian). A stone monument, found there in 1625, narrates the story of Nestorian Christianity and its first Chinese monk, Alopen. By the mid-800s there were several monasteries and communities in China, but their activity ceased in 845, with the prohibition of Buddhism and other religions. Nestorian activity began again in the Mongol period (1277–1368), and by the time of Marco Polo there were several types of Christians in China, including Armenians, Byzantine, Jacobin, and Roman Catholics, most of whom were not of ethnic Chinese extraction.

In 1556, the Portuguese established an outpost that later became their colony of Macao, and in 1583 the Jesuits were granted permission to live in mainland China and to propagate their message. They used European advances in astronomy to entice the court and scholars into discussion, but tolerated such Chinese values as ancestor veneration, until the pope denounced the Jesuits' accommodating policy in 1704, citing three concerns: the names of God used in China (*Shangdi*, *Tian*, *Taiji*), ceremonies to honour Confucius, and the practice of contributing to community festivals where non-Christian divinities were honoured. The Qing dynasty (1644–1911) initially adopted a positive attitude to Christianity, but in 1724 missionary activity became illegal, and Christianity was banned and went underground.

Nevertheless, Christian missionaries flocked to China in the nineteenth century, often supported by the imperialist aims of their home countries in Europe and North America. Host populations in turn perceived missionary activity as one of the three legs of imperialism, along with trade and military power. There were no Protestant missions to China until the Treaty of Nanking in 1842; yet by 1949 – the eve of Communist victory – there were 936,000 Chinese Protestants and 2,963 clergy. In the twentieth century, missionary orientation changed: many missionaries saw their role primarily as educators, establishing universities and private schools, and offering foreign language training and medical care.

THE OUTLOOK FOR CHRISTIANITY IN CHINA

During the Cultural Revolution, many Protestants attended clandestine 'house meetings', which later grew into more or less open networks of worshippers. The government no longer – or rarely – uses force to limit such meetings, and family meetings or prayers are of even less concern. The core of state policy towards

KAZAKHSTAN

XINJIANG UIGHUR

TIBET

NEPAL

BHUT

INDIA

BANGL
DESH

Bay o
Benga

- Roman Catholic
- Protestant
- Buddhist
- Taoist
- Muslim
- No dominant religion/no data

Major Religions of Modern China

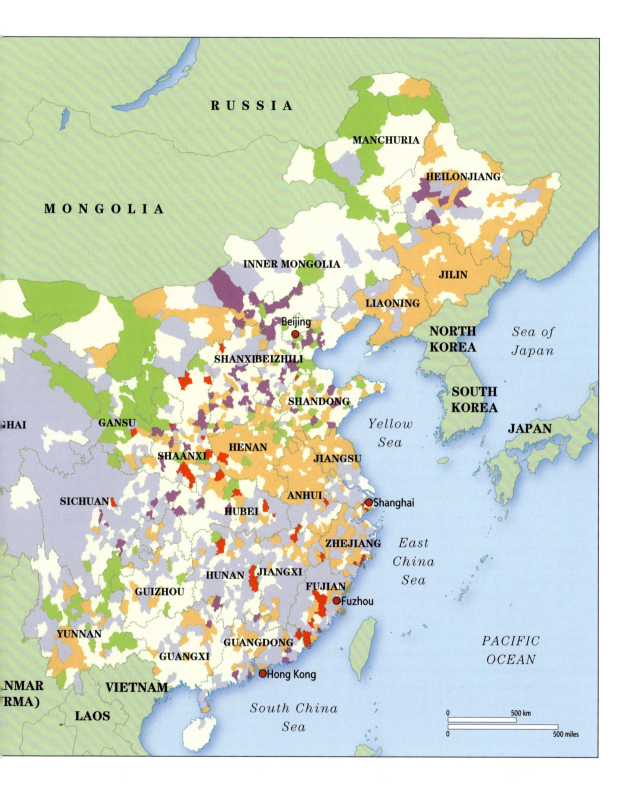

THE WORSHIP OF ANCESTORS

Ancestral worship was first introduced to China at the beginning of the Chou dynasty (1122–325 BCE). Confucius popularized this practice by his teaching on filial piety, decreeing that parents and elders are to be honoured and respected while they are alive. This sense of reverence continues after their deaths.

The Chinese believe that, at death, the soul of the deceased ancestor resides in three places: one part goes to heaven, the second remains in the grave to receive sacrifices, and the third is localized in the ancestral tablet, or shrine.

The soul has to be assisted as it journeys to heaven. Hence, at Chinese funerals, elaborate rituals are meticulously carried out to ensure that the soul is amply provided for on its course. With the help of a Taoist priest, members of the family chant prayers, offer sacrifices of food, and burn paper money – and in some cases even paper cars, planes, and servants – so that there will be no lack of provisions. Evil spirits who oppose the deceased are propitiated by appropriate sacrifices and by loud wailing.

The siting of the grave is very important. A geomancer – in Chinese *Feng shui sien sheng* – is consulted, to determine the ideal location. The tomb must be maintained, and occasional offerings are made to the part of the soul that resides in it. The heirs continue to visit it, especially during the spring festivals (*ts'ing meng*).

Within 100 days of the burial, a memorial service is held in the home of the oldest male heir.

The ancestral tablet is dedicated by a Buddhist or Taoist priest; today it normally contains a photograph of the deceased, with the name, rank, and status in life. Incense-sticks are burned and placed on the tablet, and on certain feast days food offerings are included. Newly-married couples in the family have to bow before this tablet: its presence strengthens family solidarity, and offers protection and blessing to all in the family.

Chinese Christians have sometimes been accused of not honouring their ancestors by not becoming involved in ancestral worship rites; they reply that they will always respect and honour their elders while they are alive. Many are prepared to be the first in cleaning family tombs, and some Christians have even set up halls of remembrance for their forebears. Non-Christian relatives and friends may be invited to special memorial services, where Christ is proclaimed as victor over the grave.

Chua Wee Hian

The Master said, 'At fifteen, I had my mind bent on learning.

At thirty, I stood firm.

At forty, I had no doubts.

At fifty, I knew the decrees of Heaven.

At sixty, my ear was an obedient organ for the reception of truth.

At seventy, I could follow what my heart desired, without transgressing what was right.'

Mang: I asked what filial piety was.

The Master said, 'It is not being disobedient.'

Soon after, as Fan Ch'ih was driving him, the Master told him, saying, 'Mang-sun asked me what filial piety was, and I answered him,

"not being disobedient."'

Fan Ch'ih said, 'What did you mean?'

The Master replied, 'That parents, when alive, be served according to propriety; that, when dead, they should be buried according to propriety; and that they should be sacrificed to according to propriety.'

Analects of Confucius, transl. James Legge, 1893.

INTRODUCTION TO WORLD RELIGIONS

Christianity in China today is the Three Self Policy—self-support, self-government, self-propagation — which was adopted by all officially-sanctioned religious groups in the 1950s. As one Protestant bishop stated in 1988, 'The government doesn't bother us now. They see Christians have better moral behaviour than others; they don't cause trouble.' In the 1980s some offshoots of the 'Shouters' — a network of Protestant congregations in Central China that call out words during worship — were deemed harmful 'cults' and their leaders arrested.

> No state organ, public organization, or individual may compel citizens to believe in, or not to believe in, any religion. The state protects normal religious activities. No one may make use of religion to engage in activities that disrupt public order, impair the health of citizens, or interfere with the educational system of the states.
>
> From the Chinese Constitution

The Catholic Church has a particular problem due to a rift between China and the Vatican. The officially-sanctioned Chinese Catholic Patriotic Association controls the 're-opened' churches, but in some parishes believers refuse to attend these churches, instead worshipping in private, and showing their disapproval by chanting outside a church during mass. Both Protestant and Catholic congregations suffer from a lack of trained clergy, and much local Protestant activity is beyond the control of the formal church. Christians often gather on market days, and visit private homes to pray, sometimes for days at a time. Preachers are commonly self-taught recent converts, and often there are no Bibles within a congregation.

Inevitably, China's absorption of Christianity will result in new organizational forms. Already there are several well-established indigenous churches, such as the Little Flock and the True Jesus Church, which began in China in the early decades of the twentieth century. Today both movements flourish in such locations as Hong Kong, the USA, the UK, and South-east Asia.

EDWARD A. IRONS

QUESTIONS

1. How have the concepts of yin and yang influenced religion in China?

2. Explain the importance of the 'consciousness of concern' in the history of Chinese religion.

3. Is Confucianism a religion? Explain your answer.

4. Mencius or Hsün-tzu: who was more important in the development of Confucianism – and why?

5. What are the aims and beliefs of the Taoist religion?

6. How do Confucianism and the Taoist religion differ?

7. How have Confucianism, Buddhism, and Taoism influenced each other in China?

8. How and why does Christianity in China today differ from Christianity elsewhere?

9. Explain the role of ancestor worship in China.

10. How far has Maoist Communism been responsible for shaping religion in China since 1949?

FURTHER READING

Berthrong, John H., and Evelyn Nagai Berthrong, *Confucianism: An Introduction*. Oxford: Oneworld Publications, 2000.

Ching, Julia, *Chinese Religions*. London: Macmillan; Maryknoll, NY: Orbis, 1993.

Confucius, *The Analects*. Trans. D. C. Lau. New York: Penguin, 1979.

Kohn, Livia, *Daoism and Chinese Culture*. Cambridge, MA: Three Pines Press, 2001.

Lopez, Donald S., Jr, ed., *Religions of China in Practice*. Princeton: Princeton University Press, 1996.

Miller, James, *Daoism: A Short Introduction*. Oxford: Oneworld Publications, 2003.

Oldstone-Moore, Jennifer, *Confucianism: Origins, Beliefs, Practices, Holy Texts, Sacred Places*. New York: Oxford University Press, 2002.

Yao, Xinzhong, *An Introduction to Confucianism*. Cambridge: Cambridge University Press, 2000.

PART 8
KOREAN
AND JAPANESE
RELIGIONS

SUMMARY

Korea's traditional religion, Sinkyo, has been central to Korean society throughout its history, and is grounded in the national mythology. Tangun, the mythical founder of the country, is said to have been the grandson of Hanahim, the spirit of heaven, who rewards the righteous and punishes evil. Central to Sinkyo are the opposites – the yin and the yang – in nature, whose harmonious coexistence is essential. Imbalances are restored by ritual sacrifice, led by a female shaman – the Mudang – who thus ensures success for the community. Korean tradition has borrowed much from its neighbours – Confucianism, Taoism, and Buddhism – and in recent years has been challenged by the phenomenal growth of Christianity in South Korea, as well as by repression in the Communist North.

Japan's rich and diverse religious culture is the product not only of two thousand years of history, but also of the country's peculiar geography. Inevitably, its religion has been strongly influenced by the Asian mainland; the country's location meant that almost all religious imports came by way of years of development in China or Korea. Shinto, formerly the state religion, has a history stretching back to the Yamoto period of around 300–600 CE, and is concerned with national mythology. The emperors had a special place within this narrative, as they were believed to descend from Amaterasu, the sun goddess, according them a semi-divine status that was only rescinded at the end of World War II. The religious life of Shinto is centred on its shrines, which exist for a variety of personal, local, and national reasons. Among these are sites such as the Yasukuni Shrine, in Tokyo, which commemorates the war dead, which became controversial in recent years because of their historic links with nationalism. Shinto is by no means the only tradition within Japan; Buddhism has been present almost as long, and exists in a number of forms. Unusually, it is typical for most to adhere to both Shinto and Buddhism, turning to one or the other at particular times.

CHAPTER 51

Sinkyo

KOREA'S TRADITIONAL RELIGION

Korea's traditional religion, Sinkyo, has been called 'the religion without a name'. It is not so much a structured set of uniform beliefs as a religious way of seeing the world and a person's sacred link with it – which used to be called 'animism'. Like other religions, it has five 'magnetic points':

1. **I and the cosmos**

   Humanity is in rhythm with the world. The forces of nature controlling life and death, fertility and sterility, become personified and god-like. This world is a religious arena, inhabited by spirits of heaven and the soil, water and the trees.

2. **I and the norm**

   The myth of Tangun, legendary founder of Korea, underlines that sense of cosmic norm to which the Korean must conform. Ung, the son of heaven, changed a bear into a woman. The bear-woman could find no one to marry, so Ung changed his form, married her, and fathered her child, Tangun. This myth is remembered on 'opening of heaven day' (*Kaechonjol*), an annual national holiday. Similar tales surround the archetypal tribal leaders, and mythical ancestors of present-day clan families.

3. **I and destiny**

   How do we reconcile the fact that we are active beings and also victims of fate or destiny? Borrowing from pre-Confucian roots, Sinkyo finds its answer in a cosmic pattern, where heaven, humankind, and nature make a harmony of opposites that complement each other. They are the great forces of the *yin* and the *yang*, non-being and being. The *yin* is negative, passive, weak, and destructive; the *yang* is positive, active, strong, a nd constructive. As they act and interact, harmony is achieved and recreated, again and again. Our individuality comes from these opposites: the *yin* is the

Zen door, with the yin-yang symbol at a Confucian academy in South Korea.

female, mother, soft, dark, wet; the *yang* male, father, strong, hard, bright.

Out of these opposites comes the system called 'geomancy'. 'Where shall we live?' becomes a religious question of choosing a good house-site or grave-site, in harmony with these opposites. The house or burial place, for instance, must be arranged in conformity to the cosmic workings of *yin-yang* and the harmony of the five elements: wood, metal, fire, water, earth. The interacting flow of these forces must not be disturbed.

4. I and salvation

Since this harmony is often broken, Sinkyo must also meet people's craving for salvation. When the rice paddies are ploughed in the spring, a farmers' band pacifies the spirits of the earth with music and ritual. When the ridge pole of a new house is raised, wine and food are thrown at it, while a member of the household chants, 'Please, grandfather and grandmother of the ridge pole, bless us with good luck and long life, and many sons!'

Life is under a curse, a shadow darkening the cosmic harmony. The way back to 'paradise lost' is by ritual sacrifice. Throwing a stone on a simple altar keeps you from getting sore feet on a journey; spitting on the altar is a sign of purification, and wards off evil spirits. Earth spirits must be satisfied before a corpse can be laid to rest. The 'sin' is not that of personally violating the will of a personal 'god', but the corporate breaking of cosmic unity.

The chief role in restoring unity is often played by the Mudang. Always a woman, her most important task is curing mental and physical disease. Like the shamans of Siberia, she also conducts communal sacrifice, assures the farmers of good crops, and fishermen of safe journeys and a good catch. She will produce sons for a barren woman, recall the spirits of the dead after a funeral, and lead them to the kingdom of the blessed, and pacify the spirits of those who die violent or tragic deaths. Her role is regarded as beneficial.

Sinkyo feels deep horror at the threat of death, which destroys cosmic harmony. Two thousand years ago, it was common for Koreans to bury the dead with their personal belongings, including gold and silver. With the growing influence of Confucianism in Korea from the third century CE, Sinkyo saw the spirit world in a new way. The Confucian concept of filial piety as the summit of all virtues strengthened – if it did not create – Korea's early ancestor-cult. In the following years, food was offered to kinsmen at death and at memorial times, in the hope that the ancestor would favour the descendants.

5. I and the Supreme Being

Koreans read about the gods in the great picture-book we call the cosmos. Among the spirits of nature, the spirit of heaven (Hananim, or Hanunim) has a special place. Not a 'high god', remote and supreme, he is said to bring sunlight and rain – while lightning, drought, and other disasters are his judgment on the wicked. By his favour we live and breathe. When national disaster came, the king used to appeal to Hananim, by confessing his own sins and those of his people. In some sense a 'heavenly father', Hananim was the grandfather of Tangun, the aboriginal hero of Korea.

KOREA AND JAPAN TIMELINE

1000 BCE   750 BCE   500 BCE   250 BCE   0   250 CE   500 CE   750 CE   1000 CE   1250 CE   1500 CE   1750 CE   2000 CE

552 CE   Buddhism introduced to Japan

125 BCE   Chinese culture begins to influence Korea

593–622   Prince Shotoku makes Buddhism national religion of Japan

806   Kukai brings Shingon Buddhism to Japan

1158–1210   Chinul, founder of Korean Chogye order

1173-1262   Shinran, Japanese Pure Land thinker

c 1200   Zen starts to spread in Japan

1222–1282   Nichiren, founder of Nichiren Buddhism in Japan

1603   Establishment of the Tokugawa shogunate, which rules Japan until 1868: state control of Buddhism

1730–1801   Motoori Norinaga, advocate of Shinto revival

1837   Nakayama Miki experiences trance and founds Tenrikyo

1868   Meiji Restoration ends shogunate and begins to modernize Japan

1882   Beginning of State Shinto in Japan

1937   Soka Gakkai founded

1945   Japanese surrender leads to end of State Shinto

1948   Korea divided to form communist North Korea and secular South Korea

1995   Aum Shinrikyo members release poison gas in Tokyo subway

    INTRODUCTION TO WORLD RELIGIONS

SINKYO AND THE NEW RELIGIOUS MOVEMENTS

As Korea was invaded by Confucianism, Buddhism, and Christianity, Sinkyo did not shrink, but was altered and strengthened. From Confucianism came the ethical codes surrounding the ancestor-cult. Taoism and Neo-Confucianism strengthened the magical side of Sinkyo and its geomancy. From Buddhism came a stress on suffering and pain, now linked with healing and divining.

Sinkyo has also provided the background for Korea's new religions. Chondogyo was founded in the mid-eighteenth century in reaction to the coming of Christianity, and reinforced humanity's sacred links with the universe. Sun Myung Moon, the Korean founder of the Unification Church, can be seen as the great link-man between the people and the spirit world.

HARVIE CONN

CHAPTER 52

Japanese Religions

A TAPESTRY OF TRADITIONS

Religion in Japan is a rich tapestry of diverse traditions, with a history of nearly 2000 years. Many Japanese people display some kind of allegiance to more than one religion: a person will usually be expected to have a Shinto wedding and a Buddhist funeral, though Buddhist and secular weddings are also possible. Along with this may go a personal or family interest in a particular Buddhist denomination or practice, or membership of one of the various new religions, which attract almost a third of the population.

These different forms of religion have separate organizations, buildings, festivals, sacred writings, ministers or priests and so on. However, it should be remembered that the paths of these religions have touched at many points in Japanese history, and that they still meet in the lives of many Japanese people. For this reason, it is possible to speak both of 'Japanese religions' and of 'Japanese religion' – especially as the Japanese language itself does not usually distinguish between the singular and the plural.

LAND AND RELIGION

The general pattern of Japanese religion is, in some ways, a reflection of the country's geographical position and character. Japan has received a great deal from the Asian continent, almost entirely from or via Korea and China. The major imported religions are therefore Buddhism, mainly in its Mahayana form, and Confucianism. The influence of Taoism has been largely indirect, bearing partly on divination practices, and partly on the style of Zen Buddhism. It was in reaction to the powerful Buddhist and Confucian systems, with their scholarly prestige and political influence, that Japan's native Shinto faith first became clearly organized and defined. Indeed, the impact of Chinese, and then of Western, culture, and Japan's responses to these, provide the overall cultural perspective in which Japanese religion can be understood.

FOUR ISLANDS

The fact that the country consists mainly of four great islands, spread over a vast distance from north to south, has also had its effect:

1. **Honshu**

   The most famous historic Shinto shrines and Buddhist temples are found in the southern part of the main island, Honshu. Ancient Shinto shrines which are still of national importance are located at Ise, where the sun-goddess Amaterasu is revered, and where a new prime minister usually 'reports' on the formation of the cabinet, and at Izumo, where all the gods, or *kami*, of Japan are said to return once a year. Between these two sites are the former capitals, Nara and Kyoto, which themselves boast not only well-known Shinto shrines, such as the Kasuga Shrine at Nara, but also many fine Buddhist temples and images. The thirteenth-century sectarian development of Buddhism is reflected in the temple buildings and images at Kamakura, also on the main island of Honshu, but further east, near modern Tokyo.

2. **Shikoku**

   The smaller island of Shikoku, which together with Honshu cradles the scenic Inland Sea, has never been of political importance, and so lacks major religious monuments. But it does have a famous pilgrimage route, which takes in no fewer

Zen Buddhist Kinkaku-ji Temple of the Golden Pavilion, or Rokuon-ji, Kyoto, Japan.

Major Japanese Shinto Shrines

INTRODUCTION TO WORLD RELIGIONS

than eighty-eight Buddhist temples. Today these are frequently visited by tourists, an example of the intimate link between holiday travel and religion in Japan today. Other pilgrimage routes are found in other parts of the country, the most famous being the thirty-three places in western Honshu where the Bodhisattva Kannon-sama is revered.

3. **Hokkaido**

The island of Hokkaido in the north was largely undeveloped until the nineteenth century, when young Tokyoites were sent out in a pioneering spirit to cope with its less favourable climate. The main city, Sapporo, was a centre of Protestant missionary effort at that time, although its people today practise the more usual forms of Japanese religion.

4. **Kyushu**

Kyushu, the southernmost major island, claims some of the oldest known historical sites in Japan, because of its proximity to Korea. Its importance as a maritime trading approach from the West meant that it became the main base for Roman Catholic missions in the sixteenth century, and also the scene of martyrdoms, especially at Nagasaki. Roman Catholic Christianity was suppressed partly because it was espoused by feudal lords in Kyushu who showed separatist tendencies. In a similar way, Kyushu was also the geographical base for the Shinto-inspired reassertion of imperial power in the mid-nineteenth century, when the central military government in Edo (now Tokyo) came to the end of its two and a half centuries of undisturbed rule.

MOUNTAIN SHRINES

The mountainous terrain of the country has also had a major effect on the forms of Japanese religious life. Many mountains have shrines at their summit, and not a few attract pilgrim groups seeking purification and heightened spiritual powers. The most famous is Mount Fuji itself, which is a quasi-religious symbol for the whole nation.

Buddhists had already used mountains in China as isolated retreats from the world, and this practice was carried over to Japan. The most famous example was Mount Koya, one of the leading headquarters of Shingon Buddhism (see below).

The mountain cult encouraged one of the most fascinating syncretistic movements in the history of religion, the Shugendo movement, which linked Buddhism and Shinto. This movement used ascetic exercises aiming at enlightenment in a quest for shamanic magical powers, performing spiritualist healing and fire-walking rites. It flourished in historical times, but has by no means died out, and has had considerable influence on the formation of new religions.

> Now when chaos had begun to condense, but force and form were not yet manifest, and there was nought named, nought done, who could know its shape? Nevertheless Heaven and Earth first parted, and the Three Deities performed the commencement of creation: the Passive and the Active essences then developed, and the Two Spirits became the ancestors of all things.
>
> Kojiki

SHINTO

Shinto is the name given to a wide conglomeration of religious practices with roots in prehistoric Japan. Little is known about Japanese religion before the emergence of a unified state in the Yamato period (fourth to seventh centuries CE), but in its simplest forms it was broadly animist, believing that a supernatural living force resided in natural objects such as mountains, trees, and animals.

At festivals we serve the deities by purifying ourselves, with sincerity revere the dignity of the deities, return thanks for their benefits, and offer earnest prayers.

Kokutai no Hongi

The oldest literary works in Japan were composed on the basis of the combined myths and legends of the various clans which had been forged into political unity. The oldest of these official works is the *Kojiki* (712 CE), but this was soon replaced by the *Nihongi* (720 CE), also known as the *Nihonshoki*. These two works retain to this day an honoured position in the minds of most Japanese people, and are considered especially important by the advocates of Shinto. However they are not recited – or even studied – by ordinary believers.

From the Yamato period onwards, the imperial household took a central position within Shinto. Its ancestry was traced back through legendary emperors and empresses as far as Ninigi, believed to have been the grandson of the sun-goddess Amaterasu. For this reason, the Ise Shrine has always had a close connection with the imperial household. From 1868 onwards, when the monarchy was restored to a central position in Japanese politics, under Emperor Meiji (1852–1912), up until the end of the Pacific War in 1945, the Shinto religion was focused sharply on the Ise Shrine and the emperor cult. After the war, the emperor's semi-divine status was officially denied and Shinto disestablished. Since then, religious teaching has no longer been given in state-run schools, and the observance of Shinto practices has become a voluntary matter. Nevertheless, the imperial family still enjoys very high esteem among the people, and leading Shinto shrines remain important symbols of Japanese nationhood.

SHINTO SHRINES

Shinto today is based fundamentally on each individual shrine. Although most shrines large enough to have an organizing staff are affiliated to the Association of Shinto Shrines, most people who visit a shrine, or take part in a festival, are hardly aware of this. Each shrine has some individual reason for its existence, whether it be a natural phenomenon, such as a mountain, a historical event of importance to the local community, or an act of personal devotion or political patronage. There is an endless variety: for example, the ancient shrine at Kashima, near the Pacific coast of Honshu, is patronized particularly by those devoted to the martial arts, such as swordsmanship and *kendo*. At the same time it has various sub-shrines within its grounds. One of these celebrates a spring of fresh water tumbling out of the side of a hill, and has its symbolic gate planted in the pool at the foot. Another is a fenced enclosure surrounding a mighty stone, of which only the rounded top is visible, sticking up through the sand. This stone is supposed to hold down beneath the earth the giant catfish that is believed to be responsible for earthquakes.

The god, or *kami*, of a shrine may be the natural object itself, one of the divinities mentioned in the *Kojiki* or the *Nihongi*, or a legendary or historical person. In shrines where a specific object is kept in the inner sanctuary, it is usually not known what the object is, for nobody ever sees it.

Shinto shrines have certain common features which are almost always to be seen. The first of these that the visitor will notice is a large, symbolic gate, consisting of two uprights and two crossbars, marking the entrance to the shrine. These gates (*torii*) sometimes stand quite far off, at the bottom of a busy street with shops and stalls catering for visitors; there may be two or more — or even a long line of them — leading to the shrine itself. Inside the precinct there is a large trough of clean water, usually sheltered with a roof, and provided with clean wooden ladles. Here the worshipper rinses face and hands, in a simple act of purification. The main shrine buildings, of which there are several traditional architectural types, consist of a worship hall (*haiden*), with a main hall (*honden*) standing behind. The main hall is usually smaller and is not entered, being the physical location of the *kami* itself.

> The term Kami is applied in the first place to the various deities of Heaven and Earth who are mentioned in the ancient records as well as to their spirits (mi-tama) which reside in the shrines where they are worshipped. Moreover, not only human beings, but birds, beasts, plants and trees, seas and mountains, and all other things whatsoever which deserve to be dreaded and revered for the extraordinary and preeminent powers which they possess, are called Kami.
>
> Motoori Wonnaga (1730–1801)

The worship hall is entered from time to time by small groups, for petitionary prayer. Individual visitors to the shrine simply stand outside, before the worship hall, toss a coin into the offerings box, pull on a dangling rope with a bell or clanger at the top, clap their hands twice, bow briefly in prayer, clap their hands again, and leave. The sound of the clanger and the handclap are intended to alert the *kami* to the believer's presence. The front of the worship hall is often decorated with a thick rope (*shimenawa*) and folded white paper strips, which are used to designate a sacred area or sacred object. Sometimes these are simply strung around a rock or a tree, indicating that these too are considered as shrines for the *kami* of the rock or tree.

There are three main types of shrine:

1. Shrines of purely local significance, housing the *kami* of the locality (*ujigami*);
2. Shrines of a particular recurrent type, such as the Inari Shrines, which are visited with a view to winning business success, and may be found in any part of the country;
3. Shrines of great national and semi-political importance, such as the Ise and Izumo Shrines mentioned earlier, the Meiji Shrine in Tokyo, honouring the former emperor Meiji, and the Yasukuni Shrine, also in Tokyo, commemorating the souls of Japan's

war dead. Since the end of the Pacific War, the status of Ise Shrine, and of Yasukuni Shrine, has been a matter of some controversy, because critics fear a revival of Shinto-led nationalism, if relations with political leaders, or with the imperial household, become too close or too formal.

Other types of shrine that recur throughout the country include the Hachimangu Shrines, dedicated to the *kami* of war and martial prowess; the Toshogu Shrines, sacred to the memory of the dictator-general Ieyasu (d. 1616), and reflecting the colourful pomp of his mausoleum at Nikko; and the Tenmangu Shrines, where a loyal but wrongfully banished aristocrat is revered, and believers pray for success in literature and study.

SHINTO PRACTICE

Much of Shinto practice is an individual matter, as when a person simply visits a shrine to make his or her own request – before a journey, before an examination, before some new enterprise, or perhaps because they just happen to be passing that way. In such cases the form of worship is as described earlier. Family occasions also involve visits to the shrine. It is common, though not universal, to take a newborn baby there, so that prayers may be said for its health. Shinto priests officiate at the majority of Japanese weddings, though these usually take place in a purpose-built hall, run on business lines, with reception rooms and other facilities.

Shrines are visited by particularly large numbers at New Year, especially on 1 January, but also on 2 and 3 January. Some people go just after midnight on 31 December, while others go at dawn. Some visitors to mountain shrines make a point of observing the rising sun and bathing their faces in its first rays. At the New Year visit, there is a brisk sale of feathered wooden arrows (to drive off evil), protective charms, and stiff paper strips bearing the name and seal of the shrine (*fuda*). These are taken home and kept on the *kami* shelf, if there is one, or just in a high place, for the coming year. Last year's accessories are taken back to the shrine at the New Year visit and burned on a bonfire, or handed in to be burned later by shrine staff.

Another personal charm sold in great numbers at this time of year is the papier-mâché *daruma* doll, originally a representation of the Zen Buddhist master Daruma (or *Bodhidharma*). Though Buddhist in origin, these dolls are on sale at the entrance to many shrines, and are also brought back to shrines for burning. Some Buddhist temples share in the New Year practices, by encouraging a first visit on a specified day in January, selling various kinds of talisman, and offering prayers for safety in the home, traffic safety, prosperity in business, and avoidance of bad luck.

> The magokoro or 'true heart' is pure and sincere. This links with the belief that the divine light which illuminates the kami is also found in the human heart. It is like a mirror which needs polishing and cleaning, to clear away the dust and dirt which obscure it.
>
> Ninian Smart, *World Philosophies* (1999).

SHINTO FESTIVALS

Perhaps the most important feature of Shinto practice is the festival (*matsuri*), since this is the main occasion when a particular shrine takes on meaning for all its worshippers at once. A Shinto festival usually includes a procession, or a fair with stalls and side-shows, and so easily draws large numbers of people. The more spectacular festivals bring in visitors and sightseers too, so being good for trade; for festivals which achieve national fame, special trains may be laid on, and accommodation booked months in advance. One shrine may hold several festivals in a year, but of these just one or two may be of special importance, particularly in spring or autumn.

Festivals famous throughout Japan for their huge floats hauled in procession include the Gion Festival in Kyoto, the Takayama Festival in the Hida region, and the Chichibu Festival in the mountains north-west of Tokyo. In the last of these, the vehicles — representing various parts of the town of Chichibu — are illuminated by lanterns, and drawn through the town at night, as the *kami* from the town shrine is brought to meet the *kami* of the nearest large mountain.

In many cases, the floats, or the standards and banners, are taken through the town by groups of young men wearing clothes representative of their part of the town. Sometimes they wear only a loincloth, because of the strenuousness of the work, especially if they have to wade through water. Almost always they are fortified by plenty of rice wine (*sake*), which is particularly associated with Shinto, and often offered

Shinto ritual at the Naminoue Shrine, Okinawa, Japan.

at shrines in neatly-wrapped bottles or large casks. Sometimes the processions recall a historical event, such as a battle, in which case period costumes are worn. Often the focal point of a procession is a portable shrine (*mikoshi*), which is taken from the main shrine to various points in the locality, symbolizing a journey made by the *kami*. Not all of those taking part in a procession enter the worship hall of the main shrine upon arrival. Usually only representatives go inside with the priests to present offerings, such as evergreen branches of the *sakaki* tree, and offer prayers for the safety and prosperity of the neighbourhood.

> *At that time the World-honoured One addressed the eighty thousand great leaders through the Bodhisattva Medicine-King: Medicine-King! Do you see in this assembly innumerable gods, dragon kings … human and non-human beings, as well as … male and female lay devotees … seekers after pratyeke-buddhahood, seekers after bodhisattvaship, or seekers after buddhahood? All such beings as these, in the presence of the Buddha, if they hear a single verse or a single word of the Wonderful Law-Flower Sutra and even by a single thought delight in it, I predict that they will all attain to Perfect Enlightenment.*
>
> Lotus Sutra

JAPANESE BUDDHISM

The history of Japanese Buddhism can be traced back to the early sixth century CE, when images and *sutras* (Buddhist scriptures) were sent from Korea. The first major act of patronage took place when Prince Shotoku, regent from 593–622 CE, established Buddhism as a national religion, linking it to Confucian ideals of morality and statecraft.

A stream of eminent monks brought more knowledge of the new religion from Korea and China, and the early traditions at the capital of Nara were superseded in 805 CE by a much bigger Buddhist establishment on Mount Hiei, overlooking the new capital of Kyoto. This new Buddhist centre drew its inspiration from the Chinese T'ien T'ai school, which came to be known in Japan as Tendai Buddhism.

This in turn was rapidly affected by the doctrines and practices of an esoteric form of Buddhism, not unlike that of Tibet. Almost immediately, a rival headquarters for this type of Buddhis m was set up on the then almost inaccessible Mount Koya, some distance to the south of Kyoto. This school – Shingon Buddhism – was established by the famous monk Kukai (744–835), posthumously known as Kobo Daishi, and revered as a great saint.

The Tendai and Shingon sects were rapidly supplemented by others, partly drawing on trends in Chinese Buddhism, and partly resulting from Japanese innovation. The *Lotus Sutra* had already been of great importance in Tendai Buddhism, but Nichiren (1222–82) gave it a new centrality, and his interpretative writings provided the basis for a number of sects. Among these are counted some of the most influential lay Buddhist movements of modern times. Nichirenite sects share in common the recitation of the simple formula 'Nam(u) Myoho Renge Kyo' ('Hail Wonderful Dharma Lotus Sutra'). In their various ways these sects all express significant themes in the tradition of Mahayana Buddhism, which spread from India across East Asia. While some people have a clear allegiance to one or other sect, especially in the case of the *nembutsu* sects and the Nichirenite sects, there are many features of popular devotion which cut across sectarian distinctions.

Two of the most widely revered saviour figures are the Bodhisattvas Jizo-sama and Kannon-sama. Jizo-sama is believed to care especially for children, and for infants who die during childbirth or pregnancy. Kannon-sama (*Avalokiresvara* in Sanskrit) offers many kinds of protection and solace, and is found in many places, not least in the precincts of Soto Zen temples.

BUDDHISM IN THE HOME

In the home, many families are reminded of Buddhism by the presence of a domestic Buddhist altar (*butsu-dan*). This usually contains a central Buddhist image or other symbol, tablets commemorating ancestors, a booklet with portions of Buddhist scriptures, a place for lighting incense, and various other accessories. As a morning devotion, a small offering of food may be placed on the altar, a passage recited from a *sutra*, and a stick of incense lit. Individual sects introduce many variations.

Buddhism is also particularly influential as the religion of funerals and cemeteries. Again, the different sects make slightly different provisions, though cremation and a stone memorial are universal. Thin wooden posts placed by visitors at the tombstone bear texts written in heavy black ink and reflecting the distinctive faith of the temple in question. Cemeteries are visited particularly at *higan*, which occurs twice a year, at the spring and autumn equinoxes. The other main commemoration of the dead is in midsummer at *o-bon*, which is marked by outdoor fires and dancing.

BUDDHIST FESTIVALS

To some extent, Japanese Buddhism borrows the characteristic Shinto concept of festival (*matsuri*). In early April, for example, some Buddhist temples celebrate a flower festival that centres on the commemoration of the Buddha's birthday on 8 April. At this time, a small standing statue of the infant Buddha is placed in a framework decorated with flowers, and worshippers anoint it with liquid from a bowl beneath.

Another well-known festival, climaxing at a Buddhist temple in Tokyo, is that of the forty-seven masterless Samurai (*ronin*). These forty-seven have been applauded for centuries, because they avenged the unjustly forced suicide of their master, and then committed suicide themselves, in one of the classic cases of premeditated ritual suicide (*hara-kiri*), carried out in connection with a feat inspired by loyalty. This theme is worked out in the well-known traditional drama *Chushingura*, regularly shown at the time of the festival in December. The festival itself consists of a procession re-enacting the arrival of the forty-seven Samurai at the temple to report the completion of their deed of vengeance. Following this, crowds of people light incense at their tombs.

Buddhism is linked to Japanese culture at many points: through the traditional way of the Samurai, generally known as *bushido*; through the austere *no* drama, with its

Japanese women burn incense at a traditional Buddhist ceremony.

many Buddhist themes; through the tea ceremony, which is intended to communicate simplicity and naturalness; through calligraphy and painting, and so on. The most lively aspect of Japanese Buddhism, however, remains the popular faith directed towards the various Buddhas, Bodhisattvas, and saints of the Mahayana Buddhist tradition.

NEW RELIGIONS

Innovation is an accepted feature of Japanese religious life. Many Shinto shrines are the result of some fresh religious experience, or message from a medium, long since incorporated into the general pattern of Shinto. In some more recent cases such initiatives have led to the growth of separate religious bodies.

One of the best known of these is the Religion of the Heavenly Wisdom (*Tenrikyo*), founded in the early nineteenth century by Nakayama Miki (1798–1887). This religion began with her revelations and healings, but instead of merging into the wider pattern of Shinto, it formulated its own independent sacred writings, constructed its own sacred city named Tenri, and shaped its own forms of worship, including a special dance.

Another well-known example is the popularly named Dancing Religion (*Odoru Shukyo*), which also has the longer formal name of *Tensho Kotai Jingu Kyo*, incorporating alternative names for the goddess Amaterasu and the Ise Shrine. Its founder, Kitamura Sayo (1900–67), believed that a *kami* was speaking through her abdomen, and these revelations are the basis of the religion's teaching. She also initiated a form of ecstatic dance that encourages believers to experience a state of not-self (*muga*), one of the 'three marks' of Buddhist teaching. The religion known as the Teaching of the Great Source (*Omotokyo*) is also a major independent religious group, having a Shinto background combined with belief in a new revelation of its own.

Looking all over the world and through all ages, I find no one who has understood My heart. No wonder that you know nothing, for so far I have taught nothing to you. This time I, God, revealing Myself to the fore, teach you all the truth in detail.

From the *Ofudesaki* – the revelation received by Nakayama Miki, the founder of Tenrikyo

Other new religions have moved further afield from the traditional faiths of Japan. The Syncretic House of Growth (*Seicho no Ie*) claims to overcome disease and suffering through its new teachings propounded by Taniguchi Masaharu (1893–1985), a former *Omotokyo* member. The Church of World Messianity (*Sekai Kyuseikyo*) is also loosely derived from *Omotokyo*. Its leader, Okada Mokichi (1882–1955), preached freedom from disease and from poverty, and his following grew rapidly after the Pacific War. The movement now boasts a fine art gallery. PL Kyodan, which claims a membership of about two million, sees the whole of life as art, and religion as a means of realizing this vision in the member's experience. The 'PL' in the name of this group stands for 'Perfect Liberty'. Many different explanations are offered for the appearance of new religions, but at least it is clear that they provide a kind of barometer of the needs and aspirations of much of Japan's population.

NEW BUDDHIST MOVEMENTS

Japanese Buddhism also gives scope for innovation, since the proliferation of sects and independent temple organizations is accepted as a normal feature of religious life. It is hardly surprising that several of Japan's new religions are recently developed forms of Buddhism.

The most influential are those based in some way or other on the *Lotus Sutra*, for together they claim about one fifth of the population as adherents. Of these, the Reiyukai began as a movement caring for untended tombs, and stressing the virtues of gratitude and loyalty towards ancestors. Today it boasts a huge central hall in Tokyo.

Several groups split off from the Reiyukai, however, in a series of organizational and doctrinal disputes. Of these the largest is the Rissho Kosei-kai, claiming more than six million members, strongly influenced in its beginnings by the religious messages of Naganuma Myoko (1899–1957). The dominant figure, however, was the founding president, Niwano Nikkyo (1906–99), who emphasized the exposition of the *Lotus Sutra* as the doctrinal basis of the movement. After taking over the leadership, his son Nichiko (b.1938) has also emphasized political activities, such as anti-nuclear campaigns and the promotion of world peace. It is notable that this is a lay movement, entirely independent of any previously existing monastic sect. The main emphasis is on a form of group counselling, in which the individual's problems are analyzed in Buddhist terms, though, of course, the *Lotus Sutra* is recited and studied too.

Also based on the *Lotus Sutra*, but with different doctrinal tendencies, is the lay movement commonly known as Soka Gakkai. This is linked with a monastic sect named Nichiren Shoshu, claiming a direct tradition back to Nichiren himself, and the full name is Nichiren Shoshu Soka Gakkai. Members support one of Japan's larger political parties, the Komeito (Clean Government Party), which was founded under the stimulation of Soka Gakkai leaders, although legally distinct.

PRESENT AND FUTURE

The new religions draw in many ways on the wider religious culture of Japan, which is formed mainly by traditional Shinto and Buddhism, but also influenced by Confucian ideas and values, and to a lesser extent by a Western-looking Christianity. Historically, Confucianism has provided the main moral backing for Shinto, emphasizing family duty and loyalty and extending these concepts to school, industry and state. Though Confucianism has no organization of any note, many religious bodies in Japan stress such values as loyalty or sincerity (*makoto*), gratitude, correctness of behaviour, and brightness of attitude.

Modern Christian missions have had little impact numerically or even ideologically, but have had some unintentional influence on other Japanese religious bodies. A number of Buddhist sects now run Sunday schools, for example, and some of the new religions use books looking remarkably like Christian Bibles and prayer-books, but with different contents. Christianity itself has a total membership of less than 1 per cent of the population, probably because it is strongly identified with the West. Christian churches in Japan have only the most tenuous links with the general religious culture of the country.

In spite of the startling success of several of the newer religious movements, it would be wrong to think Buddhism and Shinto have lost support in recent times. In some ways, particularly in politics and education, Japan has become remarkably secularized, and there is much ignorance about the deeper teachings of the religions. At the same time, most Japanese people are involved in various kinds of religious behaviour at certain times of the year and at the appropriate points in their lives.

MICHAEL PYE

QUESTIONS

1. Explain the importance of *yin* and *yang* in Sinkyo.

2. Why is ritual sacrifice important in Sinyo?

3. Explain the role of the Mudang in traditional Korean life.

4. How has Confucianism influenced Sinkyo?

5. How has geography influenced the development of religion in Japan?

6. What is the purpose of Shinto shrines?

7. How does Japanese Buddhism differ from varieties found elsewhere?

8. How has Buddhism shaped wider Japanese culture?

9. Why have elements of Shinto been controversial in recent decades?

10. How are the religious traditions of Korea and Japan similar – and how do they differ?

FURTHER READING

Blacker, Carmen, *The Catalpa Bow: A Study of Shamanistic Practices in Japan*. London: Allen & Unwin, 1975.

Buswell, Robert, *Korean Religions in Practice*. Princeton: Princeton University Press, 2003.

Kasulis, Thomas P., *Shinto: The Way Home*. Honolulu: University of Hawai'i Press, 2004.

Lee, Peter H., and William Theodore de Bary, eds., *Sources of Korean Tradition*. New York: Columbia University Press, 1997.

Nelson, John, *Enduring Identities: The Guise of Shinto in Modern Japan*. Honolulu: University of Hawai'i Press, 2000.

Reader, Ian T., *Religion in Contemporary Japan*. Honolulu: University of Hawai'i Press, 1991.

Tanabe, George, Jr, ed., *Religions of Japan in Practice*. Princeton: Princeton University Press, 1999.

PART 9
JUDAISM

SUMMARY

More than any other world religion, Judaism can be thought of as the religion of a particular people – or indeed as *being* that people, rather than their religion. In part, this goes back to the shared, though disputed, story of national origin transmitted to us by scripture. According to this tradition, the people of Israel are bound by a covenant as God's elect to fulfil his obligations, in return for their special status. This tradition is central to the religion today: Judaism's most popular festivals, such as Passover and *Hanukkah*, commemorate key events from this version of the community's past. The religion of the ancient Judeans, based around the maintenance of the covenant through sacrificial rites, in time gave way to the rabbinic tradition, centred upon the synagogue, serving as a place of prayer, praise, and study.

The diaspora that followed the destruction of the Temple at Jerusalem in 70 CE carried Judaism across much of the Middle East, North Africa, and Europe. During the medieval period, many Jews – especially those in Muslim lands – made significant contributions to the arts and sciences, while those living in Christendom were frequently subjected to persecution and changing royal whim. By the twentieth century, though, Jewish communities formed part of the fabric of many European states. Reform of Judaism's tradition formed one distinct strand of the European Enlightenment, and the increasing separation of church and state at this time provided a framework into which Judaism could comfortably fit. More recently of a variety of schools of thought has emerged within Judaism, maintaining different approaches to doctrine and worship, and sometimes differing over how to respond to the changes and challenges of the secular world.

Much of recent Jewish history is overshadowed by the Nazi Holocaust, and for many the memory of this event highlights the importance Jewish traditions and of the community itself. Since 1948, the state of Israel has been a centre for this community and home – along with many other countries – to the diverse schools of thought that together make it up.

CHAPTER 53

A Historical Overview

Rabbinic Judaism today sees itself as a direct development from the time of Moses, the giver of the Torah, more than 3000 years ago. To understand the developing beliefs and practices of Judaism, we need to know something of the social and political events that affected Jewish communities. We also need to observe the ideas of their neighbours in order to understand the influence of the cultures with which they came into contact. Greek thought, Christianity, Islam, medieval philosophy, and charismatic movements have all affected the intellectual activity and popular customs of Judaism.

EXILE AND AFTER

The story of the early development of Judaism is much debated. The commonly accepted narrative, largely based on the polemical biblical texts of Ezra and Nehemiah — which actually refer to 'people of Israel' rather than 'Jews' — has been important for the later development of Jewish self-understanding, but is not necessarily founded in historical reality.

This popular story of Judaism begins in the late sixth century BCE, when the Persian Empire was dominant in the Middle East. In 586 BCE, Nebuchadnezzar II, King of the

I was glad when they said to me,

'Let us go to the house of the Lord!'

Our feet have been standing within your gates, O Jerusalem!

Jerusalem, built as a city which is bound firmly together,

to which the tribes go up,

the tribes of the Lord,

as was decreed for Israel,

to give thanks to the name of the Lord.

There thrones for judgment were set,

the thrones of the house of David.
Pray for the peace of Jerusalem!

'May they prosper who love you!

Peace be within your walls,

and security within your towers!"

For my brethren and companions' sake

I will say, 'Peace be within you!'

For the sake of the house of the Lord our God,

I will seek your good.

Psalm 122, Old Testament, Revised Standard Version

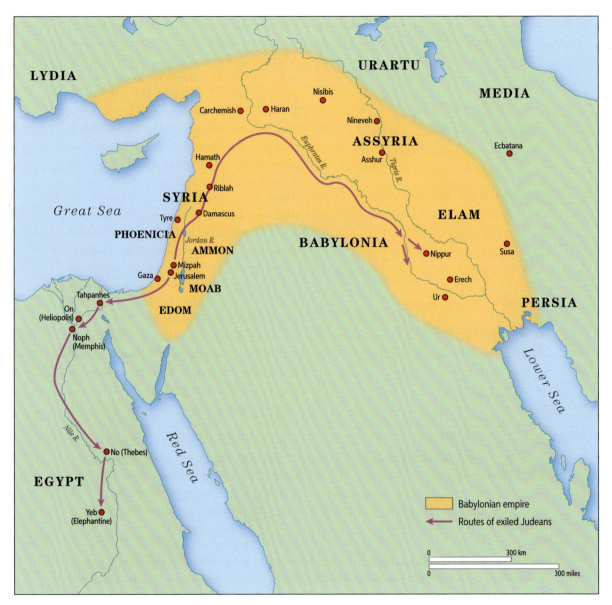

The Judean Exiles, c. 560 BCE

neo-Babylonian Empire, destroyed Jerusalem, and many its people were taken captive to Babylon, along with much of the population of Judea. In both Babylon and Egypt there were now communities of people who still considered themselves Judeans — consisting largely of mercenary soldiers and of prisoners of war and their families — some of whom were agents of the ruling power, and for that reason privileged. In Egypt, where this caused much resentment, the Judeans remained separate, following the religion and customs they brought with them.

> By the rivers of Babylon we sat
> and wept
>
> when we remembered Zion.
>
> There on the poplars
>
> we hung our harps,
>
> for there our captors asked us
> for songs,
>
> our tormentors demanded songs
> of joy;
>
> they said, 'Sing us one of the songs
> of Zion!'
>
> How can we sing the songs of the Lord
>
> while in a foreign land?
>
> If I forget you, O Jerusalem,
>
> may my right hand forget its skill.
>
> May my tongue cling to the roof of
> my mouth
>
> if I do not remember you,
>
> if I do not consider Jerusalem
>
> my highest joy.
>
> Psalm 137:1–6, Old Testament,
> New International Version

The Judeans believed there should be just a single Temple, the only place where religious sacrifice could be carried out. While they lived in Judah, it was possible for all to make the pilgrimage to this Temple in Jerusalem; but in exile this became difficult, if not impossible – though the Jews of the Dispersion apparently made great efforts to visit Jerusalem and worship in obedience to the Torah, the written teaching. To meet this obstacle, and in an attempt to maintain some continuity with the past, houses of assembly – *beitei knesset* in Hebrew, 'synagogues' in Greek – were set up in Babylon, and prayer, singing or chanting, teaching, and reading and discussion of the Torah – but not sacrifice – took place in them. Some time during this period, scribes also first appeared. Based in the synagogue, their role was to understand the Torah and interpret its rules for the contemporary situation. This 'guild of scholars' seems eventually to have evolved into the rabbis of rabbinic Judaism.

In 539 the army of Cyrus II, 'the Great', of Persia captured Babylon, and Cyrus gained nominal control of the Babylonian Empire. According to Ezra 1:3, he permitted the Hebrews to return from exile and rebuild their Temple in Jerusalem. When Hebrew religious leaders returned to Jerusalem, the city was apparently established as a Temple community, led by the priests, as Cyrus would not allow the restoration of the monarchy. According to Ezra/Nehemiah, a strict separation between Judean – 'Jews' – and non-Judean in Judah was enforced by the Hebrews' leaders, Ezra and Nehemiah, a separation apparently marked by circumcision, observance of *Shabbat* – the Jewish Sabbath – and of the Sabbatical year, recognition of the Torah (the first five books of Jewish scripture), and obligations to the Temple in Jerusalem. Rigorists also required that marriage arrangements should be made only between Judeans.

THE HELLENISTIC KINGDOMS

After Alexander the Great won the Battle of Issus in 333 BCE, an era of prosperity commenced in the region. Cities founded on the Greek pattern grew rapidly, with Alexandria becoming the leading city in Egypt within a few years of its foundation. The Judean community there was substantial, and Greek – rather than Aramaic – became their language. People even tried to look Greek! The Greek language was the medium by which Greek ideas, attitudes, and ways of reasoning were passed on. People who could read Greek – especially those living in Alexandria – might have had an opportunity to read the great Greek philosophers in the original. But it seems Greek-speaking Jews were not drawn away from their customs as much as some feared, and still visited Jerusalem to celebrate the festivals in the Temple.

After the death of Alexander, his empire broke up into smaller units, principally the kingdoms of Macedonia, Egypt, and the Seleucids. When the Parthian Empire rose to power in the third century BCE, the Seleucid Kingdom, which had included Babylon, was gradually reduced to only the Syrian region, and Babylon came under Parthian control. The Jews remaining in Babylon were now cut off from other Jewish communities, and Aramaic remained their language, adding a linguistic barrier to that of politics. The Jewish communities of Babylon and of the Greek-influenced, or 'Hellenized', kingdoms inevitably developed differently, though they were united by a common scripture and emphasis on Jerusalem and its Temple, where priests were leaders, and the high priest politically and economically powerful.

TENSION AND REVOLT

In 191–190 BCE the Romans, turning their eyes towards the East, defeated King Antiochus III of Syria; it was probably prisoners of war from this conflict who founded the Jewish community in Rome. Jews also settled in Antioch, Syria, and in Asia Minor, modern Turkey. The Romans exacted tribute from Antiochus, which meant increased taxes. Consequently tension grew between rich and poor in Jerusalem and Judah, which – along with the political and cultural divisions between those for and against Hellenism – made for a volatile situation.

The explosion came during the reign of Antiochus IV Epiphanes (175–164). When the Jews resisted his nominee for the high priesthood, he sent troops to sack Jerusalem, established pagan practices in the Temple, and attacked the Jewish religion. Some Jews submitted, but those who adhered to the Torah, especially the *Hasidim* – 'The Pious' – suffered greatly. Eventually there was full-scale revolt, led by the Maccabee family, and – against the odds – Judas Maccabeus came to terms with the Syrians in 165 BCE, marched on Jerusalem, and ritually cleansed the desecrated Temple. This victory, and the reconsecration of the Temple, is celebrated today in the Festival of Lights, or *Hanukkah*.

The Maccabee family now began a line of rulers – the Hasmonean dynasty – many of whom, ironically, became typical Hellenistic despots. However they won a measure of freedom for the Jewish realm before the Romans, under Pompey, annexed Judea in 63 BCE.

UNDER THE ROMAN EMPIRE

Judea now became a vassal of Rome. The current Hasmonean king was confirmed as the nation's leader and high priest, but the Romans refused to recognize him as king.

In 40 BCE, following a Parthian invasion of Syria and Judea, Rome gave Herod (c. 73–4 BCE), son of Antipater the Idumean, the title 'king of the Jews'. Although his personal life was disastrous, the country prospered under his rule, and Herod 'the Great' is remembered as a builder of cities such as Sebaste and Caesarea, of fortresses such as Masada and Herodium, of palaces, theatres, and amphitheatres, and of the Jewish Temple in Jerusalem. Those who opposed Rome and Hellenism hated and opposed him.

During the Roman period Jewish hopes rose for a messiah – a king of David's line, for some, a priest-king – who would rescue his people from the Romans and restore the Judean state. There were several revolts in Judea during the time of Herod and his successors, and 'prophets' attracted large followings. The most serious threat to the Jews came during the reign of the Emperor Caligula (37–41 CE), who demanded that all his subjects worship him, and ordered a statue of himself as Zeus to be placed in the Jerusalem Temple.

THE TEMPLE DESTROYED

Judea became increasingly unsettled. In the coastal cities, conflict between Greeks and Jews was constant, and tension mounted between the Roman governors and the people. Finally in 66 CE the Jews rose in revolt against Rome, but initial success was followed by crushing defeat, Jerusalem was taken, and its Temple destroyed in 70 CE.

The destruction of the Temple was decisive for the future of Judaism. The Temple, the priesthood, and the council – the Sanhedrin – were finished. No longer could Jerusalem act as a unifying force within Judaism, the focus of pilgrimage. Jewish communities now became just one group within larger communities; although distinct, they were inevitably affected by the culture of the city or nation in which they found themselves.

HELLENISTIC JUDAISM

The life of the ordinary Jew in Greek-speaking areas centred on the synagogue, where worship and practical matters of community life were conducted. Strangers were lodged,

Ptolomaic Empire

Seleucid Empire

● City with Jewish population

0 — 300 km

0 — 300 miles

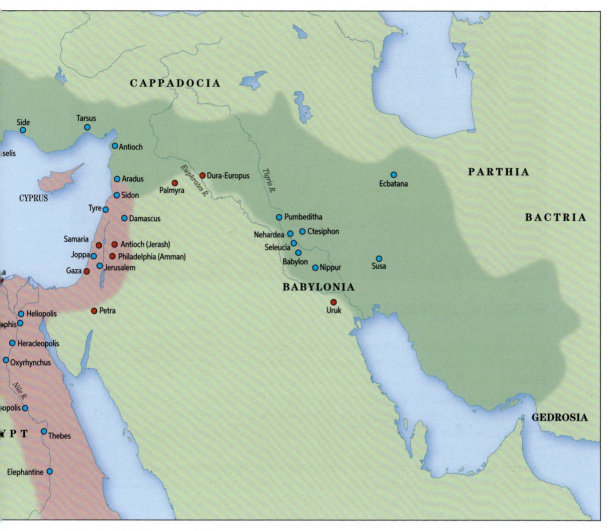

The Jewish Diaspora c. 240 BCE

the poor helped, discipline enforced, public gatherings held, and children taught in the synagogue. Visiting preachers might give a sermon, but the resident scholars probably did not. Authority was in the hands of the 'ruler of the synagogue'. Associated with the synagogue was the 'house of study' (*bet midrash*), where the Bible was studied and scholars could consult a library.

Some Hellenistic rabbis drew up rules of biblical interpretation. Philo of Alexandria (20 BCE–50 CE) attempted to explain the Bible from the point of view of Greek philosophy, presenting the great events of Israel's history as allegories of eternal truths and adopting the Stoic idea of Reason (*Logos*), which he called a 'second God', an intermediary between God and the world.

RABBINIC JUDAISM

A seemingly insignificant event provided a new direction for Judaism when Johanan ben Zakai (30–90 CE) founded a school at Jamnia, or Yavneh, Galilee, where

Jewish men pray at the Western Wall, Jerusalem, Israel. Some of the large stone blocks were part of Herod's Temple, destroyed by the Romans in 70 CE, and are therefore revered.

rabbi (master) became the formal title for teachers. Though Johanan may not have been a Pharisee, his successor, Gamaliel the Elder, was, and the school's ethos was essentially Pharisaic, the stance of emerging rabbinic Judaism. The school at Jamnia came to exercise the function of a council, and even adopted the name 'Sanhedrin'. Johanan fixed the calendar for Jews abroad – once the prerogative of the high priest – and Jews began to look to this council for advice and judgments. The rabbis of this early period are known as *Tanna* – plural *Tannaim*, 'teachers'. Their earliest surviving works are 'sayings' in the *Pirkei Avot*, sometimes known as the 'Ethics of the Fathers', and second-century written Hebrew versions of Jewish oral traditions known as the Mishnah.

Most other varieties of Judaism gradually died out. Jewish Christianity survived into the second century CE, although the rabbis tried hard to exclude Jewish Christians from the synagogues after about 90 CE. In the Greek world, Christians broke entirely with Judaism, often becoming anti-Jewish.

PERSECUTION

Jewish revolts against Roman rule continued widely and were brutally put down. The Judean revolt of 132 CE may have been ignited by the establishment of the new Roman city of Aelia Capitolina upon the ruins of Jerusalem; the Old City of present-day Jerusalem is the linear descendant of this Roman town. This revolt was led by Simon ben Kosiba, also known as Simon bar Kokhba – 'Son of a Star', who claimed to be the messiah, and who was supported by the greatest rabbinic scholar of the day, Rabbi Akiva ben Joseph (c. 40– c. 137 CE). But the uprising was hopeless, and the casualties inflicted on the Romans only made the final defeat more harsh.

The governors of Palestine – the name the Romans now gave the country – were now higher-ranking Romans than previously. Construction of Aelia Capitolina was completed, and Jews forbidden to enter the city. Galilee now became a centre of Jewish life, and several different towns in succession became the seat of the Jewish council. Judaism was not banned, but the circumcision of converts was forbidden, making conversion difficult, if not impossible.

PALESTINIAN PATRIARCHATE

Simeon ben Gamaliel II became president of the 'Great Sanhedrin' and first Palestinian Patriarch with – at least in theory – authority over all Jews of the Roman world. His son, Judah I, the Prince (b. 135) – also known as Rabbi HaQadosh – appears to have exercised considerable power. A noted scholar, during his time the Mishnah was codified and published. The Palestinian Patriarchate came to an end with the execution by the Romans of Gamaliel VI in 425, and the Sanhedrin was also dissolved as a result of Roman oppression.

The conversion of Constantine to Christianity in 313 was not auspicious for Jews. Although Judaism was never made illegal, life became difficult for Jews, as Jewish-Christian tensions grew. In Egypt, the Jewish community began to recover, though numbers were never as high as in earlier centuries. Greek culture was on the wane, and with it Hellenistic Judaism.

BABYLONIAN EXILARCHS

In Babylon, the ruler of the Jews of the Diaspora were known as an 'exilarch', or head of the exiles. This hereditary position was recognized by the state and, later, under Arab rule by the Muslims. But from the fifth century onward, relations between the Jews and the Persian authorities became difficult, and the Jews there welcomed the Arab conquerors. Similarly, in Palestine, the harshness of the Byzantine rule caused the Jews to look for help abroad, aiding the invading Persian forces in 614. However uprisings among the Jerusalem Jews in 617 were subdued by military force when the Byzantine army re-entered the city, and the Jews were once more expelled.

JUDAISM AND ISLAM

Islam arose and spread with extraordinary rapidity in the seventh and eight centuries CE. Muslim Arabs defeated the Byzantine army in 634, conquered Syria and Palestine, defeated Persia in 637, and Egypt soon after. Muslims invaded Spain in 711, and set up a Muslim state. Within a century, many Jews had come under Muslim rule. For most, living conditions improved considerably, and the Jews shared in the intellectual ferment of the Arab world. Arabs translated and studied the learning of Greece, Persia, China, and India, and drawing on these resources, Muslim and Jewish scholars made great advances in mathematics, astronomy, philosophy, chemistry, medicine, and philology. One of the greatest Jewish philosophers, Saadiah Gaon (882–942), grappled with the problem of 'faith and knowledge', discussing proofs of God's existence.

BABYLON: THE AGE OF THE GAONS

In Babylon, the authority and importance of the Gaons – the heads of the Babylonian academies – grew immensely after 600. The Gaons ensured that the Babylonian Talmud – documents compiled in the Babylonian academies between the third and fifth centuries – became accepted more widely. In the ninth century a gaonate was established in Palestine, and was recognized as authoritative by Jews in Spain, Egypt, and Italy. Under the Gaons collections of Talmudic laws were made, synagogue poetry written, prayer-books drawn up, and the text of the Bible was fixed and annotated. Most influential were the *Responsa* (Hebrew, *She'elot ve-Teshuvot* – questions and answers) – questions on matters of practice sent to the Gaons, debated in the academies, and answered in their name.

Variants from rabbinic Judaism arose. In eighth century Babylon, Anan ben David (c. 715–c. 795), and Karaite movement he possibly founded, rejected the Talmud and all forms of oral law, such as the Mishnah, taking a stand on the Bible only. It seemed the Karaites might divide the Jewish world, but the movement soon became merely a sect, which still survives today in small numbers.

SCHOLARSHIP IN SPAIN

Jews rose to influential positions at court in Spain, where 'Sephardic' Judaism developed, with its own synagogue rituals and a Spanish-Jewish dialect, Ladino. Solomon ibn Gabirol (c. 1021– c. 1058) attempted to reconcile Jewish thought with Neo-Platonism – which posits that God is separated from the world by a descending series of 'emanations' – which contributed to the development of the Jewish mystical tradition known as the Kabbalah (see below). Judah Halevi of Toledo (1085–1140) wrote a fictional dialogue between a Jewish scholar and the king of the Khazars – a Turkish tribe converted to Judaism – showing that philosophy could prove God's existence, but that revelation was then necessary to know more of him.

JEWS IN WESTERN EUROPE

From the mid-eleventh century Jewish scholars in the West became more important than the Gaons. The French scholar Rabbi Solomon ben Isaac (Shlomo Yitzhaki, 1040–1105), known, from his initials, as Rashi, produced standard commentaries on the Bible and Talmud. With additions by his successors, his commentaries are still printed in the Talmud.

In the eleventh century there was a shift in philosophical thought, as Aristotle supplanted Plato. Aristotle's science seemed to leave no room for religion, and Jewish scholars debated whether his philosophy could be reconciled with biblical religion. In Córdoba, Spain, the Rabbi Moshe ben Maimon (Moses Maimonides, 1135–1204) presented a code containing all the *halakhah* in his Mishneh Torah. Exiled from Spain to Egypt, he wrote in Arabic the great philosophical work *The Guide for the Perplexed*, discussing the difficulties Aristotle's philosophy presented for the believer. Although Judaism had been – and is – far more based on right behaviour – orthopraxis – than orthodoxy, Maimonides saw 'right belief' as of great importance, for which he was much criticized. Maimonides also drew up thirteen 'roots' of Judaism, the 'Thirteen Principles of the Faith'.

> *This God is one. He is not two nor more than two, but one. None of the things existing in the universe to which the term one is applied is like unto his unity.*
>
> Moses Maimonides,
> *Mishnah Torah*

THE RISE OF ANTI-SEMITISM

From the tenth century onwards, anti-Jewish sentiment and riots became common in France, and life in Christian Europe generally became difficult for Jews. The Crusading armies marching to the 'Holy Land' looted and slaughtered Jews as they went, and the capture of Jerusalem – hailed by Christendom as a great triumph – meant death for the Jews there. Many Jews regarded such death as martyrdom, the ultimate form of witness, or 'sanctification of the Name' (*kiddush haShem*), and some committed suicide rather than renouncing their faith. Jewish rules of conduct (*halakhah*) stated that in some situations death was preferable to the alternative – for instance to avoid idolatry, incest, or murder, or to 'sanctify the Name'.

In Europe, two vicious lies circulated: the 'blood libel' and the 'libel of desecration of the host'. The blood libel claimed Jews were guilty of ritual murder, using the blood of Christian children during Passover. The 'libel of desecration of the host' spuriously

THE THIRTEEN PRINCIPLES OF THE FAITH

- Belief in the existence of a creator and of providence
- Belief in his unity
- Belief in his incorporeality
- Belief in his eternity
- Belief that worship is due to him alone
- Belief in the words of the prophets
- Belief that Moses was the greatest of all the prophets
- Belief in the revelation of the Torah to Moses at Sinai
- Belief in the unchangeable nature of the revealed Law
- Belief that God is omniscient
- Belief in retribution in this world and in the hereafter
- Belief in the coming of the messiah
- Belief in the resurrection of the dead

JUDAISM TIMELINE

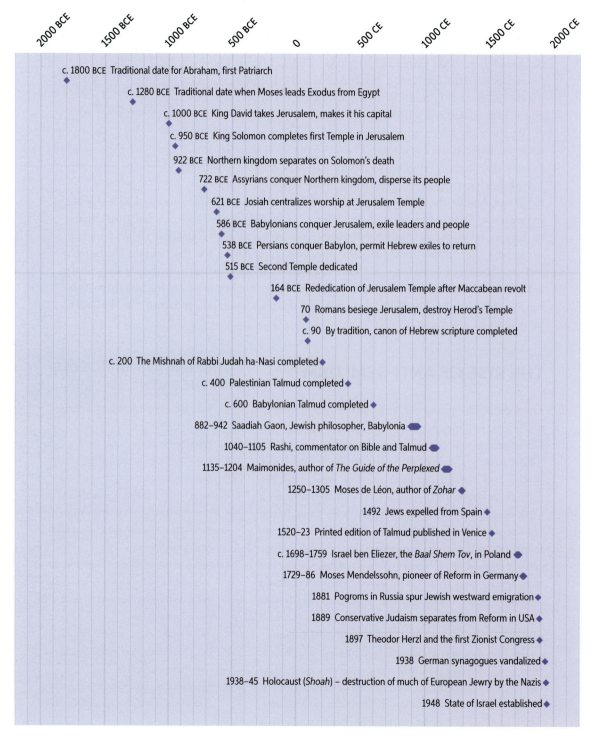

2000 BCE   1500 BCE   1000 BCE   500 BCE   0   500 CE   1000 CE   1500 CE   2000 CE

c. 1800 BCE   Traditional date for Abraham, first Patriarch

c. 1280 BCE   Traditional date when Moses leads Exodus from Egypt

c. 1000 BCE   King David takes Jerusalem, makes it his capital

c. 950 BCE   King Solomon completes first Temple in Jerusalem

922 BCE   Northern kingdom separates on Solomon's death

722 BCE   Assyrians conquer Northern kingdom, disperse its people

621 BCE   Josiah centralizes worship at Jerusalem Temple

586 BCE   Babylonians conquer Jerusalem, exile leaders and people

538 BCE   Persians conquer Babylon, permit Hebrew exiles to return

515 BCE   Second Temple dedicated

164 BCE   Rededication of Jerusalem Temple after Maccabean revolt

70   Romans besiege Jerusalem, destroy Herod's Temple

c. 90   By tradition, canon of Hebrew scripture completed

c. 200   The Mishnah of Rabbi Judah ha-Nasi completed

c. 400   Palestinian Talmud completed

c. 600   Babylonian Talmud completed

882–942   Saadiah Gaon, Jewish philosopher, Babylonia

1040–1105   Rashi, commentator on Bible and Talmud

1135–1204   Maimonides, author of *The Guide of the Perplexed*

1250–1305   Moses de Léon, author of *Zohar*

1492   Jews expelled from Spain

1520–23   Printed edition of Talmud published in Venice

c. 1698–1759   Israel ben Eliezer, the *Baal Shem Tov*, in Poland

1729–86   Moses Mendelssohn, pioneer of Reform in Germany

1881   Pogroms in Russia spur Jewish westward emigration

1889   Conservative Judaism separates from Reform in USA

1897   Theodor Herzl and the first Zionist Congress

1938   German synagogues vandalized

1938–45   Holocaust (*Shoah*) – destruction of much of European Jewry by the Nazis

1948   State of Israel established

THE KABBALAH

In the Kabbalah, God was known as the 'limitless' (*En Sof*), from whom came ten aspects of God (*Sefirot*), by which he is manifested and made known. These 'emanations' of God mediate between the *En Sof* and the world.

The most important work of the Kabbalah is the *Zohar*, attributed to Rabbi Simeon bar Yochai (Rashbi, first century CE), but in reality written in thirteenth-century Spain. The 'Talmud of Jewish mysticism', its final editor/author was probably Rabbi Moses de Léon (c. 1250–1305). Although the study of the Torah is still central in Kabbalah, the aim is to find hidden, secret meanings; the *Zohar* expounds the Torah by literal, allegorical meanings, but more importantly, by mystical insights. Astrology is also bound up in the *Zohar*: each day is influenced by one of the ten *Sefirot*.

After the Jews were expelled from Spain, the centre of Jewish mysticism became Safed, Galilee, where Rabbi Isaac Luria (1544–72) gave a new slant to the Kabbalah, using much erotic imagery, which greatly influenced later movements, such as Hasidism. In Luria's view, after the *En Sof* created the universe, he withdrew from it, leaving *Sefirot*, vessels that contain the 'divine light'. The last six *Sefirot* could not contain the light, and shattered. Some of them sank, trapping sparks of the divine light within them. This is the origin of evil; redemption will come when these sparks are returned to their source.

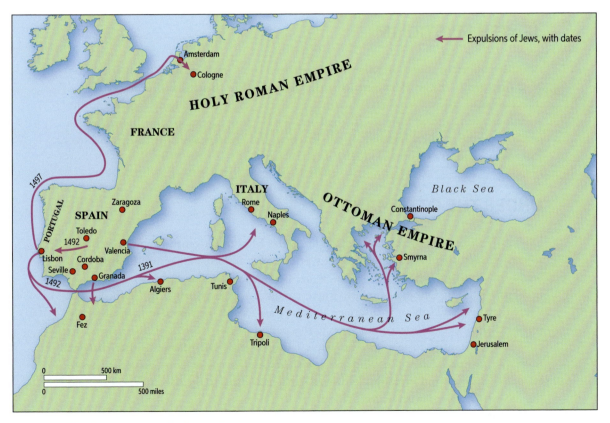

The Jews are expelled from Spain

claimed that Jews stole the host – the consecrated bread of the eucharist, believed to be the body of Christ – and stabbed or burned it, thus re-enacting the crucifixion of Jesus.

Jews entered England during the eleventh century, but were expelled in 1290, not to return until after 1650. Between 1290 and 1293, Jewish communities in southern Italy were almost wiped out and many forced conversions were made. The Jews were expelled from France in 1306, and massacres occurred in 1348. Jews were falsely accused of poisoning wells and causing the Black Death, a plague that killed off one third of the population of Europe in 1348. From Spain to Poland, Jews were persecuted and massacred.

In the twelfth century Christians attempted to recapture Spain from the Muslims. In response, the Muslim Almohades from North Africa pushed into Spain and, not showing their usual tolerance towards Jews, drove them northwards. Christian leaders at first welcomed these Jews. With other means of livelihood closed to them, many became moneylenders, since usury was forbidden for Christians. But tolerance did not last, and in Christian Spain attacks on Jews reached a peak in 1391. Many Jews professed conversion to Christianity, and were known by the insulting name of *Marranos* (swine). In 1492 Jews were offered the choice of converting or leaving; thousands fled to other parts of Europe and beyond, such as Safed in Galilee.

JEWISH MYSTICISM

Another important strand of Judaism is mysticism: belief in some kind of direct 'vision' of divine things, a way of experiencing things other than through our ordinary senses. The Kabbalah, a Jewish mystical tradition, developed in Spain, bringing together earlier traditions, such as ideas from the Talmud and the Book of Creation (*Sefer Yetsirot*), which emphasized the mystical meaning of the letters in the Hebrew alphabet and from Neo-Platonism a concept of how God related to the world.

UNDER THE OTTOMANS

During the sixteenth and seventeenth centuries, the Muslim Ottoman Empire was in the ascendant, capturing Palestine in 1515, Egypt in 1517, and expanding into Europe, until halted in Vienna in 1683. Most Jews now lived either in Christian Poland–Lithuania, or under the Muslim Ottoman Empire, where conditions were generally less difficult, but where they were still subject to arbitrary or capricious acts of the rulers. In Christian Italy, severe penalties were inflicted on the Jews in this period.

The Protestant Reformers on the whole favoured Jews, but Martin Luther changed from tolerance and defence to rabid anti-Jewish abuse. The rite of non-Sephardic Jews in Europe – especially in Germany – known as 'Ashkenazi' dates to the sixteenth century, and has its own German-Jewish dialect, Yiddish.

Anti-Jewish riots continued, but the authorities now more often protected the Jews, who were seen as useful for their money-lending and trading. In Ukraine and Poland many Jews were killed in massacres in 1648 and 1649, when Jewish leaders were seen by the peasantry to be economically and politically at one with the Polish overlords.

HOPE OF A MESSIAH

In the late seventeenth century a number of Jewish messianic movements arose, partly a product of the insecurity of Jewish life. The most important was centred on Shabbetai Zevi (1628–1716) and his prophet, Nathan of Gaza (1643–80), who called for repentance, strict ascetic practices, and mortification of the body – including fasting, bathing in freezing water, and constant prayer. Shabbetai was imprisoned in Gallipoli in 1665, and in 1666, under coercion, converted to Islam. His remaining followers were viewed with deep suspicion by the Jewish community, and the episode resulted in general disillusion with Messianism.

HASIDISM

Eighteenth century Poland saw the rise of Hasidism, a popular movement that gave hope and excitement to people who were frightened and deprived, with its emphasis on emotion and devotion. The movement focused on the individual and direct experience of the divine, and was thus accessible to ordinary labourers, who could not afford the long hours of study required by rabbinical Judaism. The key figure in the growth of Hasidism was Israel ben Eliezer (1700–60), known as the Baal Shem Tov, 'Master of the Good Name'; a dynamic, charismatic figure, widely known as a miracle worker, whose teaching contained much from the Kabbalah, especially the *Zohar*.

Many legends are told about Baal Shem Tov, and much popular belief – indeed superstition – was caught up into the movement. But at the core was a passionate devotion to God, expressed in ecstatic prayer, singing, and dancing. From outside, Hasidic life may seem a narrow existence, but it is sustained by Hasidic 'joy' – a genuine religious 'high'.

The leaders of Hasidic groups were more gurus than rabbi-like scholars. The leader, *rebbe*, or *zaddiq*, is a man who lives the life of devotion, and acts as intermediary between his followers and God. His word is absolute: his followers leave their families to be with him, and even contest for a share of the food he has touched. There are a number of different branches of Hasidism today. Women played a much more prominent role in the beginnings of the movement than they do today. Generally, Hasidism is a man's world; Hasidic women lead separate lives.

The Hasidic movement met strong opposition from the Jewish establishment, with something of a class struggle, as *rebbes* replaced the rich and learned. One of the most hostile opponents was the Gaon of Vilna, Elijah ben Solomon (1720–97), an ascetic intellectual who excoriated Hasidism. The Hasidic Jews were sometimes excluded from the community – and even betrayed to hostile authorities. Influenced by Shneur Zalman of Liadi (1745–1812), his Chabad branch of Hasidic Judaism was reconciled to Talmudic study and thus accepted by the wider Jewish community.

GO WEST

From the early seventeenth century, Jews gradually began to move from Poland and the Ottoman Empire into the cities of the West. There was a growing recognition of the value of Jewish commercial activity, and Jews began to be associated with the more developed social and economic systems. During the nineteenth century, large numbers of Jews migrated to America. Judaism remained the target for abuse and oppression, but there was a growing tolerance. During the nineteenth century equal rights were eventually obtained in many countries, though often with great difficulty.

JEWISH ENLIGHTENMENT

The 'Jewish enlightenment', *Haskalah*, pointed to another new direction within Judaism. Its founder, Moses Mendelssohn (1729–86), advocated the separation of church and state, so that religious bodies should not be able to compel, only persuade. He emphasized the universal principles of religion within Judaism, and translated the Torah into German. After his death, this movement, now led by Leopold Zunz (1794–1886), became more radical, rejecting the Talmud and traditional ideas – even the idea of revelation.

> All things that are, are in God, and must be conceived through God, and therefore God is the cause of the things which are in himself. This is the first point. Further, no substance can be granted outside God, that is, nothing which is outside God exists in itself; which was the second point. Therefore God is the immanent, but not the transcendent, cause of all things.
>
> Baruch Spinoza, *The Ethics* (1677).

At the beginning of the nineteenth century, emancipation in France, Italy, and Germany allowed Jews to leave the ghetto and – as a result of *Haskalah* – develop reformed Judaism. Emancipation also aided the assimilation of Jews – sometimes even their cultural disappearance, when Jews merged through marriage into the surrounding society. After emancipation, the lifestyle of many Jews began more closely to resemble that of their non-Jewish fellow citizens.

The dark counterpoint to increased tolerance was anti-Semitism, based on a belief in the 'soul' of a people; a contrast was drawn between the 'Semitic' nature of Jews and that of the 'Aryan' or 'Slavonic'. Strongly anti-Semitic movements were promoted in Germany and France from the 1880s, the direct consequence of which was the destruction between 1939 and 1945 of six million people in the Holocaust, simply because they were Jewish. European Jewry almost ceased to exist, and one-third of world Jewry was killed.

GEOFFREY COWLING
REVISED BY TIM DOWLEY

CHAPTER 54

Sacred Writings

The texts of Judaism have long been central to its life and culture, as can be seen in many expressions. In the Torah, Deuteronomy 30:14, we read: '… the word is very near to you; it is in your mouth and in your heart for you to observe' (literally: for you to do). Psalms and wisdom also hint at the centrality of texts. For example, the psalmist proclaims: 'I treasure your word in my heart, so that I may not sin against you … Your word is a lamp to my feet and a light to my path' (Psalm 119:11, 105).

Reading the Torah scroll using a *yad* ('hand'), a Jewish ritual pointer, to ensure the parchment is not touched by hand.

In the reign of King Josiah (c. 639–609 BCE; see 2 Kings 22–23), it is the discovery of the 'book of the Law' (an early form of Torah) that inspires Josiah's reforms. From the late biblical period until classical rabbinic Judaism, the scribe, from the copyist to the 'maker' of scrolls or books, has been regarded as something of a hero, often on a par with a sage and, eventually, a *reb* or rabbi.

A Jewish legend reflects the sacredness of texts. It tells of a Roman soldier who defaced a Torah scroll in the first century CE, and whom the authorities put to death to avoid insurrection. Since the destruction of the Temple in 70 CE, and the final revolt against Roman authorities (132–35 CE), sacrifice and pilgrimage to the Temple was replaced with the study of Scripture and other sacred texts, prayer, and works of piety.

The study of texts made Judaism a portable tradition. Jews of the diaspora, or exile, were able to worship God anywhere, and the study of sacred texts could also be done anywhere. Today, the sacredness of texts is expressed in other ways too. Since the advent of printing, Jewish writers and publishers have been at the forefront of the book industry. Modern *halakhot* (observances) include stipulations about the proper treatment of books. Judaism has always exhibited a remarkable love of the word, of manuscripts, and of books.

There are three major textual traditions:

- Tanakh (Hebrew scriptures)
- Mishnah (tractates and regulations on the Law)
- Talmud (exposition of the Mishnah and Torah)

TANAKH

In Jewish practice and theology the term 'torah' is used in three senses:

- the first five books of the Scriptures, traditionally ascribed to Moses
- the whole of the Jewish Scriptures (written torah)
- ethical teaching of the rabbis (oral torah)

This article only uses the term in the first sense, referring to the first five books. In referring to the whole of Hebrew scripture, we use the term 'Tanakh', which derives from the tradition since late antiquity of dividing the Hebrew scriptures into three distinct sections.

Much debate surrounds how and why particular books came to be included in the Jewish canon, and in what order. The order is significant. For example, in the Jewish canon the Book of Ruth is in the Writings and belongs to a group of five books (the *megillot*) that are read cyclically at festival times, Ruth being read at harvest.

In Judaism the notion of canon itself has evolved over the centuries. From the earliest records, what mattered was the pragmatic nature of texts: which texts manage to speak with immediacy — beyond the context of their composition —to the ongoing life and identity of the faith community? Once identified, those texts are 'biblical'. These are texts that, for whatever reason, accrued existential value for the community who used them.

There is one way to salvation: to go back to the sources of Judaism, to Bible, Talmud, and Midrash; to read, study, and comprehend them in order to live them … the seekers after knowledge will go back to the ancient fountains of Judaism, Bible, and Talmud and the one effort will be to obtain the concept of life out of Judaism.

Samson Raphael Hirsch,
The Nineteen Letters on Judaism
(1836), transl. B. Drachman
(New York: Feldheim, 1960).

MISHNAH

The Mishnah is a collection of tractates consisting of *halakhot*, observances which cover every conceivable area of Jewish daily life and ritual purity. Its first tractate, the sayings of the fathers, *Pirqe Avot*, begins by laying down some principles for interpretation and for practice. The first verse sets the tone:

Moses received Torah from Sinai and passed it on to Joshua, and Joshua to the Elders, and the Elders to the Prophets; and the Prophets passed it on to the men of the Great Assembly. They said three things: 'Be careful in giving judgment, raise up many disciples, and make a fence around the Torah.'

In other words, like Jewish writers after them, the authors of the Mishnah saw themselves as part of an unbroken chain of tradition. Jews who fulfilled the ordinances of the Mishnah would in turn be fulfilling the Torah, building a hedge around it in a mutually beneficial exchange: guard the Torah and it will guard you. From its inception (c. 200 CE), the Mishnah became the key reference for decision making among the diaspora Jews. However, within fifty to a hundred years large portions of it were thought to be terse and obscure, and an explanatory companion soon evolved.

TALMUD

The Talmud ('teaching'), a vast collection of writings containing the teaching of the rabbis, appeared in the rabbinic academies of diaspora Judaism out of the continuing debate about the significance and implementation of the Tanakh – especially the Torah – and the Mishnah, with tractates and groups of tractates gradually becoming authoritative through use.

There are two Talmuds: the Palestinian – also known as the Jerusalem Talmud – a record of discussion in the rabbinic schools of Galilee, especially Tiberias, during the fourth century CE; and the longer Babylonian Talmud, completed in the seventh or eighth century CE, recording the opinions of more than a thousand rabbis between 200 and 650 CE. The Babylonian Talmud was used by Jews living in the Muslim Empire, whilst the Palestinian Talmud was influential in Italy and Egypt.

These lengthy collections – the Babylonian Talmud amounts around 4 million words – contain many kinds of literature. The scholar Solomon Schechter (1847–1915) described the Talmud as 'a work too varied, too disconnected, too divergent in its elements, to be concisely defined at all, or even approximately to be described within the limits of an English sentence'. For this reason, we have to be careful about taking any particular opinion in the Talmud as 'the teaching of Judaism'. The Talmud records many views, so it is necessary to discover who said what, how authoritative it was, whether it was accepted by the later authorities, and what later commentaries said about it.

The range of topics the Talmud covers is astounding. Hyam Maccoby's anthology of the Talmud, *The Day God Laughed*, organizes its material into such categories as: Enjoying Nature, Against Asceticism, Physical Beauty, Eating and Drinking, Rejoicing, Studying; Tall Stories, The Value of Argument, Arguing for Pleasure, Arguing with God, and Privy Etiquette. The Talmud is at pains to blur any distinction between holy and profane, and is not concerned with answers. It is far more concerned with questions – and the process of answering them. One of its most celebrated passages captures this:

On that day, Rabbi Eliezer put forward all the arguments in the world, but the sages did not accept them.

Finally, he said to them, 'If the halakhah is according to me, let that carob-tree prove it.'

He pointed to a nearby carob-tree, which then moved from its place a hundred cubits, some say, four hundred cubits. They said to him, 'One cannot bring a proof from the moving of a carob-tree.' ...
[Two more miracles were performed by Rabbi Eliezer in a bid to have his argument accepted.]

Then said Rabbi Eliezer to the Sages, 'If the halakhah is according to me, may a proof come from heaven.'

Then a heavenly voice went forth, and said, 'What have you to do with Rabbi Eliezer? The halakhah is according to him in every place.'

Then Rabbi Joshua rose up on his feet, and said, 'It is not in the heavens.'
[Deuteronomy 30:12 – he goes on to explain that since the Torah has already been given on Sinai, we do not need to pay attention to a heavenly voice.]

Rabbi Nathan met the prophet Elijah. He asked him, 'What was the Holy One, blessed be He, doing in that hour?'

Said Elijah, 'He was laughing, and saying, "My children have defeated me, my children have defeated me."'

Bava Metsia 59b

In other words, God's children are grown up enough to argue with him; for the rabbi, it is even a responsibility. In this sense, the Talmud captures something essential, not just of the historical period and contexts it emerges from, but also of the ongoing life of Judaism: God is in the argument, and he may well be found in the delight of vigorous human discourse.

TEXTUAL BALANCE

In some ways, for modern Judaism the Tanakh is not the most important text. In matters of practice, the texts of classical rabbinic Judaism, of its subsequent commentators – such as the biblical *Targums* (paraphrases) and medieval texts such as the *Mishneh Torah* ('Copy of the Torah') of Maimonides, and commentaries by Rashi and Abraham ibn Ezra – and of a whole range of popular prayer books and guides to Jewish life, including the *Zohar* and *Shulhan Arukh* (c. 1565) – are often the first port of call. Yet for the composers of the Mishnah, Tanakh was the foundation not just of the laws being composed, but of life itself; and for the Talmud, Mishnah and Tanakh were foundational.

Judaism's sacred texts, then, can be envisaged as concentric circles: The innermost three circles are the Tanakh, at the very centre, Torah, followed by *Nevi'im* (the prophets), and *Ketuvim* (the writings). After that come Mishnah, Talmud, and *Midrash* ('commentary') – the ongoing tradition of commentary and critique, a potentially never-ending circle that includes all texts that manage to become, in some way, of existential value to the Jewish community.

ERIC S. CHRISTIANSON

DIVISIONS OF THE HEBREW SCRIPTURES

Torah
Genesis, Exodus, Leviticus, Numbers, Deuteronomy

Nevi'im (Prophets)
Former: Joshua, Judges, Samuel, Kings

Latter: major: Isaiah, Jeremiah, Ezekiel

Minor: the book of the twelve: Hosea, Joel, Amos, Obadiah, Jonah, Micah, Nahum, Habakkuk, Zephaniah, Haggai, Zechariah, Malachi

Ketuvim (Writings)
Psalms, Proverbs, Job, Song of Songs, Ruth, Lamentations, Ecclesiastes, Esther, Daniel, Ezra, Nehemiah, Chronicles

CHAPTER 55

Beliefs

In the Hebrew Bible, the Israelites experienced God as the Lord of history. The most uncompromising expression of his unity is the *Shema* prayer: 'Hear, O Israel, the Lord our God is one Lord' (Deuteronomy 6:4–9). According to Scripture, the universe owes its existence to the one God, the creator of heaven and earth, and since all human beings are created in his image, all men and women are brothers and sisters. Thus, the belief in one God implies, for the Jewish faith, that there is one humanity and one world.

GOD AND CREATION

For the Jewish people, God is conceived as the transcendent creator of the universe; that is to say, God is distinct from that which he has created, above and beyond the world. He is 'wholly other' than anything that is not God. Unlike creation, God is uncreated and does not depend upon anything for his existence. Thus he is described as forming heaven and earth:

> In the beginning God created the heavens and the earth. The earth was without
> form and void, and darkness was upon the face of the deep; and the Spirit of
> God was moving over the face of the waters.
>
> Genesis 1:1–2

Throughout the Bible this theme of divine transcendence is repeatedly affirmed. The prophet Isaiah proclaims:

> Have you not known? Have you not heard? Has it not been told you from the
> beginning? Have you not understood from the foundations of the earth? It is he
> who sits above the circle of the earth, and its inhabitants are like grasshoppers;
> who stretches out the heavens like a curtain and spreads them like a tent to
> dwell in.
>
> Isaiah 40: 21–2

Despite this view of God as remote from his creation, he is also viewed as actively involved in the cosmos. In the Bible, the belief that he is always omnipresent is repeatedly stressed. In the rabbinic period, Jewish scholars formulated the doctrine of the *Shekhinah* to denote the divine presence. As the indwelling presence of God, the *Shekhinah* is compared to light. Thus the Midrash paraphrases Numbers 6:25, 'The Lord make his face to shine upon you, and be gracious to you': 'May he give thee of the light of the *Shekhinah*'. In the Middle Ages the doctrine of the *Shekhinah* was further elaborated: according to Saadiah Gaon, the *Shekhinah* is identical with the glory of God, and serves as an intermediary between God and human beings during the prophetic encounter. Judah Halevi of Toledo argued in his *Kuzari* that it is the *Shekhinah* rather than God himself who appears to prophets.

Some feminists today see the *Shekhinah* as a way for women to connect spiritually to the divine, distinct from the normalized male attribute of God that occurs in many Jewish contexts.

TIME AND ETERNITY

The Hebrew Bible also depicts God as having neither beginning nor end, a teaching that was elaborated by the rabbis. According to the Talmud, there is an unbridgeable gap between God and humans:

> Come and see! The measure of the Holy One, blessed be he, is unlike the measure of flesh and blood. The things fashioned by a creature of flesh and blood outlast him; the Holy One, blessed be he, outlasts the things he has fashioned.

God's eternal reign is similarly affirmed in midrashic literature. Yet the rabbis discouraged speculation about the nature of eternity. The Mishnah states:

> Whoever reflects on four things, it were better for him that he had not come into the world: What is above? What is beneath? What is before? and What is after?

Despite such teaching, in the Middle Ages Jewish theologians debated this issue. In his *Guide for the Perplexed* Maimonides argued that time itself was part of creation; when God is described as existing before the creation of the universe, the 'time' should not be understood in its normal sense. This concept was developed by Joseph Albo in his *Ikkarim* (fifteenth century), where he argues that the concepts of priority and perpetuity can only be applied to God in a negative sense. That is, when God is described as being 'before' or 'after' some period, this only means that he was not

Whither shall I go from thy Spirit?

Or whither shall I flee from thy presence?

If I ascend to heaven, thou art there!

If I make my bed in Sheol, thou art there!

If I take the wings of the morning

and dwell in the uttermost parts of the sea,

even there thy hand shall lead me,

and thy right hand shall hold me.

Psalms 139:7–12,
Old Testament,
Revised Standard Version

non-existent before or after that time. However, terms indicating a time-span cannot be applied to God himself.

According to other Jewish thinkers, God is outside time altogether: he does not live in the present, have a past, or look forward to the future, but lives in the 'Eternal Now'. Hence, God is experiencing every moment in the past and future history of the created world simultaneously and eternally. What for us are fleeting moments rushing by are, for God, a huge tapestry, of which he sees every part continually.

OMNIPOTENCE AND OMNISCIENCE

Allied to this is the Jewish conviction that God is all-powerful and all-knowing. From biblical times the belief in God's omnipotence has been a central feature of the faith. Thus in Genesis, when Abraham's wife Sarah expressed astonishment at the suggestion that she should have a child at the age of ninety, she was criticized. Similarly, when Jerusalem was threatened by the Chaldeans, God declared: 'Behold, I am the Lord, the God of all flesh; is anything too hard for me?' (Jeremiah 32:27).

In the Middle Ages, however, Jewish thinkers wrestled with the concept of divine omnipotence. Maimonides, for example, argues in his *Guide for the Perplexed* that, although God is all-powerful, there are certain actions that he cannot perform because they are logically impossible:

Modern statue of Moses Maimonides, Rabbi Moshe ben Maimon (1135–1204), in Córdoba, Spain.

> *That which is impossible has a permanent and constant property, which is not the result of some agent, and cannot in any way change, and consequently we do not ascribe to God the power of doing what is impossible.*

Regarding God's omniscience, the Bible proclaims:

> *The Lord looks down from heaven, he sees all the sons of men ... he who fashions the hearts of them all, and observes all their deeds.*
>
> Psalms 33:13, 15

Following the biblical view, rabbinic Judaism asserted that God's knowledge is not limited by space and time. Rather, nothing is hidden from him. Further, the rabbis declared that God's foreknowledge of events does not deprive human beings of free will. Thus, in the Mishnah, the second-century sage Akiva declares: 'All is foreseen, but freedom of choice is given.' In his *Guide for the Perplexed*, Maimonides claims that God knows all things before they occur. Nonetheless, human beings are unable to comprehend the nature of God's knowledge because it is of a different order from theirs. Similarly, it is impossible to understand how divine foreknowledge is compatible with free will.

THE ELECTION AND MISSION OF ISRAEL

The Bible asserts that God controls and guides the universe. The Hebrew term for such divine action is *hashgahah*, derived from Psalm 33:14: 'From where he sits enthroned he looks forth on all the inhabitants of the earth.' Such a view implies that the dispensation of a wise and benevolent providence is found everywhere: all events are ultimately foreordained by God. Such a notion was developed in rabbinic literature, where God is depicted as the judge of the world, who provides for the destiny of individuals as well as nations on the basis of their actions.

Jews further affirm that God chose the Jews as his special people:

> *For you are a people holy to the Lord your God: the Lord your God has chosen*
> *you to be a people for his own possession out of all the peoples that are on the*
> *face of the earth.*

Deuteronomy 7:6

Through its election, Israel has been given a historic mission to bear divine truth to humanity. God's choice of Israel thus carries with it numerous responsibilities:

> *For I have chosen him, that he may charge his children and his household after*
> *him to keep the way of the Lord by doing righteousness and justice.*

Genesis 18:19

THE TORAH

To accomplish this task, God revealed both the oral Torah and the written Torah to Moses on Mount Sinai. As Maimonides explains:

> *The Torah was revealed from Heaven. This implies our belief that the whole of*
> *the Torah found in our hands this day is the Torah that was handed down by*
> *Moses, and that it is all of divine origin. By this I mean that the whole of the*
> *Torah came unto him from before God in a manner which is metaphorically*

called 'speaking'; but the real nature of that communication is unknown to everybody except to Moses.

In rabbinic literature, a distinction is drawn between the revelation of the Pentateuch – the first five books of the Bible, and Torah in the narrow sense – and the prophetic writings. Such a distinction is frequently expressed within Judaism: the Torah was given directly by God, whereas the prophetic books were given by means of prophecy. The remaining books of the Bible were conveyed by means of the Holy Spirit rather than through prophecy. According to the rabbis, the expositions and elaborations of the written Law were also revealed by God to Moses on Mount Sinai, subsequently passed from generation to generation, and through this process additional legislation was incorporated, a process referred to as 'the oral Torah'. Thus traditional Judaism affirms that God's revelation is twofold and binding for all time.

> *Before the mountains were brought forth,*
>
> *or ever thou hadst formed the earth and the world,*
>
> *from everlasting to everlasting thou art God.*
>
> Psalm 90:2, Old Testament, Revised Standard Version

According to tradition, God revealed 613 commandments to Moses. These *mitzvot* are recorded in the Five Books of Moses and classified in two major categories:

- statutes concerned with ritual performances, char acterized as obligations between human beings and God;
- judgments consisting of ritual laws that would have been adopted by society even if they had not been decreed by God.

All these laws, together with their expansion in rabbinic sources such as the Mishnah and Talmud, are binding on Jewry for all time.

Rabbinic Judaism teaches that there are two tendencies in every person: the good inclination (*yetzer ha-tov*) and the evil inclination (*yetzer ha-ra*). The former urges individuals to do what is right, whereas the latter encourages sinful acts. At all times a person is to be on guard against the assaults of the *yetzer ha-ra*.

ESCHATOLOGY

Eschatology is teaching about the 'last things', such as the end of time, the afterlife, heaven, and hell. Traditional Judaism asserts that, at the end of time, God will send the Messiah to redeem his people and usher in the messianic age. In Scripture, such a figure is depicted in various ways, and as time passed the rabbis elaborated the themes found in the Bible and Jewish literature of the Second Temple period. In the midrashim and the Talmud they formulated an elaborate eschatological scheme, divided into various stages.

First there will be the time of the messianic redemption. According to the Babylonian Talmud, the messianic age will take place on earth after a period of decline and calamity, and will result in the complete fulfilment of every human wish. Peace will reign on earth; Jerusalem will be rebuilt; and at the close of this era the dead will be resurrected and joined with their souls, and a final judgment will come upon all humankind. Those who are judged righteous will enter heaven (*Gan Eden*), whereas those deemed wicked will be condemned to everlasting punishment in hell (*Gehinnom*).

However, 'when the Messiah comes' is also a colloquial way of saying 'never', and modern Judaism has become increasingly eschatology-neutral, particularly as a result of disillusion following such messianic disappointments of Bar-Kochba and Sabbati Zevi.

CHANGING BELIEFS IN MODERN TIMES

From biblical times Jews have subscribed to a wide range of beliefs about the nature of God and his activity in the world. In modern times, these have been increasingly called into question. In the nineteenth century, reformers sought to reinterpret this belief system for modern Jews. In their view, it no longer made sense to believe in the coming of the messiah and the eschatological scheme as outlined in rabbinic sources. Subsequent movements, such as Reconstructionist and Humanistic Judaism, rejected the supernaturalism of the past, and called for a radical revision of Jewish theology for the contemporary age. In more recent times, the Holocaust has raised fundamental questions about belief in a supernatural God who watches over his chosen people. Today there is widespread uncertainty in the Jewish world about the central tenets of the faith.

DAN COHN-SHERBOK

THE COVENANT

At the heart of the Jewish religion lies a covenant between God and the people. Unlike a testament, a covenant involves a personal response on the side of the second party to make it effective. Unlike a contract, it is not a mutually negotiated affair but is offered unilaterally by one side to the other. Yet it does provide rights and obligations to both parties – which is why, for instance, Jewish protest theology is usually grounded in a covenantal framework.

The covenants we are concerned with are between God and humankind, especially Israel. But investigation of civil treaties from the adjacent Hittite culture of the fifteenth and fourteenth centuries BCE provides interesting insights. These treaties – between king and people – always included three elements:

- a historical prologue, describing the deeds of the maker of the treaty;
- a list of obligations binding the lesser of the two parties;
- a list of punishments and rewards.

The Jewish covenants generally reproduce this pattern: they are grounded in divinely ordered events; they contain a set of stipulations; and they conclude with a list of 'woes and blessings'.

God's chosen people

The first covenant referred to in the Jewish scriptures is between God and Noah (Genesis 9:8–17), the basis for which lies in God's preservation of Noah and his family during the flood. Through Noah, a promise is made to humankind and the animal world that this disaster will never be repeated. The promise has its sign – the rainbow – which is to act as a reminder, both to God and all living creatures, of this undertaking.

The covenant with Noah provides the basis for the later, more specialized, commitment to Israel, the first of which is the covenant between God and the great patriarch of Israel, Abraham. God promises to make Abraham the ancestor of a great nation (Genesis 12:1–7),

and to give him and his descendants the land of Israel (Genesis 13:14–18). This covenant (Genesis chapters 15 and 17) begins with a historical introduction, stating God is the one who brought Abraham out from Ur of the Chaldees (in modern Iraq), and then outlines obligations about living righteously and justly, which are elaborated in later books. Circumcision becomes the sign of this covenant.

More than 600 years later, the Abrahamic covenant is reaffirmed and extended at Mount Sinai, with all the people who have come out of Egypt (Exodus chapters 19–20). This covenant recalls God's historical deliverance of them from Egypt, and the accompanying promise that Israel will be God's special possession among all the nations. There is a series of obligations in the form of the Ten Commandments, and the people's acceptance of their responsibilities is also indicated.

This covenant is again an expression of both God's grace and God's demands. Even the instructions are as much a gift as an obligation, for they show Israel how they may appropriately respond to God's choice of them. And, since God later maintains both sides of the covenant, even when elements within Israel fail to obey, the fact that the covenant is based on God's grace remains transparent.

All this is nowhere clearer than in the biblical book of Deuteronomy, which is presented as the record of Moses' farewell addresses to Israel, on the eve of their entry into the promised land. Deuteronomy 5 recounts the Sinai covenant, Deuteronomy 7 refers to the covenant with the patriarchs of Israel, and Deuteronomy 29 is a renewal of the covenant with the whole people. Throughout the book, insistence on God's continued, gracious maintenance of the covenant, despite Israel's failure to fulfil its conditions, is a prominent theme.

In the historical books a more specialized covenant is recorded – with David and his descendants and, associated with this, with the Levitical priesthood (1 Chronicles 17:7, 28:4). Here again there are the standard elements:

- the prologue reminds David it was God who turned him from a shepherd into a victorious king;
- the outlining of conditions indicates that God's blessing is not automatically guaranteed (1 Chronicles 22:11);
- the promise tells of God's commitment to establish David's descendants upon the throne forever.

A renewed covenant

So naturally did the people take the covenant on which their nation was based, that, except for Hosea and Jeremiah, the great prophets rarely referred to the Sinai agreement. Only after the exile shattered Israel's confidence were the prophets less reticent about the covenant (Zechariah 9:11; Malachi 2:4), while the later

Inside one of the caves at Qumran, Israel, where some of the Dead Sea Scrolls were discovered.

historical writings also speak of significant covenant renewals (Ezra 9; Nehemiah 9).

Most significant in a number of these writings is the promise of a new covenant to replace the broken one for which Israel had been punished (see, for example, Jeremiah 31; Ezekiel 16). The new covenant will have its obligations inscribed on the wills of the people rather than exist merely as external obligations which the people must seek to observe. When this happens, Israel will receive back all they have lost – and more.

In the post-biblical writings, further changes in the understanding of the covenant take place. The idea of a new covenant either drops away altogether, or becomes simply a reiteration of the old one (Baruch 2:30). In the apocryphal writings the word for covenant refers, much more frequently than before, just to the obligations within it. This tends to push the Torah into a more prominent position and the covenant in a more contractual direction. Meanwhile the covenant with the Fathers comes to be regarded as irrevocable, leading to the use of the term for the Jewish nation itself (Judith 9:13).

Jewish apocalyptic writings preserve the same emphasis, and the term for covenant is used more often than previously for its sign, circumcision (Jubilees 15:13–14). The Torah is now said to precede the covenant, moving into a position of greater prominence (Ecclesiasticus 24:6; 44:19).

Some of the documents discovered at Qumran and known as the Dead Sea Scrolls, as well as Jewish rabbinic writings maintain the same perspective. The former take up the idea of the new covenant made with its community, but this is essentially a reaffirmation of the old covenant. The rabbinic writings occasionally suggest God's covenant with Israel rests upon their obedience as much as God's free choice.

Robert Banks

CHAPTER 56

Family and Society

According to Orthodox Jewish law, a Jew is one born of a Jewish mother, although it is possible to become a Jew by conversion. On the eighth day after his birth, a Jewish boy will be circumcised, a religious rite performed by a *mohel*, a trained and registered circumciser. When he is circumcised, the boy receives the Hebrew name which will be used at his *Bar-Mitzvah*, at his wedding, and on his gravestone.

During his early years, his mother is responsible for his religious education. As soon as he can speak, the boy is taught the words of the *Shema*. At about the age of five, he is sent to a synagogue religion class which is held after school on weekdays and also on Sunday mornings. One of the main activities of the class is to learn Hebrew and study the sacred books. For a girl, it is also important to learn how to keep a Jewish home. Increasingly in the Orthodox world, girls are also taught to study Torah, though not Talmud.

BAR-MITZVAH

At the age of thirteen, a boy becomes *Bar-Mitzvah*, 'son of the commandment'; on the *Shabbat* after his birthday he reads for the first time from the scroll of the Torah during the synagogue service. After the service, there is usually a party for family and friends. After this, he is regarded as a responsible person, is expected to fulfil all the duties of a Jew, and may count as one of the ten who are required to make a quorum for public prayer (*minyan*). A Jewish girl comes of age at twelve, and is considered to be *Bat-Mitzvah* 'daughter of the commandment'. It is increasingly the custom to hold a ceremony to mark this occasion.

PRAYER

A devout Jewish man prays three times a day — morning, afternoon, and evening — either in his home or in the synagogue. When he prays, he covers his head with an ordinary hat or a skull-cap (*yarmelka*, or *kippah*). In the morning he wears a prayer-shawl (*tallit*), which has tassels or fringes at the four corners in obedience to a command found in the Torah.

A Jewish male baby is circumcised by the *mohel*.

On weekdays he may also put on phylacteries (*tephillin*), black leather boxes containing four passages of scripture – Exodus 13:1–10 and 11–16; Deuteronomy 6:4–9 and 11:13–21 – strapped to the forehead and left upper-arm.

While Orthodox women are not obligated to time-bound *mitzvot*, or to wear prayer-shawls or lay *tephillin*, they are also strongly encouraged to pray, at least an abbreviated form of the morning and evening prayers. In other branches of Judaism, women may take on the full obligations of daily prayer, including *tallit* and *tephillin*.

When he goes out, the Orthodox Jew may continue to cover his head, as a mark of reverence towards God, in whose presence all life is lived. By the front door, both women and men pass the *mezuzah*, and touch it to remind themselves of their obligation to God. The *mezuzah* consists of a tiny scroll of parchment on which are written in Hebrew the opening paragraphs of the *Shema*: Deuteronomy 6:4–9 and 11:13–21. The scroll is housed in a wooden or metal container, and fixed to the upper part of the right-hand doorpost of the front door. A similar *mezuzah* is fixed to the doorpost of every room in the house.

KOSHER FOOD

It is the duty of a traditional Jewish housewife to safeguard the religious purity of the home, and one of her many responsibilities is to ensure the food eaten there is *kosher* – fit or clean according to Jewish dietary laws. Meat and dairy products must not be served at the same meal: if meat is eaten, there can be no butter on bread, or milk in coffee. To avoid any possibility of mixing meat with milk, the traditional housewife uses two sets of dishes, one of which is only used for meat, the other only for milk foods. She may also use two bowls for washing-up and two sets of tea-towels. In *kosher* hotels, there are two separate kitchens.

Only certain kinds of meat, listed in Leviticus 11 and Deuteronomy 14, may be eaten in a Jewish home. Lamb, beef, and chicken are among those permitted; pork and shellfish among those that are not. The animals must be slaughtered by a trained and ordained *shochet*, who follows carefully prescribed regulations that cause the blood to drain quickly from the body and ensure the creature the minimum of pain. After the animal is slaughtered, the meat must be soaked in cold water and salted, to remove all the remaining blood.

Jewish people vary a great deal in their observance of these dietary laws. Some do not observe them at all, while some abstain from food that is expressly forbidden, but are not so particular about the details of keeping a *kosher* kitchen. However, Orthodox Jews follow these regulations meticulously as an act of

A Jewish boy celebrates his Bar-Mitzvah at Jerusalem's Western Wall, Israel. Both the rabbi and the boy have *tephillin* strapped to their forehead, and the boy is wearing a cardboard *kippah*.

religious obedience, whereby the taking of food is sanctified, and the family table becomes an altar. Before each meal, a traditional blessing is recited, and though this may vary according to the food that is being eaten, the most common words are, 'Blessed art thou, O Lord our God, King of the universe, who brings forth bread from the earth.'

SHABBAT

Shabbat is considered to be the most important of all the Jewish religious festivals. It commemorates both the creation of the world, and the deliverance of the people of Israel from Egypt. It has played a significant role in the preservation of Judaism, and is a day with a special atmosphere of joy and peace. As such, it is thought of as a foretaste of the age to come.

The beginning of the *Shabbat*, sunset on Friday evening, is marked by the lighting and blessing of the *Shabbat* candles by the mother. The father attends synagogue, often with his children, and on his return blesses his children and praises his wife with the words of Proverbs chapter 31. The family then enjoys a *Shabbat* meal together, which begins with the blessing over bread and wine. The bread is a special plaited loaf called *challah*. Usually two loaves are used, in memory of the double-portion of manna that fell in the wilderness on the day before the *Shabbat*.

No work is permitted on the *Shabbat*, and Orthodox Jews have to be employed in occupations which allow them to be home before sunset every Friday throughout the year. This often means that they will be self-employed, work in a Jewish firm, or trade in Fridays and Saturdays for work on other evenings, Sundays and Christmas. No fires may be lit on the *Shabbat*, though a fire which was lit before the *Shabbat* may be left alight. Many install time-delay switches to avoid forms of work not permitted to Jews on the *Shabbat*. No long journeys may be undertaken on the *Shabbat*, though those on board ship do not have to get off. Orthodox Jews live within easy walking distance of their synagogue, since they must not drive on the *Shabbat* or use public transport.

Jewish skull-cap – *yarmelka* or *kippah* – prayer shawl – *tallit* – and Hebrew Torah.

These restrictions, far from being a burden, are seen by religious Jews as a means of releasing them from the ardours of the daily round. It is a day when they can rest completely from their ordinary work and be spiritually renewed.

At the close of the *Shabbat*, the family again gathers for a brief ceremony, called *havdalah*, 'separation'. Blessings, the '*Kiddush*', are recited over a cup of wine and a box of sweet spices, which speak of the fragrance of the *Shabbat* day, which it is hoped will be carried over into the new week.

MARRIAGE AND DIVORCE

In Judaism, marriage is considered to be a holy covenant between the bride and groom. Before the ceremony, the bridegroom signs the marriage document (*ketubbah*), in which he pledges himself to his bride. During the service the couple stand under an embroidered canopy supported by four poles (*chuppah*), which represents their future home. The ceremony ends with the breaking of a glass under the bridegroom's foot, a symbolic act thought by some to represent the idea that even times of great joy need to be balanced by moments of serious reflection. Others see it as a reminder of the destruction of the Temple of Jerusalem, a theme that constantly reappears in Hebrew prayers.

In the event of the breakdown of a marriage, the local community tries to reconcile husband and wife. If this is not possible, a *get*, or bill of divorce, may be issued by the Jewish religious court, if both partners agree. This document, written in Aramaic and signed by two witnesses, is handed by the husband to the wife and frees her from all marital obligations to him. In most countries, a civil divorce is required first, and the subsequent issuing of a *get* serves as a religious ratification of the divorce.

> *Hear, O Israel: The LORD our God, the LORD is one. Love the LORD your God with all your heart and with all your soul and with all your strength. These commandments that I give you today are to be upon your hearts. Impress them on your children. Talk about them when you sit at home and when you walk along the road, when you lie down and when you get up. Tie them as symbols on your hands and bind them on your foreheads. Write them on the door-frames of your houses and on your gates.*
>
> Deuteronomy 6:4–9, Old Testament,
> New International Version

DEATH AND RESURRECTION

The last words uttered by religious Jews when they are dying – or said on their behalf if they are too weak – are the words of the *Shema* which they first learned as children: 'Hear, O Israel, the Lord our God is one Lord...' At the funeral, close mourners make a small tear in their clothes, as a mark of grief. The funeral service, which is characterized by simplicity even among wealthy families,

A Jewish tombstone. Jews often place stones on the grave or tombstone, though the origin of this tradition is unclear. Possibly it is a symbolic act to show someone has visited the tomb, and the deceased is not forgotten.

is arranged as soon as possible – preferably within twenty-four hours of death. No prayers for the dead are offered, but *kaddish*, a prayer of praise to God, is recited in their memory. It is the particular responsibility of children to say *kaddish* on in the memory of deceased parents.

After the funeral, close relatives return home for a week of private mourning, a period known as *shivah*, or the seven days, during which those who have been bereaved sit on low stools, or even on the floor. On the anniversary of the parent's death, the children light a memorial candle and recite the *kaddish* at the end of the synagogue service.

The idea of life after death can be traced back within Judaism at least 2000 years, and is expressed in Maimonides' 'Thirteen Principles of the Faith': 'I believe with perfect faith that there will be a resurrection of the dead at a time when it shall please the Creator.' Yet Judaism is concerned primarily with this life rather than the next, and with obeying the Law of God in the present rather than speculating about the future.

DAVID HARLEY

CHAPTER 57

Worship and Festivals

An annual cycle of worship and festivals gives Judaism its distinctive form. There is a major or minor festival almost every month of the year. Beginning with *Rosh Hashanah*, New Year's Day, on the first day of *Tishrei*, and proceeding to the period of penitence that begins in the twelfth month, *Elul*, Jews are able to express and celebrate their identity through the regular re-enactment of stories that explore life's meaning and purpose. High and low points of the Jewish story are remembered year by year.

THE HEART OF JUDAISM

Maimonides' 'Thirteen Principles of the Faith' help define Judaism. They were not intended to become a creed — indeed, Judaism is based much more upon practice than belief — and can be summarized in the three great themes that underpin the Jewish religion: creation, revelation, and redemption.

At the heart of Judaism is the profound idea that human beings can bring God into the world through their everyday actions and interactions. Although Judaism acknowledges a huge distance between the infinity of God and the limitations of human beings, it believes we are called to be partners with God in the task of creation. This understanding of the divine–human relationship can be traced back to the Babylonian Talmud (*Shabbat* 10a, 119b, *Sanhedrin* 38a). The supreme moment of revelation was when the people received the commandments at Mount Sinai; hence, Jewish religious expression or worship occurs when *mitzvoth*, the commandments, are followed, as one practises *halakhah*, or 'walking in God's way'.

> Judaism is a very practical and also a very joyful religion. 'Happy are we! How good is our lot! How pleasant is our destiny! How beautiful our heritage! Happy are we who, early and late, evening and morning, twice each day declare: Hear O Israel, the Lord is our God, the Lord is One!'
>
> The Jewish Prayer Book, extract from the Morning Service.

HOME AND SYNAGOGUE

The object of greatest religious importance in Judaism is a scroll of the Law, a *Sefer* Torah. It is a moving moment when the Torah scroll is taken out of its protective ark in the synagogue during the course of a service of worship and held up before the people. The synagogue is important as a meeting place, a focus for prayer, and house of study. But it is not the only significant place of worship, in the sense in which a mosque or a church may be; Jews often refer to the synagogue simply as *shul*, school.

The home is the focus of many of the most central aspects of Jewish religious life, such as *Shabbat*, the festivals, and the dietary laws, as well as education across the generations. Every effort is made to involve children in the celebration of the major festivals. It is a child who asks the questions concerning the special night at the *Seder* celebration during *Pesach*, Passover. It is children who enjoy drowning out the sound of Haman's name whenever it is mentioned during the reading of the book of Esther at Purim. It is children who are given the best places in front of the lights of the *menorah*, candelabrum, at the festival of *Hanukkah*.

THREE PILGRIMAGE FESTIVALS

Three of the most popular biblical festivals are known as 'pilgrimage' festivals, since they recall the three annual occasions when Jews made the journey to worship in Jerusalem when the Temple played a central role in Jewish life. These are the eight-day festival of *Pesach* (Passover), *Shavuot* (Pentecost), and *Sukkot* (Tabernacles), also an eight-day festival. Together, they form an annual re-enactment of the special events that forged the relationship between the Jews and their God.

- *Pesach* (15–21/22 *Nisan*) remembers the Exodus from Egypt under the leadership of Moses, and celebrates the passage from slavery to freedom. The highlight is the first evening, with the observance of the *Seder*. Around the table in the home, Jews relive the story, often reading from the *Haggadah*, 'telling', the order of the Seder, and reflect how it must have felt to be a slave in Egypt (Exodus 13:8).
- *Shavuot* (6 *Sivan*) marked the bringing of the first fruits in the days of the Temple, and celebrates the giving of the Torah by God to Moses on Mount Sinai.
- *Sukkot* (15–20 *Tishrei*) commemorates the time when God protected the people in the desert.

In many ways, the story of the Exodus from Egypt did not end with Moses gaining freedom for a small group of people centuries ago. The theme of Passover gives a context

> The three Pilgrim festivals have in common the theme of joy in God's presence: 'And you shall rejoice on your festivals' (Deuteronomy 16:14–16) ... The festive joy is traditionally expressed in feasting with meat and drink, and with the purchase of new garments for the women. It is a joy which is only complete when allied with concern for the needy; as the verse continues, 'with ... the strangers, orphans and widows among you.'
>
> Rabbi Norman Solomon

SEDER MEAL

Through the ritual and symbolism of the *Seder* meal, Jews tell the story of how their ancestors left Egypt. The foods placed upon the often beautifully decorated *Seder* plate are symbolic and comprise: three wafers of unleavened bread, *matzot*, to symbolize the bread eaten by the Israelites when they left Egypt in a hurry (Exodus 12:39); bitter herbs, *maror*, to recall the experiences of slavery in Egypt (Exodus 1:14); a sweet paste, *haroset*, made from almonds, apples, and wine, to represent the mortar used for building in Egypt as slaves, and symbolize both the toils of slavery and the sweetness of redemption and freedom; a bowl of salt water to represent the bitter tears of slavery, with parsley used for dipping; a roasted bone, as a reminder of the Paschal lamb; and a roasted egg, as a reminder of the offering brought to the Temple for the festival with the Paschal lamb – these last two items being left on the *Seder* plate during the meal, and not eaten. It has also been the custom, since Rabbinic times, to drink four cups of wine during the *Seder* to represent the four stages of redemption, from the Exodus to the future coming of the messiah.

for exploration of the issues of freedom and slavery, and the accompanying themes of risk, choice, hope, disappointment, leadership, hardship, and sacrifice. Moses has inspired many people who have struggled to gain freedom from prejudice and oppression; issues of marginalization and possibilities for liberation in the contemporary world are often discussed during the *Seder* meal.

ROSH HASHANAH

The new year festival of *Rosh Hashanah* (1–2 *Tishrei*), as in many traditions, is a time for making resolutions about the future. However, for the Jews it is a serious occasion. A month earlier a forty-day period of penitence begins – the Ten Days of Awe, '*yamim noraim*' – and *Rosh Hashanah* marks the beginning of the last ten of these days. The foods eaten at the meal on New Year's Eve symbolize sweetness, blessings, and plenty. Bread is dipped into honey – rather than the usual salt – and the following prayer is said: 'May it be your will to renew for us a good and sweet year.' Prayers at the morning service the following day, which lasts up to six hours, focus on the characteristics of God as creator, king, and judge: the God who will show mercy and compassion to those who sincerely turn towards him, '*teshuva*'. The sounding of the ram's horn, '*shofar*', regularly through the service is literally a wake-up call to the people (see Amos 3:6).

> From the Seder liturgy
>
> *This is the bread of affliction which our fathers ate in the land of Egypt.*
>
> *Let all who are hungry come and eat.*
>
> *Let all who are in want come and celebrate the Passover with us.*
>
> *May it be God's will to redeem us from all trouble and from all servitude.*
>
> *Next year at this season, may the whole house of Israel be free!*
>
> From the *Seder Haggadah, The Union Haggadah,* ed. The Central Council of American Rabbis, 1923.

YOM KIPPUR

The Day of Atonement, 'Yom Kippur' (10 Tishrei), is a fast day marking the end of the Ten Days of Awe, and is the holiest day in the Jewish liturgical year, when Jews solemnly review their record of behaviour and literally turn to face a new year. The whole day is spent in prayer for forgiveness and for a good year ahead, and for at least part of it synagogues are full to overflowing. Yom Kippur marks one of the most emotionally charged times of the Jewish year. The theme is return to God, 'teshuva' – a major religious theme within Judaism, involving a renewed commitment to walk in the right path. Kol Nidrei – a declaration in Aramaic – forms the beginning of the synagogue service, often sung to a moving melody, and sets the tone as the congregation gathers in awe.

Work is forbidden, as on Shabbat. There are five further prohibitions, 'innuyim', or forms of self-discipline, that apply during the Yom Kippur fast, and also the fast of Tisha b'Av, discussed below. Jews must abstain from eating and drinking, anointing with oils, sexual relations, washing for pleasure, and wearing leather shoes.

The Closing of the Gates, 'Ne'ilah', is the final service, as the fast ends, and emphasizes the importance of the last hour in which the gates of heaven remain open for a returning to God. Avina Malkenu, 'our father, our king', is chanted to express the congregation's commitment to the unity of God, followed by a final blow on the shofar.

A Jewish family in Israel celebrate Passover together with the Seder meal.

Festivals of Judaism

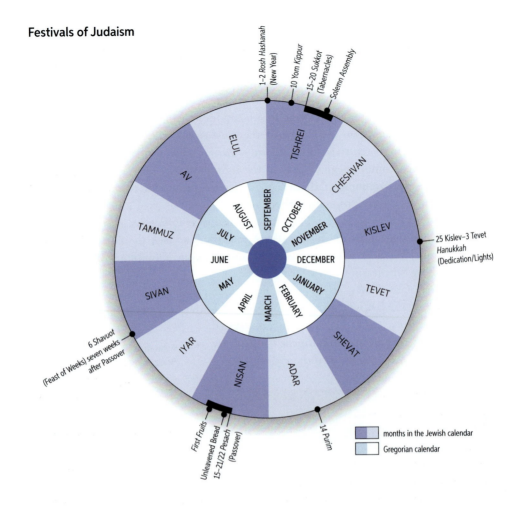

MINOR FESTIVALS

The most popular of the minor festivals are *Hanukkah* (25 *Kislev* – 2 *Tevet*), Purim (14 *Adar*), and the New Year for Trees, *Tu biShevat* (15 *Shevat*).

Hanukkah celebrates the rededication of the Temple in about 165 BCE, after its defilement by the Greeks. On each of the eight nights of the festival, a light is lit to commemorate the 'miracle of the oil'. The Hasmoneans, seeking to rededicate the Temple, could only find one cruse of oil, enough to keep the Temple *menorah* burning for a day – yet it lasted for eight. This is interpreted as symbolic of God's creative action in the world.

Between the destruction of the first Temple and the building of the second, many Jews were threatened with massacre by Haman's scheming with Ahasuerus, King of Persia, but Queen Esther and her uncle Mordechai were used by God to avert catastrophe. Purim celebrates this deliverance with parties and sending gifts of food to people in need, and the scroll of the book of Esther, *Megillah*, is read in the synagogue.

Judaism celebrates a new year for trees, *Tu biShevat*, a popular festival with the return to the land of Israel in modern times. In Israel it is marked by a school holiday and tree-planting ceremonies.

OTHER FAST DAYS

Of the other fast days the most important is 9 *Av* (*Tishah b'Av*), when the destruction of the two Temples, in 586 BCE and in 70 CE, is commemorated, as well as other tragedies of Jewish history. Reform Jews often use the day to commemorate the Holocaust.

On *Yom Kippur* and on *Tishah b'Av* people fast for twenty-five hours, instead of the twenty-four hours required for other fast days. Nothing is eaten or drunk during this time, unless there is a practical reason for not undertaking this discipline.

SECULAR JUDAISM

Many Jews who describe themselves as 'secular' nevertheless experience a sense of belonging to the wider Jewish community at times such as *Pesach* or *Yom Kippur*. Official Israeli holidays can also strengthen the links between communal identity and liturgy:

- Holocaust Day, *Yom HaShoah* (27 *Nisan*) remembers the Holocaust and the six million Jews who were murdered.
- Memorial Day, *Yom HaZikaron* (4 *Iyar*) remembers the soldiers killed defending the state of Israel.
- Independence Day, *Yom Ha-Atzma'ut* (5 *Iyar*) marks the anniversary of the founding of the State of Israel in 5708 (1948 CE).
- Jerusalem Day, *Yom Yerushalayim* (28 *Iyar*) commemorates the reunification of the city of Jerusalem in 5727, 1967 CE.
- The Israeli Declaration of Independence, proclaimed on 14 May 1948, is celebrated with social activities, in Israel and throughout the world, and special psalms and prayers are said in the synagogue, but is somewhat controversial, for both religious and political reasons.

LIZ RAMSEY

I AM A JEW

My paternal grandparents immigrated to Western Europe from Lithuania at the turn of the twentieth century to escape the effects of anti-Semitism and grinding poverty. My mother was born and brought up in Frankfurt-am-Main, Germany. She fled Germany at the end of June 1939, a refugee from Nazi persecution. She and her father were the only members of my maternal line to survive, the rest of the family are numbered among the millions of Jews murdered in the Holocaust. We live in a predominantly secular world, where religion and spiritual values are often assigned a very low priority. But, for me, my Jewish faith and family history have shaped and defined my identity. I attach great value to the traditions of democracy, freedom of speech, and equality before the law. I also feel a personal responsibility to contribute to building a better understanding and harmonious relations between the Jewish community and the non-Jewish majority among whom we live.

I also think I am incredibly lucky to be Jewish. I draw inspiration from the courage and fortitude with which my mother confronted both the difficulties of her childhood and the humiliation and poverty of being a refugee. No less inspiring is the example of friends who are Holocaust survivors. They are often the sole surviving members of their families, whose homes and communities were completely destroyed. Their suffering and loss is unimaginable. They were brutalized and terrorized solely because they were born Jewish. Yet despite all this, so many of the survivors have chosen to renew and rebuild their lives firmly rooted in the Jewish faith and tradition into which they were born. This, for me, is proof of the eternal and enduring nature of their Jewish faith. The triumph of their humanity is truly inspiring.

Many of those murdered in the Holocaust were condemned in part because of the failure of so many countries, including the Western democracies, to take in Jewish refugees. So for me, and most Jews living in the diaspora (that is, Jews who live outside the borders of Israel), Israel represents a life insurance policy, a place of safety to which we can go if we feel we are once again endangered by anti-Semitism. Israel is, therefore, very important for the worldwide Jewish community. I have visited Jerusalem twice. It is at the heart and geographical centre of the Jewish world. Synagogues around the world are all built facing Jerusalem. The festival of *Hanukkah* and the fast days of *Tevet*, *Tammuz*, and *Av* have their origin in the sieges of Jerusalem and the desecration of the Temple. Each time I prayed at the *Kotel* – formerly known as the 'Western Wall' or 'Wailing Wall' – I sobbed uncontrollably.

For me Judaism is not just a religion, but a complete and distinctive way of life. It defines my relationship with God, my relationship with other people, Jewish and non-Jewish, and my obligations as a human being. The central and defining principal of Judaism is belief in a single God who is responsible for the creation of the universe and everything in it. The foundation of Judaism is the Torah, also known as the Five Books of Moses. I remember as a five-year-old schoolboy going after school to *cheder*, where I was taught to read Hebrew. At school I had to attend assembly each morning for Christian prayers, while at home, at the synagogue, and at *cheder* I was expected to follow Jewish religious practice and traditions. For a few years I found this mixture of Jewish and Christian teaching all very confusing, especially when one day at school I was beaten up because, according to my accuser, I had 'murdered little Lord Jesus'!

Every Jew is obliged to obey the law of the land, to do all they can to preserve human life, *pikuach nefesh*, and give to charity. This includes not only donations of money or goods, but acts of kindness, the promotion of education, and caring for the sick, needy, and elderly. On *Shabbat*, Jews are obliged to refrain from all forms of work: using machines, operating mechanical or electrical equipment, cooking, handling money, and travelling in a vehicle. For me, *Shabbat* is the one day of the week to which I always look forward: it is truly a day of physical and spiritual renewal.

David Arnold

Ancient chest, or "ark", for storing the Torah scrolls in a synagogue.

CHAPTER 58

The Holocaust

The term 'holocaust' originally referred to a burnt sacrifice offered to God in the ancient Jewish Temple. Today, 'Holocaust' is widely used to refer to the destruction of Jewry under the German Third Reich (1933–45), when bodies of many victims were burnt in crematoria. Many Jews consider the term *Shoah*, 'catastrophe', more appropriate, as it is devoid of religious connotations.

THE RISE OF NAZISM

At the end of World War I, Germany became a democratic republic, based on a constitution drafted in Weimar. The regime faced opposition from the extreme right and left, and during 1922 to 1923 there was massive economic inflation. An interlude of stability and intellectual and cultural development was followed by the Great Depression: over 6 million were unemployed between 1930 and 1933. Both the Communists and their fascist rivals, the NSDAP – *Nationalsozialistische Deutsche Arbeiterpartei*, the Nazi Party – gained considerable support. The Nazis, who linked Jews with Communism, were backed by leading industrialists. After several ineffectual conservative coalitions President Hindenburg (1847–1934) appointed Adolf Hitler as Chancellor on 30 January 1933.

Once in power, the Nazi Party suspended the constitution. In the course of 1933, other political parties were eliminated, strikes were outlawed, book burnings took place, and trade union leaders were imprisoned, along with dissident scientists, scholars, and artists. In 1934 the role of Hitler's elite security forces, the SS, was expanded, and led by Heinrich Himmler (1900–45) took over many of the functions of the police, as well as running the concentration camps.

THE EXTERMINATION OF JEWS

After Hindenburg's death, Hitler became the head of state. Civil servants and members of the armed forces were required to swear an oath of loyalty to him. Jewish academics

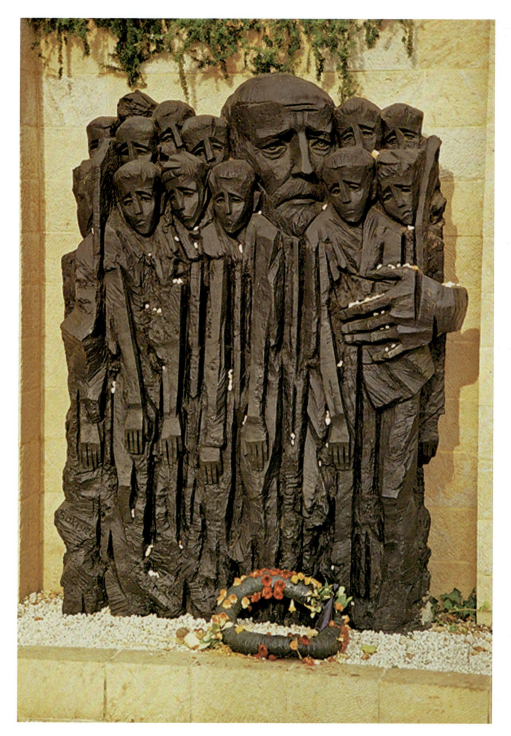

The Janusz Korczak Memorial, by Boris Saktsier, at the *Yad va-Shem* memorial to the victims of the Holocaust in Jerusalem, Israel.

lost their jobs, Jewish shops were boycotted, while the infamous Nuremberg Laws, 1935, criminalized sexual liaison between Jews and non-Jews, and prevented Jews from participating in civic life. In 1938 Jewish communal bodies were put under the control of the *Gestapo*, secret police, and Jews forced to register their property. 9 November 1938, *Kristallnacht*, the Nazis organized an onslaught against the Jewish population, killing, looting, and setting fire to homes, schools, shops, and 250 synagogues.

When the Nazis invaded Poland in 1939, in every conquered town and village the Germans forced Jews to hand over jewellery, clear rubble, carry heavy loads, and scrub floors and lavatories with their prayer shawls. Religious Jews had their beards and side-locks cut off with scissors or torn from their faces.

After the invasion of Russia in 1941, mobile task forces, *Einsatzgruppen* — murder squads of 500–900 men under the supervision of Reinhard Heydrich (1904–42) — began to slaughter Russian Jewry. Of the 4,500,000 Jews who lived in Soviet territory, more than half fled before the German invasion. Those who remained were concentrated in large cities, making it easier for Heydrich's troops to carry out their task. *Einsatzgruppen* moved in, rounded up Jews in market places, crowded them into trams, buses, and trucks and took them to woods where mass graves had been dug. They then machine-gunned them to death.

Other methods were also employed. Mobile gas vans were supplied to the *Einsatzgruppen*, and their killing operations were supplemented by the use of fixed centres, the death camps, at Chelmno and Auschwitz, in the Polish territories, and at Treblinka, Sobibor, Majdanek, and Belzec in the Polish 'General Government'. In September 1941 the first gassing took place in Auschwitz.

By September 1942 Germany had conquered most of Europe. But as the murder of Jews continued, resistance spread. The Jews of the White Russian town of Korzec set the ghetto on fire and a partisan group was formed. A former soldier in the Polish army escaped from a prison camp in Lublin with seventeen other Jews and formed a partisan group. In the Warsaw ghetto, the Jewish Fighting Organization prepared itself for action. When the Jews learned the ghetto was to be destroyed, they fought back. However, with vastly superior resources, the Germans prevailed: 7,000 Jews lost their lives in the fighting, and 30,000 were deported to Treblinka.

The murders continued without pause across Europe. By the summer of 1944, the last deportation took place, when more than 67,000 were deported from the Lodz ghetto to Birkenau. Most of these were selected for the gas chamber, but some were chosen for medical experimentation. By the end of World War II, more than 6 million Jews had lost their lives in the most terrible circumstances imaginable.

In the years since, the Jewish community has struggled with the religious perplexity of the Holocaust. Where was God at Jewry's time of dire need?

These terrible events are commemorated today on Holocaust Memorial Days, as well as in Holocaust Museums, such as *Yad va-Shem* in Israel, in an attempt to ensure that the murder of millions of Jews and others is not forgotten.

DAN COHN-SHERBOK

CHAPTER 59

Branches of Judaism

The majority of Jews throughout the world today are descendants either of the Sephardim or the Ashkenazim. Before being driven from Spain by the Inquisition in 1492, the Sephardim had been closely involved with the Muslim world, enabling them to develop a unique intellectual culture. Sephardic Jews – 'Sepharad' means Spain – created the Ladino language, a mix of Spanish and Hebrew.

The Ashkenazim came from central Europe, mainly Germany and France, and later moved to Poland and Russia. 'Ashkenaz' means the area inhabited by the Ashkenazim, who adhere to *minhag Ashkenaz* – a region that coincides with modern-day Germany, but also extends from France to the Pale of Settlement, the region within which Jews were allowed to reside by Imperial Russia. Ashkenazi Jews developed Yiddish – a mixture of Hebrew and medieval German – as their language and around it produced a culture rich in art, music, and literature. The difference in cultural background between the Ashkenazim and Sephardim is evident in Israel today, where each supports its own chief rabbi.

But the Jews are not a race, and Judaism is not an unchanging institution. Due to intermarriage, conversion, and dispersion among the nations, there has been a branching out over the centuries, and wide cultural differences between Jews have resulted. The difference between the black Falasha Jews of Ethiopia and the Indian Jews of Mexico, for instance, is immense.

In addition to these cultural groupings, several religious branches can be distinguished within Judaism today. Modern Judaism is rooted in rabbinic, or Talmudic, Judaism, and both evolved from biblical Judaism.

ORTHODOX JUDAISM

Orthodox Judaism regards itself as the only true Judaism. During the first half of the nineteenth century it developed into a well-defined movement, seeking to preserve traditional (classical) Judaism against the emerging Reform movement in East Europe.

Orthodox Jews are characterized by a 'Torah-true' approach to life, teaching that God personally and decisively revealed himself, in giving the Torah at Sinai, and that the words of the Torah are therefore divine and hence fully authoritative – the changeless revelation of God's eternal will. Every aspect of the Orthodox Jew's life is to be governed by the commandments (*mitzvot*). Jews are to study the Torah daily, and conform their lives to its propositions and rituals, including the strict rules of *Shabbat* observance, dietary laws, and prayer three times a day. In short, Orthodox Judaism is 'mitzvahcentric'.

At the start of the nineteenth century many East European Jews in rural areas lived in a close-knit community known as a *shtetl*, a stockaded, traditional culture shut off from the secular world. However, as large numbers started to emigrate to the United States, Orthodox leaders such as Rabbi Samson Hirsch (1808–88) encouraged Jews to involve themselves in the contemporary culture of the Western world, pursue secular university education, and develop philosophical thinking. Today, most Orthodox Jews believe adjustment to the modern world is legitimate, so long as it does not conflict with the teachings of the Torah.

Orthodox Jews maintain a high regard for the rabbi as teacher and interpreter of the Torah, and place a strong emphasis upon education, particularly day-schools where traditional learning can be acquired. Most Orthodox Jews are Zionist, supporting the state of Israel, and many hope for a personal messiah: an ideal man who will one day fully redeem Israel, although exactly what is meant by 'ideal' and 'redeem' is the subject of some debate. However few today would accept the divine authority of the Torah, the old test of 'Orthodoxy', and it is not uncommon for Jews to belong to both an Orthodox and a Progressive or Liberal synagogue. The term 'Orthodox' was originally used as a label for traditionalists opposed to radical change; now there are many shades of Orthodoxy, as the energy inspired by the Reform movement influences most Jewish groupings.

REFORM JUDAISM

Reform Judaism had its origins in Germany, where the Enlightenment of the eighteenth century stressed reason and progress. Emancipation in the following century opened the Jewish people to new freedoms, to equal rights as citizens, and to new opportunities to explore secular society. Jews quickly began to adapt to this new age, geared to change, growth, scientific inquiry, and critical evaluation. To meet this move away from Jewishness, Abraham Geiger (1810–74) and others declared that modern people could no longer accept the revelation of the Torah as factual and binding, and encouraged changes in ritual law and worship. Dietary laws were abandoned, prayers were translated from Hebrew into the vernacular, and synagogue worship was changed – the organ was introduced, services shortened, and the 'family pew' replaced segregation of the sexes. Some Jews even began to worship on Sunday rather than *Shabbat*.

In the USA, the Reform movement was led by Isaac Wise (1819–1900), who founded an organization of Reform congregations, and in 1875 set up the Hebrew Union College, the main seminary for training Reform rabbis. While Reform Judaism is one of the most progressive major branches of modern Judaism, active in the area of dialogue between faiths, the smaller Reconstructionist and Renewal movements are more radical in such areas as gender and political activism. Since the 1970s, Hebrew Union College has ordained women rabbis.

Liberal (Reform) Judaism[1] is still evolving – as revelation is seen to be a continuing process – and seeks to keep current with each new generation, using reason and experience to establish the relevance or truth of a proposition. Thus the ethical teachings of the prophets are emphasized rather than the ritual Law. Reform Judaism provides an individualized, non-authoritarian approach to religion; a law is observed, not because God said so, but because it is meaningful to modern religious experience.

Many Jews claim the Reform movement is now the most creative component within Judaism. With younger Jews no longer feeling that Judaism is defined by suffering and persecution, they are exploring the boundaries of cultural experience and convey a sense of expectancy for a new age of Judaism.

CONSERVATIVE JUDAISM

Many European Jews were uncomfortable with the radical changes introduced by Reform Judaism, and as a result Conservative Judaism arose at the end of the nineteenth century, emphasizing the historical elements of the Jewish tradition. As president of the newly-founded Jewish Theological Seminary, Solomon Schechter (1850–1915) led the movement in the USA, stressing commitment to tradition – with adjustments if necessary. Conservative Judaism thus has roots in Orthodoxy and Reform, and combines the ideals of both, preserving traditional Jewish practices, but holding that Jewish law can be reinterpreted in the light of modern views and trends – such as the findings of modern historical criticism.

Conservativism has maintained a strong emphasis on the people of Israel and modern Zionism. Laypeople have considerable influence: some congregations, for instance, permit the use of the organ, while others do not; some emphasize dietary laws, others do not. Conservative Judaism is possibly the largest single Jewish grouping in North America. In Israel and Britain, where it has been a more recent development, it is known by its Hebrew name, *Masorti*.

RECONSTRUCTIONIST JUDAISM

Reconstructionist Judaism is an outgrowth of Conservative Judaism, based on the work of the scholar Mordecai Kaplan (1881–1983), who stressed Judaism as an evolving culture, giving equal importance to religion, ethics, and culture. Reconstructionist Judaism doesn't fit neatly into the traditional/liberal, observant/non observant continuum. Although

---

1 In the UK, there is a difference between Liberal/Progressive Judaism, which is closer to American Reform Judaism, and Reform Judaism, which is somewhat closer to the American Conservative movement.

The Reconstructionist philosophy emphasizes our obligation as Jews to work for social justice and tikkun olam, *the 'repair of the world'. Reconstructionists reject any distinction between 'religious life' and 'real life'.*

A member of the
Jewish Reconstructionist
Congregation, Evanston, Illinois

there are few Reconstructionist groups outside the United States and Israel, the movement has influenced Judaism, contributing to a reappraisal of basic concepts such as God, Israel, and Torah. Since its inception in the late 1960s, Reconstructionism has developed the use of inclusive language, encouraged women to be fully involved in liturgical practice, and accepted people with one Jewish parent as Jewish. Reconstructionists are actively involved in developing liberal Judaism in Israel.

THE HASIDIM

The Hasidim, founded by Baal Shem Tov, have many sects around the world, each led by its own *rebbe*. However, there is – and has been historically – much controversy over whether the Hasidim inappropriately substitute the judgment of the *rebbe* for the laws of Torah.

In some Hasidic groups the men have a distinctive style of dress, including black coats and hats, and wear ear-locks. They have a joyful form of worship, involving song and dance. In the United States, the Lubavitch and Satmar sects are especially influential. Some Hasidim are ultra-Orthodox, living in isolation from the Gentile world. The Renewal Movement, with roots in the 1960s counter-culture, attempts to reinvigorate Judaism, drawing on elements from Jewish mystic, Hasidic, musical, and meditative traditions, and has been criticised by some as 'New Age'.

HUMANISTIC JUDAISM

Humanistic Judaism began in 1965 with the rejection or reinterpretation of the beliefs of traditional Judaism. For example, supernatural beliefs are denied, and the Exodus from Egypt is seen as a myth. Humanistic Jewish worship is very different from traditional worship, and rarely uses the word 'God'. Unlike traditional Judaism, Humanistic Jews 'welcome into the Jewish people all men and women who sincerely desire to share Jewish experience regardless of their ancestry.' The principal institution of Humanistic Judaism is the International Federation of Secular Humanistic Jews.

ULTRA-ORTHODOX JUDAISM

The Haredim, or Ultra-Orthodox Jews, view the total separation of Judaism from the modern world as a religious obligation. Whereas Sephardic Haredim generally support Zionism and the State of Israel, many Ashkenazi Haredim oppose both.

We believe in the value of human reason and in the reality of the world which reason discloses. The natural universe stands on its own, requiring no supernatural intervention. We believe in the value of human existence and in the power of human beings to solve their problems both individually and collectively. Life should be directed to the satisfaction of human needs. Every person is entitled to life, dignity and freedom. We believe in the value of Jewish identity and in the survival of the Jewish people. Jewish history is a human story.

Proclamation stating the ideology and aims of Humanistic Judaism

RECENT DEVELOPMENTS

The collapse of the Soviet Union led to a rapid acceleration of Jewish immigration to Israel. Due to the earlier Soviet restriction of religious freedom, however, many of these immigrants came to Israel severely limited in their understanding and practice of Judaism. Unemployment, housing needs, and political unrest among Israelis and Palestinians created additional hardships associated with return to the Land.

The increased secularization of society has continued to threaten Jewish religious and community life through assimilation and intermarriage. To help counter these and other challenges, Chabad Lubavitch launched a successful programme of outreach towards unaffiliated Jews.

MARVIN WILSON
REVISED BY TIM DOWLEY

CHAPTER 60

Judaism in the Modern World

Jewish communities can be found in most parts of the modern world, which means there are great cultural and social variations as well as religious diversity within Judaism. Out of a worldwide total of around 13 million Jews the largest groupings live in Israel – 5,000,000 or 78.7 per cent of local population – and the USA – 5,700,000 or 2.1 per cent of local population. Although Jews account for no more than 0.25 per cent of the world's population, it would be hard to find another group of people who have had so much influence on the world in so many ways over such a long time. There is little sign of this influence lessening, in spite of the challenges facing Jewish survival. In the technological and scientific developments of the modern age, Jewish knowledge and expertise have a high profile, from medicine and genetic engineering to art and architecture. Jews are also prominent in the worlds of entertainment, law and politics. It is amazing how influence on this scale has been maintained despite the appalling loss of people and centres of learning that took place between 1933 and 1945.

WHO IS A JEW?

This question is hotly debated within contemporary Judaism. The Orthodox insistence that a Jew must be born of a Jewish mother – or convert according to Orthodox criteria – is largely disregarded by Reform Jews, but can lead to painful situations concerning identity and status for partners and children. The Reform view is that a person is a Jew if one parent is Jewish and that person is raised in a Jewish community. Moreover, conversion to Reform Judaism is a much simpler process. However, the term 'Judaism' does not only refer to a religion; more than fifty per cent of all Jews in Israel today call themselves 'secular', and half of the Jews in the USA do not belong to a synagogue or temple. Jews can be described as a 'nation' or 'people' – but the question of whether Judaism is a religion or ethnicity or peoplehood is complex and hotly debated.

> 'Lo alecha ha-mamlacha ligmor,' *says the Mishnah.*
>
> *'It is not incumbent on you to complete the work (of repairing the world), but neither are you free to evade it.'*
>
> Pirkei Avot 2:16

ISRAEL

Since its establishment in 1948, the state of Israel has been the focus of the Jewish world. In this tiny strip of land, only twelve miles wide in places, Jews from more than one hundred cultures mingle. All Jews, inside or outside Israel, feel an obligation to assess their relationship with Israel. Within Israel there are serious tensions between secular, Orthodox, and Ultra-Orthodox Jews concerning their attitudes to it. Some groups of Orthodox Jews do not support the existence of a Jewish state at all, and consider the militarism involved in preserving the state to be a contradiction of fundamental Jewish values.

The Zionist movement, dating back to Theodor Herzl (1860–1904), includes many supporters who prioritize the preservation of the Jewish people over the preservation of the Jewish religion. Herzl's dream was simply to establish a Jewish homeland after centuries of exile.

A common Israeli view, shared by many Jews in the diaspora, is that Israel needs to be strong in order to provide a safe haven for Jews all over the world, to provide a feeling of security and, perhaps even more importantly, hope for the future.

A minority fundamentalist group, *Gush Emunim*, 'Bloc of the Faithful', founded in 1974 in the wake of the

Interior of Eldridge Street Synagogue, Lower East Side, Manhattan, the oldest Eastern European synagogue in the USA.

Yom Kippur War, claims a divine right to the settlement of the West Bank, the Gaza Strip, and the Golan Heights — and sometimes as far as the Euphrates — as part of Israel.

JEWISH RELIGIOUS LIFE

Religious Jews pray and study Torah. They observe the dietary laws, keep the Sabbath and the festivals, and try to apply Jewish ethics in a global context of commerce and business. Jews are keen to observe religious regulations that emphasize the importance of the family and marriage. They are also aware of the responsibilities involved in being members of a community that is international as well as local, including praying together, providing welfare support, sharing in times of sadness and joy, and becoming involved in the cycle of rituals and festivals. In so doing, the religious Jew receives a glimpse of what heaven on earth might be like.

From the first century CE onwards, the rabbinic tradition bonded the Jewish people. Today there are more Jews studying in rabbinical seminaries than at any time since the great Babylonian academies. But following the rabbinic tradition is only one way of being Jewish.

Committed Jews remain faithful because the continuing story of Judaism depends on such commitment. Traditionally, Jews have shared a strong sense that there is a divine purpose for humanity, and that they have a special role in achieving it. The covenantal relationship between the Creator and creation, described in the Torah, means that together God and human beings may embark on the task of repairing or mending the world, *tikkun olam*.

Jews and Judaism have shown an amazing capacity to adapt to changing times and circumstances, while preserving the vital traditions central to the faith — a capacity closely linked to a strong emphasis on interpretation as well as revelation. For many Jews do not view revelation as something that happened solely once and for all in the distant past, but that there are different layers of meaning of Torah that can be rediscovered and interpreted in the light of contemporary contexts and needs.

At the core of Jewish life is an immense store of moral energy. 'Social justice' is much the highest scoring factor that Jews in the United States give as relevant to what being Jewish involves. The restless drive to 'perfect the world under the sovereignty of God'

> To be a Jew means first belonging to the group ... Judaism is an evolving religious civilization.
>
> Mordecai Kaplan

remains after other practices have been abandoned. Judaism puts a high value on the dignity and responsibility of human beings, an emphasis that can provide the stimulus for creative dialogue and shared action between Jews, Muslims, and Christians with regard to the responsible stewardship and management of the world's resources, though there may never be more than an agreement to differ as far as theological issues are concerned.

INTRODUCTION TO WORLD RELIGIONS

DIVERSITY

The Jewish world reflects the pluralistic nature of the wider society in which Jews live. All Jews today contend with conflicting influences. One option is to cut off modern influences as far as possible, and seek refuge in tradition. Another is to abandon Judaism. The path that young Jews are increasingly choosing goes beyond the fractiousness between and within different groups with regard to authority, Torah, the role of women, modernity and cultural change and the state of Israel, and seeks to transform Judaism. But it is a mistake to define movements within modern Judaism as if they were sects or denominations. It is more accurate to use the term 'schools of thought'. There is a saying among Jews, 'Where you have two Jews you will have three opinions.'

THE FUTURE

The continuity of Judaism cannot be taken for granted. People are freer to be Jews than at any other time in history. They are also freer not to be. There is real concern about the continuation of the Jewish faith when in the United States one in two Jews either does not marry or marries a non-Jew. The long and painful history of anti-Semitism has understandably made some people uncertain about wanting their children to be overtly Jewish. There are many examples of people changing their name in order to hide their Jewishness.

JEWISH POPULATION FIGURES BY CONTINENT IN 2004

	Jewish Population
Africa	87,900
Asia	5,047,300
Europe	1,577,000
North America	6,114,500
South America	365,500
Oceania	103,000
Total	13,295,200

A new generation of Jews sometimes express a desire to be free of the burden of memory that has traditionally been the hallmark of being Jewish. In complex, pluralist, and multicultural societies, some argue that Jewish identity has become superfluous. However, Jews and Judaism have an incredible capacity to survive.

There is also today a greater confidence in the continuation of the story that is Judaism than there has been since the Holocaust. Jewish people have managed to outlive a succession of oppressors. At the same time, they have increased the depth and richness of Jewish spirituality. More non-Jews than ever before find inspiration from the study of Judaism, as it has entered the curriculum of institutions of higher learning.

With rising levels of anti-Semitism across the world, the need for education and dialogue is acute. Contrary to many people's perceptions, Judaism combines universalism with the exclusivity of an ethnic religion. Jewish ideas of salvation extend to the non-Jewish world. Neither Christianity nor Islam would be conceivable without Judaism. Since the Holocaust, many Christians have commenced a more positive exploration of their Jewish roots. The monotheistic religions share a distinctive ethical focus that can inspire greater efforts on the part of human beings to work together to perfect the world.

LIZ RAMSEY

QUESTIONS

1. Explain the differences between the religion of the ancient Judeans and rabbinic Judaism.

2. What were the implications for Judaism of the destruction of the Temple in 70 CE?

3. Why was medieval Europe often such an inhospitable place for Jews?

4. Explain the importance of the covenant to Judaism.

5. How important are Maimonides' Thirteen Principles of the Faith for Judaism?

6. Explain the different roles of *Tanakh*, Mishnah, and Talmud in rabbinic Judaism.

7. Why are there such different views within Judaism about the coming of the Messiah?

8. Explain the main differences between Orthodox and Reform Judaism.

9. Why is the state of Israel so important in Judaism today?

10. How is modern Judaism able to contain such diverse views on questions of belief and practice?

FURTHER READING

Barnavi, Elie, ed., *A Historical Atlas of the Jewish People: From the Time of the Patriarchs to the Present*. New York: Knopf, 1992.

Biale, David, ed., *Cultures of the Jews: A New History*. New York: Schocken Books, 2002.

Cesarani, David, *Final Solution: The Fate of the Jews 1933–1949*. Macmillan, 2016.

Friedman, Richard E., *The Bible with Sources Revealed*. San Francisco: Harper, 2003.

Gaster, Theodor H., *The Festivals of the Jewish Year*. New York: William Sloane Associates, 1952.

Newman, Louis I., ed., *The Hasidic Anthology: Tales and Teachings of the Hasidim*. New York: Scribner, 1934.

Schama, Simon, *The Story of the Jews and the Fate of the World*. London: Bodley Head, 2013.

Seltzer, Tobert, *Jewish People, Jewish Thought*. New York: Macmillan 1980.

Steinsaltz, Adin, *The Talmud, the Steinsaltz Edition: A Reference Guide*. New York: Random House, 1989.

Steinsaltz, Adin, *A Guide to Jewish Prayer*. New York: Schocken, 2002.

PART 10
CHRISTIANITY

SUMMARY

With around one third of the world's population as adherents, Christianity is easily its largest religion. This fact, though, belies Christianity's humble origins, as what was essentially a small Jewish sect. For his early followers, Jesus was a Jewish teacher commanding strong loyalty, who provided direction through his preaching and a code for life, but was also more than a mere prophet. Christianity's divorce from Judaism was the result of its acceptance of Jesus himself as the Messiah of Jewish teaching, as the Son of God, and as a sacrifice made by God to redeem his followers from sin. Jesus' message not only supersedes that of the Old Testament in Christianity, but his life also furnishes it with its distinct rituals and festivals: baptism, communion, and, above all, Easter, are all taken from the Gospels, rather than from Jewish tradition.

While the earliest history of Christianity is one of anti-establishment insurgency, a threat to both Jewish and Roman authority, much of its subsequent history is closely bound up with European high politics. Christianity rapidly advanced into Asia and North Africa, and after 324 was officially recognized in the Roman Empire, a development that eventually saw much of the church's life centred on Rome itself. This ancient church subsequently broke up during three schisms that resulted from conflicts over doctrine and authority.

If Christianity today is the world's largest religion, it is also its most diverse. This is in part due to the division of the ancient church, producing distinct Orthodox, Catholic, and Protestant branches, but also due to more recent developments, such as the adaptation of churches in the global South to the needs and cultures of their local communities. In the West, too, older churches have been shaped by their different reactions to social and scientific developments, as well as by the emergence of new trends, such as the Pentecostal and Charismatic movements. The strength of Christianity increasingly lies outside the West, however, and in much of the world it faces competition from other faiths, especially Islam.

CHAPTER 61

A Historical Overview

Christianity rapidly spread beyond its original geographical region of Roman-occupied Palestine into the entire Mediterranean area. Something of this process of expansion is described in the Acts of the Apostles, in the New Testament. For example, it is clear that a Christian presence was already established in Rome itself within fifteen years of the resurrection of Christ. The imperial trade routes made possible the rapid traffic of ideas, as much as merchandise.

THE EARLY CHURCH

Three centres of the Christian church rapidly emerged in the eastern Mediterranean region. The church became a significant presence in its own original heartlands, with Jerusalem emerging as a leading centre of thought and activity. Asia Minor, modern-day Turkey, was already an important area of Christian expansion, as can be seen from the destinations of some of Paul's letters, and the references to the 'seven churches of Asia' in the book of Revelation. This process of expansion in this region continued, with the great imperial city of Constantinople, modern-day Istanbul, becoming a particularly influential centre of mission and political consolidation.

Yet further growth took place to the south, with the important Egyptian city of Alexandria emerging as a stronghold of Christian faith. With this expansion, new debates opened up. While the New Testament deals with the issue of the relationship of Christianity and Judaism, the expansion of Christianity into Greek-speaking regions led to the exploration of the way in which Christianity related to Greek philosophy. Many Christian writers sought to demonstrate, for example, that Christianity brought to fulfilment the great themes of the philosophy of Plato.

Yet this expansion was far from unproblematic. The 'imperial cult', which regarded worship of the Roman emperor as determinative of loyalty to the empire, was prominent in the eastern Mediterranean. Many Christians found themselves penalized for their insistence on worshipping only Christ. The expansion of Christianity regularly triggered off persecutions. These were often local – for example, the Decian persecution of 249–51, which was particularly vicious in North Africa. Christianity was not given official recognition as a 'legitimate religion' by the Roman state until 313, when Constantine, a recent convert, was joint emperor. From that point onwards, Christianity became not merely a recognized faith, but in time the official religion of the Roman state.

This period of Christian history was marked by a series of controversies over the identity of Jesus Christ and the Christian doctrine of God. A series of councils was convened to resolve these differences, and to ensure the unity of the Christian church throughout the empire. The most important of these was the Council of Chalcedon (451), which set out the definitive Christian interpretation of the identity of Jesus Christ as 'true God and true man'.

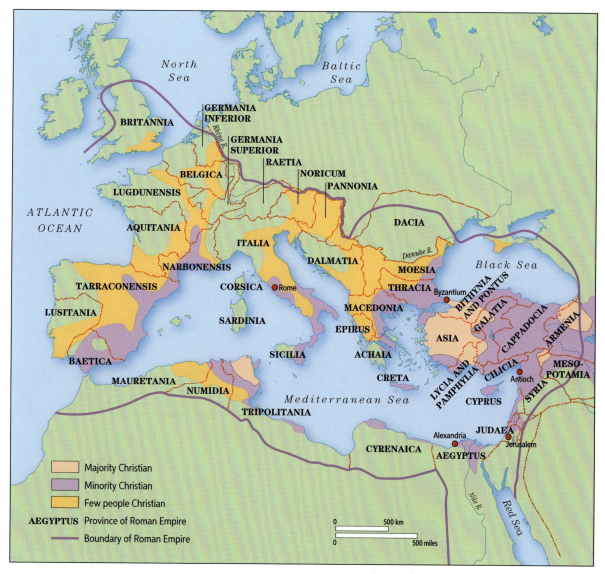

Spread of Christianity about 300 CE

CHRISTIANITY TIMELINE

0	200 CE	400 CE	600 CE	800 CE	1000 CE	1200 CE	1400 CE	1600 CE	1800 CE	2000 CE

c. 30 Death of Jesus

c. 49 Council in Jerusalem debates the status of Jews and Gentiles

c. 65 Death of the apostle Paul

c. 301 Armenian King Tiridates III baptized

312 Constantine's reported vision of the cross

325 First Council of Nicaea

354–430 Augustine of Hippo, pre-eminent theologian

451 Council of Chalcedon

476 Roman Empire falls in the West

529 Benedict establishes first monastery

638 Muslims conquer Jerusalem

842 Orthodox iconoclastic controversy ends

862 Cyril and Methodius' mission to Moravia

1054 Break between Eastern and Western Christianity

1095 Pope Urban II calls for crusade

1099 Crusaders take Jerusalem

1187 End of Latin Kingdom of Jerusalem

c. 1225–74 Thomas Aquinas, author of *Summa Theologiae*

1517 Martin Luther posts his 95 Theses

1534 King Henry VIII becomes head of Church of England

1536 Calvin's *Institutes* published

1563 Council of Trent ends

1738 John Wesley's conversion experience, London

1781 Immanuel Kant's *Critique of Pure Reason*

1830 *Book of Mormon*

1859 Charles Darwin, *On the Origin of Species*

1870 First Vatican Council ends

1910 *The Fundamentals* published in USA

1948 First assembly of the World Council of Churches

1965 Second Vatican Council ends

The fall of the Roman Empire – traditionally dated to 476 – led to widespread insecurity within the Western church. In the East, the church continued to flourish, as the Eastern Empire, based at Constantinople, was largely unaffected by the attacks from northern European invaders which eventually ended Roman power in the West. The removal of Rome as a stabilizing influence, however, gave a new role to the church in the West, and particularly to its monasteries. The founding of the first Benedictine monastery at Monte Cassino around 525 is seen as a landmark in this process. The increasingly important role of the pope as a political force also began to emerge during this period.

The major disruptions within the Roman Empire in the fifth century led to a growing rift between the Western and Eastern churches. Increasing tension over political as much as theological issues led to the 'Great Schism' of 1054. By this stage, the influence of the Eastern Church had extended as far north as Moscow. While the story of Christianity in Eastern Europe at this time is important, most attention focuses on developments in the Western church.

THE MIDDLE AGES AND RENAISSANCE

Christianity underwent a major renaissance in Western Europe during the period 1000–1500. This era – often referred to as the 'Middle Ages' – saw the renewal of church life at every level. It was a period of consolidation of the political and social influence of the church, with the personal authority of the pope to intervene in political disputes of the region reaching unprecedented levels. The form of theology known as 'scholasticism' began to develop around this time, with thirteenth-century writers such as Thomas Aquinas and Duns Scotus achieving new levels of theological sophistication.

Yet scholasticism was not universally acclaimed. The European Renaissance, which began to become a major cultural force in Western Europe during the fourteenth century, emphasized the importance of returning to the roots of Christendom through the simple language and imagery of the New Testament. The humanist movement, linked with the Renaissance, believed it was essential to study the Bible in its original languages, rather than in unreliable Latin translations, such as the Vulgate, thus creating irresistible pressure for new Bible translations. Yet it became clear that some medieval

'Prayer of St Francis'

Lord, make me an instrument of your peace.

Where there is hatred, let me sow love.

Where there is injury, pardon.

Where there is doubt, faith.

Where there is despair, hope.

Where there is darkness, light.

Where there is sadness, joy.

O Divine Master,

grant that I may not so much seek to be consoled, as to console;

to be understood, as to understand;

to be loved, as to love.

For it is in giving that we receive.

It is in pardoning that we are pardoned,

and it is in dying that we are born to Eternal Life.

Attributed to Francis of Assisi (1181–1226)

theological ideas were ultimately based on translation mistakes in the Vulgate. Some form of review of teachings was seen to be necessary, in the light of the new biblical scholarship.

The rise of Islam in the seventh century had a significant impact on Christianity in North Africa and Palestine. However, its influence seemed poised to reach new levels in 1453, when Islamic armies finally managed to take Constantinople, the city widely seen as the gate to Europe. By the early sixteenth century, Islam had become a significant presence in the Balkans, and was poised to enter Austria. Martin Luther (1483–1546) believed it was only a matter of time before Europe became an Islamic sphere of influence. In the event, a series of decisive military defeats limited this influence to the Balkans. By this stage, however, Western Europe was convulsed by new controversies, as the movement we know as the Reformation gained momentum.

REFORMATIONS

The sixteenth century gave rise to a major upheaval within Western Christianity, usually referred to as the Reformation. This movement had its origins in the Renaissance, especially its demand for a return to the original sources of Christianity in the New Testament. Alarmed at what they perceived to be a growing disparity between apostolic and medieval visions of Christianity, individuals such as Martin Luther and Huldrych Zwingli (1484–1531) pressed for reform. For Zwingli, it was the morals and institutions of the church that required reform. Luther, however, judged that a deeper level of reform was required. The teachings of the church had been either distorted or inflated during the Middle Ages, and needed to be brought back into line with Scripture. For Luther, the whole question of how we enter into a right relationship with God – technically referred to as the 'doctrine of justification' – needed radical revision in the light of the biblical witness.

Although the need for reform was widely conceded within the church, such reforming agendas proved intensely controversial. In the end, both Luther and Zwingli found themselves creating reforming communities outside the mainline church, instead of reforming that church from within, as they had hoped. By the time of John Calvin (1509–64) and his reformation of the city of Geneva, Protestantism had emerged as a distinct type of Christianity in its own right, posing a very significant threat to the Catholic Church.

In the late 1540s, the Catholic Church itself began a major process of reformation and renewal, referred to as the Catholic Reformation – previously as the Counter-Reformation. The religious orders were reformed, and many of the beliefs and practices which reformers such as Luther found objectionable were eliminated. Nevertheless, significant differences remained between Protestantism and Catholicism. In many ways, the Reformation debates defined the contours of modern Christianity, and many remain live to this day.

Christianity in Europe about 1650 CE

THE MODERN PERIOD

A period of political uncertainty developed during the eighteenth century, with major implications for the future of Christianity in the West. Growing hostility towards the church in France was one of the contributing causes to the French Revolution of 1789, which saw Christianity publicly displaced from French society. Although the French Revolution did not achieve the permanent removal of Christianity from the nation, it created an atmosphere of instability. Revolutionary movements throughout Europe sought to repeat the successes of their French counterparts, creating serious difficulties for the Catholic Church in many parts of Europe, especially Italy.

Christianity also faced new challenges in the West. During the 1840s, the German philosopher Ludwig Feuerbach (1804–72) argued that the idea of God was simply a projection of the human mind. Karl Marx (1818–83) declared that God was invented by people to console themselves in the face of social and economic hardship: all that was necessary for the elimination of religious belief was the radical alteration of the social conditions which brought it into being in the first place. Sigmund Freud (1856–1939) argued that religion was simply an illusion, a 'wish-fulfilment'. By about 1920, many had concluded that Christianity was intellectually untenable.

By then, other difficulties had arisen. Perhaps the most important of these was the Russian Revolution of 1917, which led to the establishment of the world's first explicitly atheist state. The Soviet Union actively sought to eliminate religion from public and private life, especially during the 1930s. The Allied defeat of Nazi Germany in World War II led to large areas of Eastern Europe coming under Soviet influence, and the state adoption of explicitly anti-religious policies. With the fall of the Berlin wall in 1989, a new openness towards religion developed throughout the former Soviet sphere of influence, with Christianity – especially in its Orthodox forms – and Islam experiencing a major renaissance. Yet by this stage the epicentre of Christianity had moved away from this region altogether.

WORLDWIDE EXPANSION

The sixteenth century saw the beginnings of a process which would have a decisive impact on the shaping of Christianity. During the Middle Ages, Christianity was primarily a European religion. Although it was present in parts of India and the Middle East, its numerical strength was heavily concentrated in Europe. The discovery of the Americas opened up new mission fields, and led to a new interest in spreading the gospel abroad. The Society of Jesus, the 'Jesuits', founded by Ignatius Loyola in 1540, took the lead within the Catholic Church, and sent missionaries to the Americas, India, China, and Japan.

Protestant missionary activity was later in developing. There was a surge of missionary activity from Britain during the closing years of the eighteenth century. The Baptist Missionary Society, founded in 1792 and initially known as 'The Particular Baptist

Society for the Propagation of the Gospel'; the London Missionary Society, founded in 1795, and initially known as 'The Missionary Society'; and the Church Missionary Society, founded in 1799, and originally known as 'The Church Missionary Society for Africa and the East', all played a major role in planting Christianity in Africa, India, and Oceania. American missionary societies also played important roles in establishing Christianity in various regions of the world, especially Korea.

Yet Christianity expanded by other means too. One of the most important was large-scale emigration from Europe to North America, beginning in the late sixteenth century. Initially, the immigrants were primarily Protestant refugees from England; however, these were later joined by Lutherans from Scandinavia, Anabaptists from Germany, Calvinists from Holland, and Catholics from Ireland and Italy.

Today, Christianity is primarily a faith of the developing, rather than developed, world. Although European and American missionaries played a significant role in planting Christianity in regions such as Asia and Africa, these are now largely self-sufficient. The implications of this massive shift from the West to the developing world have yet to be fully explored. It is nevertheless clear that a new phase in the history of the Christian church has begun, with momentous implications for the future.

ALISTER MCGRATH

CHAPTER 62

Jesus

Christianity is founded on the worship of Jesus Christ – 'Jesus the messiah' – as Son of God, the unique self-revelation of God to the human race. At the same time, it remembers this Jesus as a real historical figure, a man of insignificant social standing, who during his life was unknown outside the obscure corner of the Roman Empire where he lived and died.

Almost all we know about Jesus comes from the four accounts of his life, the Gospels of Matthew, Mark, Luke, and John, in the New Testament. The account that follows is based on those Gospels. Although scholars disagree at some points about the historical value of the Gospel records, the following general picture is widely agreed.

MESSIAH

Born just before the death of Herod the Great, King of Judea, around 4 BCE, Jesus lived for a little more than thirty years, scarcely travelling outside Palestine throughout his life.

The Jews were a subject people, who lived either under local princes appointed by the Roman Emperor, or under the direct rule of Rome itself. A priestly party, the Sadducees, accepted Roman rule, to which they owed their influence. The Pharisees, who later became the dominant party, were mostly less concerned with politics, concentrating on the study and application of the Old Testament law. Some stricter Jews, Essenes, opted out of Jewish society, and set up isolated communities – such as Qumran – where they could devote themselves to preserving their religious purity. But many Jews resented Roman rule, and from time to time revolts broke out, leading eventually to the disastrous Jewish War of 66–73 CE.

The Jews had long hoped for 'the day of the Lord', when God would act to save his people. There were several different hopes of a 'messiah', a saviour, whom God would send, and such hopes ran high at the time of Jesus. Some saw the messiah in spiritual terms, as a priestly or prophetic figure; but in popular expectation he was to be a political liberator, and there were occasional messianic movements centred on popular leaders. Galilee was known as fertile ground for such movements.

Jesus was born at Bethlehem, in Judea, but was brought up in Galilee, and most of his public activity was in that region. Judean Jews regarded Galilee as an uncultured, half-pagan area: Jesus' distinctive northern accent would have been conspicuous in Jerusalem. His family was respectable, if not affluent: Jesus was a carpenter, or general builder, an important figure in village life. But Nazareth was an obscure village, and Jesus' background was remote from urban culture.

The traditional location of the birth of Jesus, in a cave beneath the Church of the Nativity, Bethlehem.

BIRTH AND EARLY LIFE

Despite its provincial obscurity, Jesus' family had an honourable pedigree, so his birth took place in King David's town of Bethlehem. Owing to the overcrowding of the town for a Roman census, however, the circumstances were not regal; Luke's account of the baby, cradled in a manger in a stable, visited by shepherds, has become one of the best-known stories in the world.

But, along with the down-to-earth circumstances of his birth, the Gospels record it was far from ordinary. Angels proclaimed him the promised saviour, and it was maintained that he was not conceived by human intercourse, but by the power of God. This bringing together of earthly poverty and obscurity with a miraculous birth is typical of the Gospels' portrait of Jesus, as truly human but also uniquely the Son of God.

Virtually nothing is known of Jesus' life from his infancy until about the age of thirty. He clearly received an education in the Jewish scriptures, presumably in the local synagogue school. However, his upbringing was not academic, but in the practical work of a carpenter. The event that launched Jesus on his public ministry was the mission of his relative, John 'the Baptist', down in Judea. John called Israel to return to God, and baptized those who responded in the River Jordan. He attracted a large following, and Jesus joined him, was baptized, and himself began preaching. When John was put in prison, Jesus moved back to Galilee, and continued to preach in public.

HEALING AND PREACHING

The Gospels summarize Jesus' activity as preaching, teaching, and healing, which is how he would have appeared to his contemporaries during the three years or so of his public ministry. He and his closest followers deliberately adopted a wandering and dependent style of life. They had no permanent home, but moved around as a group, accepting gifts and hospitality when offered. Jesus spoke frequently of the danger of becoming preoccupied with possessions, and called his followers instead to an almost reckless generosity.

As a preacher, Jesus drew large crowds, who followed him constantly. He taught with a vivid simplicity, and with an authority which contrasted sharply with other Jewish religious teachers. We shall consider the content of his preaching later.

Jesus was clearly well known as a healer from the beginning of his public activity. The Gospels record his curing many different types of illness and deformity, usually by a simple word and a touch, sometimes by a word alone. There is no elaborate ritual, nor any search for patients; rather, a power which responded to physical need as he met it. He is also recorded as an exorcist, driving out demons by a word of command. It was apparently as much for his healing power as for his teaching that Jesus was sought out by the Galilean crowds.

The Beatitudes

Happy are those who know they are spiritually poor;

the Kingdom of heaven belongs to them!

Happy are those who mourn;

God will comfort them!

Happy are those who are humble;

they will receive what God has promised!

Happy are those whose greatest desire is to do what God requires;

God will satisfy them fully!

Happy are those who are merciful to others;

God will be merciful to them!

Happy are the pure in heart;

they will see God!

Happy are those who work for peace;

God will call them his children!

Happy are those who are persecuted because they do what God requires;

the Kingdom of heaven belongs to them!

Happy are you when people insult you and persecute you and tell all kinds of evil lies against you because you are my followers.

Be happy and glad, for a great reward is kept for you in heaven. This is how the prophets who lived before you were persecuted.

From Jesus' Sermon on the Mount, Matthew 5:3–12, *Good News Bible*, 1976.

Most of Jesus' recorded miracles are healings, but there are also a number of incidents where he displayed a supernatural control over nature. Again these were in response to actual needs – not mere arbitrary displays of power – as when he multiplied a little food to feed a hungry crowd, or calmed a dangerous storm on the lake by a command. The Gospels present him as one who did not go out of his way to gain a reputation as a miracle-worker, but whose personal authority extended beyond his words to a practical control over nature, which inevitably made a deep impression on those around him.

Like many other Jewish teachers, Jesus quickly gathered a group of committed followers, known as his 'disciples'. He demanded of them an absolute commitment to the ideals he preached, and to himself personally, and a total dependence on God to supply all their needs. They acted as his spokesmen, going out on preaching and healing missions of their own. An inner group of twelve disciples were his constant companions. An increasing amount of time was spent in teaching his disciples privately, preparing them to continue his mission. Jesus told them that he would soon be killed, and expected them to be the focus of the new community created by his work. He taught them to see themselves as distinct from other people, and to make it their aim to win others to be his disciples.

OPPOSITION

While Jesus was, at least at first, popular with the ordinary people of Galilee, he very quickly aroused the opposition of the leaders. His attitude was in many respects unconventional, and he posed a threat to the Jewish religious establishment.

He refused to recognize the barriers that divided people from one another in society. His habit of mixing with the ostracized classes – even of eating with them – earned him the name 'friend of tax-collectors and sinners'. Women held an unconventionally high place in his following, and not all of them were respectable. He seemed to delight in reversing accepted standards, with his slogan: 'The first shall be last, and the last first.'

Jesus did not share the general Jewish disdain for Samaritans – a despised minority of mixed blood – and even made a Samaritan the hero of one of his most famous stories, at the expense of respectable Jewish clerics. Although he seldom travelled outside Jewish territory, Jesus welcomed the faith of a non-Jewish soldier and a Syrian woman, and declared that non-Jews – the Gentiles – would even displace Jews in the kingdom of God. As for economic barriers, Jesus deliberately gave up a secure livelihood, and made no secret of his contempt for affluence. Not surprisingly, the establishment found him uncomfortable.

On religious questions he was equally radical. Jesus clashed with the religious authorities because of his liberal attitude to the observance of the Sabbath, the day of rest, and his declaration that ritual purification mattered less than purity of heart. His bold reinterpretation of the Jewish law consistently moved away from an external observance of rules to a deeper and more demanding ethic. He declared the will of God with a sovereign assurance that cut through centuries of evolving tradition, and set him on a collision course with the scribes and Pharisees, whose heartless legalism he denounced.

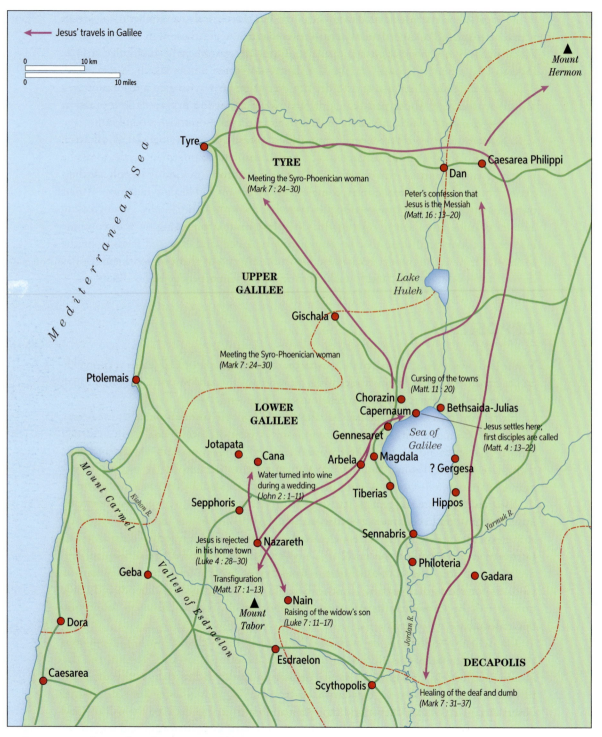

Jesus' Travels and Ministry in Galilee

Legend and labels on map:

→ Jesus' travels in Galilee

0   10 km
0   10 miles

Mediterranean Sea

Tyre

TYRE
Meeting the Syro-Phoenician woman
(Mark 7 : 24–30)

Dan

Caesarea Philippi

Mount Hermon

Peter's confession that
Jesus is the Messiah
(Matt. 16 : 13–20)

**UPPER
GALILEE**

*Lake
Huleh*

Gischala

Meeting the Syro-Phoenician woman
(Mark 7 : 24–30)

Ptolemais

Cursing of the towns
(Matt. 11 : 20)

Chorazin

Capernaum

**LOWER
GALILEE**

Bethsaida-Julias

Gennesaret

*Sea of
Galilee*

Jesus settles here;
first disciples are called
(Matt. 4 : 13–22)

Jotapata

Cana

Arbela

Magdala

? Gergesa

Water turned into wine
during a wedding
(John 2 : 1–11)

Tiberias

Hippos

Mount Carmel

Sepphoris

Kishon R.

Jesus is rejected
in his home town
(Luke 4 : 28–30)

Nazareth

Sennabris

Geba

Valley of Esdraelon

Transfiguration
(Matt. 17 : 1–13)

Philoteria

Gadara

Nain

Raising of the widow's son
(Luke 7 : 11–17)

Dora

*Mount
Tabor*

Jordan R.

Yarmuk R.

DECAPOLIS

Caesarea

Esdraelon

Scythopolis

Healing of the deaf and dumb
(Mark 7 : 31–37)

Nor could he please the Sadducees, the priestly rulers. Jesus taught that the Jewish nation was ripe for God's judgment, and even predicted the destruction of the Temple, on which their national religion was centred. In a symbolic gesture he 'purified' the Temple, by violently expelling the traders whose presence the priests encouraged. Moreover his enthusiastic popular following threatened to upset the delicate balance of the Sadducees' cooperation with Rome. All this did not diminish Jesus' popularity with the ordinary people, who soon came to see him as the expected deliverer, and even on one occasion tried to force him to be their king, in rebellion against Rome. But Jesus made it clear his idea of salvation was not a political one, so gradually his popular following dwindled, as those who wanted a military messiah became disillusioned. Even one of his twelve closest disciples betrayed him in the end, and none of them understood his real purpose until after his death.

Statue of Jesus as the good shepherd.

DEATH AND RESURRECTION

The opposition to Jesus came to its climax at the annual Passover festival in Jerusalem. Jesus rode into the city in a deliberately messianic gesture – though on a peaceable donkey, not a war-horse – and was enthusiastically welcomed by the crowds, who probably expected him now to declare himself their national leader. Instead, he carried out his demonstration against the Temple regime, and engaged in a series of increasingly bitter exchanges with the religious authorities; but he showed no sign of acting against Rome.

Eventually Jesus was arrested by the Jewish leaders, with the help of Judas – his disillusioned disciple – and tried under Jewish law on a charge of blasphemy, because he claimed to be the messiah and Son of God. A death sentence was passed, but a Roman conviction was required to make it effective. This was secured by a charge of sedition, pressed upon the Roman governor, Pontius Pilate, by the religious leaders, with popular support. So, ironically, Jesus – who had forfeited his popular following by his refusal to take up arms against Rome – was executed by Rome as a political rebel, 'the king of the Jews'.

Jesus was executed by crucifixion, the barbaric method reserved by Rome for slaves and rebels. Some highly placed followers obtained his body and buried it in a nearby tomb. The cross has become the symbol of Christianity: in Jesus' death, with all its cruelty and injustice, is the focus of salvation. He had already taught his disciples to see it that way, little as they had yet understood him. But the cross alone could have no such significance; it was the sequel that gave it meaning.

Two days later, his disciples found the tomb was empty. Their failure to understand this is not surprising – there was much about Jesus they had not understood. But the meaning of it was brought home to them by a series of encounters with Jesus himself, alive and real, though no longer bound by the limitations of time and space: he could appear and disappear suddenly even inside a closed room. For a few weeks they met him in a variety of situations, sometimes one or two alone, more often in a larger group. He explained to them again the meaning of his life and death, and the mission that he had entrusted to them. Then he left them, and they began to preach to the world that Jesus – triumphant even over death – was Lord and Saviour. It was the resurrection of Jesus that formed the focus of the earliest Christian preaching; it was the risen Lord whom they worshipped.

> *For God loved the world so much that he gave his only Son, so that everyone who believes in him may not die but have eternal life.*
>
> John 3:16, *Good News Bible.*

WHAT JESUS TAUGHT

The Gospels sum up Jesus' preaching in Galilee in the challenge: 'The time has come; the kingdom of God is near. Repent and believe the good news!' This summary is a convenient framework for setting out some of the main points of his message.

- 'The time has come': The Old Testament pointed forward to God's great work of judgment and salvation, when all Israel's hopes and the promises of God would be fulfilled. Jesus saw his mission as this time of fulfilment. In other words, however little he shared popular ideas of a political deliverer, he saw himself as the messiah, come to save God's people. He called himself the Son of man, echoing a figure in the Old Testament book of Daniel who represented the ultimate deliverance and triumph of the true people of God.
- 'The kingdom of God is near': The kingdom of God – more accurately the 'reign of God'; it is an activity, not a place or a community – is central in Jesus' teaching. It means that God is in control, that his will is done. So he called people to enter God's kingdom, to accept his sovereignty, and to live as his subjects. He taught them to look forward to the day when this kingship of God, already inaugurated by Jesus: 'Yours is the kingdom'; would find its fulfilment when everyone acknowledged God as king: 'Your kingdom come'; when Jesus himself would return in glory, and share the universal and everlasting dominion of his Father.
- 'Repent': Jesus' call was primarily to his own people, Israel. He called them to return to their true loyalty to God. He warned them of God's judgment if they refused. There was an urgency in his appeal, and, as it was increasingly rejected, he spoke of

God calling others to be his people instead. Finally, after his resurrection, he sent his disciples to call all nations into the kingdom of God. God's demands are absolute, and disobedience or disloyalty would not be overlooked.

- 'Believe the good news': Now was the time for deliverance. Jesus preached this not in a political sense, but in terms of the restoration of a true relationship with God. Those who repented would find forgiveness and a new life. And as Jesus predicted his own suffering and death, he saw this as the means of restoration; he was the servant of God whom the Old Testament prophet Isaiah had foretold, 'by whose wounds we are healed'. So he came 'to give his life as a ransom for many', to institute 'the new covenant in my blood', a new people of God redeemed from sin, as Israel had been redeemed from slavery in Egypt, to be God's special people. This was the focus of Jesus' teaching, the call to repentance, to membership of a new people of God, forgiven and restored through his atoning death. His famous ethical teaching takes second place, for it is primarily an ethic for disciples, for those who have thus entered the kingdom of God.

For them life is new. It is focused on God, their king, but also their Father, for Jesus taught his disciples to depend on God with a childlike trust. Their relations with one another were to be those of members of the same family, inspired by an unselfish, uncalculating love. In this new community, many of the world's standards would be reversed, and a concern for material security and advancement would be swallowed up in an overriding longing to see God's kingdom established. It is an other-worldly ethic which has profound this-worldly implications. Jesus expected his disciples to be clearly different, the 'light of the world', showing the world what life was meant to be like. They were to be like God their Father.

WHO WAS JESUS?

Jesus was hailed as a prophet, a man sent by God. In his preaching, teaching, and healing he matched up to that role, and as such he is one of a long and noble sequence of God's people before and since. But Christians believe, and his own life and teaching suggest, that he was much more than that.

In his appeal to Israel there was a clear note of finality. This was not just another prophetic warning, but God's last call. Its rejection would spell the end of Israel as God's

> 'I am the bread of life. He who comes to me will never be hungry.'
>
> 'I am the light of the world. Whoever follows me will have the light of life and will never walk in darkness.'
>
> 'I am the gate for the sheep … whoever comes in by me will be saved.'
>
> 'I am the good shepherd, who is willing to die for the sheep.'
>
> 'I am the resurrection and the life. Whoever believes in me will live, even though he dies; and whoever lives and believes in me will never die.'
>
> 'I am the way, the truth and the life; no one goes to the Father except by me.'
>
> 'I am the vine, and you are the branches. Whoever remains in me, and I in him, will bear much fruit; for you can do nothing without me.'
>
> Jesus' great statements about himself, from John's Gospel, *Good News Bible*.

BRANCHES OF THE CHURCH

The New Testament is witness to the vision that the church should be one – and to the reality that it is not. The history of Christianity since then is, for the most part, a history of fragmentation. Only in the twentieth century were serious attempts made to seek reconciliation between churches separated by centuries of misunderstanding and mistrust. The various branches of the Christian church owe their existence to three historic crises. The first was the splintering of Eastern Catholic Christendom in the fifth century. The second was the so-called 'Great Schism' between East and West, usually dated at 1054, that resulted in the division between 'Catholic' and 'Orthodox' Christianity. The third was the Reformation in the sixteenth century, which, together with its seventeenth- and eighteenth-century aftermath, left as its legacy Protestantism in its various forms. This article deals only with the principal branches of the church as they have emerged in the history of Christianity.

The Eastern Churches

These include the Orthodox Churches, together with those that share with them in a spiritual and cultural ethos that derives from the Byzantine Empire. The church in the East suffered its most serious divisions following the Councils of Ephesus (431) and Chalcedon (451), called to determine the orthodox Christian teaching on the relationship between the deity and the humanity of Christ. The Nestorian Church, centred historically on Persia, and the Monophysite Churches, such as those of Syria, Egypt, and Ethiopia, date from this period.

The final separation of the Eastern Churches from Western Christendom lay in their conflict with Rome over the papal claim to supreme authority, and in their rejection of the Filioque clause, added by the Western church to the original text of the Nicene Creed, in which the Holy Spirit is said to proceed 'from the Son' as well as the Father. The Orthodox Churches extend across Eastern Europe, the Slav nations, and eastern Mediterranean. The patriarchates of Constantinople, Alexandria, Antioch, and Jerusalem are given special honour, but authority belongs to the whole church, whose rich liturgical life and icon-based spirituality is seen as the living embodiment of divine love on earth. It is estimated that there are over 322 million Orthodox Christians today.

The Roman Catholic Church

Numbering around 1,200 million members, the Roman Catholic Church is the largest single Christian grouping. Roman Catholics, or simply 'Catholics', trace their lineal descent from the Western Catholic Church of the Middle Ages. They acknowledge the primacy

---

Ave Maria

Ave Maria, gratia plena,

Dominus tecum.

Benedicta tu in mulieribus,

et benedictus fructus ventris tui, Iesus.

Sancta Maria, Mater Dei,

ora pro nobis peccatoribus,

nunc, et in hora mortis nostrae.

Hail Mary

Hail Mary, full of grace,

the Lord is with thee.

Blessed art thou amongst women

and blessed is the fruit of thy womb, Jesus.

Holy Mary, Mother of God,

pray for us sinners,

now, and in the hour of our death.

One of the most popular Roman Catholic prayers. Of unknown origin, it was incorporated into the liturgy in the 15th century.

---

and authority of the Supreme Pontiff, the bishop of Rome, who is traditionally regarded as Christ's representative, or 'Vicar', on earth, and the successor of St Peter. When speaking with full authority – *ex cathedra* – and defining matters of faith or morals, the pope's utterances are regarded as infallible and binding on Catholics.

The Second Vatican Council (1962–65) resulted in far-reaching reforms, including greater emphasis on the role of bishops acting as an episcopal college, more open relationships with non-Catholic churches, and the simplifying of the liturgy.

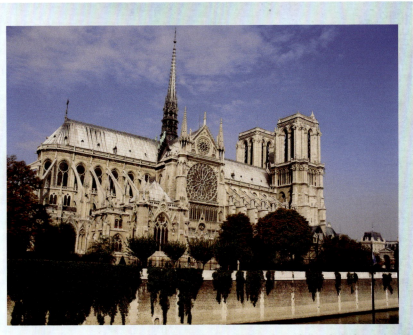

The Cathedral of Notre Dame de Paris, France, built at the peak of medieval European Christendom.

Along with the Orthodox Churches, Roman Catholicism recognizes seven sacraments: baptism, confirmation, marriage, ordination, penance – the sacrament of reconciliation, extreme unction – anointing of the sick, and, at the centre of the sacramental system, the Mass. Especially in developing countries, Roman Catholics are often prominent in supporting the struggles of the oppressed, and in the pursuit of justice and peace generally. In the early twenty-first century the church was shaken by revelations of sexual abuses committed by a number of priests.

Churches of the Protestant Reformation
The Anglican Church
The Anglican communion is a worldwide family of autonomous churches in communion with the Archbishop of Canterbury, who has presidential status amongst the heads of other Anglican Churches. Largely anglophone, its members number around 85 million. The parent Church of England has its roots both in the Celtic Christianity of the earliest Britons, and in the Roman form of the faith brought to England by Augustine of Canterbury (r. 597–604).

The Anglican Church claims to be both Catholic and Reformed, and has adhered to the Catholic threefold ministry of bishops, priests, and deacons, but with a conservatively reformed liturgy. *The Book of Common Prayer* of Archbishop Thomas Cranmer (1489–1556) retained many of the texts of the medieval church, while recasting them in a clearly Protestant direction. Nowadays, Anglicanism is an inclusive church embracing members of at least three persuasions: Anglo-Catholic, Liberal, and Evangelical, and for this reason is often seen as a 'bridge' church between Protestantism, Roman Catholicism, and Orthodoxy.

The Lutheran Churches
These represent the chief Protestant presence in Germany and Scandinavia, as well as being a significant worldwide Christian denomination, which speaks through the Lutheran World Federation. Following the

teaching of the German reformer Martin Luther (1483–1546), the doctrine of justification by faith is its central tenet, embodied in the Augsburg Confession (1530). Some Lutheran Churches have retained the Catholic threefold ministry, while others are more presbyterian or congregational in government. Like Anglicanism, Lutheranism adopted a conservative attitude to liturgy, although the preaching of the sermon has always been central, and music has always played an important part. Lutherans worldwide number around 75 million.

The Reformed Churches

Protestantism in France, Switzerland, the Low Countries, and Scotland at the time of the Reformation shared many of the central tenets of Lutheranism, but following the principles of John Calvin (1509–64), applied them in a more thoroughgoing way. The authority of the Bible is paramount, and the preaching of the Word is central to its liturgy. There are two principal forms of church organization: presbyterian – local churches grouped together under the government of a regional synod of ordained presbyters and lay elders – and congregational – local churches as independent congregations, responsible for their own life and order. Reformed churches have around 75 million members worldwide.

The Free Churches

These all derive from the various churches of the Reformation as a result of movements in subsequent centuries.

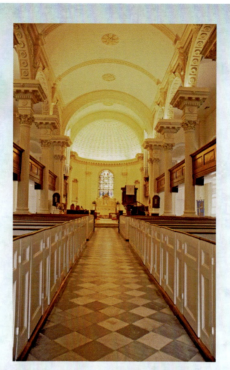

Interior of a traditional American Episcopalian church. It shares many characteristic features with other Protestant churches, with a prominent pulpit and simple altar.

The Baptist Churches are a worldwide family of independent congregations that reject the baptism of infants, claiming baptism is a sign of an adult profession of faith. Worship tends not to follow set liturgical forms. The Southern Baptists of the USA are a particularly influential conservative evangelical grouping. There are around 100 million Baptists across the world.

The Methodist Churches originate in the Evangelical Revival of the eighteenth century, and in the preaching of John Wesley (1703–91). Historically indebted to Anglicanism, which Wesley never renounced, congregational hymn-singing is one of its distinctive contributions to the church at large. Social action is emphasized. Their worldwide number is around 75 million.

The Society of Friends, or Quakers, was founded by George Fox (1624–91). It rejects all liturgical forms – including sacraments – ecclesiastical structures, and definitions of faith. Members meet for silent worship to attend to the 'inner light'. Quakers have a strong commitment to radical involvement in justice and peace issues. They number 400,000 in all.

The Salvation Army was founded by William Booth (1829–1912) as a mission to the poor of London. Now a worldwide movement, it gives equal place to the preaching of the gospel and to social action amongst the needy. Worship is informal and Bible-centred: the sacraments are not observed. Organization is along the lines of the armed forces. There are around 1.1 million Salvationists.

The Pentecostal Churches, numbering around 130 million, amongst them the Assemblies of God, date from the early twentieth century. Charismatic renewal is particularly strong in Latin America and Africa. The gifts of the Spirit, ecstatic experience, healing, and speaking in tongues, are central to church life and worship.

The Charismatic movement

This has profoundly influenced churches in most denominations, including the Roman Catholic Church.

The African Independent, or Initiated, Churches are vigorous and fast growing communities of black Christians for whom the black experience is crucial to their self-understanding. In various degrees, they are influenced by liberation theology, as a people who have known oppression, charismatic renewal, and the indigenous religion of their ancestors. They number around 40 million.

House Churches, or New Churches, are a growing phenomenon within the conservative evangelical movement. 'Restorationists' reject the institutional church with its ordained ministry, returning to what is seen as a New Testament pattern of worship in members' homes. Worship is informal, and often charismatic in style.

The Ecumenical Movement

The Ecumenical Movement, from the Greek *oikoumene*, meaning 'the inhabited world', is the product of the twentieth century. It was increasingly realized that Christian witness in the world is severely compromised by the deep historic divisions between the churches. While organic unity, or even inter-communion, between the churches remains a long way off, the churches now recognize the validity of one another's baptism. The mutual recognition of ministries, especially by Roman Catholics of non-Catholic ministries, remains problematic. All the mainline denominations are publicly committed to the task of reconciliation between Christians.

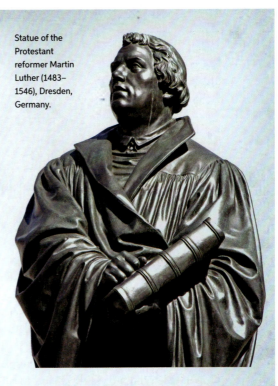

Statue of the Protestant reformer Martin Luther (1483–1546), Dresden, Germany.

The World Council of Churches was constituted in 1948 as a fellowship of churches united in their loyalty to Jesus Christ 'as God and Saviour'. The Council exists to enable the churches to debate matters of common concern, and where possible, to speak and act as one. It has been particularly vigorous – sometimes controversially so – in development work, in education, and in taking up the cause of oppressed minorities. Assemblies of the Council meet every seven years. Councils of churches exist in many places, enabling local congregations to worship, work, and study alongside one another. More formal ecumenical agreements enable sharing of buildings and ministries to take place on a regular basis.

Michael Sadgrove

special people; its acceptance would create a new people of God, in whom all God's purposes would reach their climax.

Statue of *Cristo Redentor* – Christ the Redeemer, at the peak of Corcovado mountain, Rio de Janeiro, Brazil.

The criterion was not only the response to Jesus' message, but the response to Jesus himself. He called for faith in, and loyalty to, himself, and presented himself as the final arbiter of people's destiny. He not only proclaimed forgiveness and salvation: by his own life, suffering, and death he achieved it. He is the messenger – but he is also the heart of the message. He calls people to God, but he is also himself the way to God.

During Jesus' earthly life, his disciples only dimly understood all this, though they understood enough to make them tenaciously loyal to him. But after his resurrection, they quickly came to speak of him as more than just a man, and to worship him as they worshipped his Father. Even during his earthly teaching, Jesus had prepared the way for this, by speaking of himself as the Son of God in a unique sense, and of God as his Father in an exclusive relationship quite different from the sense in which his disciples could use the term:

All things have been committed to me by my Father. No one knows the Son except the Father, and no one knows the Father except the Son and those to whom the Son chooses to reveal him.

The Father and I are one.

John 10:30, *Good News Bible.*

The worship of Jesus the man as the Son of God did not have its origin in some fanciful piety, long after his death, but in the impression he made on his disciples during the three years of his ministry. His resurrection deepened that impression and confirmed it. Without in the least doubting his real humanity, they believed that they had been walking with God.

RICHARD FRANCE

CHAPTER 63

Sacred Writings

The word 'Bible' comes from the Greek *Biblia*, meaning simply 'the Books'. The plural is significant: the Bible is a collection of books written over a period of more than 1000 years, in widely differing cultural and historical situations, and in a rich variety of styles and language. This collection has come to be regarded by Christians as a single unit, 'The Bible', as its books have been recognized as standing apart from other books.

THE OLD TESTAMENT

There are two unequal parts to the Bible. The first, and by far the larger, called by Christians 'the Old Testament', is simply the Hebrew and Aramaic scriptures of Judaism, which present the history and religious thought of the people of God up to the time when Jesus came. Christians have always regarded themselves as the legitimate heirs to the religion of ancient Israel, and so accept the books of the Hebrew Bible as fully 'canonical', or part of scripture. Without them, the specifically Christian scriptures could hardly be understood.

A number of later Jewish works in Greek are also included in Roman Catholic editions of the Old Testament, sometimes distinguished as 'deutero-canonical', of lesser importance than the Hebrew scriptures. Protestant Bibles do not include these works in the Old Testament; but they are sometimes printed after the Old Testament, as a separate section, known as 'the Apocrypha'. Protestant Christians do not accept them as Scripture.

THE NEW TESTAMENT

The specifically Christian books of the Bible, known as 'the New Testament', comprise twenty-seven writings by Christians of the first century CE, mostly quite short. While most of the writers were of Jewish origin, the books are in Greek, which was the common language of the Roman Empire.

They consist firstly of four 'Gospels', setting out from different points of view the life and teaching of Jesus, together with the 'Acts of the Apostles', which is a continuation of the Gospel of Luke telling the story of the first thirty years of Christianity. There are then thirteen letters by Paul, the great missionary leader, to churches and individuals; eight other letters by early Christian leaders; and the 'Revelation of John', a visionary work cast in the mould of Jewish apocalyptic literature.

The New Testament writings, although produced within a relatively short period compared with the many centuries of the writing of the Old Testament, are mixed in style and content; even the literary quality of the Greek varies widely. The different interests and personalities of the writers are clear on even a superficial reading.

THE INSPIRATION OF THE BIBLE

Christians have regarded these varied writings of both the Old and New Testaments as a unity, often called the 'Word of God'. They have spoken of the Bible as 'inspired', meaning not merely that it is great literature, or that it brings spiritual enlightenment, but that it comes from God. But the classic Christian belief is that what they wrote in their own language, and in their own historical setting, was directed by God, so that the result was no less his word than theirs.

So, while the biblical books must be interpreted with proper attention to their background and literary form, what they declare is, Christians believe, God's word to his people. This is why the Bible, for all its variety, is treated by Christians as a unity, progressively revealing not only God's acts, but his mind and will.

> All scripture is God-breathed and is useful for teaching, rebuking, correcting and training in righteousness, so that the man of God may be thoroughly equipped for every good work.
>
> 2 Timothy 3:16,
> New International Version.

THE AUTHORITY OF THE BIBLE

In theory, therefore, all Christians accept the Bible as authoritative, both in guiding their actions and in forming their beliefs. In practice, Christians have differed on this. The Protestant Reformation aimed to restore the Bible to a place of authority above the pronouncements of the leaders of the church and the traditions that had grown up. Within Protestant Christianity, the Enlightenment of the eighteenth century led to a new confidence in human reason as the ultimate guide to truth, and the Bible began to be treated only as a record of human religious development, not as a divine revelation.

> The Holy Scripture is the only sufficient, certain, and infallible rule of all saving knowledge, faith, and obedience.
>
> Second Westminster
> Confession (1677)

Today, while evangelical Christianity accepts the Bible as its supreme authority, more liberal Protestantism questions its importance. In Roman Catholicism, since the Second Vatican Council, there has been a resurgence of interest in the Bible.

RICHARD FRANCE

INTRODUCTION TO WORLD RELIGIONS

CHAPTER 64

Beliefs

The Christian faith is directly descended from the religion of the Jews. At the time of Jesus this had the following characteristics, as taught in the sacred book of the Jews, the Old Testament:

- Belief in the existence of one God (monotheism), the Creator and Lord of the universe, who is sovereign over all.
- Belief in the fact that human beings are made in the image of God, but have rebelled against their Creator, and stand in danger of judgment.
- Belief that God, who is the righteous judge, is also gracious and merciful. He has provided a way for people to be set free from judgment, by the penitent offering of sacrifices.
- Belief that God revealed himself to the nation of Israel and called them to be his people.
- Belief that God would some day establish his rule in a sinful world, setting his people free from their enemies, and appointing his chosen agent, the messiah, to rule over them for ever.
- The practice of a moral life, under the guidance of the Law given in the Old Testament; the maintenance of a religious ritual based on the Temple and involving the offering of sacrifice.

THE SIGNIFICANCE OF JESUS

These beliefs were decisively affected by the coming of Jesus, his followers' confident reports of his resurrection from the dead, and their receiving of the gift of the Spirit of God at Pentecost. There remained a basic similarity with the Jewish religion, but there were some fundamental changes.

The most important of these changes was due to the Christian understanding of Jesus. From a very early date, the Christians began to realize that the Jewish hope of God's chosen agent coming to set up his rule had been fulfilled in Jesus. He was the messiah whom the Jews awaited. It is the rejection of this identification by Jews that constitutes

> *I believe Christ's teaching; and this is what I believe. I believe that my welfare in the world will only be possible when all men fulfil Christ's teaching.*
>
> Leo Tolstoy, *What I Believe* (1884).

the decisive difference between them and Christians. For Christians, the coming of Jesus means that God's future plan, announced in the Old Testament, has already begun to happen. God's rule is being established in a new way.

But the way in which it has happened is different from what the Jews had come to expect. They thought that God's rule would be achieved by the military overthrow of their enemies, and would lead to their own establishment as the dominant nation. But Jesus did not speak out against the external enemies of the Jews; rather, he proclaimed the need of everybody for a change of heart. The rule of God advances by the conversion of individuals to a new way of life, and the way of violent revolution is firmly rejected.

THE DEATH OF JESUS

God's action in Jesus was also seen as including sacrifice. The death of Jesus was understood as a means of cancelling sin, provided by God himself, and displaying his love for sinners. Sinfulness must inevitably bring separation from God, or death. But Jesus died this death himself. A variety of pictures – drawn from the slave market, the law court, the Temple, and personal relationships – are used to express the fundamental belief that the death of Jesus is the means of reconciling God and human beings, and freeing them from the fear of judgment.

The effect of this understanding was to bring to an end the system of animal sacrifices, which were understood as pictures pointing forward to the spiritual sacrifice of Jesus, and now made obsolete by the offering of the perfect sacrifice. Christian worship was no longer a matter of offerings in a temple; rather it was the expression of gratitude to God for his provision of a sacrifice.

At the same time, the coming of Jesus was seen as bringing to an end the ritual Law of the Jews which regulated the Temple worship and a host of other matters. The ethical principles which lay behind the Law, seen especially in the Ten Commandments, were not abolished, but the detailed ritual and other observances were no longer needed.

In practice, the Jews had come to regard the observance of the Law in minute detail as the means of gaining and maintaining a good relationship with God and obtaining his favour. It was Paul who insisted that God's favour could not be gained by keeping the Law: all have sinned and come short of God's glory. So the proper relationship of human beings with God can only be that of faith, the grateful and obedient trust which comes to God on the basis of what he has done, in contrast to the approach of works, which insists that the individual must do something to merit God's favour.

Though Christian worship abandoned the Temple, it was deeply influenced by the synagogue, the Jewish meeting-house in which the teaching of the Law was central. But the rejection of the Law as the means of salvation led to a shift in the understanding of the Old Testament. Interest turned more to its prophetic character, as a book which looked forward to the coming of Jesus, and it was increasingly studied for what it taught about him. At the same time, other writings were increasingly placed alongside it as equally inspired and authoritative scriptures. The writings of the infant church, the letters written by its leaders, and the accounts of the actions and preaching of Jesus in the Gospels, were seen as a corpus of scriptures alongside the Old Testament. The whole collection became the Bible of the Christian church.

The recognition that observance of the Jewish Law was no longer binding on Christians, together with the simple fact that almost from the beginning non-Jews – the Gentiles – were attracted by the message, led quickly to the development of a community composed of both Jews and non-Jews. Despite initial uncertainties, it was recognized that non-Jews did not need to adopt the practices of the Jewish Law, especially circumcision and the observance of Jewish holy days, in order to become Christians. Christianity, which might have remained a Jewish sect, was thus poised to become a world faith, open to everyone on the basis of belief in Jesus.

The characteristic rites of the new faith, which roughly parallel the Jewish rite of circumcision and the festival of the Passover – which celebrated the deliverance of the people of Israel from slavery in Egypt – were baptism and the Lord's Supper. Baptism was a ritual washing with water which signified cleansing from sin, the reception of God's Spirit, the dedication of the baptized persons to God, and their entry into the new people of God. The Lord's Supper, or Eucharist – 'thanksgiving' – was a token meal of bread and wine: elements used by Jesus at his Last Supper before his death to point to his self-sacrifice and the shedding of his blood to open up a new covenant or agreement between God and his people.

THE RESURRECTION OF JESUS

> *All things are possible to him that believes, more to him that hopes, even more to him that loves, and more still to him that practises and perseveres in these three virtues.*
>
> Brother Lawrence, *The Practice of the Presence of God* (1691)

Alongside the death of Jesus, belief in his resurrection was the crucial thing for the development of Christianity. Christians saw it as God's vindication of Jesus, after he had been rejected by the Jewish leaders and put to death. It was the confirmation of his claims to be God's agent, and above all it demonstrated that he was triumphant over the power of sin and death. The resurrection was seen as the decisive stage in the ascent of Jesus to share the throne of God in heaven – to use the picture-language of the New Testament. This belief had several important consequences.

- First, it confirmed the Christian belief that God would act again in history through the return of Jesus at the end of the world. The exaltation of Jesus meant that he was the agent appointed by God to carry out final judgment and to bring in God's eternal reign in peace and justice.
- Second, it led to the conviction that Jesus was to be seen as divine. Already in his lifetime, he had displayed a unique consciousness that he was God's Son, and that God was his Father. After the resurrection, Christians recognized increasingly that all the functions of God were exercised through Jesus, and that he shared in the rule of God. He was to be regarded as the Son of God, who had 'come down' into the world in human form and then 'ascended' to be with God. The consequences of this belief were shattering: Jews and others who believed that there was one

God could not accept the Christian claim. Christians, for their part, had to revise their ideas about God, and

The ancient Christian monastery of Mar Saba is located in the Judean Hills, near Bethlehem, Israel.

recognize that, though God is one, alongside the Father there was also the Son; they were each divine in nature, yet in such a way that the Son could be regarded as dependent on the Father. The earthly Jesus was the Son of God made flesh – 'incarnate' – become a human being.

- Third, now that Jesus has been exalted to heaven, he remains active and living, in the same way as the Father is the living God. Sharing the status of the Father, Jesus is now the Lord, so that the relation of the Christian to him is not simply one of belief and trust, but also of obedience and commitment. To be a Christian is to make the confession 'Jesus Christ is Lord', a confession that he is both the Lord whom the believer obeys, and also the one to whom the whole universe will one day bow the knee.

Such faith and obedience is part of a spiritual relationship between Christians and Jesus. Christians can be said to be united with Jesus, a whole variety of metaphors from the language of personal relationships being used to express the reality of this link. The new life which they begin when they believe in Jesus is the reproduction of the life of Jesus in them. They die to their old way of life, and rise again to a new God-centred and divinely inspired life, in the same way as Jesus died and rose again by the power of God. The Christian community is a vast organism, or body, through which the spiritual life of Christ flows.

THE HOLY SPIRIT AND THE BIRTH OF THE CHURCH

After the resurrection came the third decisive event that determined the character of Christianity. The Jews already believed in the communication of God's power and guidance to particular individuals – especially the prophets – by the activity of the divine Spirit. The birthday of the church is reckoned from the day of Pentecost, when all the believers in Jesus became conscious of the gift of the Spirit given to each one personally. So universal is the gift, that a Christian can be defined as a person who has received the gift of the Spirit. The initial experience can be spoken of as a second, spiritual birth, bringing the new life of Jesus to the believer. The Spirit works in the Christian community by giving different abilities to different individuals, to enable them to lead and help the church as a whole. He also acts in the life of each Christian, to foster the qualities of love and freedom from sin which were seen in Jesus himself.

Thus the Spirit can be seen as the personal agent of God in the lives of individuals and the Christian community. This meant a further development in the understanding of God. The Spirit was recognized as being divine in the same way as the Father and the Son, so that the Christian concept of God had to recognize a fundamental 'three-ness' or 'Trinity' in the nature of God as one being who exists in three persons. Thus the understanding of God as Trinity, which in this form is peculiar to Christianity and sharply differentiates it from other religions in the same Judaic tradition – Judaism and Islam – sums up the distinctive and vital elements in Christian faith.

Christian belief takes the holiness and judgment of a righteous God seriously. This is seen in the character of the Christian message, which includes the warning that all people are sinners who have rebelled against God and therefore face judgment. It is only against this background that the Christian message makes sense as 'gospel', good news that the same God is merciful and longs for the salvation of all, and has provided the way of forgiveness and life in Jesus. Thus the gospel presents everyone with the alternatives of judgment or life.

VARIETY AND DIFFICULTY

The Christian message has naturally been subject to fresh thinking and reformulation down the ages, as theologians have tried to express the biblical teaching in ways that are philosophically acceptable and logically coherent. It is not surprising that there have been differences in understanding in different times and places, and that some expressions of Christianity have veered away from the biblical witness.

The doctrines of the Trinity and the incarnation have caused particular difficulty. Since the nature of God, who is infinite, lies beyond the scope of our finite understanding, attempts to explain his nature can lead to misunderstandings and one-sided statements. This has led to a variety of attempts to simplify the doctrine of God, by restricting full divinity to the Father, or by regarding the three persons simply as three different aspects of one God. Some theologians have found it hard to believe that Jesus is the eternal

Son of God, and sometimes he has been regarded as a separate, subordinate being. The tendency in modern times has been to deny that God could truly be united with a human being in one person, and to say that Jesus was a good man who possessed the divine Spirit to an unusual degree, or that true humanity is the same thing as divinity. Another tendency has been to regard the Spirit as less than a full person.

The Christian understanding of the work of Jesus has also been the cause of difficulty. Some Christians have denied that any sort of action is necessary to enable God to forgive sins, and have seen in the death of Jesus nothing more than a demonstration of supreme love. Others have carried the idea of sacrifice over into Christian worship, and seen the Lord's Supper as some kind of repetition of Christ's sacrifice on the cross.

At times there have been tendencies to legalism: the need to do good works in order to merit salvation has been taught. The church has on occasions claimed an authority almost equal to that of God, and developed a hierarchy, or set of graded authorities, surrounded by pomp and prestige. At other times, the doctrine of God as judge has been watered down, and replaced by a belief that God will ultimately save everyone, no matter how they have behaved in this life.

Over against such views, mainline Christianity affirms that Christian teaching must be based on the Bible, and any developments in understanding must be consistent with its supremely authoritative position as the written form of God's revelation of himself and his will for his people. It therefore insists that people must recognize that the nature of God is a complex unity in which there are three

The Nicene Creed

We believe in one God, the Father, the Almighty, maker of heaven and earth, of all that is, seen and unseen.

We believe in one Lord, Jesus Christ, the only Son of God, eternally begotten of the Father, God from God, Light from Light, true God from true God, begotten, not made, of one Being with the Father; through him all things were made.

For us and for our salvation he came down from heaven, was incarnate from the Holy Spirit and the Virgin Mary, and was made man.
For our sake he was crucified under Pontius Pilate; he suffered death and was buried.

On the third day he rose again in accordance with the Scriptures;

he ascended into heaven and is seated at the right hand of the Father.

He will come again in glory to judge the living and the dead,
and his kingdom will have no end.

We believe in the Holy Spirit, the Lord, the giver of life,
who proceeds from the Father and the Son,

who with the Father and the Son is worshipped and glorified,
who has spoken through the prophets.

We believe in one holy catholic and apostolic Church.

We acknowledge one baptism for the forgiveness of sins.

We look for the resurrection of the dead, and the life of the world to come. Amen.

persons, Father, Son, and Spirit, and that the Son became a human being in the person of Jesus. In the life and death of Jesus is seen the activity of the one God entering into the sinful plight of the world and bearing its painful consequences, so that believers might be delivered from its guilt and its power, and share in the life of God himself.

Within this basic framework of belief, as summed up in the historic creeds and confessions of the church, there is room for confession of people's inability to understand God fully, and there can be variety of understanding over matters that are of lesser significance, as the existence of the various denominations of the church shows. At all times Christians need to go back to the Bible and to test their beliefs and their practice by its teaching. Jesus himself – the Christ of the Bible and of experience – is believed to be far greater than any human formulation of dogma or teaching about him.

I. HOWARD MARSHALL

CHAPTER 65

Worship and Festivals

All institutions live by their rituals, and religious institutions are no exception. The New Testament is, from one standpoint, the history of the religious life – including the 'cultic', or worshipping, life – of the people of God: its pages record the beginnings of Christian worship.

It is recorded in the book of Acts that the infant church began a rhythm of church life which, in outline, is what would be called 'worship' today – indeed, a modern pattern for a communion service might well have the same elements. The believers gathered for the apostles' teaching, for prayer, fellowship, and 'the breaking of bread'.

EUCHARIST

The Lord's Supper, Communion, or Eucharist was the distinctive event of Christian worship. Jesus himself commanded it, and there is reason to think that the church observed it as a weekly – sometimes a daily – event from the outset. Originally, the commemoration of Jesus, especially his death and resurrection, which the 'sacramental' bread and wine signified, was held within the context of a larger meal, called an *agape*, or love-feast. But for various reasons, this context fell away in the first hundred and fifty years after the resurrection, and a ritual meal of solely bread and wine remained.

BAPTISM

The New Testament also describes what has been called the Christian initiation rite, baptism. This was certainly a means for the new convert to enter the life of the church; but in sharp distinction to contemporary mystery religions, it was open and simple. Baptism was a public 'washing', identifying the believer and his household with the death and rising again of Jesus.

Today, churches which are Baptist in conviction hold that this should only take place on confession of personal faith, at an age appropriate for the confession to be credible as the candidate's own. Others baptize not only adults and others able to confess the faith personally, but also young children and newborn infants in believing households. The intention is that such infants and children should be brought up as Christians, but they are usually expected to make a personal profession of faith at 'confirmation', or a similar rite, at a mature age.

There is other evidence in the New Testament of early church practice. Psalms and hymns were sung. To express corporate solidarity with missionaries, elders, or deacons serving the church, there was 'laying on of hands' at their commissioning. The sick were anointed and prayer made for their recovery. Money was collected for other, poorer churches. The 'ministry' of the church was divided amongst those who had the 'gifts of God's Spirit' for both practical and spiritual leadership.

There seems to have been no such concept as 'having a service'. The 'business' part of church life, such as organizing for the care of widows or the relief of famine, was all bound up with the 'worship' part, of praying, singing, and teaching.

LITURGY AND LEADERSHIP

In the post-apostolic years, patterns gradually settled down, and a clear structure of leadership emerged, in which the bishop would normally preside over the worship of the local church. Bishops wrote down for themselves the great thanksgiving prayer which they uttered over the bread and wine of communion, and these 'eucharistic prayers' began to be used regularly, and over wide areas, as others copied them.

As congregations grew, they sometimes overflowed from the homes in which they originally met. Groups started – occasionally even in times of persecution – to put up special buildings for worship. They produced an ever more detailed pattern of the church's year – not only keeping the 'week' of creation, though making the first day of the week holy in place of the seventh, but also keeping annual commemorations: first of all the Passover – when Jesus had died and risen – then – when the Spirit had come – and finally Christmas – celebrating Christ's birth – and the 'death day' of the various martyrs.

The Peace of Constantine, or Peace of the Church (313 CE), gave a new tolerance to Christians to worship freely, and also boosted church building. The assimilation of church and state that followed not only encouraged the use of pagan festivals for Christian commemorations – as happened with Christmas – but also started to shape church organization on the lines of the official civic structures. Whole communities were baptized, and the Western concept of 'Christendom' was born. Later, the natural conservatism of the followers of any institution which observes rituals ensured that Latin remained in use rather than the language of everyday speech, that fourth-century garments remained in use by those who led the worship – even though fashions changed for other uses – and that church building attracted the energies of architects and builders whilst other civic buildings were neglected.

In many ways the Eastern Orthodox Churches have remained closer than any other to the spirit of the fourth and fifth centuries. Generations of a minority position have built

Festivals of Christianity

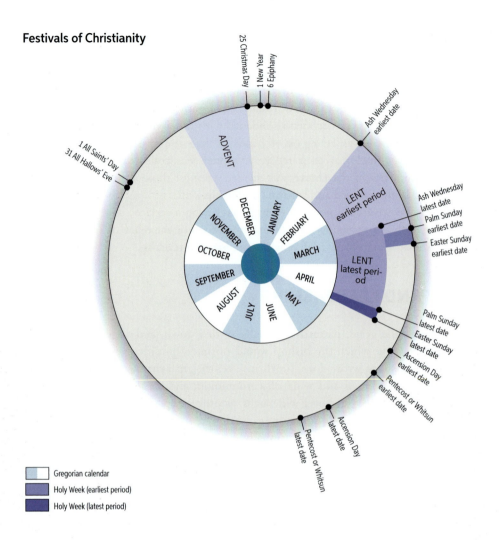

Gregorian calendar

Holy Week (earliest period)

Holy Week (latest period)

up a great regard for tradition and its conservation. The East has never had a Reformation or any equivalent of the Roman Catholic Second Vatican Council.

In the Middle Ages in the Western church, the role of the clergy became much more dominant. Celibacy added to the mystique of the clergy, who alone took an active part in worship. The concept of their special – indeed miraculous – power to transform the bread and wine into the body and blood of Christ gave them the functions of a priesthood. The part of ordinary believers was to attend Mass and to adore the presence of Christ. The people could not understand the Latin used for the Bible readings and prayers, nor did they receive communion, except at Easter, and then – from the late thirteenth century onwards – only the bread.

REFORM

The sixteenth-century Reformation, which took a stand against these perceived abuses, involved the return to God's Word written in the Bible, and a swing in ritual away from drama, colour, and movement to a word-centredness, emphasizing intelligibility and an understanding of doctrine. The reformers themselves often strove to bring the celebration of communion into the centre of church life, but the long-standing habits of their congregations defeated them. Weekly worship in most Protestant churches focused on the sermon, and in the Lutheran churches there was a growth of hymn-singing to accompany services of the Word and of prayers. The Church of England adopted a sober Prayer Book routine, in which the daily round of Bible readings, psalms, and prayers took on more importance than preaching.

The Reformation also gave birth to distinctive traditions. The Anabaptists, for example, included those who not only rejected infant baptism, but also gave voice to their emotions in worship, expressing personal piety in prayer in gatherings 'led by

The elaborate interior of St Paul's Anglican Cathedral, London, England.

the Spirit'. And in the seventeenth century the Quakers, originally quite literally, 'quaked' before God in worship.

A big change started to affect English-speaking Protestantism in the eighteenth century. The Evangelical Revival, which gave birth to Methodism, was characterized by enthusiastic hymn-singing. The hymns were objective in their rich doctrinal content, but also expressed emotions towards God. In this revival, old metrical psalters were swept aside, and the hymns of Isaac Watts and John and Charles Wesley started to take their place. Also, the Lord's Supper was more frequently celebrated.

Hymns apart, Protestantism has tended to be like Roman Catholicism, in that its worship is usually dominated by the minister or leader, and in its solemnity: for the congregation, religion is not only passive, but also serious. But in the second half of the twentieth century, a 'liturgical movement' among both Catholics and Protestants began to strive for just those ends which seem so often to have been missed – active participation by the whole congregation, understandable services, and a genuine building up of the fellowship of the body of Christ.

In the Church of Rome, this led in 1962–65 to the Second Vatican Council's reforms of the liturgy, including the admission of local languages into worship, after 1600 years of Latin. The spill over from this movement into Protestantism, along with other shifts of conviction, led to a new emphasis on the corporateness of the sacrament, and on lay participation. Many denominations gained a new sense that worship might be more than a sermon with some formal preliminaries.

As a direct result of this new openness in the Church of Rome there were many doctrinal conversations designed to clear away misunderstandings. In the area of worship, the Anglican/Roman Catholic International Commission led in 1971 to an agreed statement on the Eucharist, or holy communion. The great multilateral convergence about worship has been precipitated through the World Council of Churches' Faith and Order report, *Baptism, Eucharist and Ministry* (1982), to which churches all over the world responded in the decade following.

PENTECOSTALISM

There have always been more radical movements. The twentieth century, for instance, saw the rise of the Pentecostal denominations. These are 'Spirit-directed' rather than 'Word-directed', and the characteristic expression in worship involves a full release of feelings, a free use of body movements, and an openness to contributions – not always, but quite often, 'tongues', 'interpretation of tongues', and 'prophecies' – from all the worshippers. 'Ministries of healing' are also widely practised within public worship. In South America, for instance, Pentecostalism is the main alternative to Roman Catholicism.

A parallel, indeed related, movement has been the 'charismatic' movement, often initially called 'Neo-Pentecostalist'; here Pentecostalism, instead of separating from the historic churches, has found a strong home within the 'mainline' Protestant denominations, and even in the Church of Rome.

TODAY

The religious face of the earth is changing. Eastern Orthodoxy has resurfaced in Russia and other Eastern European nations since the collapse of Communism – whilst Islam and Eastern religions have come, largely by migration, into Western nations.

Christianity is once again in a missionary situation in the West, as Christendom fades into secularism. But the various Western forms of Christianity are not now confined to the West. Young churches flourish in Asia, Africa, and elsewhere, varying in their worship from being as traditional as the Western churches from which they sprang, to the use of their genuine freedom to be culturally relevant to their contexts, frequently showing a freshness and liveliness hard to find in Western historic churches.

COLIN BUCHANAN

I AM A CHRISTIAN

I am twenty-seven years old and live in Memphis, Tennessee, USA. My wife Emily and I have a six-month-old boy named Noah. We are members of an Evangelical Presbyterian congregation.

I was raised as a Christian in a family that took the faith seriously. I went to a Christian private school until I was fourteen. At home I was taught to read the Bible daily. I enjoyed reading it – especially the Old Testament books of Proverbs and Psalms – and read it in its entirety before the age of thirteen. My sister and I were raised on Bible stories, right behaviour, and respect for our parents and others. More than that, we were encouraged to seek God on our own. My parents held, as I do now, that beliefs must be heartfelt. A relationship with God is personal and must be freely entered into. Although instruction and example guided me in my formative years, my own public profession of faith and a personal prayer of surrender, forgiveness, and acceptance seemed to demarcate the beginning of my individual life of faith. It was then, and remains today, a life I base on the fact that God is perfect, I'm not, and Jesus makes up that infinite difference.

I feel confident in my personal relationship with Jesus, who I believe to be Lord and God, and I am continually trying to bring every element of my life under God's authority. This means, with the help of God's Spirit, continually working to understand the Bible and live by its principles, bringing my desires in line with God's guidelines, which I believe are revealed in the Bible. My aim is to live a life of gratitude for the gracious love God has shown me, living in the peace and joy that comes from knowing I am loved and accepted by my maker. I've sometimes tried to live by ideas that run contrary to what I believe the Bible teaches and, frankly, have wound up hurting myself and others.

My practice of faith is not very ceremonial or ritualistic. For me, faith is more about believing and practising what the Bible teaches. I believe Christianity is about a relationship with Jesus as a personal saviour, lord, and friend. One of my guiding principles is Jesus' commandment to love others in the same way that he has loved us. For example, after college I spent four years teaching and mentoring inner city youths. My wife and I currently live with her parents so that she can help care for her mother, who is paralysed. These experiences have taught how difficult such love and commitment can be. Following Jesus has also helped me to respect others, learn from them, and seek ways to increase their health and well-being.

Jesus' example of love has led my wife and me to tithe our earnings, sharing ten per cent of our income every month with our church and others. That said, we understand ten per cent to be a benchmark, and seek to give more. For example, having won some money on a game show, we felt strongly that at least half of it should be donated to a relief fund. Loving others means making sure that whatever I do in life – including my occupation and all other activities – I do for God's glory and the benefit of others, not primarily for my own gain, reputation, or personal satisfaction.

Because God loves the whole world, and because a person's greatest good is found in a relationship with Jesus, I feel obliged and privileged to share Jesus with believers and unbelievers, always being sensitive to the needs and rights of others.

The fact that my wife and I were both Christians was of paramount importance to us in our decision to marry, and also very important to our families. Having said that, the marriage was not arranged. Our parents were not involved in the decision-making process. However, I did formally ask my wife's father for her hand in marriage. Following this, we received the blessing and encouragement of both our families. My wife and I take our relationship of love to each other and to God seriously. We pray together frequently, discuss the Bible, and talk honestly as partners on a shared journey, never making big decisions without first seeking God's will.

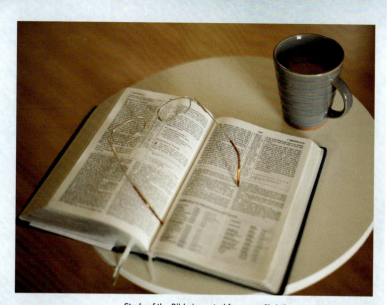

Study of the Bible is central for many Christians.

One of the most important parts of being a follower of Jesus is living in community with other Christians. I feel enormously privileged and grateful to be part of the large, global Christian family – imperfect, to be sure, but a real family nonetheless. The main gathering of our local branch is the church service on Sunday morning, which always includes thanksgiving for what God has done, prayers of petition and confession, hymns of worship, statements of belief about God and salvation, and a talk/sermon on a passage from the Bible.

Sunday is a special day to us, when we celebrate a day of rest and worship. It is the Lord's Day, a day of the week that reminds us of Jesus' resurrection. Other important celebrations are Christmas, when we celebrate the event of God becoming human in the person of Jesus, and Easter, when we remember Jesus' death on a cross for sinners and his subsequent victory over death and evil in his resurrection from the dead.

Since our church is quite large, we break down into groups for social and educational purposes, meeting on Sundays and during the week. Our group consists of newly-married couples, and within this group there are smaller 'mentor groups' which meet for intimate conversation, prayer, and Bible study. Whereas the larger groups are led by pastors, the smaller group is led by an older couple with more wisdom and experience in life than we possess. These groups and leaders are important to us. I always pray before making important decisions, and seek counsel from my group leaders, pastors, and peers.

Finally, the heart of my religion and religious experience can be summed up in the word 'love'. I celebrate the love God has for me and others, and I love God in return. My deep desire is that my love for Jesus and his love for me and others will be evident in my life in all places and at all times.

Jason Hood

CHAPTER 66

Family and Society

Jesus' teaching can be characterized as 'individualist' and 'universalist', insofar as it was directed to the smallest and the largest units of society – to the individual and to a universal 'kingdom'. In the subsequent history of Christianity, however, concern often shifted towards institutions that were intermediate between the individual and the universal, most notably the church and the family.

'BODY OF CHRIST'

In earliest Christianity the embryonic institution of the church appears to be of greater concern to Christian writers and leaders than the family. For Paul, for example, it is the church rather than the family that constitutes the 'body of Christ', and which has the stronger claim on loyalty. Not that existing family ties should be disrupted, but Paul counsels those who are not married to remain single, in order to devote themselves fully to Christ and his church. The growth of an ascetic emphasis in early Christianity served to confirm his approach. Many early Christian writers counsel against marriage, sexual intercourse, children, and family as distractions from the higher purpose of dedicating one's life to the service of God. After all, had not Jesus himself turned his back on family?

But not all early Christians were ascetics, and the growth of Christianity seems to have owed much to its ability to win over married householders. Already in the New Testament Pastoral Epistles (1 and 2 Timothy, Titus), we see the embracing of 'household codes' that counsel orderly obedience of slaves to masters, children to parents, and wives to husbands. As respectable Roman families increasingly joined the church after the conversion of the Emperor Constantine (c. 274–337), the view that family life constituted an inferior, even an ungodly, way of life became harder to sustain. Although he shared much of the ascetic sensibility, Augustine of Hippo (354–430) devoted considerable energy to a pioneering theological defence of marriage and the family as an entirely acceptable way of life for Christians. So long as sex and marriage were used instrumentally, for the begetting of children, he argued, they were acceptable in God's eyes.

THE DIGNITY OF THE FAMILY

Yet the family continued to be considered inferior, and subordinate to church and monastery, in Christian teaching right through the Middle Ages. It was the Protestant Reformation of the sixteenth century that did most to challenge this view, degrading monasticism and upgrading the family. Instead of viewing asceticism as the highest calling for a Christian, the reformers considered it dangerous and unnatural. They identified 'vocation' not with monastic calling, but with the duty to marry and have children. Their vision of the Christian family was patriarchal: the male was to be head of his household, and to take responsibility for its moral and economic welfare. Whereas men had 'vocations' to particular public roles and economic callings as well as to family life, the vocation of women was to be limited to domestic duty. Protestantism considerably narrowed the options open to its women, not only by abolishing monasticism, but by closing down the possibilities of employment in new trades. On the other hand, it lent new dignity to women's domestic 'calling', and showered praise on women who discharged it with modesty and obedience.

For Protestant Christianity then, church and family were regarded as equally important institutions. Godly Christians must be formed and moulded in both. Not only was the church the ideal family, the family was the ideal church. Although it maintained its support for monasticism and its exalted view of the church, post-Reformation Roman Catholicism soon followed Protestantism in giving a new dignity to the family. Marriage, which had once been viewed as a civil matter, was now brought inside the church – both literally and figuratively. As the early modern world gave way to the modern world, this Christian sanctification of the family gathered pace until today Christianity, both Protestant and Catholic, is regarded by many as standing first and foremost for 'family values'.

One reason why Christian support for marriage and the family intensified in the modern period may be that, as the churches' control over other aspects of society ebbed away, the domestic sphere remained the one area in which they could still witness effectively. As their control over educational institutions waned too, the task of creating the next generation of Christians fell more and more to parents and families. But these modern factors combine with a historic legacy that has always been hostile to any form of sexual relation outside marriage – although prostitution was considered a necessary evil by the Catholic Church – and which, at least since Augustine, has regarded the patriarchal household as a legitimate, or even an essential, social institution. The reason this position stands out in higher relief in modern society is not just that the church has changed, but that society has changed. For the 'sexual liberation' which characterized post-1960s society, and which was caused by a coincidence of new technology – the pill – and new values – the internalization of authority and the emancipation of women – has had far more effect on culture outside the churches than within it. In the 1920s or even the 1950s, most people would have been suspicious of contraception, sex outside marriage, one-parent families, and homosexuality. It could be argued that the churches have remained faithful to these positions, whilst the wider culture has moved on.

Yet not all modern Christians agree with 'traditional' teachings on the family. Many denominations and churches are internally divided between those who wished to defend 'traditional family values' and those who took a more liberal stance. In some denominations, such as Anglicanism and Presbyterianism, the division threatens to turn into schism. Nor is the division merely internal to Christianity: it reflects deeper disagreements within modern society as a whole – disagreements not only about gender roles and sexuality, but about the proper shape of society and the institutions which make it up.

LINDA WOODHEAD

CHAPTER 67

Contemporary Christianity

The history of the Christian movement across the centuries is full of surprises. From the very beginning this faith has displayed a remarkable ability to take root and flourish in new areas and different cultural settings, often at the very time when it faced difficulties in those lands in which it had previously been strong.

One way of explaining this is to say that Christianity is a faith capable of being translated into new languages and cultural forms. This fact is reflected within the New Testament itself, when we are told that the early believers who had been scattered by persecutions in Jerusalem went to Antioch and 'began to speak to Greeks' concerning the story of Jesus of Nazareth. This spontaneous act of witness across linguistic and cultural barriers was to have tremendous consequences. On the one hand, it resulted in the recognition that the faith could be expressed in different cultural forms, so making possible the emergence and growth of Christianity throughout the Roman Empire. At the same time, the missionary expansion around the Mediterranean actually kept the faith alive when its original base in Jerusalem was removed with the destruction of the city in 70 CE.

DECLINE OF THE WEST

What makes the situation today so interesting is that we appear to be witnessing a rerun of this pattern, in which Christianity thrives by means of missionary translation, even as it experiences decline in its previous heartlands. In this case, the churches of Europe and North America face the well-documented challenges of secularization — the process by which a society becomes increasingly secular or non-religious — while the faith grows at an extraordinary rate in very diverse cultural settings in the non-Western world. Until recently, the remarkable growth of Christianity in Africa, Latin America, and in some parts of Asia was a well-kept secret, overshadowed by both the reality of the decline of the churches in the Western world, and by the much publicized resurgence of Islam. Remarkably, at the very point in the mid-twentieth century at which the colonial empires were receding, indigenous forms of Christianity displayed considerable growth, demonstrating the extent to which the faith had put down deep roots in the soils of local cultures and languages. The outcome of this has been the emergence of what is called 'World Christianity' —

which is increasingly recognized as a central feature of our globalized world, and one which is likely to prove of great historical and social importance.

NON-WESTERN CHRISTIANITY

Non-Western forms of Christianity existed long before the modern era, although they have generally been neglected in studies of church history written from a European perspective. For example, the year 635 CE witnessed not only the arrival of Aidan on the island of Lindisfarne to commence the task of evangelizing the ancient kingdom of Northumbria, but also the entrance of a missionary bishop from Persia into the imperial capital of ancient China, where he began translating the Bible with the support of the emperor. This movement of Christianity eastwards has been a largely untold story, but its significance may increase in the coming decades, as China moves toward centre stage in the unfolding drama of world history.

Likewise, there has been an unbroken Christian presence on the African continent, stretching back across many centuries, and the symbolic importance of such traditions in modern times is reflected in the fact that large numbers of independent African congregations scattered across the south and west of the continent have affirmed their African identity by describing themselves as 'Ethiopian' churches. In this way, modern African Christians have signalled their awareness of a Christian tradition on this vast continent that long pre-dates colonization and stretches back to the earliest Christian centuries.

MODERN EXPANSION

Important as these earlier examples of non-Western Christianity undoubtedly are, the phenomenal growth of the religion across the southern continents in modern times is unprecedented. It is now possible to understand the Western shaping of the Christian faith throughout the many centuries during which it was closely linked to political power in Europe – a phase described by the term 'Christendom' – as an important period in the history of the movement, but one that has now given way to a new development, as a faith embraced by millions of non-Western believers is being reshaped through its encounter with the cultures of Latin America, Africa, and Asia.

While Western missions played a crucial role in the initial act of communicating the gospel across cultural and linguistic barriers, the key players in the spread of the faith have invariably been local Christians, who were able to express their new religion in surprising and dynamic ways, in contexts frequently marked by severe social and cultural crisis. This is the case whether we consider the role played in the evangelization of West Africa by repatriated slaves, or the contributions of thousands of ordinary Christians who – faced with the new challenge of urban living in the burgeoning cities of the south – have proved amazingly adept at sharing their faith and planting new churches. In addition, an important contribution has come from the ministries of prophetic preachers and evangelists who spontaneously applied the faith to local situations, presenting Christ in ways that resonated with the felt needs of their own people, and reaping huge harvests in the form of mass movements of converts on a scale that equals, and probably surpasses, previous revival movements in Christian history.

SHIFT OF GRAVITY

This growth of Christianity across the southern continents has resulted in a situation in which it is possible to talk of a shift in the centre of gravity of the religion, which now has its roots firmly planted in the soils of non-Western cultures. For example, in South America the extraordinary growth of indigenous forms of Pentecostal Christianity, involving the conversion of upwards of 40 million people, has taken both theologians and social scientists by surprise. Many Western scholars had argued that the decline of Christianity in Europe was merely the start of the global demise of religion, in the face of the seemingly relentless advance of secular modernity. However, inescapable evidence of the vitality and growth of churches in Latin America has exposed the shortcomings of such theoretical models, and has led to the conclusion that the secular experience of Europe – far from being the vanguard of a global trend – might actually be unusual and exceptional.

Ethiopian women pilgrims carry a cross along the Via Dolorosa, Jerusalem, at Easter, following the traditional route of Jesus to his crucifixion.

AFRICA

Young African Christians worshipping.

The continent of Africa provided even more remarkable evidence of Christian growth in the course of the twentieth century. Despite the existence of those ancient Christian traditions on this continent, the faith arrived in most sub-Saharan countries in the course of the nineteenth century. Yet so extraordinary has been the growth witnessed across this continent, that Africa is rapidly displacing Europe and North America as the chief Christian heartland. Both the Roman Catholic Church and major Protestant groupings are being transformed by these changes, as the number of their adherents in Africa dwarfs the parent churches in Europe and North America. For example, the Archbishop of Canterbury presides over a worldwide communion of around 80 million Anglicans, of whom the vast majority are to be found in the southern continents, including 20 million in Nigeria alone. One estimate suggests that the total Christian population of that country may reach 120 million by the middle of this century, and figures like this can be replicated elsewhere in Africa. Africa has also seen a plethora of Independent churches, especially in the Zionist tradition, blossom in the 1980s and 1990s especially, as well as many other charismatic and Pentecostal churches. In 1987 in South Africa, for example, there were over 4,200 distinct Zionist denominations.

ASIA

When we consider Asia, the picture appears to be rather different. In many countries across this vast region, Christians remain small minorities in contexts shaped by ancient non-Christian religious traditions. There are exceptions – notably in South Korea – where growing churches display a remarkable missionary passion, and in Singapore, and the Philippines. However, a narrow focus on percentages of Christians in the context of the vast populations of Asia may easily conceal the reality of very significant Christian movements in the context of Asian religious pluralism. A case in point would be the relatively small Christian community in Japan, which has given birth to some gifted theologians and writers. Similarly, the church in India has been able to incarnate the gospel in the context of the Hindu-shaped culture of the subcontinent, and there are indications that it is experiencing significant growth. The challenges which these churches present to their Christian friends in the West are many, but perhaps the most important concerns the extent to which Western Christianity has allowed a secular, science-based culture to set the terms of its belief and practice, thereby neglecting both the reality of the spiritual world and the social implications of the gospel.

Above all, the story of Christianity in modern China is of great significance, both in the Asian and the global context. Half a century ago, Western scholars were inclined to dismiss the church in China. Its apparently ineradicable foreignness limited its influence, and seemed to condemn it to become an ephemeral feature of colonial history. However, following the removal of Western missions after the Communist revolution, the unexpected occurred – so that scholars now speak of a 'flood' of manifestations of the revival of religion, and acknowledge that Christianity has shed its image as a foreign import and is now clearly identified as a Chinese religion. Estimates as to the number of Christian believers vary widely between 30 and 105 million; and, while claims at the top end of this range should be treated with some scepticism, there is solid evidence of a tenfold increase in the Chinese churches since 1949. This in part reflects the continuing impact of the Home Church Movement in China, where the number of congregations increased from some 50,000 in 1970 to 400,000 twenty-five years later. Such growth in this region of the world is a phenomenon of enormous importance.

WORLD CHRISTIANITY

What are the implications of the changes we have described? For Christians in the West the emergence of World Christianity demands a series of radical changes in perspective and attitude. Until recently it was possible to assume that the churches of Europe and North America could simply be transplanted to other continents, together with their inherited patterns of theology and practice. This assumption rested on the conviction that Western Christianity was a culture-free expression of the faith revealed through Christ and his apostles, and therefore possessed absolute status and importance. In the new context created by the emergence of the non-Western churches, such assumptions must

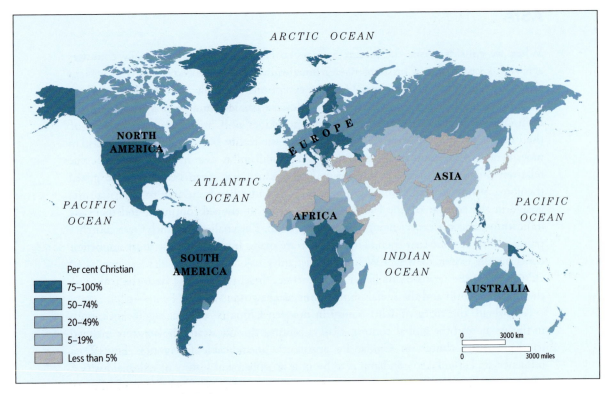

Christianity Worldwide Today

be abandoned: the church looks very different in societies which stress the importance of the community above the rights of the individual, while theology takes surprising directions in cultures relatively unaffected by Western modernity. As to Christian mission, the older approaches in which this was a one-way affair – from the West to the rest – are now replaced by a far more complex pattern, in which mission is 'from everywhere to everywhere'. Indeed, the advent of massive migrations from the southern continents into Europe and North America is resulting in the appearance of 'Southern' forms of Christianity within the great urban centres of the Western world, where they often become by far the largest and most dynamic of Christian communities. If they are wise, Western believers will respond to this situation, not with regret and anger, but with thankfulness that the baton has been successfully passed on and the biblical prize of a multinational church is more clearly in sight than ever before.

CHALLENGES

So far as non-Western Christianity itself is concerned, there is a series of daunting challenges, including the classic issue of precisely how to relate one's faith in Christ to pre-Christian cultures shaped by ancient religious traditions. What are the things from the past that can be sanctified, and what must be left at the doorway? For the vast majority of Christians in the southern hemisphere, religious pluralism is not a new experience, resulting from the collapse of the walls which previously protected one from contact with people of other faiths, it is simply part of the reality one has always known and experiences every day. Faith in Christ is confessed, and the life of discipleship is lived out, in continual interaction with one's Muslim, Hindu, Buddhist, or Confucian neighbours. This means that the growth of non-Western churches in contexts inevitably characterized by ongoing dialogue with people of other faiths holds the promise that fresh insights into the meaning of Christ and his salvation will emerge from these new heartlands in the course of the twenty-first century.

Finally, we must not overlook the fact that the non-Western churches are overwhelmingly churches of the poor, existing in social and economic conditions largely dictated by forces beyond their control, in a world shaped by the phenomenon of economic globalization. Indeed, any celebrations at the indications of growth and spiritual vitality evident in non-Western Christianity need to be tempered by an awareness of the dangers of division within the Body of Christ at a point at which we are being warned of a 'clash of civilizations'. If the dismal prospect of the fracturing of the churches along the lines of division opening up between the so-called developed world and the poorer nations is to be avoided, then Christians in the north and the south need really to listen to each other and hear what the Spirit is saying to them.

DAVID SMITH

QUESTIONS

1. Why did Christianity separate from Judaism?

2. How important was the decision in 313 CE to make Christianity the Roman state religion for the future of the religion?

3. Why is it so important in Christianity that Jesus is the Son of God, rather than merely a prophet?

4. Why is the death and resurrection of Jesus so important to Christians?

5. Explain why Jesus' teaching was so radical at the time.

6. Why is baptism important in Christianity?

7. Explain the doctrine of the Trinity, and how it differs between Orthodox and Western Churches.

8. What was the Reformation, and what did its leaders hope to achieve?

9. How do the Catholic, Anglican, and Reformed traditions differ from one another?

10. 'Christianity is no longer a European religion.' How far do you agree or disagree with this statement?

FURTHER READING

Barrett, C. K., *The New Testament Background: Selected Documents*. Rev. ed. San Francisco: Harper & Row, 1989.

Barrett, David B., ed., *World Christian Encyclopedia*. Nairobi: Oxford University Press, 1982.

Bettenson, Henry S., ed., *Documents of the Christian Church*. 3rd ed. London: Oxford University Press, 1999.

Dowley, Tim, *Christian Music: A Global History*. Minneapolis: Fortress, 2011.

Hastings, Adrian, *The Church in Africa, 1450–1950*. Oxford: Oxford University Press, 1994.

Hastings, Adrian, ed., *A World History of Christianity*. London: Cassell, 1999.

MacCulloch, Diarmaid, *A History of Christianity: The First Three Thousand Years*. London: Penguin, 2009.

McManners, John ed., T*he Oxford History of Christianity*. Oxford and New York: Oxford University Press, 1993

Noll, Mark, *A History of Christianity in the United States and Canada*. Grand Rapids MI: Eerdmans, 1992.

Pelikan, Jaroslav, *Jesus through the Centuries: His Place in the History of Culture*. New Haven: Yale University Press, 1985.

PART 11
ISLAM

SUMMARY

The history of Islam, one of the most significant cultural forces in the world today, began around 610 CE in the city of Mecca, when, Muslims believe, Muhammad began to receive revelations from God, which were recorded as the *Qur'an*. Muhammad's message – that there was only one God, who was omnipotent and merciful, and who will judge all humanity at the end of time – was initially not well received in Mecca, and he was forced out. In time, though, the new religion grew, both through conversions and – as a rising imperial power as well as a religion – military expansion. Within a hundred years of Muhammad's death, Islam dominated much of the Mediterranean world, including part of Europe. A schism had emerged, however, between the *Sunni* majority and the *Shi'a* over the succession to Muhammad.

Acceptance of the Muslim creed, which recognizes one God alone, with Muhammad as his prophet, is the first of five pillars which together shape believers' lives. The routine of daily prayers, *salah*, is the most obvious ritual element, but importantly, these are not just individual: by praying in the direction of Mecca, Muslims around the world demonstrate their unity. This sense of a community of believers is perhaps most obvious during Ramadan, the month of fasting, and in the fulfilment of *Hajj*, the duty to make a pilgrimage to Mecca at least once. Early on, Muslim scholars developed a complex legal system, *Shari'a*, to govern their community, while others made major contributions to the development of the arts and sciences.

Today Islam is thriving, not just in its traditional heartlands, but also in much of the West, as a result of significant migration since World War II. There has also been tension with the West, in part because of foreign policy questions, in part for more fundamental reasons. Some, such as the leaders of Iran's revolution of 1979, go further, seeing Western secularism as irreconcilable with Islam; while others are more comfortable with their faith's place in a pluralistic world.

CHAPTER 68

A Historical Overview

Islam began in Mecca about 610 CE. The dominant religion of Arabia at this time was a form of the old Semitic religion, with shrines of various gods and goddesses in many places. There also appears to have been a widespread belief in a high god, or supreme god, Allah. The other gods were sometimes regarded as angels, and could be asked to intercede with the supreme god on behalf of the worshippers.

Most of the Arabs were members of nomadic tribes, and believed more in human excellence than in any divine power. They believed that what happened to them was determined by Fate or Time, which they thought of, not as a being to be worshipped, but simply as 'the course of events'. Some tribes, or parts of tribes, had become Christian, and there were Jewish communities in Medina and elsewhere in western Arabia. Thus, certain Jewish and Christian ideas were familiar to many Arabs.

BEGINNINGS

Islam began, not among nomads, but among city-dwellers engaged in far-flung commercial enterprises. Towards the end of the sixth century, the merchants of Mecca gained a monopoly of trade between the Indian Ocean and the Mediterranean, which passed up the west coast of Arabia by camel caravan. Mecca had a sanctuary, the Ka'ba, which was an ancient pilgrimage centre, and the surrounding district was sacred. All this facilitated the growth of trade, but the wealth that poured into Mecca led to social tensions, especially among the younger men.

Muhammad was born in Mecca, around the year 570 CE. In about 610, he came to believe he was receiving messages from God, which he was to convey to his fellow Meccans. These messages, or revelations, revealed over 23 years, were later collected and form the *Qur'an*. They asserted that God was One (Allah), and that he was both merciful and all-powerful, controlling the course of events. On the Last Day, he would judge people according to their acts, and assign them to heaven or hell. Part of the conduct he expected of people was a generous use of wealth. In the revelations, Muhammad himself was spoken of, sometimes as simply a warner, telling of God's punishment for sinners, sometimes as a prophet, or messenger, of God. Muhammad sincerely believed these revelations were not his own composition, but the actual speech of God, conveyed to him by an angel. This is still the belief of Muslims.

Muhammad gained a number of followers, who met frequently with him, and joined him in the worship of God. But his messages were not all well received. The Meccan merchants were roused to vigorous opposition by the criticisms of their practices implied in the *Qur'an*. The merchants spoke of the old pagan gods, but the *Qur'an* came to emphasize that there is only one God – that 'there is no deity but God'. As opposition grew, the Quranic messages began to speak of former prophets who had met with opposition, and of the way in which God had preserved them and their followers, and brought disaster on their opponents. Among the stories were those of Noah and the Flood, Lot and the destruction of Sodom, and Moses escaping from Pharaoh.

> *He is Allah, besides whom there is no other god. He is the Sovereign Lord, the Holy One, the Giver of Peace, the Keeper of Faith; the Guardian, the Mighty One, the All-powerful, the Most High! Exalted be He above their idols! He is Allah, the Creator, the Originator, the Modeller. His are the gracious names. All that is in heaven and earth gives glory to Him. He is the Mighty, the Wise One.*
>
> The Qur'an, Surah 59:23–24.

EMIGRATION TO MEDINA

> *If you ask them who it is that has created the heavens and the earth and subjugated the sun and the moon, they will say 'Allah', How then are they turned away?*
>
> The Qur'an, Surah 29:61.

Muhammad's followers were now persecuted in various ways by his opponents, who were often their own relatives. Eventually it became impossible for him to carry on his religious activity in Mecca. An initial emigration of a handful of Muslims took place to the neighbouring Christian kingdom of Abyssinia, whose Christian ruler regarded kindly the message of Islam, and refused to hand over the Muslims to their adversaries from Mecca. Later, these emigrants joined the others in the main emigration of Muslims from Mecca in 622, when Muhammad, preceded by about seventy men and their families, emigrated to Medina. This emigration, the *Hijrah*, became the event that marked the beginning of the Islamic era. Medina was a fertile oasis, and the inhabitants were divided into two hostile groups. Most of them accepted Muhammad as prophet, and agreed that they and the emigrants from Mecca would form a single community or federation. Possibly they were more ready to accept Muhammad because they had heard from local Jewish clans that a messiah was expected. They were also hopeful that he would help them to overcome their divisions.

At Medina the religion of Islam took shape. The main ritual forms, modelled on Muhammad's example, were: worship (or prayer), almsgiving, fasting for the whole month of Ramadan, and the pilgrimage to Mecca, including ceremonies at neighbouring sites. The messages revealed to Muhammad at Medina included legal regulations for matters where Arab custom was unsatisfactory, such as the inheritance of wealth and the avoidance of incest.

The Jewish clans in Medina were associated with Muhammad's federation, as allies of Arab member clans, but nearly all the Jews refused to accept him as prophet. They mocked parts of the *Qur'an*, and sometimes actively opposed the Muslims. Muhammad expelled two Jewish clans from Medina, and had the men of a third executed. Until after the conquest of Mecca, he had few contacts with Christians.

At first, Muhammad had no special political powers at Medina, beyond being head of the emigrants from Mecca. After a year or two, however, all his followers there – now called Muslims – became involved in hostilities with the pagan Meccans. By 630, Muhammad was strong enough to take Mecca. He treated his enemies generously, and won most of them over to become Muslims. Many tribes all over Arabia also joined his federation and became Muslims. Because of his successes, Muhammad's authority as head of state was unquestioned.

THE FIRST CALIPHS

'He who honours Muhammad must know that he is dead. But he who honours the God of Muhammad must know that He is living and immortal.' Muhammad died in 632, and with these words his first successor, Abu Bakr (c. 573–634), encouraged the Muslim community and pointed them to the task ahead.

On his death, Muhammad left both a religion and a state. At first, the state had the form of a federation of tribes or clans, but as it expanded it became more organized. The head of state was known as the 'caliph' (*khalifa*) – the 'successor' or 'deputy' of Muhammad. Raiding their neighbours had been a normal occupation of the nomadic Arab tribes, and Muhammad and the first caliphs realized they could not keep peace within the federation unless they found some outlet for the energies of the tribesmen. They therefore organized raiding expeditions (*ghazawat*) in the direction of Syria and Iraq. The aim of these was to obtain booty, including domestic animals, and the first raids from Medina were very successful. There was a power vacuum in the region, because the two great powers of the day – the Byzantine and Persian Empires – had been almost constantly at war for half a century, and were now exhausted. In a few decisive battles, the Muslims overcame such opposition as the empires presented. Instead of returning to Medina after each campaign, they established forward base camps, so that they could go further afield in the next expedition. Following this strategy, within twelve years of Muhammad's death they had occupied Egypt, Syria, and Iraq, and were advancing westwards into Libya and eastwards into what is now Iran.

The Byzantine and Persian governors of the provinces fled, and the Muslims made treaties with the local inhabitants, giving them the status of 'protected minorities'. These groups ordered their own internal affairs, but paid tribute, or tax, to the Muslim governor. The status of protected minority was open only to 'people of the book' – communities who believed in one God and possessed a written scripture, such as Jews and Christians. The *jizya* – tax – that these protected minorities paid was in lieu of the *zakat* – poor-due – paid by Muslims, this not being required of minorities. However, the *jizya* did act as an incentive for minorities to accept Islam.

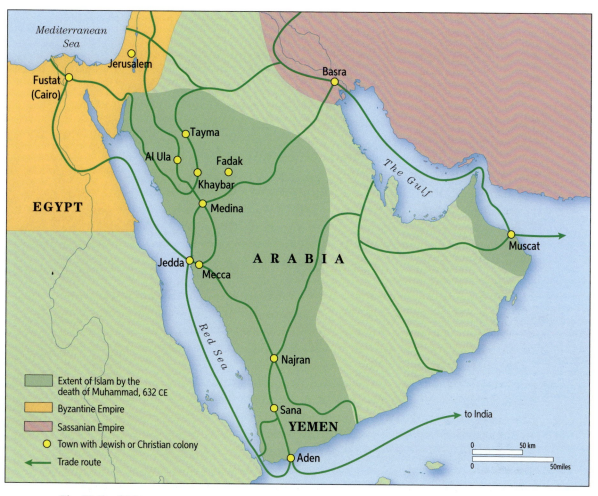

The Birth of Islam

THE EXPLOSION OF ISLAM

Apart from some periods of civil strife among Muslims, this expansion continued for a century. Westwards the Muslims occupied North Africa to the Atlantic, crossed into Spain, and for a few years held the region round Narbonne, in southern France. At the Battle of Tours, France, in 732 a Muslim raiding expedition was defeated by a French army, but this did not loosen the Muslim hold on Spain. Northwards, they raided as far as Constantinople (modern Istanbul), but failed to occupy any of Asia Minor (Turkey). Eastwards, after occupying the whole of Persia and Afghanistan, they penetrated into central Asia, and crossed the line of the River Indus in modern Pakistan. Until 750, this vast area remained a single state, ruled by the caliphs of the Ummayad dynasty.

Most of the inhabitants of these regions were not immediately converted to Islam, but became protected minorities. The military expeditions, though dignified with the title of

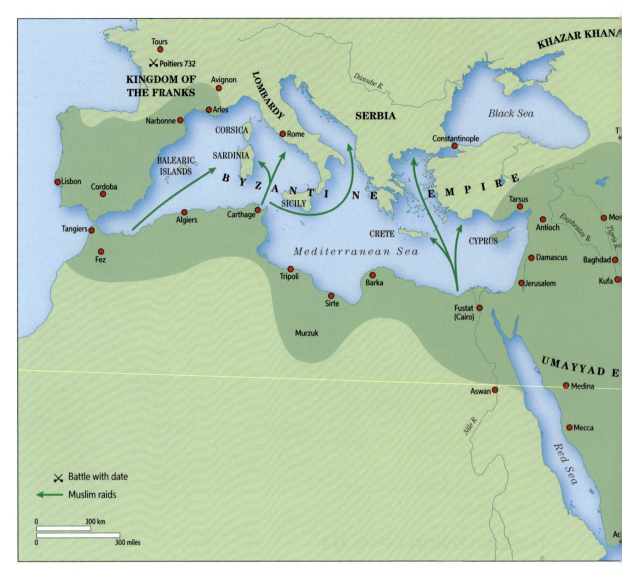

The Extent of Islam in 750 CE

'holy war' (*jihad*), were raids for booty – and not to make converts. The idea that opponents were given the choice of 'Islam or the sword' is false, except in the case of pagan Arab tribes. The protected minorities were on the whole well treated, since Muslim rulers felt it to be a point of honour that their 'protection' should be effective. Members of these minorities, however, saw themselves as second-class citizens, and over the centuries there was a steady trickle of converts to Islam. In this way Islam became the dominant religion in lands which were the original home of Christianity. In the seventh century though, Zoroastrianism – the official religion of the Persian Empire – was in decline, and conversion from it to Islam was quite rapid and extensive.

CONSOLIDATION

In 750 the Ummayad dynasty of caliphs, based in Damascus, ended, and for the next 500 years, the 'Abbasid dynasty ruled from Baghdad. They never took over control of Islamic Spain, and gradually lost authority over other outlying provinces. A local governor with a powerful army would insist on being succeeded by a person of his choice, maintaining only weak links with the caliph. In 945 the 'Abbasid caliph was even forced to delegate supreme political and military authority over Baghdad and the central provinces. However, there continued to be 'Abbasid caliphs in Baghdad, though without political power, until the destructive Mongol invasion in 1258.

Whereas the Ummayad period was one of growth and adaptation for Islam and the Arabs, the first century or two of 'Abbasid rule was marked by consolidation. All the cultural forms needed for the life of a great empire flourished. A central place was given to the development and elaboration of Islamic law, the *Shari'a*, which formed the basis of social structure. The *Shari'a* was derived in part from rules in the *Qur'an*, but to a greater extent from the example of Muhammad, known from the collections of *Hadith* — sometimes translated 'traditions' — stories about his deeds and sayings. This study of law, or jurisprudence, became the core of Islamic higher education.

Subordinate scholarly disciplines were concerned with the text of the *Qur'an*, the interpretation of the *Qur'an*, grammar, lexicology, and theological doctrine. There were also the 'foreign sciences' — Greek philosophy, medicine, mathematics, and natural science. Many Greek books were translated into Arabic, and considerable advances were made in the sciences, literature, the arts, and the skills of government and administration. Almost at the same time, scientific and mathematical advancement were further enhanced, as advances made in the Muslim East seeped back to the West, with increasing interaction between the worlds of Islam and Europe.

TO THE EAST

After 750, military expansion slowed, and almost the only advance was further into India, where the climax of Islamic power was under the Mughal emperors from 1556 until 1707, when most of the subcontinent was subject to them. Hindus were treated as 'people of the book' because their philosophers – though not most ordinary Hindus – were monotheists. Though there were group conversions to Islam, most of the population remained Hindu.

Islamic rule also spread by peaceful methods. Muslim traders with camel caravans took it into the West African steppe, and sea traders carried it to the East African coast. From India it spread – mainly through trade – to Malaysia, Indonesia, and the Philippines; and from central Asia it moved into eastern China.

Local people were impressed by the confidence and high culture of the Muslim traders, allowed them to marry local women, and often after a time decided themselves to become Muslims. Converts often kept many of their old customs, and did not immediately observe the *Shari'a* fully. But over the centuries they moved closer to standard Islam, and at the same time the number of Muslims kept increasing.

Prior to 1500 the main area where Islam contracted was Spain. Christian military pressure gradually whittled away the area under Muslim control, and in 1492 the last Sultan of Granada had to surrender. Muslims continued in Spain for a time, but were executed or driven out by the Inquisition.

THE IMPACT OF EUROPE

A new era in the history of Islam began about 1500. The Portuguese sailor Vasco da Gama (c. 1460–1524), having rounded the Cape of Good Hope and disrupted the Muslim trade on the East African coast, reached India in 1498. This was the beginning of the impact of Europe on the eastern part of the Islamic world. In the west, the Ottomans took over the caliphate, and conquered much of south-east Europe and the southern coast of the Mediterranean during the fifteenth and sixteenth centuries, and were then in military and diplomatic contact with European states, as well as having commercial dealings. The full force of the European impact, however, was not felt until after the Industrial Revolution.

The impact of Europe on the Islamic world – as on Asia and Africa generally – was many-sided: economic, political, intellectual, and religious. It began with ocean-borne trade, but went on to political interference and finally colonization. As European technology developed, in the nineteenth and twentieth centuries, richer Muslims wanted to share in its comforts and conveniences, and independent rulers wanted their countries to have railways and other forms of communication, plumbing, electricity for lighting, telephones, and so forth. Military hardware was also high on the list, and it then became necessary to train men to use it. Colonial powers also introduced Western-type education, to train men for minor administrative posts. After 1800, the Christian churches sent

The Masjid-i Jahan-Numa ('world-reflecting mosque'), usually known as the Jama Masjid, is the principal mosque of Old Delhi, India, and was built by the Mughal Emperor Shah Jahan between 1650 and 1656 CE.

missionaries to most parts of the world, but in Islamic lands they made relatively few converts; their chief contribution was to develop education and medical care.

By the early twentieth century, informed Muslims were aware of their situation. Movements for political independence grew and were eventually successful. Some industry was developed, based on Western technology. Most Muslim countries adopted an essentially Western educational system, because religious leaders were not prepared to adapt the traditional Islamic education they controlled. In many Muslim countries this has led to two parallel systems of education: a secular system inherited from Europe, and a traditional religious system of education, revolving around *madrassahs* (Islamic schools). The discovery of vast quantities of oil in the Middle East was at first exploited by Westerners, but later, when taken over by Muslim governments, became a weapon in world politics. Until the end of World War II, Muslim countries were united in their struggle to be free of colonialism. Since then, splits between 'progressive' and 'conservative' groups have become increasingly apparent; and the conservative and reactionary groups have been strengthened by the development of Islamic fundamentalism.

MONTGOMERY WATT

ISLAM TIMELINE

570 Birth of Muhammad

622 Muhammad's hijrah from Mecca to Medina: Muslim Year 1

632 Muhammad dies; leadership passes to the caliph

661 Umayyad caliphate moves to Damascus

680 Death of Hussein at Karbala; commemorated as martyr by Shi'ites

711 Islamic Arab armies reach Spain

732 Battle of Poitiers stops Muslim expansion into France

762 Mansur establishes Baghdad as Abbasid capital

1071 Seljuk Turks defeat Byzantines

1058–1111 al-Ghazali, Sufi scholar, synthesizer of faith and reason

1099 Crusaders capture Jerusalem

1165–1240 Ibn al-'Arabi, philosopher of the mystical unity of being

1258 Mongol invaders destroy Baghdad

1207–73 Rumi, Persian mystical poet

1291 Muslims expel Crusaders from Palestine

1492 Christians take Granada, final Muslim outpost in Spain

1529 Ottoman Turks reach Vienna

1703–92 Ibn 'Abd al-Wahhab, leader of traditionalist revival in Arabia

1838–97 Jamal-ad-Din al-Afghani, promoter of modern Islamic cultural revival

1924 Kemal Ataturk, modernizer and secularizer, abolishes caliphate in Turkey

1947 Pakistan formed as Islamic state

1979 Ayatollah Khomeini (1902-89) sets up a revolutionary Islamic regime in Iran

2001 Taliban, Afghanistan hardliners, demolish 1500-year-old Buddha statues in Bamiyan as 'idols'

2001 Osama bin Laden launches terror attacks in USA

CHAPTER 69

The Unity and Variety of Islam

Islam has two basic groups – the Sunni and Shi'a. Their origins can be traced back to a question which faced the first generation of Muslims: how was Muhammad, 'the Seal of the Prophets', to be succeeded as leader of the Muslim community? For Muslims this question was always a religious as well as a political one.

SUNNIS: COMMUNITY CONSENSUS

The answer of the Sunnis, who constitute the Muslim majority of approximately 85 per cent, can be summarized as follows. No one could succeed Muhammad in his nature and quality as prophet, for the *Qur'an* finalized and perfected the revelation of divine guidance, and declared Muhammad to be 'the Seal of the Prophets'. Muhammad's successor could therefore be no more than the guardian of the prophetic legacy. He would be a caliph (*khalifa*) with subordinate authority as leader of the believers, having responsibility for the administration of community affairs, in obedience to the *Qur'an* and prophetic precedent. By the process of consensus (*ijma'*), the community would select its caliph from amongst the male membership of the Quraish tribe to which Muhammad belonged.

Following Muhammad's death in 632 CE, caliphal succession passed from Abu Bakr (632–634) to 'Umar (634–644), 'Uthman (644–656), and 'Ali (656–661). These, 'the four rightly guided caliphs' are deemed to have lived so close to the Prophet that their example, together with Muhammad's, is taken to comprise the authoritative *sunnah*, or custom, for all later generations of Muslims to follow.

The Sunnis gradually developed a comprehensive system of community law, the *Shari'a*, which provided cohesion within the community, while allowing for variance between four orthodox law schools, the Malikis, Hanafis, Shafi'is, and Hanbalis. The principle of *ijma'* remained central; notionally the consensus of the whole community, though in practice that of the legal scholars.

After the 'rightly guided caliphs', the caliphate became a dynastic institution, regarded as the guardian of the *Shari'a*. But in 1924, with the demise of the Ottoman Caliphate, it was abolished. The *ijma'* of contemporary Sunni Islam seems to be that, if the *Shari'a* is observed by the national governments of Muslim states, there is no need for the transnational office of caliph to be restored.

SHI'A: AUTHORITY AND LEADERSHIP

The Dome of the Rock, on the Temple Mount, Jerusalem, built by the fifth caliph, 'Abd-al-Malik, is the third holiest place in Islam.

For Shi'a Muslims, the principal figure of religious authority is the *imam*. Muhammad completed 'the cycle of prophethood', and with it the possibility of further divine revelation. But Shi'a Muslims believe he instituted 'the cycle of initiation' for the continuing guidance of the community, by appointing as his successor an *imam*, invested with the qualities of inspired and infallible interpretation of the *Qur'an*. Accordingly, the Shi'a speak of themselves as 'people of appointment and identification'.

The first *imam* was 'Ali. As cousin, adopted son, and later son-in-law of Muhammad, by marriage to Fatima, he was not just a member of Muhammad's tribe, but also of 'the people of his house'. This intimate family relationship is significant: the Shi'a believe 'Ali inherited Muhammad's 'spiritual abilities', his *wilayah*. He was infallible in his interpretation of the *Qur'an* and leadership of the community, and passed on these qualities to the sons of his marriage with Fatima, Hasan, and Husayn, and they to their descendants in the line of *imams*. The Shi'a believe that 'the cycle of *wilayah*' will continue until the end of human history when – on the Last Day – humankind will be resurrected and judged for the afterlife.

The majority of Shi'a, known as Imamis, most of whom live in Iran, believe the cycle will be completed with the messianic return of the twelfth *imam*, often referred to as the '*imam* of the period'. He is said to have been withdrawn into 'occulation' since the third century of Islam. His guidance is still accessible through 'doctors of the law' (*mujtahidun*), of whom the most senior in Iran are the *ayatollahs*, who have the right to interpret the *Shari'a* and to make religious rulings.

The history of the Imamis has seen two important offshoots. The Zaidis, mostly found in Yemen today, do not limit the number of *imams* to twelve, and interpret their function in a manner similar to the Sunni caliph. The Isma'ilis, meanwhile, have developed highly esoteric doctrines surrounding the *imam*. They have two major groups, the Nizaris, who look to the Aga Khan as their *imam*, and the Musta'lis — more commonly known as the Bohra Muslims— who believe in a hidden *imam* who is represented on earth by their leader, the Da'i.

SUFISM

Sunni and Shi'a Islam reflect the diversity of the Muslim response to divine revelation. Sunni Islam tends to be more concerned to create and preserve structures of society within which the community may fulfil its God-given responsibilities. Shi'a Islam began in the martyrdoms of 'Ali and his son, Husayn, and has always been conscious of suffering and alienation in the human condition. It searches for answers in a more esoteric interpretation of the *Qur'an* and *Shari'a*. But there is no hard and fast distinction: Sunni Islam is also concerned with the inner life, and Shi'a with the outer. Moreover, the important mystical tradition of Sufism has seen a confluence of Shi'a and Sunni consciousness.

Sunnism and Shi'ism represent the major doctrinal varieties of Islam: Sufism denotes the inner spiritual life of both. Sufis are not a distinct group or sect; they are simply Muslims — Sunnis or Shi'as — who seek intimacy with God through a discipline of spiritual purification. The heart of Sufism is the love of God, and is built on the Quranic assurance that 'God loves the God-fearing' (*surah* 3:76), and fulfils their devotions in love. God is heard to say in a Holy *Hadith*:

> *The complete mystic 'way' includes both intellectual belief and practical activity; the latter consists in getting rid of the obstacles in the self, and in stripping off its base characteristic and vicious morals, so that the heart may attain to freedom from what is not God and to constant recollection of Him.*
>
> Al-Ghazali, *Deliverance from Error* (12th century).

> *Nothing is more beloved to Me than that my servant approaches Me with constant acts of devotion. And when I love him I am the eye by which he sees and the ear by which he hears. When he approaches a span, I approach a cubit; and when he comes walking, I come running.*

Among early Muslims remembered for their devotional insight ranks a woman from Baghdad, Rabi'a al-'Adawiyya (eighth century CE), who prayed:

> *O Beloved of my heart, I have none like unto Thee, therefore have pity this day on the sinner who comes to Thee. O my Hope and my Rest and my Delight, the heart can love none other than Thee.*

Later treatises on Sufi devotion defined love as that which 'obliterates from the heart everything except the Beloved'.

It is misleading, therefore, to think of Sufism as an 'ism'. The English word comes from the Arabic *tasawwuf*, which could be translated 'self-purification', provided we understand that human endeavour is incomplete unless fulfilled by divine love. *Sufi* (feminine, *sufiyya*) denotes a person whose heart is purified from the pollution of this world.

The prophet Muhammad is venerated by Muslims as a Sufi. Religious tradition tells of the miraculous cleansing of his heart as a child, and of his ascension to heaven (*mi raj*) by night when, through prayer, he experienced the mystery of God's all-embracing unity. Amongst his early followers were the so-called 'people of the bench' (*'ahl al-suffa*), who rarely left the mosque in Medina, due to the constancy of their prayers. They wore a simple tunic made of wool (*suf*), symbolizing their obedience to the example of the many prophets – especially Jesus son of Mary (*Isa ibn Mariam*) – who practised asceticism in rejection of worldly comforts.

Strictly speaking, a Sufi should never describe himself, nor a Sufiyya herself, by this term. They use the related word *mutasawwif* (feminine, *mutasawwifa*), 'one who tries to be a sufi'. The difference is critical. A classical Persian Sufi authority (al-Hujwiri) explained it as follows:

> *The sufi is he that is dead to self and lives by the Truth; he has escaped from the grip of human faculties and has truly attained to God. The* mutasawwif *is he that seeks to reach this rank by means of self-mortification, and in his search rectifies his conduct in accordance with the Sufis' example.*

> God dwells in the heart, according to the Tradition, 'Neither my earth nor my heavens contain me, but I am contained in the heart of my servant who believes.'
>
> Ibn al-'Arabi, *Tarjumanu al-Ashwaq* (13th century).

The way of purification through self-mortification involves the spiritual path, *tariqah*, which is modelled on the prophet's heavenly ascent. The prophet Muhammad once said that the paths are equal in number to the true believers, meaning that each person should develop his or her own spiritual practice.

As Islam developed and spread, Sufis seeing the danger of undisciplined spiritual practices, insisted that a *mutasawwif* must follow the guidance of a spiritual master (*shaykh*, *pir*). To dispense with a spiritual master is to follow the devil. So the path was institutionalized in a variety of spiritual fraternities, or orders, which followed different masters. They stretched across the medieval Muslim world, and though they varied greatly from one another, each united its followers from different continents in common spiritual disciplines.

All these orders drew a fundamental distinction in the nature of spiritual practice. Acts of self-mortification are called *mujahadat* – a word connected to the Arabic term *jihad*, which means 'striving'. The Prophet Muhammad explained that the highest level of *jihad* is the inward striving of the soul for purification. In a clear reference to the word *jihad*, referring to the personal struggle for self-purification, the *Qur'an* says that Allah 'will surely guide those who strive hard [conduct *jihad*] for Our cause.' (The *Qur'an*, surah 29:69)

DAVID KERR

CHAPTER 70

Sacred Writings

For Muslims, the *Qur'an* represents the supreme revelation of God's word in written form. It is unique among revealed books, universal in its application, and eternal in its relevance. It is extracted from a tablet on which God's word is recorded and kept in heaven. Orthodox belief among the Sunni majority considers the *Qur'an* to be co-eternal with God. According to the great Muslim scholar and jurist Abu Hanifa (d. c. 767), 'its letters, vowel points, and writing are all created, for these are the works of man; but God's word is uncreated... he who says that the word of God is created is an infidel'.

Muslims show great reverence for the *Qur'an*, handling and storing it with great care. Reading the *Qur'an* is widely considered to bring rewards, increasing with each word read; the reader will be brought closer to God through frequent reading. Memorizing the Quranic text is considered an act of considerable piety: anyone who memorizes the entire text (a *hafiz*) is highly respected. Furthermore, the pages of the *Qur'an* are considered by many Muslims to have healing qualities.

There is a supplementary body of sacred writing in Islam: the *Hadith* collections, or Prophetic Traditions, much more voluminous than the *Qur'an*, which serve as a model for Muslims around the world in their daily lives.

THE QUR'AN

> *When the Qur'an is read, listen to it with attention, and hold your peace: that ye may receive Mercy.*
>
> The Qur'an, surah 7:204.

The *Qur'an* is divided into 114 chapters. With the exception of chapter one, The Opening, these are arranged in order of decreasing length. Each chapter (*surah*) has a number and a title, which is typically based on a key word or theme in the chapter: The Women (4), The Cave (18), The Moon (54). The basic unit of a chapter is the verse (*ayah*). In all, the *Qur'an* has more than 6200 verses. The Quranic chapters are identified with two periods: those revealed to Muhammad at Mecca, and those revealed at Medina. The former tend to reflect the voice of Muhammad as protester, criticizing the Meccan status quo centred on idolatry, social injustice, and other evils. The Medinan chapters reflect Muhammad's role as community leader, addressing legal issues, matters to do with building the structures of state, inter-ethnic, and inter-religious relations.

Whatever communications We abrogate or cause to be forgotten, We bring one better than it or like it. Do you not know that Allah has power over all things?

The *Qur'an*, surah 2:106

The *Qur'an* presents a holistic theology, claiming authority over all aspects of life, allowing no separation between sacred and secular. It includes diverse themes, containing morals indicating right from wrong, as well as injunctions to obey and fear God. There are parables, or allegorical stories teaching a lesson, which Muslim scholars stress are not designed as entertainment, but rather for instruction. Passages of sheer ecstasy, relating to Muhammad's revelatory experiences, were later to become models for Islamic mystics. There are legal passages, designed to assist with the organization of the Muslim community; chapters of encouragement, especially those revealed when the embryonic Muslim community was facing dangers and challenges; sections presenting oral traditions relating to Biblical characters and events; sections including sarcasm, argumentation, response, mercy, and even ruthlessness; and biographical material, from which a life of Muhammad can be constructed.

With such diverse themes, revealed over the final twenty-three years of Muhammad's lifetime, some verses appear to contradict others. This is addressed by the *Qur'an* itself in *surah* 2:106, which explains that, where the content is contradictory, later verses abrogate earlier verses. Muslims consider this does not point to error in the earlier verse; rather, the relevance

Bronze casting of a *surah* from the *Qur'an*.

of the verse being abrogated was specific to a time or context, with the later verse addressing a broader or later context. So prayer in the direction of Jerusalem, referred to in *surah* 2:143, was abrogated by *surah* 2:144, stipulating prayer towards Mecca. This reflected the changing relationship between the emerging Muslim community and the Jewish community of Arabia.

COMPILATION AND TRANSLATION

According to the Prophetic Traditions, the first official collection of the *Qur'an* took place under the first Caliph, Abu Bakr. However, regional variations occurred in copies of the *Qur'an* written or memorized, so the third Caliph, 'Uthman, made an official collection in 649/50. Oral traditions continued to circulate and diversify, and this variety was compounded by the inadequacies of contemporary Arabic script. Further reform and standardization were considered necessary, and this was undertaken by Abu Bakr bin Mujahid (d. 936). As a result of his efforts, seven readings of the Quranic text were accepted as canonical.

The *Qur'an* in its Arabic original has been prescribed in liturgical contexts by three of the four Sunni law schools since the earliest period of Islamic history. Only the Hanafite school has shown some flexibility, with founder Abu Hanifa allowing worshippers with no Arabic to recite the opening *surah* of the *Qur'an* in Persian, a right subsequently extended to speakers of other languages. In the twentieth century, there was further liberalization of attitudes towards translation – especially in Turkey and Egypt – amongst other schools of thought besides the Hanafite school. Nevertheless, translated texts are still considered as commentaries on the *Qur'an*, not the *Qur'an* itself.

THE *HADITH*

Hadith accounts are divided into two groups. The sacred *Hadith qudsi* are considered to include God's direct words, mediated through Muhammad, as in the case of the *Qur'an*; whereas the prophetic *Hadith sharif* record Muhammad's own wise words and deeds. The influential scholar al-Ghazali (1058–1111) shows the importance of the *Hadith* collections when he says:

> **Muslim prayer**
>
> *In the name of God, Most Gracious, Most Merciful.*
>
> *Praise be to God, The Cherisher and Sustainer of the Worlds;*
>
> *Most Gracious, Most Merciful;*
>
> *Master of the Day of Judgment.*
>
> *Thee do we worship, and Thine aid we seek.*
>
> *Show us the straight way,*
>
> *The way of those on whom Thou hast bestowed Thy Grace,*
>
> *Those whose (portion) Is not wrath,*
>
> *And who go not astray.*
>
> The *Qur'an*, Surah 1, transl. Yusuf Ali, 1934.
> Used daily many times as a prayer.

God has but one word, which differs only in the mode of its expression. On occasions God indicates His word by the Qur'an; *on others, by words in another style, not publicly recited, and called the Prophetic tradition. Both are mediated by the Prophet.*

The *Qur'an* recognizes earlier sacred writings: the Torah given to Moses, the Psalms to David, and the Gospel to Jesus. However, it charges both Jews and Christians with corrupting these earlier revelations, by changing the text, or wilfully misinterpreting it. Hence, the *Qur'an* sees itself as the final, perfect revelation, supplanting those which went before. Some Islamic thinkers recognize a measure of divine authority in the earlier scriptures, but challenge their interpretation by Jews and Christians.

PETER G. RIDDELL

CHAPTER 71

Beliefs

The Arabic term *iman* is used to designate the system of belief in Islam, drawing on Quranic verses.

ONENESS OF GOD

The Islamic belief system is centred on an uncompromising monotheism, called *tawhid*, the oneness of God. Many Quranic verses provide an insight into the attributes and characteristic features of God:

> *Allah is He besides Whom there is no god, the Everliving, the Self-subsisting by Whom all subsist; slumber does not overtake Him nor sleep; whatever is in the heavens and whatever is in the earth is His; who is he that can intercede with Him but by His permission? He knows what is before them and what is behind them, and they cannot comprehend anything out of His knowledge except what He pleases. His knowledge extends over the heavens and the earth, and the preservation of them both tires Him not, and He is the Most High, the Great*

(surah 2:255).

God is supreme, eternal, and omnipotent. He sees all things and is present everywhere. He is the sole creator and sustainer of the universe, and controls life and death for all creatures. God has ninety-nine names, according to Muslim belief, representing his numerous attributes and aspects. The *Hadith* accounts provide the most important source for these names. Some relate to compassion and love, yet the depiction of God within Muslim theology is more of a God whom one reveres, of whom one is in awe, and to whom one is obedient.

The nature of God can be gleaned in part by a series of negative statements made within the Islamic sacred writings:

> *In the name of Allah, the Beneficent, the Merciful. Say: He is Allah, the One! Allah, the eternally Besought of all! Whom all creatures need. He neither eats*

*O you who believe!
Believe in Allah and His
Apostle and the Book
which He has revealed
to His Apostle and the
Book which He revealed
before; and whoever
disbelieves in Allah
and His angels and His
apostles and the Last
Day, he indeed strays off
into a remote error.*

Qur'an, surah 4:136

*nor drinks. He begetteth not nor was He begotten. And there
is none comparable unto Him*

(The Qur'an, surah 112).

God is not a trinity, but is one. God has not been created, nor is he in a relationship of father, brother, or son with any other. He depends on no one, and has no needs. Nothing resembles him. He is without imperfections.

ANGELS

Belief in angels is another important article of faith. The *Qur'an* records that angels are created from light, and are so numerous that only God knows their exact number. Angels have no offspring, being neither male nor female, and serve God in various ways. The classical commentator Tabari defines angels as: 'God's messengers between Him and His prophets, and those of His servants to whom they are sent'.

The greatest of the angels is Jibril, or Gabriel, who was, according to Muslim belief, the angel who transmitted the *Qur'an* to Muhammad. Jibril also functions as the Holy Spirit within Islamic belief. An angel was the means used by God to tell Mary of the impending birth of her son Jesus:

*When the angels said: O Mariam, surely Allah gives you good news with a Word
from Him (of one) whose name is the Messiah, Isa son of Mariam, worthy of
regard in this world and the hereafter, and of those who are made near (to Allah)'*

(The Qur'an, surah 3:45).

Angels are assigned other tasks by God, according to Islamic belief. They utter continuous praise of God, they bear his throne, and accompany believers in prayer. According to the *Hadith*, angels also record the deeds of every person. The angel Izra'il is responsible for drawing out the souls of the dying, while Israfil will sound the trumpet on the Last Day, the Day of Judgment. Other angels guard hell and direct its affairs. The *Qur'an* warns that opposing the angels is tantamount to opposing God, as they are his envoys:

*Whoever is an enemy to Allah and His angels and apostles, to Gabriel and
Michael – Lo! Allah is an enemy to those who reject Faith*

(surah 2:98).

REVEALED BOOKS

Sacred Scriptures revealed to humankind throughout history are of two types. The more substantial ones are called *Kutub* (books), while the smaller ones are known as *Suhuf* (scrolls). More than 100 works are believed to have been revealed throughout history, including scrolls revealed to Adam, Seth, Enoch, and Abraham, but now lost.

Only four revealed scriptures have survived, according to Islamic belief, and are mentioned by name in the *Qur'an*. The first is the *Tawrat*, the Jewish Torah, given by divine inspiration to Moses, according to the Quranic record: 'And before [the *Qur'an*] was the Book of Moses as a guide and a mercy...' (*surah* 46:12). This was followed by the *Zabur* (Psalms), revealed to David; the *Injil* (Gospel), revealed to Jesus; and the *Qur'an*, revealed to Muhammad. The various revealed books represented God's blueprint for people to live according to God's law.

For Muslims the *Qur'an* is the last and the definitive revelation, the repository of perfect truth, and it supplants all earlier revelations sent by God to humankind through the prophets. This is stated clearly in *Hadith* accounts anticipating events in the End Times:

> *Narrated Abu Huraira: Allah's Apostle said 'How will you be when the son of Mary [that is, Jesus] descends amongst you and he will judge people by the Law of the* Qur'an *and not by the law of Gospel?'*

(Sahih Bukhari, Vol. 4, Book 55, No. 658).

An Islamic minaret – spire of a mosque, which provides a visual feature in the landscape, and is often used for the call to prayer, *adhan*.

God thus sends his angels with revealed books to the created world. A key link in this chain is provided by messengers and prophets, who must transmit the content of the revealed books to all people. Islamic belief considers a messenger (*Rasul*) to be a prophet (*Nabi*) of a specific type. A messenger is given a new set of divine laws and a new revealed book, whereas a prophet who is not a messenger is sent to transmit and implement previously revealed dispensations. The *Qur'an* mentions some twenty-five messengers by name, while the *Hadith* collections refer to a total of 124,000 prophets, of whom 313 were messengers. All prophets, whether messengers or not, are believed to perform miracles. The *Qur'an* also mentions that prophets – who have also been labelled 'guides' (13:7) and 'warners' (35:24) – have come to 'every nation', so Muslims accept that the founders of other great religions, such as Hinduism and Buddhism, may also have been prophets in their own time and place.

The words of the prophets are not their own, but those of God. The medieval scholar Ibn Khaldun (1332–1406) portrays this prophetic role as mediator in the following terms:

> Allah has chosen individuals from among humankind whom He has honoured
> by Himself speaking to them to mould them according to His understanding,
> and to make them the mediators between Himself and His servants.

It is in this context that Islamic prophets are believed to be free from sin.

Many of the prophets named in the *Qur'an* have counterparts in the Bible:

> And We bestowed upon [Abraham] Isaac and Jacob; each of them We guided; and
> Noah did We guide aforetime; and of his seed (We guided) David and Solomon
> and Job and Joseph and Moses and Aaron. Thus do We reward the good'

> (surah 6:84).

However, this is not the case with all: for example, Hud, Salih, and Luqman are all considered as Arabian prophets.

Muhammad represents the last messenger and prophet of God. Furthermore, according to the Islamic sacred writings, he is the greatest of all the prophets, having been given special functions:

> Narrated Jabir bin 'Abdullah: Allah's Apostle said, 'I have been given five
> things which were not given to any amongst the Prophets before me'

> (Sahih Bukhari, Volume 1, Book 8, No. 429).

These comprise divine assistance in achieving victory over his enemies, the right of prayer for his followers anywhere in the world, the right to take booty after battle, a mission to all humankind, and the right of intercession on the Day of Judgment.

RESURRECTION AND JUDGMENT

The message transmitted by the prophets, contained in revealed books, borne by angels, and originating from God, warns Muslims of an impending Day of Resurrection and Judgment. The exact time of the Day of Judgment is unknown to all except Allah. All that is known is that it will be on a Friday, the tenth day of the month of Muharram.

The *Hadith* collections point to signs of the approaching Day of Judgment. These include an increase in sin in the world, widespread disobedience of parental authority and disrespect for elders, an increase in debauchery, an increase in the numbers of women vis-à-vis men in the world, and incompetent people of lowly station assuming positions of leadership.

On the Day of Judgment, all people will be judged according to their sincere repentance and good deeds, measured by the degree to which they have followed God's law (the *Shari'a*). Believers will hold a book recording their life's deeds in their right hand, while unbelievers will hold their book of deeds in their left. Everyone's deeds will be weighed on scales, and no last minute repentance will be accepted:

> And repentance is not for those who go on doing evil deeds, until when death comes to one of them, he says: Surely now I repent; nor (for) those who die while they are unbelievers. These are they for whom We have prepared a painful chastisement

> (The Qur'an, surah 4:18).

The Islamic sacred writings describe an afterlife, with the descriptions being especially graphic in the *Hadith* collections. If one earns favour from God on the Day of Judgment, according to good deeds, right belief, and sincere repentance of sins, heaven is the reward. This is a place of eternal bliss, resembling a garden with rivers, carpets, cushions, fruit, and pure maidens.

In contrast, an eternal hell awaits those who have not followed God's law, or held right belief. Hell is a place of great torment, with fire and boiling water, where skin is scalded, renewed, and scalded again. The Tree of Zaqqum provides bad fruit, and the damned are forced to eat from it:

> … the tree of Zaqqum? Surely We have made it to be a trial to the unjust. Surely it is a tree that grows in the bottom of the hell; its produce is as it were the heads of the serpents. Then most surely they shall eat of it and fill (their) bellies with it. Then most surely they shall have after it to drink of a mixture prepared in boiling water. Then most surely their return shall be to hell

> (surah 37:62–68).

ALL DECREED BY GOD

Belief in God's decrees is the final article of faith. The *Qur'an* stresses that all is decreed by God:

> And the sun runs on to a term appointed for it; that is the ordinance of the
> Mighty, the Knowing. And (as for) the moon, We have ordained for it stages till
> it becomes again as an old dry palm branch

(surah 36:38–39).

God controls the past, present, and future of each individual Muslim. Among the Muslim masses, this translates to a firm belief in God's preordination of all things, often verging on fatalism. This receives sustenance from Quranic verses such as the following:

> Wherever you are, death will overtake you, though you are in lofty towers, and
> if a benefit comes to them, they say: This is from Allah; and if a misfortune
> befalls them, they say: This is from you. Say: All is from Allah, but what is
> the matter with these people that they do not make approach to understanding
> what is told (them)?

(surah 4:78).

At the level of Islamic scholarship, this article of faith has given rise throughout history to a dynamic debate about the degree of human ability to determine events, within an overall framework of God's predestination.

PETER G. RIDDELL

CHAPTER 72

Worship and Festivals

The *Qur'an* sees men and women as religious beings. 'I created … humankind only that they might worship me,' the Muslim hears God say in the *Qur'an*. Each individual is an *'abd* of God, a term which conveys the twin meanings of 'worshipper' and 'servant' in a single word. And this description applies to all aspects of human life, all of which is lived under the command of God. There is no distinction between worship and the wholeness of human life.

SUBMISSION TO GOD

Islam understands itself fundamentally as being 'natural religion', in that every created thing exists in dependence upon God, in obedience to his creative and sustaining power, and with the purpose of expressing adoration to God. For the human, this should lead to a conscious commitment to a life of thankful and praise-giving obedience to God. The word *muslim* means one who lives his life according to God's will; Islam means 'submission to God'.

Worship (*'ibada*) and the activities of the workaday world (*mu'amalat*) are joint expressions of the character of *'abd*. The mosque cannot be separated from the marketplace. As far as worship is concerned, the *Qur'an* sees body and spirit as inseparably combined in the wholeness of human worship. Islam has no term for 'spirituality'; for its religious devotion seeks to preserve an equilibrium between the 'outward' and the 'inward' in worship. Believers' external acts of worship depend on their internal intention, and the *Qur'an* is concerned that both should be 'for the pleasure of God'. So while the holy law provides a code of practice as a framework for Muslim worship, the worship depends on the inner dynamic of thankful and praise-giving obedience, the discipline of the soul to 'remember God always'.

> *O believers, when you stand up to pray, wash your faces, and your hands up to the elbows, and wipe your heads, and your feet up to the ankles. If you are defiled, purify yourselves.*
>
> The Qur'an, surah 5:8.

> *Public worship is seventeen times better than private worship.*
>
> Al-Ghazali

THE *SHAHADAH*

The Islamic code of conduct is founded upon the bedrock of the testimony of faith, the *shahadah*. This is the first pillar of Islam. When spoken in Arabic, and with sincere intention, it is a commitment to obey God and follow the prophet.

'I bear witness that there is no god but God; I bear witness that Muhammad is the Apostle of God.' These are the first words breathed into a child's ear at birth, and the last which Muslims would utter with their dying breath – the lantern for life and the hope for the mercy of God in the life hereafter. They point to the one God, who has spoken finally through the *Qur'an*; and they point to Muhammad, 'the Seal of the Prophets', sent to all humankind to transmit and interpret the *Qur'an*. The words of the *shahadah* summon Muslims to worship throughout the world, and their meaning is the heart of prayer and meditation.

PRAYING TOGETHER

The *Qur'an* identifies a human being as 'worshipper', and also places the individual worshipper, male or female, in the context of a worshipping community.

> *Hold fast, all of you, to the rope of God, and do not separate … and may there spring from you a community who invite to goodness, enjoin right conduct and forbid indecency; such are they who are successful.*

The Qu'ran, surah 3:103

The *Shari'a* codifies and coordinates the practice of a worshipping community. Worship is a communal act, as well as one of individual commitment. To affirm the unity of God (*tawhid*) is

Muslim men, barefoot, pray together, facing Mecca.

necessarily to affirm the unity of the created order and of humankind in right worship.

This community orientation of Islamic worship is symbolized and demonstrated in the ritual of *salah*, the liturgical form of prayer, which it is the duty of all Muslims to observe at fixed hours. Prayer is the second pillar of Islam. There are five prayer times, each preceded by obligatory ritual washing: dawn, midday, mid-afternoon, sunset, and night. They serve to remind Muslims, in a regular and disciplined manner, of their status before God as 'worshipful servants'. From the moment of the *muezzin's* call, and the preliminary washings, Muslims practise *salah*. On Fridays *salah* is a communal act.

> ... *proclaim thy Lord's praise before the rising of the sun, and before its setting, and proclaim thy Lord's praise in the watches of the night, and at the ends of the day* ...
>
> The Qur'an, surah 20:130.

> *A mosque that was founded upon godfearing from the first day is worthier for thee to stand in; therein are men who love to cleanse themselves; and God loves those who cleanse themselves.*
>
> The Qur'an, surah 9:109.

Festivals of Islam

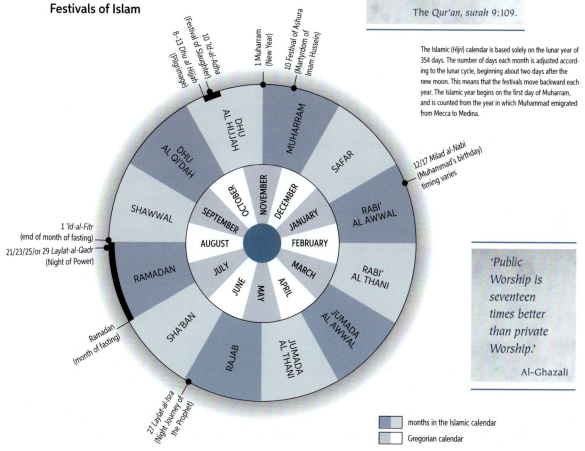

The Islamic (*Hijri*) calendar is based solely on the lunar year of 354 days. The number of days each month is adjusted according to the lunar cycle, beginning about two days after the new moon. This means that the festivals move backward each year. The Islamic year begins on the first day of Muharram, and is counted from the year in which Muhammad emigrated from Mecca to Medina.

> '*Public Worship is seventeen times better than private Worship.*'
>
> Al-Ghazali

Labels on the wheel diagram:

- 10 'Id-al-Adha (Festival of Slaughter) 8–13 Dhu al Hijjah (Pilgrimage)
- 1 Muharram (New Year)
- 10 Festival of Ashura (Martyrdom of Imam Hussein)
- 12/17 Milad al-Nabi (Muhammad's birthday) timing varies
- 1 'Id-al-Fitr (end of month of fasting)
- 21/23/25/or 29 Laylat-al-Qadr (Night of Power)
- Ramadan (month of fasting)
- 27 Laylat-al-Isra (Night Journey of the Prophet)

Islamic months: DHU AL HIJJAH, MUHARRAM, SAFAR, RABI' AL AWWAL, RABI' AL THANI, JUMADA AL AWWAL, JUMADA AL THANI, RAJAB, SHA'BAN, RAMADAN, SHAWWAL, DHU AL QI'DAH

Gregorian months: NOVEMBER, DECEMBER, JANUARY, FEBRUARY, MARCH, APRIL, MAY, JUNE, JULY, AUGUST, SEPTEMBER, OCTOBER

Legend:
- months in the Islamic calendar
- Gregorian calendar

An expression of this is the common direction – towards the Ka'ba in Mecca – in which all Muslims turn in prayer. Around the globe, all are united in direction, and in intention, within a human circle of worshippers. At a signal from the prayer leader – the *imam* – men and women assemble separately in rows, at the mosque, or in the home or place of work, taking care that each person is close to the next. Carefully following the lead of the *imam*, they pray as a single body, quietly reciting words of prayer from the *Qur'an*. At the same time, they bow their bodies in a series of ritual movements until, from an initial standing position, all are upon their knees, with foreheads touching the floor – the whole congregation enacting, as a single body, its submission before the majesty of God, and asking for his guidance and mercy. Each of the five sets of prayers includes the repetition of *Allahu akbar* – 'God is greatest' – and of the first *surah* of the *Qur'an*, itself a prayer. At the end of the prayer, each person passes the Arabic words of peace to neighbours on right and left: *as-salamu alaikum*, 'peace be upon you'. Private prayers often follow the public service.

ALMSGIVING

'O you who believe, perform the *salah* and give the *zakah*.' Prayer is linked closely with almsgiving, the third pillar of Islam, often described by modern Muslims as the pillar of social action. Externally, *zakah* is the duty of sharing one's wealth with the poor, the needy, the debtor, the prisoner, the wayfarer – all who are less fortunate than oneself, but equally part of the worshipping community and equally precious to God. The *Qur'an* is less concerned with the quantity, and more with the quality, of giving. When it is offered 'in search of God's pleasure and for the strengthening of their own souls, it is as the likeness of a garden on a hill; the rainstorm smites it and it brings forth its fruit twofold'. The inward attitude is all-important; discretion is preferred to ostentation, and reproach on the part of the giver makes the action worthless.

The *Shari'a* is meticulous in determining the amounts of alms which should be given on different categories of possessions, but contemporary practice simplifies the matter to an annual rate of 2.5 per cent of one's cash balance. However Muslim devotional literature reflects equally the inwardness of *zakah* as 'purification' of the soul. It is a mercy to the giver as much as to the recipient; a means to atone for sins which are motivated by human self-centredness, or by irresponsible stewardship of possessions.

FASTING

Special alms are given on the two main religious festivals of the Islamic calendar, the first of which, '*Id al-Fitr* or *Bairam*, marks the end of Ramadan, the holy month of fasting. Fasting (*sawm*) is the fourth pillar of Muslim worship, and involves total abstinence from food and drink through the daylight hours of the entire month, from early dawn to sunset.

In some ways this is the most obviously communal of the duties of Islamic worship. The physical discipline means that social behaviour of the whole community has to change for the duration of the month; the pace of life slows down, and there is time for reflection. It is a period when social relationships are reaffirmed, reconciliations encouraged, and the solidarity of the community is expressed. Mosque attendance swells, particularly on the Night of Power (*laylat al-qadr*), towards the end of the month, when Muslims commemorate the descent of the *Qur'an* from heaven, and the beginning of Muhammad's ministry.

The fundamental intention of fasting is thanksgiving. Inwardly, the fast is thought of as a disciplining of the soul, to wait patiently upon God who guides and provides. This inward aspect is of great importance. Muhammad is reported to have said that, of all the duties of worship, *sawm* is the most loved by God, since it is seen only by him.

THE *HAJJ*

The fifth of the fundamental duties of Islamic worship – to be fulfilled once in a lifetime if at all possible – is the *Hajj*, the pilgrimage to Mecca and its vicinity. Here are the most holy places for Muslims, full of 'memorials' of God's guidance in times past. There are associations with Muhammad, who began his life and ministry in the city, and also with his prophetic precursor, Abraham, who, according

Throngs of Muslims, clothed in white, walk around the Ka'ba, Mecca, in the first rite of their pilgrimage.

to the *Qur'an*, built the Ka'ba, helped by his son, Ishmael, as a sign of their submission to God, with the prayer that God would show them 'our ways of worship'.

A visit to Mecca has religious significance for Muslims at any time of the year. But with the twelfth month of the calendar, *Dhu al Hijjah*, the season of the *Hajj*, or Great Pilgrimage, arrives. At any other time it is known as *Umra*, the Little Pilgrimage. Pilgrims flock to Mecca, each wearing the simple pilgrimage clothing of white cloth, denoting the state of ritual purification. They congregate in the Great Mosque, and the first rite of pilgrimage is performed – the circumambulation around the Ka'ba. This is followed by running seven times between two small hills, recalling the plight of Hagar and her son, Ishmael, who, in Islamic, Jewish, and Christian tradition, were saved from certain death by a spring of water which God caused to break through the desert sands. This well is named in the Islamic tradition as *zamzam*, and from it the pilgrims may draw holy water, before journeying a few miles out of Mecca to Mount Arafat, where the *Hajj* comes to its climax. Here the pilgrims observe the rite of 'standing' from midday to sunset in meditation before God. Then they begin the return journey to Mecca, stopping overnight at Mazdalifa, where each pilgrim gathers pebbles. The following day, these are thrown ritually against three stone pillars, in the neighbouring village of Mina, recalling the moments in Abraham's life when he resisted Satan's temptations to disobey God. God had commanded him to prepare his son Ishmael for sacrifice as a test of his obedience (*islam*). The *Qur'an* tells how the child was ransomed 'with a tremendous victim', and in joyful recollection of this act of divine mercy, the pilgrims offer the ritual sacrifice of sheep or camels, the meaning of which is clearly stated in the *Qur'an*: 'their flesh and blood reach not to God, but your devotion reaches him'.

With the intention of magnifying God, and remembering him 'with a more lively remembrance', Muslims throughout the world join with the pilgrims in Mina for the Feast of the Slaughter, which brings the *Hajj* to an end. Muslims remember their corporate identity and responsibility, as a worshipping community created by Muhammad. Muhammad believed this festival was the fulfilment of the Muslim community for which Abraham is said to have prayed before the Ka'ba:

> *Our Lord make us submissive to thee, and of our seed a community submissive to thee, and show us our ways of worship, and turn towards us. Lo! thou, only thou, art the Relenting, the Merciful*

(The Qur'an, surah 2:128).

The Islamic (*Hijri*) calendar is based on the lunar year of 354 days. The number of days each month is adjusted according to the lunar cycle, beginning about two days after the new moon, which means the festivals move backward each year. The Islamic year begins on the first day of Muharram, and is counted from the year in which Muhammad emigrated from Mecca to Medina.

DAVID KERR

CHAPTER 73

The Law of Islam

Down the centuries, the traditional education of Muslims has rested on twin pillars: theology taught them what they should believe, and the sacred law prescribed how they should behave. In practice, the law has been the senior partner, for Islam has always been far more explicit about the quality of life God has ordained for his creatures than about the nature of the Creator himself. Although the role of Islamic law has changed considerably in recent years, it can still be described as 'the epitome of Islamic thought, the most typical manifestation of the Islamic way of life, the core and kernel of Islam itself'.

SHARI'A

The sacred law of Islam is called the *Shari'a* – a word which originally meant 'the way to a watering-place', but came to be used of the path of God's commandments. It is regarded by Muslims as firmly based on divine revelation, derived from four main sources:

1. The *Qur'an*, which, they believe, has existed eternally in Arabic in heaven, and was revealed piecemeal to Muhammad by the angel Jibril (Gabriel) as occasion demanded.
2. The *sunnah*, or practice of the Prophet, as enshrined in countless traditions of what he said, did, or permitted.
3. The *ijma'*, or consensus of the Muslim community, or of its leading scholars.
4. *qiyas* – analogical deductions from the first three sources.

Orientalists have, however, shown that the raw material of the *Shari'a* was provided by pre-Islamic customary – and even codified – law and the administrative practices of early Islam, systematized and Islamicized by scholar-jurists in the light of those Islamic norms which had come to be accepted. They also insist that, for a number of decades, the law was wide open to foreign influences current in the conquered territories, or ingrained in the minds of converts to Islam.

The *Shari'a* has often been classified under five categories:

1. What God has commanded
2. What God has recommended, but not made strictly obligatory

3. What God has left legally indifferent
4. What God has deprecated, but not actually prohibited
5. What God has expressly forbidden.

As such, its scope is much wider than any Western concept of law, for it covers every aspect of life. Obviously a great deal of it could never be enforced by any human court, and must be left to the Day of Judgment. But, in theory, the *Shari'a* was a divinely revealed blueprint, to which every Muslim – from caliph to slave – must attempt to approximate.

In theory, human regulations were only appropriate in those matters which God had left 'legally indifferent'. In practice, from a very early date, even the official courts allowed a number of 'devices' which eased the inconvenience of some of the *Shari'a's* precepts.

Muslim rulers, moreover, found its standards of proof too exacting for the maintenance of public order. Muslim merchants found its prohibitions too restrictive for the life of the markets, while local communities of Muslims found its rigid prescripts too alien to their age-old customs. So less rigid courts soon appeared beside the official *qadis'* courts. But the fact remains that, until little more than a century ago, the *Shari'a* remained the basic and residual law – to which lip-service, at least, was almost always paid – throughout of the Muslim world.

INTERPRETING THE LAW

But the *Shari'a* was not a system of law that was either codified or uniform. Although it is regarded as firmly based on divine revelation, it has been developed and elaborated by generations of legal scholars, who interpreted the relevant verses in the *Qur'an* and those traditions which they accepted as authentic. They also drew from these sources a plethora of analogical deductions. At first, moreover, any adequately qualified jurist had the right of *ijtihad* – going back to the original sources to derive a rule of law to cover any problem that arose.

At a very early date, the Muslim community became divided between the Sunni, or 'orthodox', majority and the Shi'a and Khariji minorities, which split into further exclusive sub-sects, while the Sunni majority divided into a number of different schools or 'rites'. As these schools and sects crystallized, the right of independent deduction was progressively replaced by the duty to accept the authority of the great jurists of the past (*taqlid*). Today, even the most learned Sunni jurists are normally considered to be under this authority. The Ithna 'Ashari sub-sect of the Shi'a, which remains the dominant sect in Iran, still recognizes *mujtahidun* who may exercise *ijtihad* in certain circumstances. It is only among the Isma'ili Shi'as that the *imam* – or, in some cases his representative, the Da'i Mutlaq – can give a wholly authoritative ruling.

CIVIL LAW

Since about the middle of the nineteenth century, the position of Islamic law has changed radically throughout the greater part of the Muslim world. First in the Ottoman Empire, next in what was then 'British India', and subsequently elsewhere, the impact of modern life has loosened the sway of the *Shari'a* in two major ways. In many spheres of life, the *Shari'a* has been displaced by new codes of law, largely derived from the Western world. In the Ottoman Empire in the 1850s and 1860s, for example, the Commercial Code, the Penal Code, the Code of Commercial Procedure, and the Code of Maritime Commerce were all based on French models. But when the Ottoman reformers came to the law of obligations – contract, tort, etc. – they debated whether again to turn to European law or to compile a comparable code derived from Islamic sources.

Eventually the latter view prevailed. So the resultant code, commonly known as the *Majalla*, completed in 1876, was compiled from the rulings of a selection of Sunni jurists – although all these opinions had received some form of recognition from the Hanafi school. The *Majalla* was thus of immense jurisprudential significance. For the first time in history, a code of law based firmly on principles derived from the *Shari'a* was enacted by the authority of the state. And for the first time, again, a compilation was made of provisions of heterogeneous origin, selected on the broad principle of their suitability to modern life, rather than their established precedent in one particular school. Moreover, all these new codes were administered in secular courts by personnel trained in modern law schools. It was only family law that continued to be applied in the age-old way in the *Shari'a* courts, uncodified and unreformed.

The second change was less obvious, but equally important. In 1915, the position of Muslim wives, sometimes tying them – even in impossible circumstances – to their husbands under the dominant Hanafi rules, virtually compelled the Sultan to intervene even in matters of family law. So he issued two imperial decrees permitting wives to request a judicial dissolution of marriage in certain circumstances sanctified by one or another of the Sunnian schools. Once this dyke had been opened, the tide came in very fast indeed. In 1917 the Ottoman Law of Family Rights was promulgated, based on an extended application of these principles.

In one Muslim country after another, much the same happened. In 'British India' the new secular codes were based on the Common Law of England, rather than the Civil Law of France. Here both secular law and the uncodified family law of different religious communities were administered by the same courts. In Turkey, by contrast, the *Shari'a* was abolished and European codes, only slightly adapted, adopted in its place.

In Saudi Arabia, on the other hand, the *Shari'a* remains dominant – though even there statutory regulations began to proliferate. Most Muslim countries, however, now have largely secular codes in all except family law – which must, they insist, remain distinctively Islamic. And even this has been codified – in whole or in part – in a way which makes it more suitable for modern life. In countries such as Somalia and the People's Democratic Republic of Yemen, the presence of Marxist influence in such codes is sometimes plain to see.

Thus the present picture is very different from that of the past. Whereas the once-dominant *Shari'a* is now, for the most part, confined to family law, the current tendency is to produce civil codes that incorporate principles derived from Islamic law alongside those of an alien origin. A few countries have, even more recently, begun to introduce some Islamic criminal sanctions and economic practices – a clear evidence of a resurgence of Islamic fundamentalism. In most Muslim countries, moreover, the law – whatever its origin – has been codified by legislative enactments. Thus the authority of the law, once implicit and transcendent, is now, in most countries, constitutional, resting on the will of the people as expressed by their executive or legislature.

NORMAN ANDERSON

CHAPTER 74

Science, Art, and Culture

Islam has produced not only successful army leaders and statesmen, but also equally talented poets and musicians, architects and builders. But above all were the Muslim philosophers and naturalists, whose achievements between the ninth and fourteenth centuries laid the foundations of modern science, on which our civilization was built.

For Muslims to start to study the world, they needed a 'supernatural' incentive. Allah was looked on as the Unapproachable, the Impenetrable, so Islam had taught that his creation was similarly unapproachable. It was Ma'mun, caliph of Baghdad from 813 to 833, who supplied that incentive. In a dream, Ma'mun saw the ghost of Aristotle, who convinced him there is no contradiction between religion and reason. Thus freed from all his scruples, Ma'mun ordered a 'house of wisdom' to be built. In the library, all available books in the world were to be collected.

The works of Greek, Persian, and Indian writers were brought together and translated into Arabic, and the knowledge obtained was examined, remodelled, and developed. So the starting-point and basis of Islamic knowledge was the Greek conviction that, behind the visible chaos of the world, there is a fundamental order, ruled by general laws and accessible to human reason. Thus scientific effort pursued primarily philosophical goals, the discovery of the 'basic laws' of the world.

DOCTORS AND MATHEMATICIANS

Muslim doctors built on the experience and knowledge of ancient Persia, and discovered the principle of the circulation of the blood, evolved treatment methods for smallpox, and practised painless operations under anaesthetics. The books of Avicenna (Ibn Sina, 980–1037), a great philosopher and physician, were used as textbooks in the universities of Europe until the seventeenth century.

In mathematics, Islamic academics learnt from India, from where they adopted the decimal system and use of the zero, which they called *sifr*, the empty one. Leonardo de Pisa, who studied with the Arabs, translated this foreign concept as '*cephirum*', and it then developed via '*zefiro*' to '*zero*'. It was the Arabs also who developed the subject of algebra, using symbols to represent unknown quantities.

In the early centuries, the Arabs had used the stars as guides in the desert. When they became familiar with the work of Ptolemy, in the eighth century, they also began to investigate the sky

Intricate Islamic stonework at the Moorish Alhambra, Granada, Spain, consisting solely of non-representational decoration.

scientifically. Star names and astronomical terms such as zenith, nadir, and azimuth are an enduring witness to this work. Scholars also collected their geographical knowledge in atlases and travel guides, which recorded the main roads of all known countries, as well as the names and positions of the large towns, and their distances one from another. They also calculated the circumference and diameter of the earth.

WORLDWIDE INFLUENCE

At the height of their culture, the knowledge of the Muslims extended to all areas, and the fascination they inspired in Europe was huge. Wherever the West met the East, the West started to learn. In Sicily, the court of Frederick II (1194–1250) became a centre of Arabian philosophy and science. In the Levant, the Crusader knights became familiar with the Eastern way of life. Above all, this contact took place in Islamic Spain. As early as the tenth century, towns were thriving. Cordoba had over 500,000 inhabitants with 700 mosques, 300 public baths, and 70 libraries. Its streets and squares were paved and brightly lit at night. Everything which made life pleasant was offered for sale: marzipan, soap and perfume, coffee, damsons and sugar, mattresses, caps and jackets, oranges, asparagus. Their influence spread right through Europe. Travelling singers brought their songs and also Arabic instruments — lute and guitar, trumpet, horn and flute. Through Muslim philosophers such as Averroes (Ibn Rushd, 1126–98,) and Avicenna, Aristotle was rediscovered in the West.

In the fine arts, calligraphy, ceramics, and architecture, Islam absorbed influences, taking the cultural inheritance of the peoples it conquered and transforming them, creating an all-embracing culture of a unique type. Islamic architecture can be seen in Cordoba, Granada, Marrakesh and Cairo, in Istanbul and Damascus, Agra and Delhi. All reflect the form and style of the country they are in, as well as the Islamic influence that unites them. The 'Islamic' style has a particular sensitivity for the decorative, and strives to turn the natural appearance of things into the abstract. The *Qur'an* teaches that an object and its image are magically united, which was probably why representational art was prohibited.

With the sack of Baghdad by the Mongol invaders in 1258, and the general decline of the Islamic world, the development of art, culture, and science in Islam halted.

LOTHAR SCHMALFUS

CHAPTER 75

Family and Society

The family is a key element of Muslim life and society, one of the cornerstones of social stability and security in the community (*ummah*). The *Qur'an* and *Hadith* abound in regulations, strictures, and caveats regarding the organization and conduct of the Muslim family, and family bonds are the strongest of all social relationships. Loyalty and commitment to the family transcend all other social loyalties.

The Muslim family is established through marriage, Islam frowning on extramarital relationships between men and women. The act of procreation is strictly within the family unit, and fornication and adultery (*zinah*) are sins for which stringent penalties are stipulated in Islamic law. Such infringements are regarded as a source of chaos (*fitnah*). Privacy and modesty are essential for the procreation and proper upbringing of children.

MARRIAGE

Marriage is strongly recommended by the *Qur'an* and the *Hadith*. Celibacy is not considered a virtue in itself, except in special cases, such as the inability to support a wife properly. Whereas marriage (*nikah*) is a social and legal contract – not a sacrament as in some other religions – the *Qur'an* and *Hadith* provide many guidelines and laws testifying to the fact that it has divine and prophetic sanction. People of marriageable age are advised to marry, rather than run the temptation of extra-marital sexual relationships.

Contrary to Western misapprehension, the consent of both male and female is required for *nikah*. According to Islamic law, the prospective bride and bridegroom are not only allowed to meet before marriage, they are advised to. There is no scriptural sanction for forced marriages, or so-called 'honour killings'.

Marriage is a public affair, not a purely private or secret act. Technically, at least two witnesses are required to the signing of

> The *Qur'an* regards the home as a microcosm of the *ummah* and the world community. It emphasises the importance of making it 'the abode of peace' through just living.
>
> Riffat Hassan (b. 1943)

> O Lord, grant us in our wives and in our offspring the joy of our eyes.
>
> The *Qur'an*, surah 25:74.

the marriage contract by the bridegroom and the bride's legal guardian, and usually a *qadi* (Islamic judge) is present. The bridegroom gives the wife a dowry (*mahr*), which can be in cash or in kind. This belongs to the woman, to use at her discretion, even if the marriage ends in divorce, unless divorce is initiated by the wife.

The *Qur'an* permits polygyny: a Muslim man may marry up to four wives – though a wife may only marry one husband. This is not a licence for unbridled promiscuity, but a concession to circumstances requiring the care of widows or orphans through marriage, such as the death of large numbers of Muslim males in war (*surah* 4:3). This message of the *Qur'an* was revealed in the context of the Battle of Uhud (625 CE), where about 10 per cent of Muslim males in the community were killed. The Prophet himself – although monogamous from the age of twenty-five to the age of fifty-two, when his wife Kadijah died – married war widows and orphans, to set an example to his disciples. The concession for polygyny came with many stipulations that make it clear that the ideal in Islam is monogamy. The injunction to treat all wives equally comes with the caveat that it is humanly impossible to do so (*surah* 4:129).

DIVORCE

Divorce (*talaq*, the untying of a knot) is permitted in Islam, but was said by the Prophet to be most hateful to God. Men have greater authority to effect divorce, but the Quranic verses permitting this power are combined with exhortations to charity, compassion, and justice to women. A waiting period of three months (*idda*) is stipulated, to ensure that the wife is not carrying a child, and the divorce can be revoked during this waiting period. Three pronouncements of *talaq* are required to make the divorce final. Though they can all be spoken at the same time, and such divorce is binding, this is considered to be irregular, or innovative, divorce (*talaq bida*), and is looked upon as offensive. Remarriage of divorcees is permitted, but when divorce has become final and irrevocable, the man cannot marry the divorcee again until she has married some other person and divorced him. This is evidently to ensure that divorcing a woman is not undertaken lightly. When the divorce process is initiated by the wife, it is known as *khula*. This involves her petitioning an Islamic court for divorce, which – if there are justifiable grounds – will be granted. In such cases, the wife will be required to return the *mahr* – the dowry she has received from her husband.

CHILDREN

The many stipulations regarding children in the *Qur'an*, the *Hadith*, and *Shari'a* testify to the importance placed on the care of children. The *Qur'an* shows particular concern for the welfare of orphans. Children are treated with great care, affection, and responsibility, and in return are expected to love, respect, and obey their parents (*surah* 6:152–54).

I AM A MUSLIM

I had my first lessons in religion – Islam – on my mother's lap, and learnt to utter a few verses from the Qur'an by heart. Her recitations of the Qur'an in the early hours of the morning left a lasting impression on me, which resounds in my ears to this day whenever I remember her. I lost my father when I was barely one year old, and my young mother had a hard time bringing up a family of six children, hence she sought refuge in religion and prayers, and took special care in our religious education. The verses she memorized carry us through in our daily prayers all our life.

During my youth and working life I was not a particularly devout Muslim. My religion has become much more important following my retirement. Part of this rekindled interest is undoubtedly influenced by my association with fellow Muslims. Even so, I wouldn't call myself a strict follower of the faith. I shun some of the practices and puritanical teachings of the so-called 'fundamentalists'. I pray daily, but wouldn't like to be coerced into religious rituals. Rather, I find comfort and solace in praying to Allah in solitude. Although praying in congregations can be inspiring, I sometimes find it too repetitive and ritualistic.

I have a family with two grown-up children, both born in the West. Being raised in a Western society made a significant difference in their upbringing. In particular, compared with my upbringing in India, they had minimal religious teaching. This concerns me, as I feel responsible for alienating them from their faith. I now believe that religious education is an essential part in moulding the character of a person, irrespective of the religion they decide to follow. The moral and religious aspects of life have become all the more important in the present-day world, where families struggle to stay together, and societies seem to be going through a period of upheaval. My wife and I are, therefore, taking extra care with our grandchildren, making sure they receive basic lessons in religious and moral education.

A few years ago I performed the Hajj pilgrimage with my family, which has left another lasting impression on me. The annual Hajj is a once-in-a-lifetime occasion for Muslims to meet fellow pilgrims from all over the world. It is an experience that tests one's patience, tolerance, and physical endurance. It also inspired a sense of fellow feeling for others.

A mosque is supposed to be a place for prayers and social contact. Unfortunately, I find there is little scope to talk with, and enquire about, others; the only other way to socialize with fellow Muslims is at private parties or weddings.

Muslims have very few religious festivals, the main two being after Ramadan and Bakrid ('Id-al-Adha), and young and old, rich and poor alike meet to celebrate these with great fervour. My recollection of 'Id (Eid) celebrations in childhood is one of rejoicing and excitement, as well as days of preparations. We all dressed in our new clothes and visited friends and relations. I remember there being plenty of delicious food, which was prepared and exchanged. The best part for the children was collecting money from the elders. and then all visiting the cinema house. Everybody knew everybody else in the town, and it was important to visit them to make up any differences. It was a time of renewing ties and friendships. Unfortunately, I find there is little community life in this country. It is probably this feeling of isolation that impels us to our religion.

Although my religion is not so important to me, at times of trouble my thoughts go automatically towards religion. A feeling of helplessness makes me submit to God Almighty. I feel my religion is my personal affair, and I don't like the intervention of a third person; but I do regard the prophet Muhammad as a good role model, who has left marvellous examples of compassion, piety, simplicity, and honesty. There is no walk of life for which he has not left guidance. Although I pray daily, I only read the scriptures occasionally. Because the *Qur'an* is in Arabic, which I hardly understand, I read translations, as well as various interpretations and commentaries.

I get comfort in submission to Allah, and thank Him for His bounty, my good health, the air we breathe, the water we drink, the sunshine, and the seasons we enjoy without our asking or paying for it. If living in a secular society means not recognizing these gifts of God, then I don't want to live in such a society. I would much rather be a religious person.

As a religious person, I observe certain food regulations. Islam has strict guidelines about what to eat and what not to eat. For example, it forbids the consumption of any intoxicating drinks. I wear Western clothes for convenience and climatic reasons, and I think it is everyone's right to wear and eat what they want. That said, I think it is good for people to dress in a way that reflects their distinctive culture. Otherwise this world becomes a monotonous and boring place to live in.

I'm not a strict follower of Islam, yet our family life is very much influenced by our faith. We follow our religion in matters relating to marriage, birth, and death. My wife performs prayers five times a day, and recites the *Qur'an* daily. My son also attends the mosque once a week, work permitting. However, living in a Western society it is not always possible to meet the requirement that a Muslim should pray five times a day. Again, there is no fixed day for our festivals and sometimes they fall on a working day, which can present difficulties. For example, during the month of Ramadan, a Muslim is supposed to fast from daybreak to sunset. Because this may mean sixteen or seventeen hours of fasting, depending on the season, it becomes very strenuous for a working person. Hence, there are limitations to following our religion in the strictest terms.

Mohammad A. Khan

A parent's first responsibility is the proper care and upbringing of children, and there are *hadith* that confirm the adage 'charity begins at home'. The care of the family takes priority even over charity for religious purposes. Contrary to common Western perception, both boys and girls are equally prized by Muslim parents. Children are looked upon as a gift from God, and there are specific injunctions in the *Qur'an* not to harm them, especially with reference to the pre-Islamic practice of burying female children alive in the sand. The father has primary responsibility for providing for the children, but in cases of divorce or separation the mother has custody.

The Quranic injunctions regarding married life make it clear that the underlying principle is equality and mutuality (*surah* 2:187 and 228).

THEODORE GABRIEL

CHAPTER 76

Islam in the Modern World

The story of the Islamic world from 1700 has often been described in terms of the 'decline of Islam' confronted by the 'rise of the West', or the struggle between a vanishing 'tradition' and a triumphant 'modernity.' This is now rejected as an over-simplified picture.

RIVAL CAMPS

The increasing political corruption and military weakness of the once powerful imperial structures of the Ottomans of Turkey, the Safavids of Iran, and the Mughals of India was paralleled throughout the eighteenth century by the economic expansion of the British, French, and Dutch empires. Economic penetration alone, however, had little immediate impact upon Muslim religious developments, which were directed at the social and moral reconstruction of Islamic societies, and a reorientation of the Sufi tradition. Sunni revival movements arose out of local conditions, while ideas of reform were disseminated by traditional means, such as the annual pilgrimage to Mecca. Indeed the holy cities of Mecca and Medina were centres of study visited by scholars from as far afield as India and Morocco.

Two outstanding – but contrasting – figures were the Indian Sufi, Shah Wali Allah (1702–62) of Delhi, and the puritan Arab, Muhammad ibn Abd al-Wahhab (1703–92). Although each stressed the *Qur'an* and the Prophet's *sunna* (model example) as binding sources for faith and law, and each rejected the blind imitation of generations of medieval legal scholarship, Wali Allah accepted the possible vision of an immanent God, while Abd al-Wahhab emphasized the transcendence of the One Unique – and unknowable – God. Their influence has come down to the present.

MODERNIZERS

By the end of World War I, the three Muslim empires lay dismembered, and European colonial powers occupied, or directly influenced, the entire Muslim world. 'Modernity', understood as a cluster of social, political, economic and cultural institutions and values,

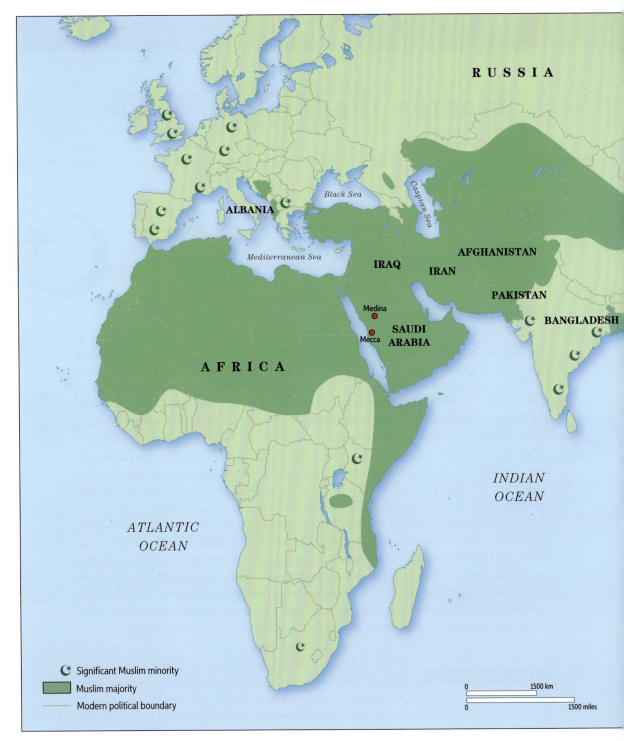

The Islamic World Today

was a transformation historically originating in Europe and North America. In the European overseas dominions, Muslims experienced modernity within a power relationship between themselves and their colonial masters, which ensured their responses to it would differ significantly. Specifically, Muslims experienced Europe's power not as secular, but as Christian power. While Muslims welcomed the material benefits of science and technology, they remained ambivalent to modern values, such as democracy, and hostile to missionary propaganda against the core of their faith. In places such as India, Algeria, and Palestine, the retreat from colonial rule down to the 1960s left much suffering and bitterness in its wake. Not surprisingly, modern Muslim reformers of the late nineteenth and twentieth centuries found it difficult to embrace either social change as secularization, or the marginalization of religion away from concerns for political, economic, or social problems.

Two early major Sunni modernist reformers were the Indian Sayyid Ahmad Khan (1817–98) and the Egyptian Muhammad 'Abduh (1845–1905), both of whom received a more or less traditional education, had an early relationship with Sufi spirituality, and later gained first-hand experience of Europe, influences which informed their efforts at social reform focused upon education and the need to modernize Islam. They held that, rather than interpreting the *Qur'an* in terms of the Prophetic Traditions (*Hadith*), revelation could be understood solely in its own terms, implicitly proposing that every Muslim could search scripture's meaning for him/herself. The banner of all modernist thought was *surah* 13:12: 'God does not alter what is in a people until they alter what is in themselves.' Rather than adhere literally to the past, Muslims must shape their future in the public interest, in order to deal with the dramatic new circumstances of the modern era. Religious debate and controversy has continued through the twentieth century to the present day.

THE RADICALS

The aim of more radical reformers was to Islamize modernity, rather than modernize Islam. Two key radicals who helped to shape movements sometimes called 'fundamentalist' or 'Islamist' were the Indian/Pakistani Abu al-Ala Maududi (1903–79) and the Egyptian Sayyid Qutb (1906–66), both of whom believed deeply that Muslims should conduct their entire lives according

to God's law. Their work also provided a strident, if not trenchant, critique of secular Western societies. A similar impulse moved Ayatollah Khomeini's revolution in Iran

Asian Muslim women pray together, their heads covered.

in 1979. Radicals became the chief target of secularists who formed the backbone of the new political elites of the new Muslim nation states following independence from colonial powers. Underlying these controversies is a contest over rival claims of authority to interpret the foundational religious sources. Some secularists even attempted to justify the separation of religion from politics by appealing to the Prophet's model community in Medina.

BEYOND 9/11

Over the past quarter of a century, Western observers and governments have noted the phenomenon of a 'resurgent Islam'. The tragic events of 11 September 2001 seemed to some to confirm fears of a 'clash of civilizations'. In this perception, two important factors have been overlooked. First, discussions among Muslim leaders worldwide, conservatives included, expressed long-held concern over the dangers of mounting religious extremism within the community, well aware that their own agendas were in danger of being hijacked by a minority. Second, extremists have articulated in religious terms current social-political problems that plague their own and other Muslim societies. Such problems include the corruption of, and repression by, regimes closely supported by Western governments, some of whose policies are widely regarded as perpetrating injustices upon Muslim peoples in areas such as Palestine, Chechnya, Afghanistan, Algeria, Iraq, and Bosnia. Effective resolution of such conflicts would help to undermine solutions proposed by extremist religious groups, and give moderate Muslim voices a forum for debate with often equally immoderate and unrepentant secularist power holders.

WOMEN AND MEN

In this multifaceted debate a growing contribution is to be expected from Muslim women. The individual's sense of the broader Muslim community is strong; men and women pray as equals in the eyes of God, and the contribution of each to community life is accepted equally by God: 'I will deny no man or woman among you the reward of their labours' (The Qur'an, surah 3:195). Whereas the spiritual equality of men and women has been traditionally agreed upon, questions of patriarchal power and social equality have been hotly contested for more than a century. Modernist thinkers, male and female – challenged by radicals, both male and female – have sought to reduce male privilege in the family, for example, by arguing that the Qur'an's true intent supported monogamous marriage, not polygyny; by raising the marriage age, and thereby abolishing union with, or between, children; by restricting the male right of divorce, and increasing the grounds upon which women may seek divorce. Yet the overall goal of change is still to preserve a harmonious and stable family life, contributing to the greater good of the community, with the relationship of its parts – men, women, and children – based upon equity. It is part of the contest over who may 'speak for God' in interpreting the divine message. Female scholars and laywomen, albeit slowly and quietly today, are insisting their voices be heard too. As the future unfolds, observers should be more attentive to what Muslims, men and women, say as well as do.

DAVID WAINES

QUESTIONS

1. Why is Muhammad so important in Islam?

2. Explain the role in Islam of traditions from other religions.

3. How and why do Sunni and Shi'a Muslims differ in their view of the succession to Muhammad?

4. Explain how decisions in *Shari'a*, the Muslim legal system, are reached.

5. How does Muslim doctrine on the *Qur'an* demonstrate its huge importance to Islam?

6. What is Sufism, and why is it inappropriate to refer to it as a 'sect' of Islam?

7. Explain *tawhid*, the Muslim doctrine of monotheism.

8. How far do the Five Pillars reflect Islam as the religion of a united community?

9. Why is Mecca so important to Islam?

10. Why do some Muslims today believe their religion to be incompatible with Western secularism?

FURTHER READING

Armstrong, Karen, *Islam: A Short History*. London: Phoenix, 2001.

Aslan, Reza, *No God but God: The Origins, Evolution, and Future of Islam*. New York: Random House, 2006.

Coulson, N. G., *A History of Islamic Law*. Edinburgh: Edinburgh University Press, 1964.

Esposito, John, ed., *The Oxford Encyclopedia of the Modern Islamic World*. New York: Oxford University Press, 1995.

Hilldenbrand, Robert, *Islamic Art and Architecture*. London: Thames and Hudson, 1998.

Nasr, Seyyed Hossein, *The Garden of Truth: The Vision and Promise of Sufism, Islam's Mystical Tradition*. New York: HarperOne, 2008.

Peters, Francis E., *A Reader on Classical Islam*. Princeton: Princeton University Press, 1994.

Qureshi, Emran, and Michael A. Sells, eds, *The New Crusades: Constructing the Muslim Enemy*. New York: Columbia, 2003.

Watt, W. Montgomery, *Islamic Philosophy and Theology*. Edinburgh: Edinburgh University Press, 1962.

PART 12
SIKHISM

SUMMARY

Of the world's major religions, Sikhism is one of the youngest. Around 1500, Nanak, the religion's founder, is said to have been transformed by God while bathing, and emerged with the words 'There is no Hindu, there is no Muslim' – a simple creed which formed the basis for Sikhism. Reflecting this idea, Sikh scripture begins by emphasizing the unity of God and his creation. Accordingly, believers are encouraged to accept all religious traditions, and to treat all humanity with equal respect – radical notions in sixteenth century Punjab, riven by conflict between Hindus and Muslims, and dominated by the social restrictions of the caste system. *Karma* and the cycle of life – *chaurasi* – are important in Sikhism: in order to escape the punishment of rebirth, one must aspire to the Guru's example. This is not achieved by asceticism, however, since the Guru was a married man, who fulfilled his obligations to both family and community. After Nanak, a line of ten Gurus, who consolidated his legacy, led Sikhism. During this period, Sikhism's primary scripture, the *Adi Granth*, was compiled, from the work of the first five Gurus. In the era of the tenth – and last – Guru, the *Adi Granth* was itself instituted as a Guru, while the *Khalsa*, the community of the initiated, was founded.

Sikhism's early development was in a Muslim kingdom. In time, Sikhs would establish their own short-lived state; but during the nineteenth and twentieth centuries had to exist under British rule, and then within the largely Hindu secular Indian republic. In the late nineteenth century, the Sikh reform movement emerged, to reassert the religion's distinct identity, which many feared was being lost. The last decades of the twentieth century saw the rise of a Sikh-Punjabi nationalist movement, which inevitably resulted in significant conflict with the Indian state, most notably during the 1980s. A significant and vocal diaspora community meanwhile has grown in the West, as a result of post-war migration.

A Historical Overview

The history of Sikhism has always been closely linked to the Punjab, the land of its origins, because of its situation in the north-west of the Indian subcontinent, always the first region of the fertile northern plains to be exposed to successive conquests by invaders crossing the great mountain boundaries through such routes as the Khyber Pass. The first such cultural inroads recorded were those of the Aryan tribes in the Vedic period, which initiated the beginnings of the Hindu tradition. The last were the invasions mounted by Muslim sultans from Afghanistan and Central Asia from early in the first millennium CE, which resulted not only in the establishment of centuries of Muslim rule over the Punjab, but also in the presence of substantial numbers of Muslims in Punjabi society, largely the product of peaceful conversion.

When Sikhism first emerged, some five hundred years ago, it appeared in a society already religiously divided. It would be quite misleading to think of Sikhism as a mechanical combination of Hindu and Muslim elements, since from its beginnings it has been self-defined as a new and independent third way. Equally, its evolution needs to be understood as a complex process of the ongoing relationship, within the Punjab and beyond, of a vigorous minority community to the two numerically larger traditions of Hinduism and Islam.

GURU NANAK

Nanak (1469–1539) is revered by all branches of the religion as the defining first Guru of the *Sikhs* (Punjabi for 'disciples'). He was by birth a Hindu of the Khatri caste — professionals with strong hereditary links to the administration — and his father was a village accountant. Nanak himself was married with a family, and had a career as an administrator working for a local Muslim nobleman. His mission began when he was around the age of thirty, with a transforming experience of the divine reality, granted to him when he entered the river to bathe. Mysteriously hidden from the view of his companions, he emerged after three days, uttering

> Great Guru whose encounter brought the Lord to mind!
>
> With his teaching as their salve, these eyes survey the world.
>
> Attached to the other, some traders left the Lord and roamed.
>
> How few have realized the Guru is the boat,
>
> Which delivers those he favours safe across.
>
> *Adi Granth 470.*

the words 'There is no Hindu, there is no Muslim,' taken as the inaugurating formula of the new religion. Nanak then embarked upon an extended series of travels, before returning later in his life to the Punjab, where he established a settled community of the first Sikhs.

Guru Nanak's teachings are embodied in his verses, hymns, and longer poetical works, which now form a substantial collection at the heart of the Sikh scriptures. In their broad thrust, these teachings are similar in content to those of other North Indian teachers of the medieval period from lower castes, such as Kabir (1440–1518) and Ravidas. They all preached that salvation was dependent upon devotion not to a divine incarnation, such as Krishna, but to the undifferentiated Formless One; and that to observe caste practices and Brahmanical authority was as futile for those who wished to be saved as obedience to the alternatives promulgated by Islam. But the subsequent, successful, independent development of Sikhism itself shows that Nanak was much more than just another teacher in this dissenting tradition of medieval Hinduism, called *nirgun bhakti* (devotion to the Formless).

Nanak's hymns combine a remarkable beauty and power of poetic expression with a distinctive coherence and ability for

Gurudwara Bangla Sahib, the most prominent Sikh gurdwara in Delhi, associated with the eighth Guru, Har Krishan, was first built in 1783.

systematic exposition, which is perhaps to be related to his professional background. Their contents embrace repeated praise of the divine order presided over and permeated by its creator, the one and only Immortal Being (*Akal Purakh*), with a penetrating analysis of the human condition, which is condemned through egotistical self-will (*haumai*, literally 'I-me') to the mechanical succession of suffering, and endless rebirths in blind unawareness of that order. In place of the false claims to offer true guidance offered by the religious specialists of the day, whether Brahmans, yogis, or Muslim clerics, Nanak sets out his own prescription for human salvation: the necessity of inner transformation through listening to the voice of the True Guru within the heart, and meditating with love upon the Divine Name. Only thus may freedom from self be gained, and escape from the cycle of transmigration be achieved, so that the liberated soul may at last join the company of saints in their eternal singing of praises at the court of the Immortal Being.

There is, however, nothing automatic about access to the path of salvation that Nanak describes. His hymns repeatedly emphasize that a righteous life is no guarantee of salvation, since the coming of the inner True Guru to any given individual depends on the favour of the Immortal Being. For this to happen, it is equally a necessary condition that the individual should have prepared him or herself for the True Guru's coming by living properly. Such a life does not entail the practice of elaborate rituals, or extreme asceticism, which are both frequently stated to be quite pointless. What is important is rather the discipline of living a normal life in this world, practising loving meditation on the divine reality, and supporting others through an honest existence, as summed up in the triple formula of 'the Name, giving, and keeping clean' (*nam dan isnan*).

THE LATER GURUS

As has been repeatedly demonstrated, the successful establishment of a religion depends not just upon the teachings of its founder, but also upon how the community created by them is subsequently organized. Besides being a teacher of outstanding force and insight, Guru Nanak was evidently a most capable organizer of his followers. He laid the foundations of some of the defining practices of the subsequent Sikh tradition, notably the establishment of daily offices of prayer (*nitnem*) and the practice of congregational assembly to hear the hymns of the Guru. Although married with two sons, Guru Nanak went outside his family to select a disciple to succeed him as the second Guru of the Sikh community, or *Panth* (path, way).

From the time of Guru Nanak's death, the Sikh Panth was led by a line of living Gurus, until the death of the tenth Guru in 1708. While rejection of the Hindu caste hierarchy was symbolically reinforced by the third Guru, Amar Das – through the institution of the *langar*, the temple kitchen offering food to all irrespective of caste – all the Gurus were from the same Khatri caste as Nanak; and from the fifth Guru onwards the succession became hereditary within a single family. Initially the centre of the community shifted with each Guru, until Guru Arjan founded the great temple at Amritsar known as the Golden Temple (*Harimandir*), which since its inauguration in 1604 has been the focal point of Sikhism.

At the same time, Guru Arjan undertook a project of still greater importance, in providing a unifying object of devotion for the Sikh Panth, through his codification of the Sikh scriptures, issued with the Guru's authority as the *Adi Granth* (original book). This is an enormous hymnal, filling 1,430 pages in the standard modern edition, and having a central place in the ritual of the Sikh temples, or *gurdwara* (gate of the Guru). Besides the compositions of Guru Nanak, the *Adi Granth* also contains those of the next four Gurus – who each used the same poetic name 'Nanak', in keeping with the belief that the transmission of the

THE TEN GURUS
Guru Nanak (1469–1539) founder of Sikhism
Guru Angad (1539–52)
Guru Amar Das (1552–74)
Guru Ram Das (1574–81)
Guru Arjan (1581–1606)
Guru Hargobind (1606–44)
Guru Har Rai (1644–61)
Guru Har Krishan (1661–64)
Guru Tegh Bahadur (1664–75)
Guru Gobind Singh (1675–1708)

SIKHISM TIMELINE

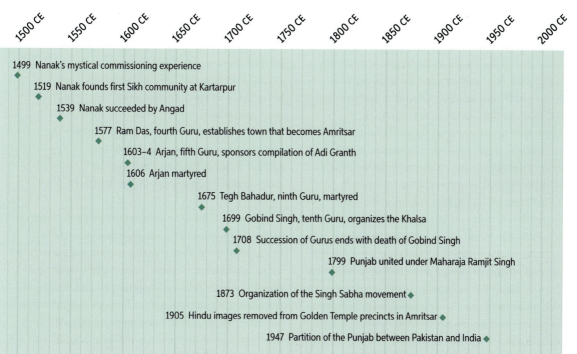

1500 CE 1550 CE 1600 CE 1650 CE 1700 CE 1750 CE 1800 CE 1850 CE 1900 CE 1950 CE 2000 CE

1499 Nanak's mystical commissioning experience

1519 Nanak founds first Sikh community at Kartarpur

1539 Nanak succeeded by Angad

1577 Ram Das, fourth Guru, establishes town that becomes Amritsar

1603–4 Arjan, fifth Guru, sponsors compilation of Adi Granth

1606 Arjan martyred

1675 Tegh Bahadur, ninth Guru, martyred

1699 Gobind Singh, tenth Guru, organizes the Khalsa

1708 Succession of Gurus ends with death of Gobind Singh

1799 Punjab united under Maharaja Ramjit Singh

1873 Organization of the Singh Sabha movement

1905 Hindu images removed from Golden Temple precincts in Amritsar

1947 Partition of the Punjab between Pakistan and India

1984 Indian government expels militants from the Golden Temple, killing hundreds of Sikhs

THE *KHALSA*

On *Baisakhi* day in 1699, the tenth Guru founded the *Khalsa*, the community of initiated (*amritdhari*) Sikhs. The nucleus of this dynamic community is popularly known as the five beloved ones (*panj-piare*), who volunteered their readiness to sacrifice their lives for the sake of the Guru on that historic day.

Thereupon the Guru prepared *amrit* ('water of immortality') – popularly known as *khande di pahul* ('water of the double-edged sword') – for the initiation ceremony. The five volunteers, who belonged to different caste groups, drank *amrit* from the same bowl, signifying their entry into the casteless fraternity of the *Khalsa*. The next most important innovation was to change their names. All five volunteers, like the Guru, had traditional Hindu names before the initiation ceremony. Now they were given a new corporate name: 'Singh'. Afterwards, the Guru received *amrit* from the *panj-piare*, and changed his name from Gobind Rai to Gobind Singh. He also admitted women into the *Khalsa*, who after the initiation received the name 'Kaur'.

According to tradition, Guru Gobind Singh prescribed a new code of discipline for members of the *Khalsa*, which includes the wearing of five emblems, collectively known as *panj kakke* (five ks), because each begins with the letter 'kakka' of the Gurmukhi script:

kes – uncut hair
kangha – a small wooden comb worn in hair
kirpan – a sword, nowadays a small one
kacha – a pair of knee-length breeches
kara – a steel bracelet worn on the right wrist

It is believed Gobind Singh also declared that members of the *Khalsa* must not smoke or chew tobacco, or consume alcohol. They should not eat meat slaughtered according to Muslim custom, and must not molest a Muslim woman. Although a turban (*pag*) is not one of the prescribed emblems, it has far greater significance for Sikhs than any other head-covering. A male Sikh is required to wear the turban in public as a symbol of commitment to Sikh ideals.

light of the guruship blended them into a seamless line of 'light blended into light' (*joti jot samai*). Guru Arjan himself is the largest single contributor, accounting for about one third of the whole. Its contents also include hymns by non-Sikh authors, such as Kabir and Ravidas, and the Muslim Farid, collectively referred to as 'devotees' (*bhagats*). The language of most of the scripture is a mixture of Old Punjabi and Old Hindi, written in the special Sikh script, *Gurmukhi*. The elaborate arrangement of several thousand hymns, itself an outstanding achievement of editorship, is not primarily by author, but by the mode (*raga*) in which they are to be sung. While no other early Sikh literature has the same canonical authority as the *Adi Granth*, popular devotion has always been fostered by the prose hagiographies of Guru Nanak – called *janamsakhis* (birth-witnesses) – which were first produced during this period.

GURU GOBIND SINGH AND THE *KHALSA*

The Panth grew significantly in numbers and membership during the time of the early Gurus, which overlapped the reign of the great Mughal emperor Akbar (1542–1605). But the strategic location of the Punjab inevitably embroiled the Gurus in imperial politics, and Guru Arjan became the first Sikh martyr, when Akbar's less tolerant successor ordered his execution. During the seventeenth century, the Panth expanded from its initial, largely professional and commercial, membership, to embrace increasing numbers of Sikhs from the Jat farming caste. At the same time, an increasingly militant policy was reflected in the proclamation under Arjan's son, Guru Hargobind, of claims to secular (*miri*) as well as spiritual authority (*piri*). Continuing conflict with the Mughals came to a further head with the execution in Delhi of the ninth Guru, Tegh Bahadur.

This led to a radical new formation of the community under the martyred leader's son, Guru Gobind Singh, the tenth and last Guru. Guru Gobind consciously adopted the role of a ruler, as well as that of guru, in his court at Anandpur, in the Punjab. His most important innovation was the re-establishment of the Guru's authority over the Panth, through the foundation of a new order called the *Khalsa*, the Guru's elite. While the Sikh Panth has always continued to contain many followers of Nanak and the gurus who choose not to become baptized members of the *Khalsa*, it is the latter who have led the Panth since the time of the last Guru. Gobind Singh's own sons were all killed in the course of his struggles against the forces of the Mughal emperor Aurangzeb (1618–1707), and he was himself killed by a Muslim assassin. After his death, the line of living Gurus came to an end, and their authority was henceforth vested in the

> Surrounded, with no choice, in turn
>
> I too attacked with bow and gun.
>
> When matters pass all other means,
>
> It is allowed to take up arms.
>
> Dasam Granth 1391.

scripture, expanded by the addition of Guru Tegh Bahadur's hymns to Guru Arjan's collection, and since revered as the *Guru Granth Sahib*.

Compositions by Guru Gobind Singh, some of which form part of the daily liturgy, and many more by others associated with him, were assembled in another volume of lesser canonical status, the *Dasam Granth* (Book of the Tenth One). A further influential set of extra-canonical Sikh religious literature also came into being at around this time, in the form of the *Rahitnamas*, simple manuals prescribing various rules of conduct (*rahit*) for the Sikhs of the *Khalsa*.

During the eighteenth century, the Punjab was fought over between the declining Mughal Empire and new Muslim invaders from Afghanistan. This was the heroic age of the Sikh Panth, which was organized into local guerrilla bands, who mounted a spirited resistance to both sets of Muslim armies, and who even in defeat are remembered for their glorious acts of martyrdom (*shahidi*). Led and manned by the Jat Sikhs, who had now become the dominant group in the community, the *Khalsa* forces achieved complete political success with the capture of Lahore, the provincial capital, which became the centre of a powerful Sikh kingdom under Maharaja Ranjit Singh (1799–1839), whose generous patronage is responsible for the splendid appearance of many of the great Sikh temples today. But Ranjit Singh's weaker successors proved unable to resist the pressure of the British, who, after two hard-fought wars, finally incorporated the Punjab into their Indian Empire in 1849.

CHRISTOPHER SHACKLE

CHAPTER 78

Sacred Writings

Sikh scripture emerged under the leadership of human Gurus, and culminated in having ultimate authority within the Sikh tradition.

SRI GURU GRANTH SAHIB

The principal scripture of the Sikhs is the *Adi Granth*, the eternal book, or original collection of compositions in book form. In everyday Sikh usage, the *Adi Granth* is reverentially referred to as the *Sri Guru Granth Sahib*, which implies affirmation of faith in the scripture as Guru. The words *Sri* (Sir) and *Sahib* (Lord) are honorific titles, indicating the highest authority accorded to the scripture. The *Adi Granth* opens with the basic creed (*Mul Mantra*), affirming the fundamentals of the Sikh faith. It begins with the phrase '*Ek Onkar*' (one God), signifying the oneness and unity of God, and affirms that the Supreme Being, or God, is 'One without a second'.

The *Adi Granth* was compiled by the fifth Guru, Arjan, in 1604, and contains the compositions of the first five Sikh Gurus, alongside the writings of Muslim and Hindu saints of the medieval period, some of whom belonged to the lowest caste group (*Shudra*). The entire collection is recorded in *Gurmukhi* script, which is also used for modern Punjabi. Because of its association with the Gurus and the scripture, *Gurmukhi* acquired a sacred status within the Sikh community.

The contents of the *Adi Granth* are respectfully referred to as *bani* (voice) and as *gurbani* (utterance of the Guru). Guru Nanak affirms the divine origin of the *bani*: 'As the *bani* of the Lord comes to me so do I proclaim its knowledge' (*Adi Granth* 722). The Guru is, in a primary sense, the 'voice' of God. Guru Nanak clarifies the distinction between the Divine Guru and the human Guru: he regarded himself as the minstrel (*dhadi*) of God (*Akal Purakh*), who openly proclaimed the glory of the divine Word (*Shabad*).

The process of identification of the *bani* with the Guru (God) began with Guru Nanak and was extended by his successors. For example, the third Guru, Amar Das, proclaimed: 'Love the *bani* of the Guru. It is our support in all places and it is bestowed by the Creator himself' (*Adi Granth* 1335). Similarly, the fourth Guru, Ram Das, says: 'The *bani* is the Guru, and the Guru the *bani*, and the nectar (*amrit*) permeates all souls …' (*Adi Granth* 982). The scripture concludes with Guru Arjan's hymn *Mundavani* (seal) which summarizes the essence of Sikh faith: 'In the platter are placed three things, truth, contentment, and wisdom, as well as the nectar of the Lord's Name [*amrit-nam*], the support of all.'

The *Adi Granth*, on its completion, was accorded the utmost sacred and authoritative status in 1604 when it was installed by Guru Arjan in the newly built Golden Temple (*Harimandir*) at Amritsar. Guru Arjan says: 'The book [*Adi Granth*] is the abode of the Supreme Lord.' From the time of Guru Nanak, the Sikh community began to use the *gurbani* in devotional singing (*shabad kirtan*) as part of congregational worship. Currently the original copy of the *Adi Granth* is in the possession of the Sodhi family at Kartarpur, Punjab.

The tenth Guru, Gobind Singh, terminated the line of human Gurus by bestowing guruship on the *Adi Granth*, to which he had added the compositions of his father, the ninth Guru, Tegh Bahadur. Since then, the *Adi Granth* has been revered as a human Guru, and is respectfully addressed as the *Sri Guru Granth Sahib*. It is placed on a high platform, under a canopy, and a ritual fan (*chauri*) is waved over it while a service is in progress. The presence of the *Guru Granth Sahib* is regarded as mandatory on almost all ceremonial and domestic occasions, such as weddings, initiation ceremonies, and naming ceremonies.

The *Dasam Granth* is the second scriptural book of the Sikhs, containing the compositions of the tenth Guru, Gobind Singh, and other poets, collected by Mani Singh after the death of Gobind Singh, and completed in 1734. The *Dasam Granth* is not installed in all *gurdwaras*, but is found at the two historic *gurdwaras* of Hazoor Sahib and Patna Sahib, popularly called *Takhat* (Throne of the Immortal Being), two of the five centres of temporal authority in Sikh society. Some of its compositions are recited during the preparation of *amrit* (water used for the initiation ceremony) and other acts of worship.

Bhai Gurdas was the scribe who wrote out the *Adi Granth*, under the direction of Guru Arjan. The collection of his writings is called *varan* (ballads), popularly known as 'the key to the *Adi Granth*', and normally sung and quoted by Sikh musicians and preachers at the *gurdwaras*.

SEWA SINGH KALSI

Guru Nanak on the Divine Name

If I could live for millions and millions of years, and if the air was my food and drink,

if I lived in a cave and never saw either the sun or the moon, and if I never slept, even in dreams

– even so, I could not estimate Your Value. How can I describe the Greatness of Your Name?

The True Lord, the Formless One, is Himself in His Own Place.

I have heard, over and over again, and so I tell the tale; as it pleases You, Lord, please instill within me the yearning for You.

If I was slashed and cut into pieces, and put into the mill and ground into flour,

burnt by all-consuming fire and mixed with ashes

– even then, I could not estimate Your Value. How can I describe the Greatness of Your Name?

If I was a bird, soaring and flying through hundreds of heavens,

and if I was invisible, neither eating nor drinking anything

– even so, I could not estimate Your Value. How can I describe the Greatness of Your Name?

Siri Ragu 2, Adi Granth 14–15.

CHAPTER 79

Beliefs

The central teaching in Sikhism is belief in the oneness of God: Sikh scripture begins with the phrase '*Ek Onkar*' (one God). All people – irrespective of caste, creed, colour, and sex – emanated from one divine source. Sikh Gurus have used a number of terms from Islamic and Hindu traditions for God, including Allah, Qadir, Karim, and Paar Brahma.

The diversity in God's creation is perceived as a divine gift, with all religious traditions regarded as capable of enriching the spiritual and cultural lives of their believers. According to Sikh teaching, all human groups evolved and developed their modes of worship and religious institutions within the context of their social environment. Reflecting on the essence and universality of religious truth, the tenth Guru, Gobind Singh, wrote:

Recognize all humankind, whether Muslim or Hindu as one. The same God is the Creator and Nourisher of all. Recognize no distinction among them. The temple and the mosque are the same. So are Hindu worship and Muslim prayer. Human beings are all one.

(Dasam Granth)

The nature of God is clearly manifested in Guru Nanak's first composition, the basic creed popularly known as the *Mul Mantra*, and in his first utterance, 'There is no Hindu, there is no Muslim.' The opening phrase of the *Mul Mantra* summarizes the fundamental belief of the Sikhs: the words '*Ek*' (one) and '*Onkar*' (God) emphasize the oneness of God. God is also believed to be the creator, from whom the universe has emanated. God is beyond the qualities of male and female; they are attributes of the creation, not the creator. Nanak says: 'The wise and beauteous Being is neither a man nor a woman nor a bird' (*Adi Granth* 1010).

Firstly God created light and then by his omnipotence, made all human beings. If we emanate from the same divine light, how can we say some are born higher than others? O, men, my brethren, stray ye not in doubt. Creation is in the Creator and the Creator is in Creation. He is fully filling all places.

Adi Granth 1349–50

As God is believed to be *ajuni*, he/she does not experience birth or die. God's having no gender further signifies the unity and equality of humankind.

Sikhism is strictly monotheistic: belief in God's incarnation and worship of idols is strongly disapproved of. Since God is without any form, colour, mark, or lineage, he/she cannot be installed as an idol. God is regarded as eternal truth (*ad sach*), without beginning and end, whereas everything else in this universe — including the sun, moon, stars, and earth — will perish. The notion of permanence applies only to God, who will remain divine truth forever.

HUKAM (DIVINE ORDER)

The term *hukam* (order, command) entered the Sikh/Punjabi vocabulary from Arabic. In Islam, God is perceived as one who gives orders, a commander (*Hakam*). In Sikhism, *hukam* is perceived as the divine order; everything in this universe is believed to be working according to God's *hukam*. The Sikh gurus used the concept of *hukam* extensively in their compositions to describe the nature of creation, the universe, and human life. Nanak refers to *hukam* as the divine hand behind the functioning of the universe, as well as behind the daily lives of human beings.

Although human beings are unique in God's creation, alone endowed with the ability to discriminate between good and evil, the most significant aspects of human existence, such as birth and death, are beyond their control. Human life (*manas janam*) is a divine gift; both birth and death occur according to *hukam*. At Sikh funerals, death is explained as eternal reality; it occurs according to the *Alahi Hukam* (divine order, Allah's order). Therefore, mortals must submit to God's will, without any doubt or questioning. Guru Nanak reflects on the concept of *hukam* by posing the question, 'How may a man purify himself? . . . This is brought about by living in accordance with God's command or will' (*Hukam Adi Granth 2*).

The concept of *hukam* raises a fundamental question. Are mortals helpless creatures in God's kingdom? Sikh teachings reject this view, and proclaim that all human beings are endowed with the ability to determine their own destiny. If someone commits evil deeds, he or she will suffer accordingly: that which one sows, that one shall reap. Ultimately, falsehood and evil will be destroyed, and truth prevail. For the attainment of truth, one needs to engage in righteous deeds.

MUKTI (SPIRITUAL LIBERATION)

The word *mukti* is the Punjabi version of the Sanskrit term *moksha* (to be free from, to release), denoting the final release, or spiritual liberation, of the soul from human existence, leading to merging with the Supreme Soul (*Parmatma*). According to the Sikh teaching, the soul (*atma*) is immortal, while the body in which it resides is perishable. After death, the body is cremated, and the *atma* either merges with the Supreme Soul, or passes from one form of life to another, depending upon one's *karma* in this world. As a religious concept, the term *karma* (literally: deeds, actions) denotes one's preordained destiny. Although Sikhs believe in the doctrine of *karma*, they do not regard human beings as helpless creatures. The notion of *jivan-mukta* (see below) transcends the limitations of *karma*, and transforms it into a dynamic force.

For the cycle of birth and death, the Sikh Gurus used the term *awagaun*, based on the doctrine of *karma* and the transmigration of souls. According to traditional Hindu belief, there are 8,400,000 forms of existence before one is reborn as a human being. Those who are sinful, and engage in evil-doing, keep going through the cycle of birth and death regarded as the most degrading state: *narak* (hell). At a Sikh funeral, the officiant recites the final prayer (*antam-ardas*) invoking God's forgiveness for the departed soul, and saving him or her from *awagaun*.

To avoid the ultimate punishment of *chaurasi* (cycle of birth and death), Sikhs are required to conduct themselves according to the teachings of the Sikh Gurus, working towards becoming Guru-oriented (*gursikh*), rather than self-oriented (*manmukh*). A Sikh is taught to live as an honest householder, a true believer in the oneness of God and the equality of humankind, while earning a living by honest means (*kirat karna*), and sharing with others (*vand chhakna*).

A Sikh who succeeds in attaining the status of *gursikh* is called *jivan-mukta*, liberated from worldly temptations such as lust (*kaam*), anger (*krodh*), greed (*lobh*), attachment (*moh*), and false pride or ego (*ahankar*). Another attribute of a *jivan-mukta* is his or her faith in *gurbani* to earn *mukti* now rather than after death. A *gursikh* transforms into a *jivan-mukta* by leading a life of detachment from worldly temptations, while actively engaged in the social and cultural enrichment of society, or *seva* (voluntary service). A *jivan-mukta* Sikh is like a lotus that remains clean, despite living in muddy water.

DHARMSAL (PRACTICE OF RIGHTEOUSNESS)

The term *dharmsal* is composed of *dharm* (religious, moral, and social obligations) and *sal* (a place of abode). Guru Nanak describes the earth as *dharmsal* (a place to practise righteousness), established by God within the universe. In this *dharmsal*, human life is regarded as the highest and most precious form, as well as a divine gift. The earth, and everything in it, is believed to carry the divine stamp.

> In pride, man is overtaken by fear. In utter commotion he passes his life. Pride is a great malady because of which, he dies, is reborn and continues coming and going.
>
> Adi Granth 592

According to Sikh teaching, Sikhs are not passive spectators, or recluses, in this world; they are expected to be active participants in human affairs, and Guru-oriented (*gursikh*). The concept of *dharmsal* implies faith in the oneness of God, and in the equality of humankind. Guru Nanak reprimanded Hindu ascetics (*yogis*) who advocated the path of renunciation, abdicating their social obligations. Apart from Har Krishan, who died aged eight, all the Sikh gurus were married men, who demonstrated their faith in their adherence to the householder's state (*grihsth-ashrama-dharma*). For a Sikh, there is no place for the renunciation of society.

GURPARSAD (GRACE AND BLESSING)

The term *gurparsad* is composed of *gur* (from *guru*) and *parsad* (Sanskrit for grace, blessing), which is also applied to the sanctified food offered to the congregation at the culmination of a Sikh service. *Gurparsad* is the last word of the *Mul Mantra*, standing for the eternal Guru (God), and affirms Sikh belief, and the way God can be realized. The Sikh Gurus used several terms to elaborate the concept of *gurparsad*, such as *karam* (Arabic), *mehar* and *nadar* (Persian), and *kirpa* (Sanskrit). It is believed that everyone's destiny is preordained, according to his or her *karma*, and ultimately one is responsible for its consequences. Guru Nanak says, 'Through grace is reached the Door of The Divine' (*Adi Granth* 145), and that, as one spark of fire can burn huge amounts of firewood, so acts of devotion and love of God may annul the consequences of bad *karma*. The Sikh Gurus repeatedly affirm that divine grace is the fruit of sincere devotion to God.

Two elderly Sikhs at the Gurudwara Bangla Sahib, Delhi. Note their long turbans and distinctive metal bangles.

THE *MUL MANTRA*

Ek Onkar	There is one God	Ajuni	beyond the cycle of birth and death
Satnam	eternal truth is his/her name	Saibham	self-created, self-existent
Karta Purakh	Creator of all things	Gurparsad	known by the grace of the Guru.
Nirbhau	without fear		
Nirvair	without enmity	Guru Granth Sahib 1	
Akal Murat	timeless, immortal, never incarnated		

NAMSIMRAN (MEDITATING ON GOD'S NAME)

The concept of *nam* (name) is one of the key doctrines in Sikhism, symbolizing the eternal truth, or God. In everyday usage, the term *namsimran* is applied to the discipline of daily meditation undertaken by devout Sikhs, during which it is common practice to use a rosary, often repeating the words *Waheyguru* and *Satnam*. Many Sikhs participate in *namsimran* sessions organized at *gurdwaras*.

The Sikh Gurus used the concept of *nam* to affirm their faith in the omnipresence of God, and impressed upon their disciples the necessity of the discipline of *namsimran*. They assert that *nam* is the creator of everything; through nam comes all wisdom and light; *nam* extends to all creation; there is no place where *nam* is not.

SEWA SINGH KALSI

CHAPTER 80

Worship and Festivals

In popular Sikh usage, the act of worship means reading from the scripture and reciting a selection of hymns (*path-karna*). In individual or congregational worship the central focus is on the utterances of the Gurus in the *Adi Granth* (*gurbani*). Sikh festivals, which are both religious and cultural celebrations, fall into two categories: *gurpurb*, an anniversary when a Guru is remembered, and *mela*, a fair. The most popular melas are *Baisakhi*, *Diwali*, and *Hola*.

INDIVIDUAL WORSHIP

The pattern of individual worship is prescribed in the Sikh code of discipline (*Rehat Maryada*), published in 1951. The daily routine (*nitnem*) comprises texts from the *Adi Granth* and rules for personal cleanliness. A Sikh should rise early and take a bath, then recite the hymns of *Japji*, *Jap*, and *Ten Sawayyas*. At sunset he or she should recite the hymn of *Rahiras*, and before going to bed recite the hymn of *Sohila* and the prayer *ardas* (petition).

Worship can be undertaken anywhere in peace and quiet, and most Sikh households have a collection of hymns normally recited during worship (*gutka*), wrapped in cloth and kept in a safe place. Many devout Sikhs also have a copy of the *Guru Granth Sahib* at home, respectfully kept in a special room, usually located on the top floor. Although any building where a copy of the *Guru Granth Sahib* is installed qualifies to be called a *gurdwara*, a family *gurdwara* is strictly a private shrine, not open to the general public.

CONGREGATIONAL WORSHIP

Congregational worship takes place at the *gurdwara*. There is no fixed day, but in the diaspora most services take place on a Sunday. The term *gurdwara* is composed of *guru* (denoting the *Guru Granth Sahib*) and *dwara* (gate or house), and is attributed to the sixth Guru, Hargobind, who is believed to have built *gurdwaras* at sites associated with his predecessors. During the period of the first five Gurus, a Sikh place of worship was known as a *dharmsala*. According to tradition, Guru Nanak established the first at Kartarpur, as a place where a congregation (*sangat*) of men and women of all caste groups would gather for communal worship and hymn-singing (*shabad kirtan*), followed by a communal meal (*langar*). The institutions of *sangat*, *shabad kirtan*, and *langar* emerged as distinguishing features of the Sikh tradition.

Historic *gurdwaras* have been built on sites linked to important events in the development of Sikhism: for example, Gurdwara Kesgarh at Anandpur, where the tenth Guru, Gobind Singh, established the *Khalsa* in 1699; and Gurdwara Sis Ganj in Delhi, built where the ninth Guru, Tegh Bahadur, was beheaded by the Mughal authorities. Community-based *gurdwaras* are autonomous institutions, established by local Sikh communities, and run by locally elected management committees, which are answerable only to their local *sangat*.

A similar pattern of service is observed at all *gurdwaras*, beginning with the recital and singing of *Asa di var* in the morning, followed by more hymn-singing from scripture. The service concludes with the recital of *ardas* by the *granthi* (reader of the scripture), while members of the *sangat* stand silently with folded hands. After the *ardas*, a randomly chosen hymn from the scripture is read out to the congregation, called *hukam-nama* (divine order for the day). The service ends with the distribution of sanctified food (*karah parshad*) to members of the congregation, symbolizing Sikh belief in the equality of humankind.

The way a Sikh expresses his or her reverence for the scripture might create the impression that the Sikhs are idol worshippers: for example, when a Sikh enters the congregational hall, he or she approaches the *Adi Granth*, makes an offering, and bows. In fact, the devotee is showing devotion towards the teachings of the Gurus, *Guru Granth Sahib*.

GURPURBS

The term *gurpurb* is made up of *gu* (short for *guru*) and *purb* (a sacred or auspicious day). Four main *gurpurbs* are celebrated by Sikhs throughout the world:
- The birthday of Guru Nanak: 26 November
- The birthday of Guru Gobind Singh: 5 January
- The martyrdom anniversary of Guru Arjan: 16 June
- The martyrdom anniversary of Guru Tegh Bahadur: 24 November

In India, *gurpurbs* are celebrated by carrying the *Guru Granth Sahib* in processions around towns and villages. In villages, the scripture is placed in a decorated palanquin (*palki*), and the procession is led by five initiated (*amritdhari*) Sikhs carrying swords, symbolizing the 'five beloved ones' initiated by the tenth Guru in 1699.

THE GOLDEN TEMPLE

The Golden Temple (*Harimandir*) at Amritsar, India, serves as a symbol of the Sikh religion, and as a visual aid to our understanding of its spiritual meaning, and how the past has influenced the present. For Sikhs this temple is the court of the Lord (*Dharbar Sahib*), and in its precincts are found peace and the possibility of access to God.

The Hindi and Punjabi hymns of the early Gurus, together with those of some non-Sikh mystics, were collected together and first installed here by Arjan in 1604. Later editions of this volume, which include the devotional poetry of the later Gurus, constitute the focal point of devotion and meditation. The hymns are sung from morning to night at the temple, and a constant stream of visitors and pilgrims comes to listen to the words, which confer a blessing on believing hearers.

The temple site consists of an outer paved area, with shaded cloisters surrounding the large pool, or tank, from which Amritsar ('pool of nectar') takes its name. At the centre of the pool stands the beautiful Golden Temple itself, in which the sacred book is placed early in the morning.

This temple has served as the basis for many interpretations of the religious life. It is, for example, like a lotus plant growing from the murky water of life, producing a beautiful flower of devotion and good works – teaching people to reach above the evil of the world, which would choke their higher desires. The outer courtyard possesses four entrances, unlike the single doorways of Muslim and Hindu shrines, expressing the universality of Sikh truth, which is open to all.

Another gold-topped building stands in the outer area, facing the long walkway to the inner holy place. This is the *Akal Takhat*, a political and community centre, where important pronouncements are made concerning the life of Sikhs. Built by the sixth Guru, it indicates the rise of political and social awareness among Sikhs, as they sought to establish a code of conduct for themselves, and a way of organizing their relations with other groups. Here, in the temple area, religion and politics are clearly distinguished.

There are four other major *Takhats* (or thrones), and many other important temples; but Amritsar provides a clear demonstration of the great unity of social and religious life which has emerged in Sikh culture.

Douglas Davies

The Golden Temple, or Harmandir Sahib, Amritsar, Punjab, India.

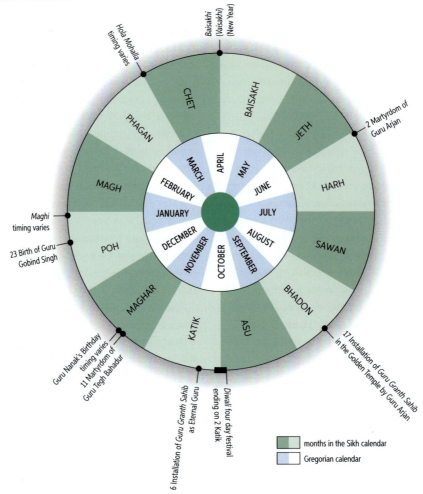

Baisakhi (Vaisakhi) (New Year)

CHET

BAISAKH

JETH

2 Martyrdom of Guru Arjan

HARH

SAWAN

17 Installation of Guru Granth Sahib in the Golden Temple by Guru Arjan

BHADON

ASU

Diwali four day festival ending on 2 Katik

KATIK

6 Installation of Guru Granth Sahib as Eternal Guru

MAGHAR

Guru Nanak's Birthday timing varies
11 Martyrdom of Guru Tegh Bahadur

POH

23 Birth of Guru Gobind Singh

Maghi timing varies

MAGH

PHAGAN

Hola Mohalla timing varies

MARCH APRIL MAY
FEBRUARY JUNE
JANUARY JULY
DECEMBER AUGUST
NOVEMBER SEPTEMBER
OCTOBER

months in the Sikh calendar
Gregorian calendar

BAISAKHI

The festival of *Baisakhi* is celebrated on the first day of the month of *Baisakh* in the Punjabi calendar, and nowadays has a special importance for the Sikhs as it marks the birthday of the *Khalsa*. In Punjab, farmers begin harvesting the wheat crop after the *Baisakhi* celebrations. Apart from religious ceremonies, a number of cultural activities are organized, such as *kabadi*, football, hockey, and wrestling. Traditional *Bhangra* dancing, when dancers dress up in colourful Punjabi costumes, is the climax of the celebrations.

HOLA

Hola takes its name from the traditional Hindu festival of *Holi*, which is celebrated by communal singing, dancing, and throwing colours on people, irrespective of caste, gender, and status. Guru Gobind Singh disapproved of the *Holi* festival, regarding it as wasteful and degrading. He summoned his followers to Anandpur to celebrate the festival of *Holi* differently: instead of merrymaking, he organized mock battles between two groups of Sikh volunteers, and trained them in martial arts, thereby giving them a new purpose in life. The title of the festival was changed to *Hola*, and the tradition of martial arts remains associated with it.

DIWALI

Diwali is one of the traditional festivals of India, popularly known as the festival of lights; its origin is traced to the homecoming of Lord Rama from exile. Hindus illuminate their homes and temples, and exchange gifts of sweets with friends and relatives. The festival has another significance for Sikhs: it is associated with the release of the sixth Guru, Hargobind, from the Gwalior Fort, where he was imprisoned by the Mughal emperor Jahangir. The Guru's arrival in Amritsar was celebrated by the illumination of the city by his followers. Nowadays, special *Diwali* services are conducted at the *gurdwaras*, celebrating the release of Guru Hargobind, and affirming a distinct Sikh identity. *Gurdwaras* and private houses are decorated with candles, and firework displays are organized. The tradition of illuminating the Golden Temple (*Harimandir*) marks the climax of the *Diwali* festivities.

SANGRAND

The first day of every month in the Hindu lunar calendar is called *Sangrand*, from the Sanskrit word *sangkrant*, denoting the entrance of the sun into a new sign of the Zodiac. In Sikhism, it is observed in a special service (*diwan*) at the *gurdwara*, with the name of the new month ritually announced from scripture. Guru Arjan composed the 'hymn of twelve months'

GURU HARGOBIND'S RELEASE

According to Sikh tradition, Guru Hargobind was imprisoned by the emperor Jahangir in the Gwalior Fort on the suspicion that he had raised a large army to fight against the government. 52 Hindu princes were already imprisoned in the fort. After several years, the authorities ordered the Guru's release, but he refused to go until the other princes were set free. The emperor agreed to the Guru's demand, and said he would release as many princes as could come out holding the Guru's garment and hands. On hearing this condition, the Guru ordered a special cloak, which had many strips of cloth, and in this way all 52 princes came out of the fort holding the Guru's garment and hands. Thus the Guru became popular as *Bandi Chhod* (deliverer of prisoners).

(*Bara Maha*), each of its twelve parts illustrating a stage of life and the journey of the soul, while directing the Sikhs to conform to the prescribed code of discipline each month. Before setting off to work on this festival

Pool, or sarovar, at the Sikh Gurudwara Bangla Sahib, Delhi, India, whose water is considered holy.

day, Sikhs visit the *gurdwara* to invoke divine grace for the well-being of their family and the whole of humankind. Listening to the recital of the name of the new month is perceived as a meritorious boon. The festival of *Baisakhi* occurs at *Sangrand* in the month of *Baisakh* (usually 14 April) and the ceremony of replacing the old covering of the flagpole with a new one (*Nishan Sahib*) takes place at the *gurdwaras* on this day.

SEWA SINGH KALSI

CHAPTER 81

Family and Society

The Sikh movement emerged in the context of a caste-ridden Indian society, in which occupation and status were ascribed and determined on the basis of one's birth into a particular caste group (*Jaat*), and there was no significant social interaction between members of different caste groups. Sikh Gurus were acutely aware of the destructive impact of the caste system on the social, religious, and cultural fabric of Indian society, and rejected the Hindu doctrine of *varnashramadharma* — laws of social classes and stages of life — which they saw as based on caste exclusiveness and institutionalized inequality.

Although Sikh teachings reject the doctrine of caste, its influence is sometimes still seen within the Sikh community. The joint family, or the extended household, is the basic unit within Punjabi Sikh society, and has a traditional occupation, such as *Jaat* (farmer), *Tarkhan* (carpenter), or *Chamar* (leather-worker).

Several domestic rites provide insight into the interaction between religious and social customs, such as marriage, birth, and death.

MARRIAGE

Marriage is regarded as the bedrock of Sikh society; Sikhism rejects celibacy and renunciation. All Sikh Gurus, except Guru Har Krishan, who died at the age of eight, were married men. They strongly advocated that Sikhs should lead as householders (*grihasthi*), recognizing their duties to parents, wife, and children — and to the wider society.

> Worthless is caste and worthless an exalted name.
>
> For all mankind there is but only one refuge.'
>
> Guru Nanak, *Adi Granth* 83.

Sikh marriage is more than the simple unification of man and a woman; it is regarded as an alliance between two families. The scriptures consider marriage to be a spiritual bond, and emphasize the concept of one spirit in two bodies (*ek jote doye murti*). The fourth Guru, Ram Das, says: 'They are not man and wife who have physical contact only. Only they are truly wedded who have one spirit in two bodies' (*Adi Granth* 788). In addition, the marital relationship is perceived as a relationship preordained by God (*sanjog*), not a social contract. However, Sikhs are permitted to remarry if a marriage irretrievably breaks down.

THE MARRIAGE CEREMONIES

The engagement ceremony (*kurmai, mangni*) begins with the recital of a prayer (*ardas*). A special hymn of *kurmai* is recited from the *Adi Granth*, and a *hukamnama* is read out for God's blessing.

The customary meeting of the heads of both families (*milni*) begins with the recital of *ardas* by the *granthi*, who prays for God's blessing on the alliance of the two families. Then the bride's father formally greets the groom's father, and makes a gift of a turban, and sometimes money.

The guests attend the *gurdwara* for the wedding ceremony (*anand karaj*), where bride and groom sit in front of the *Adi Granth*. The most popular colour for brides to wear is red. The bride usually wears a *lengha* – tunic and long skirt – made of the same material, but some wear a sari or trouser suit (*salwar kamiz*). The bride does not wear a veil, but covers her head with a long scarf (*chuni*). The groom often wears a red or maroon turban.

The *anand karaj* begins with *ardas*, followed by the ritual joining of the couple with the groom's scarf (*palla pharana*) by the bride's father. At this stage the religious musicians (*ragis*) sing *palley taindey lagi*, a hymn from the *Adi Granth* which stresses the sanctity of the marital bond. There are four wedding hymns, collectively called *lavan*. After each, the couple walks around the *Adi Granth* in a clockwise direction, the bridegroom leading the bride. The *anand karaj* concludes with the recital of the hymn *anand sahib* and *ardas*.

A young Sikh in the Punjab.

CHILDREN

The birth of a child is regarded as a divine gift (*waheyguru di dat*). Traditionally, children were given names by their grandparents, or by their paternal aunt. Nowadays, most Sikh families visit the *gurdwara* and ask for an *akhar* – usually the first letter on the page where the *Adi Granth* is opened – and a name is chosen that begins with this letter. In addition, Sikh boys are given the title *Singh* (lion), and girls *Kaur* (princess).

The turban (*pag*) is a symbol of honour, but there is no stipulation of the age when a Sikh boy starts to wear it. Usually, he will be eleven or twelve, and thus able to look after it. The turban may be of any colour, and is normally of muslin and 15 feet (about five metres) long.

DEATH

In India, funerals usually take place very soon after death, or on the next day. The body is bathed and dressed in new clothes, before cremation. It is a son's duty to light the pyre; in the absence of a son, another male relative performs this rite. Before this, a *granthi* recites *ardas* for the departed soul. Women are prohibited from helping to carry the bier, or lighting the pyre. At the death of a married woman (*sohagan*), her shroud is provided by her paternal family, and she is dressed as a bride. In the Punjab, the ashes are collected after three days, and usually deposited in running water. After the funeral, the deceased's family organize the reading of the *Adi Granth*, either at their home or at the local *gurdwara*.

If the deceased was a man, the ritual of *pagri* — transfer of paternal authority — takes place at this time. This ceremony involves the chief mourner — the oldest son — who sits in front of the *Adi Granth* and receives a turban and some money from his maternal uncle. He wears the new turban in the presence of his relatives and members of the congregation, then a senior member of the *biradari* reminds him of his new status and responsibilities. The social function of *pagri* is to facilitate the incorporation of a son into the role of his father.

SEWA SINGH KALSI

I AM A SIKH

I was born in a Sikh village called Talhan, in the state of Punjab, India. It had its own large temple (*gurdwara*). Every year, the residents of the village and the surrounding areas celebrated the important religious festivals and took part in processions, and with the other children I joined in. My early nurturing in Sikh traditions took place within my family and this village community. I knew the basic beliefs of Sikhism at a very young age.

In 1968 my family moved to Leeds, England. I was only nine, and this was quite an experience for all of us. None of us could speak English. We found it hard to socialize, and everything around us felt very different. We were fortunate to have a very helpful English family next door. They had two daughters the same age as myself. We used to play together, and their father took me to school on my first day, because my parents could not speak English. This helped us settle in at our local primary school, and made us feel at home in Leeds. At school, we began to learn English. We were very keen and worked hard, attending extra English classes for Asian children. We made lots of friends. At that time there was only one *gurdwara* in Leeds – simply called 'the Sikh temple'. Although it was a three-mile walk from our house, we attended regularly on Sundays. I also attended Punjabi classes there.

Attending the *gurdwara* on a regular basis for prayers, in the presence of the congregation, and listening to hymn-singing (*shabad kirtan*), helped me understand the meaning of 'the oneness of God'. I began to take part in voluntary help (*seva*) in the community kitchen (*langar*). Food is served to everyone attending, including visitors from other faiths and backgrounds. Importantly, all are served the same meal, as this shows equality.

Soon after we arrived in Leeds, my elder brother and I had a haircut. In our new surroundings, we were embarrassed to have long hair. When I moved to secondary school, I met a young Sikh who wore a turban. I was impressed, and soon began to grow my hair again and wear a turban. Although I am not an 'initiated Sikh', I wear a turban to identify myself as a follower. I also wear a steel bracelet (*kara*) on my right wrist. My middle name is Singh, a name given to all male Sikhs by the tenth Guru. I do not cut my hair or trim my beard, and do not drink or smoke, both of which are against Sikh teachings.

My religious discipline is based on Sikh teachings, central to which is the belief that there is only one God. My daily commitments include meditation on God's name (*nam japna*), sharing with others (*vand chhakna*), voluntary service (*seva*), and earning my living honestly (*kirat karna*). These are most important for every Sikh. Every morning before breakfast I say the morning prayer, the *Mul Mantra*. My mother taught me this when I was young, and since she passed away – more than twenty years ago – I have said it daily. I regularly participate in religious activities and festivals at the *gurdwara*, such as *Baisakhi, Diwali* and other celebrations. These bring the community and families together, enabling the younger generation, including my children, to learn more about Sikhism.

Gradually, my involvement at the *gurdwara* has increased, as has my commitment to helping others. As Sikhs, we take part in the activities of Leeds Concord multi-faith fellowship. Recently my youngest daughter lit the candles at the Peace Service, on behalf of the Sikh community. I regularly contribute towards Sikh activities, including donations towards the upkeep of the *gurdwara* and the community kitchen (*langar*). My job as a Technical Liaison Officer involves a lot of travelling. I come into contact with people of different backgrounds and faiths, and with my turban, beard and so on, I openly display my commitment to my faith. I enjoy my work and, as I do it, I apply my faith's teaching about equality and truthful living (*kirat karna*).

My wife came from India in 1983 and, having completed postgraduate studies, became a primary school teacher in Leeds. Because of my cultural tradition, I had an arranged marriage, conducted at the *gurdwara* in the presence of the Sikh holy book (*Guru Granth Sahib*) and the congregation. Verses from the *Guru Granth Sahib* were read out and sung by the priest. Not only did I marry a person of the same religion, but we also bring up our three children within the faith. Both my wife's and my own influence on the children

has encouraged them to speak Punjabi as well as English, and to attend the *gurdwara* on a regular basis. I hope that, by learning the value of prayer, by understanding the importance of helping and respecting others, and by learning the Gurus' teachings, my children will follow me in the faith and commit their lives to God.

As a family, we have visited India. As well as seeing the tourist attractions, we visited many *gurdwaras* in the Punjab and Delhi. Our visit to the famous Golden Temple at Amritsar was most exciting, and gave me a greater understanding of my religious tradition.

I have enjoyed music from an early age, particularly *shabad kirtan*. I can listen to *shabad kirtan* in the morning before going to work, as well as in the evening. I find this very helpful in my quest to learn more about the Sikh faith. It is also helpful for my children. However, we don't listen to religious music alone. We also enjoy traditional Indian music, folk music, and *bhangra* dancing.

I think the teachings of the Sikh faith have made me a better person. I thank God, who has given me so much and, in return, I want to give back to God as much of myself as I can, by committing myself to the Sikh faith.

Resham Singh Bhogal

CHAPTER 82

Sikhism Today

The evolution of Sikhism has remained closely involved with political and social developments in the Punjab, throughout a century of British rule, and since 1947 in independent India. Like many other Asian religions, Sikhism first experienced the challenges of modernity at the same time as those of nineteenth-century European colonialism. A Sikh reform movement proved remarkably successful in articulating for much of the twentieth century a reinforced Sikhism, which survived the community's traumatic experience of the partition of Punjab between India and Pakistan in 1947. More recent decades, however, have been marked by tensions between the politicized expression of Sikhism, which grew out of the reform movement, and an Indian political leadership increasingly identified with Hindu majoritarianism. The same period also saw the establishment of substantial Sikh diasporas in Britain and North America, where the challenges of adapting Sikhism to the very different circumstances of the international, twenty-first century, English-speaking world are most acutely faced.

SIKH REFORM

In the heyday of colonial rule, in the later nineteenth century, the leaders of all sections of Indian society, including the Sikhs, had to confront the linked implications of British political dominance and their dominant Victorian world view, with its strongly Christian emphasis. A path of total resistance to modernity was chosen by a few, such as Baba Ram Singh (1816–84), but his self-proclamation as Guru confined his support to the Namdhari Sikh sect which he founded.

The mainstream leadership realized, however, that a more complex process of accommodation to the new order was required for the successful survival of the Sikh community. The Sikhs' distinct religious identity was seen to be doubly threatened: by the dismantling of state-supported Sikh political institutions after the British conquest of Ranjit Singh's kingdom, and by the threat of assimilation into a resurgent Hinduism. The latter threat was forcefully articulated in the Punjab by the modernist Arya Samaj organization, founded by Dayananda Sarasvati (1824–83), whose doctrine of all truth being found in the *Vedas* was found offensively dismissive of the teachings of the Sikh Gurus.

To combat these challenges, a number of reformist associations (*Singh Sabhas*) were founded in the main cities of the Punjab. Through these associations, and making full use of the new communication systems established by the colonial state, a number of gifted lay leaders, often honoured with the title *Bhai* (Brother), came to formulate a redefinition of Sikhism which has remained the dominant orthodoxy to the present day. Like most reformers, the *Singh Sabha* activists saw the contemporary plight of Sikhism as the consequence of a falling away from the pristine ideals of an earlier age. They diagnosed an increasing reversion to Hinduism in both religious and social practice as the cause of what had gone wrong, and preached the necessity of a return to the glorious age of the Gurus, marked by uncompromising monotheism, and the adoption of a simple and devout lifestyle untainted by superstition. The title of the most famous of many tracts through which their message was disseminated, 'We are not Hindus' (*Ham Hindu Nahin*, 1898), by Bhai Kahn Singh Nabha (1867–1938), points to the cornerstone of the reformists' programme, their strenuous efforts to distinguish the Sikhs of the *Khalsa* as a community quite separate from its Hindu origins and traditionally close ties with Hinduism.

The reformists often justified their definition of Sikhism in relation to Hinduism by an analogy of the relation betweens between Protestantism and Roman Catholicism. Fitting well with imperial policies of 'divide and rule', it found particular favour with the British, as a way of ensuring the separate loyalty of their Sikh troops, who were recruited as a reliable minority, out of all proportion to their numbers in the population – and army regulations specified strict adherence to *Khalsa* practice in the Sikh regiments. At the same time, a remarkable cultural transformation was effected within the Sikh community itself, through the literary and scholarly activity of leading reformers such as Bhai Vir Singh (1872–1957). Developing Punjabi in the Gurmukhi script as a vehicle for modern communication, they produced new editions of the scriptures with extensive commentaries, and an impressive body of creative writing, which often drew upon the mythic power of Sikh history to drive home the reformist message.

SIKH POLITICAL ACTIVISM

By the end of World War I, the reformists had given the Sikhs the confidence and coherence to engage with the nationalist politics of the late colonial period. A new activist phase was launched with the *Akali* movement, established to push through the transfer of control of the major *gurdwaras* from their hereditary guardians, who administered their vast endowments, often for private profit. A programme of mass demonstrations, producing violent conflicts and fresh martyrs for the cause, eventually resulted in government sanction for the Sikh *Gurdwaras* Act of 1925, which gave control of the great *gurdwaras* of the Punjab to an elected committee of male Sikhs, the Shiromani Gurdwara Prabandhak Committee (SGPC), which became the single most important voice within Sikhism, and through its resources now supports the *Akali Dal*, the main Sikh political party. The British refused Sikh women the right to become members; however, since Indian independence in 1947, women have been elected, even to the prestigious post of secretary and president.

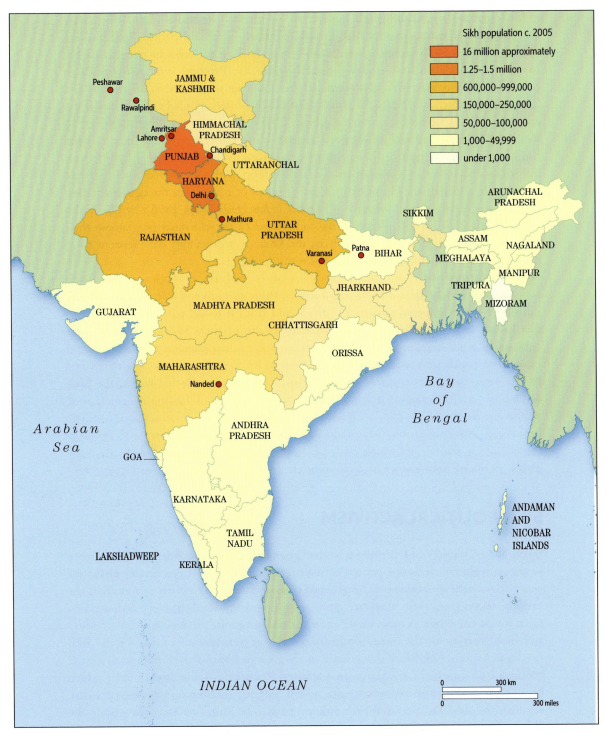

Sikhism in India Today

Sikh population c. 2005

	16 million approximately
	1.25–1.5 million
	600,000–999,000
	150,000–250,000
	50,000–100,000
	1,000–49,999
	under 1,000

For the next decades, the leaders' chief energies were devoted to the pursuit of a political settlement that would guarantee the position of Sikhs as a distinctive ethno-religious minority. The approach of Indian independence was marked by increasing polarization between Hindus and Muslims. With no realistic chance of achieving their own country, the Sikhs' lot was cast with the Hindus in 1947, when the partition of the Punjab between India and Pakistan was effected, at the cost of massive ethnic cleansing. Although this uprooted half the community that found itself on the Pakistan side, its resettlement in Indian Punjab in place of the departed Muslim population had the effect of consolidating the Sikh population territorially for the first time.

Young Sikhs at a national gathering in Italy, 2011.

From this base, and building on Sikh identification with Punjabi, the *Akali Dal* launched the *Punjabi Suba*, or Punjabi State campaign, with the aim of establishing within the Indian Union a linguistically-defined state with a Punjabi-speaking – that is, Sikh – majority. Although this was achieved with the separation of a truncated Sikh-dominated Punjab from the Hindu-majority state of Haryana in 1966, this did not halt the dangerous religio-political momentum that had been set in motion. By the early 1980s, the Punjab became a battleground, with armed Sikh activists, inspired by the ideal of establishing Khalistan as an independent Sikh country, opposed by the Indian security forces. This culminated in the notorious events of 1984 at Amritsar, when the Indian prime minister, Indira Gandhi (1917–84), ordered the army to storm the *Harimandir* – which had been occupied by the followers of the charismatic young preacher Sant Jarnail Singh Bhindranvale (1947–84). Her own later assassination by her Sikh bodyguards provoked anti-Sikh pogroms in many parts of India, killing thousands. The separatist cause eventually lost the support of most Sikhs in India.

ORGANIZATION AND AUTHORITY

The rules of reformed Sikhism are set out in the official *Guide to the Sikh Way of Life* (*Rehat Maryada*), first issued as a pamphlet by the SGPC in 1945. It defines a Sikh as any person
- whose faith is in one God, the ten Gurus and their teaching, and the *Adi Granth*
- believes in the necessity and importance of initiation (*amrit*)
- does not adhere to any other religion.

Sikhism is a religion without priests, so authority in the larger *gurdwaras* rests with the lay committees which run them, not with the 'keepers of the scripture' (*granthis*) whom they employ.

THE SIKH DIASPORAS

The necessarily rather rigid redefinitions of Sikhism first formulated by the *Singh Sabha* leaders in the late nineteenth century are beginning to be perceived as in need of adjustment, to meet the changed circumstances of the twenty-first century. With the failure of the long pursuit of solutions through political means in India, there are signs that the chief impetus for such a reformulation may come from the increasingly confident and well-established diaspora communities now settled for over a generation in Britain, Canada, and the USA, totalling about one million, and even numerically significant in relation to the fifteen million Indian Sikhs.

The Sikh diasporas remain closely linked to the Punjab, through family ties, the rituals of the *gurdwara* and the great Sikh festivals (*gurpurbs*), and regular pilgrimages to the great shrines associated with the Gurus. But they are also directly exposed to their Western environments, and relatively free from the constraints felt within an increasingly Hindu-dominated India, encouraging the emergence of a new intellectual leadership, based within Western universities and using English rather than Punjabi as its prime medium of expression.

Several emerging trends may be signalled as pointers. A new critical attention is being given to sensitive topics, notably the study of the formation of the scripture, and the interpretation of key mythic episodes of Sikh history, such as the foundation of the *Khalsa*. There is also a revaluation of the importance of other traditions within Sikhism that were marginalized by the triumph of the reformed *Khalsa*, to whom the SGPC *Rehat Maryada* almost exclusively refers, neglecting the many who follow the teachings of Guru Nanak and his successors, but do not observe the full *Khalsa* discipline. And women's voices are starting to be articulated in a religious tradition that has been so powerfully dominated by the bearded male presence. These and other trends have yet to coalesce; but it seems certain that traditional authority will become subject to increasing challenges, as Sikhism – like all other religions – grapples with an ever-changing modern world.

CHRISTOPHER SHACKLE

QUESTIONS

1. Explain the role of Guru Nanak's example in Sikhism.

2. Why does Sikhism reject asceticism?

3. Why is the *Adi Granth* so revered?

4. Why does Sikhism reject the caste system?

5. How have Hinduism and Islam influenced Sikhism?

6. How do Sikhs believe they can overcome *chaurasi* (the cycle of death and rebirth)?

7. How far was the Tenth Guru responsible for shaping Sikhism?

8. Explain the importance of the *Khalsa* in Sikhism.

9. What factors are responsible for the tension between Sikhism and the Indian state in recent decades?

10. How important is the *Rehat Maryada* to the development of Sikhism in recent decades?

FURTHER READING

Brown, Kerry, *Sikh Art and Literature*. London: Routledge, 1999.

Fenech, Louis E., *Martyrdom in the Sikh Tradition: Playing the Game of Love*. Delhi: Oxford University Press, 2000.

McLeod, W. H., *Historical Dictionary of Sikhism*. Lanham, MD: Scarecrow Press, 1995.

McLeod, W. H., *Sikhism*. London: Penguin, 1997.

Nat, J. S., *The Sikhs of the Punjab*. Cambridge: Cambridge University Press, 2008.

O'Connell, Joseph T., Milton Israel, and Willard G. Oxtoby, eds., *Sikh History and Religion in the Twentieth Century*. Toronto: University of Toronto Centre for South Asian Studies, 1988.

Shackle, Christopher ed., *Sikh Religion, Culture and Ethnicity*. Richmond, Surrey: Curzon, 2001.

Singh, Patwant, *The Sikhs*. New York: Knopf, 2000.

PART 13
RELIGIONS IN TODAY'S WORLD

SUMMARY

Throughout the modern period there has been speculation about the collapse of religious belief and rumours of the death of God. Modernity, it has been said, inevitably entails secularization. The progress of the sciences in particular leaves little room for traditional religious belief. However, while it is true that there has been, and continues to be, a haemorrhaging of people from mainstream churches, religion is still alive and well in today's world. Indeed, it is experiencing robust health in the non-Western world where faiths such as Islam and Christianity flourish. In the Western world, while many are disillusioned with traditional religious institutions, authorities and hierarchies, and have even abandoned religious belief altogether, growing numbers are finding spiritual fulfilment elsewhere. Some believe without feeling the need to belong to an institution. Others turn to the increasing number of new religions and alternative spiritualities on offer. Yet others, particularly since the 1960s, have been attracted to Eastern traditions, such as Hinduism and Buddhism. More typical of believers in today's world are those who, influenced by postmodern, consumer-oriented, religiously plural cultures, 'pick and mix' from a range of traditions, beliefs and philosophies.

CHAPTER 83

From Existentialism to Postmodernism

Much of the mood of secular thought today can be traced to a general suspicion of reason, argument, and objective truth. In historical terms, Immanuel Kant (1724–1804) was the first philosopher who went further than simply using reason, raising difficult questions about the scope and limits of reason itself. The upshot of his work was to emphasize the role of human will, rather than human reason, for issues concerning ultimate truth and value.

THE LIMITS OF REASON

In the nineteenth century, following Kant's work, thinkers assessed the role of reason in different ways. The word 'existentialism' stresses finite 'existence' as the concrete here-and-now. In this context 'existence' stands in contrast not to 'non-existence' but to 'essence', which seems to denote the inner nature of things at some profound level. But essences elude the power of human reason. On the other hand, flesh-and-blood 'existence' concerns the human will, and indeed the whole human condition; it is not – in contrast to essence – a product of some flight of reason alone.

Georg W. F. Hegel (1770–1831).

Georg W. F. Hegel (1770–1831) attempted to reinstate reason, by stressing that – although all reasoning is admittedly embedded in finite historical situations in life – it is still possible to talk about 'the Absolute' which lies behind these finite acts of reasoning.

The first existentialist thinker, Søren Kierkegaard (1813–55), rejected Hegel's philosophy as too sweeping, too optimistic, and not sufficiently concerned with human existence in all its finitude. Existentialism takes a variety of forms, but all share a deep suspicion, and often a pessimism, about the capacities of human reason. We cannot reach issues of ultimate truth by mere theory or argument, because we cannot jump outside the limits of our own point of view. I see what I see because I already stand where I stand.

In spite of their differences from one another, all whom we may call existentialists share the following perspective:

- the priority of the human will over against human reason;
- the priority of practical interest over theoretical speculation;
- the priority of the personal over the abstract;
- the priority of individual existence over general essence;
- the priority of first-hand involvement over detached objectivity.

CHRISTIAN OR SECULAR?

> *There is an infinitely qualitative difference between God and man. This means, or the expression for this is, that man is capable of nothing, it is God who gives everything, who gives man faith, and so on.*
>
> Søren Kierkegaard, *Papirer* (1849).

The most interesting feature of these characteristics is that they can lend themselves equally to a Christian emphasis (with Kierkegaard) or to secularism and atheism (with Friedrich Nietzsche, 1844–1900). Across the spectrum: Kierkegaard was a Protestant individualist; Nietzsche was a militant atheist; Karl Jaspers (1883–1969) saw value in religion, but rejected the exclusivism of traditional Christianity; Martin Heidegger (1889–1976) left no room for God; Gabriel Marcel (1889–1973) wrote as a Roman Catholic; but Jean-Paul Sartre (1905–80) and Albert Camus (1913–60) attack religious and Christian belief.

Their different use of the same perspective is easy to explain. Into the vacuum left by the absence of reason and of theory, Kierkegaard put faith, decision, venture, and obedience. Into the same vacuum, or 'abyss', Nietzsche placed self-interest, wishes, and the disguise of power-play as illusory truth-claims. Kierkegaard saw reason as a false alibi that distracted people from authentic faith and obedience to God. Nietzsche saw reason as a false alibi that allowed people to put forward claims which served their interests as if these were objective truths.

Christian existentialism, as Kierkegaard expressed, it stresses that:

- God's existence cannot be proved by argument; it must be accepted in faith.
- Christian faith is not assenting to doctrinal truths; it is commitment and obedience.
- God is far beyond human reason: truth about God entails paradox.

Atheistic existentialism, as Nietzsche expressed it, stresses that:

- Humans project a notion of God to make their own wishes and interests appear legitimate and capable of fulfilment.
- 'God' is therefore an instrumental construct, or functional cipher, to support a manipulative rhetoric: a product of decision.
- All claims to objective or ultimate truth are illusory; religion is a system of values and interests disguised as a system of truth.

EXISTENTIALIST THEMES AND THINKERS

Nietzsche has been described as the first 'postmodernist' (see below), as his views lie behind many assumptions in late twentieth-century secular ideologies. However, to complete our sketch of existentialism we must comment first on Jaspers, Heidegger, Marcel, Sartre, and Camus.

Karl Jaspers worked in psychiatry as well as philosophy, and stressed that what often passes for 'objective truth' reflects only the conventional beliefs of the day. How can one know what is genuine? He noted that in situations of crisis, in which patients came to the end of their own resources, all artificial or contrived second-hand values often fell away, leaving only that which was genuine or authentic for the patient. On one side, this approach can be therapeutic in restoring reality to a person; on the other side, what is deemed to be authentic truth still varies from person to person.

Martin Heidegger argued that even the seemingly 'general' questions of philosophy can be asked only concretely, from the standpoint of where the thinker already is. He or she can philosophize only from within their own pre-existing horizons; a thinker can never completely escape the boundaries and problems imposed by this radical finitude.

Heidegger believed that traditional philosophy had failed to take adequate account of this finitude, and of the boundaries imposed by the horizons of the individual. He followed Nietzsche, and anticipated postmodernists, in diagnosing the 'end' of philosophy – including theology – in any traditional sense, looking in his later writings for a kind of rebirth of 'listening' thinking through some kind of visionary renewal for which one might endlessly wait.

Friedrich Nietzsche.

Gabriel Marcel attempted to recapture existentialist perspectives for more positive purposes within a Christian or humanist framework. Rationality and the sciences too often viewed human persons as 'cases' or 'statistics' within some scientific theory. But a more participatory and less rationalistic approach might restore the dignity of personhood to humans who, after all, were not mere 'data' for scientists – including medical or social scientists – but active agents or subjects.

Sartre and Camus follow Nietzsche in attacking every notion of universal or objective truth as illusory. Whereas Nietzsche saw religion and philosophy as the worst culprits in disguising self-interest or group interest as truth for all, Sartre and Camus also attacked the entrapping constraints of what seemed to pass for truth in the mere conventions of society. The individual must not be deceived into imagining that society's notion of 'God', 'truth', or 'the right thing' holds any necessary validity or constraint for free-thinking individuals. All convention must be viewed with suspicion.

POSTMODERNISM

This approach reached its climax in the post-war years, especially in Paris. But by the late 1950s, a reaction had set in against the confusion between subjectivity – the human person is an agent, not an object – and subjectivism – everything is relative to the wishes and views of the individual.

If existentialism had died in the 1950s, many of its claims were renewed in a transposed form in the movement led initially by Roland Barthes (1915–80) and Jacques Derrida (1930–2004) around 1967. 'Modernity' is often associated with universal, rational truth-claims, especially those put forward by mathematics and science. By contrast, 'postmodernism' expresses a loss of confidence in any universal truth: all claims to truth are viewed as constructs which only serve the interests of particular groups. Its chief difference from existentialism lay in its recognition not simply of the radical finitude and fallibility of the individual: society as a whole cannot reach outside the values and supposed truths which it has constructed. Every power-group defines what is 'normal' for society in ways which promote its own interests.

SITUATEDNESS AND FRAGMENTATION

Following Heidegger's emphasis on what he called 'radical historical finitude', exponents of the postmodern perspective stress the 'situatedness' of every person within the pre-given historical and cultural horizons into which they were born. Our place in history and society not only conditions how we think, but also in effect constructs our view of what counts as true or useful. No single overall viewpoint is possible for everyone. We are faced with a radical fragmentation of human understanding, truth, and values. Thus the French postmodern philosopher, Jean-François Lyotard (1924–98), defined postmodernity as a suspicion of all 'grand narratives', that is, of all holistic or universal accounts of human life and history.

David Lyon tried to distinguish between postmodernism and postmodernity. Postmodernism, he argued, reflects first of all a philosophical and intellectual rejection of rationalism, and of the scientific world view of modernity. Postmodernity, by contrast, reflects a social phenomenon, in which the 'truth' becomes largely absorbed into a series of virtual reality worlds, constructed by consumer profiles, information technology, and what different classes or groups in society construct in accordance with their own norms. Many call this social constructionism. Such a distinction might serve a useful purpose, but it now seems too late to try to put the clock back, since so many use both terms indiscriminately.

CONTRASTS IN POSTMODERNISM

A significant difference emerges between more optimistic, postmodern philosophical perspectives in America, and more pessimistic, suspicious, critical postmodern philosophy in continental Europe. The first rests on pragmatism; that is, we decide what is true by what succeeds; the second is often associated with 'deconstruction'. The most notorious American postmodern pragmatic philosopher was Richard Rorty (1931–2007), whilst well known European postmodern philosophers include Michel Foucault (1926–84) and Jacques Derrida.

> God is dead; but considering the state the species Man is in, there will perhaps be caves, for ages yet, in which his shadow will be shown.
>
> Friedrich Nietzsche,
> *Joyous Wisdom.*

Rorty rejects traditional accounts of the truth: there is no such task as 'getting reality right'. All claims to truth remain entirely relative to the values and perceptions of given 'local' communities. They are relative to the practices of these sub-groups or peer groups, and to what they count as 'success' on their own terms. Although he concedes that this is relativistic, Rorty prefers to use the term 'ethnocentric' to denote what 'local' or specific social or political communities construe as useful and thereby, in effect, also truthful.

We may trace the origins of the continental European version to Friedrich Nietzsche. The phenomenon of disguise provides a key: Nietzsche argued that many claims on behalf of Christian truth or belief are, in fact, disguised bids for power over others. In the 1960s, Roland Barthes pointed out that even the choice of clothes or furniture may tell us more about someone's social aspirations or self-image than their concerns about comfort. Foucault stressed that 'knowledge' often reflects 'power'. Bureaucracies and 'regimes' claim expertise about what is right, but too readily constitute and hide an oppressive power on behalf of those in control under this guise. In hospitals and prisons we find 'the smiling face in the white coat' that controls our lives.

Derrida applies this no less radically to question the very status of philosophy, metaphysics, and traditional notions of truth and language. Following Nietzsche, Freud, and Heidegger, he diagnoses their claims to truth as 'mythologies'. They pretend to a universal status, but simply promote the power of the ruling intelligentsia, who use them as instruments to promote their own values, well-being, or power. These myths are candidates for 'deconstruction'. This exposes their disguise.

DECONSTRUCTIVE OR CONSTRUCTIVE EFFECTS

Some perceive the postmodernism of European writers as more destructive than postmodern perspectives in America. However, we may question this. Nietzsche's attack on illusion and disguise in religion – for all its cynical scepticism – may also serve to alert us to the difference between inauthentic religion, driven by selfish power interests, and genuine religious faith as a response to revelation from beyond the self. Foucault's strictures about power interests in institutions may alert us to self-serving authoritarianism, not least within churches. American postmodernity may free us from the tyranny of a supposed scientific objectivism, but it may also leave truth hostage to the mere market forces of consumerism, and to the changing criteria of 'progress'. It may merely affirm what communities choose to do, and betrays a lack of moral seriousness. Dollars and tanks may, at worst, become the sole substitutes for a lost 'ultimate'. 'Truth' quits the stage for 'winners'.

It is impossible, therefore, to pin down a neat package of postmodern beliefs. Postmodernity is more strictly a way of approach, a perspective, or a mood. David Harvey, a respected commentator on this subject, endorses a rule-of-thumb contrast between the modern and the postmodern. Whereas modernity reflects purpose, design, hierarchy, determinacy, form, and mastery, postmodernity reflects play, chance, anarchy, indeterminacy, chaos, and exhaustion or silence. This is not a bad summary of the 'feel' of the respective moods.

In religions, the contrast becomes further sharpened, as one between authority and egalitarianism; reason and rhetoric; truth and power; individual and sub-group or peer group. However, religions often challenge both secular modernity and secular postmodernity in certain respects. For example, religions tend to value traditions more highly than is the case either in modernity or in postmodernity, seeing them often, but not always, as sources of cumulative wisdom gathered through history over the generations. But postmodernity stresses disruption, and differences rather than continuities – especially in Foucault – and places a heavy emphasis on social constructionism. By contrast many religions, especially Judaism, Christianity, and Islam, often stress the 'givenness' of many beliefs, values, and practices, sometimes ascribing to them the status of divine decrees.

Postmodernity may in theory appear to promote a new-found tolerance, since no one sub-group is deemed to have the right to impose its values upon another. However, this may be illusory. Different ethnic groups, different genders, and different class and professional interests all seem to operate with different criteria of truth. But this leads to the collapse of any dialogue that crosses community boundaries. Rational argument becomes reduced to manipulative rhetoric. People look in vain for some global vision or global overview.

If claims to truth are thought to represent only the manipulative power play of interest groups, this generates – understandably – suspicion, conflict, and violence. Everything that goes wrong is blamed on the power interests of some group. Here is secular ideology, in the fullest sense of the term. Postmodernism is finally unmasked as offering, not the freedom which it claims, but conflict and uncertainty, and an invitation to blame the power interests of competing groups for all ills.

ANTHONY C. THISELTON

CHAPTER 84

New Religious Movements

The term 'New Religious Movements' (NRMs) covers a variety of religious organizations that have emerged in recent times, commonly referred to as 'cults'. The term 'cult' is inappropriate, being pejorative and lacking a clear definition. Some scholars have defined a new religion as an organization that has arrived in the West since World War II, while others regard 'new' as spanning the last 150 years. NRMs are a global, not merely a Western, phenomenon: there are some 10,000 NRMs in Africa alone, around 3000 in the USA, and 500–600 in Britain. There are an estimated 31 million followers in Japan.

NRMs tend to fall outside mainstream religion, sometimes because of doctrinal disputes, at times because of controversial practices. The mass deaths of followers of the Peoples Temple in Jonestown, Guyana (1978), and of David Koresh and the Branch Davidians in Waco, Texas (1993), and the deaths of members of the Solar Temple in Switzerland and Canada (1994), the UFO religion Heaven's Gate in California (1997), and the Movement for the Restoration of the Ten Commandments of God in Uganda (2000), and Aum Shinrikyo's sarin gas attack on the passengers of the Tokyo underground, killing twelve and injuring many others (1995), reinforced the perception that NRMs are violent, although such incidents are rare.

CHRISTIAN-RELATED NRMs

Nineteenth-century NRMs in the West were predominantly Christian. William Miller (1782–1849), an early proponent of Adventism, proclaimed that Christ's second coming was imminent. He named 1843, and subsequently 1844, as the year of Christ's return; his followers' disillusionment in 1844 became known as the 'Great Disappointment'. His ideas were nonetheless influential. Ellen G. White (1827–1915), who founded the Seventh-day Adventists in 1861, taught that Jesus had returned, but that his presence was invisible.

Charles Taze Russell (1852–1916), who co-founded Zion's Watch Tower Tract Society in 1881, also taught the doctrine of Christ's 'invisible presence', although the Jehovah's Witnesses, as Russell's successor, Joseph Franklin Rutherford (1869–1942), named them in 1931, now regard 1914 as the date of this event.

The Church of Jesus Christ of Latter-day Saints (the 'Mormons') claims a new revelation, afforded to Joseph Smith Jr (1805–44), its founder-leader. The angel Moroni

The Mormon Tabernacle, Temple Square, Salt Lake City, Utah, USA.

reportedly lent him a set of gold plates, from which he translated *The Book of Mormon* (1830), which tells of Jesus Christ preaching in the USA after his resurrection. Smith was murdered in 1844, after which Brigham Young (1801–77) took over the leadership and led the 'saints' to the Great Salt Lake in Utah, where they set up their headquarters.

Another significant movement was New Thought, or Higher Thought, which promoted the concept that Infinite Intelligence – or God – is everywhere, and emphasized health improvement through mental 'affirmations'. These ideas influenced Mary Baker Eddy's (1821–1910) Christian Science and also the Hopkins Metaphysical Association, set up by Emma Curtis Hopkins (1849–1925) in 1887. Some of Hopkins' students set up their own organizations, the best known of which is the Unity School of Christianity, or Unity Church, founded in Kansas City, Missouri in 1889.

Contact with spirits constituted a further strand. Modern spiritualism can be traced back to 'rappings' heard by the Fox sisters of Hydesville, New York, in 1848, although spiritualist churches emphasize healing as much as contact with the departed. Helena P. Blavatsky (1831–91), one of the founders of the Theosophical Society, claimed contact with a number of 'Ascended Masters', advanced spiritual beings who once lived on earth. Ascended Masters – sometimes called the 'Great White Brotherhood' – feature in other organizations, such as the Rosicrucians and the Church Universal and Triumphant, and also in the New Age 'channelling' movement.

NRMs IN THE 1960s AND 1970s

A new wave of NRMs occurred in the 1960s. Bible-based and charismatic, the 'Jesus Movement', or 'Jesus People', gained momentum within the youth counter-culture of that period, sometimes involving communal living and sharing of possessions. Converts had often previously been on drugs, and the Love Family, or Church of Jesus Christ at Armageddon, founded by Paul Erdman (b. 1940) in 1968, encouraged their use.

Of the communal groups, the best known are The Family International (TFI), previously known as the Children of God, or COG, and The Holy Spirit Association for the Unification of World Christianity, or Unification Church (UC). Founded by David Brandt Berg (also known as 'Moses David', 1919–94), COG espoused Protestant fundamentalism, but became controversial for its 'flirty fishing' – or 'FFing' – the offer of sex to seekers, mainly by female members.

Although offering an interpretation of the Bible, the Unification Church presents a new revelation, claimed by founder-leader Sun Myung Moon (1920–2012). Moon taught that Jesus was unable fully to accomplish his messianic mission, which was to marry and beget sinless children. Sun Myung Moon and his wife Hak Ja Han Moon are jointly regarded as the new messiahs, and members can be grafted into their restored family through a Blessing ceremony – the 'mass wedding'.

> Emperors, kings and presidents ... have declared to all heaven and earth that Reverend Sun Myung Moon is none other than humanity's saviour, messiah, returning Lord, and true parent.
>
> Sun Myung Moon

INDIAN-DERIVED NRMs

The first Hindu *swami* (world-renouncer) to visit the West was Ramakrishna's pupil Swami Vivekananda (1863–1902), who spoke at the World's Parliament of Religions in Chicago in 1893, and founded the Vedanta Society in New York in 1894. Several other gurus also travelled to the West, notably Paramahansa Yogananda (1893–1952), founder of the Self-Realization Fellowship in 1920; Meher Baba (1894–1969), who in 1954 declared he was the Avatar of the age; the Maharishi Mahesh Yogi (1918–2008), who developed the Transcendental Meditation (™) technique and acted as guru to the Beatles; Sri Chinmoy (1931–2007), who promoted 'inner peace'; Swami A. C. Bhaktivedanta Praphupada (1896–1977), founder of the International Society for Krishna Consciousness (ISKCON), better known as the 'Hare Krishna' movement[1]; and Prem Pal Singh Rawat (b. 1957, formerly known as Guru Maharaj Ji), leader of the Elan Vital movement and its predecessor, the Divine Light Mission (DLM).

Although Satya Sai Baba (1926–2011) never visited the West, he was well known as a miracle-worker, and his followers averred that he could materialize objects such as rings and watches. Followers made pilgrimages to his two ashrams in India to receive *darshan*: Sai

---

1 The 'Hare Krishna' mantra was introduced by the ecstatic teacher Chaitanya Mahaprabhu (1486–1534), and the movement focuses on the Hindu deity Lord Krishna.

Baba claimed to be the reincarnation of Sai Baba   Hare Krishna members on an American sidewalk.
of Shirdi (d. 1918), an avatar, spiritual saint, and
miracle worker. Less well known, but equally important, is Dada Lekhraj (1876–1969),
who founded Brahma Kumaris, a movement aiming to improve the status of women, led
by his female disciples following his death. Celibacy is encouraged and Raja Yoga – a
mental practice aimed at uniting the soul with the divine – is taught.

Bhagavan Shri Rajneesh (1931–90), later known as Osho, was born into a Jain
family in India, but taught an idiosyncratic form of Zen Buddhism. In the 1970s,
members dressed in orange or red clothes and became popularly known as the 'orange
people'. His teachings rejected authority, and extolled sexual freedom and materialism.
In 1981 Rajneesh moved to Oregon, USA, and set up his own 'enlightened city', known
as Rajneeshpuram. Following conflict with local residents, Osho was arrested in 1985
and the community disbanded, though the Osho organization survives.

BUDDHIST NRMs

After arriving in the USA in 1897, D. T. Suzuki (1870–1966) wrote prolifically on Zen. The 1960s US youth counter-culture took the Zen notion of the 'Buddha within' to mean personal licentiousness, and this anarchic counter-cultural version of Zen is sometimes known as 'Beat Zen', after the 'Beatniks' of the late 1950s. Buddhist NRMs derive from various traditions.

The Vipassana movement promotes a Theravada meditative practice aimed at seeing reality's true nature. Vipassana is an ancient practice, revived in Myanmar (Burma) and Thailand during the twentieth century, but its modern expression is taught to Western laypeople and to women.

Innovative forms of Tibetan Buddhism include the New Kadampa Tradition (NKT), founded by Geshe Kelsang Gyatso (b. 1931), which became controversial because of a ritual practice known as Dorje Shugden, opposed by the Dalai Lama.

The Soka Gakkai International (SGI), founded in 1930, derives its teachings from the Japanese teacher Nichiren (1222–82) and his favoured scripture, the *Lotus Sutra*. SGI members regularly chant the mantra *nam myoho renge kyo* – literally 'Homage to the ineffable law of the lotus teaching' – which is believed to have immense power, yielding material pragmatic benefits as well as spiritual ones.

The Friends of the Western Buddhist Order (FWBO) seek to develop a new form of Buddhism for Westerners. Founded by the Venerable Sangharakshita (Dennis Lingwood, b. 1925), it emphasizes 'right livelihood' – the fifth point of the Buddha's Eightfold Path – rather than the monastic practice of seeking alms from lay supporters.

Engaged Buddhism is based on the teachings of Thich Nhat Hanh (b. 1926), a Zen monk from Vietnam, and emphasizes active involvement in social and political issues.

BLACK POWER MOVEMENTS AND WHITE ISLAM

Some NRMs have originated from black communities.

Originating in Jamaica, the Rastafarians were initially a Black Power movement supported by the descendants of slaves. They interpreted the Bible's teachings as pointing to Ethiopia, where they believed Emperor Haile Selassie (1891–1975) was their messiah, who would herald a return to Africa. Following Haile Selassie's death, such ideas have been reappraised, and a variety of expectations now exists.

Malcolm X in 1962.

Other Black Power movements drew on Islam. The Nation of Islam (NOI) was originally a black supremacist organization, established in the 1930s, and later led by Elijah Muhammad (Elijah Poole, 1897–1975). Malcolm X (Malcolm Little, 1925–65) joined but left in 1964, having reconsidered NOI's racism.

The white population's interest in Islam tends to focus on Sufism, originally introduced to the USA in 1910 by Inayat Khan (1882–1927), and made popular by the writings of Idries Shah (1924–96).

UFO RELIGIONS

Unidentified Flying Objects (UFOs) have gained significance for a number of spiritual seekers, and the resulting organizations have come to be collectively known as 'UFO religions'. Typically, they hold that the gods are extra-terrestrials, who communicate with key individuals. The earliest UFO religion in the West was the Aetherius Society, established by George King (1919–97) in 1954 or 1955. Better known is the Raëlian Movement, whose enthusiasm for modern technology includes promoting human cloning, which they believe is the key to personal immortality. Western UFO religions are often Bible-based; Raël (Claude Vorilhon, b. 1946) contends that spaceships are frequently alluded to in Judaeo-Christian scripture, for example the chariots of Elijah and Ezekiel.

HUMAN POTENTIAL MOVEMENT

Although sometimes classified as a UFO religion, the Church of Scientology is unusual in having no obvious spiritual ancestry. Science fiction writer L. Ron Hubbard (1911–86) gained prominence in 1950 with his best-selling self-improvement classic *Dianetics: The Modern Science of Mental Health*. Dianetics claims to rid the 'thetan' (the self) of harmful 'engrams' (records of unpleasant past experiences) that impede the mind. Once these are removed, the practitioner is regarded as 'clear' and can proceed to the various levels of 'Operating Thetan', which are disclosed only to authorized students.

Scientology is one of several groups that form part of the Human Potential Movement (HPM), an umbrella term for organizations claiming to offer enhanced quality of life. Werner Erhard (b. 1935), founder of Erhard Seminar Training (*est* – now Landmark Forum) previously studied Scientology, but other groups have no such influence: for example Silva Method, PSI Mind Development, and the School of Economic Science (SES), which is influenced by Advaita Vedanta.

The Human Potential Movement is a loosely defined cluster of groups and ideas, which merges into the equally nebulous New Age Movement (NAM), characterized by eclecticism, an optimism about human nature, and a disenchantment with organized religion. From the 1980s the NRM climate changed and few new religions emerged. Falun Gong is the major significant one: founded in 1992 in China by Li Hongzhi (b. 1951), it offers a set of physical exercises similar to *tai ch'i*, with a path to becoming a Buddha. Other changes in NRMs include less community living, less proselytizing, less media attention, and greater institutionalization.

GEORGE D. CHRYSSIDES

CHAPTER 85

The Bahá'í Faith

Sayyid 'Ali Muhammad, born in Shiraz, Persia (modern-day Iran) in 1819, claimed to be a Messenger of God, and called himself the Báb, meaning 'the gate', as his mission to prepare the way for the coming of a greater Messenger. His new religious movement caused a stir, culminating in the persecution of its adherents as Islamic heretics, and he was executed in 1850. Mirza Husayn 'Ali Nuri (1817–92) from Tehran, who became a follower of the Báb in 1844, now took the name Bahá'u'lláh, meaning 'The Glory of God', and founded the Bahá'í faith.

Exiled from Persia in 1853, Bahá'u'lláh moved to Baghdad, where in 1863 he claimed to be the bearer of a new message from God, built on the previous religions of the world, and destined to take humanity to the next stage of its development: world unity. Bahá'u'lláh was subsequently exiled to Edirne, from 1863 to 1868, and then to Akko (Acre), where he died in 1892. His shrine, just outside Akko, Israel, is the holiest site for Bahá'ís, and the world centre of the Bahá'í faith is in this area.

Bahá'u'lláh appointed his son 'Abdu'l-Bahá ('Abbas Effendi, 1844–1921) to succeed him as head of the Bahá'í faith and interpreter of his writings, and between 1911 and 1913 'Abdu'l-Bahá travelled to Europe and North America, consolidating the new Bahá'í communities there. On his death, his grandson Shoghi Effendi (Rabbani, 1897–1957) succeeded as head of the Bahá'í faith. After he died, there was an interregnum until 1963, when the Universal House of Justice was elected, to spread the Bahá'í faith to all parts of the world.

During the twentieth century the Bahá'í community faced persecution in some Muslim and Communist countries, particularly in Iran in 1979 after the Islamic Revolution, when many Bahá'ís were executed and the government of Iran set out forcibly to convert its Bahá'í community. By the early twenty-first century there were more than 5 million Bahá'ís living in more than 230 countries, with the largest community in India and large communities in Latin America, Africa, and South-East Asia.

SACRED WRITINGS

During his lifetime Bahá'u'lláh wrote a number of key works, as well as many letters, known as *Tablets*, all of which are regarded as Bahá'í scripture. Most important are

the *Kitab-i-Aqdas* (the 'Most Holy Book'), which contains laws and social ordinances, and the *Kitab-i-Iqan* (the 'Book of Certitude'), which addresses theological questions, and explains how the prophecies of the Bible and Qur'an have been fulfilled spiritually and metaphorically, rather than literally. The writings of Bahá'u'lláh's forerunner, the Báb, and of 'Abdu'l-Bahá, are also regarded as scripture, although some laws and social ordinances of the Báb were repealed by Bahá'u'lláh. Shoghi Effendi's interpretations of the writings of Bahá'u'lláh and 'Abdu'l-Bahá are regarded as authoritative, but not scripture. The Universal House of Justice is regarded as head of the Bahá'í faith, and legislates in areas not covered by scripture.

Shrine of the Báb, Haifa, Israel.

THE BAHÁ'Í FAITH

BELIEFS

Bahá'ís maintain the purpose of life in this world is to show to the greatest extent possible spiritual qualities such as love, justice, patience, compassion, wisdom, purity, and trustworthiness. All human beings are capable of exhibiting these virtues, although each person exhibits them to a varying degree. Since these qualities are also attributes of the divinity, acquiring them is tantamount to drawing nearer to God. The divine potential is present in everyone, so the Bahá'í scriptures regard education as mining the gems that exist within each human being.

For Bahá'ís, salvation is a process that begins at birth and continues after death. Only God knows where each human being started on this process, what status has been attained, and the progress made. Human beings should not judge each other about these matters. To assist with spiritual progress, Bahá'u'lláh has given laws, such as a daily requirement to pray, read the scriptures, and meditate, and an annual period of fasting. From these practices are obtained the spiritual guidance which in other religions is given by leaders, since Bahá'u'lláh forbade any form of priesthood or religious leadership.

Bahá'u'lláh asserted there is a supreme reality, in Western religions called God. Since God is infinite, and our minds can only conceptualize the finite, humanity has no access to knowledge of the supreme reality. Neither the formulations of God made by Western religions, nor the descriptions of ultimate reality in Eastern religions, are adequate or accurate. The only certain knowledge human beings can gain of supreme reality is brought by intermediaries who arise from time to time to found the great world religions – such as Abraham, Krishna, Moses, Zarathushtra (Zoroaster), Buddha, Christ, and Muhammad – in the Bahá'í scriptures called 'Manifestations of God'. Bahá'u'lláh claimed to be the latest of these manifestations, who bring teachings to the world necessary for humanity's spiritual and social progress. Bahá'u'lláh asserted that now is the time for humanity to come together in world-embracing unity, that all the scriptures of the world religions include prophecies of a world saviour, and that he is the fulfilment of these prophecies.

Bahá'u'lláh stated that a human being survives after death as a spiritual entity (soul), and continues to progress in further spiritual worlds towards the goal of reunion with God. Many religions speak of heaven and hell; Bahá'ís believe these are metaphors for being near to, or distant from, God, and that one can be in heaven or hell while in this world. Humanity is reaching maturity, and much that was previously part of religion – Satan, heaven, and hell as physical entities, and practices such as confession and priestly forgiveness of sins – can be dispensed with. The belligerence of human society is also something humanity will leave behind.

WORSHIP AND FESTIVALS

There are few rituals or acts of public worship in the Bahá'í faith. At Bahá'í meetings, prayers and passages of scripture are recited. Three of Bahá'u'lláh's prayers have a ritual status, and Bahá'ís are obliged to say one of them daily. Nine Bahá'í holy days commemorate events in the life of the Báb and Bahá'u'lláh, and include the Bahá'í New Year, 21 March, the first day of spring in the northern hemisphere. If possible, Bahá'ís do not work on these days.

The Bahá'í calendar has 19 months of 19 days, and there is an annual fast of 19 days, during which Bahá'ís fast from dawn to sunset. Bahá'ís who are able go on a nine-day pilgrimage to the Bahá'í holy places in the Haifa-'Akko area, including the shrines of Bahá'u'lláh, the Báb, and 'Abdu'l-Bahá.

The Bahá'í community meets every 19 days for the 19 Day Feast. Most Bahá'í communities have meetings for enquirers, devotional meetings, study circles, and children's classes, often held in homes. Eventually each Bahá'í community hopes to be centred on a House of Worship, of which there are currently seven: in New Delhi, Sydney, Apia (Western Samoa), Kampala, Panama, Frankfurt am Main, and Wilmette (near Chicago).

FAMILY AND SOCIETY

Bahá'ís view the family as fundamental to the individual's spiritual development and to society's stability and progress, and aim for a spiritualization of the individual, society, and the whole human race. Through the teachings of Bahá'u'lláh, humankind will be united and world peace established. The Bahá'í scriptures give principles to guide all social policies and laws. People's consciousness will eventually be raised to a global level, so they no longer think of themselves in racial, religious, ethnic, or class terms, but as citizens of the world. The scriptures also stress the need to balance the masculine and feminine elements in society, in order to promote peace.

Bahá'í scriptures recommend democratic forms of government. According to Bahá'í teaching, true happiness comes from being detached from wealth and serving others. Bahá'u'lláh stated that the world's problems cannot be solved until the world is united; eventually it will be necessary to establish global institutions. Yet Bahá'í writings warn against uniformity: excessive centralization is to be avoided and decisions should be made, as far as possible, at local and national levels. The Bahá'í aim is to preserve the rich diversity of human language, culture, tradition, and thought, while removing the causes of conflict and contention.

MOOJAN MOMEN

CHAPTER 86

Secularization and Sacralization

'Secularization' names the process whereby religion declines in significance in personal life and/or society. By contrast, 'sacralization' (or 'de-secularization') names the process whereby religion grows in significance in personal life and/or society. There is normally – though not inevitably – a link between the level of significance which religion holds in personal life and in society.

SECULARIZATION AND SACRALIZATION IN THE WEST

Levels of secularization or sacralization are normally measured in terms of the numbers of active participants in religious institutions such as churches. By this measure, most Western societies have experienced secularization since the late nineteenth century, and the process has accelerated dramatically since the mid-1960s. In Sweden, for example, churchgoing is now down to just 4 per cent of the population. Rates of secularization vary by country, however, as well as by institution. Levels of congregational participation are higher in the USA than in most European countries, and in most places 'liberal' or 'mainline' denominations (both Catholic and Protestant) have declin ed faster than any other forms of Christianity.

Secularization has been more evident at the social than the personal level. The important social functions once performed by the churches in Western societies have gradually diminished, as the modern state and secular agencies have taken over responsibility for politics, education, welfare, and so on. At the national level, some modern states instigated a formal separation between church and state; and at the local level, the status and importance of the church and the clergy also diminished. In cultural terms too, Christianity has ceased to be a dominant force, being forced to compete with alternative sources and systems of meaning. At the personal level, however, religion still retains widespread allegiance. Whilst religious behaviours such as church attendance have declined, religious belief and self-identification remain high. In the 2011 census for England and Wales, for example, 59 per cent of the population identified themselves as 'Christian', whilst 96 per cent in the USA still affirm belief in God.

When personal 'Christian' belief is interrogated, however, it is often found to be 'nominal' – without accompanying commitment to churchgoing or any other form of active Christian involvement. In recent decades there has also been a noticeable shift away from a commitment to 'religion' towards a commitment to 'spirituality', and away from belief in a theistic God 'out there' towards belief in a more immanent 'Spirit'. In other words, as well as witnessing a decline in traditional religion, the late twentieth century appears to have witnessed the rise of new, more immanent, and 'holistic' forms of spirituality, which have more to do with the cultivation of unique subjective life than conformity to God-given norms. In this sense both secularization (of traditional religion) and sacralization (of new forms of spirituality) seem to be taking place simultaneously.

SECULARIZATION AND SACRALIZATION OUTSIDE THE WEST

If we move beyond the West to the rest of the world, we find evidence of sacralization of a rather different sort, namely the resurgence of traditional forms of religion. Nearly all the so-called 'world religions', including Hinduism and Buddhism, have experienced some revitalization since the 1970s, but the most dramatic growth has been enjoyed by resurgent Islam (sometimes called Islamism) and charismatic Christianity (sometimes called Pentecostalism). Journalists often bracket all these developments together, in speaking of the rise of 'fundamentalism', but the term is misleading insofar as it obscures important differences between different forms of religious revival.

Outside the West, religious resurgence is most evident in post-colonial regions, and sacralization is often bound up with the assertion of new, 'independent' identities. In the case of resurgent Islam, these identities are importantly national and pan-national, with Islam helping 'the Muslim world' establish itself over and against the cultural and economic encroachments of the West. In the case of charismatic Christianity, religion is more often mobilized at the personal and local level, where it helps individuals to establish, defend, and strengthen their identities by harnessing the power of God as Holy Spirit. In conditions of poverty, hardship, and social dislocation, these religions also have important roles to play in providing much-needed support — material, social, and spiritual.

REASONS FOR SECULARIZATION

The reasons for secularization and sacralization in the modern world are hotly debated. To date, sociologists of religion have devoted far more energy to developing theories of secularization than sacralization, mainly because the former process has been of longer duration and had greater impact in Western societies.

> *The fate of our times is characterized by rationalization and intellectualization and, above all, by the 'disenchantment of the world'. Precisely the ultimate and most sublime values have retreated from public life either into the transcendental realm of mystic life or into the brotherliness of direct and personal human relations.*
>
> Max Weber,
> *Science as a Vocation* (1919).

Five main varieties of 'secularization theory' may be distinguished, depending on which process of modernization each identifies as the salient cause:

CHURCH ATTENDANCE IN ENGLAND					
1851	1903	1951	1979	1989	2000
39%	19%	15%	12%	10%	8%

1. Theories which focus on *differentiation* argue that religion has lost significance as the process of 'functional' or 'structural' differentiation has separated functions in modern society into specialist spheres – politics, education, the law, and so on – each of which seeks to become autonomous from religion.
2. Theories which focus on *rationalization* single out the process by which modern society becomes rationalized, bureaucratized, and 'scientific' in its modes of operation as responsible for the 'disenchantment' and 'demystification' of the world.
3. Theories which focus on *pluralization* argue that beliefs are plausible when everybody one knows holds them, but become less plausible when one becomes aware that other people believe different things. The gradual pluralization of modern society therefore renders traditional belief implausible – unless it is able to sustain itself within a bounded subculture.
4. Theories which focus on *individualization* suggest that the process by which authority is internalized is damaging to religion, since the latter seeks to have authority over people, rather than let them make their own choices.
5. Theories which focus on *societalization* maintain that religion flourishes at the level of the local community, and therefore argue that the process by which wider – particularly national – society becomes more important than local societies is destructive of religion.

Although these different theories are often regarded as competitive, they may also be treated as mutually compatible, since each singles out a different aspect of the general process of modernization as responsible for secularization. In practice, therefore, they may work better in combination than in isolation. There is also a good deal more work to be done in testing these theories, to determine their power in relation to specific instances of secularization – whether by investigating historically the ways in which particular institutions have secularized, or by researching empirically the reasons why individuals drop out of religion.

CAUSES OF SACRALIZATION

Whilst there are no established 'theories of sacralization', it is possible to make some general observations about the conditions under which religion seems to do well.

Religions do best, it seems, when they are allied with dominant political and economic power – for example, the spread of Christianity from late antiquity to the Middle Ages – or when they allow peoples to resist such power – for example, the success of religion in Northern Ireland or Poland. In both circumstances religions have much to offer by way of social unity, cohesion, and strength of purpose.

But religions also do well when they offer empowerment, not at the social, but at the personal level. Historically, this is evident in the highly varied manifestations of religion that are often classified – or dismissed – as 'magic'. In the latter, individuals attempt to harness sacred power to their own ends, often for healing or prosperity. Established religions and their representatives inevitably object to 'magic', not least because it threatens their monopoly over the sacred.

In late modern capitalist contexts, we see another instance of religion growing because of what it has to offer by way of personal empowerment in the growth of 'spirituality'. Current socio-economic as well as cultural conditions encourage a 'turn to the self', in which secure structures and given roles fall away, and individuals are required to fend for themselves in the modern economy. Rather than falling back on what is 'given', individuals have to create and recreate themselves in order to survive and flourish. In this situation, it is not surprising to find that 'religion' gives way to new forms of 'spirituality' that offer the healing, enhancement, and cultivation of unique subjective lives. God is no longer seen as a being to be obeyed, but as a power, energy, or Spirit that can be harnessed to the task of 'becoming all that I can be'. Under these conditions, personal growth becomes identified with spiritual growth, and the sacred finds a new role in societies that had often been expected to become wholly secular.

LINDA WOODHEAD

I AM A RASTAFARIAN

I am a writer called Benjamin Zephaniah. My full name is Benjamin Obadiah Iqbal Zephaniah. For me, this is significant because it reflects the Muslim and Judeo-Christian religious traditions. Like the hair of Lord Shiva, the Hindu god, my hair is matted in 'dreadlocks' (or *jata*). I also practise Tibetan meditation. What religion am I? In a sense I am all of the above. But ask me what I am and I will tell you that I am a Rastafarian.

It is impossible for me to speak about Rastafarianism without talking about politics. After all, Ras Tafari was the original name of Haile Selassie I (1891–1975), the last emperor of Ethiopia. It is also impossible to talk about Rastafarianism without referring to the fact that I am black. That said, you don't have to be political or black to be a Rastafarian.

My full conversion to the faith happened when I was seventeen years old. It was a matter of life, death, and freedom. In the mid-1970s I was one of the many forgotten, unemployed, first-generation black youths who roamed the streets of London, unable to see a future, and carrying a feeling of hopelessness. Not only did we have a hopeless future, we were also told that we had a past that started with slavery. The education we were receiving seemed to suggest that black people were incapable of controlling their own destiny. Suddenly Rastafari changed all that. Here was a faith and a movement that pointed to the long, and often glorious, past of black people. It gave me pride in being black and, most importantly, it taught me that there is nothing wrong with seeing God through black spectacles – from the perspective of a black person.

I stopped walking the streets with my head held down. My head was held high, and there was a spring in my step. I now knew that my roots went back much further than Jamaica, and I started to look towards Africa. Rastafarians recognize Africa as the home of humanity, Ethiopia as its capital, and Haile Selassie as being directly in the line of Solomon. All this symbolism helped me to stand on my own feet. But most importantly, I was made aware that I could find Jah (as Rastafarians refer to God) by looking inwards. I learnt how to read any of the many holy books, or any scientific book, and apply my own intelligence. I learnt that rituals may be of some use, but that there is a way to find a direct line to Jah through meditation and inner peace. I was no longer concerned with understanding the world, I was now able to 'overstand' it. For the Rastafarian, to overstand is to apply your mind to a subject, and discern a greater meaning than the obvious one. Again, in seeking to understand a person, one overstands when one truly empathizes with that person. In other words, overstanding goes beyond basic understanding.

Rastafari is a form of black liberation theology. Although we say that we shall be liberated in heaven, Rastafarians insist that we must also be liberated here on earth. Rastafarian liberation theology has no party manifesto. It is not political in that sense. Rather, it is about social responsibility; and, if that means speaking out about the misuse of power in society, then so be it. I see it as my duty to take a stand, and to help those who are struggling to help themselves. Rastafari has given purpose to my writing. I am a scribe of Rastafari, bearing witness and writing the third testament. I am full of this sense of purpose. In interviews I have no problem answering that often asked question, 'What is the poet's role in society?' The number of books I sell, or my popularity, is of little importance to me. Making sure that what I write is written is far more important. Having said that, I do not believe that it is our job to preach. Rastafarians are not out to convert people, which is why I and many other Rasta writers don't write Rasta poetry. Rather, it is poetry about the world; poetry for the body and the soul; poetry for every body and every soul. I have found my role in life, and I am perfectly content with it. I have no great ambitions. My only ambition would be to do what I do better, and do more of it.

Many Rastafarians live in communes. However, while it is certainly good and pleasant for brethren to dwell together in unity, this is not always possible. I do not live in a commune. Although it would be very difficult for me to live a communal life, fortunately Rastafari has taught me to be at ease with my 'self' and not to fear silence, darkness, or solitude. Although I work for and celebrate the community, and value my relationship with others, there is also a great sense of liberation in not relying on the congregation to find strength. Nor do I feel the need for a building as a centre of worship. Jah is always with me. To be precise, Jah is part of me. So I have no real need to look outward for Jah. To find and worship Jah, I must look within.

I used to be very critical of Rastafarians who had children that did not wear dreadlocks, and worse still of those who did not raise their children as Rastas. I thought that if mummy and daddy were Rastas, baby should follow. But I have come to realize that it is up to me (the parent) to live a good life and be a good example to my child. My child should freely want to become a Rasta because of what he sees in me. I have found my spiritual path, and my personal relationship with Jah means a lot to me. So if my child does not become a Rastafarian, but is nevertheless influenced positively by me, I still feel that I have done well before Jah – I am still doing the work of Jah.

When it comes to religious practice, I focus on compassion, which I extend to every living thing. This means there are many practices I won't take part in. I am opposed to violence and war – except in self-defence – and the manufacture of arms. I will have nothing to do with a trade that relies on the unfair exploitation of workers or forced labour. I am also a vegan. Not only will I not eat animals – I will not even wear leather products, unless there are no alternatives. To do so, I believe, would spoil my meditation, and disturb my communion with Jah. Although I do understand that there is a time to reap and a time to sow, a time to heal and a time to kill, and so on, Jah tells me that such a time is not now. When I feel that every animal is my friend, I find that I have a direct connection with the earth, nature, and even that most abstract of things called 'the universe'. I have learned that to have a direct relationship with Jah and with creation makes for a contented guy who is at ease with his 'self'.

Benjamin Zephaniah

CHAPTER 87

Religion and Globalization

At first blush, one could be forgiven for imagining that globalization might simply be destructive of religion, or that religion would resist globalization. Are not religions bound up with ancient tradition, timeless ritual, and local experience? And doesn't 'globalization' suggest cutting-edge economies, jet-setting travellers, and instant communication by internet or smart phone?

Well, yes and no. Religious tradition does not necessarily imply looking only backwards. And the global world of fast food and transnational corporations cannot shake off religion like yesterday's fashions. For instance, the so-called Islamism that produced the attacks on the USA in September 2001 and then spawned the Islamic State is both planted in the past and has hopes for the future. It uses weaponized planes, cars vans, and social media to achieve its goals.

More broadly, we can safely say that religious activity is both a cause and effect of globalization. Among other things, missionary movements and religious territorial expansion fostered early forms of globalization. At the same time, globalization is both corrosive of, and a carrier for, religions. The multiplicity of media messages may unsettle notions of 'truth'. But online religious resources have caught on in a big way too, offering new modes of religious engagement. Thus we cannot grasp globalization without considering its religious dimensions; and we cannot reflect intelligently on religion today without considering its globalizing aspects.

These big words – religion and globalization – are notoriously difficult to define. Rather than a neat capsule of meaning, each is more like a menu or agenda. 'Religion' and 'globalization' give us an idea of what kinds of dishes we're about to eat, or what kind of topics will engage the discussion. We will start by sampling some aspects of globalization, and then suggest some ways in which religion may be understood in fresh ways in a globalized world.

GRASPING GLOBALIZATION

To many, globalization is primarily an economic process, typified by corporations, such as Microsoft, Apple, Google or Amazon that operate everywhere. These corporations not only exist as global enterprises, but also supply the means of operating over

Microsoft office in Germany.

vast distances: the world, for them, has become 'one place' for inventing, manufacturing, analyzing data, and selling. This is made possible by both rapid transport and — crucially — new communications media: these are the means of globalization, of making the world one place.

Simultaneously, though, these businesses have to acknowledge localities. Microsoft's and Amazon's headquarters are situated in Washington State, USA, and their products often have to be modified for local use. Languages differ, and so do climates and cultures. Not everyone speaks English or has air-conditioning. Such considerations indicate a demand for products suitable for distinct parts of the world. Corporations such as Microsoft have to be 'glocal' — both global and local.

Similarly, religious activities are increasingly globalized. The internet has become a key means of shrinking distances that previously separated different segments of the same religious groups. Anglican Christians in the global North, for instance, have become acutely aware of the more numerous dioceses in the global South, especially in Africa, as southern membership has mushroomed in contrast with drastic depletion in the North. Northern churches are learning from the experiences of the South, often using new means of contact. As well, every religion now has a diaspora — group members scattered well beyond their original place of activity — and Muslim, Jewish, Christian, Sikh, and Hindu diasporas can keep in touch using new technologies. In this sense, globalization draws people closer.

JIHAD v. McWORLD

Churchgoers outside Hillsong Church, Sydney, Australia at Christmas.

But globalization is paradoxical: the same forces that seem to unite also divide. Those with great promise may also present dire threat. Take Bangalore, South India. In the 'new economy' world of globalization, Bangalore is the 'Silicon Plateau' of shiny high-tech offices, a booming software industry, and affluent consumers in new shopping malls. But the surrounding state of Karnataka, including Bangalore, is predominantly rural, with high poverty rates. Landless labourers are forced to seek work in the city, so that the proportion of poor people living in huts with no services is growing faster than in other Indian cities — in fact, fewer services are available, precisely because they are overused by the sprawling science and technology parks.

A key paradox of globalization is seen in political theorist Benjamin Barber's neat phrase, 'Jihad v McWorld'. The fact that you can buy Big Macs anywhere reminds us that one fast-food company has managed to bring its products to the most remote regions. Here, globalization seems to mean 'the world as one brand'. But along with the sameness comes difference. The more the world is remade in the image of big corporations, the more people want to stress their distinctive identities and particular styles and tastes. Barber's point is that the two cannot be separated; they feed on each other, or are in tension with each other. Indeed, his phrase recalls the basic theme of religion and globalization. If McWorld offers a homogeneous diet of beef-in-bread, Jihad warns of scattered scuffles of holy war.

WORLD RELIGIONS TODAY			
Religions	Percentage of population	Population	Annual growth rate
Christian	32.29	2,229,951,315	1.2%
Muslim	22.90	1,581,765,792	1.9%
Hindu	13.88	958,695,903	1.2%
Non-religious	13.58	937,904,918	0.7%
Buddhist	6.92	478,164,008	1.3%
Chinese	5.94	409,917,596	0.0%
Other	0.85	58,613,020	0.8%
Sikh	0.35	23,990,543	1.4%
Jew	0.21	14,523,554	0.3%
Bahá'í	0.09	6,181,049	0.9%

Religions with a growth rate of over 1.2% are increasing faster than the world's population.

CULTURE CLASH

The resurgence of jihad led some, such as political scientist Samuel Huntingdon, to caution about a 'clash of civilizations' overtaking the new global world. One could say that this helpfully highlights the vital role of religions in globalization. But there is a danger of tarring all with the same brush – 'religions produce violence' – or, worse, suggesting that some religions are characterized by their worst elements, while others may be considered as basically beneficent, but with eccentric margins. The truth is that the main world religions have many manifestations, and Muslims are no happier to be lumped with Islamists than Christians with Appalachian snake-handlers or Jews with the 'fundamentalists' of Gush Emunim.

If we explore one icon of globalization, the internet, we soon find both mainstream and fundamentalist religion in cyberspace. Helpful resources from major religious organizations are available – including, curiously, re-published classics of sacred or devotional literature – as well as signs of serious spirituality and engaged faith. But strident hate-filled fundamentalist sites also abound – and these sometimes even wage cyberwar against each other – including sabotaging each other's sites! The new technologies that foster globalization may be shaped for many purposes. Outcomes are not inevitable, nor can anything be predicted simply by referring to globalization or the internet.

One can say, however, that today's fundamentalisms are produced by globalization and the cultural forces at work in its wake. Wherever one voice threatens to dominate, others will assert themselves. And wherever a babel of voices is heard, someone will issue a call back to the 'one true faith'. If this was once so with Western TV-based media, how much more is it now true of the plethora of online videos, images, and texts. Many strident voices may now be heard, rubbing salt in the wounds of decades of neglect and humiliation. So it is no surprise that, for instance, some North African and Middle Eastern countries see a future only in the past, in a revival of old verities and strict laws. In this case, religious renewal is a response to globalization. In today's West, too, there is growing nostalgia for an idealized past, often also with a religious halo.

HOPEFUL OUTCOMES

Seen both ways, the religion-and-globalization theme will not fade fast. In fact, if this analysis is correct, it will continue to be a crucial arena of activity and site of struggle for the foreseeable future. The challenge is one that must be met, if the global world is to be one worth living in. As yet, there are precious few signs that powerful corporations

I AM A SPIRITUAL SEEKER

My name is Helen Serdiville; I have been married for twenty-five years; I have a son of twenty-three, who is a trainee commercial lawyer, and a daughter of twenty-one, who is a retail manager. I have my own business in the field of accounts and business services. I do not fit into any religious category completely.

From an early age, I had strong spiritual feelings that were self-discovered, not taught by any religious denomination. Having been brought up in a divided Roman Catholic/Protestant family, I decided that, although I had been baptized a Roman Catholic, I would make my own mind up when I felt the need.

We lived out of town, in a rural area, when I was young. Always conscious of a powerful inner sense in God, I felt surrounded by him in the earth, trees, rivers, and the wind itself. As an only child, I was wrapped up in the seasons and the elements, and found inner happiness in the beautiful world that God has given us. In my dreams – or, some would say, astral adventures – I would soar above the world, and visit places and people at will. It was not until I was about eleven that I realized not everyone could do this. What I believed to be normal set me apart from my friends, and made me realize I saw the world differently from the way they did.

Now, as an adult, my spirituality has two sides to it. At least that is how it might appear to an observer. When I married my husband, I accepted his Roman Catholic faith, and over the years have found it to be a 'comfort blanket' in times of need or sorrow. I draw upon the community of the church, recognize the strength of the family of God, and value the communal spirit of worshipping with others. A Sunday homily provides helpful insights into the meaning of the Bible, and the ongoing love that God has for us. I also find the act of confession and contrition within Catholicism a cleansing process that provides renewal for my soul. The traditional church is, therefore, my 'public religious face', that I present to the world.

On the other hand, my private faith is one of spiritual searching. On the outside I say traditional prayers to God which are heartfelt and genuine. But in my inner private meditation, I delve back in time, beyond the confines of the church and the words written and formulated by men – and most were men! I look back to the creator, to the source of all life; I search for God. I long to draw upon the divine love to help me become what I am destined to be. I want to understand and accept the path chosen for me. I want God to make me a better or once-sovereign states will take the lead in shaping the global for humane ends; which leaves a – perhaps paradoxical – role for religious voices to let themselves be heard again. But they will have to become clearer about how they contribute to a world of respect, trusting relationships, and mutual care. A reading of recent history shows how quickly religious smorgasbords sour, so those voices will have to acknowledge their particularities.

For example, Christianity has too often allowed itself to become blinkered, belligerent, and bigoted – but this is not the whole story. In the twenty-first century, opportunities are open to show what contribution authentic spirituality might make to the messy everyday realities of a globalizing world. While some Muslims have resisted the world of Disney and Nike as decadent, all too many Christians have embraced consumerism without even noticing. For, while large corporations tend to direct globalization, they cannot do so without persuading the world's citizens to believe in consumerism as the

person. I want to live continually in the presence of the divine. Every day I try to find some quiet time when I can meditate. This can be anywhere at any time. Sometimes, even at work, I will take a few minutes, if I am on my own. I close my eyes and go 'inwards' to my special place, and cut out the distractions of everyday life. I may need calming if the day is stressful, or just a moment to 'touch the spirit within' for a feeling of comfort in a mad world. My meditation also has another purpose – namely self-healing – which can be both spiritual and physical. I believe that the human spirit, or life force, is connected to God and, moreover, that God is able and willing to heal the soul and mend the body.

I look for guidance. Although I do not consciously have a specific 'spirit guide', I feel there is a guardian angel that watches over me. Indeed, at times of great stress or sadness, I have been fortunate to have experienced 'spiritual cleansing' and empowerment in the form of light and colour that enters my body and gives me inner calm and peace. This experience helps me to face the future with a different outlook altogether. I feel my faith transcends cultural barriers and draws elements from many religions. I have heard this described as

'spiritual shopping' and – to a large extent – that is how I see my spiritual path. The stock on the shelves of the spiritual supermarket is extensive and varied and I want to make as much use of it as I can.

As part of my spiritual beliefs, the subject of reincarnation figures strongly. As a child I always knew – before I had even heard the term for it – that I had had a previous life. I often thought to myself, 'I already knew that from before.' And it was often said to me that I was 'an old soul'. I believe that the time spent in this life paves our way for a life ultimately in the presence of God. Through many lives, we progress spiritually and draw nearer to God.

Ultimately, I believe that, although many religious people may be spiritual, those who have a deep spirituality of their own do not need to embrace traditional religion at all. Seeking spiritual enlightenment allows our souls to soar, to escape the confines of our cerebral prison, and to search for our own truth in the light of God's love.

Helen Serdiville

route to contentment. And that, as we have seen, helps to widen the rich/poor gap, and fuel fundamentalisms.

Positively, then, Christians could revisit the gospels to find there a story to live by. This story roots humans not just in the world of forests, oceans, and cities, but as spiritual beings with material experience and real relationships. It seeks not merely to know 'who I am' but who is the other, and how should I treat her? And it sees human contentment not as an outcome of gadgets and gizmos, but from a genuine commitment to justice and to care. This perspective would oppose neither enjoyment of life's good things nor the development of the world as one place. But it would be a globalization from below, in which Gaza ceases to be an open prison, Syrian refugees are welcomed, and Bangalore's poor have a place; where hostility gives way to healing.

DAVID LYON

CHAPTER 88

Religion and Politics

From the eighteenth century, 'Western' nations have witnessed attempts to confine religion to the realm of private belief and practice, tolerated in as much as the religious commitment of individuals and groups does not impact upon the public, and therefore political, domain. As a result, a general perception has arisen that religion and politics should not mix; they belong to different spheres of human interest and activity, while an all-pervasive secularist agenda has dictated how public life should be organized and what constitutes its primary concerns. The consequent separation of church (the custodian of the sacred) and state (the political community) is a specifically Western and modern idea, stemming more from secular philosophy than from any particular religious understanding.

Nonetheless, it is difficult historically to see 'politics' and 'religion' as entirely distinct entities. In animist and tribal religions, cultic practice was intended to ensure the welfare of the group. Roman religious practice was, in part, expressed in emperor worship, while Greek religion expected citizens to undertake the civic aspects of ceremonial and sacrifice, all in pursuit of the common good. Such considerations can be discerned in subsequent history, where religion and politics have maintained a complex – if increasingly ambivalent – relationship.

SEPARATE CONCERNS

'Religion' and 'politics' have separate but related interests. Religions generally claim to answer metaphysical and existential questions, and expose human beings either to the divine call or to transcendence of the world and its concerns. Religions usually posit eternal and binding values that assist in interpreting the why and wherefore of the universe. They provide principles, morals, and laws that their adherents are to follow, but which offer little direct and pragmatic advice concerning how to respond to the exigencies of modern life. As a result, religions tend to influence politics through the teaching of certain pedagogues, through individuals as they follow their vocation in political life, or through those who would subvert existing structures, rather than by providing a blueprint for social life or the political economy.

Politics, however, is basically the way in which society is organized in order to make social life possible. Its concerns tend to be immediate, even when short-term action constitutes a policy for the establishment of long-term goals. Despite its pragmatism, often diluted by dogmatic concerns, politics remains a branch of ethics, because it is vulnerable to abuse. Political organizations can be oppressive and brutal, necessitating a commitment to commonly held values of goodness, justice, and virtue. As religious teaching often provides the source for understanding these principles, a close relationship between religion and politics can be considered almost inevitable. This is evident in the doctrine and practice of the world's three major monotheistic faiths, as demonstrated in the following brief and general accounts.

JUDAISM

Judaism emerged out of the biblical history of a chosen people and promised land. The Hebrew people had a specifically religious identity: they were Yahweh's elect people, whose life, socially and individually, was to reflect Yahweh's Torah (law). The result was a political identity that was indelibly linked to religious belief and practice. While officially secular, the modern state of Israel contains many who wish to see the theological understanding of land and people enshrined in political institutions. Some, such as the Gush Emunim (Bloc of the Faithful), have seen the expansion of Israel's territory as the fulfilment of biblical promises, while some rabbis have been keen to confirm the Jewish status as a chosen people, and thus beneficiaries of certain privileges and rights. Nevertheless, others resident within it, such as members of Neturei Karta (Guardians of the City), see the modern state of Israel as a sacrilegious human trespass on the divine prerogative. For them, it is God, not human beings, who will restore the nation of Israel.

CHRISTIANITY

From its inception, Christianity differentiated between religious and political authority, partly because of its emergence as a weak and vulnerable social group, partly because of ambiguity in the interpretation of Jesus' injunction to 'Give to Caesar what is Caesar's, and to God what is God's' (Matthew 22:21), and partly because of the influence of the Emperor Constantine and the role of the church following the collapse of the Roman Empire. The Augustinian and Magisterial Reformation traditions have asserted that believers belong to two states or cities: the sacred city, which has its home in heaven, and the earthly city, which is ruled over by princes and governments. However, this is not strictly the separation of the secular and the sacred, because the state – the earthly city – is ruled by those whose vocation under God is to govern, and whose rule must consequently conform to the divine will. In Christian thought, politics is both the legitimate concern of each believer, to act and live in a way pleasing to God, and the specific task of keeping the peace under God's law. Part of the church's task is to prick the state's conscience, but the assumption that the state is governed by Christians committed to act as stewards belongs to the medieval conception of Christendom far more than to contemporary secular, multicultural, religiously plural societies.

ISLAM

Islam knows no separation between the sacred and the secular. All aspects of human life are to be drawn under the direct influence of the law of Allah, to which the only response is obedience. In its traditional forms, Islam views political leadership as a succession descending from the Prophet, practised by those who are selected as caliphs (Sunni) or imams (Shia). These leaders implement Shari'a law, but are expected to seek Shura, or consultation with those under their governance. In all Islamic traditions the need to rebuke the unjust ruler remains a primary responsibility, though — as in other religious systems — this is more difficult to achieve in practice than to uphold in theory. Nevertheless, the obedient life, in all its aspects, individual and social, spiritual and civic, internal and external, should express the divine will. As a result, there is no value in the separation of religion and spirituality, on the one hand, from politics and social practice on the other.

RELIGION AND POLITICS

Religions have historically exercised a potent influence on politics. The relationship of church and state, primarily through the established Church of England and its privileged status in parliament, influences British society to the present day, though in the twenty-first century this is more implicit than explicit. The Puritan founders of the USA inspired a later generation, influenced by deistic and rationalistic traditions, to exalt freedom, choice, and individual conscience as basic rights, even in matters of religion. Hindu traditions played an important role in forging an Indian political identity, prior to that country's independence in 1947. Pakistan was founded in the same year, as an Islamic state, and, over time, has attempted to modernize, while also upholding Shari'a law. Buddhism was an important factor in anti-colonialist movements in Myanmar, while liberation theology assisted many in Latin America in opposing unsatisfactory secular regimes — although poverty remains at significant levels on the subcontinent. All these examples hold a common view of religion in its various guises as exercising a liberating influence, influencing politics for the better, and challenging corruption and injustice.

POLITICIZATION

From the mid-twentieth century, a renewed association developed between religion and politics, resulting from disillusionment with secular values and dissatisfaction with policies of modernization. Hindu traditions became a significant force in Indian politics, particularly manifest in the Bharatiya Janata Party (BJP) and its association of land, religion, and national identity. In Thailand and Sri Lanka, the prima facie other-worldly and pacifist convictions of Buddhism seemed to be set aside as particular groups on occasion embraced violence in order to preserve a political system congenial to their own survival. Although from the time of the sixth Guru, Hargobind (1595–1644), Sikhism has maintained that state and religion are natural allies, it has emerged as a political force in India, particularly following the declaration of the Sikh state, Khalistan, in 1986. In the USA, Christians have exercised a political influence through organizations such as the Moral Majority and the Christian Coalition, as they opposed the liberalization of US society and its abandonment of what they saw as core Christian values, especially regarding the family unit and procreation.

FUNDAMENTALISM

Much of this renewed political interaction can be attributed to the rise of religious fundamentalism, which achieved its first institutional expression when the Iranian revolution of 1979 swept the Shah from power and installed the Ayatollah Khomeini as national leader. Islamic militancy increased throughout the 1970s, and following this takeover became a far more potent force in the Middle East and Africa, reaching an infamous expression in the Taliban regime in Afghanistan. The attack on the World Trade Center, New York, on 11 September 2001 ('9/11'), perpetrated by al-Qaeda against what was perceived to be the corrupting influence of the West, has had far-reaching consequences. The 'war on terror' initiated by the US government and its allies largely failed in its goal of establishing Western-style (and inevitably secular) democracies in the Middle East, facing instead the rise of so-called 'Islamic State', which in 2014 declared a worldwide caliphate from its base in Syria and Iraq.

Some have seen the inspiration for Islamic State in the ultra-conservative Salafi, or Wahhabist, tradition, which traces its history to an eighteenth-century Islamic jurist, Muhammad ibn 'Abd al-Wahhab (1703–92), who campaigned to restore pure monotheistic worship instead of popular, but idolatrous, practices. The movement gained potency through its political pact with the House of Saud and the support given to its teaching by successive governments in Saudi Arabia. Others have seen the work of Sayyid Qutb (1906–66) as justifying Islamic State's aggression towards those considered to be enemies of Islam, both those belonging to the Muslim faith and those who do not. Either way, while radical Islamic movements such as Islamic Jihad and al-Qaeda appear to have considered violence to be a modus operandi, for Islamic State it has been a modus vivendi. Its prominence on the world stage is largely the result of the threat it poses to the West, especially through direct acts of terror and attempts to control oil reserves. Possibly Boko Haram, based in Nigeria, and active in Chad, Niger, and Cameroon, fully encapsulates this violent reaction against Western influence (its name can be translated as 'Western education is forbidden'). Aligned with Islamic State, this group was declared the deadliest terrorist group in the world in 2015, having killed more than 20,000 people and displaced a further two million.

Perhaps more than any other religion, Islam has been criticized for its political associations, and the willingness of its most militant followers to take extreme measures to achieve their goals. As a result, the concern of many that religion and politics had too close an association has, in the twenty-first century, given way to the fear that religion, at least in some of its forms, has too close an association with terrorism.

Responses to fundamentalism

The response to this situation has been mixed. In France, since 2004 a ban has been placed on the wearing of religious symbols in state schools, and since April 2011 a ban on concealment of the face in public, whether by mask, helmet, balaclava, niqab, or burqa. In the UK, the Racial and Religious Hatred Act (2006) attempted to prevent prejudicial and violent acts against religious groups, which increased particularly against the Muslim population after 9/11. This act's definition of 'religious hatred' as 'hatred against a group of persons defined by reference to religious belief or lack of religious belief' led some to allege that the Bible and the Qur'an were thus rendered illegal documents, while others worried about freedom of speech, especially in the context of comedy and satire. Such policies are at best paradoxical, involving the state's direct intrusion into what it previously considered to be private belief and practice. The right of the state to dictate the extent of religious expression appeared to be upheld when the European Court of Human Rights agreed with the French government's argument that the ban on the veil was based on a particular idea of what social life and acceptable public engagement might mean. The suppression of religious symbols has stemmed from a dubious sense that shared secular values can lead to a common sense of national identity that can properly be imposed on citizens regardless of their personal convictions.

Removing militant Islamic graffiti in Indonesia.

In the USA, the apparent failure of President Jimmy Carter (b. 1924) to deal effectively with the crisis that saw fifty-two diplomats held hostage in Tehran for 444 days after the ascent to power of the Ayatollah Khomeini became a catalyst which saw evangelical Christians transfer allegiance from the Democrat to the Republican cause. Conservative Christianity has aligned itself with conservative politics, especially the reduction in welfare spending, reactionary approaches to perceived attacks on the traditional family such as rights for homosexuals or access to abortion, promotion of the right of individuals to defend themselves or carry arms, support for the state of Israel, and strong – even aggressive – foreign policy when US interests are perceived to be jeopardized. The alignment of conservative Christianity with right-wing politics has influenced a number of presidential campaigns, resulting in a significant impact on contemporary global politics.

Government and religion

Historically, religion has related to politics in several ways. Governments and subversive groups can claim direct religious inspiration for their policies and initiate a theocracy where the state is governed by a priestly caste; religion can hold a theological view of political institutions, where the state and its organs are divinely ordained to maintain order; religion can act as the political conscience of a society, with religious institutions criticizing political policy and calling for action when those policies are perceived as contradicting eternal values; religion can oppose the political status quo for being too compromising. In the West, governments have often sought to appropriate religious conviction in order to promote the social good, though 'religion' is often homogenized, and, when religious commitment overrides any sense of a shared national identity or common humanity, it is rarely understood. Nevertheless, in all instances, the association of religion and politics holds the potential to do both good and harm – the latter being most prominent when religious practitioners fail to live up to the highest ideals of their own creed.

ROBERT POPE

CHAPTER 89

Women and Religion

WOMEN AND WORLD RELIGIONS

The dominance of men in society and religious structures appears almost universal, across the globe and from the beginning of recorded human history. While there are a few important exceptions amongst traditional African religions, for example, all of the so-called 'world religions' have evolved in patriarchal cultures. It is predominantly men who have formulated their religious beliefs, recorded, transmitted, and interpreted religious texts, created and led institutions, controlled rituals and worship, and, importantly, written the histories of their traditions. There are recorded instances where women have played prominent roles in these traditions, but these are isolated, and usually exist as anomalies alongside a mainstream culture where only men are the educated decision-makers. So in Islam, all accepted legal rulings have been made by men; in Buddhism, the most senior nun must defer to the most junior monk; and in Hinduism, the Brahmanic priesthood (like the traditional Christian priesthood and Orthodox Jewish rabbinate) has been the sole preserve of men. This male dominance of religious institutions, which for the most part continues until this day, went largely unchallenged until the latter half of the twentieth century.

In Europe and North America – 'the West' – it could be said that the successes of the movement for women's equality have been in spite of religious traditions rather than because of them. Societal change in this regard has come, albeit very slowly, as a result of a predominantly secular women's movement. This movement has been aided by the loosening of women's confinement within the domestic sphere, brought about by industrialization, war, the availability of contraception, and increased access to education for women. Religious structures have generally functioned as a conservative force in society, upholding traditional roles for women and men. In those instances where greater equality has been granted to women within religious institutions, the change has usually been vigorously resisted, as with the Anglican Communion's decision to include female priests and bishops. Within traditional religions, views on gender are often underpinned theologically by texts and teachings about the God-willed or 'natural' order of things, meaning that change will only take place as a result of considerable scholarly and theological effort.

WOMEN AND THE STUDY OF WORLD RELIGIONS

The Western study of 'world religions' has its roots in Orientalism, the study of non-Christian cultures and religions, which developed in tandem with the colonial enterprise to 'the Orient' in the eighteenth and nineteenth centuries. At that time, very few women were highly educated or had the opportunity to travel, and therefore the discipline consisted for the most part of male scholars studying male-dominated traditions, generally oblivious to the missing voices and experiences of women. Moreover 'religion', for these early pioneers, was viewed through a thoroughly Christian lens: they were concerned primarily with texts, theological beliefs (as opposed to practice), and the structures of authority. Women, by and large, had no prominent role in any of these, and so Orientalist scholars found no cause to question their androcentric presuppositions. Forms of religion, such as Shamanism, where women were more prominent were dismissed as magic or superstition. In those few instances where women were implicated in the object of inquiry, women's voices were still not heard. A case in point can be found in the nineteenth-century British debates around the Hindu practice of sati – the ritual burning of a Hindu widow on her deceased husband's funeral pyre – a practice abolished by the British in 1829. This debate was not informed by the experiences of women, but instead endeavoured to establish whether the practice was sanctioned by the authoritative Vedic texts.

These Orientalist scholars assumed themselves to be involved in a scientific, objective study of other religions, as is evident in the classic text, F. Max Müller's Introduction to the Science of Religion (1882). However, the notion that it is possible to engage in an objective study of anything was increasingly called into question during the twentieth century. Critical theory highlighted the inevitable influence of bias on all the choices made by the scholar, conscious and unconscious. Orientalism, from which the supposedly position-neutral discipline of 'Religious Studies' had evolved, was exposed as a form of colonialism (see Edward Said's Orientalism, 1978). With the increase in the number of women at universities, and the rise of feminist thought in the 1970s, 1980s, and 1990s, female scholars increasingly exposed the male bias (androcentrism) in evidence in the discipline of Religious Studies, as well as in theological scholarship and in religious traditions themselves. As renowned feminist scholar Carol P. Christ remarked: 'We are slowly beginning to realise that the religious lives of one-half of humanity have never adequately been studied.'

FEMINISM AND THE STUDY OF RELIGIOUS TRADITIONS

Feminist and gender-critical approaches, which have developed since the 'second wave' feminism of the 1960s, have been slow to make inroads into the domains of theology and religious studies. This is in part due to the potentially huge implications of such scholarship, both for the study of religion and for the religious traditions themselves. They call into question what counts as religion, the methods adopted, the content to be explored, and the validity of firmly-held religious narratives. The percentage of scholars in religious studies and theology adopting gender-critical approaches is low, as is that of feminist scholars from other disciplines who see religion as an essential aspect of their study. Yet those engaged in gender-critical studies of religion have produced some of the most exciting and ground-breaking work in their field in the last forty years. Many have also pioneered an approach that breaks down the distinction between theology and religious studies, and have been important drivers behind the development of interreligious and comparative studies. Although feminist studies are still most developed within, or with reference to, Christianity and Judaism, by the 1980s feminist studies of religious traditions had extended to include Eastern traditions too.

FEMINIST SCHOLARS OF RELIGION: REFORMISTS AND REVOLUTIONARIES

Those who have engaged in a feminist study of religion can be broadly divided into two categories – 'revolutionaries' and 'reformists' – though these terms have also been resisted. On the one hand are those who believe traditional religions are fundamentally and inescapably patriarchal, and therefore to be abandoned. The revolutionaries, largely from Christian and Jewish backgrounds, have focused on the male imagery of the biblical God as beyond reform, as in Mary Daly's *Beyond God the Father* (1973), for example. These scholars often move on to explore non-traditional, minority, or 'heretical' sources, or New Religious Movements, which can perhaps better express and embody the equality and importance of women, often through a focus on goddess spirituality. (See, for example, Carol P. Christ's *Rebirth of the Goddess*, 1997.)

One the other hand there are those who argue that it is the message of liberation that is basic, or essential, to the tradition, and that this has been overlaid by the patriarchal culture within which the tradition emerged. They point to elements within the tradition which, they argue, show real potential for reform, such as important female figures and non-canonical texts that have hitherto been obscured, as well as re-interpretations of traditional texts and teachings. It has been argued, for example, that the Buddha, Jesus, Muhammad, and Guru Nanak (the founding figures of Buddhism, Christianity, Islam, and Sikhism respectively) were all radical in according greater roles and/or rights to women than were afforded to them in their time. Feminist exegesis of scriptures has been particularly important within Judaism, Christianity, and Islam, where they play a central and authoritative role within the tradition. Studies of classic texts has been less critical for reformers within Buddhism, Hinduism, and the Chinese traditions. Across all these traditions, many feminist scholars have also shifted their attention to religious practice, recognizing that it is in the realm of ritual and religion as an everyday activity that women are perhaps best seen as having agency in their religious lives.

GENDER STUDIES AND RELIGION

Some see feminist discourse as unable to tackle the gender inequality in religion and in the study of religion which it has successfully identified. Feminist discourse has at times been accused of championing the interests of white, Western, middle-class, educated, straight women, without recognition of all those women whose voices have been denied or simply assumed.

Some African-American scholars, arguing that white feminists have too often been blind to the ways in which race and class informed and shaped women's experiences of oppression, have preferred to describe themselves as 'womanist' rather than feminist. Many Muslim women do not identify with the label 'feminist', associating it with the imposition of distinctly Western values and norms. They have attempted to define a distinctive 'Islamic Feminism', or chosen to eschew the term all together. These scholars point out, for example, that Western feminists have often rushed to critique practices such as arranged marriage and dress codes that require modesty as damaging products of a patriarchal system, without taking time to listen to women who argue for the benefits of these practices for women.

Turning to the future, it seems more scholars may be comfortable under the umbrella of 'Gender Studies', which is thoroughly post-colonial in its outlook, as defined by leading feminist scholar of religion Ursula King. Gender Studies also has the potential to reach out beyond the perception that the issues involved are 'women's issues'. Gender studies has been primarily focused on women because of their historical voicelessness, but King stresses that it is important to consider not only the construction of femininity, but also that of masculinity, within religious traditions. (See, for example, deSondy's ground-breaking work, exploring the construction of masculinity in Islam.) It is within this broader conception of Gender Studies that gender-critical scholars of religion stand to make the biggest impact in their fields.

MAGDALEN LAMBKIN

QUESTIONS

1. Explain the differences between Christian and atheistic existentialism.

2. Why did postmodernism pose problems for traditional religion in the twentieth century?

3. What factors do you think explain the growth of new religious movements (NRMs) since the late nineteenth century?

4. Explain the core beliefs of the Bahá'í faith.

5. Why is engagement with political issues so important in the Bahá'í faith?

6. What factors explain the decline of traditional religion in the West?

7. What factors explain the growth of religion outside the West in recent years?

8. Can religion and politics ever be entirely separated?

9. How has globalization shaped religion since the late twentieth century?

10. 'Fundamentally, religion and modern secularism are incompatible.' Discuss this statement with reference to at least three religious traditions.

FURTHER READING

Castelli, E. A. ed., *Women, Gender, Religion: A Reader*. New York: Palgrave, 2001.

Chang, Maria Hsia, *Falun Gong: The End of Days*. New Haven, CT: Yale University Press, 2004.

Chryssides, George D., *A Reader in New Religious Movements: Readings in the Study of New Religious Movements*. London: Continuum, 2006.

Dawkins, Richard, *The God Delusion*. New York: Houghton Mifflin, 2006.

Heelas, Paul, *The New Age Movement: Celebrating the Self and the Sacralization of Modernity*. Oxford and Cambridge, MA: Blackwell, 1996.

Smith, Peter, *A Concise Encyclopedia of the Bahá'í Faith*. Oxford, UK: Oneworld Publications, 2000.

Sutcliffe, Stephen J., *Children of the New Age: A History of Alternative Spirituality*. New York: Taylor and Francis, 2002.

York, Michael, *The Emerging Network: A Sociology of the New Age and Neo-Pagan Movement*. Lanhan, MD: Rowan & Littlefield, 1995.

FURTHER READING ON WORLD RELIGIONS

Bowker, John, ed., *Oxford Dictionary of World Religions*. Oxford: Oxford University Press, 1997.

Eliade, Mircea, ed., *The Encyclopedia of Religion*. 16 vols. New York: Macmillan, 1987.

Oxtoby, Willard G., and Alan F. Segal, *A Concise Introduction to World Religions*. Don Mills, Canada: Oxford University Press, 2007.

Smart, Ninian, ed., *Atlas of the World's Religions*. Oxford: Oxford University Press, 1987.

Smith, Jonathan Z., ed., *The HarperCollins Dictionary of Religion*. New York: HarperSanFrancisco, 1995.

Woodhead, Linda ed., *Religions in the Modern World*. London and New York: Routledge 2002.

Rapid Fact-Finder

This fact-finder was written by Angela Tilby and John-David Yule, revised and expanded by Christopher Partridge in 2005, and further revised and expanded for this new edition.

The terms include some that do not appear in this book. These are common terms included to give additional information to readers.

Words printed in small capitals indicate cross-reference.

A

'Abbasid dynasty (750–1258 CE) The second great Islamic dynasty, and third caliphate, which ruled from Baghdad. Under the 'Abbasids the empire enjoyed a period of increased prosperity and trade. Libraries and centres of learning were established throughout the Islamic world.

Abhidhamma Pitaka THERAVADA Buddhist scripture on techniques of mind-training. The aim is to eliminate the idea of the self. It is the key work of Buddhist psychology.

Abraham, Isaac, and Jacob The three PATRIARCHS who are continually remembered in the Jewish liturgy as the original recipients of God's promise and blessing. According to tradition they are buried in the tomb of the patriarchs in the cave of Machpelah in the modern town of Hebron.

Absolute, The Term for GOD or the divine often preferred by those who conceive of God predominantly in abstract or impersonal terms.

Abu Bakr MUHAMMAD's father-in-law and traditionally his earliest convert. He was elected CALIPH after the PROPHET's death and ruled for two years, fighting tribes who were trying to break away from the Islamic community. According to some traditions, he began the compilation of the QUR'AN.

Adi Granth Sacred book of Sikhism. It is regarded as the eternal GURU for the SIKH community. It is the central focus of the Sikh home and of the GURDWARA. The tenth GURU, Gobind Singh, said that after him the final and perpetual guru would be the Adi Granth, to be known as Guru Granth Sahib.

Adonai *see* YHWH.

Advaita ('non-dualism') The monist (*see* MONISM) doctrine of SHANKARA, that all reality is fundamentally one and divine.

Æsir Plural of '*as*', meaning 'god'. The collective noun used in Norse literature for the pantheon of deities. More particularly, it is used of a particular majority group that share a common origin, which includes principal deities such as Odin, Thor, and Tyr. (*See also* VANIR.)

African Independent Churches African churches which have risen in the past 100 years and offer a synthesis of CHRISTIANITY with traditional INDIGENOUS RELIGIONS. Many have prophetic or charismatic founders and emphasize spiritual healing and communication with ancestors. Some have been a focus of nationalistic aspirations.

Afterlife Any form of conscious existence after the death of the body.

Agadah/Aggadah A moral or devotional Jewish teaching derived from the midrashic exposition of a Hebrew text (*see* MIDRASH). There are many of them in the Talmud where they take the form of narrative tales, poems, and metaphysical speculations.

Agape Greek word for 'love' that has come to express the Christian understanding of God's love which does not depend on any worthiness or attractiveness of the object of his love. Christians are taught to demonstrate this love to each other in the Christian FELLOWSHIP, and to others.

Agni Indian fire god of Vedic times (*see* Vedas). As sacrificial fire, Agni mediates between gods and people and is especially concerned with order and ritual.

Ahimsa Indian virtue of non-violence. It usually applies to abstention from harming any living creature and hence to

vegetarianism. The doctrine was developed in JAINISM, BUDDHISM, and some HINDU sects. In Jain belief violence carries severe penalties of KARMA. MAHATMA GANDHI applied the idea to the political struggles of the oppressed in his practice of non-violent non-cooperation.

Ahmadiyya sect Offshoot of ISLAM founded in India by Mirza Ghulam Ahmad (died 1908), who is believed to be the MESSIAH, the Shi'a MAHDI. The sect denies the authority of the 'ULAMA', IJMA', and JIHAD. It is a missionary sect and has gained converts in Asia and Africa.

Ahriman *see* ANGRA MAINYU.

Ahura Mazda/Ahrmazd ('wise lord') ZOROASTER's name for God. He demands ethical and ritual purity and he judges human souls after death. His symbol is sacred fire.

Akhenaten Name adopted by Amenophis IV, king of Egypt c. 1353–1335 BCE, in honour of ATEN ('the sun disc'), whose cult he promoted to the exclusion of all others in a short-lived reform of Egyptian religion. He built a magnificent new capital at el-Amarna.

Akiva, Rabbi (c. 50–135 CE) Jewish teacher who developed the MISHNAH method of repetitive transmission of teachings. He began the work of systematizing the available interpretations of the TORAH, laying the foundations for the work of JUDAH HANASI. He was also famous for his use of MIDRASH, investing every detail of the Hebrew texts with significance.

Albigensians The Cathars of southern France who flourished in the late twelfth and early thirteenth centuries. Their theology was a dualism that has been compared with that of the Manichaeans, although they were probably unconnected. They saw Christ as an angel whose teachings had been corrupted by the Catholic clergy. Their most rigorous adherents, the *perfecti*, abstained from marriage and avoided animal products.

Alchemy Mystical science of chemical manipulation which *seeks* to change base metals into gold, find the universal cure for illness, and discover the secret of immortality. Its study passed from Hellenistic Egypt through the Arabs to medieval Europe. It is also important in Taoism.

Al-Ghazali (1058–1111 CE) Orthodox Muslim legal expert who renounced his post and became a Sufi (*see* Sufism). He attacked the incursions of Greek thought into Islam and defended the teaching of the Qur'an. He also defended the Sufi experience of God but denied the possibility of human deification.

Al-Hallaj (died 922 CE) Sufi MYSTIC who was crucified because of his confession 'I am the real,' which was taken as a claim to divinity. He considered JESUS OF NAZARETH as the supreme example of human deification and at his death forgave his enemies in imitation of the passion of Jesus.

'Ali Cousin and son-in-law of MUHAMMAD. SUNNI Muslims claim he was elected fourth CALIPH in 656 CE; Shias that he was the first Imam, and that he and his descendants are Muhammad's rightful successors. War broke out between 'Ali and the governor of Syria, who claimed 'Ali had plotted 'UTHMAN's death. In 661 CE 'Ali was murdered and his son, Hasan, succeeded and ruled briefly before renouncing any claim to the caliphate.

Allah The Muslim name for God. Allah is one; there are no other gods. As pure, undivided spirit, Allah is the creator and sustainer of all that is known to human beings in the revelation of the divine will in the Qur'an. Throughout the Qur'an, Allah is declared to be 'the merciful' and 'the compassionate'.

All-India Muslim League Organization founded in 1906 CE to promote the interests and political aspirations of Indian Muslims.

Almsgiving The giving of free gifts, usually of money, to the poor. In Islam it is obligatory (*see* zakah). In Theravada Buddhism the lay community is linked to the sangha by their provision of food for the monks, which is collected on a daily almsround. Jain ascetics also rely on alms from the laity.

Alternative spiritualities One of the more significant developments in particularly Western religious adherence has been the emergence of private, non-institutional forms of belief and practice known as 'alternative spiritualities'. There has been a move away from traditional forms of belief which have developed within religious institutions towards forms of belief that focus on 'the self', on 'nature', or simply on 'life'. Although there may be particular traditional teachings that are valued by the individual *seeker*, or particular groups to which the individual belongs, generally speaking there is a suspicion of traditional authorities, sacred texts, churches, and hierarchies of power.

Amida *see* AMITABHA.

Amidah ('standing') The principal Jewish daily prayer, also known as the Eighteen Benedictions, recited standing. Today it actually comprises nineteen benedictions, including prayers for the restoration of ISRAEL and for peace.

Amitabha ('infinite light') Celestial Buddha worshipped in China and Japan (where his name is Amida). He is believed to live in a 'pure land' in the far west where those faithful to him go after death (*see* JODO SHINSHU; NEMBUTSU; PURE LAND BUDDHISM).

Amritsar Site of the Golden Temple, the holiest shrine of the SIKH religion, completed by Arjan, the fifth GURU.

Analects One of the four books of the so-called Confucian canon. It contains the essence of CONFUCIUS's teaching and was probably compiled about seventy years after his death.

Ananda One of the most prominent members of the BUDDHA's SANGHA. Traditionally he was the Buddha's cousin and many of the sayings are addressed to him, including the words of comfort shortly before the Buddha's death. He helped to fix the canon of Buddhist SCRIPTURE.

Anatta/Anatman Meaning 'not-self', a Buddhist term indicating that there is no permanent self or ego. All beings are merely a series of mental and physical states. *Anatta* is one of the three characteristics of existence.

Ancestor veneration The practice in INDIGENOUS RELIGIONS of making offerings to the spirits of the dead and expecting to communicate with them through DREAMS.

Angels Spiritual beings who in JUDAISM and CHRISTIANITY act as the messengers of GOD. They have two primary functions: to worship God, and to support and encourage human beings. In ISLAM the Archangel GABRIEL (Jibril) is associated with the giving of the QUR'AN.

Anglican churches Worldwide groupings of churches which recognize the primacy among equals of the Archbishop of Canterbury. They include both catholic and reformed elements and retain BISHOPS.

Angra Mainyu/Ahriman The chief spirit who is opposed to AHURA MAZDA in Zoroastrian belief. His nature is violent and destructive. He created the demons, he rules in hell and has opposed God from the beginning.

Anicca/Anitya Buddhist term for the impermanence and changeability which characterizes all existence.

Animism A term formerly used to describe pre-literary religions. It was dropped because its meaning, 'spiritism', was felt to be misleading. (*See* INDIGENOUS RELIGIONS.)

Anthroposophy Spiritual system invented by Rudolf STEINER. It stresses the threefold nature of humanity as physical, etheric, and astral body and proposes a programme for spiritual education which includes techniques of MEDITATION.

Anu The sky god of ancient Sumerian religion and high god of the Sumerian pantheon. He had little to do with human affairs and delegated his authority to ENLIL. From about 2000 BCE he was called King of Gods and Father.

Anubis Jackal-headed god of ancient Egypt who conducted souls to judgment and weighed them in the great balance. Known as 'the embalmer', he watched over mummification and was the guardian of tombs and cemeteries.

Aphrodite Greek goddess of love and patroness of beauty and sexual attractiveness. Her cult was imported from the Near East. The Greeks thought of her as vain and cruel but the Romans identified her with VENUS and honoured her as the mother of Aeneas, ancestor of the Romans. In Cyprus she was worshipped as the MOTHER GODDESS.

Apocalyptic Genre of writing in CHRISTIANITY and JUDAISM, concerned with hidden truths, pointing to the ultimate triumph of faith and the judgment of nations. Daniel and Revelation are examples in the BIBLE.

Apocrypha Historical and wisdom writings found in the Greek version of the Hebrew scriptures but excluded from the canon of the HEBREW BIBLE. The Roman Catholic Church and Eastern Orthodox churches accept its authority, but Protestant churches distinguish it from inspired SCRIPTURE.

Apollo A major god of both Greeks and Romans, though Greek in origin. He is sometimes seen as the sun and is the patron of the arts (especially music), or prophecy, of divination, and of medicine. He was the inspiration of the DELPHIC ORACLE.

Apostle (1) 'One who is sent', name for the twelve original followers of JESUS OF NAZARETH, also PAUL. The 'apostolic age' is a time of great authority for the Christian CHURCH. (2) Title of MUHAMMAD.

Apostles' Creed A statement of faith used by Western Christian churches and often repeated in services. Introduced during the reign of Charlemagne (c. 742–814). (*See* CREED.)

Aquinas, Thomas (1225–74 CE) Dominican theologian and philosopher whose teachings form the basis of official Roman Catholic theology. He taught a fundamental distinction between faith and reason, asserting that God's existence can be proved, but that the doctrines of the TRINITY and the INCARNATION are revealed and must be accepted on faith.

Archetypes Term invented by C. G. JUNG to describe the concepts held in common by different people at different times and in different places. He believed that the concept of GOD was the archetype of the self and that it was the object of each individual to discover it.

Arianism Fourth-century Christian heresy of Arius, who denied the divinity of Christ, claiming that the Son of God was created and not eternal. It was condemned at the Council of Nicea in 325 CE but flourished until the Council of Constantinople in 381 CE. (*See* ECUMENICAL COUNCILS.)

Aristotle (384–322 BCE) Greek philosopher and scientist who taught on every branch of knowledge valued in his time. His work is characterized by acute observation, close reasoning, and orderly exposition. His work was rediscovered in the Middle Ages and laid the basis for the theology of Thomas AQUINAS and for the HUMANISM of the Renaissance.

Ark (1) Israelite religious artefact, probably in the form of a portable miniature temple, which was carried into battle as evidence of the presence of God (*see* YHWH). In Solomon's Temple the ark lived in the Holy of Holies. (2) A cupboard in the wall of a synagogue that faces Jerusalem, where the handwritten parchment scrolls of the Torah are kept.

Artemis Greek goddess and patroness of virginity, hunting, archery, and wild animals. She was also the protector of the newly born and the bringer of death to women. At Ephesus in Asia Minor, she was worshipped as the mother goddess. (*See also* DIANA.)

Arthur Legendary hero of Celtic Britain who may have originated as a Romano-British chieftain. His legends were gradually worked into a coherent Christian framework in which he became the medieval ideal of a Christian king.

Aryan Word describing the Caucasian people who invaded India around 2000 BCE and who gradually imposed their language and culture upon the earlier inhabitants. Related peoples settled in Iran and Mesopotamia.

Asceticism Austere practices designed to lead to the control of the body and the senses. These may include FASTING and MEDITATION, the renunciation of possessions, and the pursuit of solitude.

Asgard The home of the gods in Norse religion. It is a mountainous region rising out of Midgard and separated from it by a rainbow bridge.

Ashkenazim One of the two main cultural groups in Judaism which emerged in the Middle Ages. Their tradition is from Palestinian Jewry and they live in Central, Northern, and Eastern Europe. They developed Yiddish as their language, which is a mixture of Hebrew, Slav, and German. *See also* SEPHARDIM.

Ashram In Indian religion, a hermitage or monastery. It has come to denote a communal house for devotees of a GURU. It functions as a centre for building up the commitment of believers and for transmitting the guru's message.

Astral plane The intermediate world, according to THEOSOPHY and SPIRITUALISM, to which the human consciousness passes at death. Some psychics and visionaries are able to project themselves there at will.

Astrology The study of the influence of the stars on the character and destiny of human beings. The locations of the planets in the field of the zodiac at the time of the subject's birth are the key date considered in the astrologer's analysis.

Aten The sun in ancient Egyptian religion. In the reforms of AKHENATEN he was worshipped as the one true God.

Athanasius (296–373 CE) Bishop of Alexandria who strongly resisted the teachings of ARIANISM and developed the Christian doctrines of the INCARNATION and the TRINITY.

Athena One of the great Greek goddesses of Mount OLYMPUS who sprang fully armed from the head of her father, ZEUS. She is the patroness of war, of the city of Athens, and of many crafts and skills. She is usually portrayed in full armour, with an owl on her shoulder, and the Gorgon's head painted on her shield. Her Roman counterpart is Minerva.

Atman Sanskrit word meaning soul or self. The Upanishads teach that *atman* is identical to brahman, i.e. the soul is one with the divine.

Atonement (1) Ritual act which restores harmony between the human and the divine when it has been broken by SIN or impurity. (2) In CHRISTIANITY, reconciliation between God and humanity required because of the absolute holiness of God and the sinfulness of men and women. As human beings are incapable of achieving atonement, it is a work of God's GRACE, through the death of Jesus Christ, for human sin.

Atonement, Day of *see* YOM KIPPUR.

Augustine (354–430 CE) Bishop of Hippo in North Africa who was converted to CHRISTIANITY from the teaching of the MANICHAEANS. He stressed the absolute

GRACE of God in men and women's SALVATION and the depravity of human beings through ORIGINAL SIN.

Augustus Title of the first Roman emperor, formerly known as Octavian, who ruled 31 BCE–14 CE. He pacified and unified the empire, thus facilitating the later spread of CHRISTIANITY. While he was still alive he was declared a god and after his death he was worshipped throughout the Empire.

Austerity Ascetic practice in which one exercises self-restraint or denial, for example, the restriction of food during a fast.

Avalokiteshvara ('regarder of the cries of the earth') Celestial BUDDHA worshipped by Tibetans and in Korea, Japan, and China. The DALAI LAMA is believed to be an emanation of him. This Buddha is known under male and female forms and is depicted with a thousand arms symbolizing endless labour for the welfare of humankind.

Avalon Celtic island of immortality replete with miraculous apple trees. Here the hero ARTHUR was taken to recover from his mortal wounds.

Avatar ('one who descends') In popular HINDUISM, Lord VISHNU appears on earth at intervals to assert ancient values and destroy illusion. The main tradition refers to ten descents, nine of which have already happened. KRISHNA is the most famous *avatar*. Some modern cults claim to worship a living *avatar*.

Averroes *see* IBN RUSHD.

Avesta The scriptures of Zoroastrianism. It includes the *Gathas*, a series of poems reminiscent of the hymns of the Vedas, which may go back to Zoroaster himself. They may have been used as a liturgy to ward off Angra Mainyu and his evil spirits.

Ayatollah ('sign of God') Term for a great MUJTAHID who has authority in the SHI'A MUSLIM community.

Ayn Sof *see* EIN SOF.

Aztec new fire ceremony Ritual which took place at the end of every AZTEC cycle of fifty-two years. It was performed at night on a volcanic hill visible from many parts of the valley of Mexico. When the constellation Orion's Belt reached the middle of the sky, the priests signalled that the world would

continue for another cycle of fifty-two years. A human victim was sacrificed and a new fire was kindled in his chest cavity.

Aztecs An indigenous people whose empire in central Mexico flourished from the late twelfth century CE until the coming of the conquistador Hernando Cortes in 1519. Their religion centred around a sacred calendar and featured human sacrifice in which the heart torn from a living victim was offered to the gods. (*See also* HUITZILOPOCHTLI; QUETZALCOATL; TEZCATLIPOCA; TLALOC; XIPE TOTEC; XIUHTECUHTLI.)

B

Baal Divinity of ancient Canaanite or Phoenician fertility religion. The name means 'lord'.

Baal Shem Tov (1698–1760 CE) Jewish MYSTIC who founded the movement of HASIDISM. His name means 'Master of the Good Name' and it is often shortened to the Besht. His original name was Israel ben Eliezer. At the age of thirty-six he developed powers of healing and prophecy. He taught a kind of mystical PANTHEISM. He was greatly loved and became the source of many Yiddish legends and miracle stories.

Babism *see* BAHÁ'Í FAITH.

Babylonian epic of creation The story of the god MARDUK's fight with the primordial ocean, Tiamat, who is presented as a sea monster. Marduk slit Tiamat in two and made heaven and earth out of the pieces. This MYTH was probably re-enacted every spring at an enthronement festival.

Babylonian flood story A parallel to the story of the flood in the BIBLE going back to a Sumerian original but best known from the EPIC OF GILGAMESH. It tells the story of a wise king, Ut-napishtim, who survived the flood caused by the god ENLIL by taking refuge in a huge boat with his wife and various animals. He was rewarded by Enlil by being transported to a land of immortality.

Bahá'í faith A religious movement that arose out of the Persian Islamic Babi sect, led by the 'Báb' ('gate', 1819–50). Founded by Bahá'u'lláh (1817–92), it is based on the idea that there has only ever been one divinely revealed religion, which has been progressively revealed by the teachings of the founders

of the world's religions, the most recent of whom is Bahá'u'lláh. Bahá'u'lláh appointed his son 'Abdu'l-Bahá (1844–1921) to be his successor and also the interpreter of his writings. He was succeeded by Shoghi Effendi (1897–1957) in 1921. Following the death of Shoghi Effendi in 1957, there was an interregnum until 1963, when the Universal House of Justice, an institution that had been ordained in the writings of Bahá'u'lláh, was elected. This is now the supreme administrative body of the Bahá'í faith.

Balder The son of ODIN and FRIGG, the wisest and most beautiful of the Norse gods. He was killed by the wiles of LOKI but could not be restored to ASGARD because Loki refused to weep for him. His name means 'lord' and he may be connected with the Middle-Eastern dying and rising gods, Adonis and TAMMUZ.

Baptism The SACRAMENT of entry into the Christian CHURCH (I). By washing in water in the name of the TRINITY, it symbolizes the person's identification with CHRIST's death and resurrection, in dying to sin and being raised to new life. In the case of infants, promises are made on behalf of the child for later CONFIRMATION.

Baptist churches Protestant churches emphasizing the BAPTISM of adult believers by total immersion.

Bar Mitzvah ('Son of the Commandment') Ceremony by which Jewish boys, at the age of thirteen, accept the positive commandments of JUDAISM and are counted as adult members of the community.

Bat Mitzvah ('Daughter of the Commandment') Ceremony, mainly in non-ORTHODOX communities, by which Jewish girls, at the age of twelve, accept the positive commandments of Judaism and are counted as adult members of the community.

Barth, Karl (1886–1968 CE) Swiss Calvinist theologian who reacted against Liberal Protestantism in theology and declared theology's central theme to be the WORD OF GOD.

Beautiful names of God Ninety-nine names which characterize the will of ALLAH in ISLAM. The most important are Al-Rahman and Al-Rahim, 'the merciful' and 'the mercy-giver'.

Beltane Celtic spring festival and origin of May Day. The name means 'shining fire' and it is likely that sacred fires were lit for the people to dance around, encouraging the growth of the summer sun.

Benares/Varanasi/Kashi The most holy city of HINDUISM, situated on the banks of the GANGES. It is a centre for the worship of SHIVA and attracts a million pilgrims every year. The BUDDHA preached his first sermon here, traditionally in the deer park on the outskirts of the city.

Benedict (c. 480–550 CE) Monk and reformer who wrote a Rule of monastic life which has been followed by MONKS and NUNS of the Western church ever since.

Bhagavad Gita ('song of the lord') A section of the MAHABHARATA in the form of a battlefield dialogue between the warrior prince Arjuna and KRISHNA, disguised as his charioteer. Arjuna is unwilling to fight his kinsmen but Krishna encourages him, teaching him that wisdom requires him to fulfil his proper role while at the same time renouncing the consequences of his actions.

Bhagavan/Bhagwan Indian title meaning 'lord' or 'worshipful'. It is frequently used of VISHNU. It is also a title of honour used by devotees of holy men.

Bhagavan Shree Rajneesh (1931–90 CE) Indian spiritual teacher and philosopher who founded his own ASHRAM at Pune (Poona) in India. His daily talks and reflections have been transcribed and widely published in the West.

Bhajana An Indian song or HYMN in praise of God usually sung communally at devotional gatherings and accompanied by musical instruments.

Bhakti Love of, or devotion to, God. It is one of the Hindu paths to union with God (see yoga). It is expressed in popular religion in which the worshipper develops a sense of personal relationship to God, responding to him as though to a father, mother, friend, lover, or child, and looking to him for grace.

Bible The book of CHRISTIANITY, comprising the Hebrew OLD TESTAMENT and the NEW TESTAMENT which, Christians believe, together form a unified message of God's SALVATION.

Bishop The most senior order of ministry in the Christian CHURCH (1) with authority to ordain PRIESTS (2). Many REFORMED CHURCHES do not have bishops.

Black stone Sacred object set in the wall of the Ka'ba sanctuary in Mecca. Tradition asserts that it was received by the biblical Ishmael from the archangel Gabriel (Jibril). During the rites of pilgrimage (see HAJJ) the faithful try to kiss or touch the stone.

Blavatsky, Helena Petrovna (1831–91 CE) Founder in 1875 of the Theosophical Society (see Theosophy), who claimed to have received the 'ancient wisdom' after seven years in Tibet being taught by various Mahatmas. She wrote books defending spiritualism and various occult teachings.

Bodhi In various schools of BUDDHISM, 'awakening', or 'perfect wisdom', or 'supreme ENLIGHTENMENT' (1).

Bodhidharma Traditionally the first teacher of Ch'an Buddhism who moved from southern India to China in c. 520 CE. He introduced the methods of sharp questioning and paradox found today in Japanese ZEN.

Bodhisattva In Mahayana Buddhism a saint or semi-divine being who has voluntarily renounced NIRVANA in order to help others to salvation. In popular devotion *bodhisattvas* are worshipped as symbols of compassion.

Bon/Bön A branch of Tibetan VAJRAYANA.

Book of Mormon Sacred SCRIPTURE of MORMONISM which was revealed to Joseph SMITH. It describes a conflict between two branches of a family which had emigrated under divine guidance from JERUSALEM to America in 600 BCE. The Mormons regard it as the completion of the biblical revelation.

Book of the Dead Name given to various collections of spells, often illustrated, buried with the dead of ancient Egypt to assist their souls through the judgment. Commonly the soul is depicted as weighed in a balance against *ma'at*, a conception of 'right order' (depicted as an ostrich feather), by the god Anubis while the scribe Thoth records the result and Osiris presides. (*See also* TIBETAN BOOK OF THE DEAD.)

Book of Shadows A term used in contemporary WICCA of the book in which rituals, invocations, and spells are recorded. While some are kept secret, many allow other

witches to copy their contents in order to share good practice. It is believed by some witches that, traditionally, the Book of Shadows was burned when the witch died.

Booths/Tabernacles/Sukkot Jewish festival marking the end of the harvest. Branch- or straw-covered booths remind JEWS of God's protection during their forty-year journey through the wilderness.

Brahma The creator god of HINDUISM. With VISHNU and SHIVA, BRAHMA belongs to the TRIMURTI of classical HINDU thought.

Brahman In HINDUISM, the divine, absolute reality.

Brahmins *see* CASTE SYSTEM.

Breviary Liturgical book containing instructions for the recitation of daily services as followed by the Christian clergy, MONKS and NUNS of the Western church, with the proper hymns, psalms, and lessons for each service.

Brighid Celtic goddess of poetry, prophecy, learning, and healing. The Romans associated her Gaulish equivalent with Minerva. She was absorbed into Irish Christianity as St Brighid, whose feast day coincides with a Celtic spring festival.

Buber, Martin (1878–1965 CE) Austrian–Jewish theologian whose religious roots were in HASIDISM. Although a Zionist, he was critical of the politics of ZIONISM and of Talmudic tradition (see TALMUD). He believed that the central task of JEWS was to build up God's kingdom on the basis of the Jewish belief in an essential dialogue between God and humanity. He has influenced Christian spirituality and social teaching.

Buddha ('the one who has awakened'/'enlightened one')
(1) Siddhartha GUATAMA, a sage of the SHAKYA tribe who lived in India in around the sixth century BCE, the founder of BUDDHISM. There is little doubt that there was a historical figure at the source of Buddhism, though some branches of MAHAYANA regard this as unimportant.
(2) Any human being or celestial figure who has reached ENLIGHTENMENT (1).

Buddhaghosa Buddhist writer of the fifth century CE who wrote many commentaries on the scriptures and one original work, *The Path of Purification*. The Burmese believe he was a native of Myanmar (Burma) but other traditions hold that he was an Indian who worked in Sri Lanka (Ceylon).

Buddha image Representation of the BUDDHA used in all forms of BUDDHISM. The Buddha is most commonly portrayed in the LOTUS POSTURE, but there are also versions of him standing or lying on one side. The various postures and position of the hands symbolize the defeat of evil, the achieving of ENLIGHTENMENT, the preaching of the DHAMMA, and the final NIRVANA. The images are psychological aids rather than objects of worship, though in MAHAYANA Buddhism they act as a focus for devotion.

Buddhism The religion which developed from the teaching of the BUDDHA and which spread from India into south-east Asia, later expanding into northern Asia, China and Japan. The two principal divisions are the THERAVADA (HINAYANA) and the MAHAYANA. Special features are found in TIBETAN BUDDHISM, also known as VAJRAYANA.

Butsudan A Japanese domestic altar to the BUDDHA which contains images or objects of worship and memorial tablets to ancestors. There may be lights, flowers, and incense and it is the focus of daily prayer chanting and the offering of food and drink.

C

Caliph ('deputy' or 'representative') Title of the leaders of the MUSLIM community after the death of MUHAMMAD. The first three caliphs ruled from MEDINA; the UMMAYADS from Damascus, and the 'ABBASIDS from Baghdad. SUNNI Muslims revere only four Caliphs. From 1517 CE the caliph was based at Istanbul. Kemal Ataturk abolished the caliphate in 1923. SUNNI and SHIA differ over the caliphate: Sunnis say 'ALI was the fourth caliph; Shias say he was the first IMAM, and he and his descendants are MUHAMMAD's rightful successors.

Calvin, John (1509–64 CE) French theologian who organized the REFORMATION from Geneva. He emphasized justification by faith and the sole authority of the BIBLE and in particular that each person's eternal destiny was decided irrevocably by God and only those destined for salvation would come to faith.

Cao Dai Religious and political movement which started in southern Vietnam around 1920. It is sometimes called the 'Third Amnesty'. Firmly nationalistic, its teachings are a mixture of BUDDHISM and TAOISM.

Cardinal Member of a college of ordained high officials in the ROMAN CATHOLIC Church who, since 1059, have elected the POPE. Cardinals are appointed by the pope.

Cargo cults Term used for new religious movements of Melanesia and New Guinea which imitate European ritual in the hope of thereby receiving European-type material wealth – 'cargo'. They look for the arrival of a MESSIAH who will banish illness and distribute the cargo among the people.

Caste system The division of a society into groups reflecting and defining the division of labour. In Hinduism, caste is traditionally seen as the creation of Brahma, each caste emerging symbolically from different parts of his body. There are four chief groups (*varnas*): Brahmins, priests, come from Brahma's mouth; Kshatriyas, warriors, come from Brahma's arms; Vaishyas, commoners, come from Brahma's thighs; Sudras, servants, come from Brahma's feet. Groups of no definite caste were regarded as Untouchables and were banished from society.

Catechism (1) Instruction on Christian faith; for example, instruction in question and answer form given to those preparing for BAPTISM or CONFIRMATION. (2) A popular manual of Christian doctrine.

Catechumen Candidate in training for Christian BAPTISM.

Cathars Members of a medieval heretical Christian sect which flourished in Germany, France, and Italy before their suppression in the thirteenth century. (*See also* ALBIGENSIANS.)

Catholicism CHRISTIANITY as practised by those who emphasize a continuous historical tradition of faith and practice from the time of the APOSTLES (1) to the present day.

Celts Population group occupying much of Central and Western Europe during the first millennium BCE. They included the ancient Gauls and Britons. They worshipped the mother goddess and various local and tribal deities. Evidence from skulls excavated in Celtic sacred places suggests that they practised human sacrifice. Their priests were the Druids. *See* DRUIDRY.

Cernunnos ('the horned one') Celtic horned god associated with the earth and fertility, and protector of the animal kingdom. Usually portrayed sitting cross-legged, he is often accompanied by a stag, or a horned serpent or a bull.

Chac Rain god of the MAYA (3). He is portrayed as an old man with a long nose and weeping eyes. He is in quadruple form and faces in all directions. Benevolent and a friend to humanity, his name was invoked at planting ceremonies.

Chakras According to Indian thought and many contemporary alternative spiritualities, there are seven (sometimes six) chakras (meaning 'wheels') or spiritual energy centres located in the human body. They are: at the top of the head; between the eyebrows; at the throat; at the heart; at the navel; at the genitals; and at the base of the spine, where KUNDALINI, the serpent-energy, lies coiled. The chakras are sometimes called 'lotus centres'.

Chant Type of singing in which many syllables are sung on a single note or a repeated short musical phrase. Many religions use chanting in worship. Jews and Christians chant the PSALMS; Buddhists and others their own sacred SCRIPTURES. The repetitive nature of chanting can aid MEDITATION.

Characteristics of existence In the BUDDHA's teaching all existence is marked by the three characteristics: ANATTA; ANICCA; DUKKHA.

Charismatic movement Renewal movement in Catholic and Protestant churches stressing the work and manifestation of the HOLY SPIRIT in the life of the church and of the individual believer.

Chela In Indian religion, a disciple, student, or follower of a GURU.

Chi In Chinese thought, chi is a universal energy, which manifests in the negative and positive polarities of *yin* and *yang*. The manipulation of chi is central to a form of Chinese yoga known as Chi Gung (Chi Gong, Quigong, Chi Kung) to some forms of acupuncture and martial arts, such as t'ai chi.

Chinvat bridge The bridge of judgment in the teaching of ZOROASTER. Good souls found it broad and easy to cross but wicked souls slipped off as it narrowed, and fell into a chasm of torment.

Chorten *see* STUPA.

Christ Greek word for MESSIAH. First applied to JESUS OF NAZARETH by his followers, who believed him to fulfil the hopes of ISRAEL, it later became more a proper name of Jesus than a title.

Christadelphians Christian sect founded by John Thomas (1805–71 CE) in the USA, which claims to have returned to the beliefs and practices of the original DISCIPLES. They accept the BIBLE as infallible and are particularly interested in the fulfilment of prophecy. They reject the doctrines of the TRINITY and INCARNATION and have no ordained ministry.

Christian Follower of JESUS OF NAZARETH, the CHRIST, a member of the Christian CHURCH (1).

Christianity Religion based on the teachings of JESUS OF NAZARETH, the CHRIST, and the significance of his life, death, and RESURRECTION.

Christian Science Christian sect founded in the USA by Mary Baker EDDY in 1866. It began with a small group fathered 'to reinstate primitive Christianity and its lost element of healing'.

Christmas The festival of the birth of CHRIST celebrated in Western Christendom on 25 December (which is not necessarily the date believed to be the actual date of his birth). The date suggests that it was intended to replace the Roman festival of the birth of SOL INVICTUS in the fourth century CE.

Christology Teaching about the nature of the person of CHRIST.

Chuang Tzu Chinese Taoist teacher who lived in the fourth and third centuries BCE. He commended a way of life according to nature which disregarded the conventions of CONFUCIANISM. His writings stress spiritual discipline which should lead to MEDITATION on the formless Tao. *See* TAOISM.

Chu Hsi (1130–1200 CE) Chinese philosopher who expounded a system rather similar to that of PLATO. He believed that by quiet daily MEDITATION one could see through diversity to the supreme reality behind all phenomena.

Church (1) The community of all CHRISTIANS, seen in the NEW TESTAMENT as the 'body of Christ', of which he is the head.

(2) Building used for Christian WORSHIP.
(3) A local group, organized section, or 'denomination' of the church (1).

Circumcision The cutting off of the prepuce in males or the internal labia in females as a religious rite. It is widely practised in traditional African religion, either shortly after birth or at puberty. In JUDAISM boys are circumcised at eight days of age in commemoration of ABRAHAM's COVENANT with God. Male converts to Judaism undergo this rite. Circumcision is also practised in ISLAM.

Civil religion Religion as a system of beliefs, symbols, and practices which legitimate the authority of a society's institutions and bind people together in the public sphere.

Conciliar process The decision making of the CHURCH through the resolutions of specially convened councils or synods in which the will of CHRIST is revealed to the gathered body. Since the second VATICAN COUNCIL member churches of the WORLD COUNCIL OF CHURCHES have pledged themselves to work towards a common stand on important issues in the hope that this would lead to the restoration of a universal council which would speak for all Christians.

Confirmation Christian rite involving the laying on of hands on those who have been baptized, with prayer for the gift of, or strengthening by, the HOLY SPIRIT. It is often the sign of becoming a communicant member of the CHURCH (1). In Orthodox churches it is performed at BAPTISM. Roman Catholics are confirmed at about seven years of age. Other churches that accept confirmation offer it at puberty or later.

Confucianism The system of social ethics taught by CONFUCIUS and given imperial recognition in China in the second century CE. Opinion is divided on whether or not Confucianism should be regarded as a religion. (*See* FIVE RELATIONSHIPS; LI.)

Confucius/K'ung Fu-tzu (551–479 BCE) Chinese civil servant and administrator who became known as a teacher, opening his classes to everyone regardless of wealth or class. His teachings, especially the idea of LI, became the basis of a system of social ethics which greatly influenced Chinese society after his death.

Congregationalists *see* INDEPENDENTS.

Conservative Judaism Movement which tries to stand midway between Orthodox and PROGRESSIVE JUDAISM. It claims to accept the Talmudic tradition (*see* TALMUD) but to interpret the TORAH in the light of modern needs.

Conversion A moral or spiritual change of direction, or the adoption of religious beliefs not previously held.

Coptic Church The Church of Egypt, a more or less tolerated minority in Egypt since the coming of ISLAM in 642 CE. The Church is 'monophysite', i.e. it rejects the teaching about the INCARNATION OF CHRIST agreed at the ECUMENICAL COUNCIL of Chalcedon.

Corroboree Ceremony of the Australian Aboriginals comprising festive and warlike folk dances.

Cosmology (1) The study of the nature of the cosmos. (2) In religion, cosmologies concern the relationship between the divine and the natural world. This relationship is usually described in MYTHS or stories of how God or the gods had brought the world, humanity, and particular peoples into existence and how they continue to relate to them. Cosmologies form the frameworks within which reality is interpreted.

Councils of the Church *see* ECUMENICAL COUNCILS.

Counter-Reformation The revival and reform of the Roman Catholic Church as a reaction to the REFORMATION. Its reforms included those of the Council of Trent (1562–63 CE).

Covenant A bargain or agreement. In JUDAISM the chief reference is to that made with MOSES at SINAI: GOD, having liberated his people from Egypt, promises them the land of ISRAEL and his blessing and protection as long as they keep the TORAH. This confirms the earlier covenants with ABRAHAM and with Noah. The term is also used of God's special relationship with the house of DAVID. With the defeat of the Kingdom of Judah in 586 BCE, Jeremiah's prophecy of a new covenant written on the people's hearts came into its own. In the Christian NEW TESTAMENT the sacrificial death of JESUS OF NAZARETH marks the sealing of a new covenant between God and the new Israel, the Christian CHURCH, which completes and fulfils the old covenant.

Cranmer, Thomas (1489–1556 CE) Archbishop of Canterbury under Henry VIII who helped overthrow papal authority in England and created a new order of English worship in his *Book of Common Prayer* of 1549 and 1552.

Creation The act of GOD by which the universe came into being. Hence also refers to the universe itself. In JUDAISM, CHRISTIANITY, and ISLAM creation is usually thought of as being *ex nihilo*, from out of nothing that existed before. In HINDUISM it is believed that the universe has been outpoured from God and will contract into him at the end of the age.

Creation myth A story that explains the divine origins of a particular people, a place or the whole world. In some INDIGENOUS RELIGIONS and ancient religions it is ritually re-enacted at the beginning of each year.

Creation Spirituality Initiated in 1977 by the Dominican theologian Matthew Fox (b. 1940), it is highly critical of traditional CHRISTIANITY, which is described as the 'Fall–Redemption' tradition, emphasizing original sin and the fundamental badness of humanity and the created order. Such theologies are, it is claimed, anti-emotional, anti-sensual, hierarchical, patriarchal, and destructively dualistic. Creation spirituality, instead of emphasizing ORIGINAL SIN, speaks of 'original blessing', and seeks to provide a life-affirming celebration of humanity and creation. Drawing liberally on the mystical traditions (particularly Christian MYSTICISM), NEW AGE thought, INDIGENOUS SPIRITUALITIES, and contemporary eco-spiritualities, it speaks to many Westerners who are disillusioned with mainstream Christianity.

Creed Formal statement of religious belief. In CHRISTIANITY, the two creeds used most commonly today are the APOSTLES' CREED and the NICENE CREED.

Crusades The military expeditions undertaken by Christian armies from Europe from the eleventh to the fourteenth centuries intended to liberate the Holy Land from ISLAM.

Cybele Phrygian MOTHER GODDESS whose ecstatic rites included a bath in the blood of a sacrificial bull. Her consort was the youthful Attis. Her cult spread to Greece in the fifth century BCE and to Rome in around 210 BCE, though here it was virtually banned until the late first century CE because of the scandal caused by her oriental eunuch priests.

Cynic Follower of the eccentric Greek philosopher Diogenes (c. 400–325 BCE) who taught that people should seek the most natural and easy way of life, ignoring conventions. He was nicknamed *Kyon* ('dog') and the name stuck to the beggar philosophers who followed him. Some historians believe that JESUS OF NAZARETH may have been influenced by the radical lifestyle and pithy wisdom of the cynics.

D

Dakhma Persian term for the TOWER OF SILENCE of ZOROASTRIANISM.

Dalai Lama Former religious and secular leader of Tibet, widely held to be the reincarnation of AVALOKITESHVARA. Since the Chinese takeover of Tibet the Dalai Lama has lived in India. He is still regarded as the spiritual leader of Tibetan Buddhists. (*See also* LAMA.)

Daruma Japanese name for BODHIDHARMA. It is also the name of a doll used by Japanese children which resembles Daruma.

Dasara An Indian festival usually celebrated in October. Different parts of India celebrate the festival in different ways and focus on different deities. The celebrations vary from a day to nine days to a month. Those who celebrate it as '*Dussehra*' worship the goddess DURGA or celebrate RAMA's victory over RAVANA.

Dastur Parsi priest who is responsible for the rituals of the FIRE TEMPLES and wears a white turban. The priesthood is hereditary. (*See* PARSIS.)

David King of the Israelite tribes around 1000–962 BCE who united them and extended their territory. He stormed the city of the Jebusites and made it his capital, JERUSALEM. He was a musician and poet, to whom a number of psalms in the BIBLE are ascribed. The belief is common to JUDAISM and CHRISTIANITY that the MESSIAH would be a descendant of David.

Deacon Junior minister in the Christian CHURCH. The word means 'servant' and the deacon's functions originally included the distribution of ALMS to the poor.

Dead Sea Scrolls Sacred writings of a breakaway Jewish sect which were discovered in 1947 at Qumran on the western shore of the Dead Sea. The several scrolls and fragments include much of the HEBREW BIBLE as well as hymns, treatises, and rules for the life of the sect. Many scholars identify the sect with the ESSENES.

Death of God theology Radical American movement of the 1960s seeking to reconstruct Christianity on the basis of atheism. Its two tenets were that God had 'died' in human experience but that it was still possible to be a follower of JESUS OF NAZARETH. Later developments of Death of God theology are NON-REALISM and the attempt to blend Christian teaching with Buddhist rejection of a personal God.

Deists Followers of a movement for natural religion which flourished in seventeenth-century England. They rejected the idea of revelation and held that the Creator did not interfere in the workings of the universe.

Delphic Oracle Most authoritative source of prophecy and political advice in Ancient Greece. Run by the priests of APOLLO, its prophet was a woman, the Pythia ('pythoness'), who uttered her oracles in a state of induced frenzy. The message was then interpreted by the priests and delivered in a cryptic, often ambiguous, form.

Demeter Greek goddess of fertility and growth. Worshipped throughout the Greek world, she was identified with the Egyptian ISIS, the Phrygian CYBELE, and the Roman Ceres as the MOTHER GODDESS. Her MYTH concerns the abduction of her daughter Persephone by HADES; yearly, in autumn, the earth becomes barren while she searches for her child. She initiated her own MYSTERY RELIGION – the ELEUSINIAN MYSTERIES – at Eleusis near Athens.

Demiurge Term used in GNOSTICISM to describe the creator god, seen as wilful, passionate, and ignorant. His creation is a cosmic disaster which traps in material existence the divine sparks that emanate from the true God.

Demonology Teaching about the demonic and all forms of personified evil.

Dervish Islamic MYSTIC belonging to one of the orders which induce ecstasy by movement, dance, and the recitation of the names of God.

Devadatta Cousin of the BUDDHA, and one of his earliest disciples. In some texts he is in conflict with the Buddha and leads a schismatic movement. He was condemned to a period in hell for his misdeeds.

Devil Term generally used to describe an evil spirit. In CHRISTIANITY the devil (SATAN) is the personification of evil who is permitted to tempt and accuse human beings within the overall providence of God.

Dhamma The teaching of the BUDDHA – his analysis of existence expressed in the FOUR NOBLE TRUTHS and his cure as outlined in the NOBLE EIGHTFOLD PATH. Dhamma is sometimes represented as an eight-spoked wheel. (*See also* DHARMA.)

Dhammapada One of the best-known texts of the PALI CANON expounding the essence of THERAVADA Buddhist teachings. It encourages Buddhist disciples to achieve their own salvation, relying on no external saviour or authority.

Dharma In HINDUISM, cosmic order, the law of existence, right conduct. Also, in BUDDHISM, the teaching of the BUDDHA (*see* DHAMMA).

Diana Italian goddess who was associated with wooded places, women, childbirth, and the moon. She became identified with the Greek ARTEMIS. The centre of her cult was a grove on the shore of the volcanic Lake Nemi.

Diaspora (1) The geographical spread of a people who share a common culture. (2) The term was originally used to describe the spread of the Jewish nation, the dispersion from the land of ISRAEL. The dispersion of the JEWS came about partly as a result of war and exile, partly as a result of travel and trade.

Dietary laws Rules about food and drink that are characteristic of a particular religion. Thus JUDAISM prohibits the simultaneous preparation or eating of milk and meat products, bans totally the eating of, for example, pork and shellfish, and regulates the ritual slaughter of other animals for meat. ISLAM proscribes pork and alcohol. JAINISM bans all animal products.

Digambara ('sky-clad') Member of a major sect of JAINS who followed MAHAVIRA in believing in the virtue of total nudity. Numerous in the warm south of India, they tend to wear robes in public.

Dionysus Greek god of wine and of liberation, a dying and rising god identified with OSIRIS. His cult probably came from Thrace or Phrygia. He is associated with vegetation and fertility and appears surrounded by satyrs, nature spirits pronouncing fertility. He is followed by a host of maenads, frenzied women leading orgiastic rites. Dionysus punishes unbelief with terrible vengeance. In the late Hellenistic world (*see* HELLENISM) the cult of Dionysus became an important MYSTERY RELIGION.

Disciple Followers of a religious leader or teaching. In CHRISTIANITY it refers to the original followers of Jesus in the NEW TESTAMENT and is widened to include all Christian 'followers' throughout history.

Divali *see* DIWALI.

Divination The art of the DIVINER.

Divine kingship The belief that kings and queens are descended from the gods and rule with their authority. The ritual purity of the divine king guarantees the community's welfare. Notions of divine kingship are found in some INDIGENOUS RELIGIONS. (*See also* INCA; PHARAOH.)

Diviner One who tells the future either by reading the signs of nature in the weather, stars, or the flight of birds, or by the manipulation of objects such as sticks, stones, bones, or playing cards. An important figure in ancient Roman religion, Chinese religion, and many INDIGENOUS RELIGIONS (*see* I CHING; TAROT CARDS). Diviners may also share the powers of a MEDIUM or SHAMAN.

Divinities Name given to minor gods or spirits in INDIGENOUS RELIGIONS who rule over an area of the world or some human activity – e.g. storms, war, farming, marriage. Divinities are usually worshipped formally with special RITUALS and festivals.

Diwali Festival of light celebrated by HINDUS, JAINS, and SIKHS. For Hindus it marks the return of RAMA from exile and his reunion with SITA as told in the RAMAYANA. For Jains it is the beginning of a new ritual and commercial year and celebrates Mahavira's transcendence to MOKSHA and the

enlightenment of his disciple Gautama. For Sikhs it is a commemoration of the release from prison of the sixth GURU and his return to the city of Amritsar.

Doctrine A religious teaching or belief which is taught and upheld within a particular religious community.

Dravidian Word describing the pre-Aryan civilization based in the Indus valley. It was overturned by Aryan invaders around 2000 BCE. Today Dravidian peoples inhabit southern India.

Dreams One of the chief sources of revelation to the individual in INDIGENOUS RELIGIONS. Dreams may contain warnings or commands or promises of blessing.

Dreamtime In Australian INDIGENOUS RELIGION, the mythical period in which, according to Aboriginal tradition, ancestral beings moved across the face of the earth forming its physical features. The Dreamtime is recreated in art, painting, chanting, dancing, and cult ceremonies.

Druidry (1) The priestly caste of Celtic society. It is likely that they presided at sacrifices, made and enforced legal decisions, and passed on the traditions of learning, magic, healing, and ritual. (2) Since the late eighteenth century, in Wales and Cornwall, self-identified Druids, many of whom were Christian, established national philanthropic and cultural events. Such cultural events, designed to encourage national pride, are still enormously important, particularly in Wales. (3) In the twentieth century there was a revival of specifically Pagan Druidry. It is now a growing and important Pagan tradition, including numerous groups and 'orders'. Worship focuses on ancient pre-Christian sites, such as Stonehenge.

Dualism (1) The belief that reality has a fundamentally twofold nature. Opposed to MONISM it describes the belief that there is a radical distinction between God and the created world. (2) The belief that there are two fundamentally opposed principles: one of good, the other of evil. This moral dualism is the basis of ZOROASTRIANISM. (3) The belief that the mind and the body are fundamentally different yet act in parallel.

Duat *see* TUAT.

Dukkha Buddhist term for unsatisfactoriness or suffering. Birth, illness, decay, death, and REBIRTH are symptoms of a restless and continuous 'coming-to-be' which marks all existence as *dukkha*.

Durga ('the inaccessible') In HINDU tradition, the consort of SHIVA in one of her terrifying forms.

Dussehra *see* DASARA.

E

Easter The festival of the RESURRECTION of CHRIST, the greatest and oldest festival of the Christian CHURCH (1). Its date is fixed according to the paschal full moon and varies from year to year.

Eastern Orthodox churches Family of self-governing churches looking to the Ecumenical PATRIARCH, the Patriarch of Constantinople, as a symbol of leadership. (*See also* GREAT SCHISM.)

Ecclesiology Teaching about the church.

Eco-feminism A movement which seeks spiritual enlightenment through a synthesis of feminism with concern for the environment.

Ecumenical councils Assemblies of Christian BISHOPS whose decisions were considered binding throughout the Christian church. These ended with the GREAT SCHISM, though the Roman Catholic Church has continued to assemble councils into the twentieth century. The most important of the Ecumenical Councils were held at Nicaea (325 CE, condemning ARIANISM), Constantinople (381 CE), Ephesus (431 CE, condemning NESTORIANISM), and Chalcedon (451 CE, concerning the INCARNATION OF CHRIST).

Ecumenical movement Movement for the recovery of unity among the Christian Churches. It dates from the Edinburgh 'World Missionary Conference' of 1910 and today focuses in the WORLD COUNCIL OF CHURCHES.

Eddy, Mary Baker (1821–1910 CE) American spiritual teacher and founder of CHRISTIAN SCIENCE. She believed that orthodox CHRISTIANITY had repressed CHRIST's teaching and practice of spiritual healing and that healing was not miraculous but a natural expression of the divine will. She founded the First Church of Christ Scientist in Boston in 1879; it remains the mother church of Christian Science.

She wrote the authoritative work of the movement – *Science and Health with Key to the Scriptures* – and founded the newspaper the *Christian Science Monitor*.

Eid *see* 'ID AL-'ADHA, 'ID AL-FITR.

Ein Sof Name for God used in Jewish MYSTICISM, in particular in the KABBALAH, meaning the endless, the absolute infinite whose essence is unrevealed and unknowable.

El Great god and 'creator of creation' among the Canaanite and Phoenician peoples.

Elder An officer of the church in the PRESBYTERIAN and INDEPENDENT CHURCHES. Teaching elders also deal with pastoral care; ruling elders help in church government and administration.

Election God's choice of ISRAEL to be his people as expressed in the COVENANT at Mount SINAI and manifested in the gift of the land of Israel. In JUDAISM the election of the JEWS carries responsibility. They are to bear witness to the reality of God in the world by keeping the TORAH. In Christian theology, the concept is widened to include GENTILE converts to CHRISTIANITY who spiritually inherit the promises made to the PATRIARCHS and to MOSES.

Eleusinian Mysteries MYSTERY RELIGION of DEMETER, centred at Eleusis near Athens. The Greater Mysteries were held at the time of the autumn sowing and went on for nine days. The myth of Demeter was probably re-enacted and the climax may have been a revelation of a reaped ear of corn. But only initiates were admitted and the exact nature of the mysteries was kept a secret.

Eliezer, Israel ben *see* BAAL SHEM TOV.

Elohim Plural form of the Canaanite word for a divinity (*see* DIVINITIES), usually translated 'God' and used as a name of God by the HEBREWS (*see also* EL). It is sometimes treated as a common-noun plural, 'gods' or 'angels'. (*See also* ANGELS.)

Elysium Paradise of Greek religion. It was held to be either far away across the sea, or a section of the underworld ruled not by HADES, but by Kronos, one of the ancient Titan race.

Emperor, Japanese Since the reign of the legendary JIMMU TENNO the emperors of Japan claimed divine descent from Amaterasu Omikami. SHINTO thus became an expression

of imperial power and nationalism. The divinity of the emperor was formally repudiated in 1945.

Enki The water god of ancient Sumerian religion.

Enlightenment (1) Full spiritual awakening. (2) In BUDDHISM, the realization of the truth of all existence which was achieved by the BUDDHA in his meditation at Bodh Gaya. Enlightenment or final enlightenment also refers to the passing into NIRVANA of anyone who follows the Buddha's way and attains release from the cycle of birth and REBIRTH. (*See also* BODHI.) (3) Eighteenth-century European movement of philosophy and science which stressed the supremacy of reason over revelation and tradition.

Enlil The wind god in ancient Sumerian belief. He persuaded the other gods to plan the destruction of humankind in a great flood. He rewarded the flood's only survivor with the gift of immortality.

Epic of Gilgamesh Babylonian poem, the earliest versions of which date to the eighteenth century BCE. It tells the story of Gilgamesh's vain quest for the secret of immortality and includes the BABYLONIAN FLOOD STORY.

Epicureanism Philosophical school founded by Epicurus (341–270 BCE) and holding an atomic theory of the universe. It teaches that the gods are irrelevant to human life, the chief end of which is happiness. Fulfilment comes from the prudent and restrained cultivation of pleasure.

Epistle (1) Letter in the NEW TESTAMENT to a Christian community or individual usually from one of the APOSTLES. (2) Letter on doctrine or practice addressed to a Christian community in post-apostolic times.

Eros Greek god of love, Cupid to the Romans, the son of APHRODITE. In Greek literature his cruelty to his victims is emphasized, also his omnipotence. In the Christian era 'cupids' became angelic beings symbolizing divine benevolence and compassion.

Eschatology Teaching about the 'last things'. In Christianity this includes discussion of the end of the present world order, the SECOND COMING/PAROUSIA, the final judgment, PURGATORY, HEAVEN, and HELL.

Esoteric Word meaning 'inner', suggesting something (e.g. a knowledge or a teaching) that is available only for the specially initiated and secret from outsiders and perhaps even from ordinary believers.

Essenes Jewish group which withdrew to live a monastic life in the Dead Sea area during the Roman period. Most were celibate and they stressed the importance of ASCETICISM. They also performed exorcisms and rites of spiritual healing. Many scholars believe that the DEAD SEA SCROLLS were the scriptures of an Essene community.

Eucharist ('thanksgiving') The central act of Christian worship instituted by CHRIST on the night before his death. It involves sharing bread and wine which are sacramentally associated with the body and blood of Christ. (*See* SACRAMENT.)

Evangelicals CHRISTIANS of all denominations who emphasize the centrality of the BIBLE, justification by faith, and the need for personal conversion. In Germany and Switzerland, the term refers to members of the Lutheran as opposed to the Calvinist churches.

Evangelism The preaching of the Christian GOSPEL to the unconverted.

Exile (1) The period between 597 BCE and around 538 BCE when leading JEWS from the former Jewish kingdoms were held in captivity in Babylon. (2) The condition of Jewish life in the DIASPORA, away from the land of ISRAEL.

Exodus The flight of the people of ISRAEL from Egypt under the leadership of MOSES.

Exorcism Removal of sin or evil, particularly an evil spirit in possession of someone, by prayer or ritual action.

Ezra Scribe of the Babylonian EXILE who was sent with a royal warrant from the Persian king to reform religion in JERUSALEM. Traditionally he arrived in 458 BCE and embarked on a programme to purify the Jewish faith and install the TORAH as the central authority in Jewish life.

F

Faith Attitude of belief, in trust and commitment to a divine being or a religious teaching. It can also refer to the beliefs of a religion, 'the faith', which is passed on from teachers to believers.

Fall of Jerusalem The capture of JERUSALEM and the final destruction of the TEMPLE OF JERUSALEM by the Roman general Titus in 70 CE at the end of a revolt which broke out in 66 CE.

Family Federation for World Peace and Unification Another name for the Holy Spirit Association for the Unification of World Christianity, commonly known as The Unification Church, or, after the name of the founder, the Moonies. It was founded in Seoul, South Korea, in 1954 by Sun Myung MOON. Central to Unificationism is an emphasis on the important of the family unit within society.

Fasting Total or partial abstinence from food, undertaken as a religious discipline. In INDIGENOUS RELIGIONS it is often a preparation for a ceremony of INITIATION. In JUDAISM and CHRISTIANITY it is a sign of mourning or repentance for SIN. It is also more generally used as a means of gaining clarity of vision and mystical insight.

Fatwa An authoritative legal declaration or religious opinion made by a Muslim scholar, or MUFTI, applying SHARI'A to a particular situation. There is no central authority that issues a fatwa.

Fellowship The common life of Christians marked by unity and mutual love, a creation of the HOLY SPIRIT.

Feminist theology A movement developed first in the USA which uses the experience of being female in a male-dominated society as a basis for critical reflection on Christian thought, tradition, and practice.

Feng Shui Literally translated as 'wind' and 'water', it is the Chinese art of living in harmony with one's environment in order to ensure happiness and prosperity. It emerged during the Han dynasty (206 BCE–220 CE) and, by the twelfth century, had been developing into the quasi-science of geomancy. Based on the notion that there are five basic elements (earth, fire, metal, water, wood) and two fundamental forces (YIN and YANG), it studies the interaction between these

in order to discover the most auspicious and powerful places. Hence, for example, feng shui is used to make wise decisions about the location of buildings, furniture, and gardens, all of which are believed to contribute to human well-being.

Fire sermon One of the BUDDHA's most famous sermons traditionally preached at Gaya to 1000 fire-worshipping ascetics, in which he explained that all that exists is burning with lust, anger, and ignorance.

Fire temples Parsi temples where the sacred fire of AHURA MAZDA is kept continually burning. The fire is kept in a censer on a stone slab hanging under the central dome of the temple. There are no images: the fire symbolizes the purity and goodness of Ahura Mazda. (*See* DASTUR; PARSIS.)

Five pillars of Islam Five duties binding upon every Muslim and signifying commitment to Islam. They are: the SHAHADAH (the Islamic creed); SALAH (ritual prayer); SAWM (fasting in the month of RAMADAN); ZAKAH (almsgiving); and HAJJ (undertaking the pilgrimage to MECCA).

Five precepts Ethical restraints for Buddhists, who are to refrain from: taking life, stealing, wrong sexual relations, wrong use of speech, drugs and intoxicants.

Five relationships The codification and application of CONFUCIUS's teaching to the five basic relationships of human life. These are father and son; older brother and younger brother; husband and wife; elder and younger; ruler and subject. The inferior should show proper deference, the superior proper benevolence. The stress is on reciprocity and Confucius believed that such correct behaviour would weld society in 'the way of heaven'.

Four noble truths The BUDDHA's analysis of the problem of existence – a four-stage summary of his teaching:
(1) all that exists is unsatisfactory;
(2) the cause of unsatisfactoriness (DUKKHA) is craving (TANHA);
(3) unsatisfactoriness ends when craving ends; (4) craving can be ended by practising the NOBLE EIGHTFOLD PATH.

Four rightly guided caliphs SUNNI ISLAM accepts ABU BAKR, 'UMAR, 'UTHMAN and 'ALI as legitimate successors to MUHAMMAD.

Four stages of life HINDU outline of a man's ideal spiritual life. There are four stages (ashramas): student, the Hindu boy learns the scriptures in the house of his GURU and lives a life of chastity; householder, he marries, has children and earns his living; retired life, when his family are grown up he gradually begins to withdraw from everyday life; renounced life, where he cuts all earthly ties and seeks liberation, often as a wandering beggar.

Francis of Assisi (1182–1226 CE) Founder of the Franciscan monastic order who lived by a simple rule of life, rejecting possessions, ministering to the sick and having a special concern for nature.

Freemasonry Originally a religious brotherhood of English masons founded in the twelfth century. In the sixteenth century it spread to the European mainland where in Roman Catholic countries it became associated with Deism (see DEISTS). In the UK and USA today it is a semi-secret society which retains certain mystical symbols and ceremonies. Members are committed to a belief in GOD as 'the great architect of the universe', symbolized by an eye.

Frey Norse god of beauty with power over rain and sunshine and the fertility of the earth. His name means 'lord'.

Freyja Norse goddess and sister of FREY; her name means 'lady'. She is patroness of love and sorcery and drives a chariot pulled by cats. She possesses half the corpses of those who are slain in battle, the other half going to ODIN.

Friends, Society of see QUAKERS.

Frigg Chief of the Norse goddesses and wife of ODIN; the goddess of love and fertility. She knows the fates of people but cannot avert destiny.

Fundamentalism The doctrine that the BIBLE is verbally inspired and therefore inerrant and infallible on all matters of doctrine and history. The bases of fundamentalism were set out in twelve volumes, *The Fundamentals*, published between 1910 and 1915.

G

Gabriel (1) An archangel named in both the Old and New Testaments. In the Gospel of Luke he foretells the births of John the Baptist and Jesus.

(2) In ISLAM Gabriel (Jibril) is associated with the 'faithful spirit' by whom the QUR'AN was revealed to MUHAMMAD. Jibril also transported Muhammad from MECCA to JERUSALEM and from there to the throne of God during the NIGHT JOURNEY.

Gaia Greek name for MOTHER GODDESS, now revived by the hypothesis originated by J. E. Lovelock according to which all living beings on earth are part of a single living organism.

Gandhi (1869–1948 CE) Leader of the Indian independence movement and the greatest spiritual and political figure of modern India. Disowning violence, he advocated political change through non-violent resistance. After independence he tried to reconcile the Hindu and Muslim communities. He also campaigned against the social exclusion of UNTOUCHABLES. He was assassinated by a Hindu nationalist.

Ganesha Elephant-headed god much loved in popular HINDUISM, especially in western India. He is the god of good beginnings and is a symbol for luck and wealth in business and daily life.

Ganges The holy river of India whose waters are sacred for all HINDUS. It is thought to flow from the toe of VISHNU. Pilgrims wash away evil in its waters and the ashes of the dead are thrown into it.

Gautama/Gotama Family name of the BUDDHA. Legend depicts him as a great prince born into a royal household. Modern scholars think that his father was probably the head of an aristocratic family living in the town of Kapilavastu.

Gemara Part of the Jewish TALMUD that takes the form of a series of rabbinical commentaries on the MISHNAH.

Genius (1) In occult religion, a guardian spirit or familiar. (2) In Roman religion, the spirit of a man, giving rise to his maleness. A LIBATION was poured to the genius of the reigning emperor at every banquet.

Gentile Person who is not a JEW.

Ghat ('holy place') In HINDU use, a word which can refer to a range of hills, a ritual bathing place, or a cremation ground.

Ghost dance A dance which sprang out of a religious movement of the 1870s among Native Americans. It was believed that the dance would lead to the resurrection of all

dead Native Americans on an earth free of disease and death. The movement was destroyed at the Battle of Wounded Knee in 1890. (See also WOVOKA.)

Glossolalia Expression in unknown tongues by people in a heightened spiritual or emotional state. In the Christian CHURCH (1) it is used to express WORSHIP to GOD and prophetic messages, in other religions to express a state of religious ecstasy.

Gnosticism Movement of ESOTERIC teachings rivalling, borrowing from and contradicting early CHRISTIANITY. Gnostic sects were based on MYTHS which described the creation of the world by a deluded DEMIURGE and taught a way of salvation through *gnosis*, 'knowledge' of one's true divine self. Gnostics contrasted their 'knowledge' with faith, which they considered inferior.

Gobind Singh, Guru (1666–1708 CE) The tenth GURU of the Sikh community. He formalized the Sikh religion, requiring Sikhs to adopt a distinctive name and dress. He also shifted the focus of authority from the Gurus to the sacred scripture, the ADI GRANTH.

God (1) The creator and sustainer of the universe; the absolute being on whom all that is depends. (2) A being with divine power and attributes; a deity, a major DIVINITY.

Goddess (1) Female form of god.
(2) The supreme being conceived as female as in some modern Pagan religious movements. Worshippers of the Goddess claim that they are continuing the ancient religion of the MOTHER GODDESS who was a personification of nature.

Good Friday The Friday before EASTER, in CHRISTIANITY, kept by the CHURCH (1) as a holy day, sometimes including FASTING, penance, and witness, in memory of the crucifixion of Jesus CHRIST.

Gospel (1) One of the four accounts of the 'good news' about Jesus in the NEW TESTAMENT. (2) The Christian message, proclamation of 'good news', referring especially to Jesus' teaching about the KINGDOM OF GOD and to the preaching of the CHURCH about Jesus.
(3) The ritual reading of a set portion from the Gospels (1) in the context of the EUCHARIST. (4) A partial account of the life

and teaching of Jesus, usually ascribed to a New Testament figure but rejected by the Church as heretical.

Gospel of Thomas Syriac text of a collection of sayings of Jesus discovered at Nag Hammadi in Egypt in 1947. It has many parallels with the sayings of Jesus in Matthew and Luke, and some scholars consider it to be as authentic as the canonical Gospels. Its teaching, though, is GNOSTIC.

Gotama *see* GAUTAMA.

Grace (1) Unmerited favour, especially in the divine salvation of the unworthy. An essential concept in CHRISTIANITY, where it is contrasted with merit, Christians believe that nobody receives SALVATION because he or she deserves it but only by God's grace. (2) A prayer or blessing before a meal.

Great Schism The SCHISM declared in 1054 CE between the Eastern and Western Christian churches resulting from disagreements over the POPE's claim to supremacy, and the doctrine of the HOLY SPIRIT.

Gregory of Nyssa (c. 330–395 CE) Christian theologian who helped develop the doctrine of the TRINITY and expounded the BIBLE as a spiritual path leading to the perfect contemplation of God.

Ground of Being Phrase used by German-US theologian Paul Tillich (1886–1965 CE) to describe GOD. It stresses the immanence of God as depth or ground rather than his transcendence as creator.

Gurdjieff, George Ivanovich (1873–1949 CE) Spiritual teacher whose book *Meetings with Remarkable Men* relates his search for wisdom. He invented a system of non-identification with the ego which he believed led to the realization of man's true essence. He was influenced by SUFISM. In 1922 he founded an Institute for the Harmonious Development of Man which attracted a number of Western intellectuals.

Gurdwara SIKH temple and meeting place, consisting of a worship area which houses the GURU GRANTH SAHIB, and a cooking and eating area, the *langar*, for the meal which ends Sikh worship.

Guru ('teacher') A spiritual teacher or guide who, in Indian religion, awakens a disciple to a realization of his or her own divine nature.

In SIKH religion it refers to the ten teachers, from Guru NANAK to Guru GOBINDH SINGH, who ruled the community.

Guru Granth Sahib *see* ADI GRANTH.

H

Hades (1) Greek god of the dead and ruler of the UNDERWORLD. He was connected with growth and vegetation and the production of wealth. Because it was considered unlucky to speak his name, he is often referred to as Pluto (the 'rich'). (2) Greek name for the underworld, the abode of the dead. In the Septuagint version of the HEBREW BIBLE it translates *sheol*. In Christian usage it is sometimes used for the interim abode of the departed as distinguished from HELL, the abode of the damned.

Hadith Traditions of MUHAMMAD's words and actions, many of which complement or elucidate the directions of the QUR'AN. There are many spurious Hadith; one of the major tasks of MUSLIM lawyers has been to categorize Hadith into likely degrees of authenticity.

Hagadah/Haggadah Prayer-book used by Jews on the eve of PASSOVER for the SEDER ritual.

Hajj Pilgrimage to MECCA which is one of the FIVE PILLARS OF ISLAM and which MUSLIMS are obliged to make at least once in a lifetime. *Hajj* must be performed in *Dhu al-Hijjah* (the last month of the Islamic *Hijri* calendar). *Umrah* ('lesser' Hajj) can be performed at any time. On arrival at Mecca, pilgrims make seven anticlockwise circuits of the KA'BA and, if possible, kiss the BLACK STONE.

Halakhah (from HEBREW verb 'to walk') A legal teaching based on the midrashic exposition of a Hebrew text (*see* MIDRASH).

Hamartiology Teaching about sin.

Hammurabi (eighteenth century BCE) Mesopotamian ruler who produced a law code laying down punishments for various transgressions and enunciating principles for the conduct of business and social life. The breaking of his code incurred the enmity of the Babylonian gods.

Hanukkah ('dedication') Eight-day Jewish festival marked by the lighting of ritual

candles which celebrates the rededication of the TEMPLE OF JERUSALEM by JUDAS MACCABEUS in 164 BCE.

Hanuman Monkey-god of popular HINDUISM. In the RAMAYANA he led a monkey army against a host of demons. He can fly and cover huge distances at great speed.

Hara-Kiri Japanese expression meaning 'belly cutting' which is used for the Japanese traditional practice of ritual suicide among the warrior classes.

Hare Krishna Mantra used by devotees of KRISHNA to induce ecstatic union with the divine. The most familiar version is a two-line chant, invoking both Krishna and RAMA. (*See also* INTERNATIONAL SOCIETY FOR KRISHNA CONSCIOUSNESS.)

Hasidim ('the pious') Followers of BAAL SHEM TOV, who taught a new kind of HASIDISM in the eighteenth century CE.

Hasidism Jewish mystical movement with roots in the KABBALAH which arose in the eighteenth century in response to the teachings of BAAL SHEM TOV after a period of persecution by the Cossacks. It stressed the presence of God in everyday life and the value of prayer. Chanting and dancing were used as aids to ecstatic communion with God. The movement was popular and had a wide appeal among ordinary JEWS.

Heathenism Also referred to as 'The Northern Tradition' or 'Asatru' ('faith in the deities'), Heathenism is a form of contemporary Paganism which focuses on Anglo-Saxon, Norse, and Germanic traditions. Runes are used as powerful magical and meditative symbols. Popular Heathen teachings include the belief that this world, MIDGARD/Middle Earth, is one of nine linked by the 'World Tree', YGGDRASIL. There are two groups of deities, the ÆSIR and the VANIR. A popular form of Heathenism is Odinism, the spirituality of which focuses on the Norse god ODIN.

Heaven (1) The realm of God or of the gods. (2) In CHRISTIANITY the dwelling place of God and the ultimate home of the saved, regarded both as a place and as a state.

Hebrew (1) A member of the Semitic tribes which emerged as the people of ISRAEL. (2) The (Semitic) language of the ancient people of Israel, of the HEBREW BIBLE, and of the modern state of Israel.

Hebrew Bible The Jewish SCRIPTURES which comprise the Books of the Law (*see* TORAH), the PROPHETS, and the WRITINGS. According to tradition, the canon was fixed at the Synod of Jamnia or Yavne about 100 CE.

Heimdall White god and watcher of the gods in Norse religion.

Hecate An earth goddess who probably originated in Asia Minor. Connected with magic and death, she was sometimes known as the ARTEMIS of the cross-roads. She is shown with three faces, carrying torches, and followed by baying hounds. A popular deity in contemporary Paganism.

Hell Realm where the wicked go after death. Religious teachings differ over whether this punishment is reformatory or eternal. In CHRISTIANITY, it is total separation from God. Most religions describe a place or a condition for the wicked following death. ZOROASTRIANISM, JUDAISM, and ISLAM all describe such a state following divine judgment after death. Even religions which have a doctrine of reincarnation, such as Buddhism and Hinduism, include teachings about hells (although the belief in reincarnation makes them quite different from the teachings of Christianity and Islam).

Hellenism The adoption of the Greek language, culture, philosophy, and ideas, particularly around the Mediterranean, from the time of Alexander the Great (356–323 BCE). It was the dominant cultural influence during the rise of CHRISTIANITY.

Hera Greek goddess, the wife of ZEUS and queen of heaven. She was the protectress of women and marriage and is presented as a model of chastity. She was worshipped throughout the Greek world. Her special bird was a peacock, a symbol of pride. Her Roman counterpart was JUNO.

Heresy The denial of a defined doctrine of the Christian faith. The word means 'chosen thing' and refers to the heretic's preference for an individual option over the consensus of the CHURCH (1).

Hermes Greek messenger god and son of Zeus, protector of travellers, bringer of luck, and god of thieves and merchants. He is usually portrayed as a young man in winged hat and sandals, carrying a staff twined with snakes.

Hermeticism Mystical movement based on a collection of Egyptian scriptures from the first to third centuries CE. The writings drew on Greek and Eastern ideas, and were ascribed to Hermes Trismegistus (thrice-great HERMES), who is identified with the god THOTH.

Herzl, Theodor (1860–1904 CE) Leader of the Zionist movement (*see* ZIONISM). He argued that a national homeland for the JEWS was a necessity. He travelled widely raising support from Christian governments for the Zionist cause and convened the First Zionist Congress in 1897 which formulated a political programme for the return to Palestine.

Hesiod Greek poet, probably of the eighth century BCE, whose THEOGONY sought to draw together the ancestries of the Greek gods, understanding creation in terms of procreation.

High Priest Traditional head of the Jewish priesthood and organizer of TEMPLE worship. His function was to enter the Holy of Holies and offer sacrifice on the DAY OF ATONEMENT. This was a key political appointment under the Seleucids and Romans. Talmudic tradition criticizes the corruption of some who held the office, which ceased at the destruction of the Temple in 70 CE.

Hijrah ('going forth') The migration of MUHAMMAD, preceded by some of his followers, from MECCA to MEDINA in 622 CE. This was the decisive event for the development of ISLAM for it was in Medina that Muhammad established himself as a religious and political leader and organized his followers as an Islamic community. The MUSLIM calendar, the *Hijri* calendar, counts years 'after *Hijrah*'.

Hillel Pharisaic Jewish teacher of the first century CE. He was known for his humane and lenient interpretations of the TORAH, in contrast to his chief opponent, the stern and religious Shammai.

Hinayana ('lesser vehicle') Buddhist term used to indicate the doctrine of salvation for oneself alone, in contrast to MAHAYANA. Most Buddhists of south-east Asia prefer the term THERAVADA to describe this school of BUDDHISM.

Hindu Word used by Arabs to describe people living beyond the Indus Valley. Today it refers generally to people practising Indian religion who are neither Muslim, Sikh, Parsi, nor Jain, and also to their religion, Hinduism.

Hinduism A term coined by Europeans for a religious tradition and social system that emerged in India. It has no founder, no set creed, no prophets, and no single institutional structure. It is actually an umbrella term for an enormous range of beliefs and practices, from the worship of local village deities to the thought of a great philosopher such as Shankara. There are, however, some common beliefs which are basic to most strands of Hinduism. There is an emphasis on DHARMA (the right way of living) rather than assent to particular doctrines. Also found throughout Hinduism is the notion of MOKSHA, or release from the eternal cycle of birth, death, and rebirth (SAMSARA) to which one is bound by KARMA. Linked to this set of beliefs is the social stratification known as the caste system. The three chief Hindu deities are BRAHMA, VISHNU, and SHIVA, who together form a triad known as the TRIMURTI. Numerous other deities are worshipped, but all are aspects of the universal spirit, BRAHMAN. Hindus' concepts of God are complex and largely depends upon the Indian traditions and philosophy followed.. (*See also* BHAGAVAD GITA; BRAHMAN; UPANISHADS; VEDANTA; VEDAS.)

Hoa Hao Offshoot of the Vietnamese CAO DAI movement. It is Buddhist-based and has been strongly nationalistic.

Holi HINDU spring festival which celebrates the love of KRISHNA and RADHA. It is marked by boisterous games which are reminders of Krishna's amorous pranks with the cow-girls as told in the MAHABHARATA.

Holiness The sacred power, strangeness, and otherness of the divine. In the BIBLE and the QUR'AN the term has moral implications and refers to God's purity and righteousness as well as to that which invokes awe. In CHRISTIANITY, believers are called to reproduce God's holiness in their own lives with the help of the HOLY SPIRIT.

Holocaust (from the Latin BIBLE's word for 'whole burnt offering') The name given to Hitler's extermination of six million Jews in the Nazi death camps in Europe from 1941–45. Mass destruction was envisaged as the 'final solution' to the 'problem' of the Jews. The memory of the Holocaust is the key to modern Jewish theology and made the founding of the state of Israel an event of profound significance. The Holocaust is also referred to by many Jews as as the *Shoah* (catastrophe).

Holy Communion Name widely used by Anglicans and some Protestants for the Christian EUCHARIST.

Holy Spirit The third person of the Christian TRINITY. In the BIBLE the Holy Spirit is the instrument of divine action and is portrayed as fire or wind. In this sense the Spirit is acknowledged in JUDAISM and ISLAM. The divinity of the Holy Spirit was agreed at the Council of Constantinople in 381 CE. The Holy Spirit is the source of faith and new life in the believer and the church, giving 'spiritual gifts', guidance, and holiness.

Holy Spirit Association for the Unification of World Christianity *see* FAMILY FEDERATION FOR WORLD PEACE AND UNIFICATION.

Homer Author of the Greek epics the *Iliad* and the *Odyssey*, which date from between the tenth and eighth centuries BCE. According to the historian Herodotus, Homer was the first to detail the characters and functions of the gods of Mount OLYMPUS.

Honen (1133–1212 CE) Japanese teacher of PURE LAND BUDDHISM. He taught that repetition of the word NEMBUTSU is all that is necessary for salvation. He is said to have recited it 60,000 times a day.

Horus Egyptian hawk-headed sky god, associated with the king. The son of ISIS, conceived on the dead OSIRIS, he defeated the evil SETH and assumed the earthly rule Seth had usurped from Osiris.

House churches/New churches Networks of charismatic, non-denominational churches which started in the 1960s. Members claim that they are restoring the conditions of the primitive church, which met for worship in members' houses. *See* RESTORATIONISM.

Hsün-tzu Chinese Confucian scholar of the third century BCE who blended the philosophies CONFUCIANISM and TAOISM. He believed in the correct observance of ceremonial which helped to improve evil human nature. He was critical of superstition and reinterpreted popular religious practices in rationalistic terms.

Huaca Any of the multitude of DIVINITIES recognized by the INCAS; also, an Inca holy place, shrine, or temple.

Huiracocha *see* VIRACOCHA.

Huitzilopochtli AZTEC god of war and the sun. His name means 'hummingbird wizard' and he was perpetually at war with darkness and night.

Hui Yuan *see* PURE LAND BUDDHISM.

Humanism Way of life based on the belief that what is good for human beings is the highest good.

Hus, Jan (1374–1415 CE) Bohemian reformer who, under the influence of WYCLIFFE's writings, denounced the worldliness of the clergy. When he was burnt at the stake he was declared a MARTYR and national hero in Prague. His thought influenced the REFORMATION.

Hymn A sacred song sung in the context of communal worship; a PSALM of communal praise. Hymns are particularly important in Christian and Sikh worship and in the gatherings of the Hindu BHAKTI cults (*see* BHAJANA).

I

I Ching/Book of Changes One of the five classics of Chinese literature which was originally attributed to CONFUCIUS but is now thought to be much earlier. It gives instructions and interpretations for a form of DIVINATION using six sticks which can fall in sixty-four significant hexagrams.

Ibn Rushd (1126–98 CE) MUSLIM philosopher, known in the West as AVERROES, who was greatly influenced by PLATO and ARISTOTLE. He believed that the Greek heritage was compatible with ISLAM. His synthesis, however, seemed suspicious to the orthodox and he was banished and his books burnt.

Icon A likeness of a divine figure or SAINT painted on wood or inland in mosaic and used in public or private devotion.

'Id al-'Adha The great festival of the MUSLIM year, commemorating Ibrahim's preparedness to sacrifice his son, Isma'el. It coincides with the offering of the pilgrim sacrifice at Mina near MECCA.

'Id al-Fitr The MUSLIM feast which ends the fasting month of RAMADAN. Greetings cards are exchanged, presents are given, and sugary sweets are eaten.

Ijma' The consensus of opinion of the MUSLIM community. It is an important principle of Islamic law-making.

Ijtihad A way for the Islamic community to develop its law to deal with new situations. It is a ruling given by one MUSLIM teacher, rather than by general consensus (*see* IJMA'). It is controversial whether Ijtihad is always valid or whether the completion of SHARI'A will render it unnecessary.

Imam Meaning 'model' or 'example', the term refers to three types of leader within Islam. (1) The leader of ritual prayer in the local community. He is also a Qur'anic scholar and is therefore respected and often fulfils a leadership function within the local community.
(2) Used in a more exalted sense, the term refers to leaders of particular Islamic schools of thought. For example, the founders of the schools of Islamic law are referred to as imams. Similarly, it is an honorific title given to great Islamic scholars (e.g. AL-GHAZALI). (3) It has a special significance in the Shi'ite community. The term refers to a unique intercessor with exceptional spiritual authority, knowledge, and charisma. Imams are agents of divine illumination, indispensable for understanding the relevance of divine revelation for the contemporary community.

Immortals Various beings who live in the Realm of Great Purity, according to the teachings of TAOISM. Best known are the 'eight immortals' who are portrayed with a variety of individual characteristics and symbols and feature in Chinese art and drama.

Inanna The MOTHER GODDESS as worshipped in ancient Sumer.

Inca The divine king who ruled over the INCAS.

Incarnation (1) The Christian doctrine that GOD became human in Jesus CHRIST, so possessing both human and divine natures.
(2) A term sometimes used for the HINDU doctrine of the AVATAR.

Incas Empire centred on Cuzco in modern Peru from around 1100 CE until the Spanish conquest (1532 CE). From the late fourteenth century the empire expanded to include parts of modern Ecuador, Bolivia, Chile, and Argentina. The first INCA, Manco Capac, was created by and given absolute authority by the SUN GOD. (*See also* HUACA; PACHACAMAC; VIRACOCHA.)

Incense Sweet-smelling smoke used in worship, made by burning certain aromatic substances.

Inclusive language A response to feminism which tries to eradicate the assumption in speech and writing that maleness is more normally human than femaleness. Churches adopting it modify their hymn, liturgy, and Bible translations.

Independence, Day of Jewish festival of thanksgiving on the anniversary of the birth of the state of ISRAEL (4). The liturgy includes prayers for the victims of the HOLOCAUST.

Independents/Congregationalists CHRISTIANS who uphold the authority and independence of each local church, claiming this system to be the earliest form of church order.

Index of prohibited books The official list of books which members of the Roman Catholic Church are forbidden to possess or read, first issued in 1557. The *Index* was abolished in 1966.

Indigenous religions The preferred term for religions which are sometimes referred to as 'primal', 'tribal', 'traditional', 'primitive', and 'non-/pre-literate' religions. That said, indigenous religions are often developments of the traditional religions of tribal and aboriginal cultures. The problem with the earlier terminology was that it suggested simple, undeveloped, non-progressive, and archaic belief systems. Contemporary indigenous religions include Native American religion and Australian Aboriginal religion.

Indra ARYAN god of war and storm. There are 200 hymns to him in the RIG VEDA (*see* VEDAS). He faded from significance in later HINDUISM.

Indulgence The remission by the Christian church of a period of correction in PURGATORY. The sale of indulgences by unscrupulous 'pardoners' was one of the abuses which led to the REFORMATION.

Initiation Ceremony marking coming of age, or entry into adult membership of a community. It is also used of the secret ceremonies surrounding membership of the MYSTERY RELIGIONS. (*See also* CONFIRMATION; NAVJOTE; RITES OF PASSAGE; SACRED THREAD CEREMONY.)

Inquisition Papal office for identifying heretics, founded by Pope Gregory IX and staffed by the Franciscan and Dominican religious orders. Torture became an approved aid to interrogation in 1252.

Intercession Prayer offered on behalf of others by a believer on earth or by a SAINT in HEAVEN. In CHRISTIANITY, supremely the work of CHRIST, who intercedes for men and women before GOD.

International Society for Krishna Consciousness (ISKCON) Founded in 1965 by A. C. Bhaktivedanta Swami Prabhupada (1896–1977), and popularly known as the Hare Krishna movement, ISKCON is a modern BHAKTI cult which has been successful in Europe and America. Shaven-headed orange-robed devotees chant the MANTRA '*Hare Krishna*' as a way of reaching ecstatic union with God.

Inti The SUN GOD of the INCAS.

Ishtar Babylonian goddess, mother, and wife of TAMMUZ and associated with the fertility rites of death and resurrection. In mythology she is responsible for the great flood which almost destroyed the earth (*see* BABYLONIAN FLOOD STORY). Worshipped in various forms all over the Ancient Near East, she was known as Astarte to the Phoenicians and as Ashtoreth to the Hebrews.

Isis Great Egyptian goddess of motherhood and fertility. The sister and wife of OSIRIS, she restored him to life after he was murdered by SETH. Sometimes represented as cow-headed, she had a great temple at Philae.

Isis cult MYSTERY RELIGION based on the MYTH of ISIS and OSIRIS which became particularly popular in the Roman world from the first century CE. Its sacred drama and liturgy express the experience of salvation from sensuality which is open to initiates through the grace of the goddess.

Islam (infinitive of the Arabic verb 'to submit') Teachings derived from the QUR'AN, which is the revelation to MUHAMMAD, a religion of submission to the will of Allah. (*See also* ALLAH; MECCA; MUSLIM; FIVE PILLARS; SUNNI; SHIA.)

Isma'ilis A group of SHI'A Muslims who accept the legitimacy of Ismail and his son as the sixth and seventh Imams (*see also* MAHDI; TWELVERS).

Israel (1) Name given by GOD to Jacob the patriarch and hence to his descendants, the 'people of Israel'.
(2) The land promised by God to Abram (ABRAHAM) in the early traditions of JUDAISM.
(3) The Northern Kingdom of Israel which seceded from Solomon's kingdom in 922 BCE and was destroyed by the Assyrians in 722 BCE. (4) The modern state of Israel, founded in Palestine as a Jewish state in 1948 CE.

Izanagi The sky god in SHINTO, and the father of Amaterasu. With his consort, Izanami, he created the islands of Japan.

J

Jade Emperor The supreme divinity in TAOISM, who came into prominence about the tenth century CE. He presided over life and death and kept account of human actions.

Jahannam MUSLIM name for HELL which is frequently mentioned in the QUR'AN as a place of scorching fire and black smoke. Sometimes it is personified as a great monster appearing at the Day of Judgment.

Jain ('one who has conquered') A follower of the religion known as JAINISM.

Jainism Religion of India that derives its name from Jina (conqueror). This term (and the related term Tirthankara) is used of a religious teacher who is believed to have attained enlightenment and omniscience. The most recent Jina was MAHAVIRA, who is regarded as the founder of Jainism. Early in its history Jainism separated into two main sects: DIGAMBARA Jainism and SHVETAMBARA Jainism. (*See also* DIGAMBARA; JINA; JIVA; MAHAVIRA; PARSVA; SHVETAMBARA.)

Janus Roman god of beginnings whose name derives from *janua*, 'entrance' or 'gate'. He is portrayed with a two-faced head, facing both ways. In Julius Caesar's reform of the calendar, his month became the first of the year.

Jarovit Slavic war god.

Jehovah *see* YHWH.

Jehovah's Witnesses Christian sect founded in the 1870s by C. T. RUSSELL. It propagates its

INTRODUCTION TO WORLD RELIGIONS

own version of the BIBLE (The New World Translation), which it regards as inspired and inerrant, and stresses the imminent return of CHRIST. Members are pacifists and are forbidden to have blood transfusions.

Jerome (c. 342–420 CE) Translator of the BIBLE into Latin (the 'Vulgate' version). He wrote many commentaries on the text.

Jerusalem Fortified city captured by DAVID in the c. 1000 BCE which became the capital and principal sanctuary for the people of ISRAEL. It has remained the focus of Jewish religious aspirations and ideals (see TEMPLE OF JERUSALEM). It is a holy city for CHRISTIANS because of its association with the passion, death, and RESURRECTION of JESUS OF NAZARETH. For MUSLIMS it is the holiest city after MECCA. The Mosque of the Dome of the Rock stands over the site of Muhammad's NIGHT JOURNEY.

Jesus of Nazareth Teacher, prophet, and worker of miracles in first-century Palestine and founder of Christianity. He taught the coming of the KINGDOM OF GOD with forgiveness and new life for all who believed. His claims to be the promised MESSIAH (or CHRIST) roused opposition from the religious authorities and he was put to death by crucifixion, but after his death his followers claimed that he was risen from the dead and he was seen alive by many. CHRISTIANS, members of his CHURCH (1), believe him to be fully divine and fully human, and await his promised SECOND COMING, which will bring the fulfilment of the KINGDOM OF GOD.

Jew (1) A person who is regarded as a member of the Jewish race. According to Jewish religious law Jewishness is inherited through the female line. (2) A person who identifies with JUDAISM, the religion of the Jews.

Jihad ('striving') A much-misunderstood concept, jihad is the relentless fight against worldliness. Muslims are exhorted to wage holy war only in their defence.

Jimmu Tenno Traditionally the first Japanese EMPEROR, who began his reign in 660 BCE. He was thought to be a great grandson of the sun goddess Amaterasu, and was credited with the unification of Japan and the establishment of its government under the guidance of the gods (see KAMI).

Jinas Also called '*Tirthankaras*' ('ford-makers'), *Jinas* ('conquerors') are Jain religious teachers who have attained enlightenment and omniscience by conquering SAMSARA (the continuous cycle of birth, death, and rebirth to which those with KARMA are bound).

Jinja The SHINTO sanctuary. They vary in size from roadside shrines to beautifully located halls surrounded by trees and entered through traditional arched gateways (see TORII). They include halls for ceremonial dances, offerings, and prayer rooms.

Jinn Spiritual creatures in Islamic belief who are made of smokeless flame. They are capable of belief and unbelief: the good ones are regarded as MUSLIMS.

Jiva A soul or 'life monad' according to JAIN belief. Jivas are infinite and omniscient but in this world KARMA weighs them down into a material existence. Jivas are liberated by acquiring omniscience, and this makes them float up to the summit of the universe.

Jodo Japanese name for PURE LAND BUDDHISM.

Jodo Shinshu ('True Pure Land Sect') A refinement of PURE LAND BUDDHISM founded by SHINRAN. It was characterized by the doctrine of salvation through faith alone and the abolition of the SANGHA.

Johanan ben Zakkai Creator of the academic SANHEDRIN in Jamnia after the FALL OF JERUSALEM in 70 CE. He led the work of Jewish reconstruction within the limits of Roman law and ensured, through the Sanhedrin, that the Jewish community was represented before the Roman authorities.

Judah HaNasi ('The Prince', 135–217 CE) Leader of the academic Jewish SANHEDRIN in Galilee. He was responsible for compiling the MISHNAH, which helped the Jewish community in developing a source of ritual authority in religious teaching.

Judaism The religion that developed from the religion of ancient ISRAEL and has been practised ever since by the JEWS. It is an ethical MONOTHEISM based on the revelation of GOD to MOSES on Mount SINAI and his giving of the Law (see TORAH). (See also ASHKENAZIM; CONSERVATIVE JUDAISM; ORTHODOX JUDAISM; PROGRESSIVE JUDAISM; SEPHARDIM.)

Judas Maccabeus (d. 160 BCE) Jewish revolutionary who opposed the Hellenizing Seleucid emperor Antiochus Epiphanes, who had set up an image of Olympian ZEUS in the TEMPLE OF JERUSALEM. Under Judas sporadic guerrilla revolt became full-scale war. In 165 BCE Antiochus was defeated and in the following year the temple was rededicated (see HANUKKAH). Though he achieved religious freedom, he failed to establish a free Jewish state.

Judgment The divine assessment of individuals and the settling of their destinies, a notion found in many religions. Christianity teaches that judgment is based on the individual's response to Christ.

Jumis Latvian harvest god.

Jung, C. G. (Carl Gustav) (1875–1961 CE) Swiss psychiatrist who invented the theory of ARCHETYPES. He investigated the significance of MYTHS, symbols, and DREAMS, and found in them evidence for a 'collective unconscious' which was at the root of religion.

Juno Roman goddess, counterpart of the Greek HERA, and wife of JUPITER. She was the patroness of women, marriage, childbirth, and family life.

Jupiter/Jove Principal god of the Romans, identified with the Greek ZEUS. He controlled the weather, particularly lightning and rain, and was worshipped throughout Italy as almost a national god.

K

Ka The guardian spirit of each individual which, according to Egyptian belief, survived death and lived on in the next world, where it was reunited with *ba*, breath.

Ka'ba ('cube') The sanctuary in MECCA to which all MUSLIMS turn in prayer. Set in its eastern corner is the BLACK STONE. A pre-Islamic holy place, all its religious images were removed in 630 CE by MUHAMMAD when he purified it to be the central sanctuary of ISLAM. The QUR'AN associates Abraham and Ishmael with the building of the *Ka'ba*.

Kabbalah Jewish mystical tradition which flourished in the teaching of two schools: the practical school based in Germany which concentrated in prayer and MEDITATION; the speculative school in Provence and Spain in the thirteenth and fourteenth centuries. The tradition originates in Talmudic speculation on the themes of the work of creation and the divine chariot mentioned in the biblical book of Ezekiel. The most famous Kabbalistic book is *Zohar* ('splendour'), a MIDRASH on the PENTATEUCH. (*See* MYSTICISM; TALMUD.)

Kabir (c. 1440–1518) Indian poet and hymn writer who influenced the development of early Sikhism. He attempted a synthesis of ISLAM and HINDUISM, rejecting the CASTE SYSTEM and CIRCUMCISION, but teaching the love of God, rebirth, and liberation.

Kali Consort of the HINDU god SHIVA, a black goddess who is portrayed with a necklace of human skulls and fangs dripping blood. She is both the goddess of destruction and the Great Mother, giver of life.

Kalki In HINDU tradition, the last AVATAR of VISHNU who will descend on a white horse, with a sword, to kill the wicked and bring the world to an end.

Kami Powers of nature which are venerated in SHINTO. They are beneficent spirits who help in the processes of fertility and growth. They were generated by the gods and the Japanese people are descended from them according to Shinto mythology.

Kamma PALI word for KARMA.

Karaites ('readers of scripture') Heretical Jewish school of the eighth century CE which denied the validity of the TALMUD and the oral tradition. They held to a literalist view of the TORAH. By the tenth century they had spread throughout the Middle East and Spain. They refused to mix with other JEWS. Under attack by SAADYA BEN JOSEPH, the movement gradually disintegrated.

Karma SANSKRIT word for work or action. In Indian belief every action has inevitable consequences which attach themselves to the doer requiring reward or punishment. Karma is thus the moral law of cause and effect. It explains the inequalities of life as the consequences of actions in previous lives. The notion of karma probably developed among the DRAVIDIAN people of India. In MAHAYANA Buddhism the concept is transformed by the idea of the BODHISATTVA. Merit can be transferred by grace or faith, thus changing the person's karma.

Karo, Joseph (1488–1575 CE) Jewish legal teacher and MYSTIC. He produced the *Shulshan Aruch* (1565), which is one of the most important and cohesive authorities in JUDAISM, and is considered to be in accord with the purest Talmudic tradition (*see* TALMUD). His work is characterized by a devotional tone unusual in legal works.

Kashrut The code in JUDAISM according to which food is ritually clean or unclean. It refers particularly to meat, which must be slaughtered so as to ensure the minimum of pain and the draining off of blood.

Kashi *see* BENARES.

Khalsa Originally the militant community of SIKHS organized by Guru GOBIND SINGH in 1699 CE. Now it is the society of fully committed adult members of the Sikh community. Membership is signified by the 'Five Ks': uncut hair, a comb worn in the hair, a small dagger, shorts, and an iron or steel bracelet.

Khandha *see* SKHANDHA.

Kharijites MUSLIM party of seceders from 'ALI, the fourth CALIPH. They opposed the UMMAYAD DYNASTY, believing that the succession should be based on a democratic vote. They were puritans strongly critical of the moral laxity that developed as Ummayad power increased. Their stance inspired later reforming movements.

Khnum Creator god of ancient Egypt.

Kingdom of God The rule of God on earth. In JUDAISM God is king of the universe, the sole creator and ruler. The JEWS are his witnesses and their task is to work and pray for the fulfilment of his rule among all people. The kingdom will be brought by the MESSIAH and will include the restoration of ISRAEL. In CHRISTIANITY, JESUS of Nazareth proclaimed the arrival of the kingdom in himself. Christians share in the kingdom now, and it will be completed and fulfilled at his SECOND COMING.

Kitab-i-Aqdas Meaning 'the most holy book', this is one of the most important works of Bahá'u'lláh. It contains most of the laws and many social ordinances of Bahá'u'lláh.

Kitab-i-Iqan Meaning 'the book of certitude', this is one of the most important works of Bahá'u'lláh. It addresses a range of theological questions and provides interpretations of the BIBLE and the QUR'AN.

Koan Technique used in RINZAI ZEN to bring about SATORI. It is a mind-bending question given by a teacher to a pupil to help him or her break through the prison of mental concepts and achieve direct awareness of reality.

Kojiki SHINTO scripture which is the oldest book in the Japanese language, though it is written using Chinese characters. It contains MYTHS and legends about the creation, the founding of Japan and the ceremonies and customs of the Japanese people.

Koko Spirits of dead ancestors in the popular cults of the Zuñi people of northern Mexico. The spirits are represented in ceremonial dances in which all participating males wear god-like masks.

Kol Nidrei *see* YOM KIPPUR.

Kook, Abraham Isaac Rabbi (1868–1935 CE) First Chief Rabbi of the Holy Land. He believed the Zionist movement to be essentially religious and that the restoration of ISRAEL was necessary for the redemption of the world. He influenced orthodox JEWS in favour of ZIONISM, though he was also tolerant of secular Jews.

Koran *see* QUR'AN.

Kotel *see* WESTERN WALL.

Krishna The eighth incarnation of VISHNU according to HINDU tradition. His name means 'black'. Though of noble birth, he was brought up as a cowherd. Eventually he obtained his inheritance and ruled in justice. He was also a great lover: the MAHABHARATA describes his romances with the cow-girls which are seen as a type of God's love for the SOUL (1). He is also the main character in the BHAGAVAD GITA, where he appears disguised as the charioteer of Prince Arjuna.

Krishnamurti, Jiddhu (1895–1986) Indian spiritual teacher who was brought up by a leading Theosophist, Mrs Annie Besant, who proclaimed him as a World Teacher. He renounced this role in 1929 and became a solitary traveller, teaching liberation from dogma and organized religion by the rejection of belief in the individual ego. (*See also* THEOSOPHY.)

Kshatriya *see* CASTE SYSTEM.

Kuan-yin Chinese name for the great BODHISATTVA Avalokiteshvara, especially when thought of in female form.

INTRODUCTION TO WORLD RELIGIONS

Kukai (774–835 CE) Japanese Buddhist teacher who tried to reconcile BUDDHISM with SHINTO. He is sometimes regarded as a manifestation of the Buddha VAIROCANA. Some believe he exists in a deep trance from which he is able to perform miracles and that he will return one day as a saviour.

Kundalini Energy that is coiled like a serpent at the base of the spine according to TANTRISM. When awakened by YOGA it leaps up the spine to the brain giving an experience of union and liberation re-enacting the sexual union of SHIVA and SHAKTI.

L

Laity (from Greek *laos*, 'people') The non-ordained members of a religious community (*see* ORDINATION), or those with no specialist religious function.

Lakshmi Lord VISHNU's consort. She appears in the *Rig Veda* (*see* VEDAS) as good fortune. In the RAMAYANA she rises out of the sea holding a lotus. She is involved in Vishnu's descents to earth as an AVATAR. Some associate her with SITA and RADHA, the consorts of RAMA and KRISHNA.

Lama Tibetan religious leader, a title formerly applied only to abbots, but later used of any monk. Lamas have been credited with magical powers which are said to be attained through years of arduous training. Their most common feat is telepathy, but they are also reported to be able to leave their bodies at will, cover huge distances at great speed, and know the time and place of their own death. (*See also* SHAMAN.)

Lao-tzu Traditionally the author of the TAO TE CHING and a contemporary of CONFUCIUS. His name means 'old master', which could have applied to any wandering teacher.

Lares Roman agricultural spirits who were worshipped at crossroads and in the home as household gods.

Latter-Day Saints, Church of Jesus Christ of *see* MORMONISM; SMITH, JOSEPH.

Lectisternium A Roman feast in which food was offered to images of the gods which were placed on couches (*lecti*) like human guests.

Lent In CHRISTIANITY, a forty-day period of FASTING and penitence before EASTER,

originally a period of training and examination for those who were baptized at Easter.

Ley lines Straight geological lines of spiritual force which some adherents of NEW AGE RELIGIONS believe were discovered and used in the NEOLITHIC PERIOD. Their existence is said to be demonstrated by the many alignments between religious sites, MEGALITHS and unusual topographical features. There is no archaeological or statistical support for this view.

Li CONFUCIUS's concept of propriety or reverence which he believed should direct all relationships between members of society. Correct application of *li* was a guarantee of social welfare and harmony.

Libation The RITUAL outpouring of drink as an offering to DIVINITIES or ancestor spirits.

Liberation Theology Originating in Latin America, associates SALVATION with the political liberation of oppressed peoples. Its insights have been used by black Christians and feminists to understand sexism and racism. It is marked by a stress on the challenges to social action contained in the BIBLE, especially the prophetic books and the NEW TESTAMENT, and the reality of the KINGDOM OF GOD as a coming event.

Limbo According to Roman Catholic doctrine, the dwelling place of souls (e.g. of unbaptized children) excluded from HEAVEN but not subjected to HELL or PURGATORY.

Liturgy ('public service') (1) Any regular prescribed service of the Christian Church. (2) The EUCHARIST, especially in ORTHODOXY.

Logos Greek for word or principle. In STOICISM it identified the principle of reason, immanent in nature. Speculations about the logos were developed by the Jewish philosopher PHILO OF ALEXANDRIA. The Prologue to St John's GOSPEL identifies CHRIST with the pre-existent logos of God.

Loki The opponent of the ÆSIR in Norse mythology who is bent on their downfall and the overthrow of the world order. His name may mean 'light' and he is associated with destructive fire. For his part in the death of BALDER he is fettered to underground rocks and poisoned by serpents until the day of RAGNARÖK. His agonies cause earthquakes and volcanoes.

Lord's Supper Name for the Christian EUCHARIST favoured by the Protestant reformers who saw the Eucharist primarily as a memorial of CHRIST's death.

Lotus Type of water lily, a Buddhist symbol of ENLIGHTENMENT. The roots of the lotus are buried in the earth while the flower opens out above the water.

Lotus posture Style of sitting upright and cross-legged, used as a position for MEDITATION in Hindu and Buddhist practice.

Lotus Sutra MAHAYANA Buddhist scripture in the form of a sermon preached by the BUDDHA (I) to a vast throng of gods, demons, rulers, and cosmic powers. It contains the essence of Mahayana teachings on the eternity of the Buddha, the universal capacity for Buddhahood, and the compassion and power of the BODHISATTVAS. It is especially revered in Japan and is the basic scripture of the NICHIREN Buddhist NEW RELIGIONS.

Lucretius (c. 100–55 BCE) Roman poet and philosopher who expounded the materialist and rationalist doctrines of EPICUREANISM in his poem '*De rerum natura*' ('On the nature of things'). He accepted the existence of the traditional gods but located them far away from our world and believed that they had no interest in or influence over events on earth.

Lugh (Irish: 'The Shining One'; Welsh: *Lleu*) Most honoured of the Celtic gods, a war god, the patron of commerce and moneymaking, and prototype of human beings. Skilful in all arts and crafts, he is often portrayed as a youthful traveller. His Gaulish name is unknown, but Julius Caesar compared him to the Roman MERCURY.

Luria, Isaac (CE 1514–72) Jewish teacher from Spain who developed the Kabbalistic teachings of the *Zohar* (*see* KABBALAH). He believed in reincarnation and taught that the dispersion of the JEWS was providential and would lead to universal salvation. His teachings inspired devotional poetry and hymns.

Luther, Martin (1483–1546 CE) Founder of the German REFORMATION. He held that people could only be justified before God by faith in JESUS CHRIST, not by any 'works' of religion. So, the priesthood and the 'mediating' role of the church are unnecessary.

Lutheran churches Important churches in Scandinavia, other parts of Western Europe, and the USA. They value theological study and emphasize the weekly sermons.

M

Maccabees The family and supporters of Judas Maccabeus. They were the forerunners of the Zealots in fighting a holy war against alien rulers.

Madhva (1197–1276 ce) Indian philosopher who founded a dualist school (*see* DUALISM) in opposition to the MONISM of Shankara. He was a devotee of Vishnu, and believed that God was eternally distinct from the natural world. He may have been influenced by Christian teachings.

Magi Priestly class of ancient Persia who at first opposed the spread of Zoroaster's teachings. By the fourth century bce they had been drawn into the service of the new religion and stressed the ritual and magic elements of it.

Magic The manipulation of natural or supernatural forced by SPELLS and RITUALS for good or harmful ends.

Mahabharata One of the two great epics of the Hindu scriptures compiled by the third or second century bce. Ascribed to the sage Vyasa, it tells of the war between two families, the Kauravas and the Pandus. The divine hero of the epic is the AVATAR Krishna.

Maharishi Mahesh Yogi *see* TRANSCENDENTAL MEDITATION.

Mahatma Sanskrit title of great respect or veneration meaning 'great soul'.

Mahatma Gandhi *see* GANDHI.

Mahavira Great Jain teacher who traditionally lived 599–527 bce, though this is disputed. He abolished the distinctions of the CASTE SYSTEM and tried to spread his teaching among the Brahmins. He starved himself to death at the age of seventy-two, having spent his last years totally naked.

Mahayana ('large/great vehicle') The form of Buddhism practised in Nepal, China, Tibet, Korea, and Japan. Mahayana accepts more scriptures than Theravada, and has developed various forms of popular devotion based on the doctrine of the BODHISATTVAS.

Mahdi 'The guided one' who according to Shi'a teaching will come at the end of the world. The Mahdi is identified with Muhammad al-Mahdi who disappeared in 880 ce and is believed to be hidden until his reappearance. There have been a number of false Mahdis in the Shi'a community.

Maimonides, Moses (1135–1204 ce) Jewish philosopher who lived in Spain and later Egypt and attempted a synthesis of Aristotelian and biblical teaching. He listed the Thirteen Principles of belief which have been treated in Judaism as a creed and are found in the Jewish Daily Prayer Book.

Maitreya The Buddha-to-be, or the next Buddha to appear on earth according to Mahayana teachings. He is at present a bodhisattva awaiting his last rebirth.

Mana Polynesian word for the invisible spiritual power which permeates all things. It has been adopted as a general term in the study of INDIGENOUS RELIGIONS. It is not necessarily a personal power, though it can be focused in particular individuals, places, and objects.

Mandaeans Members of a Gnostic sect teaching redemption through a divine saviour who has lived on earth and defeated the powers of darkness. The sole surviving practitioners of Gnosticism, about 15,000 still live in Iraq and Iran.

Mandala A visual aid in the form of a series of coloured concentric circles used in Buddhism and Hinduism. Segments of the circles portray different aspects of the Buddha's compassion. Concentration on the *mandala* enables the disciple to see himself in relation to the Buddha's compassion and thus to achieve ENLIGHTENMENT.

Manichaeans Followers of Mani (around 216–276 ce), a Persian teacher whose strict ascetic system was designed to release the divine spark trapped in every person by the wiles of Satan. Their teaching influenced Augustine.

Manitou Name used by the Algonquin Indians of North America to refer to spiritual powers. It can apply to all kinds of NATURE SPIRITS or DIVINITIES, friendly or unfriendly.

Mantra A symbolic sound causing an internal vibration which helps to concentrate the mind and aids self-realization, e.g.

the repeated syllable 'om', and in Tibetan Buddhism the phrase OM MANI PADME HUM. In Hinduism the term originally referred to a few sacred verses from the Vedas. It came to be thought that they possessed spiritual power, and that repetition of them was a help to liberation. A mantra is sometimes given by a spiritual teacher to a disciple as an INITIATION.

Mara In Buddhism, the evil one, temptation.

Marduk Babylonian deity who superseded the Sumerian god Enlil. He was associated with the sun and with vegetation. He was addressed as Bel, the Supreme Lord.

Marriage, sacred A religious rite involving real or simulated sexual intercourse which represents the marriage of earth and sky in the fertilization of the soil and the growth of the crops.

Mars Roman war god, regarded second only to Jupiter. Soldiers sacrificed to him before and after battle. Originally he was probably a god of agriculture.

Martyr ('witness') Title originally applied to Christians who died rather than renounce their faith during times of persecution. Now a term applied to anyone who dies for a religious belief.

Mary, the mother of Jesus Because of her role in the divine plan of salvation, Mary is honoured by all Christians and venerated by Roman Catholic and Eastern Orthodox Christians. The Gospels describe her as divinely chosen to be the mother of the Saviour. Roman Catholic churches have attributed an intercessory role to Mary, and developed other doctrines concerning her nature.

Masoretes A group of Jewish scholars from the Babylonian and Palestinian schools who from the seventh to the eleventh centuries ce supplied the text of the Hebrew Bible with vowel points and divided it up into sentences and paragraphs. They also tried to exclude copyists' errors and noted all the variant readings they found.

Mass Name for the Christian Eucharist derived from the words of dismissal. The standard Roman Catholic term, it emphasizes the sacrificial aspect of the rite.

Matsuri Japanese name for a solemn celebration intended to invoke worship of the

SHINTO gods and obedience to their moral will. They take place at stated intervals in Shinto sanctuaries.

Maya (1) Illusion or deception in HINDU thought. *Maya* is concerned with the diverse phenomenal world perceived by the senses. It is the trick of *maya* to convince people that this is all that exists and thus blind them to the reality of BRAHMAN and the oneness of existence. (2) Legendary mother of the BUDDHA (1). (3) People of an ancient Central American empire which spread from Yucatan to El Salvador. Mayan civilization was at its height around 300–900 CE and was finally broken up by the Spaniards in the sixteenth century. The Maya developed a complex calendar and a form of writing. Their gods were linked with nature symbols, the most important of which was a double-headed snake. (*See also* CHAC.)

Mecca Holy city of Islam, in Saudi Arabia, the birthplace of MUHAMMAD, and later the base for his MUSLIM state after its conquest in 630 CE. Pilgrimage to Mecca, HAJJ, is one of the FIVE PILLARS OF ISLAM and all Muslims are required to face Mecca to perform ritual prayer five times a day.

Medicine man *see* WITCH DOCTOR.

Medina Formerly Yathrib, city 100 miles/169 km north of MECCA, the political base for MUHAMMAD from 622 CE until his conquest of Mecca. Pilgrims from Medina were among the first to accept and spread Muhammad's message. The city contains the site of Muhammad's tomb.

Meditation Deep and continuous reflection, practised in many religions with a variety of aims, e.g. to attain self-realization or, in theistic religions, to attain union with the divine will. Many religions teach a correct posture, method of breathing, and ordering of thoughts for meditation.

Medium One who is possessed by the spirit of a dead person or a DIVINITY and, losing his or her individual identity, becomes the mouthpiece for the other's utterance.

Megaliths Large stone monuments dating from the late NEOLITHIC PERIOD. Their original function is uncertain but they mark burial mounds and temples and they may have served as a calendar of times and seasons.

Meher Baba (1894–1969 CE) Indian spiritual leader, regarded by his followers as an AVATAR. From 1925 until his death he did not speak once.

Mencius (b. 371 BCE) Confucian teacher who expanded and developed CONFUCIUS's teachings. He believed that the universe followed a moral order and that knowledge of this order could be attained by MEDITATION.

Mendelssohn, Moses (1729–86 CE) German Jewish rationalist philosopher who taught that the three central propositions of JUDAISM are: the existence of God; providence; the immortality of the soul. He believed these to be founded on pure reason and to be the basis of all religion. The revelation to the Jews preserves the JEWS as an ethnic entity. He translated the PENTATEUCH into German and encouraged Jews to become more involved in European culture.

Mercury Roman messenger god, identified with the Greek HERMES. He presided over trade.

Merit In BUDDHISM the fruit of good actions which can be devoted to the welfare of other beings. The idea develops in MAHAYANA, where it is believed that the BODHISATTVAS have acquired almost infinite supplies of merit which they can transfer to believers.

Merlin Bard and magician in the romances of the CELTS, later the mentor of ARTHUR. He has become a popular figure in some forms of contemporary Pagan spirituality.

Messiah ('anointed one') A HEBREW word referring to the person chosen by God to be king. (1) After the end of the Israelite monarchy it came to refer to a figure who would restore ISRAEL, gathering the tribes together and ushering in the KINGDOM OF GOD. JUDAISM has known several false messiahs (*see* ZEVI, SHABBETAI). Modern Jews are divided as to whether the messiah is a symbolic or a representative figure and whether the founding of the Jewish state is in any way a prelude to his coming. (2) In the Christian NEW TESTAMENT, JESUS OF NAZARETH is described by messianic titles, e.g. messiah, CHRIST, 'the King', 'the One who Comes'. The account of Jesus' entry into JERUSALEM is deliberately phrased in messianic terms. Jesus himself was cautious about claiming to be messiah, probably because of its political overtones.

Methodist churches Churches deriving from those which joined the Methodist Conference, first established in 1784 by John WESLEY. They are now spread worldwide, promoting EVANGELISM and social concern.

Mezuzah ('doorpost') Parchment (often cased) and inscribed with the SHEMA placed on the door frame of a Jewish house.

Middle Way The BUDDHA's description of his teaching as a mean between the extremes of sensuality and asceticism. It is designed to lead to NIRVANA.

Midgard/Middle Earth The home of human beings according to Norse cosmology. Made from the body of the primeval giant, Ymir, it was defended by Thor from attack by giants. Midgard is the middle of the nine worlds. It is now part of contemporary HEATHEN belief. It has also been popularized in J. R. R. Tolkien's *The Lord of the Rings*.

Midrash A method of exposition of HEBREW texts designed to reveal the inner meaning of the TORAH. Great attention to detail was paid because the texts were believed to be of divine origin. The method was originally oral; the most important midrashim were recorded and written down.

Mihrab Semi-circular recess in the wall of a MOSQUE which indicates the direction of the holy city MECCA, which is the direction for MUSLIM prayer.

Mimir In Norse mythology, the fount of wisdom who guards the well of knowledge at the root of YGGDRASIL. He is ODIN's mentor. In one version of his MYTH, Odin comes to drink from the well and has to sacrifice an eye to do so; in another Mimir's head is cut off and brought to Odin, who preserves it as a talking head which gives him advice.

Minaret (from the Arabic for lighthouse) A tower attached to a MOSQUE from which the call to prayer, *adhan*, is broadcast to the MUSLIM community.

Mindfulness Buddhist method of contemplative analysis. It has two uses in MEDITATION, where it refers to the practice of observing the arising and passing away of different mental states until one arrives at detachment; in daily life, where it refers to a quality of carefulness in thought, speech, and action which prevents the accumulation of bad KARMA.

Ming Chinese emperor (first century CE) of the Han dynasty who, according to tradition, introduced Buddhist scriptures from north-west India. According to tradition he had a dream of a golden man, which he took to be a revelation of the BUDDHA.

Minister (I) A lay or ordained Christian who has been authorized to perform spiritual functions (ministries, literally 'service') in the CHURCH. (2) General title for any member of the clergy, especially those of Protestant denominations.

Minoan religion Religion of the Bronze Age civilization of Crete. The Minoans probably worshipped the MOTHER GODDESS and reverenced SACRED SNAKES and SACRED BULLS.

Miracle An event which appears to defy rational explanation and is attributed to divine intervention.

Mishnah A compilation of Jewish oral teachings undertaken by Rabbi JUDAH HANASI in around 200 CE. It quickly became second in authority only to the HEBREW BIBLE and formed the basis of the TALMUD. The Mishnah helped Jewish teaching to survive in a period of persecution when the future of the SANHEDRIN was in doubt.

Missal Liturgical book containing all that is said or sung throughout the year at the celebration of the MASS. It also includes appropriate directions.

Mission The outreach of a religion to the unconverted. Whereas understandings of mission vary from faith to faith, the various aims of mission usually include spiritual conversion. However, mission is often conceived more holistically and concerns, not just spiritual conversion, but the transformation of all areas of life. It addresses injustice, suffering, poverty, racism, sexism, and all forms of oppression.

Missionaries Those who propagate a religious faith among people of a different faith. BUDDHISM and CHRISTIANITY have been the most notable missionary religions.

Mithra Originally a god of the Indo-Iranians, he was worshipped in the Hindu VEDAS as Mitra and was an important figure in ZOROASTRIANISM, where he was particularly associated with ideas on judgment and the priesthood. To this day, the term for Zoroastrian FIRE TEMPLES is *dar-i Mihr*,

'courts of Mithra'. To the Romans he was the god Mithras of MITHRAISM. (*See also* SOL INVICTUS.)

Mithraeum In MITHRAISM a cave-like sanctuary housing a statue of MITHRA slaying the bull.

Mithraism Religion of MITHRA which flourished throughout the early Roman empire, but concentrated in Rome, the Rhine Valley, and what is now Hungary and Romania. Popular among soldiers, it stressed the ethical values of courage and endurance. It was not open to women. (*See also* SOL INVICTUS.)

Moderator MINISTER of the PRESBYTERIAN CHURCH appointed to constitute and preside over one of the courts that govern the life of the church.

Mohammed *see* MUHAMMAD.

Moksha SANSKRIT word meaning liberation from the cycle of birth, death, and rebirth. Permanent spiritual perfection experienced by an enlightened soul after the physical body has died. No further incarnations will be endured.

Monism The belief that there is only one basic reality in spite of the appearance and experience of diversity. It applies particularly to the beliefs of the HINDU philosopher SHANKARA. (*See also* ADVAITA.)

Monk A member of a male religious community living under vows which usually include poverty, chastity, and the wearing of a distinctive form of dress. Monastic orders are found in Christianity, Buddhism, Hinduism, and Jainism. The Buddhist monk is a member of a SANGHA and, additionally to the FIVE PRECEPTS, vows to eat only at set times, not to handle money, use a high bed, use scent, or go to stage performances. (*See also* BENEDICT.)

Monotheism The belief that there is one supreme GOD who contains all the attributes and characteristics of divinity.

Moon, Sun Myung (1920–2012) Korean engineer, businessman, and founder of the FAMILY FEDERATION FOR WORLD PEACE AND UNIFICATION. He claimed to have authoritative visions of Jesus. Members of the federation accorded him a high, if publicly ill-defined, status.

Moonies *see* FAMILY FEDERATION FOR WORLD PEACE AND UNIFICATION.

Moravians Protestant pietist Christians continuing the simple ideals of an earlier, mid-fifteenth century group, 'The Bohemian Brethren' or Unity of the Brethren. After Count Nikolaus Ludwig von Zinzendorf allowed Moravian refugees to live on his land in 1722 CE they became particularly active MISSIONARIES.

Mormonism Unorthodox Christian sect founded in 1830 CE in the USA on the basis of the visionary experiences of Joseph SMITH. Under its second leader, Brigham Young (1807–77 CE), the Mormons journeyed to found Salt Lake City (1847), where they developed into a strong missionary community. Mormons accept the BIBLE and the BOOK OF MORMON and some other revealed writings. The Mormon Church, officially the 'Church of Jesus Christ of Latter-day Saints', has about 14 million members, half of them in the USA and Canada.

Moroni *see* SMITH, JOSEPH.

Moses The father of JUDAISM who received the TORAH from God on Mount SINAI, having led the people of ISRAEL out of captivity in Egypt. The first five books of the Hebrew BIBLE are traditionally ascribed to him.

Mosque MUSLIM place of public worship, consisting usually of an outer courtyard for ablutions and a large unfurnished inner area where Muslims kneel, sit, or prostrate themselves in worship. On Fridays special prayers are offered in the afternoon and the IMAM delivers the sermon. Many mosques have gender segregation.

Mother goddess/Great Mother The personification of nature and the natural processes of fertility and growth connected with the earth. Worship of a mother goddess was universal in the Ancient Near East, Asia, and Europe (*see* CYBELE, DEMETER, INANNA, ISHTAR, ISIS). Her worship continues in HINDUISM, where the consorts of SHIVA (DURGA, KALI, PARVATI) have some of her characteristics. There is some revival of her worship in feminism, ECO-FEMINISM, and among adherents to the GAIA hypothesis and practitioners of WITCHCRAFT.

Muezzin Person who calls the MUSLIM faithful to prayer.

Mufti A canon lawyer in ISLAM who gives formal legal advice on questions brought to him in accordance with the QUR'AN, the SUNNAH, and the law schools.

Muhammad (c. 570–632 CE) Prophet and apostle of ISLAM, the final messenger of God whose message, the QUR'AN, sums up and completes the previous revelations to the Jews and Christians. Muhammad saw the expansion of ISLAM in terms of military conquest and political organization and he was outstandingly successful as a commander and ruler in MEDINA and later MECCA.

Muharram A commemoration by Shi'ite MUSLIMS (see SHI'A) of the murder of Hussein ibn 'Ali, Muhammad's grandson, on the tenth day of the month Muharram. A passion play is performed depicting the martyrdom.

Mujtahid MUSLIM teacher who gives a ruling, legal decision, or deduction on the basis of his own learning or authority (see IJTIHAD). In Shi'a Islam, a *mujtahid* has great authority.

Mullah An Arabic word which means a 'teacher' or 'scholar' – an exponent of the sacred law of ISLAM.

Muslim 'One who submits' to the will of God, a follower of ISLAM.

Muslim brotherhood Egyptian organization founded in 1928 CE by Hasan al-Banna. The brotherhood was influential after World War II and worked against ZIONISM and Westernization. It is active in Egypt and in many other Middle Eastern and North African countries.

Mystery religions Cults based on ancient MYTHS which flourished in Greece, in Rome and throughout the Roman empire. Initiates went through a dramatic and secret ceremony in which they identified with the divinity at the centre of the myth and experienced salvation and the assurance of immortality.

Mystic One who seeks direct personal experience of the divine and may use PRAYER, MEDITATION or various ascetic practices to concentrate the attention.

Mysticism The search for direct personal experience of the divine. There is a distinction between seeing mysticism as leading to identification with GOD (as is common in HINDUISM) and as leading to a union with God's love and will (as in ISLAM, JUDAISM, and CHRISTIANITY).

Myth A sacred story which originates and circulates within a particular community. Some aetiological myths explain puzzling physical phenomena or customs, institutions and practices whose origin in the community would otherwise be mysterious. (See also CREATION MYTH.)

N

Nagarjuna (c. 150–250 CE) MAHAYANA Buddhist philosopher who taught that the truth of reality was void or emptiness.

Nakayama Miki (1798–1887 CE) Founder of the Japanese religion TENRIKYO. In 1838 she was possessed by a divine being who announced he was the Creator and true God and gave her a series of revelations. Nakayama Miki gave away all her money and practised spiritual healing. Her teachings attracted a wide following. Adherents believe she is still alive, in non-physical form, in the shrine built on the site of her home at the city of Tenri.

Namu Myoho Renge Kyo Formula coined by NICHIREN as the essential truth of the LOTUS SUTRA. It means 'Reverence to the wonderful truth of the *Lotus Sutra*' and it is used by a variety of sects based on Nichiren's Buddhist teachings.

Nanak, Guru (1469–1539 CE) Indian religious teacher and founder of the SIKH religion. He intended to reconcile HINDUS and MUSLIMS and travelled widely preaching a monotheistic faith (see MONOTHEISM) which was influenced by BHAKTI and SUFISM. He appointed a successor to continue his teachings.

Native American Church Religious organization of Native Americans founded in the 1880s. It teaches a synthesis of native religion and Christianity. Its rituals include the ceremonial use of peyote, a spineless cactus containing the hallucinogenic substance mescaline.

Nature spirits Spirits of trees, hills, rivers, plants, and animals which are acknowledged with prayers and offerings in most INDIGENOUS RELIGIONS.

Navjote INITIATION ceremony of the PARSIS at which a child is invested with a sacred shirt and thread symbolic of 'new birth' to adulthood.

Near-death experience Visionary sequence of events occasionally reported by those resuscitated. Features include a sensation of being OUT OF BODY, a journey down a long tunnel, the appearance of a being of light who is sometimes identified as CHRIST or an ANGEL, and a flashback of one's past life. Feelings of bliss and oneness, which remain for years afterwards, are common.

Nembutsu ('Hail to the BUDDHA AMIDA') The formula of faith taught by the Japanese Buddhist teacher HONEN.

Nemesis Greek goddess who personified the retribution due to evil deeds. Her vengeance was regarded to be inevitable and exact.

Nemeton 'Sacred place' in Celtic religion, usually an enclosed woodland grove.

Neolithic period The New Stone Age, from about 10,000 BCE until the Early Bronze Age.

Neo-Platonism Religious and philosophical movement from the third to the sixth centuries CE. It used the teachings of PLATO as a basis for ascetic practices and mystical experience. Its principal architect was PLOTINUS.

Neptune Italian water god who became associated with POSEIDON and acquired his mythology.

Nestorianism CHRISTIAN HERESY that claimed that two separate persons, human and divine, existed in the incarnate CHRIST (as opposed to the orthodox view that God assumed human nature as one person in Christ). Although condemned in 431 CE it continued to flourish in Persia. A few groups of Nestorians survive in the present day.

New Age With roots in particularly Theosophy, the term refers to alternative spiritualities which emerged in the mid-1960s principally on the west coast of the USA and spread throughout North America and Europe. The movements are characterized by a concern to realize the spiritual potential of the individual self, which is often believed to be divine. Also common is the belief that, as we move from the astrological age of Pisces into the age of Aquarius, we are witnessing a spiritual renaissance, a New Age of non-hierarchical, non-patriarchal, eco-friendly self-spirituality. Drawing from discoveries in physics and cosmology, their teachings claim to revive ancient mystical traditions of East and West. They emphasize healing, a healthy and balanced lifestyle, and expansion of self-awareness through meditation and personal counselling.

New religion There is a scholarly debate over the precise definition of a 'new' religion. Some scholars limit the definition to those religions that have emerged since 1945 (i.e. since the end of World War II) or, indeed, even later (i.e. since 1960). However, this excludes many older new religions such as the JEHOVAH'S WITNESSES. Hence, other scholars prefer the following general working definition: a religion, sect, or spirituality that has emerged or that has arisen to prominence during the twentieth century.

New Testament The second division of the Christian Bible, comprising the GOSPELS, the Acts of the Apostles, the Revelation of John, and various EPISTLES.

New Year, Jewish *see* ROSH HASHANAH.

Nibbana PALI word for NIRVANA.

Nicene Creed The fullest version of the orthodox Christian CREED, compiled to counter Christological heresies in the fourth century.

Nichiren (1222–1282 CE) Japanese Buddhist reformer who taught that the LOTUS SUTRA contained the ultimate truth and that it could be compressed into a sacred formula: NAMU MYOHO RENGE KYO. He denounced all other forms of Buddhism. When the Mongols threatened Japan he preached a fiery nationalism, urging the nation to convert to true Buddhism. His teachings have provided the inspiration for some modern Buddhist sects (*see* NEW RELIGIONS).

Night Journey The journey of MUHAMMAD from the temple in MECCA to the TEMPLE OF JERUSALEM, which is described in the QUR'AN. Tradition asserts that he travelled on a winged horse accompanied by GABRIEL (Jibril). By the sacred rock of Abraham, Muhammad met Abraham, Moses, and Jesus. Then he ascended up a ladder of light into the presence of ALLAH. He returned bringing instructions for the faithful.

Nihongi SHINTO scripture which contains the Japanese CREATION MYTH and legends of the gods. It was originally written in classical Chinese.

Ninigi The son of Amaterasu in SHINTO belief. At a time of chaos in heaven Amaterasu sent him down to rule the islands of Japan, making him the first Japanese EMPEROR.

Nirvana ('going out', 'becoming cool') In BUDDHISM, the state when DUKKHA ceases because the flames of desire are no longer fuelled. It is a state of unconditioned-ness and uncompounded-ness beyond any form of known or imagined existence.

Nkulukulu ('the old, old one') Zulu name for God.

Noble Eightfold Path In BUDDHISM, the way to extinguish desire by adopting right views; right resolves; right speech; right action; right livelihood; right effort; right mindfulness; right concentration/meditation.

Non-realism Movement arising from DEATH OF GOD theology which claims that religious doctrines refer only to human sources of value and do not refer to objective reality.

Norns The Fates of Norse religion. Of giant origin, they are immensely powerful, controlling the destiny of people. They tend and water the trunk of YGGDRASIL. The names of the three norns mean Past, Present, and Future. Their association with time makes them more powerful than the immortal gods of ASGARD, since even they are bound to predestined fate.

Numen In Roman religion, the divine power suffusing nature. From this concept Rudolf Otto developed the idea that the root of religion was a sense of holy power. This he termed the 'numinous'.

Nun A member of a religious community of women, as found in CHRISTIANITY, BUDDHISM, HINDUISM, and JAINISM. Nuns live under vows usually including poverty, and chastity and often the wearing of a distinctive form of dress. (*See also* BENEDICT.)

Nut The sky goddess of Egyptian mythology whose body is lined with stars. Every evening she swallows the sun and gives birth to it again each morning.

O

Obeah Religious and magical practices of the West Indies which are usually of West African origin. (*See also* VOODOO.)

Occult Teachings, arts, and practices that are concerned with what is hidden and mysterious, as with WITCHCRAFT, ALCHEMY, and DIVINATION.

Odin Chief of the Norse gods. Originally he was a wild wind god who led the spirits of the dead through the air. The Romans associated him with MERCURY. In later mythology he visits the earth as The Wanderer. There are two myths of his search for wisdom: the first that he sacrificed an eye as the price for his drinking from the well of MIMIR; the second that he hanged himself upon YGGDRASIL. He is associated with the gallows and there is evidence that victims were hanged on trees in sacrifice to him. As Allfather, Odin watched over the nine worlds and was brought daily reports by two ravens. Variants of his name include Woden (Anglo-Saxon) and Wotan (German).

Odinism *see* HEATHENISM.

Ohrmazd *see* AHURA MAZDA.

Old Catholic churches A group of national churches which have separated from Rome. Since 1932 they have been in communion with the Church of England.

Old Testament The HEBREW BIBLE as the first division of the Christian BIBLE.

Olympus, Mount The highest mountain in Greece (9572 feet/2917m), held to be the home of the twelve greatest Greek gods under the leadership of ZEUS.

Om mani padme hum ('the jewel in the LOTUS') Tibetan mantra whose six syllables are held to correspond to the six worlds of Tibetan Buddhist teaching: om, 'gods'; ma, 'anti-gods'; ni, 'humans'; pad, 'animals'; mi, 'hungry ghosts'; hum, 'hell'. Each world is present as a state of the human mind. The mantra sums up the whole of human existence and is an indispensable aid to self-realization.

Omnipotence All-powerful.

Omniscience All-knowing. Simultaneous knowledge of all things.

Option for the poor Decision of Latin American churches following Medellín

Conference of 1968 and Puebla Conference of 1978 to adopt the tenets of LIBERATION THEOLOGY by insisting that God chose the poor and willed social justice.

Ordination Rite in the Christian CHURCH by which chosen individuals are authorized as MINISTERS of the Word of God and the SACRAMENTS. In BUDDHISM the term denotes entry into the SANGHA.

Origen (c. 184–c. 254 CE) Theologian who tried to present biblical CHRISTIANITY using the ideas of HELLENISM. He believed that all creatures would eventually be saved, a view condemned as heretical in 553 CE.

Original sin The SIN of Adam and Eve, the first human beings, in eating from the forbidden tree in the Garden of Eden, expressing independence from God. In Christian teaching the inevitable consequence is seen as separation from God; human creatures inherit Adam and Eve's 'fallen' state, resulting in the need for SALVATION.

Orphism Religious movement which began in Thrace and flourished in the sixth century BCE. It was based on MYTHS of DIONYSUS and Orpheus, who was the supreme minstrel of Greek mythology. It taught a way of liberation through ASCETICISM and held also a doctrine of REINCARNATION.

Orthodox Judaism Traditional JUDAISM which is Talmudic (*see* TALMUD) in belief and practice, and is the largest of the modern groupings .

Orthodoxy CHRISTIANITY as practised by the Eastern Churches after the GREAT SCHISM. Orthodox Christians are found mostly in Eastern Europe, the Balkan States, and Russia.

Osiris Egyptian vegetation god, the force behind the cycle of growth and decay. Mythology tells how he had originally lived on earth as a king. He was murdered and later dismembered by his jealous brother, SETH. His wife, Isis, searched for the pieces of his body and restored him to life. As a symbol of death and resurrection, Osiris became associated with life after death and the judgment of individual souls.

Ottoman Empire (1453–1918 CE) The empire of the Ottoman Turks who were converted to ISLAM. It stretched from the Middle East to the Balkans and at its height to the frontiers of Austria. The Ottomans supported SUNNI orthodoxy against heterodox DERVISH movements. The empire went into slow decline in the eighteenth century and its religious life stagnated. Muslim communities in the Balkans have been vulnerable since the fall of Communism in Eastern Europe.

Out-of-body experience Sensation of separation of the self from the body occasionally reported in mystical or drug-induced trance, or as part of a NEAR-DEATH EXPERIENCE.

P

Pachacamac Leader of the gods in the religion of the INCAS. A great shrine was built for him near the modern city of Lima, Peru.

Pachamama MOTHER GODDESS in the INDIGENOUS RELIGION of the Andes.

Pagan/Paganism The word 'pagan' (derived from the Latin term *pagus*, which literally means 'from the countryside' or 'rural') was first used in a general religious sense by the early Christians to describe the non-Christian gentile religions. It is now generally used to refer to a broad range of nature-venerating religious traditions. Whilst the term 'Neo-Paganism' is sometimes used by academics and even by some devotees, particularly in the USA (e.g. the Church of All Worlds), practitioners generally prefer the simpler term 'Paganism'. Because many contemporary Pagans do seek to learn from indigenous culture, there are some continuities between the two forms of religion. While there are many forms of Paganism, arguably there are three principal traditions. The largest and most influential of these is WICCA. A second contemporary Pagan tradition is DRUIDRY. Finally, within contemporary Paganism there is a tradition often referred to simply as the 'Northern Tradition'. Northern Tradition Pagans often prefer the appellative 'Heathen' rather than 'Pagan'. 'Heathen' means roughly the same as 'Pagan', but is derived from Germanic languages rather than Latin – it is also a term that has been used pejoratively by Christians. The Northern Tradition/HEATHENISM draws inspiration principally from Anglo-Saxon, Norse, and Icelandic pre-Christian mythology, religion, and culture.

Pagoda A Buddhist building in south-east Asia built over Buddhist RELICS and often characterized by a series of superimposed spires. It is an evolution of the ancient STUPA.

Palaeolithic period ('Old Stone Age') The prehistoric age covering from around 2.6 million years ago to c. 10,000 BCE.

Pali Vernacular language of northern India in the BUDDHA's time, and hence the language of early BUDDHISM and the THERAVADA SCRIPTURES. It is related to SANSKRIT.

Pali Canon The basic Buddhist SCRIPTURES – the only scriptures valid among THERAVADA Buddhists. Traditionally the collection began soon after the BUDDHA's death when his followers met to receive the TIPITAKA/TRIPITAKA or 'three baskets' of his teaching. The precise wording of the canon was fixed at a council in 29 BCE.

Pan Arcadian fertility god, patron of shepherds and herdsmen, usually portrayed with goat's horns and legs.

Panchen Lama Title given to one of the leading abbots of TIBETAN BUDDHISM, whose authority paralleled that of the DALAI LAMA, though its emphasis was more on spiritual matters. The Panchen Lama was believed to be a reincarnation of AMITABHA.

Pantheism The belief that all reality is in essence divine.

Parousia *see* SECOND COMING.

Parsis Descendants of the ancient Zoroastrian Persians (*see* ZOROASTRIANISM) living in India, mostly near Mumbai (Bombay). They practise an ethical MONOTHEISM with a RITUAL life that expresses the purity of AHURA MAZDA. The roughly 200,000 Zoroastrians in the world today are divided into groups that differ over the religious calendar.

Parsva Important figure in JAINISM. Born a prince around 850 BCE he renounced his throne and became an ascetic, finally gaining omniscience. He is considered to be the twenty-third JINA.

Parvati ('mountaineer') Consort of SHIVA, in HINDU mythology, like Shiva both beautiful and terrifying.

Passover Seven-day Jewish spring festival marking the deliverance from Egypt (*see* EXODUS). Since Talmudic times (*see* TALMUD) the festival has begun with a service in the home where unleavened bread, wine, and bitter herbs symbolize the joys and sorrows of the Exodus. There is then a meal and the evening concludes with psalms and hymns which look to God's final redemption of Israel.

Patriarch (1) 'Father-figure'; especially in family and community; in Judaism and Christianity, refers to the founders of the faith such as Abraham, Isaac, and Jacob. (2) Head of one of the Eastern Orthodox churches. The Ecumenical Patriarch of Constantinople is a figurehead for Orthodox Christians.

Paul Apostle of Christianity who established new churches throughout Asia Minor and Macedonia. Originally a Pharisee, he was converted by a vision of Christ on the road to Damascus. He wrote several New Testament epistles. Tradition asserts that he was beheaded at Rome under Nero.

Penates Spirits or gods who protected the Roman household and family and were guardians over the household stores.

Pentateuch *see* Torah (1).

Pentecost (1) Hellenistic name for Jewish harvest festival, fifty-two days after Passover. More usually called *Shavuot* or the Festival of Weeks. (2) Christian festival marking the coming of the Holy Spirit upon the apostles fifty days after Easter. The second most important Christian festival, it commemorates the beginning of the church (1).

Pentecostal churches Churches which have formed from a renewal movement which started in the USA in the early 1900s. They teach the experience of 'baptism in the Holy Spirit' which shows itself in speaking in tongues (*see* glossolalia) and other 'spiritual gifts'.

Perkons/Perkunas/Perun Supreme god of ancient Russia, particularly associated with thunder and lightning.

Peter Apostle and close follower of Jesus of Nazareth, from whom he received the name Peter, meaning 'rock' in Greek. He held a position of leadership among the early apostles. Tradition asserts that he was martyred in Rome.

Pharaoh In the Bible, the title of the king of Egypt. The reigning king was identified with the god Horus, and was held to be responsible for the fertility of the land. On death the king became Osiris, his body being mummified and buried in a tomb which from the Third Dynasty to the end of the Middle Period might be a pyramid.

Pharisees Jewish anti-nationalistic party that emerged in the time of the Maccabees. They believed that God was universal and taught the individuality of the soul and the resurrection. They prepared the way for the survival of Judaism after the Fall of Jerusalem in 70 ce.

Philo of Alexandria (c. 25 bce–40 ce) Jewish philosopher who tried to reconcile Greek philosophy with the Hebrew scriptures. His commentaries used allegorical devices to penetrate the meaning of scripture. He developed the Greek doctrine of the Logos or Word of God into the status of 'a second God'. His speculations were widely studied by the early Christians.

Philosophy of religion The branch of philosophy which investigates religious experience considering its origin, context, and value.

Phylacteries *see* tephillin.

Pilgrimage A journey to a holy place, undertaken as a commemoration of a past event, as a celebration, or as an act of penance (*see also* hajj). The goal might be a natural feature such as a sacred river or mountain, or the location of a miracle, revelation, or theophany, or the tomb of a hero or saint.

Pilgrim Fathers Puritan Christian group who left England for America in the Mayflower in 1620 ce and founded the colony of Plymouth, Massachusetts.

Plato (c. 427–347 bce) Greek philosopher and pupil of Socrates. He taught the theory of Forms or Ideas, which are eternal prototypes of the phenomena encountered in ordinary experience. Above all is the Form of the Good, which gives unity and value to all the forms. Plato also taught the immortality of the soul.

PL Kyodan ('Perfect Liberty Association') One of the new religions of Japan, founded in 1924 It is based on Shinto but accepts karma from Buddhism and teaches that the ancestors have an influence on the lives

of believers. Its motto is 'life is art' and it sponsors games centres and golf clubs as well as shrines and temples.

Plotinus (c. 205–69 ce) Philosopher and author of Neo-Platonism whose speculations influenced early Christianity. He dealt with the relationship between the world and the soul and blended Platonic teaching with oriental mysticism. His teachings influenced Augustine.

Polytheism The belief in and worship of a variety of gods, who rule over various aspects of the world and life.

Pontifex High priest of Roman religion and member of a guild of priests whose president was the *pontifex maximus*. From the fifth century ce the title was applied to Christian bishops, usually the pope.

Pontius Pilate Roman procurator of the province of Judea 26–36 ce under whose authority Jesus of Nazareth was crucified. Some Eastern Orthodox traditions assert that he killed himself out of remorse.

Pope Bishop of Rome, Vicar of Christ, and head of the Roman Catholic Church, regarded as the successor of Peter. Since the First Vatican Council his pronouncement on matters of faith and doctrine issued *ex cathedra* have been regarded as infallible.

Poseidon Greek god of the seas and waters, usually presented as a tall bearded figure carrying a trident. He is responsible for sea storms and earthquakes and is also 'Lord of Horses'.

Prayer The offering of worship, requests, confessions, or other communication to God or gods publicly or privately, with or without words; often a religious obligation.

Prayer wheels Wheels and cylinders used by Buddhists in Tibet and northern India. They are inscribed with the mantra 'Om mani padme hum', the powerful effect of which is multiplied as the wheels turn.

Preferential Option for the Poor *see* Option for the Poor.

Prehistoric religion Religions dating from the period before the development of writing.

Presbyter ('elder') Term for a Christian minister used in the New Testament interchangeably with bishop. Later it was

INTRODUCTION TO WORLD RELIGIONS

held that the authority of the presbyter (from which comes 'PRIEST') derived from the bishop.

Presbyterian churches REFORMED CHURCHES whose teachings and order of worship reflect Calvinism. They are governed by a pyramid of elected, representative courts.

Priest (1) One authorized to perform priestly functions including mediation between God or gods and humanity, the offerings of SACRIFICE and the performance of RITUAL in many religions. (2) A Christian MINISTER, the term deriving from PRESBYTER.

Progressive Judaism Term covering the Liberal and Reform movements which emerged in JUDAISM in nineteenth-century Europe. Both movements are critical of the Talmudic fundamentalism of ORTHODOX JUDAISM and welcome scientific research on the Bible. They also tend to use the vernacular in worship and interpret the dietary laws more liberally than do the Orthodox.

Propaganda Sacred Congregation for the Propagation of the Faith, a ROMAN CATHOLIC body concerned with MISSION in non-Christian countries. It dates from the COUNTER-REFORMATION, and is now known as the Congregation for the Evangelization of Peoples.

Prophet One who speaks for or as a mouthpiece of God or a god. (1) The Old Testament prophets were social and religious reformers of ISRAEL (3) and Judah and of the people of God in EXILE. They proclaimed God's prospective judgment of Israel; they recalled the people to obedience to God, some offering a hope of a future vindication. (2) In ISLAM the Prophet is MUHAMMAD, who brings the word and judgment of God to final utterance. The authority of the Prophet is an article of the MUSLIM confession of faith, the SHAHADAH.

Prophets, The The second division of the HEBREW BIBLE, including the histories and the prophetic books.

Protestantism Christian faith and order as based on the principles of the REFORMATION. It emphasizes the sole authority of the BIBLE; justification by faith; the priesthood of all believers. Since the nineteenth century it has embraced liberal trends which have stressed the subjective side of religion.

Psalm A sacred song or poem. The Book of Psalms in the BIBLE provides the basis for much Jewish and Christian worship.

Ptah The chief god of Memphis in ancient Egypt, usually depicted bearded, in mummified shape, and carrying three sceptres. He was a creator-god, the patron of craftsmen. Merged with Sokar and OSIRIS, he came to have a role in the rituals ensuring the survival of the dead.

Puja ('reverence') Refers to temple and domestic worship in BUDDHISM and HINDUISM, and to the keeping of rites and ceremonies prescribed by the Brahmins (*see* CASTE SYSTEM).

Puranas A vast corpus of sacred writings (c. 350–950 CE), which include mythologies of Hindu deities and AVATARS of VISHNU, the origins of the cosmos, and of humanity, pilgrimage, ritual, law codes, caste obligations, and so on. There are eighteen principal Puranas, each exalting a member of the *Trimurti* (BRAHMA, VISHNU, SHIVA). They are very important in popular HINDUISM, JAINISM, and BUDDHISM, the most popular being the *Bhagavata Purana*, which deals with Krishna's early life and encourages devotion to him (BHAKTI).

Pure Land Buddhism Buddhist sect founded by a Chinese monk, Hui-Yuan (334–416 CE) who was called the First Patriarch of Pure Land Buddhism. It is characterized by faith in the BODHISATTVA AMITABHA, the creator of a 'pure land' in the west. Through faith his devotees hoped to be transported there after death.

Purgatory In Roman Catholic teaching, the temporary state of punishment and purification for the dead before their admission to heaven. Its existence was denied by the Protestant reformers.

Purim ('lots') Joyful Jewish festival celebrating the story of Esther, wife of the Persian king Xerxes, who defeated the anti-Jewish plot of the king's steward, Haman.

Pyramid Type of Egyptian royal tomb, usually tapering to the top from a square base, constructed between about 2630 and 1640 BCE. Pyramid-shaped structures are also found in Mesoamerica.

Pythagoras (c. 570–500 BCE) Greek philosopher, musician, and mathematician who taught that number was the basis of reality and that mathematics offered insight

into the invisible world. He was influenced by ORPHISM, and taught REINCARNATION and a strict vegetarianism.

Q

Qiyas ('analogy') Principle of Islamic lawmaking by which the answer to a problem concerning a *hadith* may be inferred from the answer to an analogous problem in the QUR'AN or the SUNNAH.

Quakers Members of the Religious Society of Friends, deriving from a puritan group which formed around George Fox in the 1650s. They have no SACRAMENTS and no ordained ministry. Instead authority derives from the 'inner light of the living Christ' in each believer.

Quetzalcoatl Mythological figure in MAYA and AZTEC religion. He may have been a king of a pre-Aztec civilization. He is associated with the rediscovery of the complex Mayan calendar. His name derives from the sacred Quetzal bird. In mythology he is a god of the air who descended to earth and taught humanity the arts of civilization. He opposed the practice of human SACRIFICE. His activities aroused the wrath of another deity and he fled in a boat made of serpent skin. He is often symbolized by a feathered serpent. The name Quetzalcoatl was given to the high priests of Aztec religion.

Qur'an The central sacred text in Islam – the Muslim holy scripture. Muslims believe the Qur'an, meaning 'recitation', was revealed to the PROPHET MUHAMMAD, piecemeal, by God via Jibril (Gabriel) and is written in Arabic. All Muslims believe the Qur'an to be divine in origin. It is literally divine thought and law in words, preserved in the 'Mother of the Book' (also called 'the Preserved Tablet') inscribed in heaven. It was revealed bit by bit to Muhammad.

Quraysh The tribe of MUHAMMAD, who opposed his attack on idolatry because they were the traditional custodians of the KA'BA. They were defeated in Muhammad's attack on MECCA in 630 CE.

R

Ra *see* RE

Rabbi ('my master') Jewish religious teacher and interpreter of the TORAH. In modern Judaism he or she is a minister to the community, a preacher, and a leader of synagogue worship. Not all Jewish traditions accept female rabbis.

Rabbinic Judaism The religion of the rabbis who – beginning from the second centruy ce – expanded the interpretation of the Talmud and produced authoritative codes of laws, responses, views, and judgments, mostly in the form of correspondence with particular communities.

Radha In Hinduism, friend and love of the god Vishnu as his avatar Krishna. The love of Krishna and Radha is a frequent theme of bhakti devotion where it is seen as a type of the love between God and the soul. The frank eroticism of the stories of Radha is not welcomed by all Hindus.

Radhakrishnan, Sarvepalli (1888–1975 ce) Indian philosopher who became vice-president and then president of India. He taught that there is a basic unity of all religions and that Hinduism is a useful meeting ground because of its breadth and tolerance.

Radical Theology Term sometimes used for theology committed to left-wing politics or for theology that tends towards Non-realism.

Ragnarök The doom of the Norse gods, the end of the world order. Odin and the gods ride out with the dead heroes of Valhalla against Loki and the hosts of Hel. A great wolf swallows Odin and the whole creation is dissolved in fire. Out of the chaos emerges a new heaven and a new earth. There are Christian influences in some accounts of Ragnarök.

Rama The seventh incarnation of Vishnu according to Hindu tradition. His exploits in love and war are described in the Ramayana. He is the epitome of righteousness and moral virtue.

Ramadan Islamic lunar month in which Muslims are obliged to fast from food and water between sunrise and sunset. The old and sick, pregnant women, and nursing mothers are exempt, though they are expected, if possible, to make it up later.

Ramakrishna (1834–86 ce) Hindu Brahmin (*see* caste system) who taught that all religions are paths to the same goal. He laid the foundation of Hindu universalism. He was a devotee of Kali, though philosophically he adhered to the teaching of Shankara.

Ramakrishna Mission Indian religious order founded in 1897 by Vivekananda. Its aims are to teach Vedanta and to care for the sick and needy. It has dispensaries, libraries and welfare centres throughout India and has teaching branches in Europe and the USA.

Ramanuja (d. 1137 ce) Indian philosopher who opposed Shankara's stress on the oneness of being and denied that the divine lord belonged to a lower order of reality. He believed God and the world were related like body and soul, inseparable but distinct. He was a devotee of Vishnu, and believed in the validity of personal devotion to God.

Ramayana One of the two great epics of the Hindu scriptures compiled in the second or first century bce. Ascribe to the sage Valmiki, it tells of the life of the avatar Rama.

Rammohan Roy (1772–1833 ce) Hindu reformer who founded the Brahmo Samaj, an ethical organization with monotheistic tendencies, in opposition to the idolatry of popular devotion. He believed the Vedas taught monotheism, though he also used Christian and Muslim ideas.

Rastafarianism Religious and political movement centred in the Caribbean. It is a cult of Ras Tafari, better known as Haile Selassie (1892–1975 ce), Emperor of Ethiopia (1930–74). Many Rastafarians (not all) are distinguished by keeping their hair in 'dreadlocks' and by their use of cannabis in worship. Some prefer the term Rastafari or Rastafari Movement. They are linked with the reggae style of music, which they use to express their political and religious aspirations. The singer Bob Marley has become one of the heroes of the movement.

Re Sun god and supreme god of the religion of ancient Egypt.

Rebirth Buddhist modification of reincarnation in the light of the anatta teaching. The karmic (*see* karma) residue of one's life and actions are reclothed in the attributes and qualities acquired in the previous life. After a while this karmic 'bundle' is reborn.

Redemption God's saving work of buying back or recovering what is his. In Judaism it refers to the restoration of Israel; in Christianity to the ransoming of sinners from the power of sin and death.

Red Hats Unreformed branch of Tibetan Buddhism whose practices owe much to the former Tibetan religion of Bon, or Bön.

Reformation The movement within Western Christianity between the fourteenth and the seventeenth centuries which led to the separation of the Protestant churches from Rome. The main issue was the authority of the Pope, but doctrinal issues such as the precise meaning of the Eucharist and the authority and accessibility of Scripture were also important.

Reformed churches Churches which inherit the Calvinist Protestant tradition, including Presbyterians, Independents, Calvinistic Methodists, and Congregationalists.

Reiki The term is often translated as 'Universal Life Force Energy'. It is a method of spiritual healing founded in Japan by Mikao Usui (1865–1926) and introduced into the West by Hawayo Takata. It teaches the existence of a universal energy, *ki*, which is similar to the Chinese notion of *chi*. When the flow of this energy is blocked, the result is a range of ailments, both psychological and physical. Reiki practitioners are able to channel and manipulate this energy by laying their hands on (or over) a person's body.

Reincarnation The belief that individual souls survive death and are reborn to live again in a different body, thus passing through a series of lives. Held in pre-Aryan India, the belief is associated with the doctrine of karma. Some traditions believe rebirth is possible only in human bodies, others envisage hellish or heavenly states, while others suggest a transmigration in which human souls are tied to animal or vegetable forms. Some Hindu apologists explain the doctrine as a mythical way of speaking about the continuity of the human race.

Relics Bones or remains of saints, venerated and accredited with miraculous powers in many religions.

Religion (from Latin *religare*, 'to tie something tightly') A system of belief and worship, held by a community who may express its religion through shared MYTHS, DOCTRINES, ethical teachings, RITUALS, or the remembrance of special experiences.

Renunciation Giving up ownership of material possessions. In some religions, such as Buddhism, renunciation extends to psychological detachment from material possessions, including one's own body.

Restorationism Movement to restore the CHURCH to a pristine state in which the KINGDOM OF GOD is established through a charismatically ordained ministry. Restorationists see themselves as EVANGELICALS and Pentecostalists, but with a new edge to their commitment. Many HOUSE CHURCHES promote a Restorationist theology.

Resurrection (1) The Christian belief that JESUS OF NAZARETH was raised from death by God the Father who thus vindicated him as MESSIAH and revealed his defeat of death and SIN. (2) The raising of all the dead for JUDGMENT as taught in JUDAISM, CHRISTIANITY, and ISLAM.

Rinzai Zen School of ZEN which employs startling techniques (e.g. KOANS) to induce SATORI.

Rissho Kosei Kai An offshoot of the Reiyukai movement which is spreading the teachings of NICHIREN Buddhism beyond the boundaries of Japan. The sect claims over 6.5 million members.

Rita The cosmic order as understood in the Hindu VEDAS. It is the principle of ethical and physical organization throughout the universe and is the work of the sky god VARUNA.

Rites of passage Religious ceremonies which mark the transition from one state of life to another. In many religions these transitional periods are felt to be dangerous and to require spiritual protection. Examples include birth rites, INITIATION rites, marriage rites, and funeral rites.

Ritual Religious ceremonial performed according to a set pattern of words, movements, and symbolic actions. Rituals may involve the dramatic re-enactment of ancient MYTHS featuring gods and heroes, performed to ensure the welfare of the community.

Roma The personification of the city of Rome, worshipped by the Romans as a goddess.

Roman Catholic Catholic CHRISTIAN who recognizes the authority of the POPE, the Bishop of Rome.

Rosh Hashanah The Jewish New Year, celebrated as the anniversary of creation. The liturgy is penitential in tone and looks forward to the KINGDOM OF GOD and the MESSIAH. The blowing of the ram's horn, *shofar*, proclaims God as king of the universe.

Rosicrucianism Mystical system founded in seventeenth-century Germany and based on an account of a secret brotherhood founded 'to improve mankind by the discovery of the true philosophy'. Several societies came into being based on this originally fictitious 'Meritorious Order of the Rosy Cross' with its private language and magical alphabet. They applied themselves to studies such as ALCHEMY.

Rugievit Slavic god with seven faces from the island of Rügen.

Rumi, Jalal al-Din (d. 1273 CE) Sufi MYSTIC and poet, author of the *Mathnavi*, and founder of a DERVISH order. He was a nature mystic and often used love and wine as allegories of the experience of the divine.

Russell, C. T. (Charles Taze) (1852–1916 CE) US Bible scholar who started a periodical called *Zion's Watchtower* after being influenced by speculation about the return of CHRIST. This grew into the JEHOVAH'S WITNESSES movement.

Russian Orthodox Church The principal church of Russia since 988 CE.

S

Saadia Ben Joseph (892–940 CE) Head of the Jewish academy at Susa in Babylon. He defended the cause of RABBINIC JUDAISM against the KARAITES and the doctrine of the oneness of God against the Christian TRINITY. He was the first Jewish systematic theologian and he believed in the unity and divine origin of both revelation and reason.

Sabbath (*Shabbat*) Jewish day of worship and rest lasting from Friday sunset to Saturday sunset. The Sabbath is holy because it commemorates God's rest on the seventh day of creation and reminds JEWS (2) of the deliverance from Egypt.

Sacrament 'an outward and visible sign of an inward and spiritual grace' (Book of Common Prayer). REFORMED CHURCHES count only BAPTISM and the EUCHARIST as sacraments, both being instituted by CHRIST. Roman Catholic and Orthodox Churches add CONFIRMATION, marriage, ORDINATION, penance, and extreme unction (the anointing of the sick).

Sacred bears In PREHISTORIC RELIGION ritual veneration of the slain bear. It remains common especially in Arctic and sub-Arctic regions. The Japanese Ainu tribe have bear rituals, as do the Lapps, Finns, Inuit, and Native Americans. Eskimo SHAMANS receive the Great Spirit disguised as a polar bear. Bear worship is frequently associated with the recognition of the constellation Ursa Major; MYTHS concerning the constellation are found among the Greeks and other European and Asian peoples.

Sacred birds Often a symbol of transformation. In Greek mythology ZEUS disguises himself as a swan in pursuit of amorous adventures. The CELTS revere the swan as a symbol of divine transformation and also recognize ravens as appearances of war goddesses. Native peoples of South and Central America venerate the plumed quetzal (*see also* QUETZALCOATL). The mythical phoenix of Arabia symbolized the cycle of death and rebirth, the ancient Egyptians finding in the similar bent a manifestation of the god Re-Atum worshipped at Heliopolis. A bird often symbolizes the departing SOUL (1) freed from the shackles of earthly life. In the BIBLE, the HOLY SPIRIT is described as being like a dove.

Sacred bulls Symbols of power and strength. They were connected with the worship of the MOTHER GODDESS, especially in the MINOAN RELIGION of ancient Crete where they gave rise to the MYTH of the Minotaur, a bull-like monster who had to be placated with human sacrifices. The slaughter of a bull was important in some forms of Roman religion.

Sacred snakes Frequently associated with the MOTHER GODDESS especially in MINOAN RELIGION. Because they shed their skin they are symbols of immortality. They are also associated with wisdom and healing. In Chinese religion dragons replace snakes as sacred animals. In Norse mythology a Great Serpent, son of the evil LOKI, surrounds the earth. In CHRISTIANITY the snake is a symbol of evil and deceit, especially connected with the biblical MYTH of the Garden of Eden.

Sacred Thread ceremony INITIATION ceremony performed on HINDU and BUDDHIST boys. A sacred thread is placed around the neck indicating that the boy is one of the twice-born and has entered the first stage of life. (*See also* NAVJOTE.)

Sacred trees Objects of religious significance since they connect the earth to the sky. In Celtic religion tree species were sacred to particular tribes: Irish literature speaks of a sacred ash, a yew, and an oak, among others. The connection of DRUIDS with the oak is likely but unproved. (*See also* YGGDRASIL.)

Sacred wells Springs, rivers, and natural wells often have religious significance, particularly in Celtic religion. Regarded as passages to the UNDERWORLD, votive offerings such as brooches, bracelets, and even severed human heads were deposited there. The custom of throwing coins into water may reflect these ancient practices.

Sacrifice The ritual offering of animal or vegetable life to establish communion between humans and a god or gods.

Sadducees Aristocratic Jewish party which emerged in the times of the MACCABEES. They rejected the oral law and late doctrines like the RESURRECTION. They were nationalists and collaborated with the Romans to ensure the survival of the Jewish state. The party collapsed after 70 CE.

Sai Baba (1926–2011 CE) Spiritual teacher from south India who is regarded by his followers as an AVATAR. Probably the most popular and influential GURU in present-day India, he specialized in curing illness and materializing gifts for his disciples.

Saint (1) Holy person or dead hero of faith who is venerated by believers on earth and held to be a channel of divine blessing. The Protestant reformers rejected the practice of devotion to saints. (2) In the NEW TESTAMENT and some Protestant churches, a term for any believer.

Salafiyya Puritan Sunni Islamic party which emerged in nineteenth-century Egypt. It accepted the authority only of the QUR'AN and the SUNNAH and rejected the 'ULAMA'.

In time it grew closer to the WAHHABI MOVEMENT. It published a journal, *Al-Manar*, which circulated in the Middle East.

Salah Islamic ritual prayer which is carried out five times a day, facing MECCA and using ritual movements to accompany the words. Salah is one of the FIVE PILLARS OF ISLAM.

Salvation (1) In the BIBLE, deliverance of God's people from their enemies, and especially from SIN and its consequences, death and HELL, hence also the whole process of forgiveness, new life, and final glorification for the believer. (2) In Eastern religions, release from the changing material world to identification with the ABSOLUTE.

Samhain Celtic festival marking the beginning of winter, celebrated on 1 November with feasting and carousals. Regarded as a period outside the normal flow of time when the dead could freely return to communicate with the living, it was the subject of many MYTHS and legends, mainly concerning death. It is celebrated today by contemporary Pagans.

Samsara ('stream of existence') Sanskrit word which refers to the cycle of birth and death followed by rebirth as applied both to individuals and to the universe itself.

Sanctuary A place consecrated to a god, a holy place, a place of divine refuge and protection. Also, the holiest part of a sacred place or building. Historically, in some cultures, a holy place where pursued criminals or victims were guaranteed safety.

Sangha Community of Buddhist MONKS which started with the BUDDHA's first disciples. The functions of the *sangha* are to promote through its own lifestyle the best conditions for attaining individual salvation and to teach the DHAMMA to all people.

Sanhedrin Jewish supreme council of seventy which organized religious life during the period of independence following the revolt of the MACCABEES. Under Herod the Great the Sanhedrin was divided: the SADDUCEES dealt with political matters; the PHARISEES concentrated on the interpretation of the TORAH. After the Fall of Jerusalem (70 CE) an academic Sanhedrin was organized in Jabneh to reorganize Jewish life.

Sannyasi ('one who renounces') The last of the Hindu Four STAGES OF LIFE.

Sanskrit The language of the ARYAN peoples and of the Hindu scriptures. It is an Indo-European language related to Latin, Greek, and Persian.

Sarasvati In HINDUISM, the goddess of truth and consort of BRAHMA, the Creator.

Satan In the BIBLE, the personification of evil and identified with the DEVIL.

Satanism Sometimes referred to as 'devil-worship'. It should be distinguished from Paganism. Most Pagans do not recognize a being called Satan, which they identify with Christian belief. That said, Satanists will claim that their religion too is not simply an inversion of Christian teaching. Indeed, not all Satanists believe in the existence of a being called Satan, but rather focus on him as a powerful, alternative symbol.

Satguru (1) In SIKHISM, GOD, the true and eternal GURU. (2) In popular HINDUISM a term for a revered teacher such as SAI BABA.

Satori ENLIGHTENMENT in ZEN BUDDHISM.

Saturnalia Roman festival of Saturn, a mythical king of Rome and father of the god JUPITER, which began on 17 December. A time of banquets and present-giving, some of its characteristics were transferred to the festival of CHRISTMAS.

Sawm *see* FIVE PILLARS OF ISLAM.

Schism A deliberate division or split between Christians that disrupts the unity of the CHURCH.

Scribes Officials who organized the religious life of the Jewish community after the EXILE of 586 BCE. They regulated the observance of the SABBATH, communal prayer, and fasting and were the interpreters of the Law. Some copied manuscripts, but this was not necessarily part of their job.

Scripture Writings which are believed to be divinely inspired or especially authoritative within a particular religious community.

Sebek Egyptian god associated with water and death.

Second Coming/Parousia The personal second coming of CHRIST which, Christians believe, will be a time of judgment and the inauguration of the KINGDOM OF GOD in its fullness.

Sect A group, usually religious (but it can be political), which has separated itself from an established tradition, claiming to teach and practise a truer form of the faith from which it has separated itself. It is, as such, often highly critical of the wider tradition which it has left. For example, the JEHOVAH'S WITNESSES and the SEVENTH-DAY ADVENTISTS are sectarian Christian organizations.

Sefirot According to the teachings of Jewish Kabbalistic MYSTICISM (*see* KABBALAH), the potencies and attributes by which God acts and makes himself known.

Sephardim One of the two main cultural groups in JUDAISM which emerged during the Middle Ages. Sephardic Jews lived in Spain and Portugal and their traditions go back to Babylonian Jewry. They developed Ladino as their language.

Serapis State god of Ptolemaic Egypt whose worship spread throughout the Mediterranean. He took over many characteristics from the ancient Egyptian OSIRIS, but was also associated with the bull god Apis, in turn associated with PTAH. He was both a healing god and a ruler of the UNDERWORLD.

Seth The evil brother of OSIRIS in Egyptian mythology. He murdered his brother and seized his earthly rule until in turn, defeated by HORUS. He became the god of war, storms, deserts, and disorder.

Seven Precepts of the Sons of Noah The obligations placed on all men and women, regardless of race or faith, according to Jewish teaching. They comprise abstinence from idolatry, blasphemy, incest, murder, theft, the eating of living flesh, and the implementation of justice.

Seventh-Day Adventists Christian sect which emerged from a number of nineteenth-century groups stressing the imminent return of CHRIST. In line with Saturday being the original seventh day of the Judeo-Christian week, they observe Saturday as the Sabbath. They accept the BIBLE as infallible and require a lifestyle of strict temperance.

Shabbat *see* SABBATH.

Shahadah *La ilaha illa Allah.* The first four words of the MUSLIM confession of faith, 'There is no god but God', which continues 'and MUHAMMAD is his prophet'. To accept this creed is to be a Muslim. It is the first of the FIVE PILLARS OF ISLAM. Its words form part of the call to prayer, the adhan, which is broadcast from the MOSQUE five times a day in Muslim communities.

Shaivism Worship of the Hindu god SHIVA and his family. It is particularly strong in southern India and appeals to extreme ascetics.

Shakti ('energy', 'power') A feminine word, particularly associated with SHIVA and his consorts (*see* DURGA; KALI; PARVATI). In TANTRISM *shakti* is universal creativity and exists in people as a latent energy located at the base of the spine (*see* KUNDALINI). In tantric YOGA this energy is awakened to travel up the spine and unite with Shiva, who is present as mind.

Shakyamuni ('The wise man of the SHAKYAS') One of the names of the BUDDHA.

Shakyas Tribe to which the BUDDHA's family belonged. They occupied territory in the Himalayan foothills.

Shaman (1) An ecstatic priest-magician among the Tungu people of Siberia. (2) By extension, a similar figure in other INDIGENOUS RELIGIONS and ancient religions. Shamans induce a trance experience in which they are believed to leave the body and visit other worlds. The shaman's role is to convey sacrifices to the gods, to escort the dead to their destination and to return with divine prophecies.

Shamash Babylonian sun god and lord of justice who rewards honesty and loyalty and brings retribution on the wicked. He is depicted as giving a ring and sceptre to the lawgiver HAMMURABI.

Shammai *see* HILLEL.

Shankara (788–820 CE) The best-known exponent of classical HINDU philosophy. Developing the thought of the UPANISHADS, he declared that only the eternal being is real; the diverse, phenomenal world is an illusion of MAYA (1). Even the notion of a personal God is part of maya. Liberation comes from realizing oneness with the ABSOLUTE, which is defined as Being, Consciousness, and Bliss. (*See also* VEDANTA (2).)

Shari'a ('path') Body of law for the MUSLIM community which derives from the QUR'AN, the SUNNAH, and other sources, the legitimacy of which is debated in the different schools of law. Shari'a is regarded as divinely authoritative.

Shavuot *see* WEEKS, PENTECOST.

Shaykh/Sheikh/Shaikh (1) An Arab tribal leader. (2) Sufi spiritual teacher (*see* SUFISM), somewhat analogous to the Hindu GURU.

Shekhinah The presence or manifestation of God as described in the TARGUMS and later Jewish writings. It came to refer to the indwelling of God in creation. In KABALLAH the Shekhinah is exiled from the eternity of God, EIN SOF, because of human SIN and will only be restored at the final REDEMPTION.

Shema The Jewish confession of faith, recited in the morning and evening service. '*Shema*' is the opening word in HEBREW of the confession: 'Hear, O Israel, the Lord our God, the Lord is One …' Three passages from the TORAH confirm that there is one God and that Israel is chosen to witness to him.

Shi'a/Shi'ites A minority group in ISLAM, comprising 15 per cent of MUSLIMS. They reject the first three CALIPHS, believing 'ALI to be MUHAMMAD's true successor and first IMAM. They also hold that authority resides in the Imams, who are the infallible messengers of God in every age. The Shi'a live mostly in Iraq, Iran, Lebanon, Pakistan, and India. The two main Shi'a divisions are the ISMA'ILIS and the TWELVERS.

Shingon 'True Word' sect of Japanese Buddhism founded in the ninth century CE and characterized by a complex sacramental and magical ritual which may have been influenced by TANTRISM and by indigenous SHINTO practices.

Shinran (1173–1263 CE) Disciple of HONEN and founder of the Japanese Buddhist sect JODO SHINSHU.

Shinto The indigenous nature religion of Japan which has provided a focus for nationalistic aspirations. (*See also* EMPEROR, JAPANESE; IZANAGI; JIMMU TENNO; JINJA; KAMI; KOJIKI; MATSURI; NIHONGI; NINIGI.)

Shirk ('association') In ISLAM the greatest sin, that of ascribing equals to God. (*See also* TAWHID.)

Shiva One of the great gods of HINDU devotion. He is a god of contrasts, presiding over creation and destruction, fertility and asceticism, good, and evil. He is the original Lord of the Dance who dances out the creation of the universe. As god of ascetics he is portrayed as a great *yogi*, smeared with ashes, holding the world in being through meditation. His symbol is a phallus-shaped pillar denoting procreation.

Shoah *see* HOLOCAUST.

Shotoku, Prince Japanese ruler who introduced BUDDHISM as the state religion. During his reign (593–622 CE) he built a Buddhist academy and temple near the state capital at Nara.

Shudras *see* CASTE SYSTEM.

Shulhan Aruch *see* KARO, JOSEPH.

Shvetambara ('white-clad') Member of a major JAIN sect who rejected the DIGAMBARA stress on the virtues of nudity. They are numerous in the north of India.

Siddhartha Personal name of GAUTAMA the BUDDHA.

Sikh ('disciple') Follower of the Sikh religion which developed in the fifteenth century CE in northern India as a synthesis of ISLAM and HINDUISM. (*See also* ADI GRANTH; GOBINDH SINGH; GURDWARA; KABIR; KHALSA; NANAK; SINGH.)

Sin (1) An action which breaks a divine law. (2) The state of rebellion against God which, in Christian teaching, has been the human condition since the Fall of Adam and Eve and their expulsion from the Garden of Eden.

Sin Babylonian moon-god and guardian of the city of Ur. He usually appears riding on a winged bull. He is the father of the sun, SHAMASH, and god of vegetation.

Sinai, Mount Mountain in the south of the Sinai peninsula where, according to tradition, God revealed himself to MOSES and gave him the Ten Commandments.

Singh Surname used by SIKHS when they become a member of the KHALSA. It means 'lion' and expresses the militant stance which Guru GOBINDH SINGH impressed upon the Sikh community.

Sinkyo Traditional religion of Korea.

Sita Consort of RAMA in Hindu tradition.

Skandha/Khandha Term referring to the five factors which compound human personality according to Buddhist teaching. They are form, sense perception, consciousness, intellectual power, and discrimination. The relation between them is continuously changing in accordance with the action of KARMA.

Skilful means Buddhist practice of compassion in sharing the DHAMMA with the unenlightened. Tradition describes the BUDDHA explaining the Dhamma at different levels to different people. In the LOTUS SUTRA tricks and deceptions are among the skilful means employed to lead the lost to salvation.

Smith, Joseph (1805–44 CE) Founder of MORMONISM who claimed to be the recipient of a divine revelation to the former inhabitants of America in the form of golden plates inscribed in ancient languages. With the help of the Angel Moroni, he translated these and they became the basis of the BOOK OF MORMON. Ordained priest by the heavenly messenger, he founded the Church of Jesus Christ of Latter-day Saints in 1830. He died at the hands of a mob.

Socrates (469–399 BCE) Greek philosopher and teacher and mentor of PLATO. He taught by a method of question and answer which sought to elicit a consistent and rational response and hence to arrive at a universally agreed truth. He was executed in Athens for corrupting the youth and introducing strange gods.

Soka Gakkai 'Value-creating society' of lay members of the Japanese Buddhist sect NICHIREN. It was founded in 1930 in a wave of new cults. It is evangelistic, exclusive, and highly organized. It runs its own political party and has schools and a university.

Sol Invictus ('unconquered sun') A name for MITHRA. From the time of the emperor Aurelian (270–275 CE) until displaced by CHRISTIANITY, his was the official imperial cult of Rome.

Soma The juice of the Indian *soma* plant, which may have been fermented or had hallucinogenic properties. It was drunk by gods and men in the VEDAS, and was regarded as a mediating god with power over all plants and as a conveyor of immortality.

Son of Man Title used by Jesus Christ to refer to himself, traditionally used to describe Christ's humanity. Its meaning in the New Testament is much debated.

Sorcerer A practitioner of harmful MAGIC. In INDIGENOUS RELIGIONS sorcerers are sometimes believed to be able to kill others through magic.

Soteriology Teaching about SALVATION.

Soto Zen School of ZEN Buddhism which teaches a gradual and gentle way to SATORI.

Soul (1) The immortal element of an individual man or woman which survives the death of the body in most religious teachings. (2) A human being when regarded as a spiritual being.

Spell A formula of words with or without accompanying RITUAL actions which is believed to have the power to manipulate natural or supernatural forces for good or evil ends. The exact form of the spell is often the secret of the practitioner. In contemporary WICCA, spells are recorded in the *Witch's Book of Shadows*.

Spiritualism Any religious system or practice which has the object of establishing communication with the dead. Most modern spiritualist churches derive from a movement which grew up in mid-nineteenth-century America. Spiritualists seek to communicate with the dead through such means as table-turning and automatic writing. All mainstream Christian churches denounce the practices of spiritualism.

Steiner, Rudolf (1861–1925 CE) Founder of ANTHROPOSOPHY. He originally followed THEOSOPHY and ROSICRUCIANISM, but he broke with these groups and developed his mystical ideas into an educational, ecological, and medical programme for spiritual progress. He founded a number of highly successful schools which cater for some 120,000 pupils.

Stoicism Philosophical school founded by Zeno of Citium (c. 335–263 BCE) and named after the porch or *stoa* where he taught in Athens. Stoics believed that the world order reflected the divine intelligence – the LOGOS which was present in all creation. Human beings could attain virtue – harmony with the universe – by learning self-sufficiency and behaving with courage and self-control.

Stonehenge Megalithic monument (*see* MEGALITHS) on Salisbury Plain, England. It may have been a sanctuary for sun worship or regulated an agricultural and astrological calendar.

Stupa Tibetan Buddhist shrine, found by roadsides, in fields, and at gateways. It is shaped as a pointed dome, often with a spire crescent and disc at the top, and built on a square base. The construction represents the five elements and may contain RELICS or images or texts of sacred scripture. Many stupas in India date from the reign of king Asoka.

Subud Spiritual teaching of the Javanese Muslim teacher Pak Subuh (1901–87 CE). It emphasizes submission to the Life Force through a course of spiritual training designed to open up the individual to the reality of God and to mastery over the lower nature. The Subud training is open to members of all faiths.

Sufism Islamic mystical movement that gained prominence in the eighth century CE as a reaction to the worldliness of the UMMAYAD DYNASTY. Sufis claimed direct experience of ALLAH through ascetic practices. The orthodox rejected them at first, but today Sufi orders are accepted among SUNNIS and SHI'AS. (*See also* ISLAM.)

Sukkot *see* BOOTHS.

Sundance Four-day ceremony which grew up among Native Americans Plains in the 1870s as a reaction against white attempts to break up the traditions and beliefs of the people. It was held in the summer inside an immense circular area. The ceremony was crushed by the US army and regulations were imposed against such rituals.

Sun God In the INCA religion, the creator of Manco Capac, the first Inca, and father to all the Inca rulers. His names include INTI and Punchau.

Sunnah ('trodden path') The source of authority in Islamic lawmaking which is second only to the QUR'AN. It refers to the words and actions of MUHAMMAD and, in a lesser degree, to the words and actions of the first four CALIPHS.

Sunni The majority group in ISLAM, comprising about 85 per cent of MUSLIMS. They accept the authority of the FOUR RIGHTLY GUIDED CALIPHS and the developing process of lawmaking guided by the community's legal experts. Sunni Muslims live in the Arab states in North, West, and East Africa, and in India and Indonesia.

Sutta Pitaka An important collection of THERAVADA Buddhist SCRIPTURES. It consists of sermons of the BUDDHA, including the DHAMMAPADA.

Suzuki, Daisetz T. (1870–1966 CE) Japanese ZEN scholar who played a major part in introducing Zen Buddhism to the Western world. He was a member of the RINZAI sect and was sympathetic to CHRISTIANITY.

Swami General term for a HINDU holy man or member of a religious order.

Swaminarayan (1781–1830 CE) Gujarati preacher and founder of a popular sect which attracted Sikh and Hindu followers.

Swedenborg, Emmanuel (1688–1772 CE) Swedish scientist who became a MYSTIC and visionary. He taught a kind of pantheistic THEOSOPHY (*see* PANTHEISM) centred on Jesus Christ, in whom he found a Trinity of Love, Wisdom, and Energy. He founded the New Church.

Synagogue Jewish meeting place for worship and study. Synagogues grew out of the TORAH schools of the SCRIBES during the EXILE. After the destruction of the TEMPLE OF JERUSALEM (70 CE), synagogues became the centres of Jewish life. They are built to face JERUSALEM and contain an Ark (2) in which the scrolls of the law are displayed before a perpetual lamp. Worship in synagogues includes readings from the TORAH, psalms, sermons, and communal prayers.

Syncretism The growing together of two or more religions making a new development in religion which contains some of the beliefs and practices of both.

T

Tabernacles, Festival of *see* BOOTHS.

Taboo Polynesian word applied to an object, place, or person which is prohibited because of its holy or dangerous character. It may include the sense of being 'marked off' and therefore separate from everyday usage.

Tagore, Rabindranath (1861–1941 CE) Bengali poet, playwright, musician, and Nobel prize-winner, whose passionate espousal of Bengali culture influenced the cause of Indian nationalism. His devotional verses were popular in Britain in the Edwardian era.

T'ai Chi (1) The 'Transcendent Absolute' or 'Great Ultimate' which is the underlying cause and unity of all things in early Chinese Taoist and later neo-Confucian thought. It is the nearest equivalent to GOD in Chinese thought. (2) The name of a martial art often practised as a form of spiritual development. It takes the form of slow, graceful movements, designed to align the practitioner with the natural flow of the universal Chi.

Tallit Jewish prayer-shawl fringed at the four corners and used during morning prayer, SHABBAT, and Jewish festivals including YOM KIPPUR.

Talmud The written interpretation and development of the HEBREW scriptures. It is based on the MISHNAH of JUDAS HANASI, with the addition of some excluded teachings and commentary recorded from the debates and controversies of the Schools of Babylon on Palestine. There are two versions: the Palestinian, compiled while the Jews were under duress from the Christian Church, and the Babylonian which is more detailed and complete.

Tammuz Babylonian/Syrian fertility deity. A young god who, in mythology, died and was resurrected after the pattern of the Egyptian OSIRIS.

Tanha ('craving') The main cause of suffering as analyzed by the BUDDHA in the FOUR NOBLE TRUTHS.

Tantrism Tibetan Buddhist practices which aim at direct experience of the enlightened self through symbols, visual images, repetition of sounds, prescribed movements, breath control, and ritualized sexual intercourse.

Tao ('way') In TAOISM, the underlying principle of reality.

Taoism Chinese philosophy outlined in the TAO TE CHING. Its aim is to achieve harmony with all that is by pursuing inaction and effortlessness. Taoism gradually evolved an elaborate mythological system and incorporated notions of spirit possession, ALCHEMY, and DIVINATION. (*See also* JADE EMPEROR; LAO-TZU.)

Tao te ching Chinese religious work compiled in the fourth century BCE and ascribed to LAO-TZU, though it is probably the work of several writers. It describes the TAO as the underlying principle of reality which can only be attained by passivity.

Targum A (usually) Aramaic translation of a HEBREW scripture reading. The translator was expected to make a free interpretation. Some of these have become famous in their own right and are used by pious JEWS alongside the appointed text.

Tarot cards Deck of seventy-eight cards marked with various symbolic figures which are shuffled and dealt as a form of DIVINATION.

Tat tvam asi ('you are that') Phrase from the UPANISHADS which expresses the claim that BRAHMAN, the divine power sustaining the universe, and ATMAN, the soul, are one.

Tawhid ('asserting oneness') The essential MUSLIM doctrine of the unity of God. He is oneness in himself without parts or patterns.

Tephillin/Tefillin ('phylacteries') Small boxes containing scriptural texts written on parchment. They are worn by JEWS (2) on the head and arm during daily prayer.

Temple Building designed for WORSHIP of God or gods, usually containing a SANCTUARY or holy place where SACRIFICE may be offered.

Temple of Heaven Great Chinese temple in Peking where the Chinese emperors received the mandate of heaven (*see* T'IEN) to rule over the Chinese people. It is still used for great state occasions.

Temple of Jerusalem/Holy Temple TEMPLE first built by Solomon on a site bequeathed by DAVID. It was divided into the Holy Place and the Holy of Holies where dwelt the presence of YHWH. This temple was destroyed in 586 BCE. The second temple was dedicated in 515 BCE. It was desecrated by the Hellenistic Seleucid king Antiochus Epiphanes but rededicated by JUDAS MACCABEUS. Rebuilding was begun under Herod the Great in 20 BCE. The temple was virtually completed in 62 CE, but destroyed by Titus in 70 CE.

Ten Gurus In SIKHISM GURU NANAK and his nine successors who are seen as sharing the same essential insights into the nature of God.

Tendai Japanese Buddhist sect based on a former Chinese sect T'ien-t'ai, and founded

in the ninth century CE. Tendai was an attempt at a synthesis between MAHAYANA teachings which stressed MEDITATION and those that stressed devotion.

Tengri The supreme god of the Mongols. It was also used as a collective name for gods.

Tenrikyo 'Religion of Heavenly Wisdom' founded in Japan by NAKAYAMA MIKI, and based at the city of Tenri, near Nara, at the site of the founder's home. This is believed to be at the centre of the world and it is the place of divine homecoming for the sect's two million adherents.

Tetragrammaton *see* YHWH.

Teutates, Esus, and Taranis Gaulish gods mentioned by the Roman writer Lucan (39–65 CE). They required to be appeased by bloody sacrifices. Teutates in particular may have been a god of war, healing, and fertility and the guardian of his people.

Tezcatlipoca ('that which causes the Black Mirror to shine') AZTEC god of night and the north, a magician, symbolized by a jaguar. He was one of the most important of the Aztec gods.

Theism The belief in one supreme GOD who is both TRANSCENDENT and involved in the workings of the universe.

Theocracy ('divine government') Term describing a state which is constituted on the basis of divine law. It is an important concept in ISLAM, where it is sometimes believed that the law of the land should be identical with the SHARI'A. The regime of CALVIN in Geneva was also theocratic.

Theodicy The defence of God as both good and omnipotent, which accounts for the existence of suffering and evil. The term was coined in 1710 by Gottfried Leibniz.

Theology (1) A systematic formulation of belief made by or on behalf of a particular individual or CHURCH or other body of believers. (2) The critical study of RELIGION, particularly CHRISTIANITY, with regard to its origins, SCRIPTURES and other texts, DOCTRINES, ethics, history, and practices.

Theophany A divine appearance, revelation, or manifestation, usually inducing awe and terror in those who witness it. Examples are the appearance of God to MOSES on Mount SINAI amidst thunder, lightning, smoke, and

trumpet blasts; the appearance of KRISHNA in his divine form, 'like a thousand suns', as described in the BHAGAVAD GITA.

Theosophy ('divine wisdom') A term applied to various mystical movements but which refers particularly to the principles of the Theosophical Society founded by Madame BLAVATSKY in 1875. These comprise a blend of Hindu, Buddhist, and Christian ideas, together with particular stress on REINCARNATION, immortality, and the presence of GOD in all things. Theosophists also believe in a series of World Teachers ('Ascended Masters') who are incarnated to express the divine wisdom.

Theravada ('the doctrine of the elders') The form of BUDDHISM practised in Sri Lanka, Myanmar (Burma), Thailand, Cambodia, and Laos, which sticks firmly to the teachings of the VINAYA PITAKA and rejects the doctrine of the BODHISATTVAS.

Thirteen Principles Articles of Jewish faith which were formulated by Moses MAIMONIDES in the twelfth century CE. They assert faith in God as creator, as formless unity, First and Last, and only hearer of prayer. They also affirm the words of the PROPHETS, the unchanging nature of TORAH, the Creator's knowledge of humanity, the judgment, the coming of the MESSIAH, and the RESURRECTION of the dead. The Thirteen Principles are found in the Jewish Prayer Book.

Thomas, John *see* CHRISTADELPHIANS.

Thor Norse god of thunder and lightning. He is portrayed as wild and red-haired, wielding a great hammer. Thor is the son of Mother Earth and his wife, Sif, is a corn goddess. He is associated with agriculture and is the protector of MIDGARD against the giants.

Thoth Ibis-headed Egyptian god, patron of writing and counting, who recorded the weighing of souls in the judgment after death.

Three Body doctrine MAHAYANA Buddhist teaching that the BUDDHA exists in three aspects. His human existence was his 'transformation body'. In his celestial existence he appears in his 'enjoyment body'.

But the ultimate basis of his Buddhahood is his 'truth body' which unites all three bodies. This is identical with ultimate reality.

Three refuges Brief dedication used by Buddhists and traditionally given by the Buddha himself: 'I go to the Buddha for refuge; I go to the Dhamma for refuge; I go to the Sangha for refuge.'

Thunderbird A totem (*see* TOTEMISM) found widely among Native Americans of North America. It represents the eagle, the great bird of the eastern doorway of the world. It also represents thunder spirits who bring rain; the clap of its wings sounds the thunder and the flash of its eyes symbolizes lightning. The Thunderbird is frequently found at the top of Native American TOTEM POLES.

Tibetan Book of the Dead Book of instructions and preparations for death and rites to be performed for the dying. In TIBETAN BUDDHISM the dying must train in advance, helped by a spiritual teacher, to face the clear light of the Void, reality itself, in such a way as to avoid REBIRTH, or at least to ensure a human rebirth.

Tibetan Buddhism/Vajrayana A mixture of BUDDHISM, TANTRISM, and the ancient Bön religion of Tibet. The two main groups are the RED HATS and the YELLOW HATS. (*See also* CHAKRAS; CHORTEN; DALAI LAMA; LAMA; MANDALA; PANCHEN LAMA; PRAYER WHEELS; TIBETAN BOOK OF THE DEAD.)

T'ien ('heaven') Chinese term sometimes used for the supreme GOD. From around 1000 BCE the Chinese emperors were believed to rule by mandate of heaven.

Tipitaka The 'three baskets' of the BUDDHA's teaching, the canon of SCRIPTURE for THERAVADA Buddhists, comprising the VINAYA PITAKA, the SUTTA PITAKA, and the ABHDHAMMA PITAKA.

Tirthankaras *see* JINA.

Tlaloc AZTEC god of rain and vegetation. His name means 'he who makes things sprout'. He is portrayed with long fangs and rings around his eyes.

Tongues, Speaking in *see* GLOSSOLALIA.

Torah (1) The five books of the Law (the PENTATEUCH) revealed to MOSES; the first division of the HEBREW BIBLE. (2) 'The teaching', the correct response

of ISRAEL to God, outlined in the rules for purity and social justice. It is God's gift to Israel and the way for Israel to fulfil God's call for holiness. (3) The cosmological principle of order which embraces moral and religious instruction as well as the physical ordering of the universe by God.

Torii Gateway to a SHINTO shrine which consists of two vertical posts supporting two horizontal bars, the higher of which is often curved at each end towards the sky.

Totemism (from a Native American word meaning 'relative') The belief in some INDIGENOUS RELIGIONS that particular animals or sometimes plants or other objects have a special relationship with the tribal group and act as its guardians.

Totem poles Tall decorated posts, found especially among Native Americans, which display tribal relationships with ancestors and guardian spirits.

Towers of Silence Parsi mounds used for the disposal of corpses. In the belief of the PARSIS, sacred fire must not be polluted by contact with the dead. Corpses are exposed on the mounds where the flesh is eaten by birds of prey. The bleached and disintegrated bones are finally washed away.

Transcendent That which is above or beyond common human experience or knowledge.

Transcendental Meditation/TM MEDITATION technique taught by Maharishi Mahesh Yogi which has flourished in the West since the 1960s. Practitioners need no religious beliefs. They are taught to meditate for fifteen to twenty minutes twice a day; this reduces stress and aids relaxation. In some states in the USA it has been ruled that Transcendental Meditation is a religion, of Hindu origin.

Transfiguration The occasion of CHRIST's appearance in glory to three of his disciples during his earthly ministry. It is celebrated as a feast in the Eastern Churches and by many in the West.

Transmigration of souls The belief held by some Hindus that souls are detached from their bodies at death and are attached to other human, animal, or vegetable bodies. What the new body will be depends on the individual's KARMA.

Trimurti The three principal deities in HINDUISM — BRAHMA, VISHNU, and SHIVA, who are believed to control the three activities — creation, preservation, and destruction — inherent in the created cosmos.

Trinity Christian doctrine of GOD as three Persons, equally God: the Father, the Son, and the HOLY SPIRIT, constituting the divine unity.

Tripitaka (1) Sanskrit spelling of the (Pali) word TIPITAKA. (2) The SCRIPTURES of THERAVADA BUDDHISM, which include translations of THERAVADA texts, SANSKRIT MAHAYANA texts, and some Chinese additions and commentaries. Also called the San-tsang.

Triple gem The BUDDHA as teacher, the DHAMMA as his teaching, and the SANGHA as the community who live by his teaching. The 'triple gem' is the core of the Buddhist faith.

Tuat/Duat The other world in Egyptian mythology, a land of gloom and darkness which is divided into twelve areas, one for each hour of the night. The souls of the dead have to cross this region to enter the judgment hall of OSIRIS.

Twelvers The majority group among SHI'A Muslims who hold that the twelfth IMAM, Muhammad al-Mahdi, will reappear as the MAHDI on the last day. (*See also* ISMA'ILIS.)

Tyr The oldest of the Norse gods. Originally a sky god like ZEUS or VARUNA, his attributes were taken over by ODIN. The Romans compared him with MARS because he became a war god, an inspirer of warriors. He is portrayed as having great strength and courage.

U

UFO ('unidentified flying object') The subject matter for many speculative groups since the 1950s. Members consider the spiritual and practical significances of UFO sightings.

'Ulama' The doctors of the law in ISLAM. They are the interpreters of the SHARI'A and the upholders of Islamic orthodoxy. They exist in SUNNI and SHI'A communities.

'Umar Caliph after the death of ABU BAKR, 634–644 CE. His rule was a period of dramatic expansion for ISLAM, into

Mesopotamia, Persia, and Lower Egypt. He was assassinated by the Persians in the MOSQUE OF MEDINA.

Ummayad dynasty (661–750 CE) The Islamic dynasty based on the Meccan family Ummaya. The caliphate was based in Damascus. Under the Ummayads ISLAM spread through North Africa to Spain and as far east as the Indus. There were fourteen CALIPHS until the Ummayad period ended in military defeat and the succession of Abu al-'Abbas as first caliph of the 'ABBASID DYNASTY.

Ummah The MUSLIM community; those who have received God's revelation through MUHAMMAD and live in submission to it.

Underworld The abode of spirits after the death of the body. In many religions the underworld is a shadowy half-real place presided over by a god of death. (*See also* HADES; HELL; TUAT.)

Unification Church *see* FAMILY FEDERATION FOR WORLD PEACE AND UNIFICATION.

Unitarianism Dissenting movement which spread in Britain, Poland, and Hungary from the sixteenth century. Unitarians reject the Christian doctrines of the TRINITY and INCARNATION and defend a reason-based ethical THEISM.

Untouchables Indians who belong to no caste (*see* CASTE SYSTEM) and are therefore banished from normal social life. MAHATMA GANDHI called them 'children of God' and worked for their acceptance in Indian society.

Upanishads The last books of the Indian VEDAS which were written in SANSKRIT between 800 and 400 BCE. They develop the concept of BRAHMAN as the holy power released in sacrifice to the point where it becomes the underlying reality of the universe. The soul, ATMAN, is identified with the holy power, Brahman. They include speculation on how the soul can realize its oneness with Brahman through contemplative techniques.

'Uthmān ibn 'Affān Son-in-law of MUHAMMAD who succeeded 'UMAR as CALIPH in 644 CE. He was regarded as weak, and was murdered in 656 after a period of rebellion. Under his caliphate the final authoritative version of the QUR'AN was produced.

V

Vairocana A title for the sun in ancient HINDU mythology. In MAHAYANA Buddhism it became a title for one of the great Buddhas. He is regarded as supreme BUDDHA in Java and in the Japanese SHINGON sect. He was said to be identical with the SHINTO sun deity Amaterasu.

Vaishnavism Worship of, or devotion to, the Hindu god VISHNU. Devotees regard him as the sole deity, of whom other gods are mere aspects.

Vaishyas *see* CASTE SYSTEM.

Vajrayana ('diamond vehicle') An expression sometimes used for Tibetan Buddhism, a form of MAHAYANA Buddhism which has distinctive doctrines and practices.

Valhalla ('hall of the slain') The part of ASGARD in Norse mythology reserved for dead heroes waiting for the final battle RAGNARÖK. It had 540 doors and 800 men could march, shoulder to shoulder, out of each door. The dead heroes spent their time drinking, playing games, and fighting.

Valkyries ('choosers of the slain') Female servants of ODIN in Norse mythology who choose which side is to have victory in battle and which warriors are to die. They conduct the dead to VALHALLA and wait on them with food and drink. Some MYTHS portray them as witch-like beings, exulting in blood and death.

Vampyr/vampire Spirit of a dead person in Slavic folklore who lives by sucking the blood of the living.

Vanir ('shining ones') Divine beings of Norse mythology who at first fought with the ÆSIR and later allied with them and came to live in ASGARD.

Varanasi *see* BENARES.

Varuna Indian sky god of the Vedic period (*see* VEDAS). He produced the cosmic order and was seen as a heavenly ruler and lawgiver as well as a moral guardian of the earth.

Vatican Councils The first was convened by POPE PIUS IX in 1869–70 CE. It resulted in the dogma of Papal Infallibility and attacks on 'modern' thought. The second (1962–65 CE) was called by John XXIII. It led to a

drastic modernization of Roman Catholic worship and improved relations with other churches.

Vedanta (1) 'The end of the VEDAS'. A name for the UPANISHADS, which close the period of HINDU revelation. (2) Indian philosophy based on the teachings of SHANKARA. Its basic tenet is that only BRAHMAN, the Absolute, is fully real. The world of sense experience is contradictory and dreamlike because it is spun from the illusions of MAYA (1). Release from illusion comes from recognizing the sole reality of Brahman.

Vedas Scriptures which express the religion of the ARYAN people of India. They comprise HYMNS, instructions for RITUAL, and cosmological speculations. There are four divisions: *Rig Veda*, hymns to the Aryan gods who are personifications of natural forces; *Sama Veda*, verses selected for chanting (*see* CHANT); *Yajur Veda*, prose instructions on matters of ritual; *Atharva Veda*, rites and SPELLS in verse, especially concerned with curing illness.

Venus Roman goddess of love, identified with APHRODITE and thus honoured as the mother of the Roman people.

Vesta Roman goddess of the hearth and protectress of domestic life. She was regarded as the guardian of the Roman nation. Her cult was under the supervision of six Vestal Virgins who tended the undying flame (traditionally from Troy) which burned in her temple.

Vestments Special garments worn by the Christian clergy during liturgical services (*see* LITURGY).

Vinaya Pitaka One of the oldest Buddhist scriptures consisting of the rules of discipline for the SANGHA, and related commentaries.

Viracocha/Huiracocha The uncreated creator-god in the religion of the INCAS. He was god of the ancient city of Tiahuanaco and the giver of civilization. Pachacutec, the ninth Inca, exalted him as supreme deity over even the SUN GOD.

Vishnu In HINDUISM, the divine as preserver and life-giver, the creator of the cosmos. He and SHIVA are the two great gods of Hindu devotion. As lawgiver and moral guardian,

Vishnu appears on earth from time to time as an AVATAR to reawaken people to knowledge of truth.

Vivekananda (1863–1902) Follower of RAMAKRISHNA and founder of the RAMAKRISHNA MISSION in 1897. An apologist for VEDANTA, he criticized the dogmatism of CHRISTIANITY. Attending the World's Parliament of Religions in Chicago in 1893, he commended Vedanta as the highest form of religion.

Voodoo Religion of estimated 75 per cent of the people of Haiti – in spite of the official domination of Christianity – as well as others in the West Indies and parts of South America. The name derives from a West African word for GOD. In practice Voodoo is highly syncretistic. West African DIVINITIES are worshipped, often as Christian SAINTS, and their sanctuaries are closed during the Christian season of LENT.

W

Wahhabi movement Puritanical SUNNI ISLAM movement founded by Muhammad ibn 'Abd al-Wahhab of Arabia (1703–92 CE). Wahhabi advocated the right of individual Muslim scholars to go directly to the QUR'AN and the HADITH revelation. The movement has revived in the twentieth century and is the dominant religious influence in Saudi Arabia.

Wailing Wall see WESTERN WALL.

Wandering On In Buddhist thought the continual cycle by which the KARMA of past actions causes the coming-to-be of new mental and physical states which in turn produce more karma and further phases of existence.

Wandjina Spirit beings of the Australian Aboriginal DREAMTIME who are believed to have left their shadows on rock and cave walls in paintings and engravings. They are regarded as kindly beings who care for the people, ensure fertility, and bring rain.

Weeks/Shavuot Jewish feast celebrated seven weeks after PASSOVER. It has become associated with the giving of the Ten Commandments on Mount SINAI. Also known as PENTECOST.

Werewolf Human being who has been transformed into a wolf in Slavic folk tradition.

Wesley, John (1703–91 CE) Founder of the METHODIST movement. He travelled through Britain on horseback preaching the 'new birth'. Although loyal to the Church of England, he was eventually forced to ordain his own ministers.

Western Wall/Wailing Wall/Kotel Site in JERUSALEM used by Jews to lament the FALL OF JERUSALEM and the continuing suffering of the Jews and to pray for restoration. It is believed to be part of the original Herod's Temple, the only part left standing after the destruction of 70 CE. (*See* TEMPLE OF JERUSALEM.)

Wicca Also called 'the Old Religion', 'witchcraft', 'wisecraft', or simply 'the Craft', the term is taken from the Anglo-Saxon *wicce*, meaning 'witch' or 'wise woman'. Many contemporary practitioners of witchcraft prefer the term Wicca for their religion. While some claim that it has ancient origins, many would argue that contemporary Wicca was founded by Gerald Brosseau Gardner (1884–1964), who claimed to have been initiated into the 'Old Religion' in 1939. Although there are many Wiccan paths, it is generally agreed that there are five principal ones: Gardnerian Wicca, Alexandrian Wicca, Hereditary Craft, Traditional Craft, and Feminist Craft.

Witch doctor/Medicine man A healer in INDIGENOUS RELIGIONS. The terms are rarely used today as they are felt to have misleading connotations.

Word of God Christian term for the BIBLE or part of it.

World Council of Churches Body including many Protestant and Orthodox churches, first constituted at Amsterdam in 1948 (*see* CONCILIAR PROCESS, ECUMENICAL MOVEMENT).

World Fellowship of Buddhists Society founded in 1950 in Ceylon (Sri Lanka) by G. P. Malalasekera to bring together Buddhists of all traditions and nations with the common intention of spreading Buddhist teaching throughout the world.

Worship Reverence or homage to God or a god which may involve PRAYER, SACRIFICE, RITUALS, singing, dancing, or chanting.

Wovoka (1856–1932 CE) Paiute Native American PROPHET and MYSTIC who, reacting against white domination, urged his followers to live in peace, fighting the whites through the power of the GHOST DANCE. His hope of imminent regeneration spread among the Native American Plains. The movement was destroyed at the Battle of Wounded Knee in 1890.

Wrath The righteous anger of God against SIN.

Writings The third and final division of the HEBREW BIBLE, comprising the Wisdom literature (such as Job and Proverbs), the Psalms, the later histories, and other material.

Wycliffe, John (c. 1320–84) English religious reformer who appears to have condemned the POPE as Antichrist. He and his associates translated the Vulgate (Latin) into English.

X

Xipe Totec ('the flayed one') In Mexican mythology, the god of the west and of agriculture, who skinned himself like the maize. He was represented by the mask of a skinned human face.

Xiuhtecuhtli ('turquoise lord') The ancient Mexican fire god. His fire burned in every home and temple and he was regarded as a form of the supreme god.

Y

Yahweh see YHWH.

Yama In the VEDAS the primordial man who crosses through death and becomes immortal. He is therefore god of death who judges men and consigns them to heaven or hell. His significance as judge faded as the pre-ARYAN doctrine of SAMSARA became established.

Yasna The form of public worship in ancient ZOROASTRIANISM, elements of which are retained by the PARSIS. Part of the AVESTA, it teaches the presence of the divine in all things and refers to many lesser divine beings alongside AHURA MAZDA.

Yellow Hats Reformed branch of TIBETAN BUDDHISM whose leader is the DALAI LAMA. (*See* BUDDHISM.)

Yggdrasil The great ash tree which unifies the creation according to Norse mythology. Its three roots reach ASGARD, MIDGARD, and Niflheim, the UNDERWORLD. The tree holds together the nine worlds of giants, dwarfs, human beings, light elves, dark elves, ÆSIR, VANIR, the dead, and the home of the world-destroyers. The tree of knowledge, it is simultaneously being nourished and destroyed. It is also a symbol of the generation of life: the first man in Norse myth is named Ash.

YHWH The 'tetragrammaton', the sacred name of the God of ISRAEL which was revealed to MOSES. The name means 'I am'. It could not be spoken and the Hebrew '*Adonai*' ('the Lord') was substituted when the scriptures were read aloud. The MASORETES put the vowel points for *Adonai* into the name YHWH, which gave rise to the malformation 'Jehovah'.

Yin and Yang The polarity of energies in Chinese philosophy. *Yang* is masculine, dynamic, bright, and good; *yin* is feminine, passive, dark, and bad. Their production and interplay is represented in a circular diagram (*see* T'AI CHI). *Yin* and *yang* produce the elements and the cycle of the seasons. They also provided the theoretical basis for the Taoist practice of ALCHEMY (*see* TAOISM).

Yoga A way to union with GOD in HINDU philosophy. It also forms one of the six classical systems of Indian thought. Traditionally there are eight stages of yoga: restraint, discipline, posture, breathing, detachment, concentration, meditation, and trance. In the Bhagavad Gita the three paths to spiritual fulfilment are: jnanayoga (the path of knowledge/wisdom), karmayoga (the path of work/action), and bhaktiyoga (the path of devotion).

Yogi Indian holy man who has reached ENLIGHTENMENT through yogic practices (*see* YOGA). (*See also* TRANSCENDENTAL MEDITATION.)

Yom Kippur/Day of Atonement Jewish day of FASTING and repentance, the most solemn day of the Jewish year. The LITURGY includes a solemn chant, the Kol Nidrei, which challenges Jews who have strayed from religion to return to faith.

Z

Zaddiq/Zadik Jewish teacher in the later Hasidism The zaddiq was *seen* as the perfectly righteous man who was in mystical communion with God. The zaddiq's house became the meeting place for the HASIDIM.

Zakah A 'poor tax' charged at the rate of 2.5% of a person's total income for the year, in ISLAM. It is levied on all who can afford it, and distributed among the poor and needy. It cannot be used for any other purpose.

Zarathushtra *see* ZOROASTER.

Za-Zen Japanese term for the form of MEDITATION practised in ZEN monasteries. It involves a sitting posture designed to accompany reflection on a KOAN.

Zealots Jewish nationalistic party in Roman times who believed that the Roman presence was a defilement of the land and a flouting of TORAH. In 66 CE they revolted. The war which followed led to the destruction of JERUSALEM and its Temple in 70 CE. The last stand of the Zealots was at Masada, where 960 of them died in 73 CE.

Zen Japanese Buddhist movement which developed from the Chinese Ch'an school in the twelfth century CE. It is characterized by the teaching that ENLIGHTENMENT is a spontaneous event, totally independent of concepts, techniques, or rituals. Zen aims at harmony in living and uses secular arts such as tea-making and calligraphy to develop effortless skills.

Zeus Supreme ruler of the Greek gods. Described by HOMER as 'Father of gods and men', he may have originated as a storm god and continued to be regarded as controller of the weather. Although there were many MYTHS about him he did not appear in drama, which suggests that he was held in special awe. Sometimes the name Zeus stood simply for God, as supreme deity.

Zevi, Shabbetai (1628–76 CE) Kabbalistic RABBI from Smyrna who became the centre of a messianic movement which spread throughout the Jewish world (*see* KABBALAH). In 1665 he proclaimed himself MESSIAH. He was later imprisoned and, to the horror of his followers, converted to ISLAM. There were attempts to argue that the sin of the messiah was a necessary part of redemption, but the movement disintegrated.

Ziggurat Ancient Babylonian TEMPLE in the form of a tower rising from a broad base to a narrow top.

Zionism The movement to establish a national and permanent homeland for JEWS. In 1897 the First Zionist Congress was organized in Basle by Theodor HERZL in the wake of a wave of European anti-Semitism. Gradually the movement became determined that Palestine was the only realistic place to establish the Jewish state and Jews were encouraged to emigrate and acquire property there.

Zohar Most important writing of the Jewish KABBALAH.

Zombie Term used in Haiti and South America for the 'living dead'.

Zoroaster/Zarathushtra Prophet and founder of ZOROASTRIANISM. He lived in Persia, possibly as early as 1200 BCE. At the age of thirty he had a revelation of AHURA MAZDA which drove him to preach against polytheism. According to one tradition he was murdered at the altar by the Turanians.

Zoroashtrianism The religion of ancient Persia, founded by ZOROASTER, possibly related to the Vedic religion of India (*see* VEDAS). It was strongly ethical: Zoroaster taught that AHURA MAZDA would judge each individual soul after death. Later there developed a complex doctrinal system speculating about the inner nature of the universe. The expansion of ISLAM drove Zoroastrianism out of Persia (*see also* AVESTA; PARSIS; ZURVANISM).

Zurvanism Zoroastrian heresy according to which an absolute being called Zurvan ('time') was the origin of good and evil and the source of the two spirits AHURA MAZDA and ANGRA MAINYU.

Index

Numbers in **bold type** indicate pages with illutrations.

Picture Acknowledgments

Bible Land Pictures: p. 73

Dreamstime: pp. 6, 19, 31, 34, 48, 57, 82, 93, 97, 100, 108, 120, 138, 146, 162, 164, 173, 198, 202, 204, 241, 251, 257, 266, 274, 278, 281, 293, 296, 300, 310, 315, 321, 324, 373, 381, 405, 423, 429, 446, 450, 463, 499, 504, 511, 516, 518, 523, 525, 526, 539

Illustrated London News: pp. 3, 22, 28, 187

Israel Government Tourist Office: pp. 357, 359, 367, 371

Photolink: pp. iii, 15, 51, 54, 77, 78, 194, 195, 205, 219, 222, 223, 229, 236, 238, 249, 361, 362, 399, 403, 404, 406, 419, 455, 460, 470, 480, 529

Pixabay: pp. 136, 430, 540, 549

Tim Dowley Associates: pp. 25, 52, 59, 68, 103, 111, 112, 212, 336, 345, 352, 360, 395, 412, 443, 485, 495, 502

Wiki Commons: p. 171